JOHN LEWIS KRIMMEL

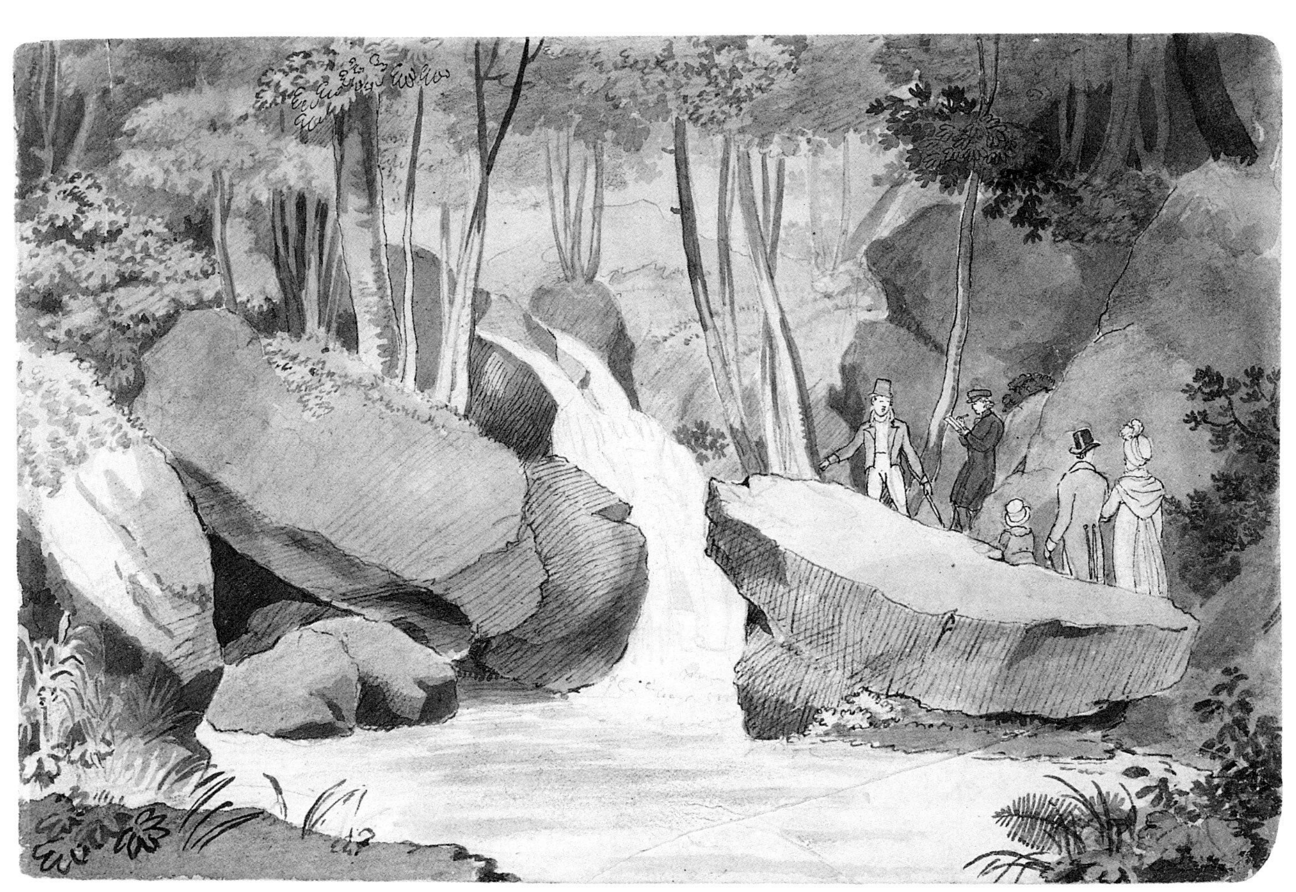

John Lewis Krimmel

GENRE ARTIST OF THE EARLY REPUBLIC

Anneliese Harding

A Winterthur Book
Winterthur, Delaware
1994

The publication of this book is supported in part by funds from the National Endowment for the Arts.

Library of Congress Cataloguing-in-Publication Data

Harding, Anneliese.
John Lewis Krimmel : genre artist of the early Republic / Anneliese Harding.
p. cm. —(A Winterthur book)
Includes bibliographical references and index.
ISBN 0-912724-25-0
1. Krimmel, John Lewis, 1786–1821—Criticism and interpretation.
2. Genre painting—19th century—Pennsylvania. I. Title.
ND237.K69H37 1994
759.13—dc20 94–014906
CIP

Printed and bound by Arnoldo Mondadori Editore S.p.A., Verona, Italy

ISBN 0-912724-25-0

Frontspiece: Waterfall, *probably June 1818. From Krimmel sketchbooks; see fig. 207.*

Contents

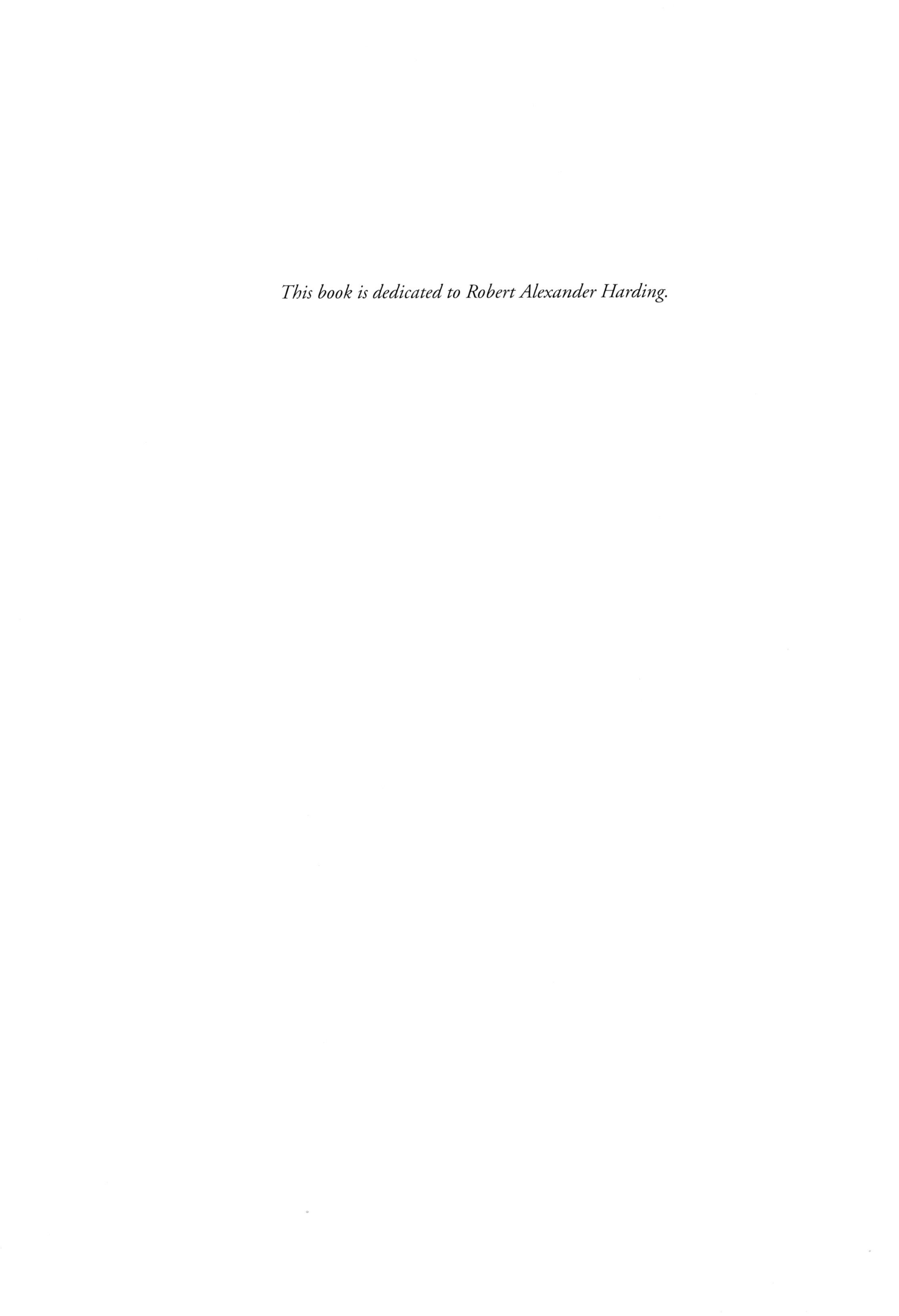

This book is dedicated to Robert Alexander Harding.

Acknowledgments

Many individuals and institutions contributed to the making of this book. My initial interest in Krimmel grew out of research on German-American artists, which I pursued in my work as art historian of the Goethe Institute Boston. Special thanks for their support go to the institute's director Dr. Erhard Staedtler and his successor, Dr. Gerhard Kirchhoff, and chief secretary Ilse Kohli. During several visits to the artist's German home region, I benefited most from the meetings with Dr. Walter Stettner, the municipal archivist of Albstadt-Ebingen and an authority on the history of the town. His information on Krimmel's background clarified the context of his education and emigration. Among others who were helpful to me in Germany, I thank Dr. Ulrike Gauss of Staatsgalerie Stuttgart, and Hertha Beck, Edeltraut Brockmüller, and Ernst Adolf Groz of Albstadt.

At the Henry Francis du Pont Winterthur Museum, I am primarily indebted to Ian M. G. Quimby, former director of Publications and a scholar of American material culture, who commissioned this book on Krimmel in 1978. His active participation in the initial research got the project well under way. I was further helped by his editorial assistant, Catherine H. Maxwell, and by librarians Beatrice K. Taylor, Eleanor McD. Thompson, E. Richard McKinstry, and graphics and paintings curator E. McSherry Fowble. The person who contributed most to this book is its editor, Catherine E. Hutchins, who took the project over in 1983. While giving me important leads and information, her probing questions always challenged me to substantiate my statements as far as possible. She graciously adapted herself to the peculiarities of an author educated in Europe, tolerantly amending any of my inadequacies in the English language with her skillful editing. On my trips to Winterthur she extended herself as a friend, joining me in looking at Krimmel pictures in collections as far away as Washington, D.C., and New York City in order to resolve problems of attribution. I thank Lisa L. Lock who handled the organization and editing of the book in the final stages and coordinated production. I am also grateful to professor William T. Oedel for his perceptive critique and helpful suggestions as outside reader of the manuscript.

To those experts in the field of American art whom I consulted over the years and who generously shared with me of their time and knowledge, I express my thanks here: in Boston, Theodore E. Stebbins, Jr., and Carol Troyen of Museum of Fine Arts and John Kirk of Boston University; in Worcester, Georgia Barnhill of the American Antiquarian Society; in Philadelphia, Frank H. Goodyear, Jr., of the Pennsylvania Academy of the Fine Arts; in New York, Elisabeth Roth of New York Public Library, Jay E. Cantor of Christie, Manson, and Woods International, and Kevin J. Avery and Karl Kusserow, Department of American Paintings and Sculpture, Metropolitan Museum of Art. I am grateful to the following institutions for having made their resources available to me: at Winterthur, the research library and the manuscript collection;

at Harvard University, the Houghton Library, the Fogg Art Library, and the Widener Library; at Wellesley college, the Art Library; at Boston Public Library, the Manuscript and Rare Book Collection; the Archives of American Art in Boston; the Boston Athenaeum; the American Antiquarian Society; the Historical Society of Pennsylvania; the American Philosophical Society; the Pennsylvania Academy of the Fine Arts; the Frick Art Reference Library; the National Gallery of Art; the Metropolitan Museum of Art; Württembergisches Landesmuseum, Staatsgalerie Stuttgart, Württembergische Staatsbibliothek; Salzburger Landesarchiv; Stadtarchiv Albstadt-Ebingen; and Heimatmuseum Golling. For bringing previously unknown or unlocated Krimmel pictures to my attention, I am sincerely grateful to Dr. Friederike Zaisberger, Salzburg, Austria; Melinda Browne, New Caanan, Connecticut; Art Cohen, Baltimore, Maryland; Robert Lang, Rye, New York; Milton Luria, Verona, New Jersey; Sumpter Priddy, Richmond, Virginia; and the staffs of Sotheby's and Christie's, both in New York.

On a personal note, I thankfully acknowledge the help and comments of my friends Dr. Ilse Fang and Nancy Salzman and the assistance and advice of my son Dr. Christopher Harding. My deepest thanks go to my husband Robert who patiently endured my absences during the time it took to research and write this book.

FEBRUARY 1994

Introduction

Whenever the present insensibility to the interests of the fine arts shall have passed away, and the American public have learned to appreciate the labours of the pencil, Krimmel's name will rank high as an artist of great ingenuity of design, and truth and delicacy of delineation.

ANALECTIC MAGAZINE, December 1820.

The flowery prediction about the eventual renown of genre painter John Lewis Krimmel at last seems to be coming true. After 170 years of neglect and periods when his name was all but totally forgotten, the artist is gaining recognition for his superior artistic talent, especially as a draftsman, and his progressive contributions to American art. Extensive research has substantiated the claim that Krimmel was the first genre painter in the new republic, and that he helped to bring American painting out of its provincial restrictions and dependence on English models into the mainstream of Western art. Although his initial models were the pictures of Wilkie, Hogarth, and West, after he revisited Europe in 1817–18, Krimmel returned to Philadelphia inspired by the concepts of German romanticism and with an increased appreciation for French neoclassical painting as a compositional source. These influences affected his ensuing projects. The artist died suddenly, only 35 years old, just after he had received his first large commission that would do justice to his remarkable talent. For a long time it appeared that the paintings he had left were too few in number to make him a significant artist. He was generally known in art history for two or three paintings, *View of Centre Square on the Fourth of July*, *Country Wedding*, and *Quilting Frolic*, all from his early period.

The recent rise in Krimmel's reputation stems in part from the general increased respect for American art. Milo M. Naeve's master's thesis for the University of Delaware 1954 was the first scholarly research on Krimmel's life and work. In the last decade the dramatic increase in the value of American pictures has caused long unlocated Krimmel paintings to come on the art market and has prompted private owners to let the existence of a Krimmel picture in their collection be known.

My research in Krimmel's home region in Germany, as well as the investigation of all the available materials on the artist in the United States, brought forth hitherto unknown facts and pictures. The most comprehensive and illuminating information about Krimmel I gained from the study of the seven sketchbooks, now in the library of Winterthur. The books contain about seven hundred separate drawings, ranging from quick pencil sketches to finished watercolor pictures, and served a key function in developing my understanding of the artist's professional development and in the reconstructing of his conceptual processes. While a number of these sketchbook images have been published before, they have not been illustrated in nearly complete form, nor have they been used as a tool for understanding Krimmel's evolution as an artist.

The chronological order of the sketchbooks and the images in them has been established through Krimmel's own dating system and notes written in them, mostly in German. Because the artist also used his sketchbooks as diaries, calendars, and address books as well as for shopping lists and calculations, they are a fortuitous record of the painter and his work. When compared to one another, they show clear distinctions in subject matter and drawing style, commensurate to the changes in his paintings. Each book seems to represent a new phase in Krimmel's professional evolution and reveals another dimension of his talent. The numerous studies of figures and faces demonstrate that the artist was primarily interested in types of Philadelphia's middle and working classes, which explains his frequent inclusion of black people. It is the intimate and personal aspect, the painstaking exactness that make these drawings so appealing and the information they give so authentic. By producing and storing such images in his sketchbooks, the artist prepared for himself a reservoir of visual information of which he later could avail himself when he composed his paintings. He also resolved in these drawings many of the problems he had to confront as a painter, such as the issues of composition and the detailed studies of shapes and colors. While the areas of drawing and painting constantly interacted and complemented each other in Krimmel's work, they never produced identical images. Since the extant paintings, the large finished watercolor pictures, and the prints made from his drawings provide only sporadic information, the sketchbooks, through their exceptional continuity over a period of more than ten years, supply sufficient evidence to reconstruct Krimmel's growth as an artist.

From Amateur to Professional Artist

Johann Ludwig Krimmel was born May 30, 1786, in Ebingen, a small town in the Schwäbische Alb, a scenic area traversed by a spur of the Jura mountains in the south German duchy of Württemberg.[1] The region was marked by an inclement climate and stony soil that combined to limit farming and favor sheepherding and forestry. Ebingen, which had been granted a town charter in 1285, enjoyed periods of prosperity, the most recent of which coincided with the late seventeenth-century introduction of textile manufacturing using wool shorn from locally raised sheep. Because town privileges included the right to hold regional markets, Ebingen possessed an important advantage in trade and commerce that encouraged the growth of a variety of shops and businesses.[2]

One of the town's tradesmen was Krimmel's father, Johann Jacob Krimmel, a prosperous Conditor (a baker specializing in fine pastries), whose store and workrooms were located on the lower floors of the handsome half-timbered building in which he and his family lived next door to the Rathaus (town hall) on Market Street. His stock-in-trade were sweet breads, cakes, and cookies. The first two were labor intensive products that required a good deal of creativity in both the artful shaping of dough and the skillful decoration with icing; gingerbread cookie designs were individually imprinted with intricately carved wooden molds, which at the end of the eighteenth century featured whimsical and humorous motifs such as street vendors, musicians, dancing couples, fine ladies, dandies, and even drunkards.[3]

Conditor Krimmel's business profited handsomely from the weekly markets and seasonal fairs that attracted many customers, and many of the ingredients that his confectionery needed probably came directly or indirectly from the numerous garden plots, large pasture, and stand of timber that he owned on the outskirts of town. On these he and his family raised bees, poultry (for eggs), cows (for milk); cultivated beets (for sugar) and herbs; and maintained a supply of fuel.[4]

The Krimmels were a long-established family in Ebingen; relatives and ancestors included a mayor, several millers, taverners, and brewers. Within Johann Jacob's family, Johann Ludwig, the future painter, was the fourth of six children and the youngest of three sons. But the 1790s brought unexpectedly hard times. The youngest daughter, Agatha Rosina died in 1794, followed two years later by 7-year-old Regina Catharina. Even more calamitous in 1796 was the death of the father, 46-year-old Johann Jacob. This left his widow, Elisabetha Katharina, and four children between the ages of 10 and 21 to run the bakery.[5]

Georg, the oldest child, seems to have been uninterested in taking over the family business. Within a few years he left Ebingen to work at a mercantile house in Switzerland, probably in Basel. Johann Ludwig, the youngest son, was still in school, attending the local Lateiner from which he was graduated in 1801. He immediately began borrowing small sums of money

1. Geburts- und Taufregister [birth and death register], Stadtarchiv [municipal archives], Rathaus [town hall], Albstadt-Ebingen, Germany. (In 1975 Albstadt-Ebingen was made a district town encompassing what had been nine separate communities.) Seelenregister der Evangelischen Kirchengemeinde Ebingen, Familienbuch A2, p. 273, Evangelisches Kirchenregisteramt [Index of the Ebingen Protestant congregation, Office of Protestant church records], Spitalhof, Albstadt-Ebingen. In 1786 the south German duchy of Württemberg was bordered on the west by the Duchy of Baden and on the east by the Duchy of Bavaria.

2. French Huguenots introduced textile industries to Württemberg in the 1600s. Ebingen gained a modest reputation for inexpensive woolen fabrics and stockings. During the 1700s their manufacture became a major source of employment for Ebingeners of all ages who did spinning and weaving in small workshops and at home; the textiles were exported to Switzerland, Austria, other duchies of Germany and Italy, and German-speaking Alsace and Lorraine, France; Walter Stettner, *Ebingen, die Geschichte einer Württembergischen Stadt* (Sigmaringen, Ger.: Jan Thorbecke Verlag, 1986), pp. 148, 154, 229, 233–34. Other town privileges included the right to be self-administered by an elected council and the right to fortify and thus erect a town wall.

3. Living quarters are described in Grundbesitzurkunde [real estate documents], Stadtarchiv, Albstadt-Ebingen. Anneliese Harding, *The Edible Mass Medium: Traditional European Cookie Molds of the Seventeenth, Eighteenth, and Nineteenth Centuries* (Cambridge: Busch-Reisinger Museum, Harvard University, 1975), pp. 4–9; Stettner, Ebingen, pp. 154, 204.

4. The extent of the property is detailed in cases 139–44 in the Kaufprotokolle, Stadtarchiv, Rathaus, Albstadt-Ebingen, 1817–18. The Krimmel half of the double house included the confectionery, a brewery, family living quarters, and outbuildings all valued at 1,200 guilders; several gardens—herb, cabbage, sugar beets, and grapes—valued at 155 guilders, timberland and a large field valued at 44 guilders, a flax garden valued at 36 guilders, a vegetable garden valued at 15 guilders, and another one which was sold for 13 guilders.

5. Stettner, *Ebingen*, p. 154; Geburts- und Taufregister.

from Georg: 5, 6, and 7 guilders in June, September, and November of 1801, probably to pay a local tutor, such as a *Stadtschreiber* (town scribe), who routinely taught youths the skills needed in the mercantile world—bookkeeping, letter writing, and elementary French, the international language of the period.[6]

When Krimmel graduated, external pressures were increasingly affecting his family and life in Ebingen. Napoleon's invasion of the German territories brought hard economic times and military conscription. In 1802 Frau Krimmel sold part of the family land to come up with the 100 florins needed to hire a substitute to serve in the military in Georg's place, which suggests that she was also unwilling to send either of her sons to serve in his stead. Then, in 1803, both she and her middle son, Johann Jacob, died.

As the only son in Ebingen 17-year-old Johann Ludwig had a seemingly assured future; however, like his eldest brother, this young man apparently did not intend to become a conditor or remain in Ebingen. In March 1805, four months after his sister Christiane, then age 26, married Paul Daser, a trained confectioner who was the son of a Lutheran pastor in a nearby community, a legal division of the Krimmel property was finally made. The three surviving heirs, Christiane, Johann Ludwig, and Georg each received a third of the property. More important, from then on Daser was to manage the confectionery and to have the option of purchasing the shares, over time, of his two brothers-in-law. On June 9, 1805, the second anniversary of their mother's death, Johann Ludwig again borrowed money from Georg, this time the substantial sum of 508 guilders, and apparently soon after moved to Stuttgart, the capital of Württemberg. During the next four years he rose to the level of a commercial clerk and worked briefly (at least during the spring of 1809 and possibly before then) in England, probably as the employee of a Stuttgart firm. Little else is known about his activities during these years.[7]

Conditions in Europe were greatly unsettled. The French Revolution had upset the traditional social order and the concept of divinely ordained absolute monarchies. Principles of liberty and equality and the notion that the supreme power of the state might properly rest with the people were concepts affecting the thinking of many Europeans. In Germany this had been most apparent in cultural and intellectual circles, prompting, for example, Ludwig van Beethoven to conclude his Ninth Symphony with a choral singing the words of Friedrich Schiller's "Ode to Joy" espousing the ideals of liberty and brotherhood of men. In France the reign of terror and the failure of the leaders to develop and establish a stable republican government had facilitated Napoleon Bonaparte's rise to power and his use of revolutionary ideals to achieve his own imperialistic political and military ends. By 1798 his armies were moving across Europe.

Württemberg was caught in a reckless power game that its ruler, Duke Frederick II (1754–1816), played with Napoleon for several years. Initially the duke joined in the war against France, and when the French invaded Württemberg, he took refuge outside his duchy until a peace treaty was concluded (Peace of Lunéville, 1801). In 1802 Frederick made a separate treaty with France, giving up his claim to territories west of the Rhine in exchange for additional lands east of the Rhine, and in 1803 Napoleon granted Frederick the title "elector." In 1805 Frederick joined Napoleon in the war against the Third Coalition—Great Britain, Austria, Russia, and Sweden, and later Prussia. Following the dissolution of the Holy Roman Empire in 1806, Napoleon

6. Through age 14 children attended either the Deutsche or the Lateiner. The former had large classes and taught students basic reading, writing, and arithmetic; the latter had smaller classes and a demanding curriculum that included Latin, geometry, drawing, and ancient history in addition to the 3Rs; see Stettner, *Ebingen*, pp. 279, 318, 60; Julius B. Hartmann, *Johann Baptist Pflug (1785–1866): Gemälde und Zeichnungen* (Biberach, Ger.: Verlag Biberacher Verlags druckerei, 1985), p. 5. Krimmel's sketchbooks and paintings demonstrate he knew geometry and drawing; his persistent use of "7bris" (September) and "9bris" (November) when dating images in his sketchbooks shows knowledge of Latin and the Julian calendar. Georg's loans are evidence of special tutoring, for were Johann Ludwig learning a trade as an apprentice/journeyman, no money would have changed hands. Two later loans of 158 guilders (April 1803) and 508 guilders (June 9, 1805) were probably for lessons that prepared Johann for entry into the mercantile business, for relocation, and for job-hunting. For Georg's 1821 claim against his brother's estate to recover the loans, see estate of John Lewis Krimmel, Administration no. 187, Department of Wills, County Court House, Philadelphia, a document the staff termed "temporarily unfound" in 1987; Milo M. Naeve, *John Lewis Krimmel: An Artist in Federal America* (Newark: University of Delaware Press, 1987), p. 29 n. 10, summarizes these bills, and Milo Merle Naeve, "John Lewis Krimmel: His Life, His Art, and His Critics" (Master's thesis, University of Delaware, 1955), pp. 175–76, has a transcription. I am indebted to Naeve for preserving this record.

7. Christiane received the jewelry and women's clothes and Johann Ludwig the men's clothes. Geburts- und Taufregister; Ehebuch der Evangelischen Kirchengemeinde Ebingen vom Jahre 1804, Spitalhof, Albstadt-Ebingen; Inventuren und Teilungen, vol. 1184, Stadtarchiv, Albstadt-Ebingen. Most records in Stuttgart were destroyed during World War II, but Krimmel's residency there is documented by Ebingen court records of March 27, 1806. A businessman from Tübingen filed a claim against the Krimmel confectionery. The issue of the suit dated back to 1795. Daser knew nothing about the claim, but offered to ask his brother-in-law, Johann Ludwig, who he said was then living in Stuttgart. At the second session of this case on July 17, 1809, Daser stated Krimmel was then working in England as a *"Kaufmanns-Diener"* (commercial clerk). Krimmel had visited Ebingen during the interim but since he was 9 years old in 1795 could be of little help in the suit; see Gerichtliches Protoll [record of court hearings], 1806 and 1809, Stadtarchiv, Albstadt-Ebingen.

elevated the former duke to kingship. King Frederick II of Württemberg, then brought his country into the Confederation of the Rhine, which supported Napoleon and supported the treaty of Tilsit (1807), bringing all of Germany under French rule. Napoleon redistributed these lands and in 1809 bestowed additional territories upon Frederick, who in return again joined Napoleon's campaign against Prussia, Austria, and Russia. This was the situation when Krimmel—23 years old and quite possibly facing military conscription—left for the United States.

Leaving Europe presented its own problems. In 1806 Great Britain had established a naval blockade to prevent any supplies from reaching France. France responded by declaring a blockade of the British Isles. Ships attempting to sail to either nation were at risk, a situation that severely damaged transatlantic commerce and further strained relations between England and the United States. Political tensions had been high since Britain began stopping American ships and confiscating cargo that might aid France in 1803. Aggravating the situation was the British policy of impressing English-born sailors serving on ships flying the United States flag. Late in 1807 the United States Congress passed the Embargo Act forbidding American ships to sail to foreign ports; however, this so injured trade and shipping that two years later it was replaced by the Non-Intercourse Act prohibiting trade with only France and England.

The oldest Krimmel son, Georg Friedrich, his wife Susana, and their 5-year-old daughter had immigrated to Pennsylvania in the summer of 1807, sailing on the *Frederick Augustus* from Amsterdam just before the Embargo Act was passed. He established himself in Philadelphia as a merchant and agent for Haus Balthasar Dietrich Bankhard, a Swiss trading firm based in Basel and in September 1809 became a naturalized citizen of the United States. Concerned about the worsening conditions in Europe, George (as he now called himself) encouraged his brother to follow suit and join him in business.[8]

Johann Ludwig, soon Americanized to John Lewis or perhaps simply Lewis, arrived in Philadelphia about the first of November 1809. He roomed with George, Susana, and their three children (the youngest of whom was only weeks old) and reportedly worked for his brother's firm. Sometime during the spring of 1810 Krimmel decided instead to become an artist, and by February 1811 he had begun sharing quarters with Alexander Rider, a painter of miniatures, a fellow German with whom Krimmel had sailed across the Atlantic, and quite possibly the man who persuaded him to change careers.[9]

Krimmel was 24 years old. His decision to become an artist displays an independent spirit and a self-confidence that may well have been rooted in his middle-class upbringing. He must have believed that intensive work would allow him to turn an avocation into a vocation, and he may well have embraced the lofty ideals of personal freedom that had affected intellectual currents in Europe and North America for more than forty years.

What fostered Krimmel's more specific movement toward genre art—as opposed to more traditional art such as history painting and portraiture—may have been a combination of his adopted city's visual stimulation and his own personal inclinations. The diverse ethnic population, their dress, and their habits struck the newcomer's heightened senses as picturesque. The early images in his sketchbooks indicate that he was focusing on the ordinary facets of life, drawing people of all ages as they went about their daily routines on the city streets. This approach was common in England and continental

8. "List of Passengers on Board Ship Frederick Augustus, Capt. Robinson Potter, from Amsterdam, Sept. 15, 1807," *Pennsylvania Archives*, ed. William H. Egle, 2d ser. (Harrisburg, 1890), 17:661; Naturalization Record 582, District of Pennsylvania, U.S. District Court Records, Philadelphia; Abraham Ritter, "Recollections of the Village of Nazareth, Northampton Co., in the More Primitive and Unsophisticated Times of 1809–10 and 11," 1855, p. 120, microfilm, Historical Society of Pennsylvania, Philadelphia. St. Michael's and Zion Lutheran Church, Philadelphia, Verzeichnis der Tauf- Trauungs- Begräbnis Register . . . , microfilm, Historical Society of Pennsylvania, notes the death of George and Susana's child J. Krimmel, age 11, in July 1813; William Dunlap, *A History of the Rise and Progress of the Arts of Design in the United States*, 3 vols. (rev. ed.; Boston: C. E. Goodspeed, 1918), 2:392. Dunlap's account, based largely upon interviews with those who had known Krimmel, is essentially correct and has been confirmed by evidence in the sketchbooks, both visual and written; letters written during Krimmel's lifetime; and archival records. Many of Dunlap's sources for the account in *History* can be determined by using *History* in conjunction with William Dunlap, *Diary of William Dunlap (1766–1839)* . . ., (1930; reprint, New York: Benjamin Blom, 1969).

9. Klaus Wust and Heinz Moos, eds., *Three Hundred Years of German Immigrants in North America, 1683–1983* (Baltimore: Heinz Moos Publishing Co., 1983), p. 63. Dunlap, *History*, 2:392. A note in Krimmel's sketchbook 1, leaf 22 verso reads "Received Febry 28th 1811 of Mr. Rider fifteen Dollars in full for one quarters rent due 13th instant—Jacob Smith $15.00." That the receipt mentions Rider's name but was written in Krimmel's book is evidence that the two Germans lived in the same lodgings and possibly shared rooms. Krimmel lived with his brother at least until July 6, 1810; Naeve, *Krimmel*, p. 176.

Europe where many artists considered aspects of everyday life suitable topics for their work, but it was uncommon in the United States. Indeed, in Philadelphia no local painter had yet taken genre art as his specialty. Krimmel may well have believed that his inclinations to create genre images would allow him to carve out a niche in his adopted city; to have reached this decision, he must have believed that the middle class in the United States, as in Europe, would be attracted by an art aimed specifically at them.[10]

At the time, Philadelphia was the creative center of cultural and intellectual life in the United States. With a population of about 92,000, this the largest city in the new republic had led the way in the development of art, science, and literature. For decades its active cultural life had attracted a large group of artists with diverse skills. In 1805 these artists had expectantly looked to the newly founded Pennsylvania Academy of the Fine Arts, which announced its purpose was "to promote the cultivation of Fine Arts," throughout the new nation. But, generally speaking, the academy sought to serve what its laymen-dominated board perceived to be the interests of the wider community. In its first five years, the institution's only major achievement was the acquisition of a collection of plaster casts of classical sculpture to assist aspiring artists in drawing the human form. Much to the disappointment of the local professional artists, the academy did not address the pressing need that many of them had for further instruction and did not mount an exhibition of their works. In May 1810 Joseph Hopkinson, one of the directors, admitted to members and the public that the institution's policies ensured that many of the nation's distinguished painters were still forced to go abroad for training that the academy should have been able to provide them in Philadelphia. He urged remedy of this situation, reminding his listeners that artists needed patronage, that the public tasks needed cultivation, and that, "the fine arts are of great importance to the morals of the community."[11] Artists may have found this new sensitivity to their concerns gratifying, but most felt that they still had to help themselves.

The same month that Hopkinson made his remarks sixty Philadelphia painters, engravers, sculptors, and architects formed the Society of Artists of the United States, "a national institution with the purpose of giving character to the Fine Arts in the United States of America." The society's objectives were "to teach the principles of art, improve the taste of the public through exhibitions, to encourage the exchange of ideas between artists on a national scope and provide a fund for the financial relief of artists in extreme circumstances, [and] in the event of an artist's death, relief for his widow and children." After gaining support from a large number of artists (membership in the society swelled to nearly a hundred within six months—Krimmel was a participant at the associate level) the society proposed to the academy that the two groups join forces; however, the fees the academy wanted to levy on individual artists were onerously high. A compromise was struck. "For a consideration of two thousand dollars . . . the members of the society became entitled to free admission to the academy in like manner with the members there of" and received "the right of using the specimens of art" and "the right of making their annual exhibition in the rooms of the academy for six weeks . . . [at] which time the academy [was] also to be open" to the public.[12]

Within a year the Society of Artists organized drawing classes for its members at the academy. On January 29, 1812, Irish-born John James Barralet was named professor of the antique department and instructor for drawing

10. Albert Boime, *Art in the Age of Revolution, 1750–1800* (Chicago: University of Chicago Press, 1987), pp. 24, 16–51. Boime points out the connection between the emergence of genre art and the growth of a strong middle class in England and Holland by 1700; in France he sees the connection between genre art and enlightenment thought. Despite its acceptance in public circles, genre art was given a lesser ranking by the artists who controlled the academies; they maintained that history painting was more important because it involved more expenses, time, and practice. William T. Oedel, *Philadelphia Portrait, 1682–1982: Catalogue of an Exhibition Celebrating the Three Hundredth Anniversary of Philadelphia* (Philadelphia: Historical Society of Pennsylvania, 1982), pp. 9–56.

11. Joseph Hopkinson, May 13, 1810, "Annual Discourse" retitled "The Pennsylvania Academy of the Fine Arts," *Port Folio,* supplement [1810]: 11; Edgar P. Richardson, *Painting in America: The Story of 450 Years* (New York: Thomas Y. Crowell Co., 1956), p. 135. Of the twelve original directors of the Pennsylvania Academy of the Fine Arts (PAFA), Charles Willson Peale and William Rush were the only artists; see Charles Coleman Sellers, *Charles Willson Peale* (New York: Charles Scribner's Sons, 1969), p. 321.

12. George Murray, Address of August 1, 1810, as transcribed on December 19, 1810, Minutes of the Society of Artists, PAFA, p. 18, microfilm; John Melish, *Travels in the United States of America in the Years 1806 and 1807, and 1809, 1810 and 1811 . . .* (Philadelphia, 1812), 2:5–7; Dunlap, *History,* 2:107. Murray, an emigrant from Scotland and one of Philadelphia's eminent engravers, played a leading role in establishing the society.

sessions, and Denis Volozan, a French-born artist who had worked in Philadelphia since 1806, was named professor of the elementary—a beginner's class in drawing human figures, architecture, and landscape.[13]

On May 6, 1811, the Society of Artists opened the first annual public exhibition at the academy. Professionals and amateurs submitted their works, and the committee in charge of selecting and hanging works gave precedence to contemporary, original paintings rather than copies after works by European or ancient artists. The exhibition attracted considerable public attention, and admission fees raised $1,860 within six weeks.[14]

Nonetheless, the artists' efforts to gain public stature and have their art readily accepted met only limited success. In 1811 architect Benjamin Henry Latrobe spoke to the Society of Artists, of which he was vice-president, with thinly veiled frustration:

> For we cannot disguise from ourselves, that, far from enjoying the support of the general voice of the people, our national prejudices are unfavourable to the fine arts. Many of our citizens who do not fear that they will enervate our minds and corrupt the simple and republican character of our pursuits and enjoyments, consider the actual state of society as unfit for their [the arts'] introduction: more dread a high grade of perfection in the fine arts as the certain indication of the loss of political liberty, and of the concentration of wealth and power in the hands of a few. Many despise the arts and their professors as useless, as manufacturing neither food nor raiment, nor gathering wealth by the enterprise of foreign commerce. . . . Inasfar as these prejudices, the only real obstacles to the triumph of the fine arts, grow out of the political constitution of society in the United States, the attempt to remove them suddenly by argument will be vain. . . .
>
> [Further] that among the numerous pictures and drawings [by Philadelphia's artists], there are many which would not dishounour the walls of the London and Parisian galleries. . . . And in this is our superiority . . . our strength is our own. It is not hotbedded by imperial and royal patronage, nor even by the nobility of wealth: it is the concentrated force of individual genius and industry, and of the encouragement of private and unproclaimed protection.[15]

During these early years of the second decade, when American artists were changing their approaches to art, they stopped emulating the English school and began incorporating ideas from the Continent, especially from France. In architecture, French and Italian models were gaining currency, and in literature, philosophy, and music, Germanic influences were growing.[16]

Locally some of these changes may have been a consequence of Philadelphia's history and its current conditions. The city's prominence in political and cultural affairs had long made it a destination of visiting and emigrant Europeans. Germans had made important contributions to the economic, scientific, religious, and cultural life of southeastern Pennsylvania beginning with the very early settlement of Germantown in 1683, some seven miles from Philadelphia along Wissahickon Creek. Soon after, settlement immigrants were cultivating flax, which allowed textiles to become a regional industry, and in 1690 William Rittenhouse established another important industry: papermaking. Although many of the German settlers were farmers or rural-

13. Edward J. Nygren, "Art Instruction in Philadelphia, 1795–1845" (Master's thesis, University of Delaware, 1969), pp. 60, 61, 66, 64; Philadelphia Museum of Art, *Philadelphia: Three Centuries of American Art* (Philadelphia, 1976), p. xvii; Minutes of the Board of Fellows, January 11, 1812, PAFA.

14. Dunlap, *History*, 2:107–8; Rembrandt Peale, "Resolutions Adopted by the Committee of Arrangements and Inspections," April 22, 1811, Peale Papers, microfiche 6:A-2. The exhibition was housed in an 1809 neoclassical building at 10th and Chestnut streets designed by amateur architect and member of the academy board, John Dorsey.

15. B. Henry Latrobe, "Anniversary Oration Pronounced before the Society of Artists of the United States," *Port Folio*, separately issued with n.s., 5, no. 6 (June 1811): 4–5, 31.

16. The Germanic influence is further explored in Henry A. Pochmann, *German Culture in America: Philosophical and Literary Influences, 1600–1900* (Madison: University of Wisconsin Press, 1957); Günter Moltmann, ed., *Germans to America: 300 Years of Immigration* (Stuttgart and Bonn-Bad Godesberg: Institute for Foreign Relations and Inter Nationes, 1982); Anneliese Harding, comp., *John Quincy Adams: Pioneer of German-American Literary Studies* (Boston: Goethe Institute, 1979).

based craftsmen who moved to the arc of land stretching from Northampton County to Lancaster County in southeastern Pennsylvania, there were also townspeople who established or settled in thriving communities, such as Bethlehem, Easton, Reading, and Philadelphia, and opened shops.

During the eighteenth century the sheer number of Germans in Pennsylvania caused a degree of apprehension among the dominant Anglo-American populace. In 1753 Benjamin Franklin worried that Germans would soon "so outnumber us that the advantages we have will, in my opinion, be not able to preserve our language, and even our government will become precarious." The fears proved unfounded in spite of the large areas of Lancaster and Berks counties in which Germans clung to their native language, culture, and customs. Although German-language books, almanacs, and newspapers were printed throughout southeastern Pennsylvania, in many areas and especially in Philadelphia Germans rapidly and successfully adapted themselves to the English-speaking community. Further, after coming through the 1793 yellow fever epidemic unscathed, Germantown and Bethlehem became summer retreats for many Philadelphians of English descent.[17]

Krimmel apparently acclimated himself in Philadelphia easily and quickly. His circle of acquaintances soon included Anglo-Americans, as his few surviving letters and numerous notations in his sketchbooks attest. German-born Rider may have remained his closest friend, but within two years Krimmel was also sketching or drawing at an easel alongside Rembrandt Peale, Thomas Sully, and Charles Bird King.[18]

In 1812 Krimmel publicly identified himself as a painter in the city directory, yet the watercolor and wash drawings that fill the first of his seven sketchbooks indicate he was actively working as an artist two years prior to that. Because many images in sketchbook 1 are dated and marked with an astrological sign for the day of the week, it is possible to trace his endeavors to perfect his craft. He used his first sketchbook from May 1810 until at least July 1812, filling it with a variety of images, most of which are delineations of the human figure. These range in size from tiny vignettes, drawn in any open space that was left on a page, to full-page pictures. They are produced in various ways, most often with a pencil or a very fine brush. Krimmel used a well-sharpened implement for precise linear definition—such as the outlines of a face, a figure, an arm, or a hand—and a duller one or piece of graphite for soft hatching, shading, or surface structure—as in a sleeve or a backdrop. For modeling he made hatchmarks, generally holding the graphite on its side, and these marks vary from straight to inclined and from long to short, depending on the effect he desired. Individual images, some of which are ten to a page, range from swiftly and spontaneously drawn sketches to elaborate detailed renderings that the artist later traced in ink or to which he added wash or watercolor.

The majority of drawings are of subjects in his immediate environment (fig. 1). Both in draftsmanship and in composition they indicate that Krimmel was still very much an amateur but one who already knew how to handle watercolor (fig. 2). Given the recency of his arrival, it is likely that Krimmel had obtained his watercolor instruction while clerking in England, a nation in which amateurs avidly practiced this medium and where, in 1802, they had founded the Watercolour Society of Dilettanti; German-trained amateurs preferred pencil and ink wash.[19]

According to artist-turned-historian William Dunlap, who wrote a biographical sketch of Krimmel in the 1830s that relied on the reminiscences of

17. Pochmann, *German Culture in America*, p. 41. The extent of the assimilation has been well discussed in many histories, including Kenneth W. Keller, "Cultural Conflict in Early Nineteenth-Century Pennsylvania Politics," *Pennsylvania Magazine of History and Biography* 110, no. 4 (October 1986): 512, 515–17. See also Oswald Seidensticker, *The First Century of German Printing in America, 1728–1830* (1893; reprint, Millwood, N.Y.: Kraus Reprint, 1966); William Henry Egle, *An Illustrated History of the Commonwealth of Pennsylvania* (Harrisburg: De Witt C. Goodrich, 1876), p. 1048; see also Stephanie Grauman Wolf, *Urban Village: Population, Community, and Family Structure in Germantown, Pennsylvania, 1683–1800* (Princeton, N.J.: Princeton University Press, 1976).

18. December 1812, Thomas Sully, Journal of May 1792–1846, New York Public Library (Archives of American Art [AAA], microfilm).

19. Philadelphia also had many well-trained watercolor artists from England, such as John Rubens Smith and Benjamin Henry Latrobe; see Donelson F. Hoopes, "The Emergence of an American Medium," in *American Traditions in Watercolor: The Worcester Art Museum Collection*, ed. Susan E. Strickler (New York: Abbeville Press, 1987), pp. 21–24; Theodore E. Stebbins, Jr., *American Master Drawings and Watercolors: A History of Works on Paper from Colonial Times to the Present* (New York: Harper and Row, 1976), p. 53; Edward C. Carter II, John C. van Horne, and Charles E. Brownell, eds., *Latrobe's View of America, 1795–1820: Selections from the Watercolors and Sketches* (New Haven: Yale University Press, 1985), pp. 17–27. Dunlap, *History*, 2:392; Dunlap, *Diary*, pp. 683–703. Following a discussion with Rider several years after Krimmel's death, Dunlap noted in his diary "Seeley the name of Krimmels teacher at home. His excellence—dismissed by Duke of Wirtemberg—Bonaparte employs him." In his later biographical sketch of Krimmel, Dunlap omitted Seele's name and any mention that Krimmel had been a painter in Germany, quite probably because he discovered that the story of a direct connection between the two was spurious. Furthermore, Seele remained the court painter of the Duke and never worked for Napoleon. Krimmel probably had taken drawing in school and learned to handle wash then or while working as a clerk in Stuttgart; Seelenregister, p. 273; underneath Krimmel's name in the register is a brief sentence, written a few years after his death, which sums up Ebingeners' understanding of his life—*"Johann Ludwig Krimmel, Kaufmann und Conditer (geb) 1786 Mai 30 nach Nordamerika gegangen, Maler geworden und ertrunken bei Philadelphia"* [John Ludwig Krimmel, merchant and pastry baker, born May 30, 1786, went to North America, became a painter, and drowned near Philadelphia].

Krimmel's friends and acquaintances, during these early years in Philadelphia Krimmel gained enough proficiency that he did portraits "of the master and mistress of his boarding house [in exchange for rent], and the boarders who were its inmates introduced [him to other sitters]. . . . these portraits were miniatures in oil, somewhat in the size like those Mr. Trumbull commenced his career."[20] A number of small, more-or-less finished portraits in the first three sketchbooks confirm the small scale in which he worked, and some look like sketches for small portraits, although none are in oil. Most others delineate only the face of a person and were later incorporated in Krimmel's genre scenes. All are clearly done from life (figs. 3, 4).

Krimmel's lack of professional training became apparent when he strove to invent his own composition, specifically when he had to relate several figures in a scene. One instance of this is the drawing he did for a religious-allegorical engraving that became the frontispiece for the second issue of *Evangelisches Magazin*, a short-lived serial published in Philadelphia under the supervision of the German Lutheran Synod. The drawing probably dates early to mid 1811, and most likely it was his first commission. The scene has four females symbolizing the three cardinal theological virtues—Faith, Hope, and Love (Charity)—and one human attribute—Knowledge (fig. 5). The church may have stipulated the didactic content of the image, for it provided the accompanying verse printed in the margin below the image and detailed explanatory text on the facing page:

> The sun is a metaphor for the light that is spread through the Bible. The moon by itself would be a dark body if it would be deprived of the sun's rays. For this reason, it is here represented as a metaphor of Human Knowledge which without the enlightenment of the Holy Scriptures gropes in the thickest darkness.
>
> Faith sits on an immovable rock, carrying the Cross in one and the Bible in her other hand. At her right, one can see Hope resting on an anchor—at her left is Love with two children for whom she cares most tenderly. These three sisters are seated without fear, secure and in blissful peace under the reviving and warming rays of the sun. On the opposite side, under the moon one can see the allegory of mere human knowledge on a swampy ground overgrown with the reeds of her own ideas. She has her arts scattered by her side and around her—squinting at the sun; but since the rays are too strong for her weak eye, she covers it up, and despite all her assumed arts, she still remains in darkness and on a slippery ground, close by the River of Time which carries her and her arts along into the Sea of Oblivion.[21]

Krimmel pictorialized these concepts in an easily graspable manner and vaguely based his figures on the classical statues in the academy's collection of plaster casts and on some of his life sketches, but his ineptitude in delineating anatomy is unmistakable.

To remedy his artistic deficiencies, Krimmel had already begun studying at the academy. A seated Venus and *Venus of the Bath*, both of which were part of the academy's collection of plaster casts, were among the first models he drew early in 1811 (figs. 6, 7). He also copied prints of classical nudes (fig. 8) and oil paintings, including one that was exhibited in 1811 (figs. 9, 10).[22]

20. Dunlap, *History*, 2:392.

21. *Evangelisches Magazin unter der Aufsicht der Deutsch-Evangelisch-Lutherischen Synode* 1, no. 2 (January–March 1812), verso of title page (translation by the author).

22. Some plaster casts and busts were purchased in Paris. Others were a gift of Joseph Allen Smith of South Carolina who thought that his collection of pictures and plaster casts of classical sculpture executed in Italy would be appreciated in Philadelphia. Among these were *Dying Gladiator, Meleager, Venus of the Capitol,* and *Venus of the Bath*; Smith also gave a large number of engravings and a collection of medals, guns, and intaglios. Robert Fulton and P. G. Lechleitner deposited "a number of paintings" at the academy; Oliver Oldschool, "Pennsylvania Academy of the Fine Arts," *Port Folio*, n.s., 1, no. 6 (June 1809): 461–62. Many casts were destroyed in a fire in 1845; see *In This Academy: The Pennsylvania Academy of the Fine Arts, 1805–1976* (Philadelphia, 1976), pp. 17–18, 25. William Kneass's engraving of Blake's *Hercules and Apollo* appeared in Abraham Rees, *Cyclopaedia; or, Universal Dictionary of Arts, Science, and Literature* (Philadelphia, 1810–24). For Robert Fulton's role in acquisitions of art, see *In This Academy*, pp. 18–19; for Fulton's loan of the Molinari painting to the Pennsylvania Academy, see *American Daily Advertiser*, November 27, 1807, p. 3; it is listed as by an unknown artist. For Molinari see Thieme and Becker, *Allgemeines Lexikon*, 25:165. I thank Naeve (*Krimmel*, pp. 126, 127, 131–32, 135) for pointing out the sources for the Hercules and Adam and Eve sketches.

FIGURE 1
Rooftops and trees, 1810. Watercolor, ink inscription. Sketchbook 1, leaf 1 recto. Krimmel's earliest dated sketch. The text translates "Thursday, May 10, 1810. Overcast with light rain in the evening, clear in the morning."

FIGURE 2
Poplars, ca. 1810. Watercolor. Sketchbook 1, leaf 2 recto.

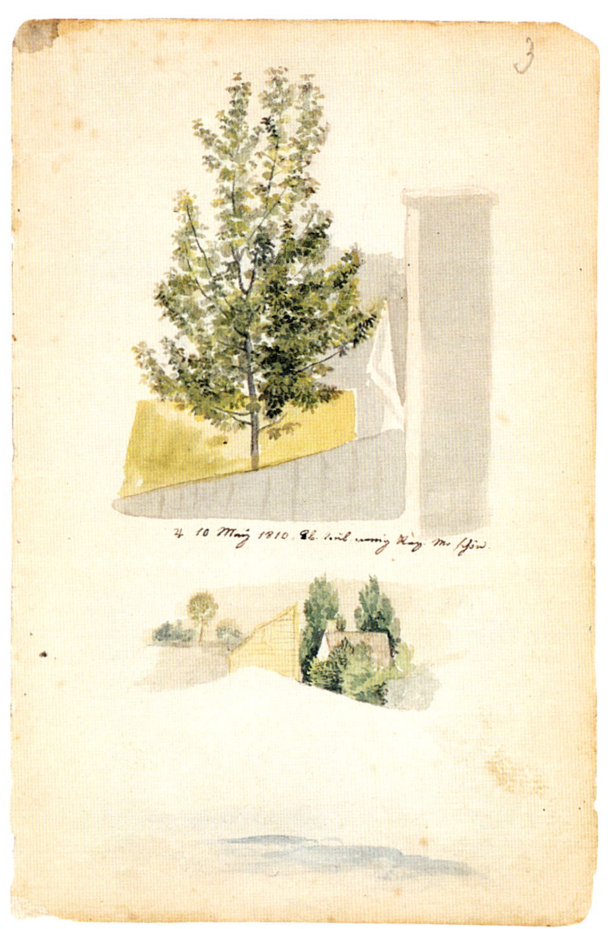

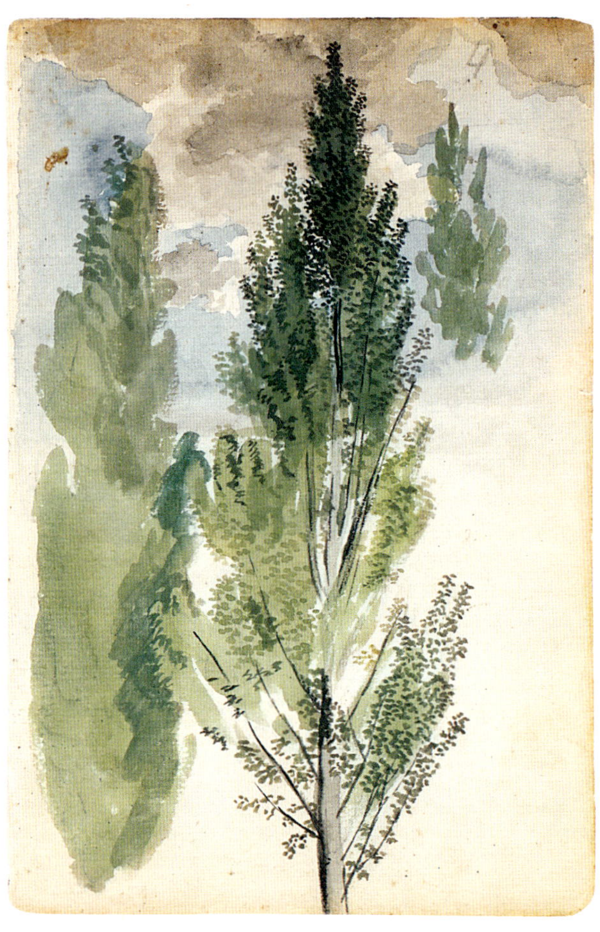

FIGURE 3

Portrait of child, ca. 1810. Pencil. Sketchbook 1, leaf 4 recto. In this early effort, the painter sought to capture the psyche of the sitter by giving attention to the expression of the eyes and mouth; the smock is only roughly sketched, and the delineation of the arms and legs is anatomically incorrect.

FIGURE 4

Sketch of young woman, ca. 1812. Pencil. Sketchbook 1, leaf 18 recto. The color notes in German at the bottom of the page suggest this sketch was the basis for a finished watercolor or oil portrait.

FIGURE 5

John Lewis Krimmel, artist, and William Kneass, engraver, allegorical print, Evangelisches Magazin *1, no. 2 (January–March 1812), frontis. Krimmel's drawing dates early or mid 1811. (Photo, American Antiquarian Society, Worcester, Mass.) The accompanying verse translated from the German reads:*

Faith in the Word that generates Love and Hope
Is refreshed by the eternal light of the sun.
The Wisdom of this World, inclined to vanity,
Covers her proud face before this radiance.
The moon—but dear reader, look at the picture more closely,
You still will find much more than can be said here.

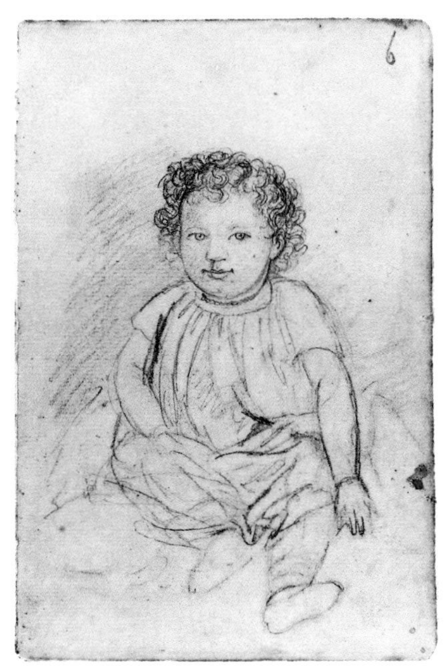

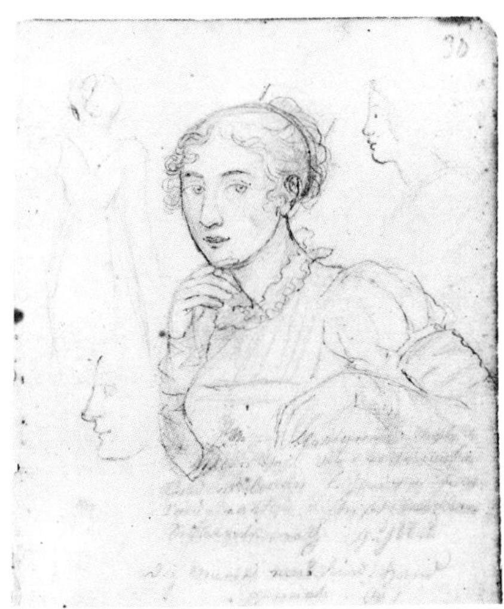

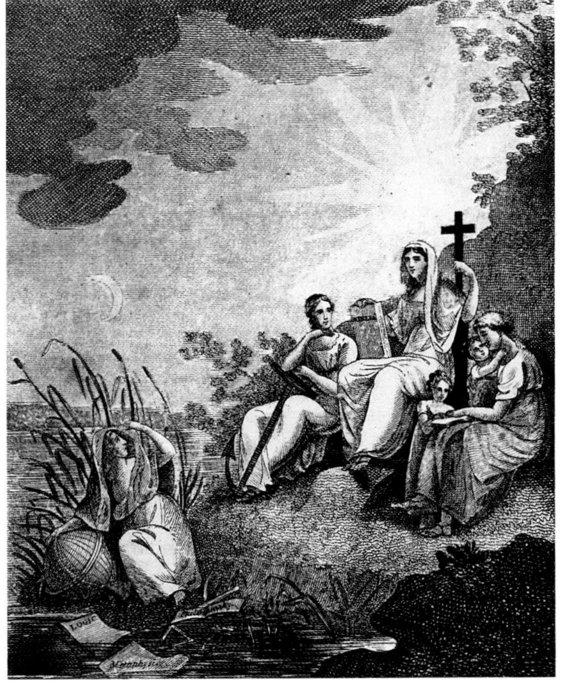

FIGURE 6
Study of seated Venus, January 1811. Pencil. Sketchbook 1, leaf 17 recto.

FIGURE 7
Study of Venus of the Bath, *Thursday, January 3, 1811. Ink tracings and ink wash over pencil. Sketchbook 1, leaf 16 recto. Probably Krimmel's first finished drawing of a classical nude. The cast was acquired by the academy in 1806.*

FIGURE 8
Study of Hercules, 1811 or 1812. After William Blake's, Hercules and Apollo Contending for the Tripod from the Villa Albani. *Pencil. Sketchbook 1, leaf 9 recto. Krimmel subsequently adopted contrapposto to convey energetic motion in his genre scenes.*

FIGURE 9
Study of Adam and Eve, *1811 or 1812. After Antonio Molinari,* Adam and Eve. *Pencil with wash. Sketchbook 1, leaf 18 verso. Krimmel delineated the forms and poses of the figures and only indicated the serpent and the fruit. Pencil lines are partially retraced, and the ink wash makes the figures stand out like a bas-relief.*

FIGURE 10
Antonio Molinari, Adam and Eve, *ca. 1690. Oil on canvas; 49 ½ x 59 in. (Ball State University Museum of Art, Muncie, Ind., museum purchase with funds provided by the Joseph Johnson Charitable Trust and Richard and Dorothy Burkhardt.)*

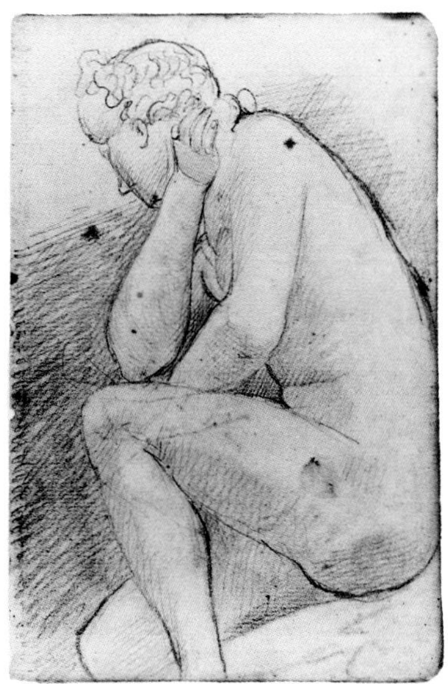

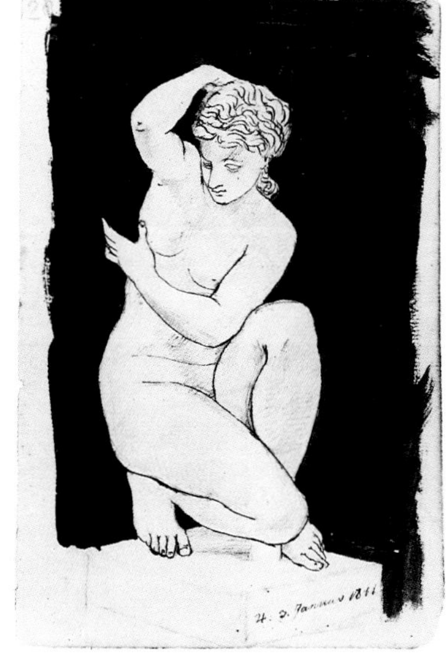

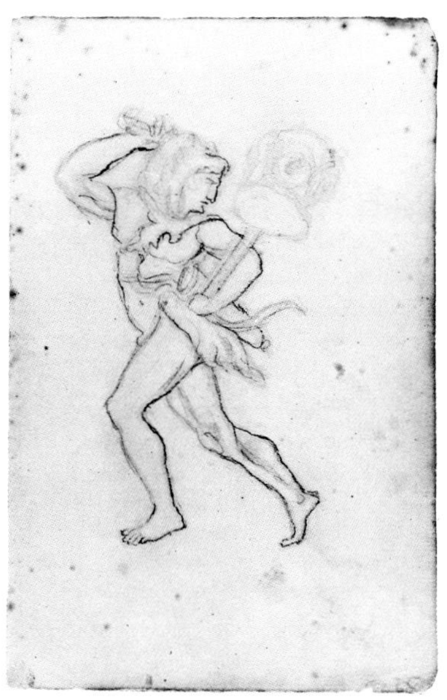

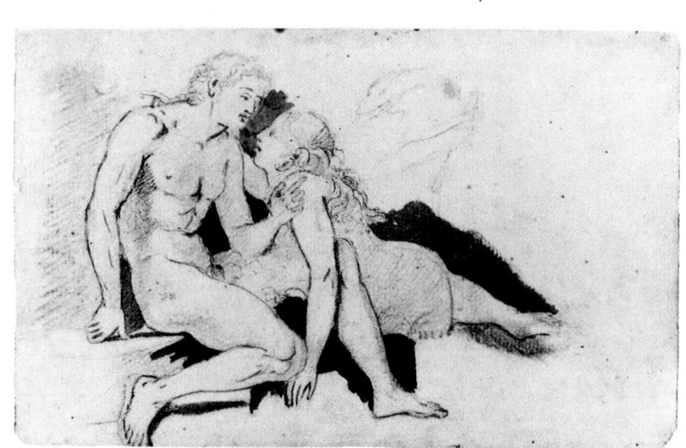

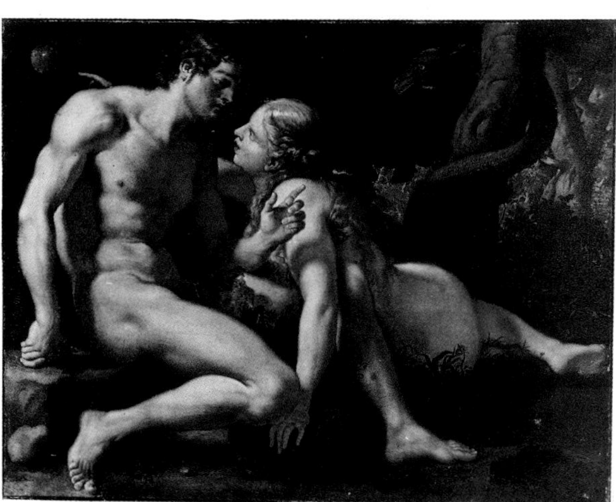

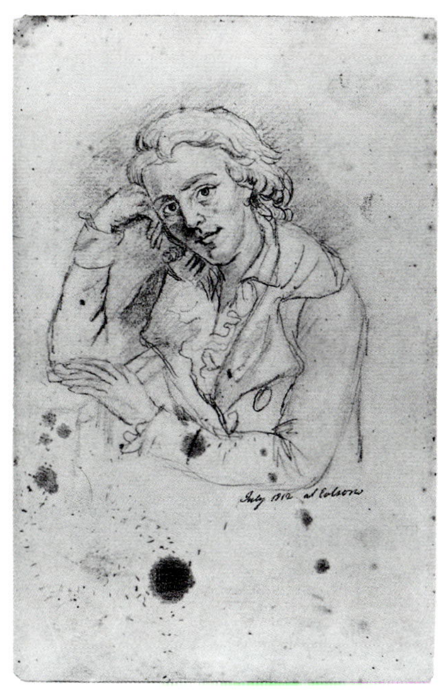

FIGURE 11
Portrait of young man, July 1812. Pencil. Sketchbook 1, leaf 7 verso. The flowing design, the inclined head, and the position of the arms relate to the poses of the Vesalius skeletons; the arms and hands are correctly and gracefully defined.

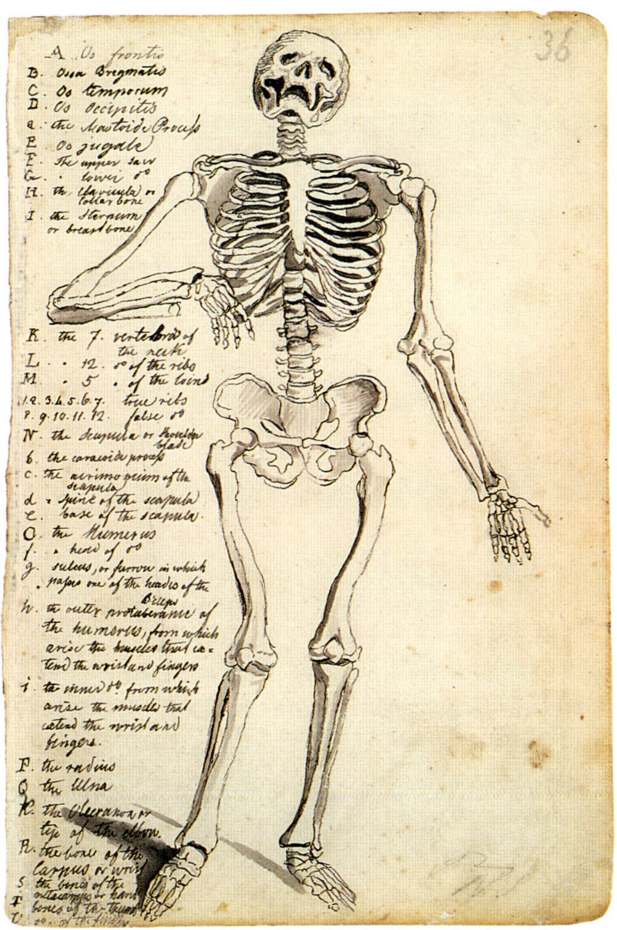

FIGURE 12
Human skeleton, front view, mid 1812. After Vesalius. Wash over pencil. Sketchbook 1, leaf 21 verso.

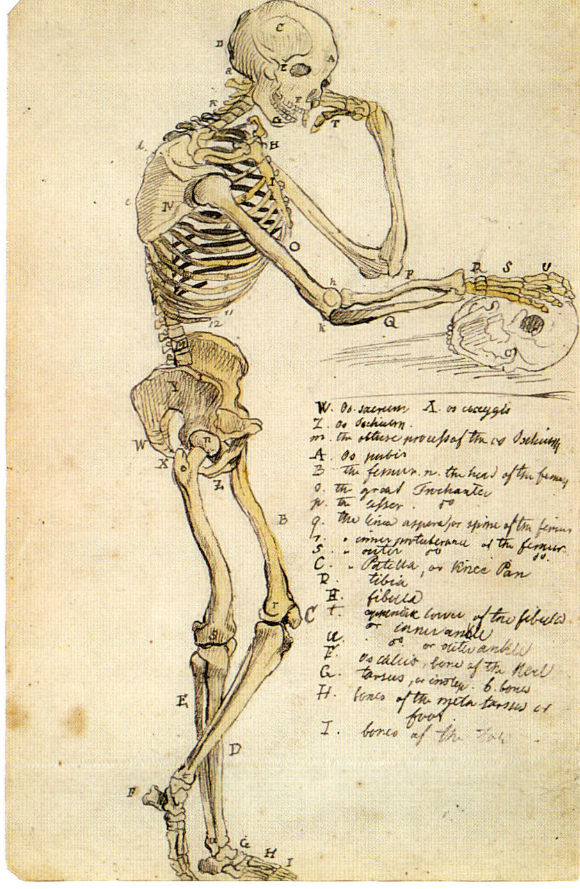

FIGURE 13
Human skeleton, side view, mid 1812. After Vesalius. Ink with wash over pencil. Sketchbook 1, leaf 22 recto.

He also enrolled in the first anatomy classes offered at the academy, which were taught by Dr. Chapman beginning in May 1812. By July 1812 his understanding of anatomy had improved considerably (fig. 11; an example of his earlier handling of anatomy is fig. 3). His copies of well-known engravings by Andreas Vesalius, a sixteenth-century Flemish artist and professor of anatomy whose studies of the human body served as standard teaching material at every art academy in Europe and America, are probably the result of these classes (figs. 12, 13).[23]

If quantity of drawings is an accurate index, Krimmel's interest increased when he began taking classes that used live models. These classes were taught by John S. Dorsey, professor of anatomy, beginning in January 1813. The fifteen students who enrolled in this initial course included Thomas Birch and Charles Bird King. The fee was $8 per quarter, and classes were held twice weekly for two hours in the evening. In addition to drawing the live model, students also copied plaster casts, paintings, and medals in the academy's collection. The model was male, and the society had advertised for one who was "athletic, well proportioned, with no bodily defect, steady, and temperate." Krimmel's drawings indicate that the model had at least the first three qualities; they also suggest that the method of instruction was quite similar to that used in European academies. Initial sessions stressed mastering the depiction of parts of the body. Thus in one class students concentrated on drawing the left leg and foot; in another session they focused on the upper torso, and in still others on the arms, hands, and face (figs. 14, 15). What Krimmel learned in this course probably prompted him to assemble a "Port folio of studies from the human body drawn from life" that he kept in his studio, probably as a reference tool, for the rest of his career.[24]

Instruction in painting proved harder to obtain. Neither the Pennsylvania Academy nor the Society of Artists had taken steps to initiate such classes, and the former provided only a few paintings from which students might make copies in an effort to teach themselves color and composition. Yet this situation was not unusual. Even in Europe, the emphasis in artistic training remained completely on drawing—whether from casts or from life. The academy in Copenhagen was the first to introduce a painting class in 1816. The Royal Academy in London also added a school of painting in 1816, and in it students copied old masters, a system that London's British Institution had used for several years. To acquire professional instruction in oil painting a student had to study with an artist. Fortunately for Krimmel, Philadelphia had several painters who were willing to share their methods with those who wanted to learn. They allowed themselves to be observed while painting and generously explained their working processes step by step, as Charles Robert Leslie later recalled: "[Thomas Sully] began a copy of a picture in my presence, and then put his palette and brushes into my hand, telling me to proceed in the same way with a copy of my own. The next day he carried his work further, and I again followed him, and so on, until the copies were both finished; thus explaining to me at once the processes of scumbling, glazing, etc."[25]

Whether Krimmel received similar instruction from Sully is unrecorded. Some small portraits in Krimmel's early sketchbooks are much like Sully's work in design, and a double portrait of a woman with a child in sketchbook 1 (fig. 16) is an exact copy of a Sully painting that was exhibited at the academy in May 1812. In general Sully possessed a broader, more loosely

23. *In This Academy*, p. 59. For self-instruction, especially in drawing hands and feet Krimmel could have used *Elements of Drawing Illustrated by Eleven Elegant Copper Plates* (New York: John Low, 1804) because his earliest hand drawings show the same gestures as the examples in that book. Andreas Vesalius came from a family of physicians and studied medicine at the University of Louvain and Montpelier. His plates of the human body, based on direct observations while serving as professor of anatomy at University of Padua, were prized for their artistic quality and anatomical accuracy. His first book, *De humani corporis fabrica*, was published in Basel in 1543.

24. *Poulson's American Daily Advertiser*, January 8, 1813; Krimmel estate sale, *Poulson's American Daily Advertiser*, August 14, 1821; Nygren, "Art Instruction," pp. 64–70; Rembrandt Peale, "Communication from Council of Academicians," January 13, 1813, and "Draft [to] Mr. Voorhes April 30, 1813, paid him $10.00 for serving as model for the class for 10 nights," Minutes of the Society of Artists, January 6, February 24, 1813, Peale Papers, microfiche 6:A-2. Specific reference to the life class is in Krimmel to Birch, [n.d. but clearly 1812 or 1813], Charles Henry Hart Autograph Collection (AAA, microfilm); Albert Boime, *The Academy and French Painting in the Nineteenth Century* (London: Phaidon Publishers, 1971), pp. 3–16, esp. p. 4: drawing was seen as "the theoretical element uniting all the branches of art." By controlling instruction in drawing, the artists at each academy thus controlled style.

25. Charles Robert Leslie, *Autobiographical Recollections*, ed. Tom Taylor, 2 vols. (Boston: Ticknor and Fields, 1860), 1:27; Sully probably used the same technique with other students. Stebbins, *American Master Drawings*, p. 83; William T. Whitley, *Art in England*, 1800–1820, vol. 1 (New York: Macmillan Co., 1928), chap. 17. See also Nygren, "Art Instruction," p. 89.

FIGURE 14
Study of man's leg, torso with arm, 1812/13. Ink and wash, pencil and wash. Sketchbook 1, leaf 20 recto.

FIGURE 15
Studies of hand and arm movements, 1812/13. Pencil. Sketchbook 1, leaf 19 verso. This is one of several drawings in sketchbook 1 to which Krimmel often referred as he delineated gestures in genre scenes.

FIGURE 16
Woman and child, 1812 or 1813. After Thomas Sully. Pencil. Sketchbook 1, leaf 17 verso. Krimmel elongated and chose not to copy the pattern of the lace.

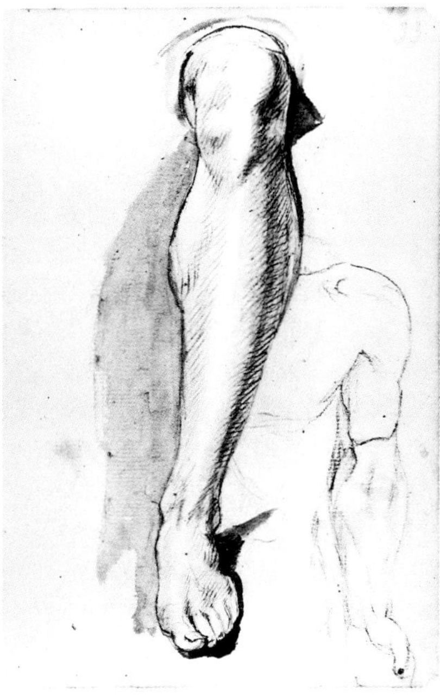

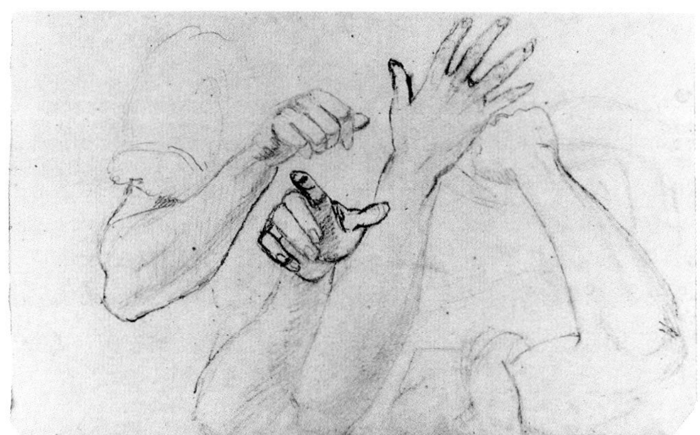

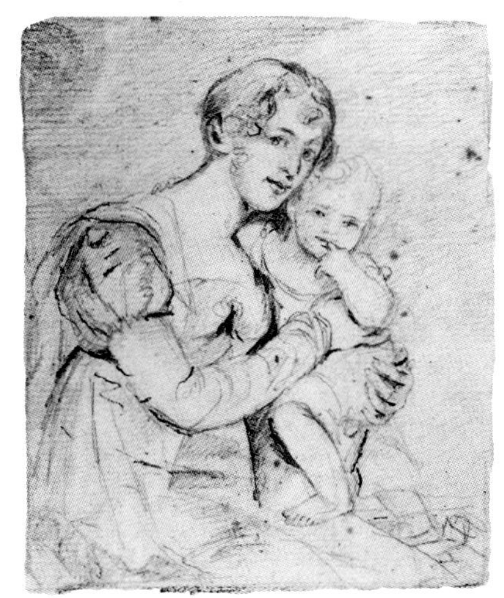

brushed style that was more coloristic and more idealizing in the rendition of the face than Krimmel, who applied his colors with finer brushes and worked on a painstakingly small scale. Although both artists' delineation of anatomy were at times faulty, Sully's portraits are designed with drama and verve, even with a theatrical flair.[26]

A sense of Krimmel's determined efforts to become an accomplished painter can be gained from the pictures that he entered in the first two annual exhibitions held at the academy and from his first sketchbook drawings. For the exhibition that opened May 6, 1811, only a year after Krimmel started out as an artist, he had four paintings accepted. Three are only known through the descriptions in the catalogue, from a general understanding of the topics, and from the artist's decision to list himself in the exhibition as a "fancy painter," a term designating an artist who painted images of his own conception. *Celadon and Amelia* was inspired by an episode in "Summer," one of four sections of James Thomson's immensely popular poetic series *Seasons* about the affection and tragic end of two young lovers. *Aurora* probably depicted the goddess of Dawn, possibly as a classical nude, in which case Krimmel may have been making direct use of his recent studies of antique sculpture. According to the catalogue, the third painting, *Raspberry Girls of the Alps of Wirtemberg*, was a nostalgic homage to his homeland and depicted two girls who had lost themselves in the woods and were rescued by a boy. The fourth image, *Pepper-Pot: A Scene in the Philadelphia Market*, was a contemporary scene, the "first effort of this kind which attracted public attention to the young stranger" (fig. 17), and was based on what historian Dunlap termed "an article of food known no where else in the United States but in Philadelphia"—a thick, spicy soup made of vegetables and tripe that was eaten in the streets but not served in the private homes of respectable citizens.[27]

Krimmel may have been the first Philadelphia painter to give this common scene the status of a painting, but he was not the first artist to be drawn to the subject. A woodcut entitled *Pepper Pot, Smoking Hot* had appeared in 1810 as one of several illustrations for *The Cries of Philadelphia*, a primer describing street vendors and their cries, and the accompanying text provided details about the vendor, her product, and her customers: "Strangers who visit the city cannot but be amused with the cries of the numerous black women who sit in the market house and at the corners, selling a soup which they call pepperpot. It is made chiefly of tripe, ox-feet and other cheap animal substances, with a great portion of spice. It is sold very cheap, so that a hungry man may get a hearty meal for a few cents. . . . excepting to weak stomachs, it is a very pleasant feast."[28]

The woodcut depicts a heavyset black woman pouring soup from a pitcher and closely surrounded by five customers all of whom are black. Standing further off, a white boy looks longingly at the pepper pot. The clothes worn by most of the people including the vendor give the impression that this is a winter scene. The setting is unspecific in composition and figure characterizations, and there are no parallels between the woodcut and Krimmel's painting. In the painting, only the pepper pot woman is black and the event takes place within the Philadelphia market house. The season is summer, and the barefoot pepper pot woman is young and slender and about to ladle a bowl of her soup.

Some of Krimmel's stock figures appear for the first time in this painting, such as an old man with a balding pate and long white hair and a strong young man with curly hair and long sideburns, types that will reappear in

26. *Second Annual Exhibition* . . . (1812); Sully's portrait remained in private hands and unknown to scholars until very recently when it came into the possession of PAFA. The identification of Krimmel's sketch as a copy of the Sully painting was graciously made by Frank Goodyear, director of the academy. Sully's work has been most recently discussed in Monroe H. Fabian, *Mr. Sully, Portrait Painter: The Works of Thomas Sully (1783–1872)* (Washington, D.C.: Smithsonian Institution Press, 1983), p. 14; Beatrice B. Garvan, Federal Philadelphia, 1785–1825: *The Athens of the Western World* (Philadelphia: Philadelphia Museum of Art, 1987), pp. 30–31.

27. Dunlap, *History*, 2:392. In 1788 Joshua Reynolds labeled Thomas Gainsborough's pictures of beggar children in arcadian settings "fancy pictures." The term subsequently was more generally applied to pictures that fell between portraiture and genre art, especially rural scenes in which the subjects, generally peasants, behave as if in a studio rather than the country; see Harold Osborne, ed., *The Oxford Companion of Art* (Oxford: Clarendon Press, 1975), p. 401; *First Annual Exhibition* . . . (1811), p. 6; James Thomson, *The Seasons*, issued in four parts between 1726 and 1730. The poem remained popular for a century. Alexander Lawson issued engravings of scenes from it soon after settling in Philadelphia in 1794; see Mantle Fielding, *American Engravers upon Copper and Steel* (Philadelphia: Burt Franklin, 1917), p. 177.

28. *The Cries of Philadelphia* (Philadelphia: Johnson and Warner, 1810), p. 15. With the exception of the pepper pot image, the other woodcuts also appeared in *The Cries of New York* (1808), and *The Cries of London* (ca. 1800); inspired in turn by illustrations in Pierce Tempest's *Cries of the City of London* [ca. 1688]. Stanley Fisher, *Dictionary of Watercolor Painters, 1750–1900* (London: W. Foulsam, 1972), p. 11.

FIGURE 17
John Lewis Krimmel, Pepper-Pot: A Scene in the Philadelphia Market, *1811. Oil on canvas; 19½ x 15½ in. (Sumpter Priddy III.)*

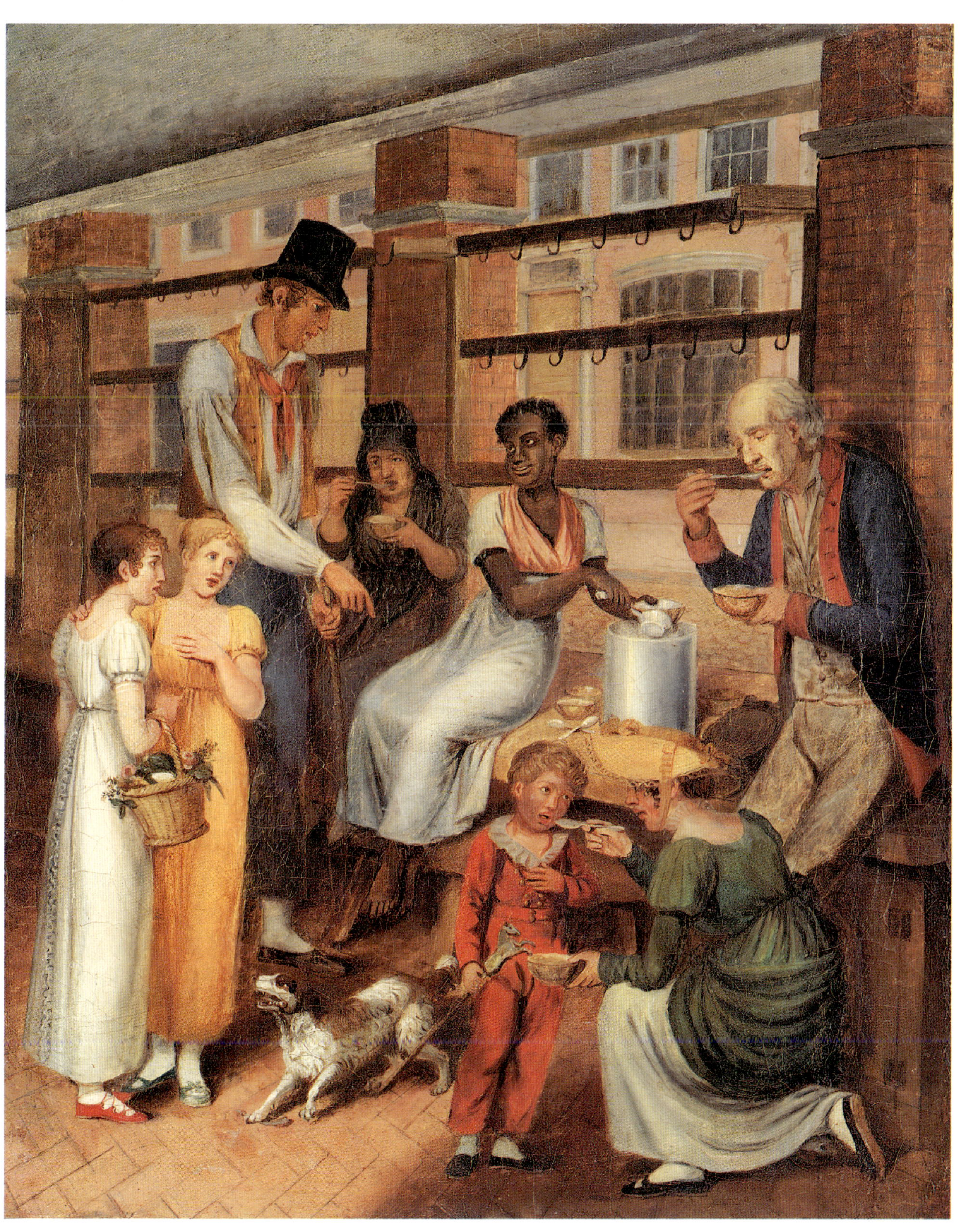

different roles in his later genre scenes. The English springer spaniel carrying a bone in his mouth is the first example of what was to become a Krimmel trademark. In nearly all of his subsequent genre scenes, certainly in all of his known oil paintings, the artist included at least one animal (most often a dog) and sometimes two or three. In *Pepper-Pot* the dog plays the role of a compositional tie between the foreground figures and the midground, and it is the only believably moving, figurative element among the less skillfully delineated figures, which seem frozen in their particular poses.

Compared with the other figures, the extraordinarily tall man is completely out of proportion, and the head of the pepper pot woman seems not to harmonize with her body. The posture of the mother is based on Krimmel's January 1811 study of Venus (see fig. 7), which suggests the pepper pot painting was painted between January and May when the exhibition opened. That Krimmel's ability to design figures was still limited in 1811 also explains why he repeats the essentially same arm position in four of his eight figures and why he gives the blonde girl and the boy the same tilt of the head. Nevertheless, the artist succeeded in making an interesting picture by clearly differentiating the figures in their age, behavior, social class, and emotions. The picture's perspective is faulty—the floor seems to rise, and yet a measure of pictorial depth is created through the grouping of the figures and the strong architectural elements, regardless of their imperfect rendition. At this early stage Krimmel demonstrates with the brick pillar on the right his intent to stabilize the design by means of a single vertical component that extends the full height of the picture.

Genre scenes such as this had long been a very popular branch of painting, particularly in the countries north of the Alps. Their origins lay in details of religious paintings; but since the 1560s, images featuring scenes of everyday life had been an independent specialty. Among the best known were Pieter Brueghel the Elder's peasant scenes, many of which had an underlying allegorical or moral meaning. During the 1600s, genre painting flourished in the southern and northern Netherlands. Flemish painters, foremost among them Adriaen Brouwer and David Teniers the Younger, depicted raucous peasant dances and dingily lit tavern scenes that emphasized the "low life," while their Dutch contemporaries, Jan Vermeer, Gerard Terborch, and Pieter de Hooch, painted scenes that featured the bourgeoisie in light-filled, rationally constructed interiors, and Jan Steen portrayed people of all social levels in scenes richly animated with humor and anecdotes. After this golden age, the quality of genre painting declined as artists contented themselves with repeating established motifs. Nonetheless their pictures helped keep alive the influence of Dutch and Flemish genre scenes in other countries. In the 1730s William Hogarth, inspired by French and other models, gave genre depiction a powerful new application as he began satirizing contemporary English life. English artists who followed Hogarth either strongly emphasized the ridiculous in their genre representations, as did Thomas Rowlandson and George Cruikshank, or tempered it with a sentimental naturalism, as did Francis Wheatley and George Morland. In the second half of the eighteenth century Jean Baptiste Greuze became the master of sentimental bourgeois scenes in France and Daniel Chodowiecki produced more than two thousand engravings of scenes of everyday life in Germany.

Until 1811 most genre art in America had been limited to shop signs and banners. Charles Willson Peale's 1787 *Accident on Lombard Street*, an image of a young woman who has dropped a pie as she rushes along, was planned as the first of a series of etchings with which Peale hoped to win a share of the emerging printmaking and printselling business. The print did not sell well so Peale abandoned the project. In 1806 Peale made a second foray into genre art with *Exhumation of the Mastodon* (1806–8), which depicted a particular event, a specific location, and even more readily recognizable figures. Although the image was better received than *Accident*, Peale decided against pursuing genre painting at that point in his career.[29]

In 1800 William Russell Birch, a miniaturist and engraver from England, and his son Thomas had published *Views of Philadelphia*, a series of topographical engravings featuring the important streets and most impressive buildings of the city. Many had included groups of people but merely as staffage to give scale and animation to the architecture. Only one of the images was a genre scene: *High Street from the Country Marketplace Philadelphia with the Procession in Commemoration of the Death of General George Washington, December 26, 1799*.

Perhaps more so than their European counterparts, American artists believed that "professional artists" limited their canvases to portraiture, history painting, and landscapes. So while they often turned to English and Netherlandish conventions for their portraits, landscapes, and still lifes, Americans ignored the genre tradition.[30]

Given the lack of a local genre tradition upon which to draw Krimmel turned to recently published engravings based on English art, including images of David Wilkie's popular paintings and Hogarth's engravings. These he supplemented with Benjamin West's pictures, illustrations in the *Port Folio* (the locally published cultural journal), and the few prints by contemporary Philadelphia artists to learn how to excerpt pictorial ideas for his own compositions of American life. With *Tending the Rabbit Hutch* (fig. 18) he chose an unpretentious contemporary scene, this time of rural life—as subject for a painting. It shows a young family in the yard of their farmstead, parents and children participating in the same chore. As in *Pepper-Pot* four figures hold their left arms at an almost identical angle; their movements seem forced. The father, who is reaching inside the hutch, is in a sitting pose derived from Krimmel's sketch of a seated Venus (see fig. 6). His shirt resembles that worn by the tall man in *Pepper-Pot*. The peculiar tilt of his head suggests a tie to David Wilkie's genre scene *The Jew's Harp*, painted in 1809 and engraved by John Burnet in the same year (see fig. 106), as does the figure of the girl, the large pitcher, and the upright barrel. Because the figures are clearly still at a beginner's level, the scene is of the artist's own conception, but the setting, which shows such an advanced awareness of the principles of good design, suggests that Krimmel was working from a print—possibly a Dutch or Flemish one, given the lines of the thatched roof, the type of dovecote, and the glimpse into a wooded landscape.[31] Specific elements demonstrate that the attention to design is well thought out (much better than Krimmel's own design for the allegorical image for *Evangelisches Magazin*; see fig. 5). The lower right portion of the composition is visually strung together through a number of still-life elements that seem to demonstrate a growing knowledge of perspective and geometry. The bucket and wooden tubs are realistically drawn and positioned so that their volumetric shapes visually connect with the rain barrel. The diagonal lines of the wheelbarrow, the bundle of faggots, and the spade intersect with one another in a manner

29. Edgar P. Richardson, Brooke Hindle, Lillian B. Miller, *Charles Willson Peale and His World* (New York: Harry N. Abrams, 1983), p. 79; Sellers, Peale, chap. 22.

30. Hermann Warner Williams, Jr., *Mirror to the American Past: A Survey of American Genre Painting, 1750–1900* (Greenwich, Conn.: New York Graphic Society, 1973), pp. 40, 26, 31.

31. Christie's evaluated the painting in 1986 but apparently did not sell it; Jenny Long to A. Harding, March 25, 1986; Debra Neel to A. Harding, January 28, 1991. A similar setting is in Jacques de Gheyn's *Landscape with Dilapidated Farm House* (1603); see Peter C. Sutton, *Masters of Seventeenth-Century Dutch Landscape Painting* (Boston: Museum of Fine Arts, Boston, 1987), p. 86.

FIGURE 18
John Lewis Krimmel, Tending the Rabbit Hutch, *Philadelphia, 1811/12. Oil on canvas; 11¾ x 15½ in. (Photo, Christie, Manson, and Woods, Intl., New York.) Signed "J. L. Krimmel," lower right corner.*

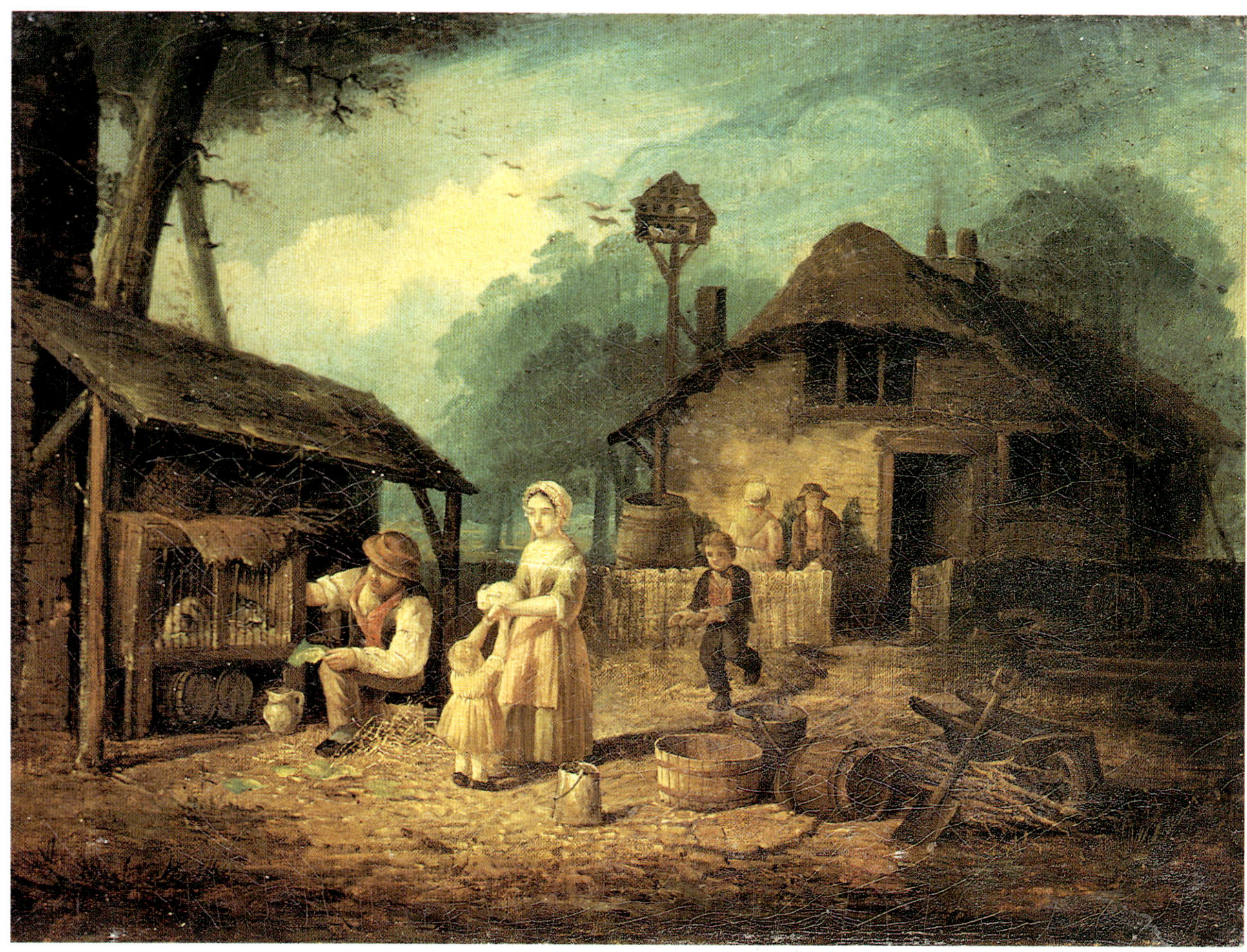

FIGURE 19
John Lewis Krimmel, View of Centre Square on the Fourth of July *(now called* Fourth of July in Center Square*), Philadelphia, 1811/12. Oil on canvas; 23 x 28½ in. (The Pennsylvania Academy of the Fine Arts, Philadelphia, Pennsylvania Academy purchase from the estate of Paul Beck, Jr.)*

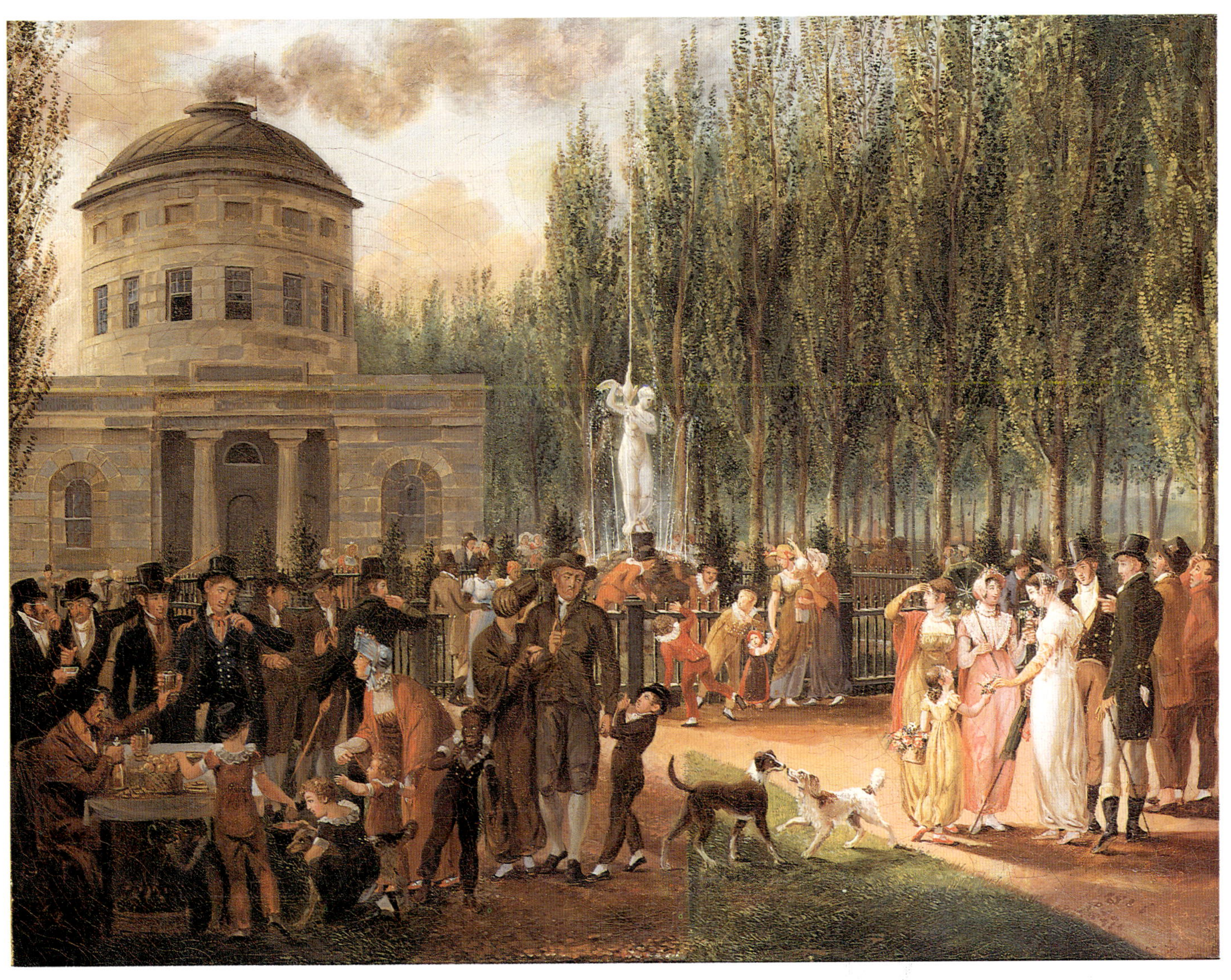

that harmonizes with the outlines of the cottage roof. The high brick chimney on the left is a use of the same composition-steadying device Krimmel had introduced in *Pepper-Pot*; however, here he has employed a horizontal format instead of an upright one.

Krimmel's distinctive style, one that emphasizes figural composition rather than architecture or picturesque location, and one that has a strong story-telling quality, is exemplified in a painting of a scene at the waterworks in Philadelphia's center square, the first of his genre scenes to receive a formal review. The site's handsome new building, a pumphouse designed in 1799 by Benjamin Henry Latrobe, had attracted other artists, but the celebrations held there had not. In *View of Centre Square on the Fourth of July* Krimmel uses the building as background and makes the activities of the people gathered for the holiday the subject (fig. 19). He first displayed the painting at the academy in May 1812, at the second annual exhibition of the Society of Artists, along with *The Accident* and *The Contrast*, which seem to have been watercolors of smaller dimensions, given that they attracted less attention.[32]

View of Centre Square on the Fourth of July is carefully composed with neoclassical precepts: balance, repetition of shapes, and symmetry. The sixty-two–foot tall pumphouse looms importantly, and its strong horizontals are balanced by the verticals of the poplars on the right. The shape of the building's drum is consciously echoed in the foreground emphasis that Krimmel gave to the numerous top hats. But overall Krimmel gave primacy to the behavior of the people. The figures extend across the fore- and middle grounds like a frieze; within this they are separated into small groups portraying different social strata. Wealthier celebrants are on the right, among them are a trio of women in a pose reminiscent of classical representations of the Three Graces. Behind them are the country bumpkins staring in amazement at the nude statue that is William Rush's *Water Nymph with Bittern.*[33] Close to the middle of the picture is a somberly dressed Quaker family. The wife clings to her husband's arm as she casts a curious, almost furtive glance across his shoulder at the fountain. The husband is giving stern instructions to their son, as if inveighing against joining the boys who are clambering over the fence encircling the sculpture. A small group of blacks, two women and a man, lean against the fence, their clothes and demeanor emphasizing the success that a limited number of the city's numerous blacks had achieved. The only visible commercial aspect is an old woman selling refreshments. Her customers are largely men, but a woman and three children have just arrived. The eldest child selects their peaches while his brother, in a posture derived from *Venus of the Bath*, holds out his hat as a basket to carry them and simultaneously holds their dog in check. Brought to eye-level with the underside of the table, he gapes with surprise at the lad crouched there, guzzling cider or beer from the bottle in his hand; a second boy withdraws in amusement.[34]

The scene is lively and natural, but individual figures are awkward. Elongated proportions—relatively long bodies and small heads—are a reflection of the prevailing neoclassical style, as are the location of Rush's statue at the visual axis of the image and the balanced positioning of the crowd, yet parts of their bodies are unsuccessfully executed and remain unintegrated. The young girl shown from the back relates to the girl with the basket in *Pepper-Pot* and—to a lesser degree—the girl in *Tending the Rabbit Hutch.* The portrayal of light, the view of the building, the glimpse into the woods, and the definition of the sky and the picture space are also similar to those elements in

32. Frederic Trautmann, "Pennsylvania Through a German's Eyes: The Travels of Ludwig Gall, 1819–1820," *Pennsylvania Magazine of History and Biography* 105, no. 1 (January 1981): 39, 42–43, provides descriptions of the city and its public spaces; an engraving of the waterworks was published in the July 1812 *Port Folio* two months after Krimmel's painting was exhibited but is generally thought to have been issued in 1810, so it may have helped Krimmel construct the background of his painting. Over the years the title of Krimmel's painting has been variously modified; see Anna Wells Rutledge, comp. and ed., *Cumulative Record of Exhibition Catalogues: The Pennsylvania Academy of the Fine Arts, 1807–1870; The Society of Artists, 1800–1814; The Artists' Fund Society, 1835–1845* (Philadelphia: American Philosophical Society, 1955), p. 117; Naeve, "Krimmel," pp. 59–62. Paul Beck, Jr., an eminent merchant, philanthropist, and warden of the port, lent the painting to the academy in 1843. He died in 1844, and the academy acquired the painting for $115 at the 1845 sale of his estate. The disposition of *The Accident* and *The Contrast* after 1811 remains unknown.

33. This life-size figure carved of pine and painted white was made by Rush in 1810. He copied the arm positions from *Venus of the Bath*, the same classical cast Krimmel sketched on January 3, 1811.

34. In 1810 Philadelphia had 9,656 blacks and a total population of 91,877. See Gary B. Nash, *Forging Freedom: The Formation of Philadelphia's Black Community, 1720–1840* (Cambridge: Harvard University Press, 1988), pp. 134–245, for an incisive discussion of the gains and losses made by Philadelphia's blacks in the opening decades of the century. For the moralizing aspects of this image, see William Oedel, "Review Essay: Krimmel at the Crossroads," *Winterthur Portfolio* 23, no. 4 (Winter 1988): 275–77; James Edward Fox, "Iconography of the Black in American Art, 1710–1900" (Ph.D. diss., University of North Carolina at Chapel Hill, 1979), p. 83.

Tending the Rabbit Hutch. The general stiffness of the figures is evidence of Krimmel's level of skill immediately prior to enrolling in Chapman's anatomy classes in May 1812, the same month Krimmel exhibited the Fourth of July picture at the academy.

While the Society of Artists' second exhibition at the academy was still on display, *Port Folio* reviewed a select number of the paintings, including *View of Centre Square.* Praising the painting's truthful reflection of life and the young artist's choice of such a well-known setting, the writer, G. M., gave it a fulsome treatment. "There are few people (if any) who visit the Academy, who are not perfectly acquainted with the scene of which this is so familiar and pleasing a representation. It is truly *Hogarthian,* and full of meaning, the figures are amply varied, and the character highly diversified. The artist has proved himself no common observer of the tragi-comical events of life that are daily and hourly passing before us, many of which leave impressions upon the *few* and pass unmarked by the *million.*" But, the author continued, the "picture is crude in its colouring, and deficient in effect, and disposition of light and shade. In fact, the artist is greatly wanting in the mechanical part of his art, which, by the by, he has yet had but little opportunity of acquiring, and which can only be gained by unremitting industry and application." Charles Willson Peale, after visiting the exhibition voiced "admiration for the genre paintings, so pointed, spirited and contemporary, of the young German John Lewis Krimmel."[35]

The painting also caught the eye of a young Russian naval attaché named Pavel Svinin, who was writing a book about the United States. He was so taken with the scene that he either made (or commissioned a local artist to make) a watercolor copy of it to take back to his homeland along with fifty-one other watercolors of mixed authorship, all of which have American motifs. Among these were fourteen by Krimmel.

The evidence in Svinin's portfolio of watercolors and Krimmel's sketchbooks suggests that the two men enjoyed a mutually satisfying business relationship (see appendix 3). Svinin needed pictures to illustrate his book about life in the United States, and Krimmel was eager to sell his pictures to earn a living as an artist. In all probability the two men began dealing with each other in May or June of 1812 and continued to do so until Svinin sailed for Europe a year later. Svinin, although opportunistic, was working in a well-established tradition. For the published account of his travels, he planned to use illustrations derived from various sources. Krimmel undoubtedly saw Svinin's desire to have a copy of his Fourth of July painting a flattering affirmation of his newly acquired professional status and his painterly talents. Svinin's offer to purchase other watercolors of Krimmel's American scenes must have been a much needed source of income for the aspiring artist.[36]

The images Krimmel sold to Svinin can be roughly dated by their level of competence, how they relate to the dated drawings in Krimmel's sketchbooks and to his early paintings. *Stage Coach Travel on the Trenton Diligence* may be the earliest of these watercolors; the figures are ineptly drawn and their parts are not naturally combined (fig. 20). The arm hanging outside the coach does not convincingly reach for the falling hat, is disproportionately long for the torso to which it is attached, and is less well done than is the arm in a sketch Krimmel dated August 1811 (fig. 21). Similarly the baby in the arms of the woman in the back seat is neither well drawn nor persuasively positioned. The leg of the passenger in the front seat is better drawn, and probably post-

35. G. M., "Review of the Second Annual Exhibition," *Port Folio* 8, no. 1 (July 1812): 24; Sellers, *Peale,* p. 384. The source of the assertion cited by Sellers is not apparent in the microfiche edition of the Peale Papers.

36. That Krimmel's brother laid claim against the estate in 1821 for loans made to John Lewis Krimmel in 1801, 1803, and 1805 only suggests that Krimmel, even in the 1810 to 1812 learning period, had found it possible to earn enough money to support himself. Dunlap (*History,* 2:392) also suggests he earned money by painting and selling miniatures.

FIGURE 20
John Lewis Krimmel, Stage Coach Travel on the Trenton Diligence, *1811. Watercolor on paper; 6⅞ x 9¾ in. (The Metropolitan Museum of Art, New York, Rogers Fund, 1942.)*

FIGURE 21
Man seated at table, August 15, 1811. Watercolor over pencil. Sketchbook 1, leaf 22 verso.

FIGURE 22
Men seated on ground, ca. 1811. Pencil and wash. Sketchbook 1, leaf 6 recto.

FIGURE 23
Horse in harness, September 17, 1811. Ink over pencil, wash. Sketchbook 1, leaf 23 recto.

FIGURE 24
Horse harnessed to wagon, 1811. Pencil and wash. Sketchbook 1, leaf 12 recto.

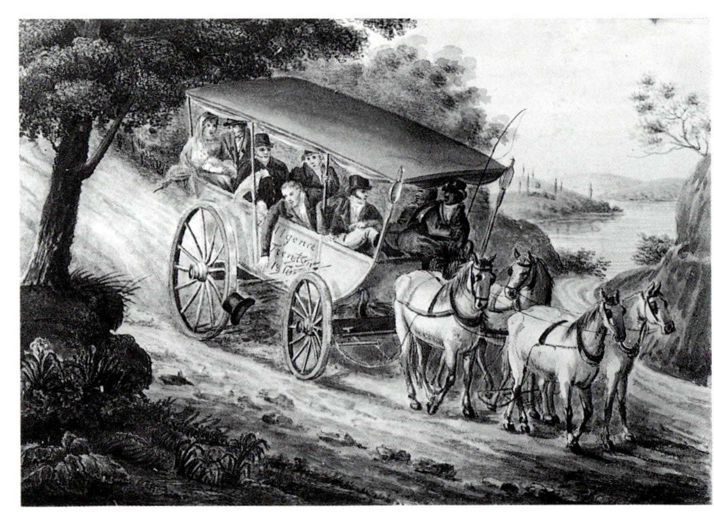

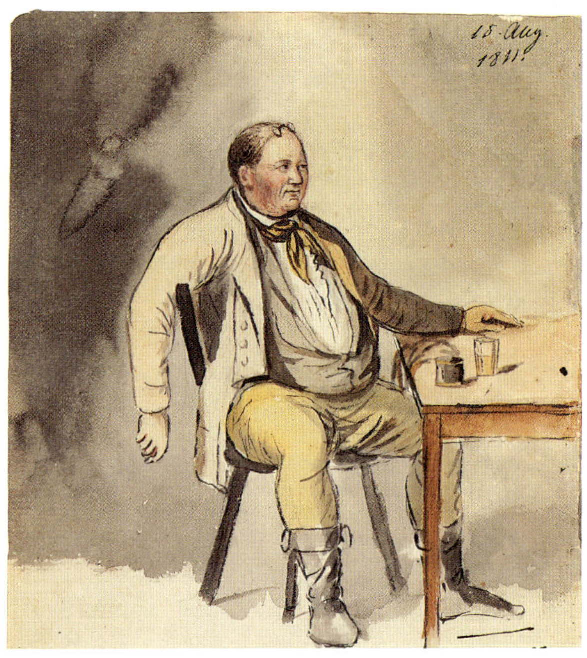

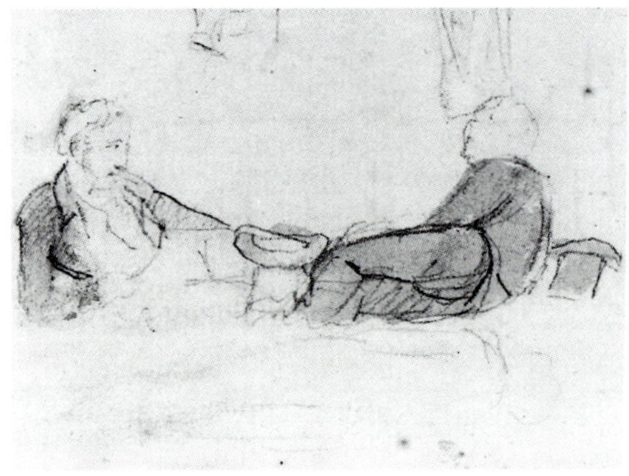

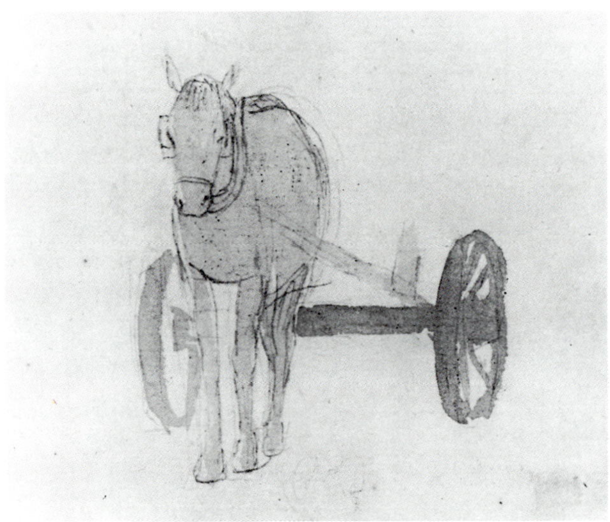

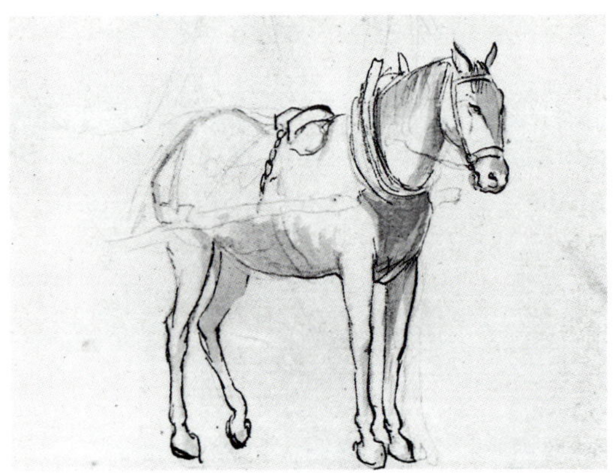

FIGURE 25
John Lewis Krimmel, Anabaptist Baptism, *ca. 1812. Watercolor on paper; 7 x 9¾ in. (The Metropolitan Museum of Art, New York, Rogers Fund, 1942.)*

FIGURE 26
Details of hats, foot gear, seated women, 1811/12. Wash and ink. Sketchbook 1, leaf 12 verso.

FIGURE 27
Man seated on chair, ca. 1812. Pencil. Sketchbook 1, leaf 15 recto.

FIGURE 28
Man seated on tipped chair, 1811 or 1812. Pencil and wash. Sketchbook 1, leaf 9 verso.

FIGURE 29
Man seated on box, 1811 or 1812. Pencil and wash. Sketchbook 1, leaf 9 verso.

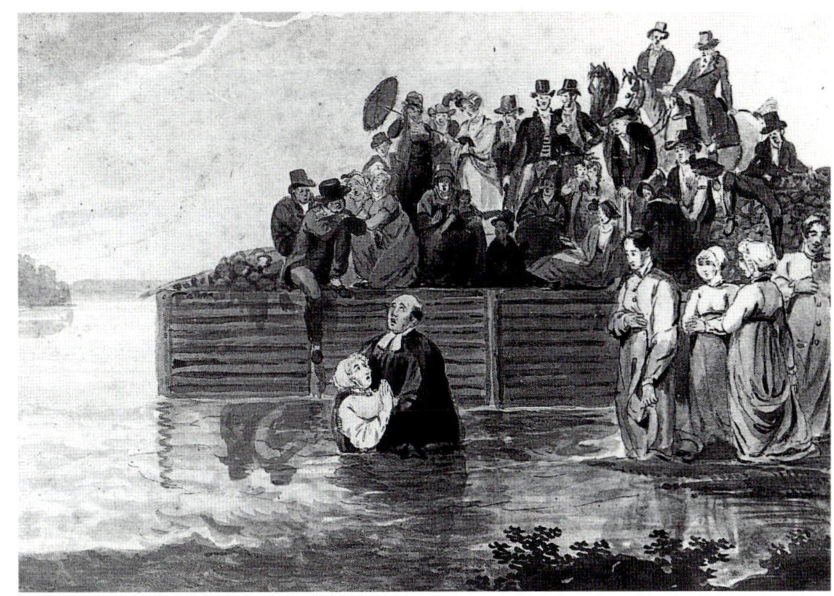

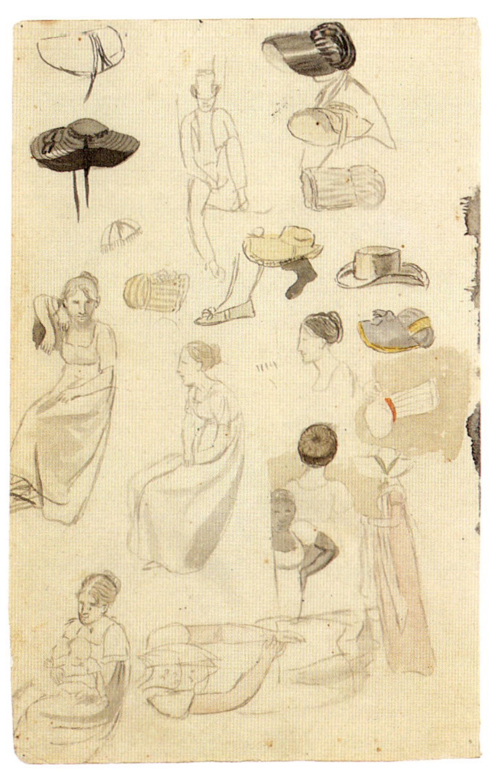

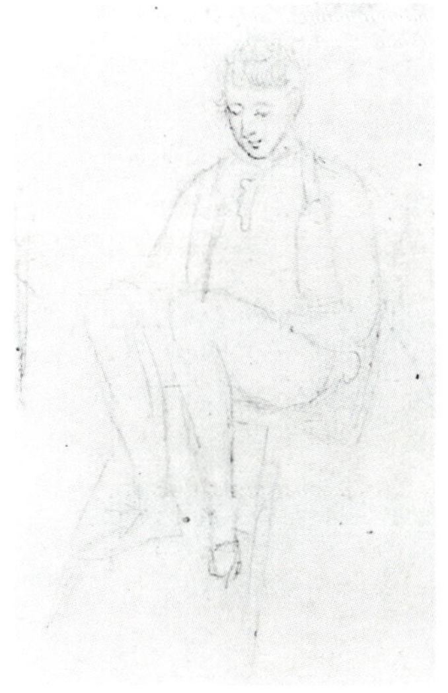

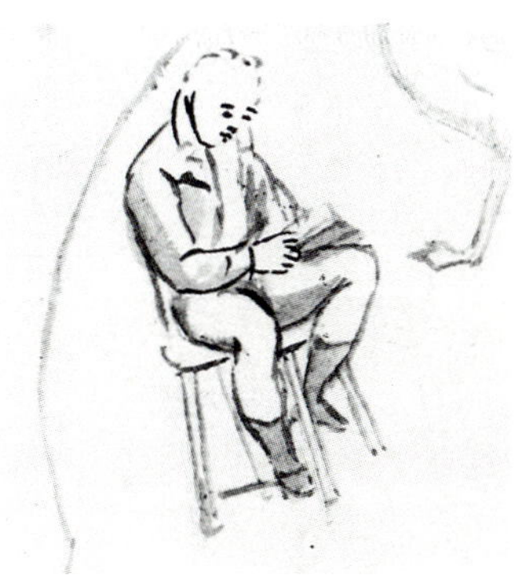

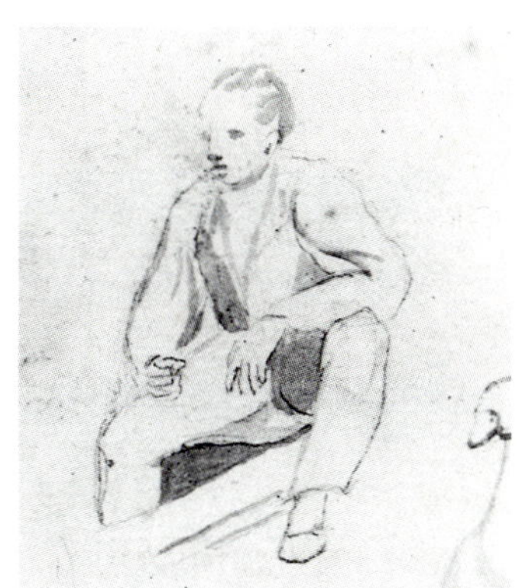

dates a similar but less well-executed study in the sketchbook (fig. 22). The painting also displays the artist's difficulties in composition. The carriage, seemingly small for the figures, is well defined in its parts but not as a whole. The horses are rather static, perhaps because Krimmel had not attempted to draw horses in motion before this (figs. 23, 24).

In contrast the composition of *Anabaptist Baptism* is more polished, suggesting a date of 1812 because like *View of Centre Square*, it is based on dominant horizontals and verticals (fig. 25). Although the figures are smaller, more numerous, and tightly packed, they too are arranged in the manner of a neoclassical frieze—aligned on two levels that run parallel to each other. As in the Fourth of July painting, all figures are individualized in expression and pose. To achieve this Krimmel relied on his sketches for details of dress and stance, but the anatomy lacks the polish apparent in later studies (compare figs. 26–29 with 14 and 15).

The genesis of *Sunday Morning in Front of Arch Street Meeting House*, another watercolor sold to Svinin, is a wash drawing Krimmel made of an elderly Quaker couple preceded by two young women walking along the street (fig. 30). To develop his rapidly drawn observations into a genre scene, the artist added more figures, taking details from his other sketches (figs. 31–34). The exact correspondences between elements in the detailed sketches and the final watercolor picture indicate that by 1812 the artist had developed a system that synthesized various elements to create the effect of a spontaneously observed scene. That the Sunday morning watercolor predates the Fourth of July scene is indicated by its overall effect, which, despite the boy's outstretched hand, is basically static. As in the other early images, the figure types are restricted and their poses not fully resolved, yet their varied and lively hand and arm movements echo the hand studies in sketchbook 1. The architectural setting although carefully drawn, lacks the more advanced handling of perspective seen in the Fourth of July painting.

A watercolor of a sudden encounter between an elegantly dressed white couple and two black chimney sweeps and their master at a corner (fig. 35) is a strongly vertical picture similar to the composition of *Pepper-Pot*, and in contrast to the Fourth of July painting in which the balanced horizontals and verticals create a clearly structured picture that conveys the relaxed spirit of a holiday celebration, this scene has tension. Krimmel achieved this by squeezing the figures into a narrow and shallow space diagonally transversed by the curbstones. Krimmel used this compressed setting to strengthen the expressions of surprise and dismay. Yet he still maintained a neoclassical balance and symmetry: the brick building on the left balances the steel lantern on the right, the vertical grate of the cellar window visually echoes the iron fence, and the architectural lines of the brick building in the foreground parallel those of Christ Church in the background. Aside from the rich couple's clothing, which is generally comparable to that of the fine ladies and gentlemen in the Fourth of July painting, a specific detail—the woman's shoes—are identical in both pictures and had also been pictured in *Pepper-Pot*. With such detailed renderings of stylish clothing, the artist identified the figures as members of the wealthy class. In the two oil paintings, *Pepper-Pot* and *View of Centre Square*, Krimmel made his comment on the different social ranks quietly and unobtrusively, but in the watercolor, he juxtaposed rich and poor in such a striking, although slightly comical, manner that the stark contrast can be interpreted as a form of social criticism.

FIGURE 30
John Lewis Krimmel, Sunday Morning in Front of Arch Street Meeting House, *late 1811–early 1812. Watercolor on paper; 9 x 7⅜ in. (The Metropolitan Museum of Art, New York, Rogers Fund, 1942.)*

FIGURE 31
Three Quakers walking, 1811/12. Pencil and wash. Sketchbook 1, leaf 7 recto.

FIGURE 32
Sketches of women and children, 1811 and 1812. Wash and ink. Sketchbook 1, leaf 13 recto. The young black woman and the Quaker woman were added to the page after the other images were drawn.

FIGURE 33
Quaker woman, 1811/12. Pencil. Sketchbook 1, leaf 6 recto.

FIGURE 34
Study of elderly man's face, 1811/12. Pencil and wash. Sketchbook 1, leaf 9 verso.

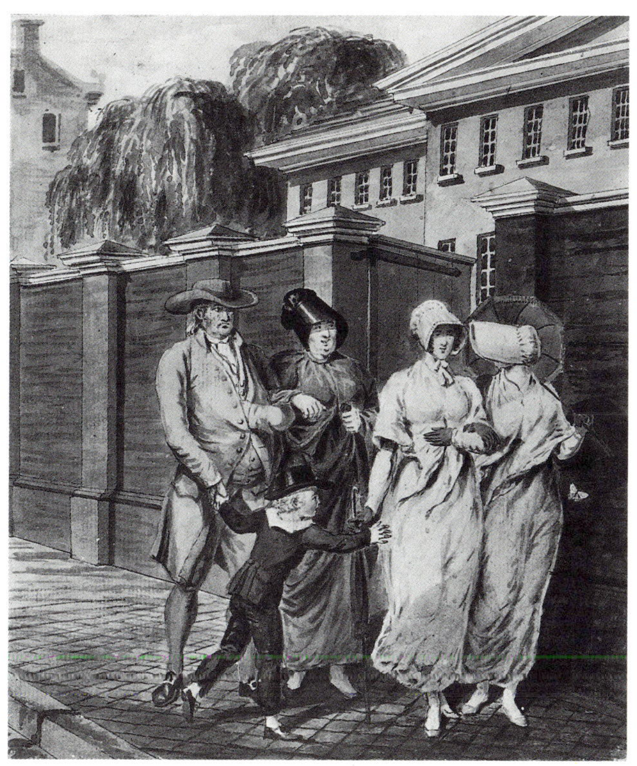

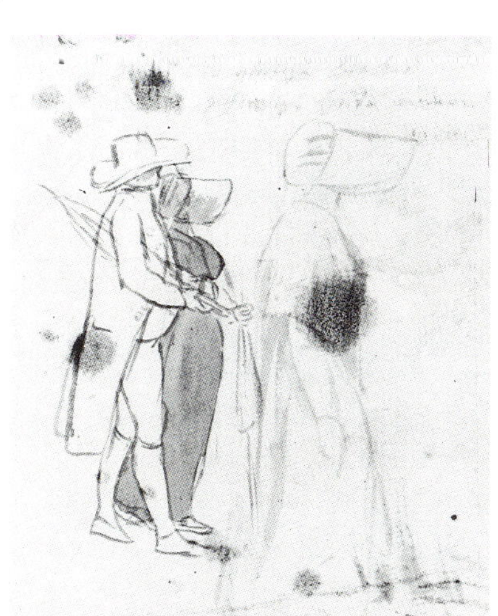

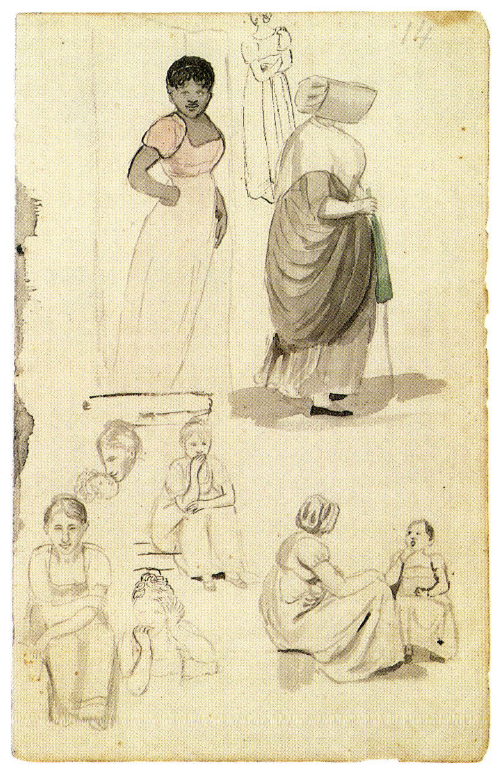

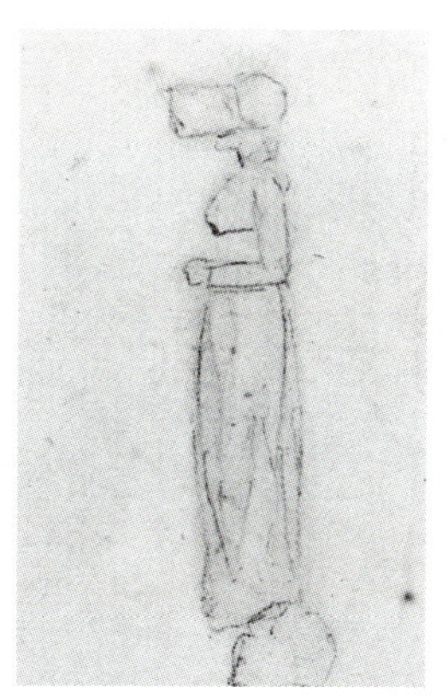

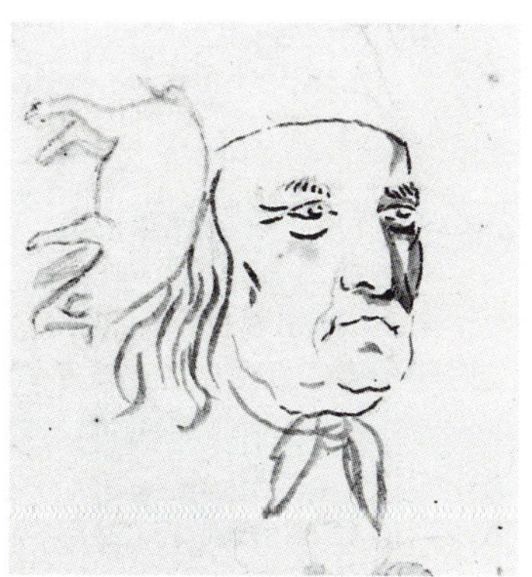

Elegant Couple Meets Chimney Sweeps illustrates a figure type Krimmel had settled upon for depicting young black boys. From 1811/12 on, the figures and their clothing are largely unchanged, and the specific detail of their strong bare feet is based on Krimmel's drawing of a plaster cast at the academy (fig. 36). The idea of using chimney sweeps in a painting may also have come from a woodcut in *The Cries of Philadelphia.* It shows a man wearing a wide-brimmed hat walking behind two barefoot youngsters dressed in rags and carrying large brushes, an arrangement that Krimmel's grouping resembles, although the context is very different.

That same penny book also contains a woodcut of an oyster vendor with his wheelbarrow and a single customer. The accompanying cry is "Oysters. Here your beautiful oysters; here your fine, fat salt oysters." Krimmel's interpretation of the theme, *Oyster Barrow in Front of Chestnut Street Theatre,* produced a much richer image (fig. 37). The men who patronize an oyster vendor after a theater performance savor the tidbits while standing around the barrow; however, women, according to Krimmel's picture, did not eat oysters in the street. A young woman has come to the stand to fetch oysters on a plate.

Oyster Barrow was most likely executed after *View of Centre Square.* The figures are arranged about the barrow in a manner similar to the group Krimmel had placed around the vendor's table in the Fourth of July painting. The resemblances are strongest in the foreground figure whose back is to the viewer (similar in pose to the boy at the vendor's table and in leg position the same as the rich merchant with the cane) and the woman with the candle (similar in type to the woman shading her eyes), but other similarities include the same peculiar hand movements used for the man pointing to the oysters and for the man holding a glass. The clothing, hats, and gestures are based on drawings in sketchbook 1 (fig. 38; see also fig. 26).

In terms of skill, the watercolor's figural composition and the reflections of the candle are well done, but foreground and background are not unified. As in most of Krimmel's early works the building behind is like a stage setting, carefully, even precisely rendered, yet not part of the story played out in the foreground. The precision with which this and other buildings are drawn in the early images, suggests that Krimmel on occasion resorted to using a camera obscura as early as 1811 and quite probably by 1812.[37] This device allowed easy and accurate copying on an enlarged or reduced scale, and facilitated perspective drawing and viewing a landscape. The artist could project an image onto a flat surface and then trace it. Such a technique would then have allowed Krimmel to use a very fine brush to delineate the elements of the buildings, especially outlines of bricks and details of architecture.

Krimmel's genre scenes attracted the attention of Svinin and fellow artists in the city precisely because they were unusual in the United States. His contemporaries (and later writers) often drew parallels between Krimmel's work and Hogarth's, and "Engravings from the works of Hogarth" were listed among the effects of Krimmel's estate in 1821; however, close study of Krimmel's early oil paintings and watercolors reveals that the young artist self-consciously absorbed other influences as well.[38] Part of this may have been because by 1812 Hogarth's images were more than a half century old and their crowded, irregular compositions and baroque perspectives outmoded. Krimmel studied Thomas Rowlandson, whose vividly drawn satirical scenes, for example *Vauxhall Gardens* and *Tour of Dr. Syntax in Search of the Picturesque* (both of which harkened back to Hogarth), incorporated clear, frieze-

37. The apparatus was a shuttered box, a darkened chamber (camera) with a convex lens at one end to admit light, and a mirror or screen at the other end, onto which the image of an exterior object was thrown so that the outlines could be traced. Krimmel owned a camera obscura (estate sale, *Poulson's American Daily Advertiser,* August 14, 1821), and given the architecture in his Fourth of July painting, he may have owned it as early as 1811.

38. Dunlap *(History,* 2:394) claims, "[the Fourth of July painting] is said to rival Hogarth in truth, nature, and humor"; Ritter ("Recollections," p. 119) states, "[Krimmel's] pencil was, as tho' dip'd in the autumn sunset of Hogarth." Joseph Jackson, "Krimmel, the American Hogarth," *International Studio* 93, no. 385 (June 1929): 33–36, used the sobriquet, "the American Hogarth," to describe Krimmel.

FIGURE 35
John Lewis Krimmel, Elegant Couple Meets Chimney Sweeps in Front of Christ Church, *late 1811–early 1812. Watercolor on paper; 9 ¼ x 6 ⅞ in. (The Metropolitan Museum of Art, New York, Rogers Fund, 1942.) This image may have been* The Contrast, *which was displayed at the annual exhibition of 1812.*

FIGURE 36
Foot of the Farnese Hercules, 1811/12. Pencil. Sketchbook 1, leaf 19 recto.

FIGURE 37
John Lewis Krimmel, Oyster Barrow in Front of Chestnut Street Theatre, *ca. 1812. Watercolor on paper; 9 ¾ x 7 in. (The Metropolitan Museum of Art, New York, Rogers Fund, 1942.)*

FIGURE 38
Hand, 1811/12. Pencil. Sketchbook 1, leaf 19 recto.

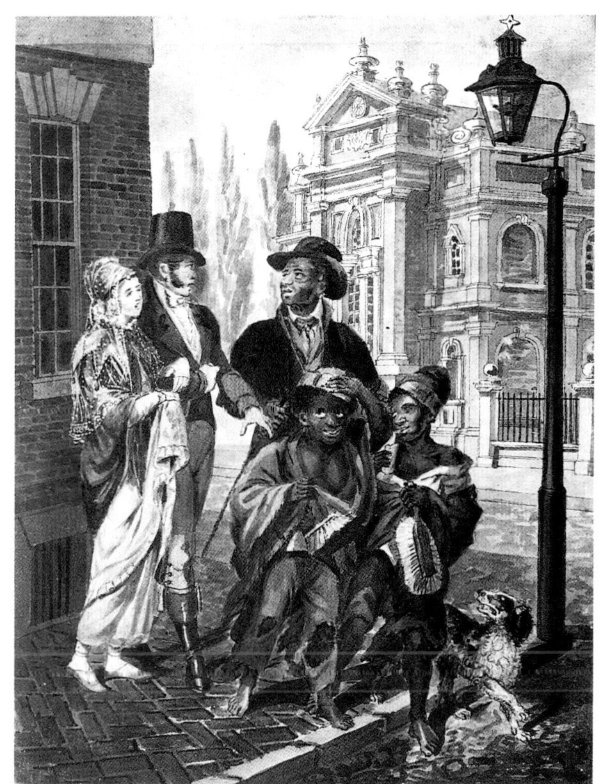

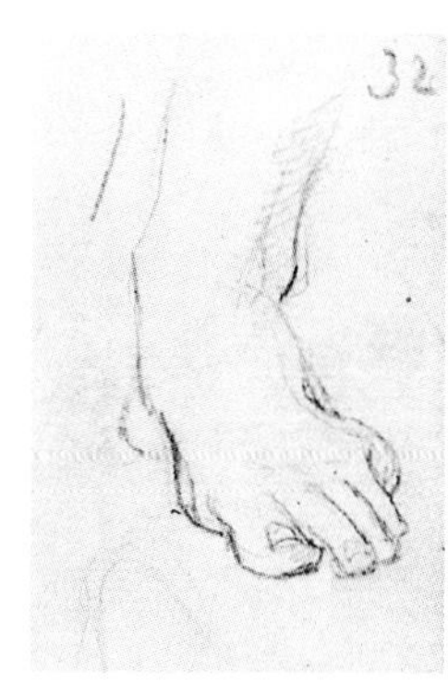

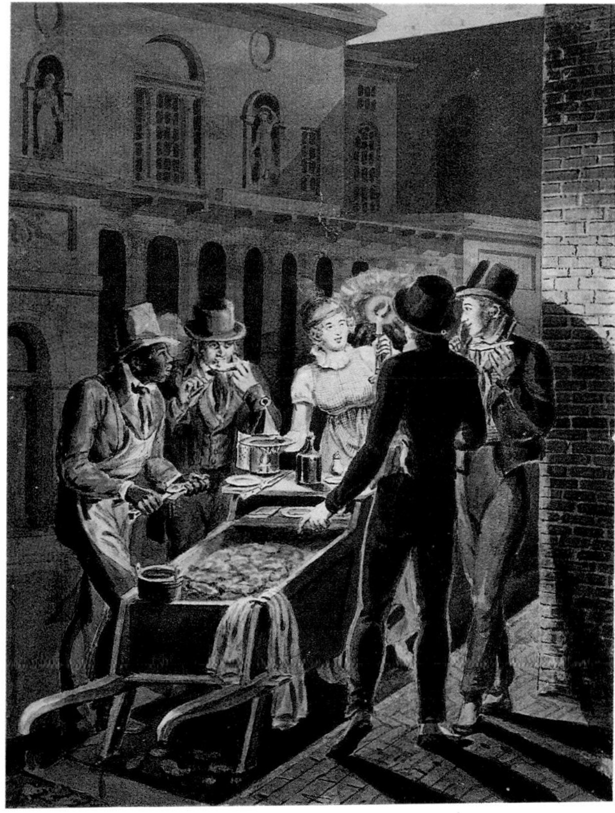

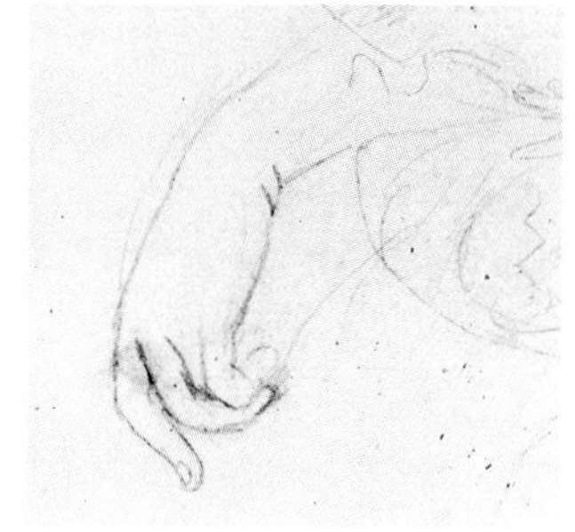

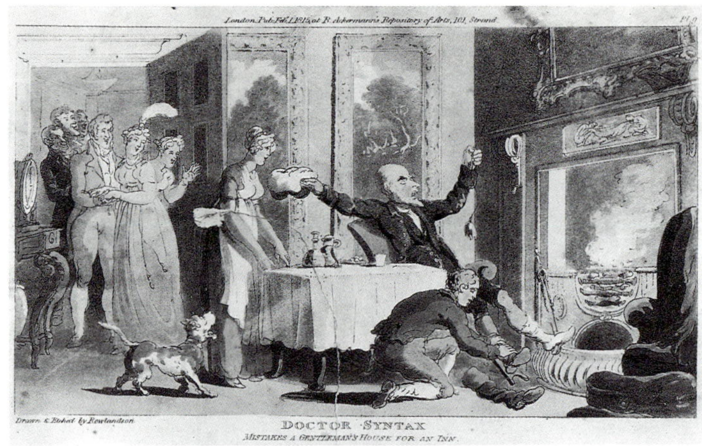

FIGURE 39
Thomas Rowlandson, Doctor Syntax Mistakes a Gentleman's House for an Inn, *London, February 1, 1815. Hand-colored etching; 5½ x 8½ in. (Photo, Winterthur.) This is one of the prints in the three "Tours of Doctor Syntax in Search of the Picturesque" series, 1812–21, published by Robert Ackermann.*

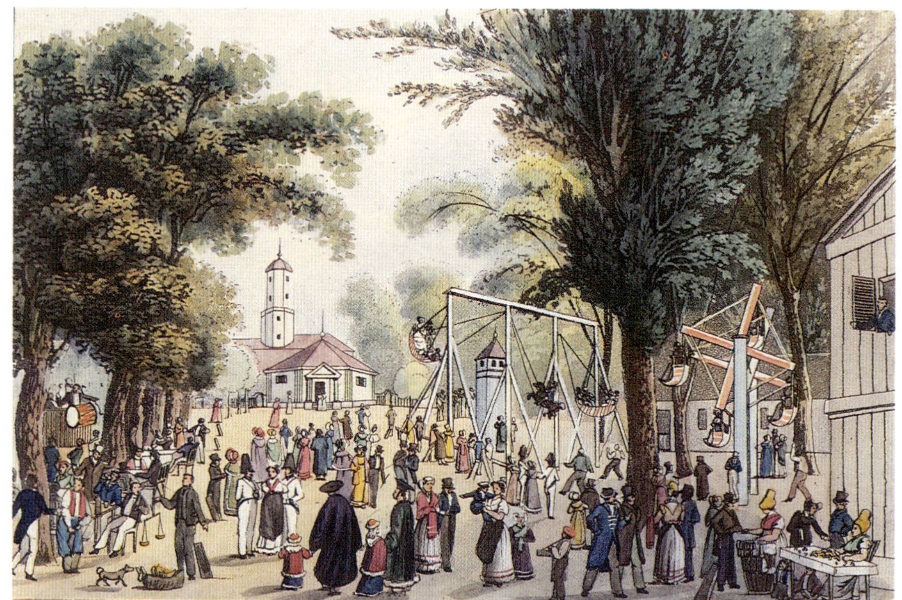

FIGURE 40
Bey den Wirthshäusern. Aux Guinguettes *[Near the taverns. Near the taverns], 1810–15. Hand-colored etching; 4¾ x 5⅞ in. [image 3⅝ x 5⅜ in.]. (Private collection.) The image depicts people of various social levels and backgrounds enjoying themselves at the restaurants and playgrounds of Vienna's Prater, a large wooded park between the banks of the Danube River and the Danube Canal.*

like arrangements of figures (fig. 39). But as with Hogarth, Rowlandson had a cursory and deliberately distorted style in the treatment of anatomy and proportions and an overblown sense of the ridiculous. Thus Krimmel turned to contemporary German artists, who placed their genre scenes against city views and topographical vistas—prints of which were sold as travel souvenirs (fig. 40). He added ideas drawn from famous European paintings, many of which he probably found in the "Sketches from Ancient Masters" drawn by Adolph Ulrich Wertmüller that he purchased in May 1812. These included useful study copies of important classical pictures, perhaps even those by Nicolas Poussin and Jacques-Louis David that influenced Krimmel's images in 1813 and later.[39]

Krimmel's earliest surviving genre scenes are Germanic in their astutely observed portrayals of behavior but English in their themes and formal construction; a combination of English and German components was a result of more than a century of interaction by artists from these different nations. In the early nineteenth century English art was widely considered to be superior to most art being produced on the Continent, especially in Germany. The south German and Austrian artistry that had produced brilliant architectural masterpieces decorated with spectacularly painted ceilings and altars in the late baroque period had been eclipsed by French and English artists who enjoyed more profitable patronage. German-born artists had taken advantage of the cultural links with England that had been initially forged by the marriage of duke (later elector) Ernest Augustus of Hanover to Sophia, granddaughter of James I of England.Their son George was crowned king of England in 1714, and Hanover and Great Britain shared rulers until 1837. The marriage of his son George to Wilhelmina Caroline of Anspach and of his grandson George III to Augusta of Saxe-Gotha had further strengthened these connections. The portrait style of the English school came to influence German artists, particularly Friedrich August Tischbein (1750–1812) in Leipzig; Anton Graff (1736–1813) in Dresden and Berlin; and Heinrich Friedrich Füger (1751–1818) in Stuttgart. Among the German-born painters who worked in England and affected English art were Sir Godfrey Kneller (1646?–1723), Henry Fuseli (1741–1825), Angelica Kauffman (1741–1807), and John Zoffany (1735–1810). The long accepted interaction between German and English artists made it easy for a budding artist from Germany early in the nineteenth century, such as Krimmel, to accept English modes of pictorial organization and subject matter.[40]

The integration of Germanic and English elements is also apparent in Krimmel's distinctive female figure: a smallish head; a short upper and a long lower torso; very high, full, and round breasts; long legs with relatively large thighs, the shapes of which are visible through the clinging muslin dresses; feet that are too small; and arms and hands that are sometimes too big. This female is at once neoclassical and naturalistic. She is closer to female types painted by German painters Philipp Otto Runge, Philip Friedrich Hetsch, and Gottlieb Schick than to those by American and English artists such as Sully and Sir Thomas Lawrence.

Once Krimmel had taken the step from amateur to professional artist, he almost immediately veered in the direction that became his specialty. After fewer than two years as a painter his genre scenes won critical acclaim. The strong contemporary spirit that viewers discerned in Krimmel's genre pictures is, as Krimmel's first sketchbook indicates, a consequence of his observations of people.

39. The Wertmüller drawings are listed in the 1812 sale held by Wertmüller's widow, and then again at the sale of Krimmel's effects in 1821; see Michael Benisovich, "The Sale of the Studio of Adolph-Ulrich Wertmüller," *Art Quarterly* 16, no. 1 (Spring 1953): 27–28; Krimmel estate sale, *Poulson's American Daily Advertiser*, August 14, 1821.

40. The works of composer George Frederick Handel (1685–1759) best exemplify the close cultural relationship between England and Germany that developed during the Georgian period after the German ducal house of Hanover succeeded to the English throne in 1714. By 1800 German and English painting were close in style and spirit.

Late in 1811 *Port Folio* published a lengthy essay on the nature of genre painting. In contrast to history painting, the writer observed, genre painting "admits a choice of subject, *ad libitum,* [that] is particularly favourable to mediocrity, as its models are within the reach of every amateur of the *easel;* nor does it refuse its aid to genius, when genius sinks to its level." He continued,

> on a canvass not too extensive, it is much easier to attend to the detail of outline, and to produce all the magic of colouring, than in a picture on a large scale. Pictures which are designed for a near point of view, lose nothing of the fine touches of the pencil, or of the illusions of colour; so that whilst genius is necessary to form the historical painter, a certain taste, or turn of mind, will enable the man even of moderate talent to please in that species of painting now under discussion. . . .
>
> Though it has been said that this style of painting requires not absolute perfection, or even an approach to it like the others, yet that must be understood with respect to the grand principles of the art, to the grandeur of outline, and the correctness of the drawing; for with respect to *colouring,* there no deficiency must exist. In colouring then, we ought always to meet with that exquisite velvet touch which may almost be felt, and which leaves nothing for the eye to desire; in short, that elegance which calls for, and bids defiance to the magnifying glass.[41]

Although Krimmel had made great strides in his art between mid 1810 and mid 1812, beyond Svinin he found few, if any, purchasers for his scenes of contemporary American life. In Philadelphia a cautious attitude toward art prevailed, but Krimmel remained undeterred. Committed to the specialty of genre art, he continued to draw, paint, and study.[42]

41. "Illustrations of the Graphic Art: Exemplified by Sketches from the National Museum at Paris," *Port Folio,* n.s., 6, no. 6 (December 1811): 568–75.

42. Dunlap, *History,* 2:393.

A Maturing Talent 1812–1816

Encouraged by the attention his oil painting had received in the exhibition of 1812 yet conscious of the deficiencies in his art and his lack of training, Krimmel seized opportunities to improve his skills. Before the year was out he was practicing compositional sketching as one of seven members of a group that Thomas Sully described as "a club for the purpose of making designs." The members—Sully, Rembrandt Peale, Charles Bird King, Gideon Fairman, William Greene "of the Virginia Theatre," John Clifton, and Krimmel—"met once a week in Mr. Sully's painting room, and from some passage read by one of the club, from the work of some author promiscuously taken up, a design was executed by each one of the company. Two hours were allowed."[1]

Sully's sketch club is presumed to have been the first of its kind in America and was modeled after English examples. When the sketching sessions actually began or how long the club existed is not known; however, three members—Sully, Peale, and Fairman—had resigned from the Society of Artists in the spring of 1812 when relations between the society and the academy became strained. They were among the twenty-four painters, sculptors, engravers, and architects, all members of the academy, who were promptly elected to a new group called *Pennsylvania Academicians*.[2] Given the artists' general concern about increasing the opportunities for refining their skills, Sully's decision to invite a small group of fellow artists to form a "club for the purpose of making designs" is not out of the ordinary.

The members of this small group were a diverse lot. English-born Sully (1783–1872) had come to America as a boy and had worked as a portrait painter first in Virginia, briefly in New York, and then in Philadelphia. In 1809 he went to London to study with Benjamin West but found the facile brush stroke and more coloristic style of Sir Thomas Lawrence more to his taste. Sully returned to Philadelphia in the spring of 1810 well equipped to paint in the current mode of English portraiture and quickly emerged as a dominant leader in Philadelphia's artistic community, becoming a founder of the Society of Artists and a member of the board of directors of the academy. He excelled in the rendition of feminine prettiness and in the likenesses of his male sitters conveyed a particular ease and elegance—major reasons why he quickly became the city's most popular portraitist. In May 1812 he moved his studio to Philosophical Hall on Independence Square, Charles Willson Peale's former rooms. There he held the sketch club sessions.[3]

An equally distinguished member of the sketch club was Rembrandt Peale (1778–1860), second son of Charles Willson Peale, a founding member and director of the Pennsylvania Academy and probably the most experienced artist in the group. Although a portrait painter of a rank equal to Sully, he preferred history painting. He too had studied abroad: twice in England (1802–3 and 1808), and an extended stay in France (1809–10) before returning to Philadelphia in 1810. One of his first major works, *Roman Daughter*, showed the

1. December 1812, Sully Journal; Sully wrote this next to a drawing entitled "Gertrude of Wyoming" that was probably inspired by Thomas Campbell's 1809 poem of the same name. Any drawing Krimmel made of this massacre in the Wyoming Valley of eastern Pennsylvania in 1778 has since disappeared.

2. The dispute is detailed in Linda Bantel, "William Rush, Esq.," in *William Rush: American Sculptor* (Philadelphia: Pennsylvania Academy of the Fine Arts, 1982), pp. 17–18. Academicians received stockholders privileges, established a life class, and administered the academy's annual exhibitions; see Frank H. Goodyear, Jr., "A History of The Pennsylvania Academy of the Fine Arts, 1805–1976," in *In This Academy: The Pennsylvania Academy of the Fine Arts, 1805–1976* (Philadelphia, 1976), p. 18.

3. Edward Biddle and Mantle Fielding, *The Life and Works of Thomas Sully (1783–1872)* (1921; reprint, New York: Kennedy Graphics and DaCapo Press, 1970); Minutes of the Board of Directors, PAFA, microfilm; Fabian, *Sully*.

strong influence of French neoclassical history painting. When he exhibited it in May 1812 critics quickly voiced their admiration, but in a matter of days their applause was tempered by a slanderous charge levied by Russian attaché and amateur artist Pavel Svinin questioning the originality of the composition (see appendix 3).[4]

The third outstanding member of this group was King (1785–1862), portrait and still-life painter. King was financially independent and had trained under and worked with distinguished painters for more than a decade. During seven years in London as a pupil of and studio assistant to West, he was befriended by Washington Allston and David Wilkie and came to admire seventeenth-century Dutch and Flemish painting. He returned to the United States shortly before war was declared in June 1812, lacking a mastery of portraiture. His images were correctly painted and won praise for their flesh tones but did not convey the sitters' sense of ease or expressions of feelings.[5]

Another member of the sketch club was Fairman (1774–1827), a banknote engraver of high repute who had worked in Albany and New York City before moving to Philadelphia and becoming a partner in a successful firm of engravers.[6] In 1812 Fairman, age 38, was an academician greatly respected for his detailed work, who regularly exhibited his and his firm's work at the academy. His figural images, although done in small scale, were stylistically close to Sully's.

Less is known about two members of the sketch club. Clifton left no trace as an artist. Greene "of the Virginia Theatre" may have been actor William Green who intermittently worked in Philadelphia from the early 1790s on, possibly the comedian Sully painted in miniature in 1804. If so, he may have done the dramatic readings for the artists in the sketch club.

Sketching with these well-trained artists was certainly to Krimmel's great advantage and may explain why during 1813 his style became more fluent. Sketchbook 2, a nearly square book with only eleven leaves, seems to have been used in the two-hour sessions held in Sully's studio. With the exception of a few portrait sketches its content is limited to compositional exercises, often crowding two or more of them to a page.[7] The images give the impression that they are invented pictures (in contrast to the observed imagery in sketchbook 1), and the complex subject matter and often hasty drafting style suggest they were executed under special circumstances. Many groupings are defined only in outline but are clearly recognizable as genre subjects. Most were drawn with a quill pen, a pliable implement that produced a flexible ink line that varied in thickness and strength according to the speed and pressure applied. The best-defined images have areas of exceptionally strong hatching freely and boldly handled; the closely spaced parallel strokes enliven various images even when they extend beyond individual figures. The more fully developed designs in the sketchbook have watercolor and wash, media Krimmel used after his conceptual process had reached an advanced stage. The majority of these sketches are done in a cursive, very loose style that Krimmel had not practiced before. The compositions usually involve several figures and recognizably relate to Krimmel's known pictures. They chronicle the successive stages through which a scene evolved before the artist arrived at a version close to the one he painted in oil. As such, they clearly communicate Krimmel's work process and show how he experimented with shifting figures and movements to achieve the rhythms of a final composition (figs. 41–47). Compared to the drawings in sketchbook 1, the graphic style of these sketches

4. Carol Eaton Hevner, *Rembrandt Peale, 1778–1860: A Life in the Arts* (Philadelphia: Historical Society of Pennsylvania, 1985); Lillian B. Miller, "In the Shadow of His Father: Rembrandt Peale, Charles Willson Peale, and the American Portrait Tradition," and Lois Marie Fink, "Rembrandt Peale in Paris," *Pennsylvania Magazine of History and Biography* 110, no. 1 (January 1986): 33–64, 77–90.

5. Andrew J. Cosentino, *The Paintings of Charles Bird King (1785–1862)* (Washington, D.C.: Smithsonian Institution Press, 1977), pp. 16–28, notes that Sully shared King's lodgings and painting room at Buckingham Palace.

6. Dunlap, *History*, 2:177–79.

7. My reading of sketchbook 2 is that the drawing sessions began with cursory images and ended with quite finished drawings; such is discernible in *Country Wedding*.

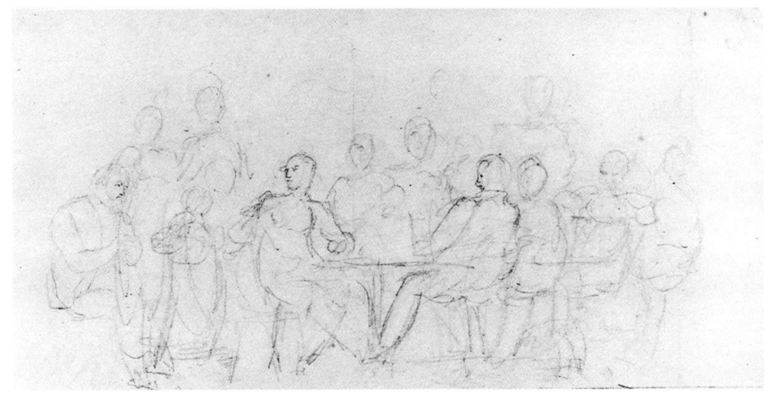

FIGURE 41
Compositional sketch, ca. 1812. Pencil. Sketchbook 2, leaf 6 recto. This may later have been developed into The Tea Party, *a "sketch in oil" listed among the effects at the sale of Krimmel's estate, August 14, 1821, and in the sale of Doggett's Repository of the Fine Arts in Boston on November 22, 1821. The location of* The Tea Party *is unknown.*

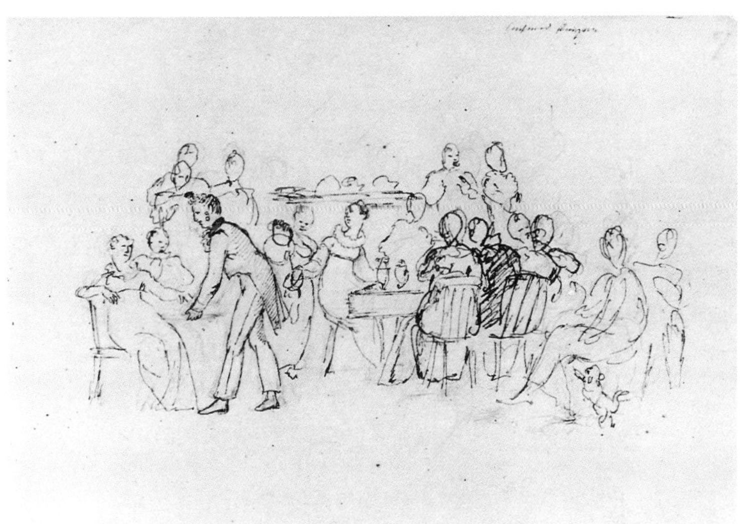

FIGURE 42
Compositional sketch, 1812 or 1813. Ink over pencil. Sketchbook 2, leaf 12 recto. This is the most advanced of the drawings that may have been sketches for The Tea Party.

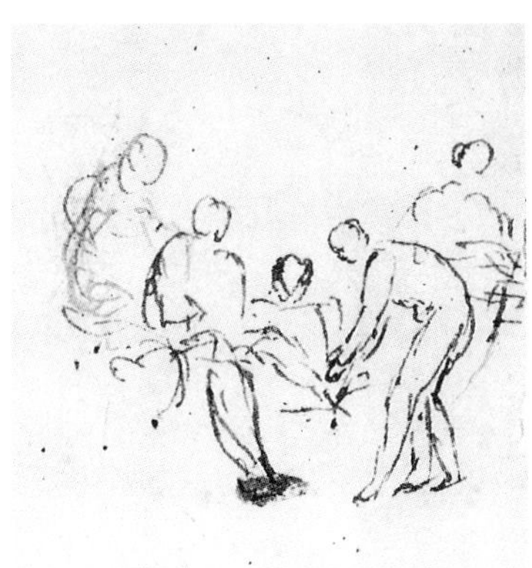

FIGURE 43
Compositional sketch, ca. 1812. Ink. Sketchbook 2, inside front cover.

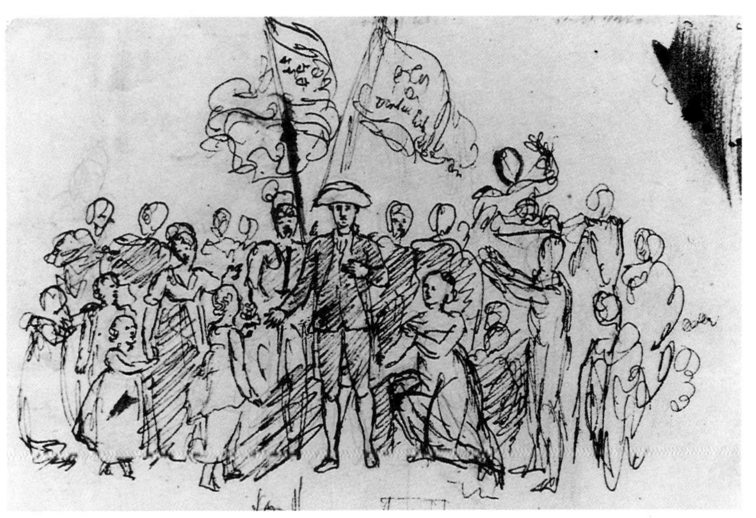

FIGURE 44
Compositional sketch, ca. 1812. Ink and ink wash over pencil. Sketchbook 2, leaf 7 verso. This scene of people crowded in homage around a man—possibly Washington—is stiffly and symmetrically composed and lacks variety in design.

FIGURE 45
An artist and his family confronted by a bill collector, ca. 1813. Ink and ink wash over pencil. Sketchbook 2, leaf 4 recto. This mildly satirical scene alludes to the plight of many artists. Charles Bird King's 1813 The Poor Artist's Cabinet *is a trompe l'oeil still life expressing the same basic concern.*

FIGURE 46
Concertizing amateurs, 1812–13. Ink and ink wash over pencil. Sketchbook 2, leaf 5 recto. This well-designed, imaginatively balanced composition may be related to "A Music Party," listed in the auction of the Krimmel pictures in Devaltooth's estate in 1825.

FIGURE 47
Courtroom scene, ca. 1813. Ink over pencil. Sketchbook 2, leaf 10 recto. The young man before the judge is apparently involved in a paternity case; another defendant awaits his turn in the doorway.

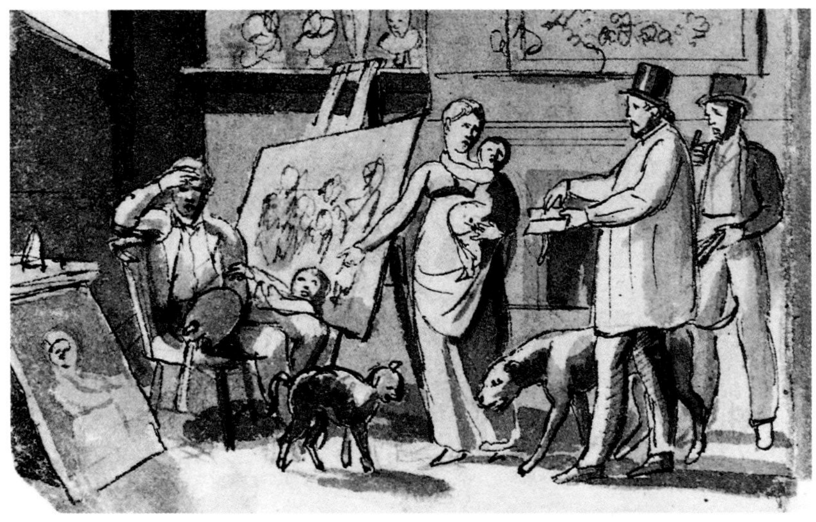

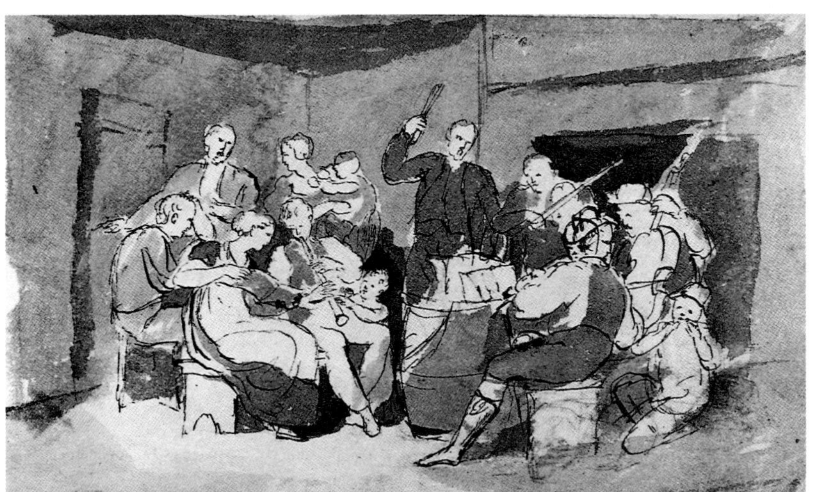

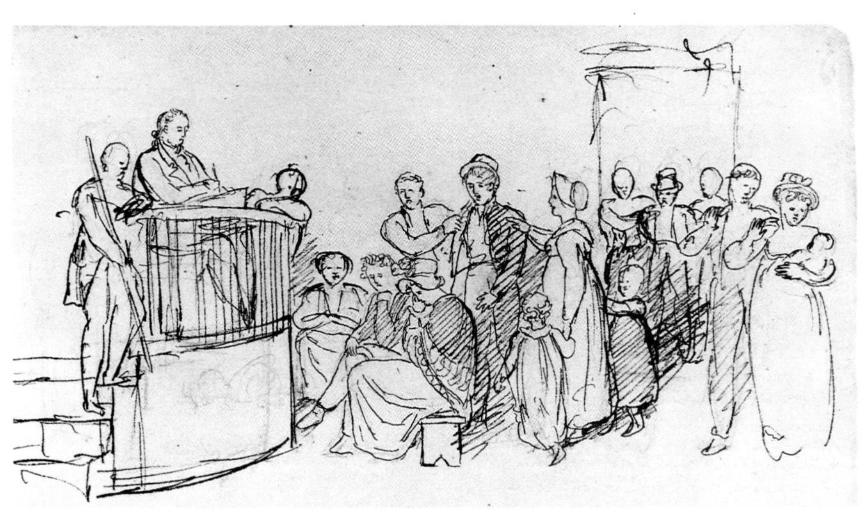

is looser, more cursive, more uniform, and more complex. These compositional drawings represent a considerable advance in the artist's ability to delineate movement and the interaction of several—even many—figures. Krimmel's rapid progress may be explained by the sketch club, for it brought him into close association with a group of Philadelphia's best painters, including three who had recently trained in Europe and who could convey to him the most current pictorial conventions.

Of the few portraits in sketchbook 2, one is an excellent likeness of a man, apparently done from life, and another is of a woman. The color notes on the latter and the outline suggest that it is either Krimmel's copy of a Sully painting or his attempt to do a portrait in the Sully style (figs. 48, 49).

Krimmel continued to carry sketchbook 1 with him to make quick studies as he walked about the city. On one such outing to the academy he made a copy (fig. 50) of Charles Leslie's *Musidora Bathing*, which was in turn a copy of West's *Arethusa Bathing*. (The same painting inspired Sully, who painted two copies of it.)[8]

Small watercolor pictures were another aspect of Krimmel's work in 1812 and 1813, and for many of these designs he drew adaptively on other artists' works. He turned to two of West's paintings, *William Penn's Treaty with the Indians* and *The Death of General Wolfe*, for discrete elements in *Indian Council* and *Tableau of Indian Faces* (figs. 51–54). *Penn's Treaty* provided the design precepts for *Indian Council*, specifically the neoclassical frieze and the use of isocephaly, and influenced his depictions of the clothing and body language of the leaders; *The Death of General Wolfe* was the source for the left foreground figure. Krimmel's *Tableau of Indian Faces* is a franker copy of the heads of the young mother and two children and several of the other Indians that populate West's *Penn's Treaty*.[9]

West was just one of the artists whose work Krimmel turned to for ideas in 1812 and 1813. He also became interested in Wilkie's paintings, which were available in the United States through engravings. Wilkie (1785–1841) had soared to sudden fame after moving to London in 1805, where his scenes of Scottish country life, painted in the manner of seventeenth-century Dutch genre paintings, met instant success. Late in 1811 an engraving of his *Blind Fiddler*, a painting that Wilkie completed as a private commission in 1806 and exhibited briefly at the Royal Academy in 1807, was issued. The engraving probably was exported to the United States shortly after it was released (fig. 55), and Krimmel, "delighted . . . [to find] a composition congenial to his taste and feeling," decided to make a copy of it in oil, which he entered in the joint Columbian Society of Artists/Pennsylvania Academy exhibition of 1813.[10] He replicated the engraving with absolute fidelity and invented a sympathetic color scheme that in contrast to the vivid reds and dark browns in the Wilkie painting relied on a cautious blending of large areas of light brown, blue green, muted red, and rose that gave the image a quiet effect (fig. 56).

The review of the exhibition that appeared in *Port Folio* termed Krimmel's copy a "beautiful little picture." It continued: "Although the design, composition and effect of this picture are not the production of our young artist, yet we must give him great credit for his beautiful and harmonious colouring, and for the masterly manner in which he has preserved the character of the original." Adding that it was "impossible . . . to pass over this copy without noticing the extraordinary merits of the original," the commentator described the scene in detail. Then he added:

8. Helmut von Erffa and Allen Staley, *The Paintings of Benjamin West, 1738–1820* (New Haven: Yale University Press, 1986), p. 229. Biddle and Fielding, *Sully*, p. 372. *Musidora Bathing* refers to a passage in James Thomson's "Seasons"; an analogous story is that of Arethusa in Ovid's "Metamorphoses." In both a beautiful young bather is spied upon by a young man. Leslie's version was displayed at Pennsylvania Academy in 1813.

9. Krimmel sold *Indian Council* and *Tableau of Indian Faces* to Svinin; see appendix 3. Krimmel's studio effects in 1821 included engravings of the most celebrated works of Benjamin West; *Poulson's American Daily Advertiser*, August 9, 1821.

10. Dunlap, *History*, 2:392; H. A. D. Miles, "Catalogue of Paintings," in William J. Chiego et al., *Sir David Wilkie of Scotland (1785–1841)* (Raleigh: North Carolina Museum of Art, 1987), p. 115; *Third Annual Exhibition* . . . (1813), p. 21.

FIGURE 48
Man, ca. 1813. Pencil. Sketchbook 2, leaf 1 recto.

FIGURE 49
Woman, 1812–13. Watercolor over pencil. Sketchbook 2, leaf 1 recto.

FIGURE 50
Woman seated, 1813. After Charles Leslie, Musidora Bathing *(1813), after Benjamin West,* Arethusa Bathing *(1802). Watercolor over pencil. Sketchbook 1, leaf 15 recto.*

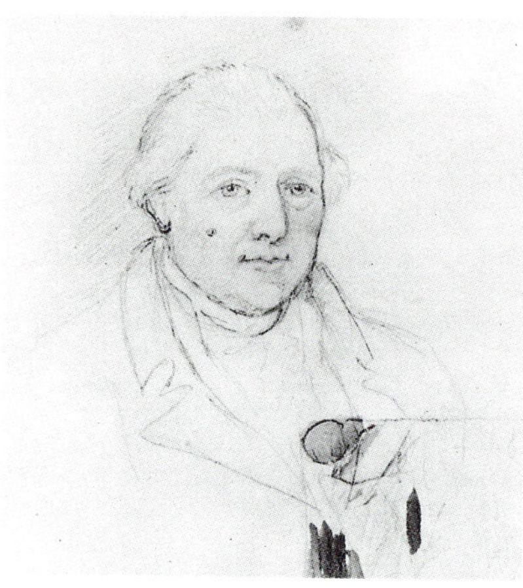

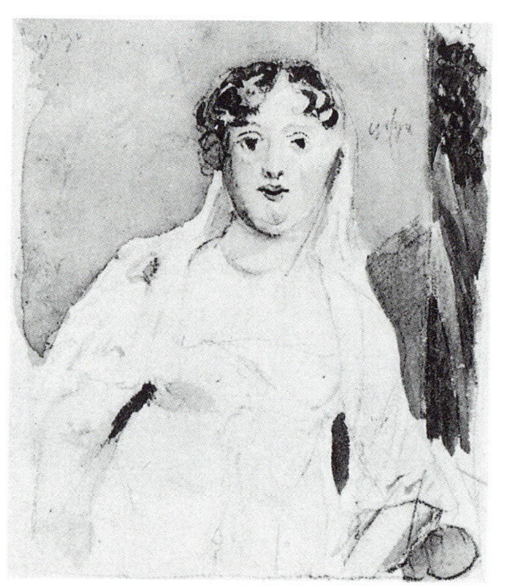

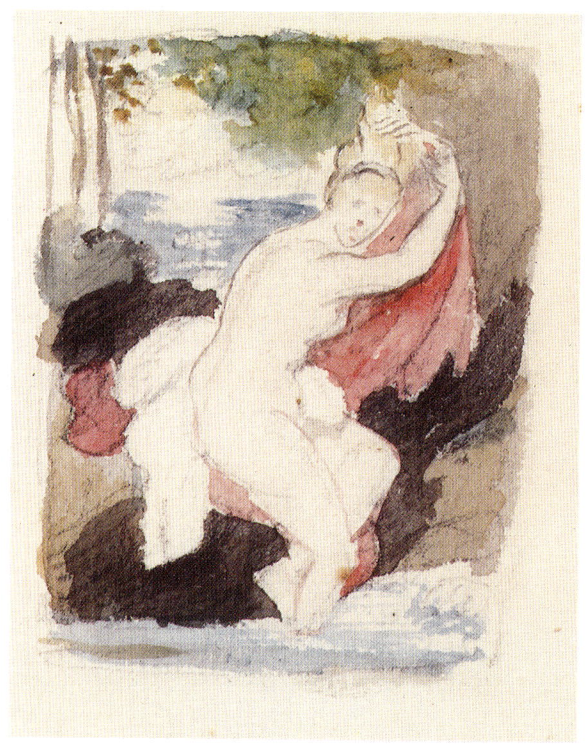

FIGURE 51
Benjamin West, William Penn's Treaty with the Indians, *1771–72. Oil on canvas; 75½ x 107¾ in. (Joseph Harrison, Jr., Collection, The Pennsylvania Academy of Fine Arts, Philadelphia, gift of Mrs. Sarah Harrison.)*

FIGURE 52
Benjamin West, The Death of General Wolfe, *1770. Oil on canvas; 60 x 84 in. (National Gallery of Canada, Ottawa, transfer from the Canadian War Memorials, 1921, gift of the 2nd Duke of Westminster, Eaton Hall, Cheshire, 1918.)*

FIGURE 53
John Lewis Krimmel, Indian Council, *1812/13. Watercolor on paper; 7 x 9¼ in. (The Metropolitan Museum of Art, New York, Rogers Fund, 1942.)*

FIGURE 54
John Lewis Krimmel, Tableau of Indian Faces, *1812/13. Watercolor on paper; 9¼ x 7 in. (The Metropolitan Museum of Art, New York, Rogers Fund, 1942.)*

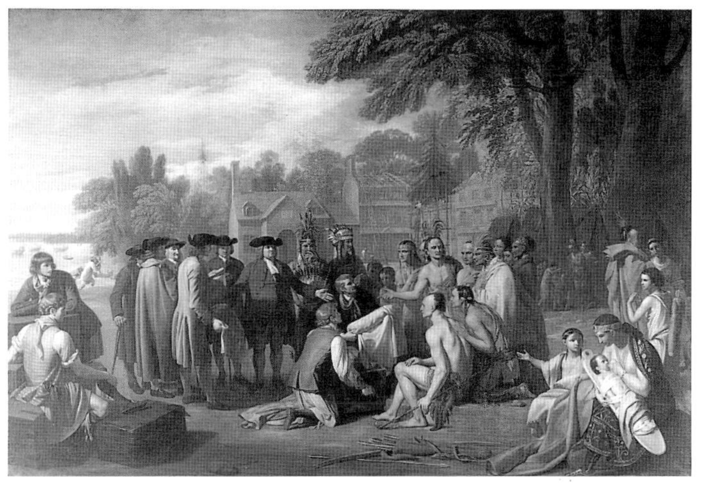

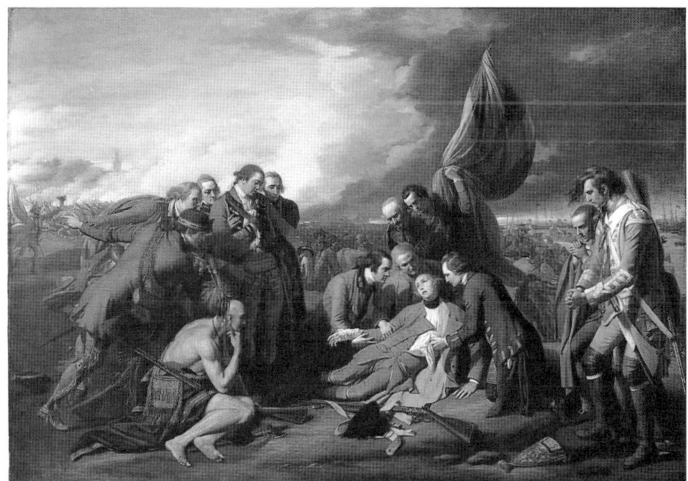

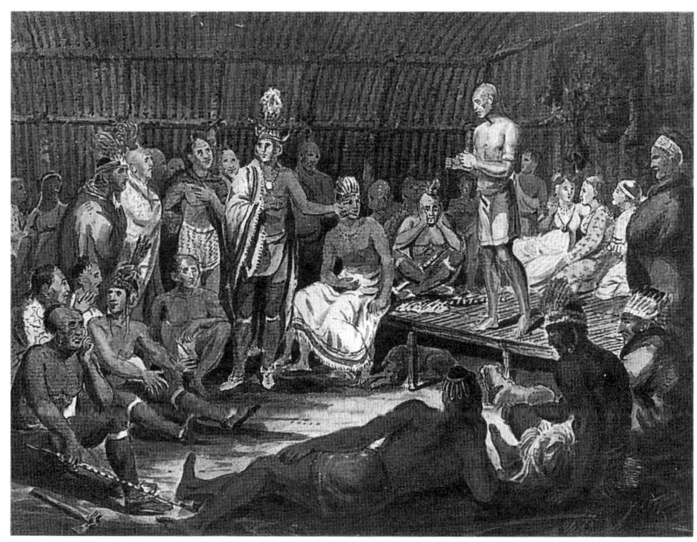

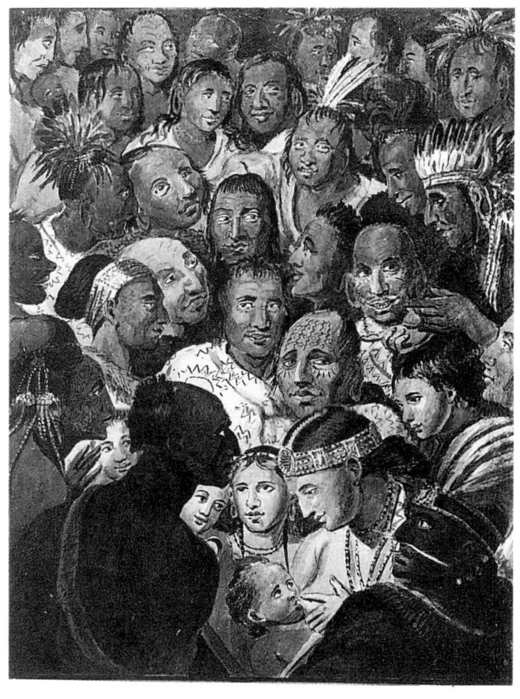

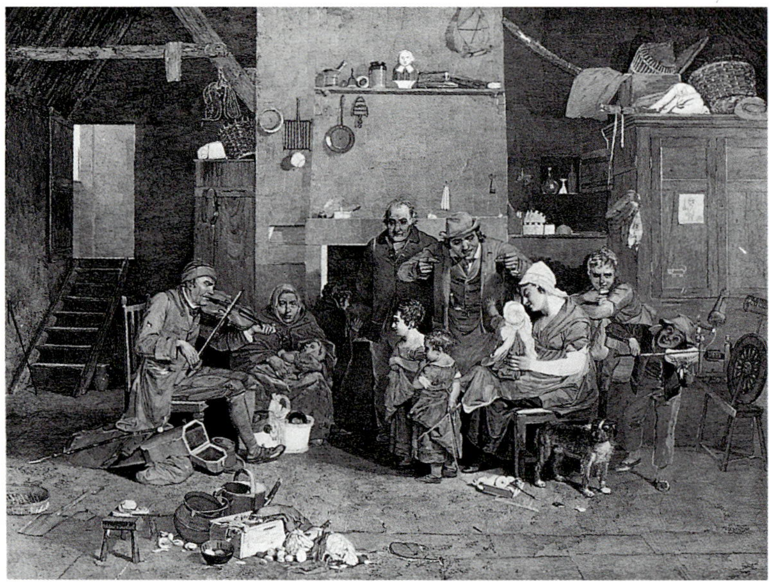

FIGURE 55
John Burnet after David Wilkie, The Blind Fiddler, *London, 1811. Engraving; 19½ x 24¼ in. Published by Boydell and Company. (Prints and Photographs Division, Library of Congress.)*

FIGURE 56
John Lewis Krimmel after John Burnet after David Wilkie, The Blind Fiddler, *Philadelphia, 1812. Oil on canvas; 16⅜ x 21⅞ in. (Berry-Hill Galleries, New York.)*

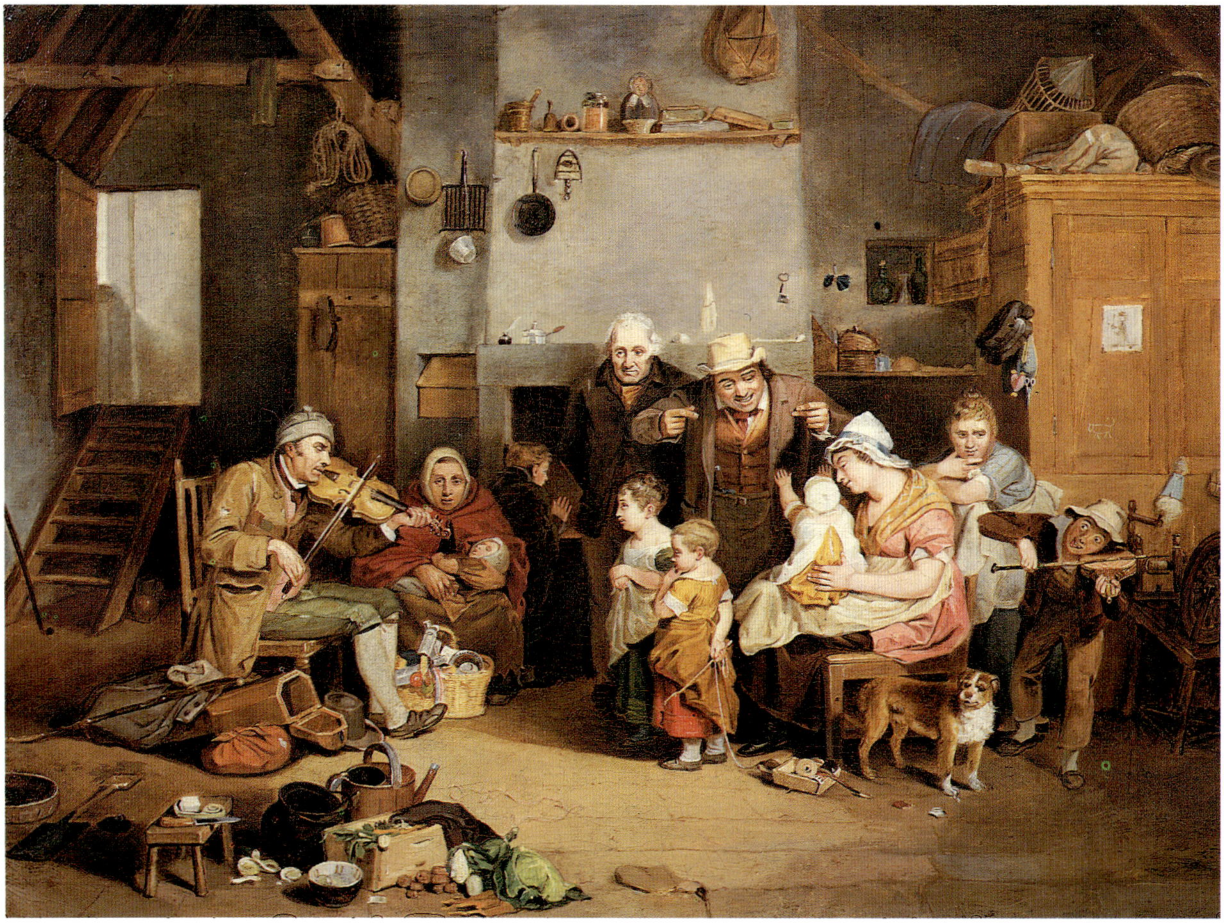

> Mr. Wilkie . . . copied nature very closely, without her deformities: he has given all the character and finish of *Teniers* without his vulgarities. His pictures are equally interesting to the learned and ignorant—they are faithful, chaste, and dignified representations of nature, conveying at the same time pleasure and instruction. . . . We believe his school of painting is well fitted for our republican manners and habits, and more likely than any other to be appreciated at present. Instead of mounting on the wings of *imagination* and ascending into the regions of *fancy*, our artists may exercise their talents to more advantage by representing real objects.[11]

That the critic stressed that realistic images were well suited to the nation's republican ethos may have given Krimmel encouragement, for such images were certainly the subject matter he was partial to and could depict in a singular way. Ideas of republican virtue had informed intellectual debates since the 1760s, yet in art much of its impact had been to spur artists to choose classical or biblical topics to illustrate such ideals. Wilkie's realistic images relied on contemporary topics and were republican in that they focused on the ordinary citizens, but they were not optimistic; poverty was readily apparent. Krimmel's decision to make a copy of Wilkie's *Blind Fiddler* suggests that he found the simplicity appealing, yet when Krimmel composed his own images he chose to emphasize another brand of realism, one that celebrated family ties and the prosperity of an emerging, often rural, middle class in his adopted country, as another canvas he submitted to the 1813 exhibition demonstrates.

Krimmel's second entry, *Quilting Frolic* was his interpretation of family hospitality. The title alludes to an informal party that will celebrate the completion of a major sewing project, a quilt that was probably intended as part of the dowry for one of the young women (fig. 57). In contrast to Wilkie's sentimental and slightly pathetic scene of home life on a poor farm, Krimmel's scene is lighthearted and lively and is painted with a greater variety of color, larger applications of white, a more animated play of light, and stronger surface textures. To the critic who lavished so much space on Krimmel's copy of *The Blind Fiddler*, *Quilting Frolic* was equally worthy of comment:

> This is an original and very excellent picture, and [is] no doubt intended as a companion to his copy of Wilkie's blind fiddler. Throughout the whole of this charming and very interesting subject we can perceive strong marks of the genius of the painter. The composition, drawing, colouring and effect, display much knowledge of the true principles of art: the style is evidently his own. Mr. Krimmell is a pupil in the *school of Nature,* and he has already given sufficient proofs that he has not studied in vain. His figures are graceful, easy, and well drawn. On first viewing this picture we were inclined to believe that the objects were rather crowded; but on mature consideration, we changed our opinion. The subject represents a sort of entertainment, or *tea-party and dance,* given at the close of what is called a *quilting frolic.* It is very natural to suppose that a small room would not only be full, but crowded, and that every thing wanted on the occasion would be in requisition—the tea-cups, &c. are placed on a small tray close together (evidently for the want of a larger.) The bustle throughout this entertaining scene is very visible, and managed by the artist with great dexterity. The subject is good and executed with great judgment.[12]

11. M., "Review of the Third Annual Exhibition of the Columbian Society of Artists and Pennsylvania Academy of Fine Arts," *Port Folio*, n.s., 2, no. 2 (August 1813): 138, 139. In spring 1813 the Society of Artists formally became the Columbian Society of Artists.

12. M., "Review of the Third Annual Exhibition," p. 140.

FIGURE 57
John Lewis Krimmel, Quilting Frolic, *Philadelphia, 1813. Oil on canvas; 16⅞ x 22⅜ in. (Winterthur.)*

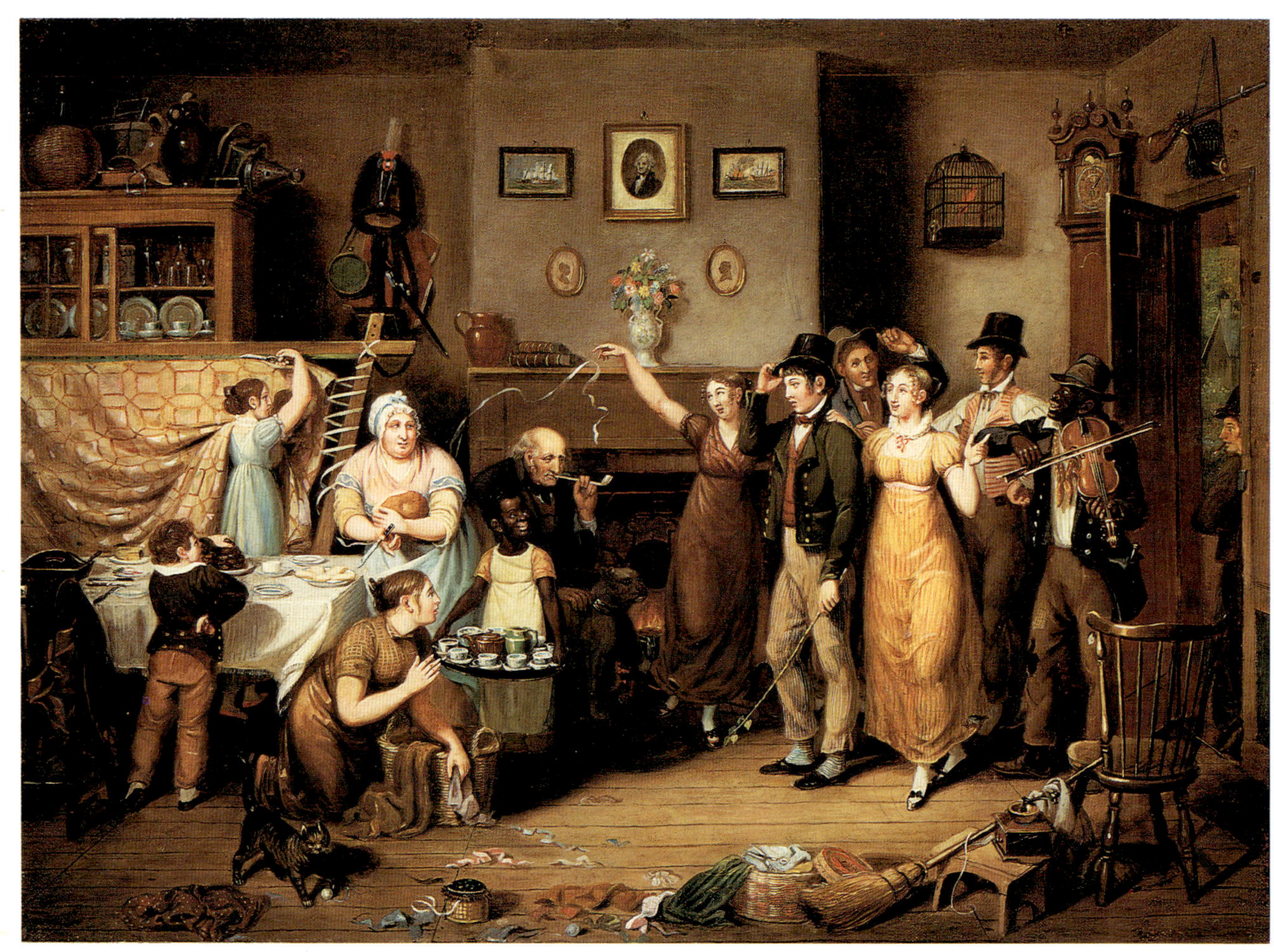

In this painting Krimmel demonstrates an improved knowledge of anatomy and better ways of delineating movement. He renders facial expressions, gestures, and poses so skillfully that each figure has a different emotional charge. This is particularly well realized in the kneeling girl, whose right hand expresses surprise and affection as she glances at the young man who tips his hat while looking into her face, a gesture through which the artist hints at the tender feelings that these two young people hold for each other. Rounding out the circle are the mother's guarded expression and the father/grandfather's bemused one.

The type of furniture and the many objects in the room—the tall-case clock, the ornate vase with flowers and the books on the mantle, the birdcage, the dishes and glassware, the tablecloth, and the five pictures above the fireplace—indicate that the family enjoys a measure of prosperity but is not wealthy. Instead of portraits, two silhouettes, probably of family members, hang on the wall below three prints that have patriotic connotations: an image of George Washington is flanked by two images of sea battles, direct references to the ongoing War of 1812. The print on the right may represent USS *Constitution* (Old Ironsides) defeating HMS *Guerrière*, a battle that had taken place August 19, 1812, and was commemorated by a large number of paintings and prints. The other print may depict the *Wasp* defeating the *Frolic*, a battle that occurred October 18, 1812, or the *United States* capturing the *Macedonia* on October 25, 1812. The handsome still-life motif provided by the soldier's hat and gear hanging on the wall to the left of the fireplace also refers to the war and functions as a decorative detail that visually balances the birdcage holding a cardinal on the right.[13]

In contrast to the strong reliance on obvious verticals and horizontals and the stiffness that had characterized Krimmel's 1812 images, *Quilting Frolic* has rounded shapes, and the figures move more naturally. The general design is based on Wilkie's formula: a central fireplace and a balanced composition that is set in a Dutch-box space with the background wall parallel to the picture frame. As in Wilkie's pictures, light emanates from an unseen source in front of the picture, and some still-life details are invested with a deeper meaning much as they were in seventeenth-century Netherlandish paintings of tavern and domestic scenes.[14]

Krimmel's reliance on Wilkie can easily be overstated, for there were other artists exploring still lifes who may have influenced Krimmel's decision to include such elements. Foremost among them in Philadelphia was Raphaelle Peale (1774–1825), Charles Willson Peale's oldest son. In the exhibitions of 1811 and 1812 he had established himself as the first professional still-life painter in America and demonstrated that still life was highly rewarding subject matter for professional as well as amateur artists. He worked from the tradition established by seventeenth-century Flemish and Dutch masters, but his arrangements, generally of fruits and unpretentious objects, were composed with a neoclassical plainness and an exquisite sense for pictorial order in keeping with contemporary taste.[15]

Krimmel trod a middle ground between Wilkie and Peale as he chose the still-life elements to enrich his scenes. The items in *Quilting Frolic* have a dual function: they serve as compositional devices, and they reinforce the subject of the picture. Thus the disorderly array of commonplace household goods in the foreground serves as a *repoussoir* conveying pictorial depth and realism; subtle but effective highlights and reflections on glass, glazed ceramics, metals,

13. For silhouettes as inexpensive and popular art, see Desmond Coke, *The Art of the Silhouette* (1913; reprint, Detroit: Singing Tree Press, 1970); Raymond Lister, *Silhouettes: An Introduction to Their History and to the Act of Cutting and Painting Them* (London: Pitman, 1953). Inexpensive prints of Washington were widely available; see Charles Henry Hart, *Catalogue of the Engraved Portraits of Washington* (New York: Grolier Club, 1904). Britain had not stopped impressing American sailors, had continued her trade blockade, and had incited Native Americans against the United States; the young nation had declared war on England on June 19, 1812, even though unprepared. United States troops did not win many battles; the navy was more successful.

14. Herman Bauer, *Niederländische Malerei des 17. Jahrhunderts* (Munich: Verlag F. Bruckmann, 1982); Sam Segal, *A Prosperous Past: The Sumptuous Still Life in the Netherlands, 1600–1700* (The Hague: SDU Publishers, 1988).

15. Peale's work did not reflect the great disarray of his personal life; see Richardson, *Painting in America*, pp. 130–31; Nicolai Cikovsky, Jr., with Linda Bantel and John Wilmerding, *Raphaelle Peale Still Lifes* (Washington, D.C.: National Gallery of Art, 1988), pp. 25–26, 100–101.

and woods increase these qualities. The items also look ordinary and necessary: a sewing basket, scissors, ribbons, and scraps; a table set for an informal party; a serving tray with teapot, pitcher, and cups; objects inside and on top of the sliding-door cupboard; and items above the fireplace communicate specific information about the day's work, the nature of the party that will be held, and the general life-style of the family living in this home.[16]

Quilting Frolic also demonstrates how well the artist had learned to integrate his own observations with the pictorial concepts he borrowed from other artists whose works he admired. The lively figure of the fiddler clearly is modeled after the boy in Wilkie's *Blind Fiddler* who pretends to fiddle on a bellows and wears a similar floppy hat. The arm position of the girl removing the quilt is derived from West's *Arethusa* (see fig. 50). The design for the young boy at the cookie plate is based upon the figure of Hercules holding the apples of the Hesperides which had appeared in Rees's *Cyclopaedia* (fig. 58). The design of the corpulent mistress of the house who holds a round loaf of bread in her left arm is based on Wilkie's symmetrically outlined figure of the woman in *The Blind Fiddler*, who cradles a sleeping child in her left arm (see fig. 55) and on the face of a woman Krimmel had drawn in sketchbook 3 (fig. 59). The young people's lively gestures and dancelike stances are reminiscent of figures in Hogarth's prints, and their arm and hand movements can be directly traced to studies in sketchbook 1 (see fig. 15). Yet in spite of these frank adaptations and amalgamations, in his combination of them Krimmel constructed a scene that achieves a convincingly original and contemporary quality and projects a distinct sense of place.

Three watercolors that are structurally similar to *Quilting Frolic*, and thus date from late 1812 or early 1813, demonstrate Krimmel's efforts at improving his handling of axial symmetry and centripetal movements. Two are small, well-executed watercolors in sketchbook 2 that present an interior of a house in which a family celebrates Christmas Eve in a Moravian fashion; the third is among the watercolors he sold to Pavel Svinin.

The Moravians, officially members of the Renewed Unitas Fratum, the Protestant United Brethren of the Augustan Confession, were in some respects a curiosity because of their evangelicalism. Members of the church had emigrated from Europe to Pennsylvania and North Carolina in the eighteenth century, and they established several communities. They stressed the subjective aspects of religion and promoted celebratory expressions of piety at a time when most other religions stressed solemnity. For example, at Christmas Moravians often hung images relating to the birth of Christ on a wall and placed a *putz*, which included a creche, magi, and town and farm buildings, at the base of a cut tree or on a table, and thus joyfully celebrated the birth of Christ. Krimmel's drawings are of such a scene and are quite similar in details. In one there is a single ornamented tree; in the other there are two, but both images have a *putz*, the carved figures of which reinforce the religiosity conveyed by the picture of the Holy Family on the chimney breast (figs. 60, 61).[17] While Krimmel experimented with the props and design in the two scenes, he retained the same spatial structure—a shallow stage with a central fireplace. The shadows unify and enliven the scene, but in both drawings most figures gesture and move toward the center of the picture, making the design seem obsessively symmetric.

Krimmel used the same structure to create *Black People's Prayer Meeting* (fig. 62), an image that also reveals his fascination with the blacks in Philadel-

16. The profusion and type of goods set this apart from the furnishings found in a home or rooms of the lower sort; the lack of high-style furniture, portraits, and fashionable clothes distinguish this from a home of the well-to-do. High-style furniture can be found in books such as Charles F. Montgomery, *American Furniture: The Federal Period in the Henry Francis du Pont Winterthur Museum* (New York: Viking Press, 1966); and Gerald W. R. Ward, *American Case Furniture in the Mabel Brady Garvan and Other Collections at Yale University* (New Haven: Yale University Art Gallery, 1988). For social history see Nash, *Forging Freedom*, pp. 134–246; Billy G. Smith, *The Lower Sort: Philadelphia's Laboring People* (Ithaca: Cornell University Press, 1990).

17. James Henry, *Sketches of Moravian Life and Character* (Philadelphia: J. B. Lippincott, 1859), pp. 158–61; Joseph Mortimer Levering, *A History of Bethlehem, Pennsylvania, 1741–1892 . . .* (Bethlehem: Times Publishing Co., 1903), pp. 66, 183; Adelaide L. Fries, *Customs and Practices of the Moravian Church* (rev. ed.; Winston-Salem, N.C.: Board of Christian Education and Evangelism, 1964), pp. 39–41.

FIGURE 58
J. Yeager, detail of Drawing, *from Abraham Rees,* Cyclopaedia; or, Universal Dictionary of Arts, Science, and Literature *(Philadelphia: Samuel F. Bradford & Murray, Fairman and Co., 1810–24), pl. 234. (Photo, Winterthur.)*

FIGURE 59
Woman's head, 1812–13. Watercolor over pencil. Sketchbook 3, leaf 1 recto.

FIGURE 60
Christmas Eve 1, 1812/13. Ink and ink wash over pencil. Sketchbook 2, leaf 7 recto. Although this is the less finished of the two Christmas scenes, it is the more naturally composed and livelier one. The child in the high chair playing with the dog is a particularly engaging detail.

FIGURE 61
Christmas Eve 2, 1812/13. Ink and ink wash over pencil. Sketchbook 2, leaf 8 recto. This more finished design is overly symmetrical and lacks the freshness of fig. 60. These two watercolors may be the earliest representations of a Christmas tree in American art.

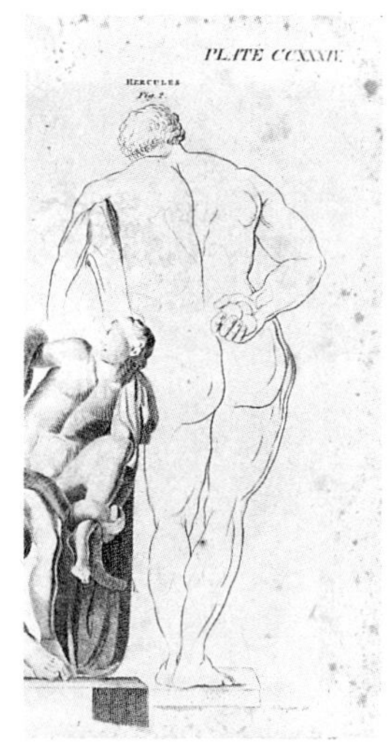

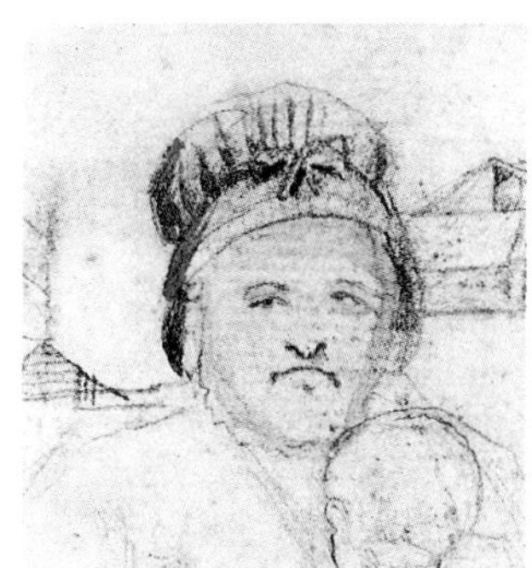

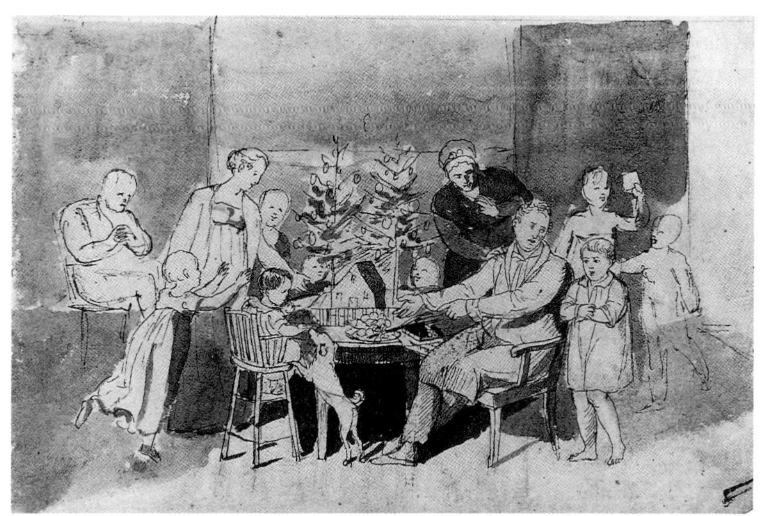

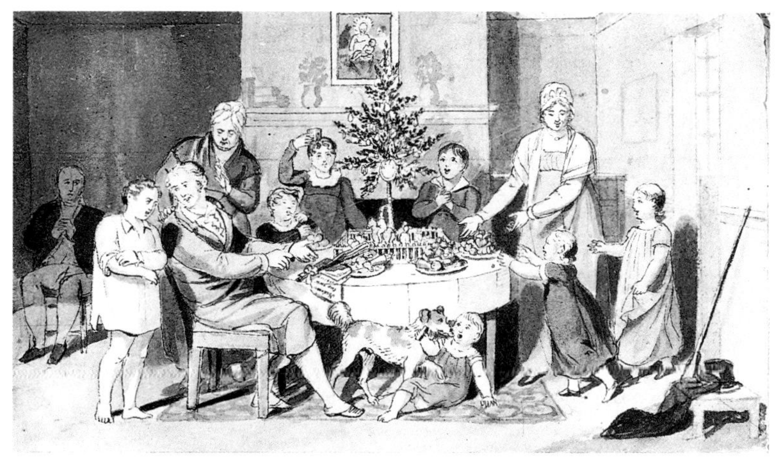

FIGURE 62
John Lewis Krimmel, Black People's Prayer Meeting, *1813. Watercolor on paper; 6 5/8 x 10 in. (The Metropolitan Museum of Art, New York, Rogers Fund, 1942.)*

FIGURE 63
Seated man, ca. 1812. Pencil. Sketchbook 1, leaf 6 recto.

FIGURE 64
Hand and arm movements, ca. 1812. Pencil. Sketchbook 1, leaf 23 verso.

FIGURE 65
Man's legs, 1811/12. Pencil. Sketchbook 1, leaf 11 verso.

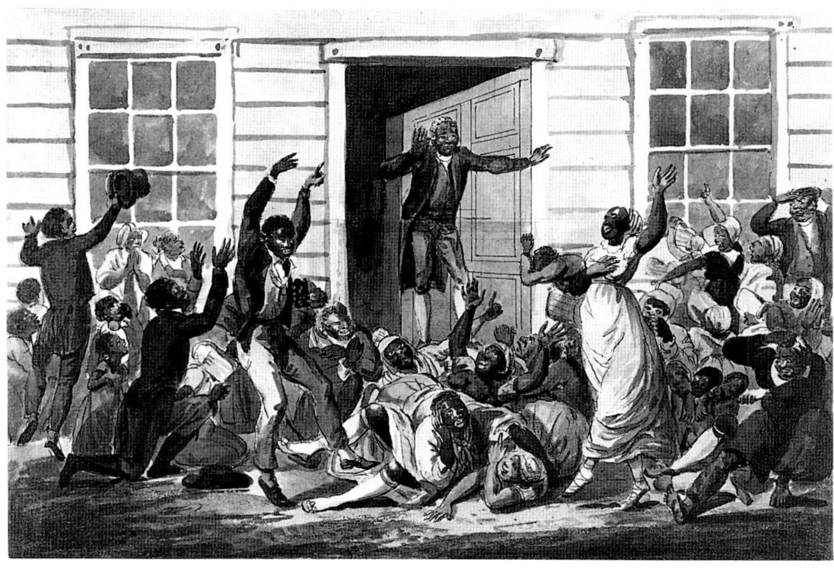

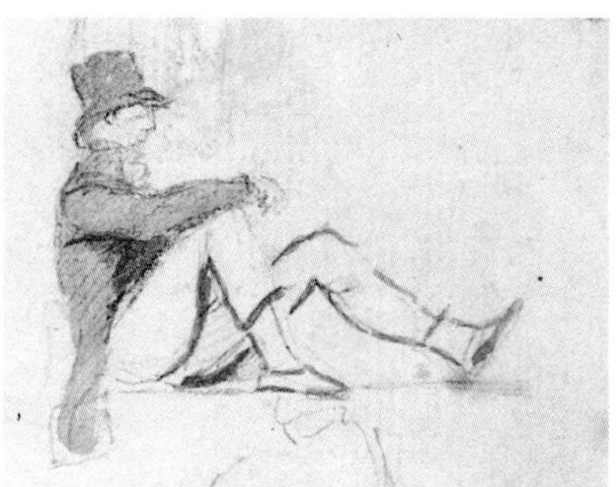

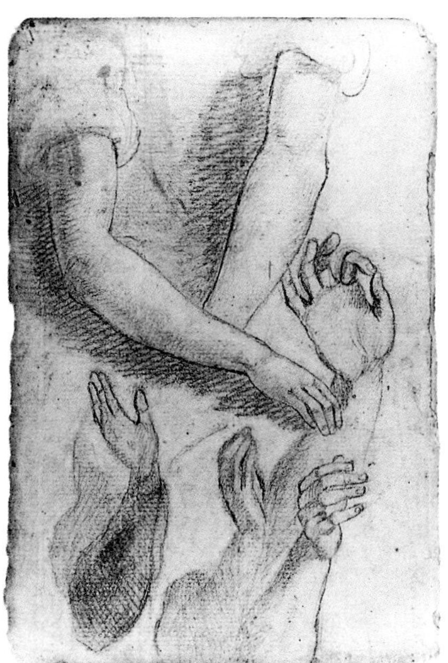

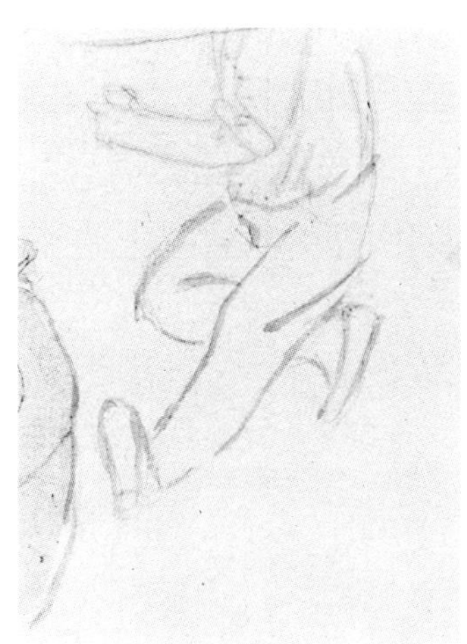

phia.[18] Compared with the two Christmas images this not fully finished watercolor has a greater variety of movement and pose, an effect that minimizes the strong axial symmetry. The scene is designed with great devotion to neoclassical principles: pure horizontals and verticals provide a firm background. The regular lines of the broad clapboards extending to the edges of the image stabilize the design; the figures are aligned in a frieze and exist in a shallow space. Although the congregants give an impression of frenetic behavior, the individual ecstatic gestures and positions are quite close to Krimmel's life studies in sketchbook 1 and to the figure types he used in *View of Centre Square on the Fourth of July* (1812), and *Quilting Frolic* (1813) (figs. 63–65). Good examples of this are the two men on the extreme right who touch their foreheads in the same manner as a man and woman in the right side of the Fourth of July painting, a gesture that Krimmel also worked on in Dr. Dorsey's life study class. The axial, bilateral construction and emphatically symmetrical distribution of figures suggest a temporal relationship to *Quilting Frolic*, which also has lively gesturing figures placed against a pronounced horizontal and vertical background. The figure type of the dancing girl also appears in *Quilting Frolic*, and her red shoes are identical to those on girls in *Pepper-Pot* and in the Fourth of July painting and on the elegant woman in the chimney sweep watercolor (see fig. 35).

Other Krimmel watercolors in the Svinin Portfolio demonstrate aspects of his artistic growth in the months between his completion of *View of Centre Square* and the beginning of *Quilting Frolic*. One is *Members of the City Troop of Philadelphia* (fig. 66). The idea for this image probably came in summer 1812 as the soldiers assembled near Philadelphia following the declaration of war. Its figure types are richly varied and individualized but have the same elongated proportions and picturesque shadows as the Fourth of July painting; they are also aligned in the same tight, vertically packed manner and stacked in three parallel horizontal friezes. Indeed the correspondences are strong: for example, the rippling movement in the flag is analogous to the plume of steam, and the officer's sword and the closed parasol and the walking stick function similarly. Krimmel based the stances of the soldiers on drawings in sketchbook 1 (fig. 67; see also figs. 12, 13) and the military equipage on an image he had drawn in sketchbook 3 (fig. 68) which he subsequently used in *Quilting Frolic*.

In another watercolor, *Winter Scene with the Bank of the United States in the Background* (fig. 69), Krimmel expanded a sleigh motif he had initiated in sketchbook 2 and also explored ways of conveying children's actions more effectively than he had in the Fourth of July painting. Although the perspective of the building in the background is not well resolved—a recurrent problem in his early works—its position suggests that Krimmel was experimenting with ways of creating a balanced composition that was not symmetrical and achieving more success than he had in the chimney sweeps watercolor. Conversely, the way the composition of the winter scene is handled, the quality of the design, and the delineation of the figures suggest that the scene predates *Quilting Frolic*.

The watercolor *Dance in a Wayside Inn* evinces the contemporary way of life in a charming manner, and like *Pepper-Pot* it is an interior genre scene with an informative vista of the outside world. It features a small stagecoach station in which four young people dance to the tunes of a fiddler while another couple flirts on a bench, and an open door reveals two large, covered

18. For discussions of blacks and religion see Dee Andrews, "The African Methodists of Philadelphia, 1794–1802," *Pennsylvania Magazine of History and Biography* 108, no. 4 (October 1984): 471, 479; Nash, *Forging Freedom*, pp. 109–11, 191–202, 227–35, 260–67.

FIGURE 66
John Lewis Krimmel, Members of the City Troop of Philadelphia, *1812/13. Watercolor on paper; 9 x 7¼ in. (The Metropolitan Museum of Art, New York, Rogers Fund, 1942.)*

FIGURE 67
Men's legs, 1812/13. Pencil. Sketchbook 1, leaf 6 verso.

FIGURE 68
Men in military uniforms, young boy, 1812/13. Pencil. Sketchbook 3, leaf 14 verso.

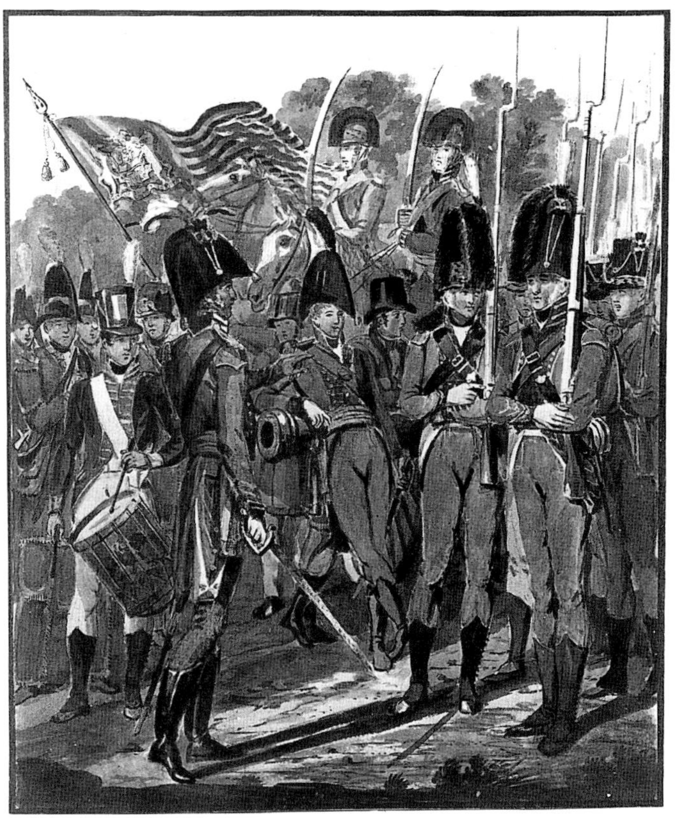

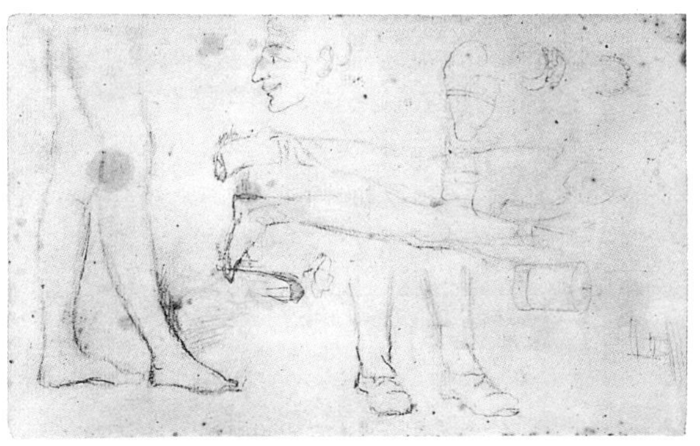

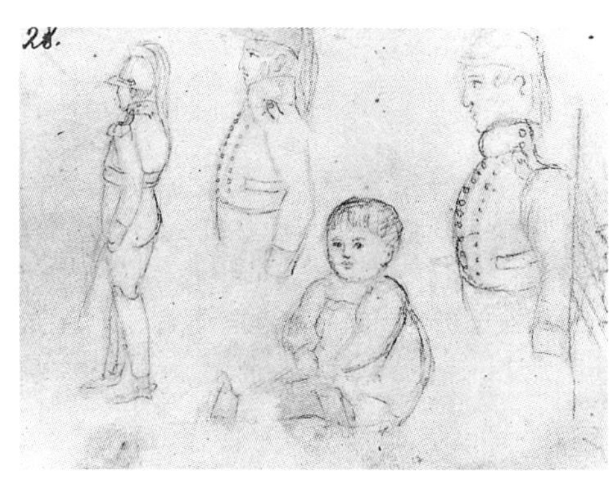

FIGURE 69
John Lewis Krimmel, Winter Scene with the Bank of the United States in the Background, *1812/13. Watercolor on paper; 7 3/8 x 9 3/4 in. (The Metropolitan Museum of Art, New York, Rogers Fund, 1942.)*

FIGURE 70
John Lewis Krimmel, Dance in a Wayside Inn, *1812/13. Watercolor on paper; 7 1/8 x 9 1/8 in. (The Metropolitan Museum of Art, New York, Rogers Fund, 1942.)*

FIGURE 71
Covered wagon, 1811/12. Pencil. Sketchbook 1, leaf 1 verso. The "h. blau" signifies light blue.

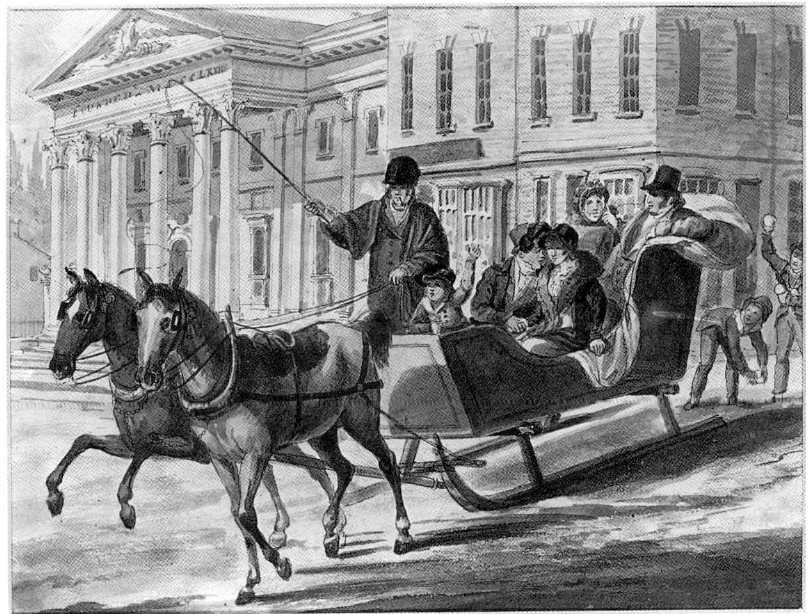

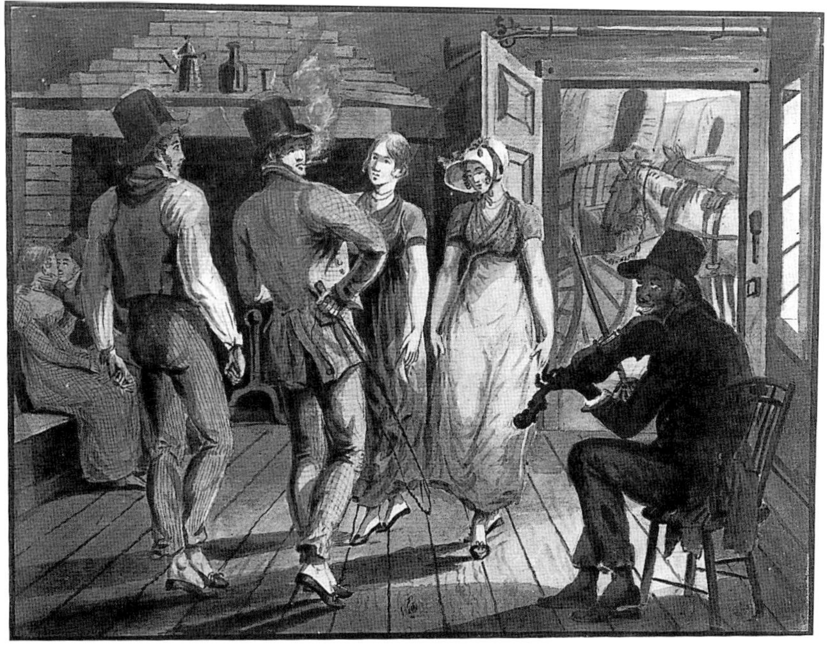

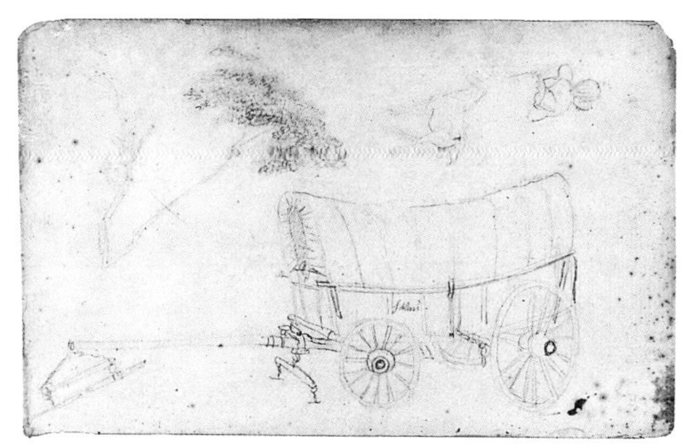

wagons that have come to a halt (figs. 70, 71). The fiddler, the girl with the hat, and the glimpse through the open door balance the five figures on the left. The props and figure types and gestures are familiar (compare, for example, the open door and the rifle to those in *Quilting Frolic*). The rural couple and city couple are distinguishable by their clothes and mannerisms—a variation of the same theme Krimmel used in *Pepper-Pot* and his Fourth of July oil painting and in his watercolor of the chimney sweeps. As in *Pepper-Pot*, one girl is blonde, the other dark-haired; the city girl's dress is similar to that of the *Pepper-Pot* woman. Following a by-now-established procedure, Krimmel selectively adapted details from his paintings and sketchbooks. The dancing girl wearing a hat for example, in dress and arm position, is similar to the woman standing near the fence in front of the fountain in the Fourth of July painting. Her hat is based on two hat studies in sketchbook 1 on the same page with the hat studies Krimmel turned to for many of his watercolors and paintings (see fig. 26). The arms are based on a pencil study and the foot position on a watercolor sketch (figs. 72, 73). The figures of the dancers, their foot positions and hand movements, their shoes, and the fabric of the seated girl's dress are remarkably similar to those in *Quilting Frolic*. Another connection to that oil painting is the similarity of the arm and hand position of the city-bred male dancer to that of the boy swiping cookies. The outfit of the country lad closely resembles that of the very tall man in *Pepper-Pot*. Although the idea of the fiddler may have come from Wilkie's *Blind Fiddler*, Krimmel's figure is distinctive—only the back of the fiddle and part of the bow are visible, the fiddler taps his heel not his toe, and his eyes follow the dancers' movements. In this advanced watercolor Krimmel also paid considerable attention to the role of light and shadow, much more so than he had in *Pepper-Pot*. He also experimented with conveying greater depth by running the floorboards perpendicular to the picture plane. Although this can be an effective way of conveying space, it was beyond his skills; the floor seems to rise up in back. Having failed to master this problem of perspective, in his next several interior scenes starting with *Quilting Frolic*, Krimmel chose to run the floorboards horizontally.

By the start of the second decade of the nineteenth century, steam-powered boats had become a regularly used form of transportation. To most people they epitomized the best of American ingenuity and were hailed as an important contribution to modern technology. It is not surprising that Krimmel, who repeatedly had exercised a progressive bent, was among the first artists depicting this newest mode of transportation. In sketchbook 2 he made a very quick drawing of a steamboat in the distance, and a subsequent page includes a genre scene of steamboat travel (fig. 74). Although a humorous reference to the new mode of travel, this sketch supports most written accounts, such as that by John M. Duncan, a Scotsman traveling in the United States, who stressed the cleanliness, the painted decks, the quality of the berths, the food (served on china), and the speed with which the vessels traveled. In sketchbook 3, Krimmel's approach to steamboat travel was different: trying to render correct information, he made a full-page watercolor of the *Car of Neptune*, Robert Fulton's rebuilt and renamed *Clermont*, the inventor's first steamboat, which in 1812 was operating as a companion to *Northern Star*, navigating the Hudson River between New York City and Albany as a scheduled conveyance for passengers and freight (fig. 75).

FIGURE 72
Arm, 1812. Pencil. Sketchbook 1, leaf 8 recto.

FIGURE 73
Young woman in dancing pose, 1811/12. Watercolor and wash. Sketchbook 1, leaf 10 verso.

FIGURE 74
Steamboat travel, 1812–13. Ink and ink wash over pencil. Sketchbook 2, leaf 6 recto.

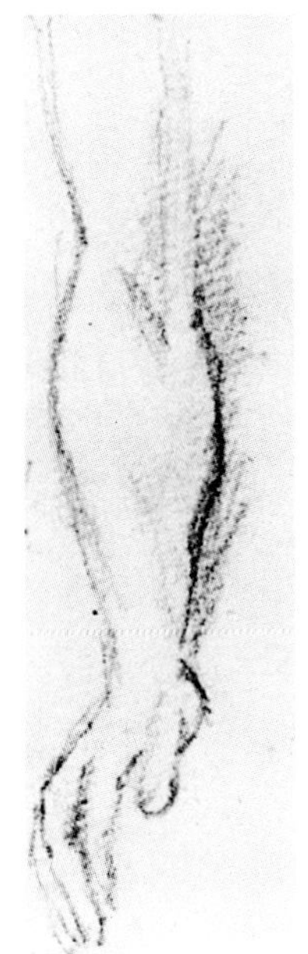

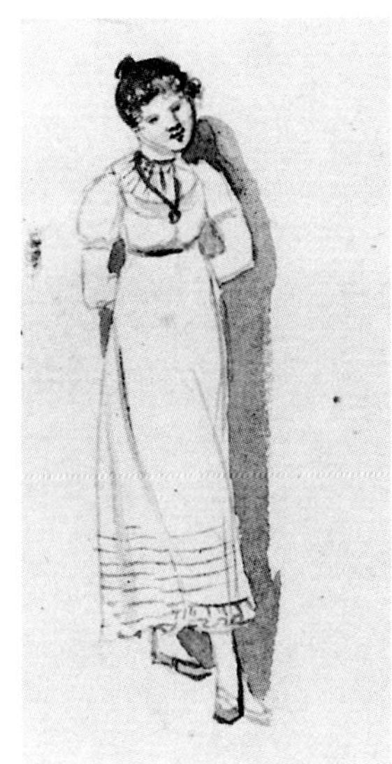

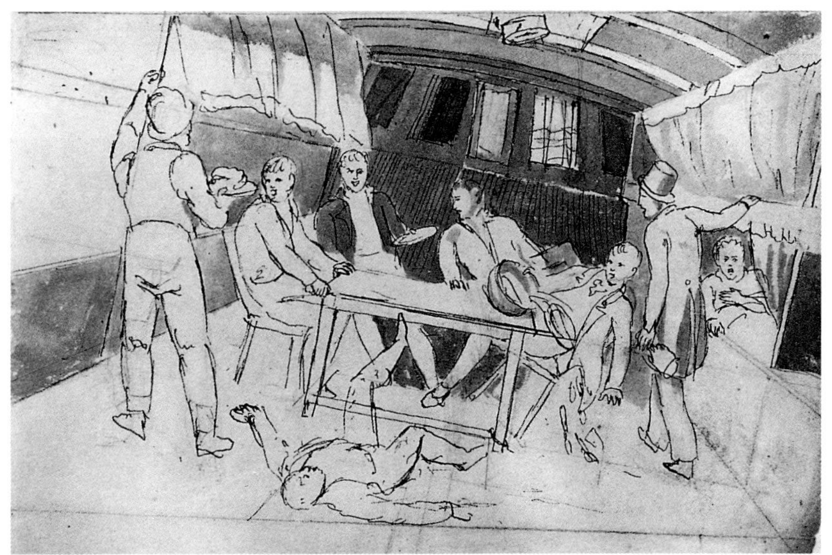

Of no less interest to the artist were the steam-powered ferryboats such as those traversing the relatively short spans of water separating New York and New Jersey or Pennsylvania and New Jersey. Their rounded bows and sterns permitted docking at either end and easy disembarking of passengers, horses, and wagons (fig. 76).

Krimmel's most finished and informative image of steamboat travel was the relatively large watercolor he sold to Svinin (fig. 77). It shows a steamboat cutting through choppy waters on the Hudson, and as in his image of the *Car of Neptune* he depicts the vessel broadside, the flag flying in the wind and steam puffing from the stack. It also shows life on deck but in a much expanded manner: well-to-do passengers sit in the middle section of the deck, the most stable part of the vessel; next to them the officers chart the ship's course while the crew measure the depth of the waters and work on the riggings of the auxiliary sails. A traveler seated close to the railing is fishing, another is stretched out in the sun, and two boys watch with amusement as a dog chases a cat. The boat is not identified by name, and Fulton's newest steamship, *Paragon* (1811), did not have auxiliary sails. Descriptions of *Northern Star* suggest that this may be the vessel in the watercolor.

Krimmel's artistic progress did not go unnoticed by fellow artists. In August 1813, Krimmel was elected an academician. He also took a sketching trip to the Lehigh Valley, a picturesque locale that had attracted many of his fellow artists, where he filled sketchbook 3 with landscape drawings and detailed studies of nature. Many convey an immediacy of observation and are precisely dated. They indicate that Krimmel spent the latter part of August and early September in the region. On August 22, 1813, he sketched a spectacular sunset near Bethlehem; regrettably he did not identify the other sites with such specificity. His drawings display two different approaches in the delineation of landscape as well as two distinct watercolor techniques. In his carefully finished topographic views depth is achieved through a succession of receding planes, and a tree or rock is often in the foreground to frame the vista. In these images Krimmel adhered to traditional design formulas, and these views owe more to early European landscape painting than to nature. Accordingly, he applied watercolor thickly and statically in a rather conventional manner (figs. 78–81).

In contrast Krimmel's sketches of intimate spaces—slices of nature in close view—and of atmospheric phenomena show a modern vision that favors a more open design (figs. 82–85). In these images he demonstrates an interest in geological structure, botanical growth, the shape of a tree, its root system, and its type of leaf. He also made precise studies of flowers and plants and more transient spectacles such as a sunset sky. More in line with romanticism, the artist applied watercolor thinly and fluently. The speed and technical simplicity of the watercolor medium suited him particularly well for making fast records of quickly changing impressions. With these types of sketches Krimmel was building up a vocabulary of nature elements for use in his paintings. Significantly, these nature views and pure landscapes were made more than a decade before the emergence of the Hudson River School, the first native school of American landscape painting. All express the artist's excitement and wonder at the marvels of nature and match an enthusiastic description of the countryside that infuses an undated letter he wrote to Thomas Birch.

FIGURE 75
Car of Neptune, *1812/13. Watercolor and ink over pencil. Sketchbook 3, leaf 12 verso.*

FIGURE 76
Steam-powered ferry boat, 1812/13. Watercolor and ink over pencil. Sketchbook 3, leaf 13 verso.

FIGURE 77
John Lewis Krimmel, Steamboat Travel on the Hudson River, *1812/13. Watercolor on paper; 10 x 14 ¼ in. (The Metropolitan Museum of Art, New York, Rogers Fund, 1942.)*

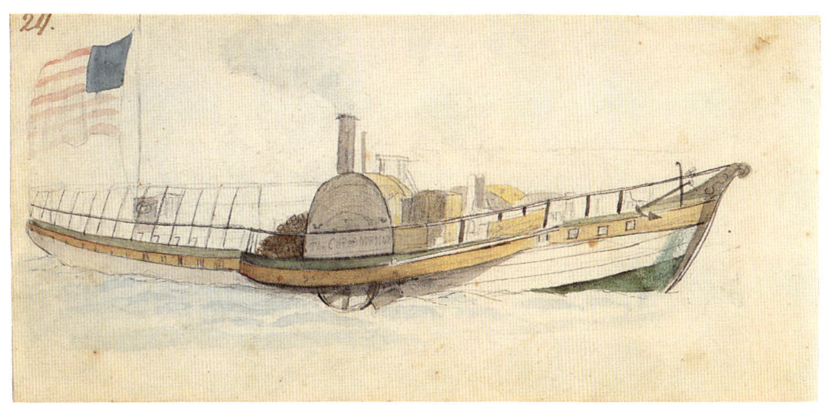

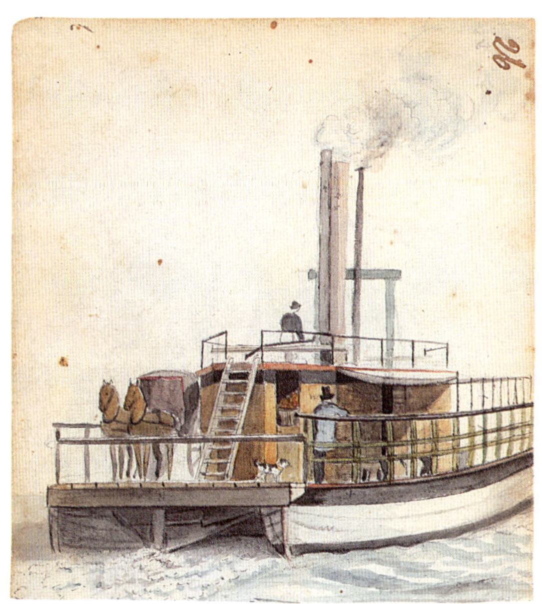

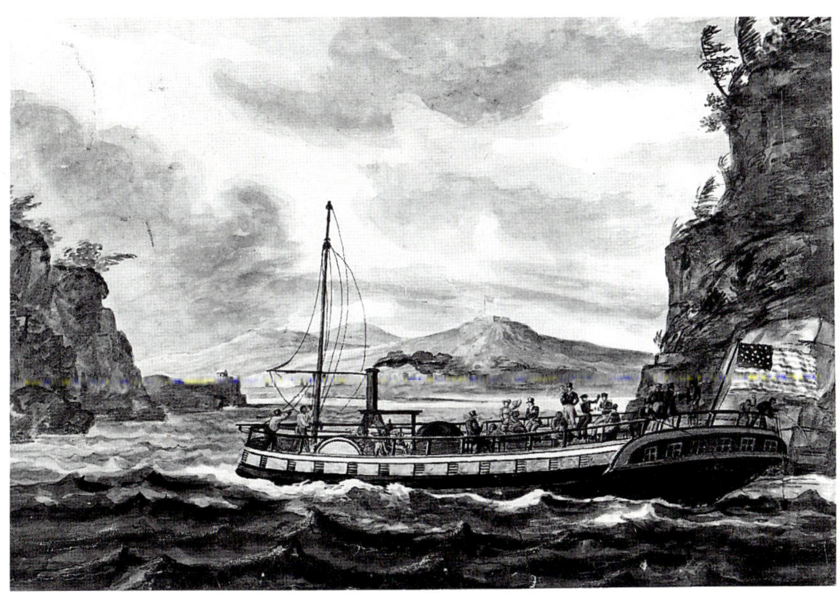

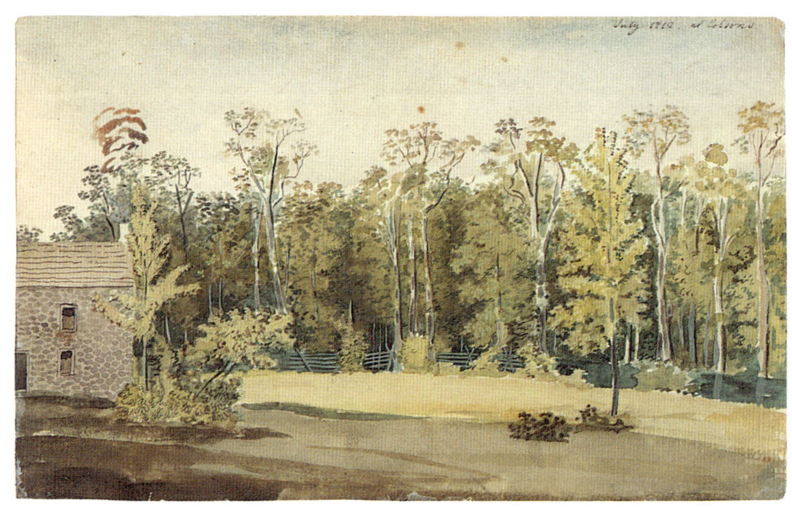

FIGURE 78
At Colsons, July 1812. Watercolor over ink, ink inscription. Sketchbook 1, leaf 5 verso. In this image Krimmel has imposed a neoclassical style on a landscape.

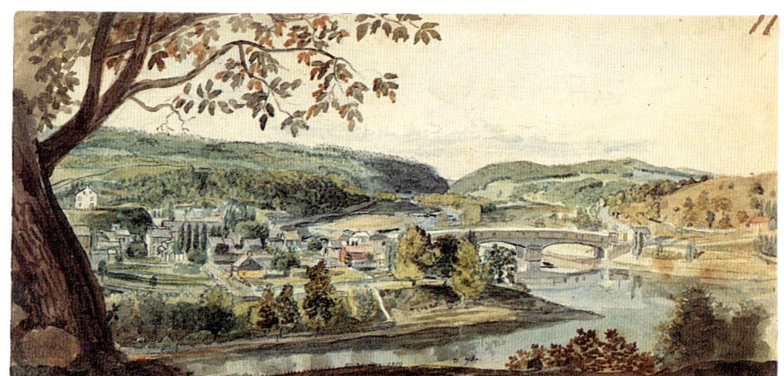

FIGURE 79
View of Easton, August 30, 31, and September 3, 1813. Watercolor and ink over pencil. Sketchbook 3, leaf 6 recto. Easton was a sizable town near Bethlehem located at the junction of the Delaware, Lehigh, and Bushkill rivers. This view shows the Lehigh water gap in the background, one of the more impressive sights in eastern Pennsylvania.

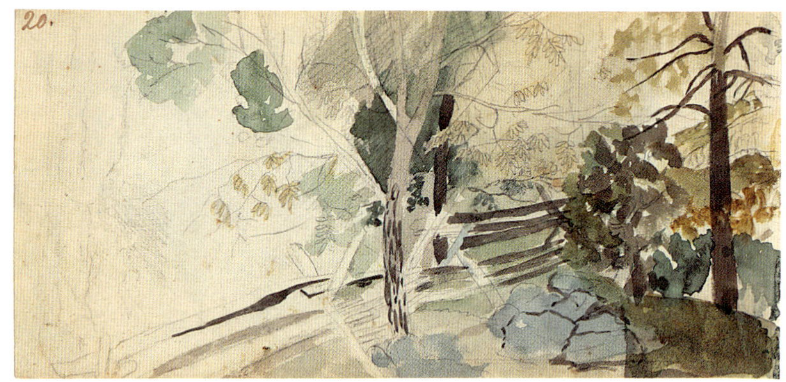

FIGURE 80
Trees and rocks near a split-rail fence, ca. 1813. Watercolor over pencil. Sketchbook 3, leaf 10 verso.

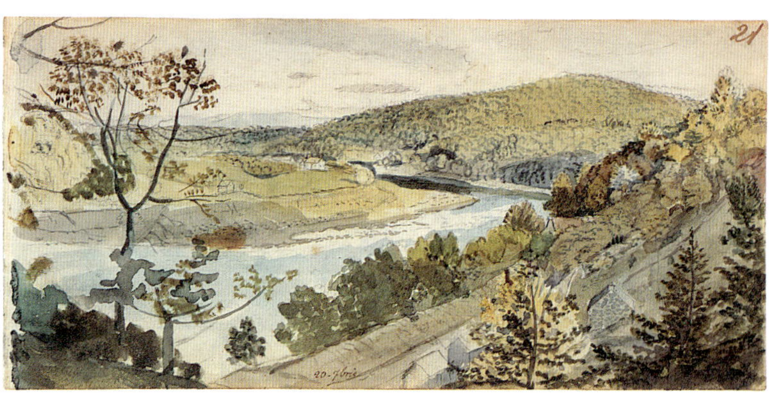

FIGURE 81
Pennsylvania landscape, September 20, 1813. Watercolor over pencil. Sketchbook 3, leaf 11 recto.

FIGURE 82
On the banks of the Lehigh River, Sunday, September 5, 1813. Watercolor over pencil. Sketchbook 3, leaf 7 verso. This simple sketch of a river view is made more picturesque by the sunlight reflected on the foliage and the large dark split in the tree trunk.

FIGURE 83
Schneider's meadow, Tuesday, September 7, 1813. Watercolor and ink over pencil. Sketchbook 3, leaf 8 recto. The meadow was located near Easton, for on the same day Krimmel also made a watercolor of the bridge over the Lehigh River there.

FIGURE 84
River valley with rocky slope in foreground, September 11, 1813. Watercolor and ink over pencil. Sketchbook 3, leaf 10 recto.

FIGURE 85
Cattle watering in river, Friday, August 21, 1813. Watercolor over pencil. Sketchbook 3, leaf 3 recto. A Krimmel painting titled Cattle Watering *was exhibited at the Boston Athenaeum in 1828 and may have been based on this image.*

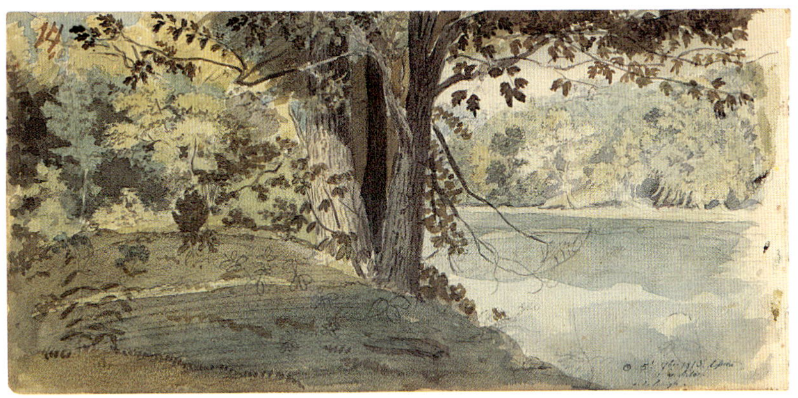

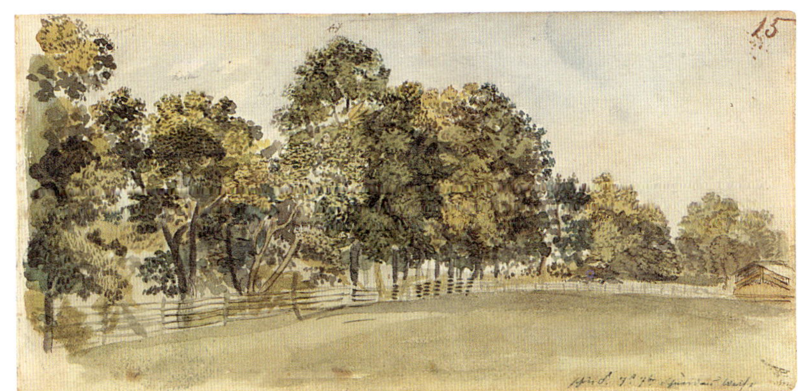

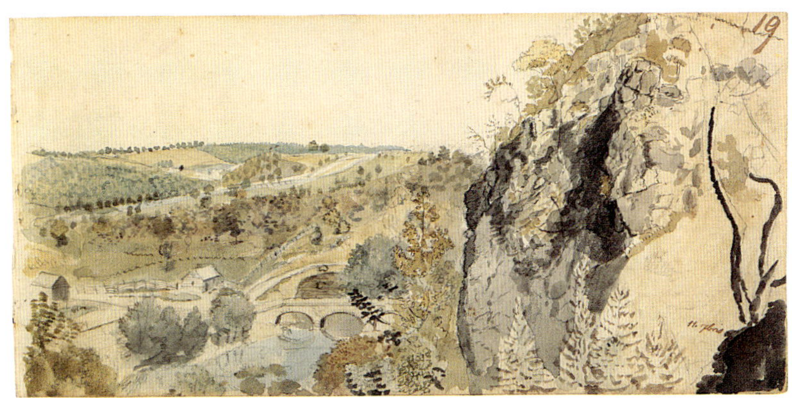

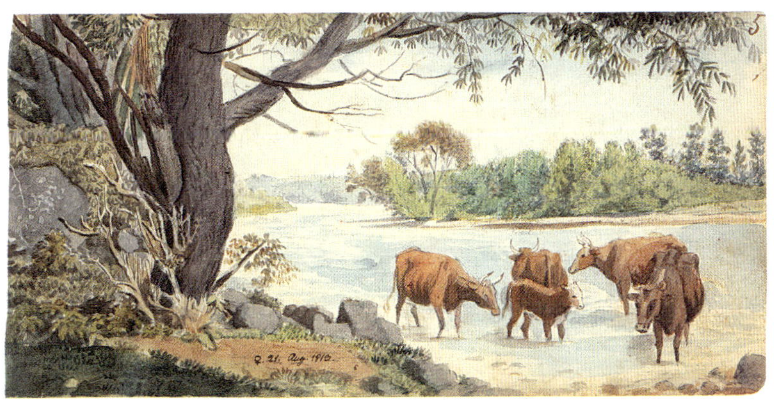

Dear Birch

Although I expected, You would make up your mind, and take a trip to this place, I had not the pleasure, to see You yet. Indeed If you knew, what a beautiful Scenery surrounds this place, You would not hesitate to come. To convince Yourself more, ask Mr. Sansom or Mr. Rash. Both were here, a few weeks ago, and expressed several times, that this would be one of the finest [two words marked out] countrys for You, to study from,—I am sure there are very few places in the United States, who offer so much Variety at so little trouble to a landscape Painter, for where ever you go, You find something, worth to be sketch'd. The expense, which is the only thing to deter you, cannot amount to a great summ, since boarding in the Hotel here, cost's only $3 a week, the first week cost's $3 ½; and the benefit which You receive not only for Your health, but for Your art will repay You a hundred fold.

Now then Birch do, come, and if possible with my friend Mr. Floegel, since I intend to leave this place in a short time, for Your sake I shall stay longer. Should you, which I hope not, be not able, to go, please to tell my friend, when the "Life Academic" begins;—

I am with Esteem
Yours
J. Lewis Krimmel

P. S. Mr Rider sends [page torn] respects to you.[19]

Birch, keeper of the academy, was probably involved with the efforts to set up another life study class, but Krimmel's tone suggests he was also a friend rather than just a colleague. If the letter dates from 1813, it was probably written during late August or early September when, as Krimmel's dated sketches indicate, he was in the Lehigh Valley north of the city, indulging in a joyful devotion to nature and escaping the oppressive heat, humidity, and yellow fever that yearly gripped Philadelphia. Like many other tourists he may have been staying at Sun Tavern in Bethlehem, which the Moravians ran as an inn for tourists and sightseers.[20]

Sketching tours in the country had been regular artistic activities in England during the second half of the eighteenth century and were widely practiced in Germany and America early in the nineteenth century. Krimmel's 1813 visit to the Lehigh Valley enabled him to make spontaneous sketches of dramatic sunsets and idyllic spots in the woods. These types of images, in which he experimented with freer applications of watercolor and more modern choices of motifs, resemble those of English and German artists who during the last decade had begun depicting nature more directly and with greater insight and respect. Watercolor served him well for detailed studies such as a tree trunk, an ornamental bush, or a particular rock, and Krimmel treated each element as an individual phenomenon with its specific imperfections (figs. 86–91)—an approach that became the hallmark of romanticism.[21]

Krimmel showed less ingenuity in his carefully drawn topographic views for which he seems to have resorted to drawing book instructions. Such books, initially imported from England and more recently published in New York and Philadelphia, had become extremely popular and were instrumental in introducing the topographical watercolor tradition to America. Although they provided an excellent method for self-instruction, most treated

19. Krimmel to Birch, [1812 or 1813], Hart Collection; Dunlap, *History*, 2:392. Samson may be Joseph Sansom (1767–1826), a member of the Columbian Society of Artists who did silhouettes of prominent Philadelphians in the 1790s, an art collector and a connoisseur who had sufficient wealth to travel frequently and widely; see Charles Coleman Sellers, "Joseph Sansom, Philadelphia Silhouettist," *Pennsylvania Magazine of History and Biography* 88, no. 4 (October 1964): 395–438. "Rash" is probably sculptor William Rush. "Floegel" (or Flegel or Voegel—both Germanic variants) is not listed in the city directories.

20. For Birch's appointment to the position of keeper, see Cincinnati Art Museum, *Masterpieces of American Painting from the Pennsylvania Academy of the Fine Arts* (Cincinnati, 1974), p. 22. For more on the roles of Birch and his father in advancing English ideas of landscape representation, see William H. Gerdts, *Thomas Birch, 1779–1851: Paintings and Drawings* (Philadelphia: Philadelphia Maritime Museum, 1966); Edward J. Nygren, *Views and Visions: American Landscape before 1830* (Washington, D.C.: Corcoran Gallery of Art, 1986), p. 58. That the life class continued in late 1813 or 1814 is established in Minutes of the Society of Artists, Peale Papers, microfiche 6:A-2. For the Lehigh as a vacation spot, see Ellis Paxton Oberholtzer, *Philadelphia: A History of the City and Its People; A Record of 225 Years* (Philadelphia: J. S. Clarke, 1912), 2:48.

21. William B. Vaughan, *German Romanticism and English Art* (New Haven: Yale University Press, 1979); Hugh Honour, *Romanticism* (New York: Harper and Row, Icon edition, 1979). In these sketches Krimmel comes close to drawings by contemporary German and English romantic artists and invites comparison with Caspar David Friedrich and Thomas Constable, not in quality of execution but in the early date of these observations.

FIGURE 86
*Skoke or Pokeweed (*Phytolacca Americana*), ca. 1813. Watercolor over pencil. Sketchbook 3, leaf 11 verso. A second watercolor of this tall, wild growing plant is dated September 11. The purple berries served as dye.*

FIGURE 87
Studies of large leafed plant, steer's head, man's head, flock of geese, September 8, 1813. Watercolor over pencil, partially traced in ink; pencil and watercolor. Sketchbook 3, leaf 2 verso.

FIGURE 88
Rock overgrown with grass and flowers, Saturday, September 4, 1813. Wash and ink over pencil. Sketchbook 3, leaf 6 verso.

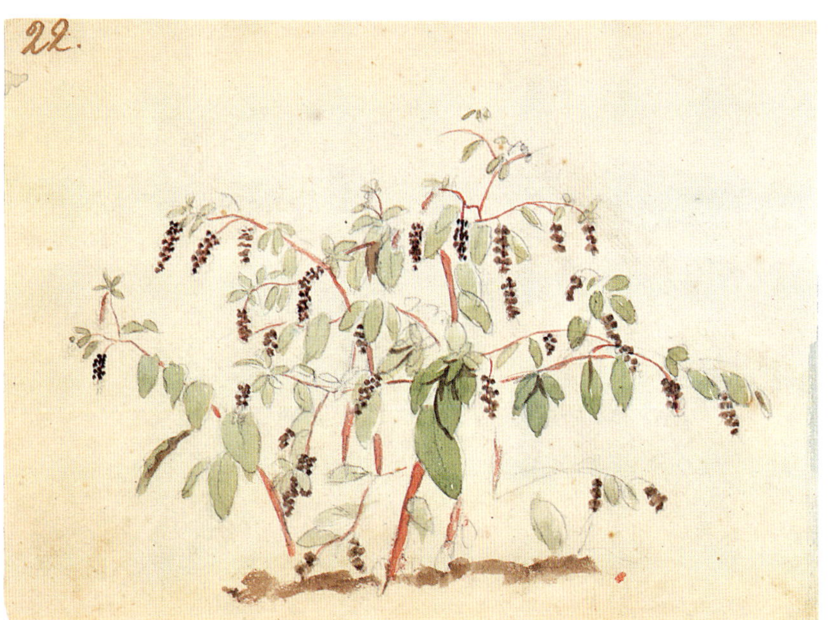

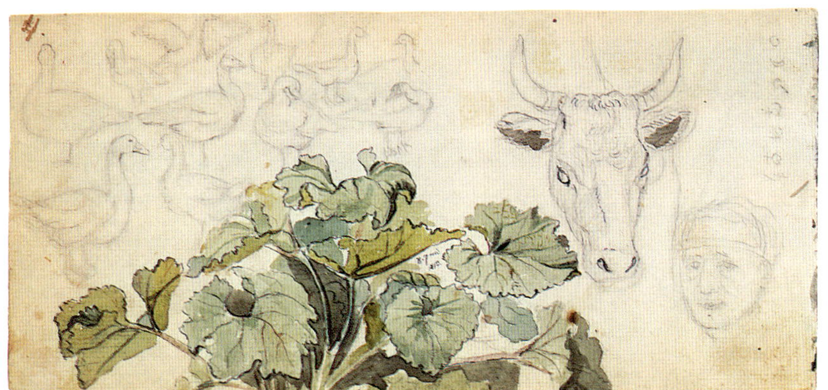

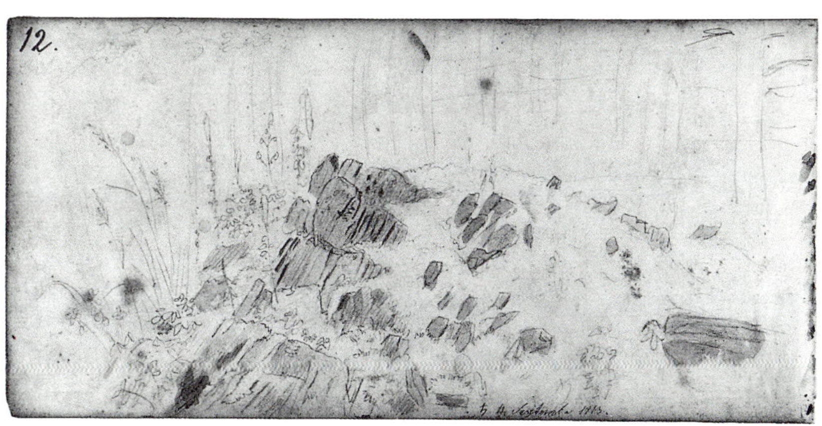

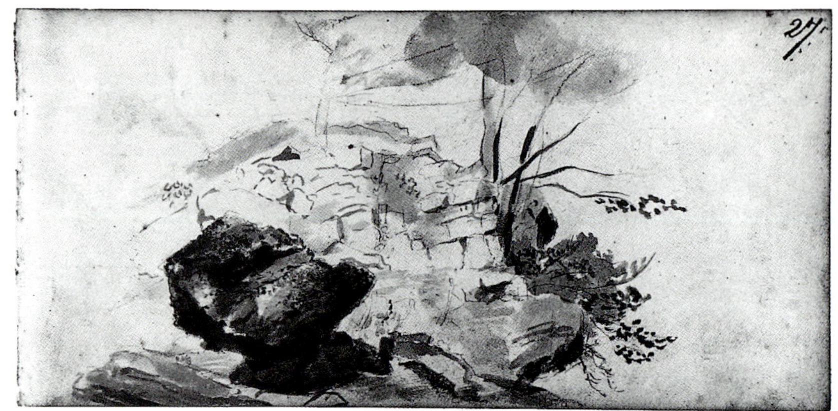

FIGURE 89
Top of rocky hill, ca. 1813. Watercolor over pencil. Sketchbook 3, leaf 14 recto.

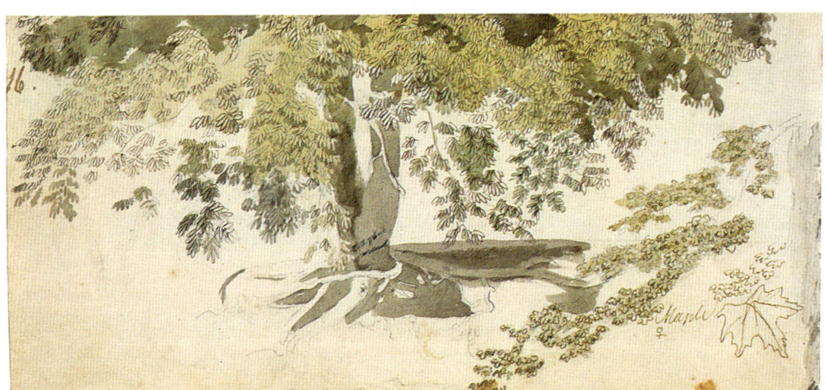

FIGURE 90
Large walnut tree, Wednesday, September 8, 1813. Watercolor and ink over pencil. Sketchbook 3, leaf 8 verso. On Friday (probably September 10) he sketched the outline of a single maple leaf.

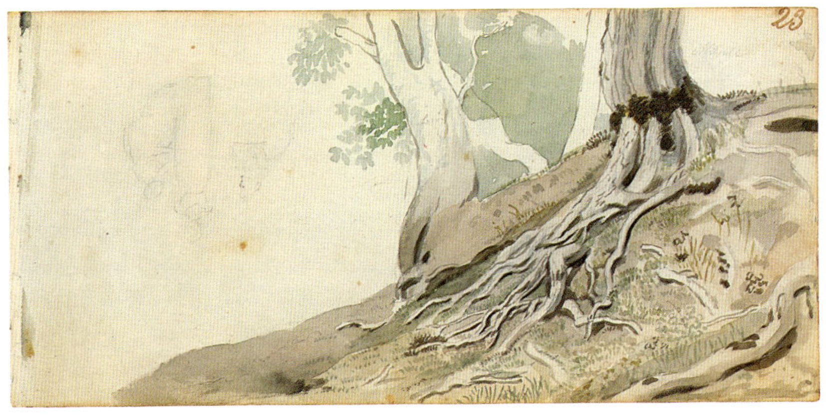

FIGURE 91
Lower trunks and surface roots of two trees, ca. 1813. Watercolor over pencil, pencil inscription. Sketchbook 3, leaf 12 recto. At left, "Bergahorn" translates as sycamore.

nature in a stereotypical manner. Reliance on these models would explain why Krimmel's 1813 topographical landscape views are uncharacteristically traditional. This also may explain why Krimmel hoped that Birch, who did landscapes so much better, would join him, even though it seems unlikely that Krimmel would have adopted Birch's manner—an approach derived from seventeenth-century Dutch models rather than the English tradition Krimmel's other Lehigh watercolors emulated.[22]

Sketchbook 3 also includes a number of figure studies and small portraits of people of different ages and color. In freshness and directness, these strikingly lively images surpass most characterizations Krimmel achieved in his paintings or final pictures (figs. 92–94). Several focus on little girls who may have been his nieces (figs. 95–99).[23] Such life studies in sketchbook 3 as well as some in sketchbook 1 (fig. 100; see also figs. 27–29) helped Krimmel create another genre scene, *Interior of an American Inn*, an oil painting that he may have started by autumn 1813 and which he exhibited under the title *Village Tavern* at the academy in May 1814.

Early in the nineteenth century, taverns and inns were way stations of great importance, especially for travelers but also for residents of rural regions. In addition to beer and other alcohol, hot and cold beverages and simple hot foods were served, newspapers and broadsides were available, rooms were obtainable for overnight stay by travelers (often sleeping dormitory fashion), and stables were available for grooming horses and sometimes for smithing work.

To paint a broad description of life at an inn Krimmel experimented with design options and decided to group most of the twelve figures around a rectangular table in the barroom (figs. 101, 102). The composition centers on a young wife, who implores her husband to stop drinking and go home, and a barefoot daughter, who puts a pleading hand on her father's knee while holding onto her mother's apron with the other.[24] Two young men entering the room—one shouting excitedly as he waves his hat, the other carrying a big basket full of bread and a leather duffle bag—provide a counterpoint. The almanac on the wall is dated 1814, and the dates of the week chalked above the bar indicate the month is May. This tempts the conclusion that the two men are bringing news of the May 6 fall of Fort Oswego; however, Krimmel more likely was making a general reference to news from the war and his choice of the days in May was a demonstration to viewers at the academy exhibition (which opened in May) that his genre scenes were indeed contemporary.

The war is a subtheme in the painting nonetheless, and an effective one. Pennsylvania had mustered more men for the militia and regular forces than had any other state, and Philadelphia's status as the largest port city in the nation and a shipbuilding center made its residents well aware of the threats posed by the British attempts to blockade Delaware Bay. During late 1813 and early 1814 most American victories had occurred on the Great Lakes, to which the prints of naval battles and a map of the region tacked to the back wall allude. Emphasis on current events is reinforced by the intensity with which two men are reading newspapers and the excited emotion with which a third gestures and shouts at either the man next to the bar who has raised his hand in appeasement or the men who have just entered with news.

Krimmel experimented in sketchbook 2 with various ways of blending the elements of his scene. Once he had determined the composition he did a small watercolor (fig. 103). Before completing the final version he experimented with details from his previous pictures: for example, the arm and

22. One such book was Archibald Robertson and Alexander Robertson, *Elements of the Graphic Arts or the Art of Sketching* (New York, 1802), cited in Stebbins, *American Master Drawings*, p. 52; another is *Drawing Book of Landscapes* (Philadelphia: Johnson and Warner, ca. 1810). See also Carl W. Drepperd, *American Pioneer Arts* (Springfield, Mass.: Pond-Ekberg, 1942), pp. 16, 21. For Birch's art see Gerdts, *Birch*.

23. Susana had borne at least six and probably seven children by 1814; four were still alive. George (Jr.) died in 1812, aged 4 months; "J" (presumed to be a daughter) died in July 1813, aged 11. Heinrich was born in 1807, Catharina in 1809, Frederika in 1812, and Susana in 1814. The gap between the birth of "J" in 1802 and Heinrich (later called Henry) in 1807 make it probable that a child was born in Europe and died before Susana and Georg emigrated in 1807; see St. Michael's and Zion Lutheran Church, Verzeichnis Register.

24. Krimmel's allusion to the temperance movement may have been timely; however, the theme was an old one among artists.

FIGURE 92
Two sketches of same man wearing a hat, 1813 or 1814. Watercolor over pencil. Sketchbook 3, leaf 4 verso.

FIGURE 93
Woman, ca. 1813. Watercolor over pencil. Sketchbook 3, leaf 4 recto.

FIGURE 94
Man, September 18, [1812?]. Watercolor over ink over pencil. Sketchbook 3, leaf 9 verso.

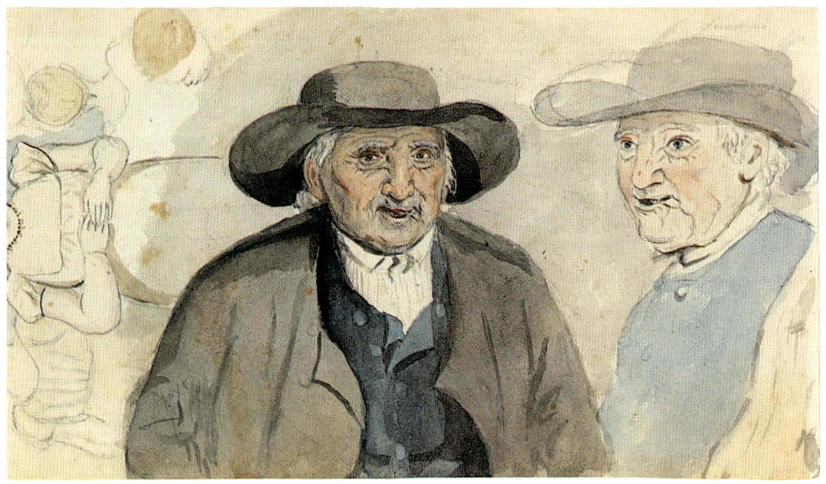

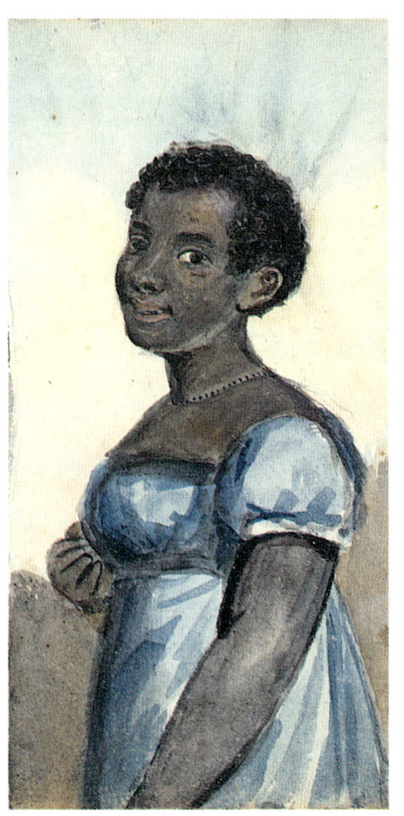

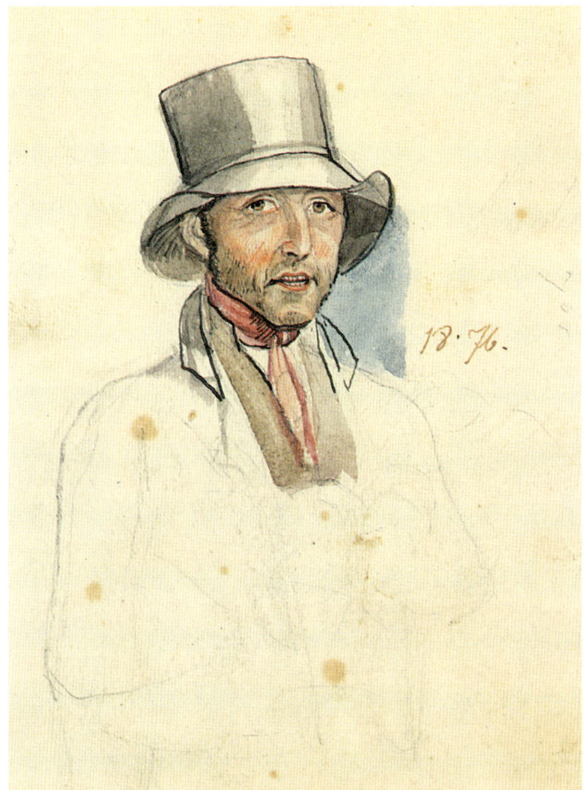

FIGURE 95
Two seated girls; two grazing cows; heads of two children; September 1, 1813. Pencil and watercolor over pencil. Sketchbook 3, leaf 3 verso.

FIGURE 96
Girl holding apple, September 17, 1813. Watercolor over pencil. Sketchbook 3, leaf 1 recto.

FIGURE 97
Outdoor studies of girls, September 17, 19, 20, 1813. Watercolor over pencil. Sketchbook 3, inside front cover.

FIGURE 98
Two girls seen from behind, 1813–14. Pencil and watercolor over pencil. Sketchbook 3, leaf 19 recto. These sketches are more polished and have a three-dimensionality lacking in earlier sketches.

FIGURE 99
Studies of girls, September 1, 1813. Watercolor and ink over pencil, pencil. Sketchbook 3, leaf 4 verso.

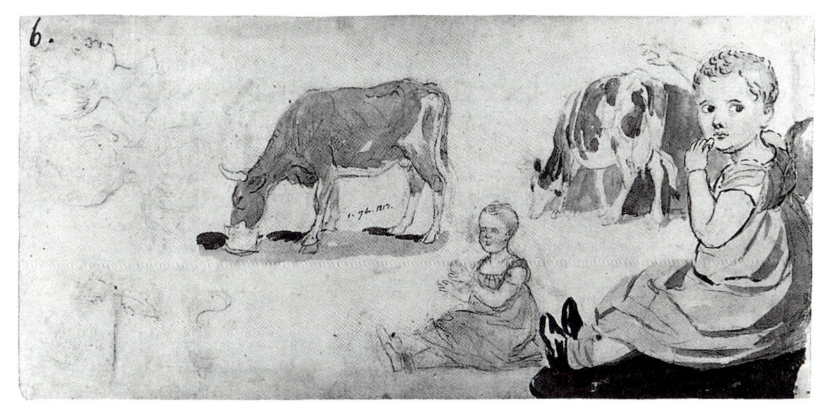

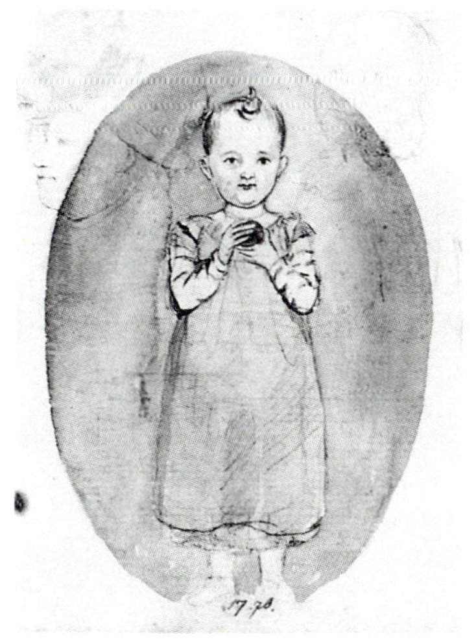

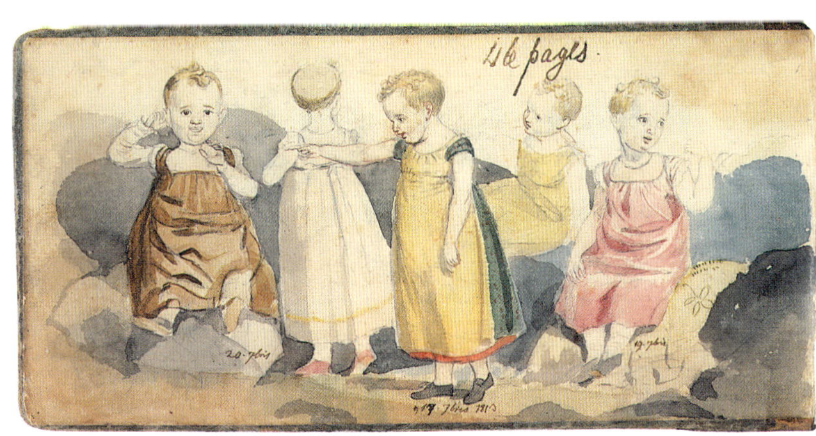

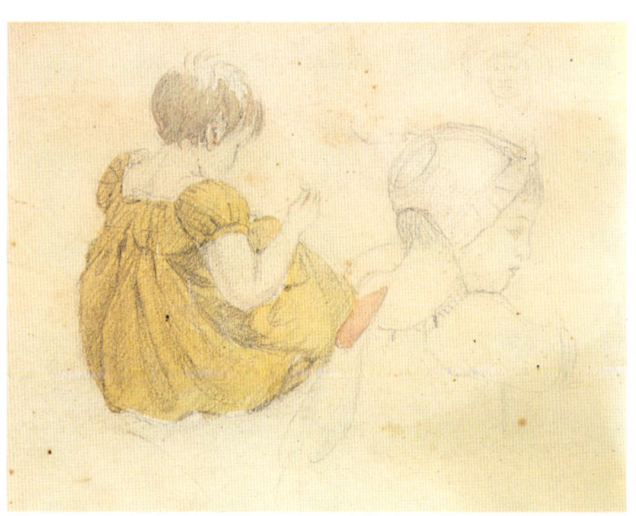

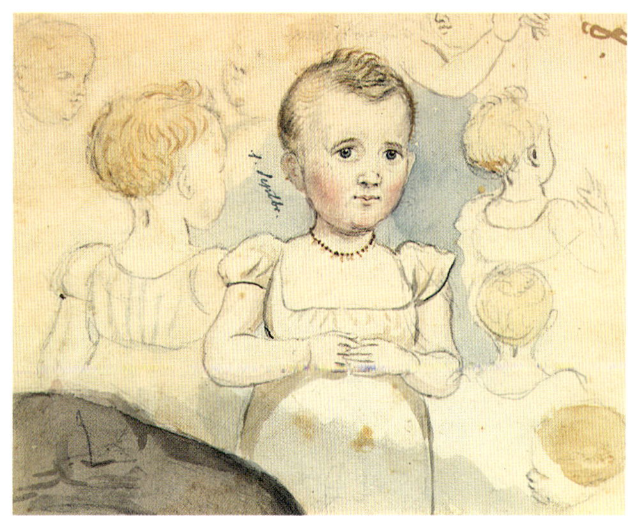

FIGURE 100
Group at a table, 1813/14. Pencil. Sketchbook 3, leaf 20 recto.

FIGURE 101
Compositional sketch for Interior of an American Inn, *1813/14. Ink and ink wash over pencil. Sketchbook 2, leaf 2 recto.*

FIGURE 102
Compositional sketch for Interior of an American Inn, *1813/14. Ink and ink wash over pencil. Sketchbook 2, leaf 2 recto.*

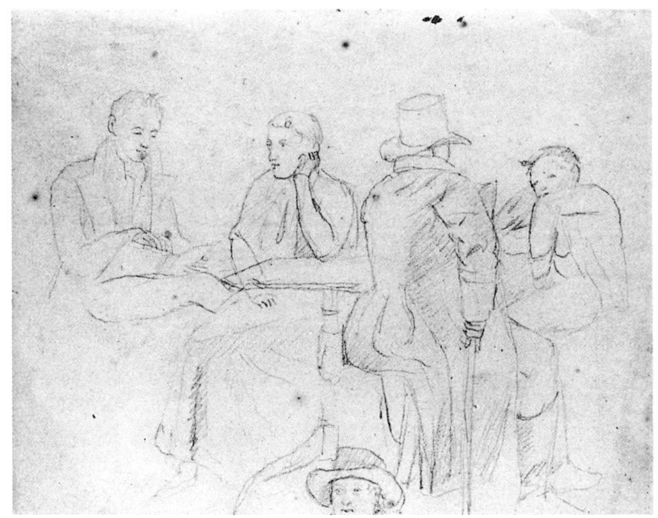

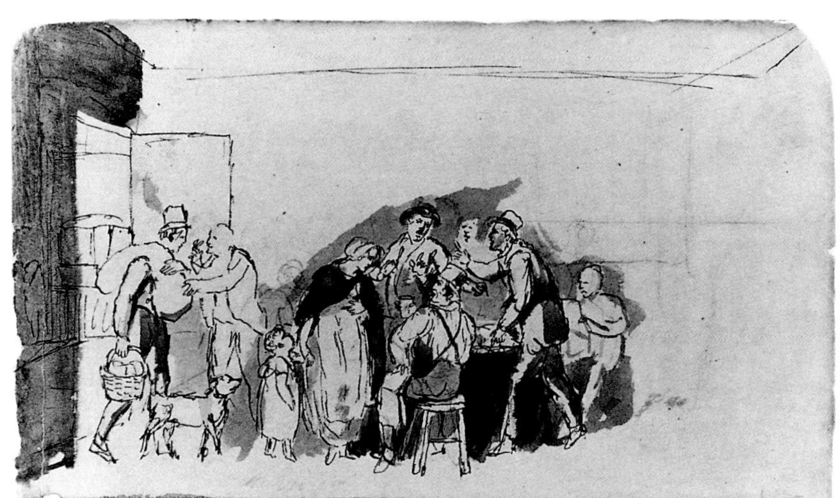

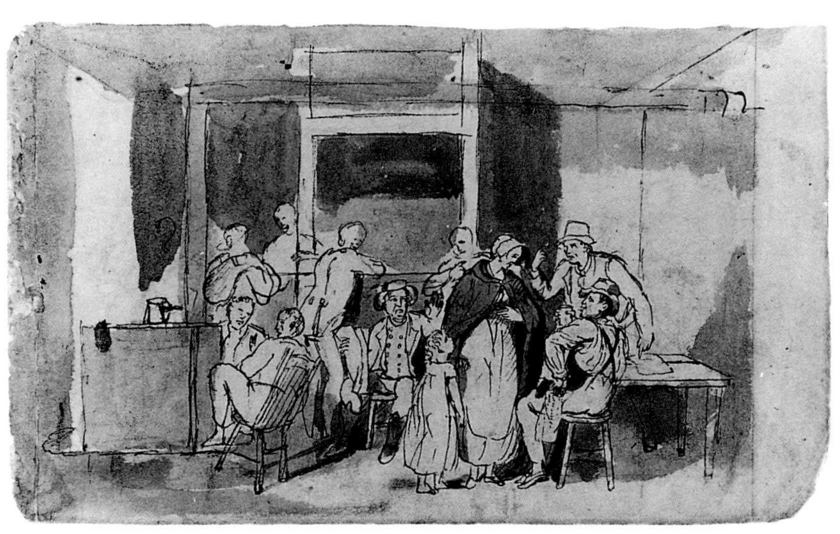

FIGURE 103
Preparatory drawing for Interior of an American Inn, *probably 1814. Watercolor on panel; 8¾ x 11¼ in. (Private collection: Photo, Winterthur.)*

FIGURE 104
Abraham Raimbach after David Wilkie, The Village Politicians, *London, 1814. Engraving; 19⅞ x 24 in. Published by David Wilkie and A. Raimbach. (Paul Mellon Collection, Yale Center for British Art, New Haven.)*

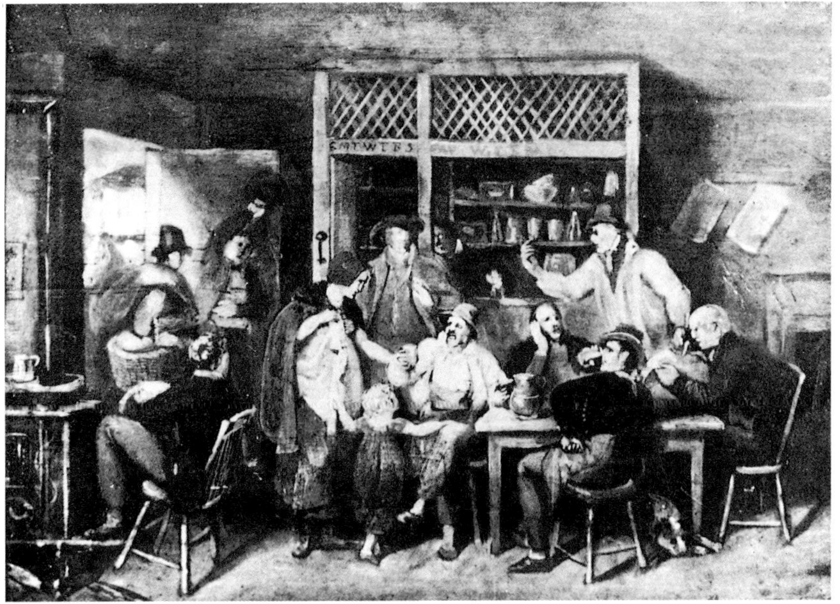

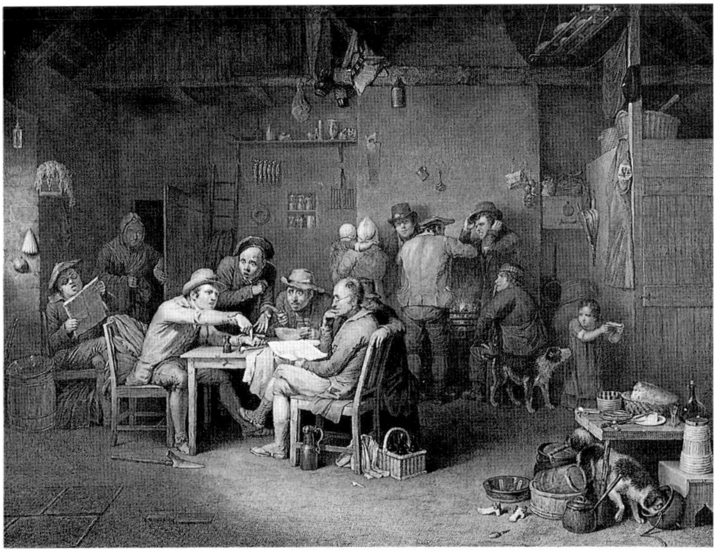

FIGURE 105
John Lewis Krimmel, Interior of an American Inn, *1814. Oil on canvas; 16 7⁄8 x 22 1⁄2 in. (Toledo Museum of Art, Toledo, Ohio, gift of Florence Scott Libbey.) Signed "ILK" on table apron.*

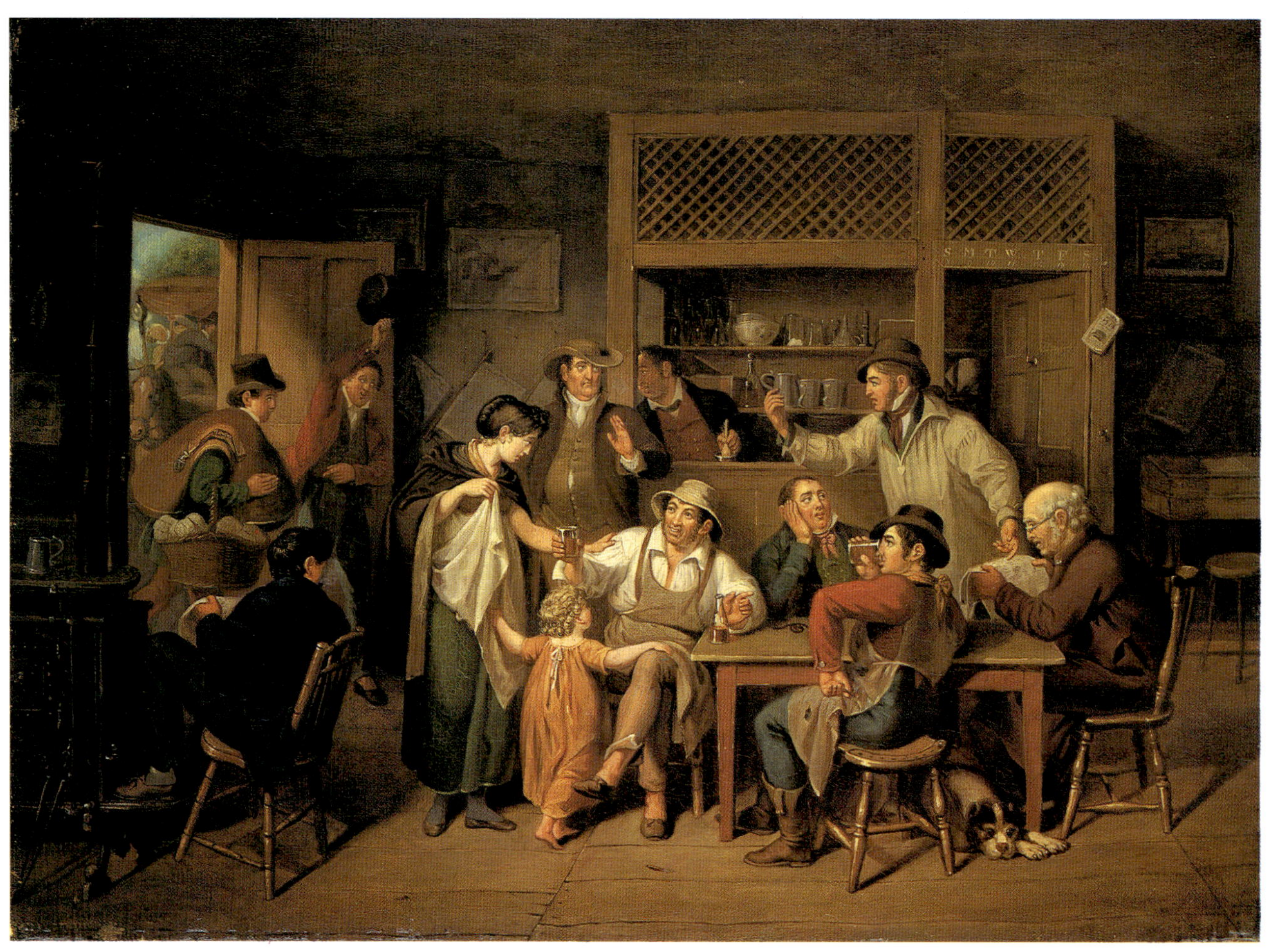

hand position of the aproned tradesman seen from the back and the hand of the hat-swinging messenger are taken from *Dance in a Wayside Inn* (1813). Furthermore, the structure of the image is based on Wilkie's *Village Politicians* (1806), an engraving of which had been published in London on January 1, 1814 (fig. 104), of which Krimmel painted a (now lost) copy.[25]

The similarities between *Village Politicians* and *Interior of an American Inn* (fig. 105) are too striking to be coincidental. In both the backgrounds have clear vertical and horizontal lines, and the middle-ground tables are parallel to the picture frame. Both have a bespectacled newspaper reader, a man who sits with his legs crossed, a man who rests his face on his hand, and two men who sit with their backs to the viewers but with their heads shown in profile.

Despite the similarities to Wilkie's image, Krimmel's scene and figures are fresh characterizations that convey completely different meanings. Krimmel's tavern scene has a firmer, tauter structure and is set in a much shallower space than Wilkie's. Most of the activities take place either parallel or perpendicular to the picture plane. The figures are in a more coherent design and are neatly grouped into three triangular arrangements, the first one inverted. Within this tripartite composition, the people are linked by movements and gestures. The figural design undulates across the width of the picture through foreground and background figures that turn away from the viewer or gesture toward the foreground. By refraining from overlapping the figures and by bathing the primary ones in a well-defining light, Krimmel enhanced the clarity and sculptural qualities of his design and increased the legibility of the story. Because the main scene is close to the viewer, Krimmel dispensed with the still-life repoussoir, but to compensate for the shallow depth of the picture stage, he placed an open door at the back to provide a glimpse of the larger world outside, suggested by the stagecoach from which the driver and passengers are still disembarking.

Although the tavern setting harkens back to Dutch seventeenth-century genre scenes, the painting is emphatically neoclassical in its reduction of pictorial depth, strict parallelism between the background wall and the painting's surface, and reinforcement of the rear plane by the taproom's clear geometric lines. The depiction of four of the men and the young mother in profile is a typical neoclassical convention. So too is the treatment of the woman—in the preparatory sketches she was clad in an ordinary street cloak and hat, but in the painting she is an idealized classical type in appearance, clothing, and deportment.

As he designed the scene, Krimmel also turned to another Wilkie picture, *The Jew's Harp* (1809), which had been engraved by John Burnet (fig. 106). Krimmel painted a copy of the image and then used its compositional scheme in the tavern scene. Wilkie's three figures—two children listening to the man playing a harmonica—are a pyramidally structured group. This strongly symmetrical and well-unified design so appealed to Krimmel that in his final version of *Interior of an American Inn* he abandoned a more realistic composition and created two pyramidally structured groups; he repositioned the young child with her back to the viewer, angled the father's hat and shoulders, and added the recumbent dog.[26]

Krimmel also painted *The Cut Finger* in 1813 or 1814 and entered it in the exhibition of 1814, but the current location of the painting is unknown, and no description survives. Two small compositional sketches in sketchbook 2 explore the visual representation of a story focusing on a small boy who has cut

25. "Krimmel's Picture—*Return from Boarding School*," *Analectic*, n.s., 2, no. 6 (December 1820): 508, specifies that Krimmel's copy of *The Village Politicians* belonged to "A[lexander] Murray." Late 1813 or early 1814 is the likely date of execution because the design discernibly influenced Krimmel's design for *Interior of an American Inn*.

26. Naeve ("Krimmel," p. 45) first noted the similarity of the posture and position of the younger child in Wilkie's *Jew's Harp* to those of the child in Krimmel's *Interior of an American Inn*.

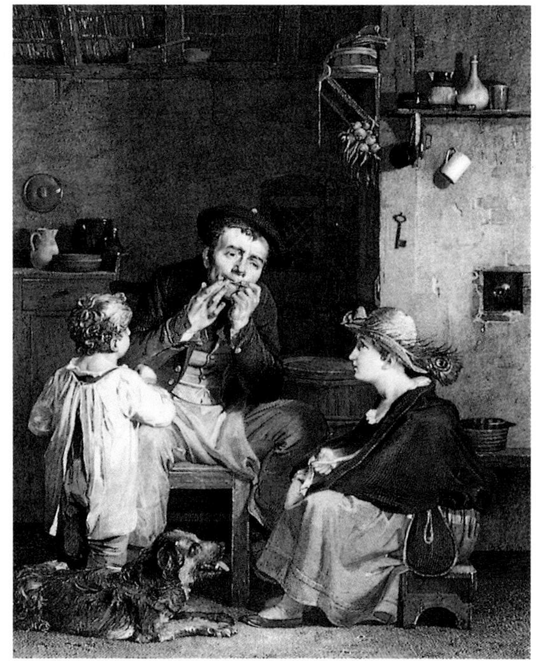

FIGURE 106
John Burnet after David Wilkie, The Jew's Harp, *London, 1809. Engraving. (British Museum.) This was the first collaboration between Burnet and Wilkie.*

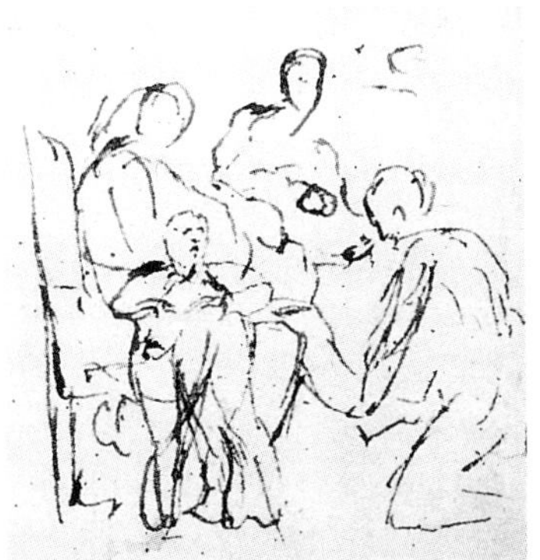

FIGURE 107
Compositional sketch, 1813. Ink. Sketchbook 2, inside front cover.

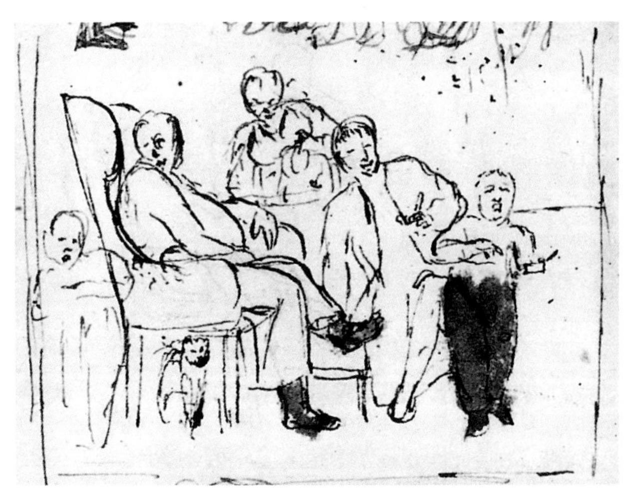

FIGURE 108
Compositional sketch, 1813. Ink and ink wash. Sketchbook 2, inside front cover.

his finger (figs. 107, 108). Two adults rush to help the sobbing boy who stands near a large armchair in which a grandfatherly figure is seated. Whether the final design of this scene is much like the sketches or was further influenced by the designs Wilkie used is undetermined. It is, however, highly unlikely that Krimmel based his image on the Wilkie painting of the same name. Wilkie's 1809 image depicted a grandmotherly figure bandaging a boy's finger as two other children look on; however that painting went immediately into private hands and was not engraved for nearly a decade. Because both artists used essentially the same subject, it is possible that both based their pictures on the same anecdote.[27]

Another 1814 Krimmel painting bearing a title identical to a contemporaneous Wilkie painting but decidedly different in story and design is *Blind Man's Buff* (fig. 109). Wilkie's version takes place in a large tavern and everybody present—about two dozen people, mostly adults—joins in the game (fig. 110).[28] Krimmel's version takes place at home, and the participants are children who are under the supervision of parents; of the twelve figures in Krimmel's painting only two are adults.

Krimmel's sustained preference for neoclassical design is discernible in the geometric clarity of the background furnishings, the run of the floorboards and the ceiling beams, and most important in the succinctly outlined and close-knit frieze of figures. It is further conveyed by the horizontal spread of the blindfolded girl's arms, a pose that is strikingly similar to those of two of the principal figures in Nicolas Poussin's *Rape of the Sabines* and to the sweeping gesture of the main figure in Jacques-Louis David's *Sabines*, which was based on Poussin's design (figs. 111, 112). Both these famous paintings—one an icon of French baroque classicism, the other of French neoclassicism—place an active figural scene against a geometrically firm background, and both were widely known through engravings.[29]

Krimmel also turned to Poussin and David for other elements. The fleeing girl, who at first suggests a classical or Renaissance source such as a dancing Maenad in a bacchanal and has been linked to Gianlorenzo Bernini's *Daphne Being Pursued by Apollo*, is a composite of elements from three different figures in Poussin's picture: the parallel movement of her raised arms and the motion of her hands are like that of a Sabine in the right background; the peculiar baroque draping of her dress resembles that on a Sabine in the left background; and the turn of her head and her loose curly hair is much like that of a Sabine in the left foreground.[30] The squatting boy with the footstool may be derived from the figure of the kneeling Sabine. The stance of the boy who is stopping him is like one in David's picture at the same spot in the figure frieze. The resemblance between the fallen and crying boys in the two pictures is also particularly close. The sheer number of correspondences further suggest Krimmel made a careful study of the images, possibly at the urging of Rembrandt Peale, a fellow sketch club member who in 1812 or 1813 had recently returned from France.

As was becoming customary for him, Krimmel also drew on other artists' imagery at the compositional stage of *Blind Man's Buff*. Wilkie's *Jew's Harp* once more served as a model for a pyramidal arrangement of the group that included the parents. Krimmel retained the same basic placement of the figures: the man's head is the apex of the pyramid, the child shown from the back stands to the left, and the female figure sits on a low seat to the right. *The Blind Fiddler* provided him with specific details—the mother holding on

27. Wilkie's picture of the same name, painted in 1808–9 as a private commission was briefly displayed in 1809 at the Royal Academy but was not engraved until 1819. There is only a slight possibility that Krimmel saw the painting while working in England in 1809. It is unlikely Krimmel made a copy of it from a five-year-old memory, so I presume the canvas was an original composition.

28. Dunlap (*History*, 2:392–93) pairs Krimmel's *Blind Man's Buff* and Krimmel's copy of Wilkie's *Blind Fiddler*. As librarian of the American Academy in New York, Dunlap probably saw the pictures together in the 1820 exhibition at that institution. The two paintings have almost the same measurements. The superficial similarities may be of significance since the two paintings were presumably held as companion pieces by their private owners. Wilkie's *Blind Man's Buff* stands in marked contrast to his earlier quiet and sentimental pictures—it is an amusing and risque image designed for a cosmopolitan audience. The authorized engraving of the painting was published June 1, 1822. For a European perspective on Wilkie's *Blind Man's Buff*, see *Zweihundert Jahre englische Kunst* (Munich: Haus der Kunst, 1976), p. 345. Although the correct title of the game and the painting is *Blind Man's Buff*, nineteenth- and twentieth-century authors have often misidentified it as "Blind Man's Bluff."

29. "The Fine Arts; . . . The Modern French School: Life of David," *Port Folio*, 3d ser., 1, no. 4 (April 1813): 388–89, was accompanied by one illustration of his work, *Brutus and His Return Home after Condemning His Sons;* David's *Bonaparte Crossing the Alps* appears in *Port Folio*, 3d ser., 1, no. 5 (May 1813): 509. Among the German neoclassical artists who studied with David were Stuttgart painters Friedrich Hetsch and Gottlieb Schick; see Herbert von Einem, *Deutsche Malerei des Klassizismus und der Romantik: 1760 bis 1840* (Munich: C. H. Beck, 1978).

30. "The Fine Arts; . . . The Life of Poussin," *Port Folio*, 3d ser., 1, no. 1 (January 1813): 52–59; "The Fine Arts; . . . David," pp. 388–89. For the Bernini link see the commentary on the Krimmel painting in Christie, Manson, and Woods, Intl., *Important American Paintings, Drawings, and Sculpture of the Nineteenth and Twentieth Centuries*, sale of December 9, 1983, p. 14.

FIGURE 109

John Lewis Krimmel, Blind Man's Buff, *Philadelphia, 1814. Oil on canvas; 16 ⅝ x 22 ¹/₁₆ in. (Terra Museum of American Art, Chicago: Photo, © 1994.) Signed and dated on chair at lower left.*

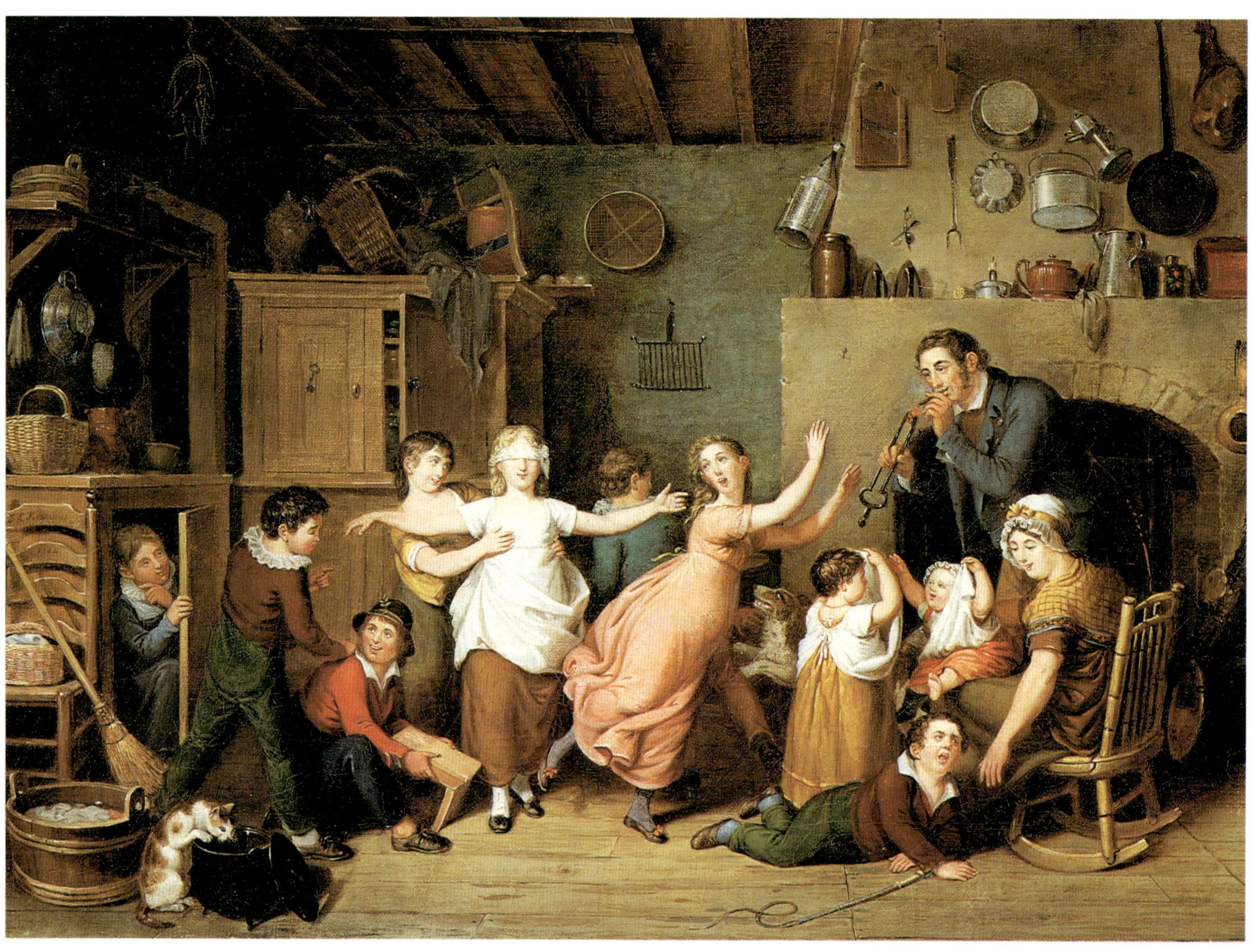

FIGURE 110
Abraham Raimbach after David Wilkie, Blind Man's Buff, *1822. Engraving; 19 7/8 x 25 1/4 in. (Paul Mellon Collection, Yale Center for British Art, New Haven.)*

FIGURE 111
Nicolas Poussin, Rape of the Sabines, *Rome, 1635. Oil on canvas; 60 7/8 x 82 5/8 in. (The Metropolitan Museum of Art, New York.)*

FIGURE 112
Jacques Louis David, The Sabines, *Paris, 1799. Oil on canvas; 144 3/4 x 204 in. (Museé du Louvre, Paris: Photo, © R. M. N.)*

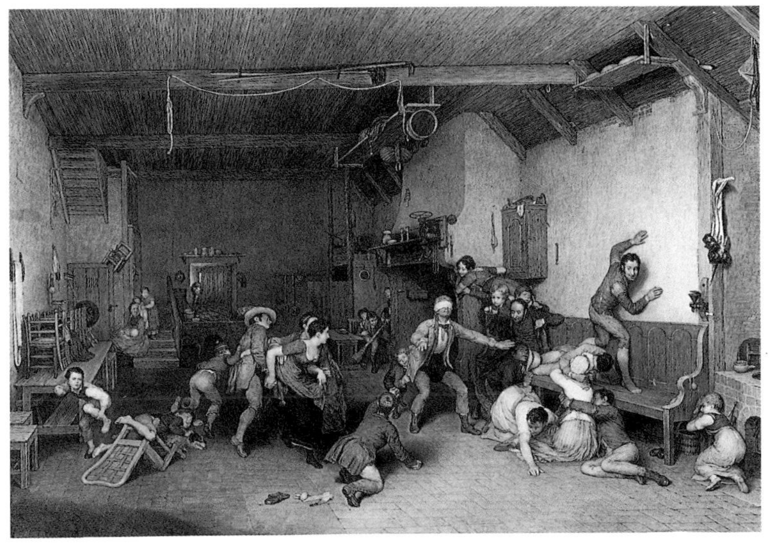

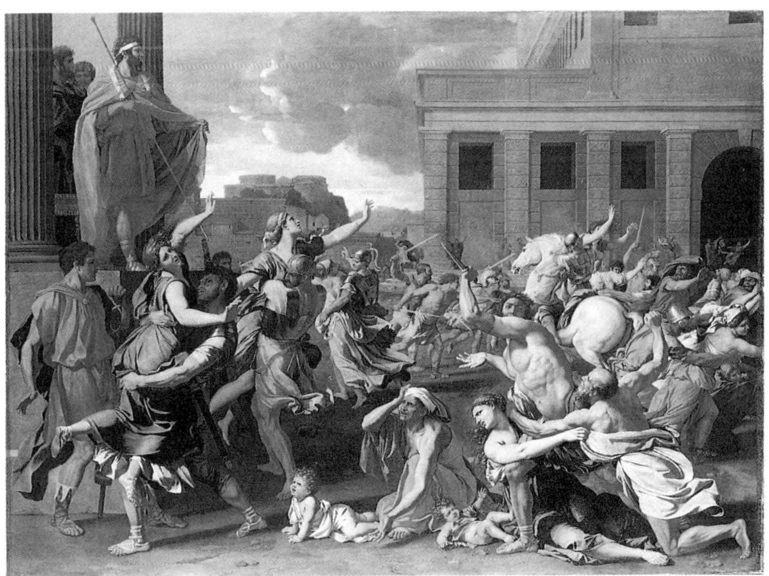

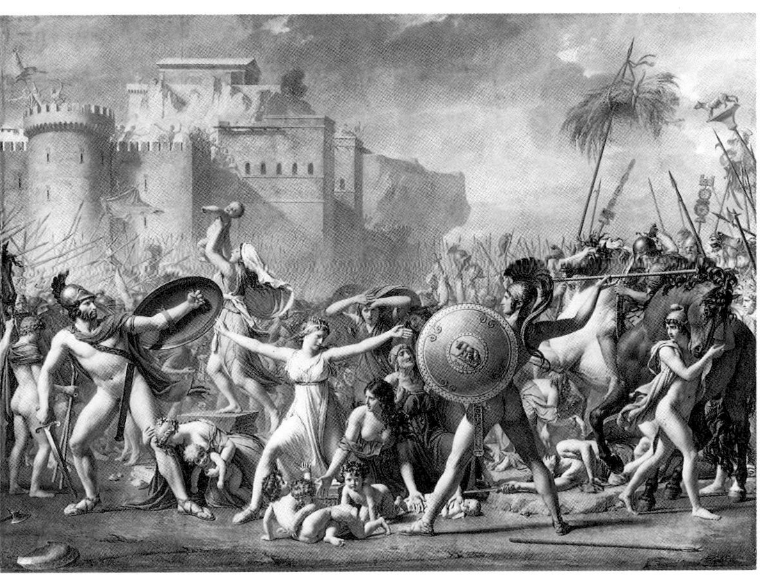

her lap the baby girl with outstretched arms, the father standing behind them, and the numerous household items in the foreground and background (see fig. 55). In Krimmel's scene the family is comfortably fixed and its members interact. Thus the young mother is not merely holding the baby, she is about to console the boy who has fallen on the floor. The children play with one another. Further, the furnishings are part of the scene; indeed some, such as the footstool and cabinet, are integral to the story.

Like Wilkie, Krimmel included a variety of round, cylindrical, and angular shaped household items. He even picked some of the same ones, such as the flour sieve and the iron grill hanging on the back wall, the coiled rope hanging from a ceiling beam, and the smoked meat hanging over the fireplace. But the elements function differently in the two pictures. Indeed Krimmel's *Blind Man's Buff* is seemingly a public demonstration that he could improve on the Scotsman's genre designs, as a comparison of the left section of both paintings reveals. In Krimmel's composition, Wilkie's open door into the room becomes the doors—both ajar—of the two cupboards, the ladder becomes the ladder-back chair, the flat round dish on the floor becomes the large wooden laundry tub filled with clothes, the iron kettle becomes the object of the cat's curiosity, and the fiddler's walking stick becomes the corn broom.

The fundamental differences in the designs of the two paintings are also significant. In Wilkie's *Blind Fiddler* more than half the figures are static, but in Krimmel's painting each person and pet stirs in a lively, individualized manner. Krimmel's shallower picture space brings the scene close to the viewer. His figures are arranged into three small units that form a continuous friezelike composition that moves from left to right in fast cadence. Although verticals prevail in Wilkie's design, verticals and horizontals are balanced in Krimmel's picture; as a result, the two pictures, although of almost identical dimensions, appear to be different in size and format. Perhaps what gives *Blind Man's Buff* a modern edge and adds to its vitality is the greater variety of geometric lines and stereometric forms achieved in the different angle of the mother's chair, the open doors of the cupboards, the arch of the hearth, and the rich array of household equipment that is volumetrically better defined. Krimmel's sophistication in perspective calculations suggests that by 1814 he owned the "case of mathematical instruments" that were later listed among the items in his estate.[31]

Another painting that influenced the design of Krimmel's *Blind Man's Buff* was John Burnet's *Young Bird* (1812), of which Krimmel painted a copy in 1812 or 1813. The copy was first exhibited in May 1817 (figs. 113, 114).[32] *The Young Bird* has three figures, a man and two children. The man balances a hungry bird on the thumb of one hand and offers it food on the tip of a small stick held in the other. A smiling boy watches and dips a second stick into the food cup. A smaller child, back to the viewer, kneels on a small chair and reaches into a straw basket that serves as the bird's temporary nest. The paraphernalia that frames the figures creates a crowded picturesque disorderliness much indebted to eighteenth-century tastes.

The gentle, natural behavior of the figures and Burnet's coherent composition probably enticed Krimmel to use *The Young Bird* as a model, even though in his own compositions he relied less on the picturesque. Indeed it is possible that the composition also affected *Quilting Frolic* (1813) with which there are specific correspondences—a basket with an attached cover pushed to the side, a reaching figure presented from the back, and the positioning of a foreground chair—which in turn suggest that Krimmel may have copied *The*

31. Estate sale listing, *Poulson's American Daily Advertiser*, August 14, 1821.

32. The painting was exhibited at the American Academy in New York along with Krimmel's copy of Wilkie's *Jew's Harp*.

FIGURE 113
John Burnet, The Young Bird, *London, 1812. Engraving; 10 x 7⅞ in. (© British Museum.) Burnet was both artist and engraver of this work.*

FIGURE 114
John Lewis Krimmel after John Burnet, The Young Bird, *1813–16. Oil on wood; 10⅝ x 8⅜ in. (Private collection.) The inscription "J. L. Krimmel / 1820" on the back is in a later hand.*

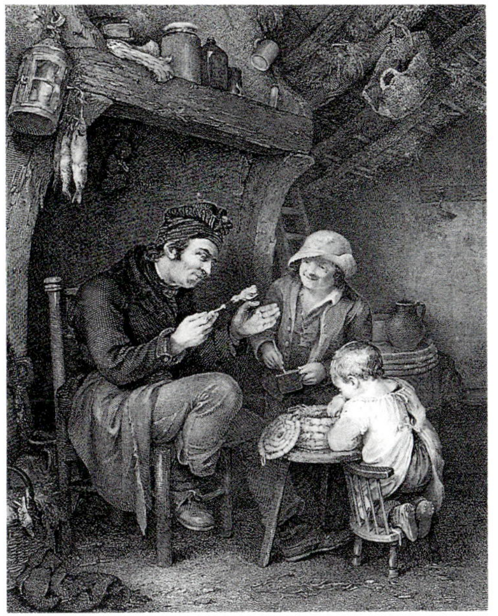

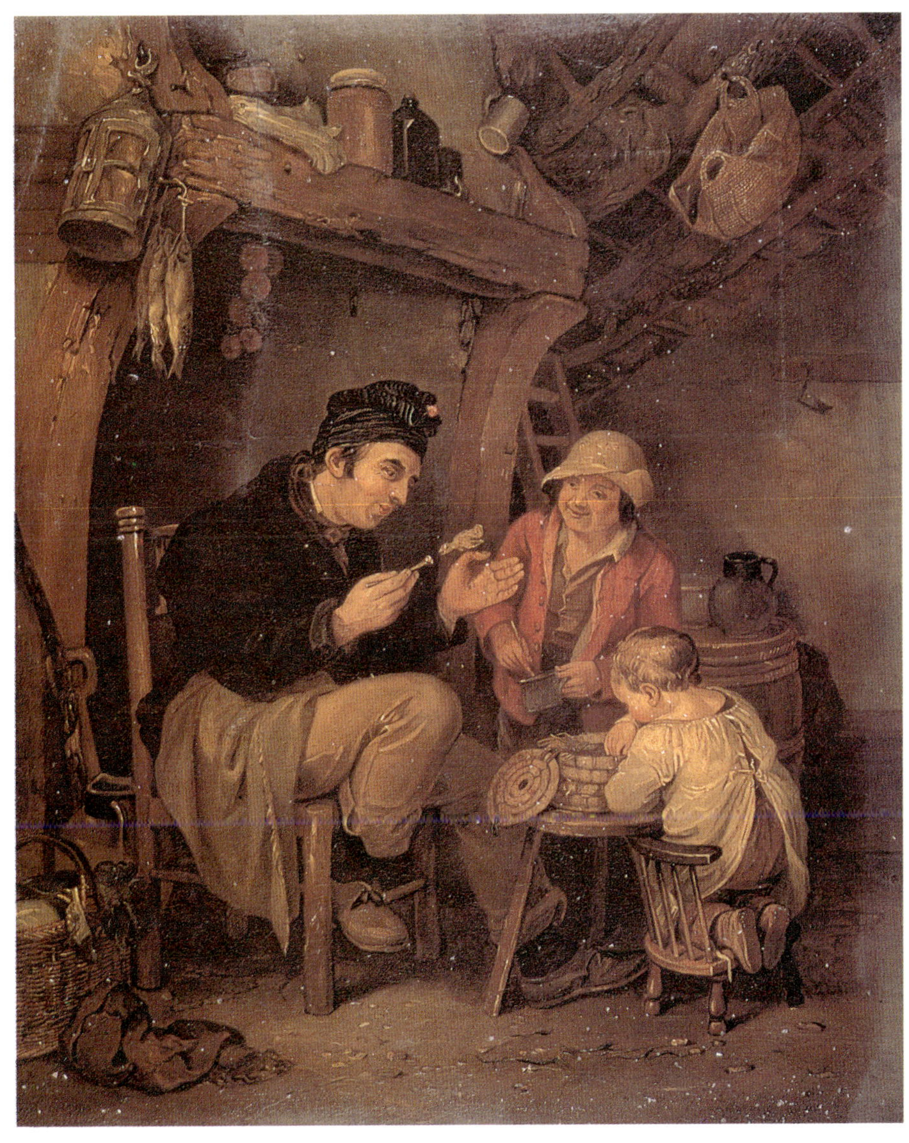

Young Bird in late 1812 or early 1813. In *Blind Man's Buff* the correspondences are stronger still. He restated Burnet's motifs of a father concentrating on the area in front of his hands, a full-face view of a smiling boy wearing a short-brimmed hat, a child turned away from the viewer, and a foreshortened view of the child's foot. He also translated Burnet's ideas into his own idiom. Thus instead of a child investigating the basket, Krimmel has a cat inspecting the kettle; the picturesque draping of the man's apron becomes the folds of cloth at the cupboard.[33]

By 1814 Krimmel was a mature painter using a rich palette, but he never used many different colors. His increased competence with colors is apparent when *Quilting Frolic* and *Blind Man's Buff*, painted a year apart, are compared. The latter painting beguiles the viewer with its more saturated, more eye-filling, more memorable colors. Krimmel blended the hues in vivid yet harmonic and pleasing combinations and introduced large areas of rose, bright red, moss green, and a variety of warm browns. He excelled in the use of white especially as the main color of the central player; he applied it selectively to other figures—in a collar, an apron, and a cap—to enliven the adjacent colors and visually unify the composition. Another 1814 painting, *Country Wedding*, possesses many of these same color qualities (fig. 115).

Country Wedding depicts the celebration of one of the important stages in a family's life, but many of its details are reminiscent of *Blind Man's Buff*: the young girl with blonde hair, the face and bonnet of the mother, a standing girl shown from the back, a young boy with a whip, a horizontal run of floorboards, a small stool, and a snooping cat. The wedding takes place in the main room of a home in which twelve persons are assembled. The figure of the minister is based on the same grandfatherly type with a balding pate, long white hair, and distinctive profile depicted in *Pepper-Pot* as an old soldier, in *Quilting Frolic* as a grandfather, in *Interior of an American Inn* as a newspaper reader, and even in *Indian Council* as an old Indian standing in the right foreground. The consistent inclusion of this stock figure into most of his paintings from 1811 to 1814, always in a new role, raises the possibility that the model was a personal friend of the artist. To underscore the significance of the event Krimmel carefully positioned two background details, a print bearing the French title *Mariage*, and a pair of white doves billing and cooing in the birdcage attached to the wall nearby.

As in *Quilting Frolic*, the furnishings and the clothing indicate that the family is comfortable but not wealthy. The walls are decorated with a print and silhouettes rather than paintings. The ornate tall-case clock represents a sizable investment, but the large cupboard and straight-leg table lack the embellishments of high-style forms and were less costly. The stiles and legs of the chairs are embellished with grooves and balls, but these elements were quickly shaped on a lathe, which meant these windsor chairs were generally inexpensive. The clothing is similar to that worn by women Krimmel drew in his sketchbooks (figs. 116–118, see also figs. 26, 32), but lacks the stylishness of the latest fashions that were shown in monthly magazines such as Rudolph Ackermann's *Repository of Arts, Literature, Fashions, &c.*

Preparatory sketches for *Country Wedding* are in sketchbook 2 and make it possible to follow the artist's steps as he strove to give the story a pictorial interpretation (figs. 119–121). Krimmel explored various movements, figures, positions, and background elements until he found a design that pleased him

33. The cumulative evidence shows that Krimmel had acquired engravings of *The Jew's Harp*, *The Young Bird*, *The Blind Fiddler*, and *The Village Politicians* by 1814, for he had made copies of them and then freely adopted and adapted their motifs and specific design elements into his own paintings.

FIGURE 115
John Lewis Krimmel, Country Wedding *(now titled* Country Wedding: Bishop White Officiating*), Philadelphia, 1814. Oil on canvas; 16¾ x 22½ in. (Paul Beck Collection, The Pennsylvania Academy of the Fine Arts, Philadelphia.)*

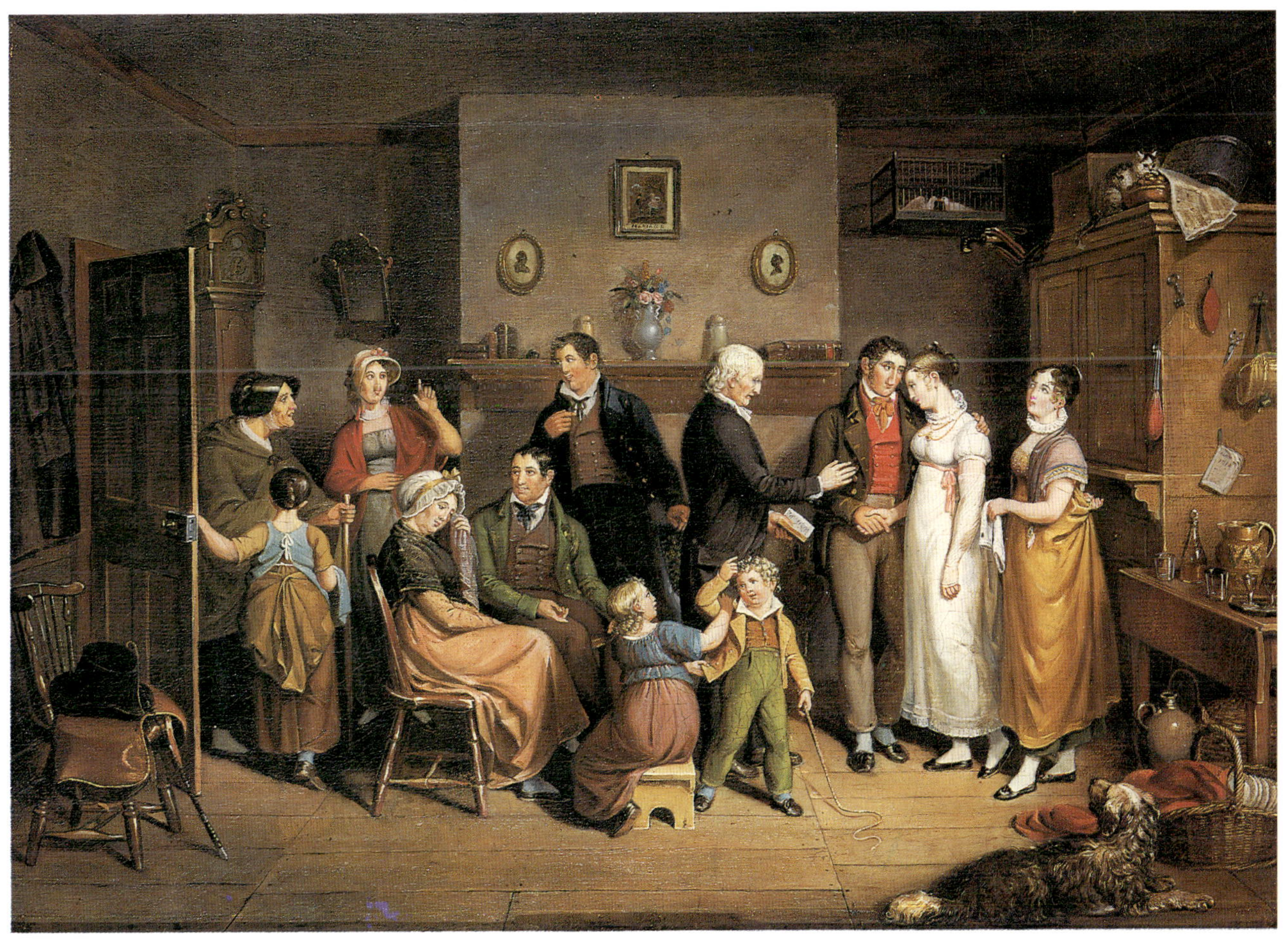

FIGURE 116
Woman, 1813/14. Pencil and watercolor over pencil. Sketchbook 3, leaf 15 verso.

FIGURE 117
Woman, 1813/14. Pencil. Sketchbook 3, leaf 15 verso.

FIGURE 118
Woman, 1813/14. Watercolor over pencil. Sketchbook 3, leaf 16 verso.

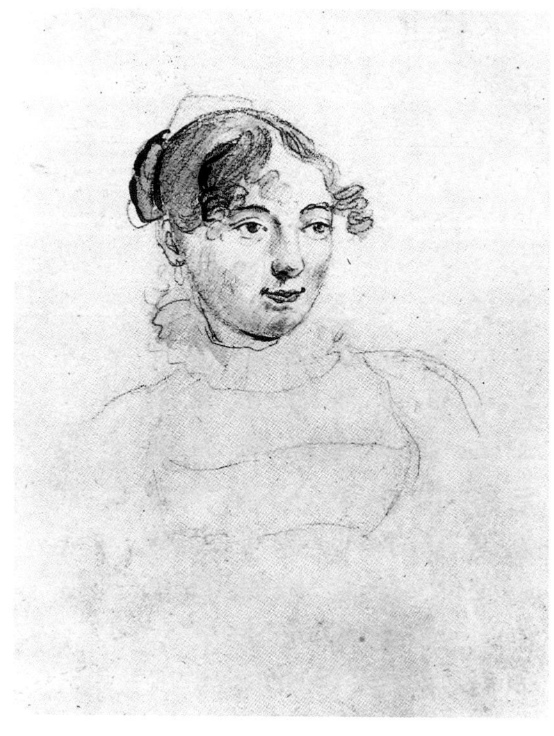

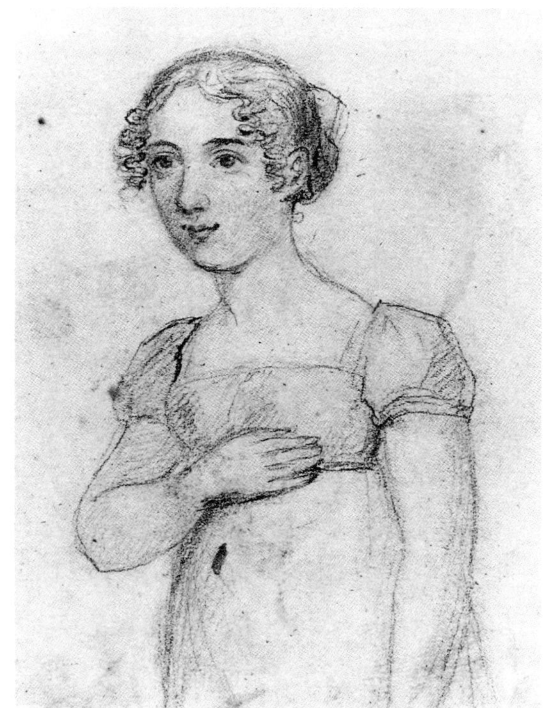

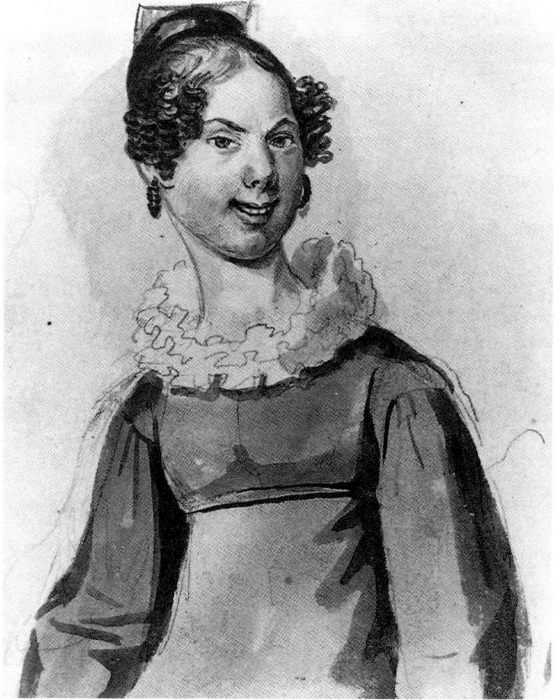

FIGURE 119
Compositional sketches for Country Wedding, *1812 or 1813. Ink. Sketchbook 2, leaf 3 verso.*

FIGURE 120
Compositional sketch for Country Wedding, *1812 or 1813. Ink over pencil. Sketchbook 2, inside front cover.*

FIGURE 121
Preparatory drawing for Country Wedding, *ca. 1813. Watercolor over pencil. Sketchbook 2, leaf 4 recto.*

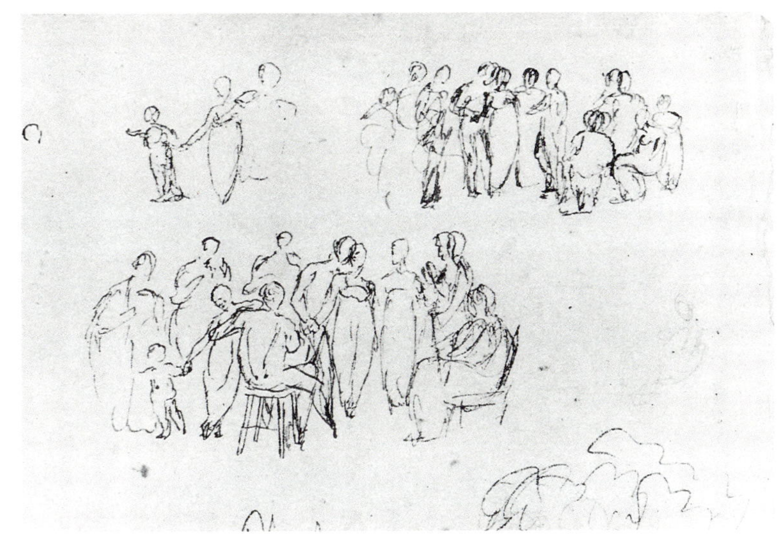

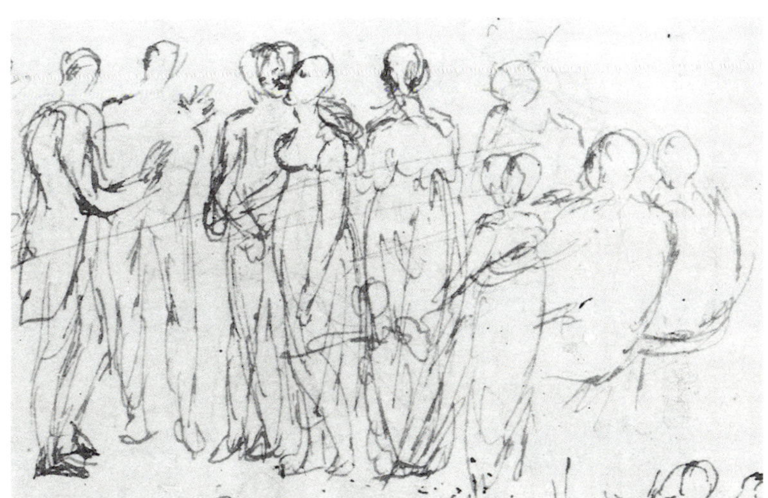

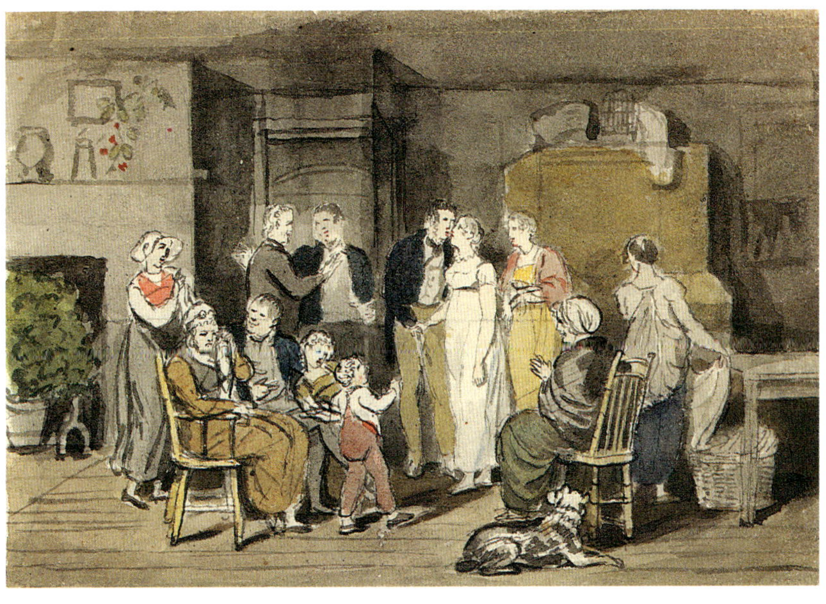

in rhythm and expression. Next he did a more finished watercolor study that is close but by no means identical to the final design of the oil painting.[34] In the painting only, Krimmel incorporated Wilkie's general pictorial structure and added specific gestures (such as the man pointing to his chest and the woman pointing out of the scene), elements that reiterate the main theme of the story in a Hogarthian manner.

Overall *Country Wedding* is a companion piece to *Quilting Frolic*, but a close comparison of the two works further demonstrates the rapid strides Krimmel made in a single year. *Country Wedding* is painted with finer brushes and more delicate brushwork; on its more closed and polished surface the strokes are hardly visible. The figures are more fully rounded, have more expressive faces, and are arranged in an evenly spaced, continuous design that avoids the middle axis orientation so obvious in *Quilting Frolic*. Colors are richer, and more highlights enliven the textures of hair, garments, furniture, and household items. Hand and arm movements are less obviously taken from the artist's life-class sketches and are more convincingly integrated into the story even though the composition has a staged character.

Commander Alexander Murray, a retired naval officer who served in the revolutionary and Tripolitan wars and the War of 1812, purchased *Country Wedding*. He may have done so soon after it was painted, possibly as a companion piece to *Quilting Frolic*, which he had also purchased along with Krimmel's copy of Wilkie's *Village Politicians*. If so, that might explain why Krimmel did not enter *Country Wedding* in any exhibitions at the academy. Indeed the first public notice of the painting's existence came in 1820 when a line engraving of it was published in *Analectic*, a periodical with wide distribution. Although the scene contains nothing to indicate a rural setting, the accompanying caption in the magazine commended Krimmel for producing "a true portraiture of nature in real, rustic life."[35]

Murray's purchase of Krimmel's art was an exception; Krimmel's plight as an artist was shared by many. Most American artists found it difficult to interest the general public in their art, although they tried mightily. Even magazines that supported the advance of the arts and the development of a separate American identity did so unevenly. *Port Folio*, which was published in Philadelphia, featured biographical sketches of famous European artists rather than Americans, indeed other than reviews of the initial exhibitions at the academy, the editor gave scant attention to American art. The first serious analysis of American painting appeared in a Boston magazine—an 1816 issue of *North American Review*. Turning to genre art, the unnamed author asked

> Have we in fact enough that is peculiar in this country, to trust one's reputation exclusively to its delineation? . . . Further, have our peasantry individuality enough to insure the artist, who may study and delineate their habits, a lasting fame. Is there enough that is peculiar in their costume, their manners, their customs and features, to enable an observer at once to recognize them in a picture? The great claim of delineations of this kind, consists in their striking truth; or in their novelty, their originality. We can ascertain their truth by our knowledge of their originals only. But for them to delight us by their truth and originality, their correctness will perhaps not be taken into account, they must be new to us, and still bear a resemblance to what has, or does, exist. We are interested in the new costume and new countenance because they in some sort

34. Patricia Hills, *The Painters' America: Rural and Urban Life, 1810–1910* (New York: Praeger Publishers, 1974), p. 5, implies that Jean Baptiste Greuze's *Village Bride* (1761) influenced Krimmel. The subject matter is almost the same and some narrative elements are similar; however, the two pictures are distinctly different in style and spirit. Home weddings were frequent in early nineteenth-century America, and Krimmel may have been steered to the subject matter more by a wedding he had attended than by a print; see Charles Sealsfield (Karl Anton Postl), *United States of North America as They Are* (1828; reprint, New York: Johnson Reprint Corp., 1970), pp. 132, 133.

35. Untitled commentary accompanying plate in *Analectic*, n.s., 1, no. 2 (February 1820): 175–76. "American Biography—For the Port Folio: Life of Commodore Murray," *Port Folio*, 3d ser., 3, no. 5 (May 1814): 399–409. *Country Wedding* was exhibited at PAFA in 1822; Paul Beck acquired it during the next two decades, and in 1843 or 1844 it came into the possession of PAFA; see *Eleventh Annual Exhibition* . . . (1822), p. 17, no. 412; *Catalogue of the Exhibition* . . . (1843), p. 3, no. 25; *Catalogue of the . . . Exhibition* . . . (1845), p. 10, no. 166.

> extend our knowledge of human society. And when the foreign artist descends to the detail of the amusements and mechanical occupations, to the domestick economies of his countrymen, we are still more indebted to him for the new acquaintance to which he has introduced us. He becomes in short a most interesting historian, of all that most delights us in the outside of human nature. Now many of these sources of interest must be wanting to the native artist, who confines himself to our own country. His pictures will want novelty—They will not extend our knowledge. And unless we have observed the inhabitants of our village with more than a casual glance, unless we have caught their faint, but distinctive characteristics, the whole claim of native peculiarity will be wanting, and the painter, or us, will have gleaned them in vain.[36]

Recognizing the genre painter's prerogative not to confine himself to mere imitation but to aim to reproduce the more perfect ideas of beauty fixed in his mind in accordance with the philosophy of aesthetic idealism as propagated by Reynolds and West, the writer maintained that a genre artist's "imagination will not be allowed to repose because his eye meets new objects on every side it turns. He must be true and at the same time original"—a description that well applies to Krimmel.[37]

Among the Philadelphia sights that had piqued Krimmel's interest was yet another of street vendors—a cherry seller, which he used to create a genre scene with a moralizing aspect by presenting two opposing inclinations of human nature: selfless kindness and callous selfishness to reiterate the assessment that society is made up of the "haves" and the "have nots." This was a theme he had used in his watercolors but that he had only obliquely referred to in his oils.

Cherry Woman with Children is an outwardly simple scene (fig. 122). The vendor sits on the sidewalk next to a basket containing three varieties of cherries—black, red, and yellow—and has attracted three young people. Two are paying customers, the third is penniless. As the woman weighs out a quantity of fruit, the teenage girl takes pity on the poor boy and offers him a few cherries. The other customer, a young boy, is less compassionate; he munches on his cherries with relish while he ridicules the penniless lad.

Three compositional sketches and one preparatory drawing for *Cherry Woman with Children* are in sketchbook 2. Three are drawn on the same pages as the preliminary sketches for *Country Wedding*, each carefully boxed off in a manner that suggests the artist was simultaneously working out the designs for the two paintings. The preparatory drawing is on a page by itself and is an intermediate image in which Krimmel explored ideas for both composition and facial expressions (figs. 123–126). After these four sketches Krimmel made further stylistic refinements, quite probably after restudying *The Jew's Harp* (see fig. 106), that inspired him to a more pyramidal arrangement.[38]

The four preliminary drawings and the oil painting are a good record of the developmental progress toward the final design. Krimmel at first drew a symmetrically spread-out composition that depicted the vendor from the back. Then he tightened the structure by arranging the four figures in a triangle. To achieve this he turned the vendor to one side, increased the bend in her position, and lowered the outstretched arm of the girl. To strengthen the group's coherence, he adjusted the core of the design by reversing the positions of the kneeling boy's arms. He shifted the angle of the beam scale

36. "For the North-American Journal: On the Fine Arts," *North American Review and Miscellaneous Journal* 3, no. 8 (July 1816): 198–99.

37. "For the North-American Journal," pp. 196–97, 199.

38. Krimmel's copies of *The Jew's Harp* and *The Young Bird* were exhibited at the newly reorganized American Academy of the Fine Arts in New York in 1817 while Krimmel was in Germany; therefore, both must have been completed before Krimmel's October 1816 departure.

FIGURE 122
John Lewis Krimmel, Cherry Woman with Children *(now titled* Cherry Seller*), Philadelphia, 1814 or 1815. Oil on canvas; 14 ¼ x 12 ¼ in. (The Reading Public Museum and Art Gallery, Reading, Pa., gift of Mrs. William L. Savage, 1921.)*

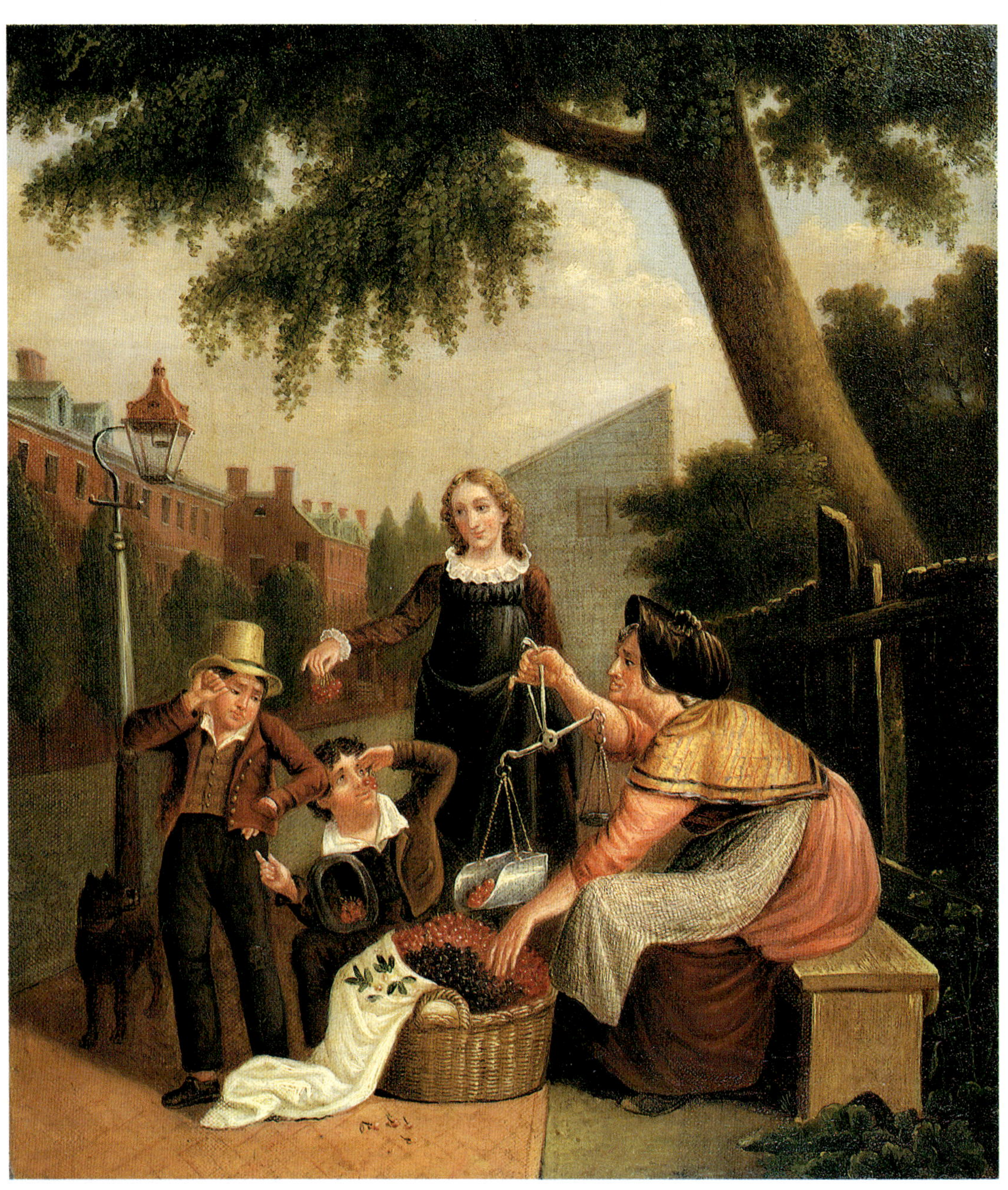

FIGURE 123
Compositional sketch for Cherry Woman with Children, *ca. 1813. Ink over pencil. Sketchbook 2, leaf 3 verso.*

FIGURE 124
Compositional sketch for Cherry Woman with Children, *ca. 1813. Ink over pencil. Sketchbook 2, leaf 3 verso.*

FIGURE 125
Compositional sketch for Cherry Woman with Children, *ca. 1813. Ink and watercolor over pencil. Sketchbook 2, leaf 5 verso.*

FIGURE 126
Preparatory drawing for Cherry Woman with Children, *1813. Ink and ink wash over pencil. Sketchbook 2, leaf 4 recto.*

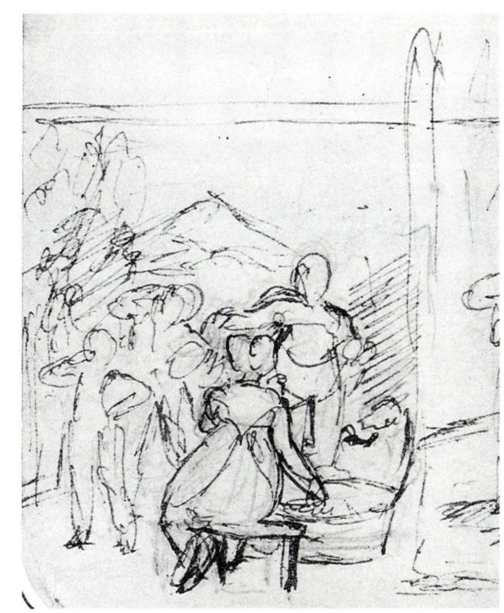

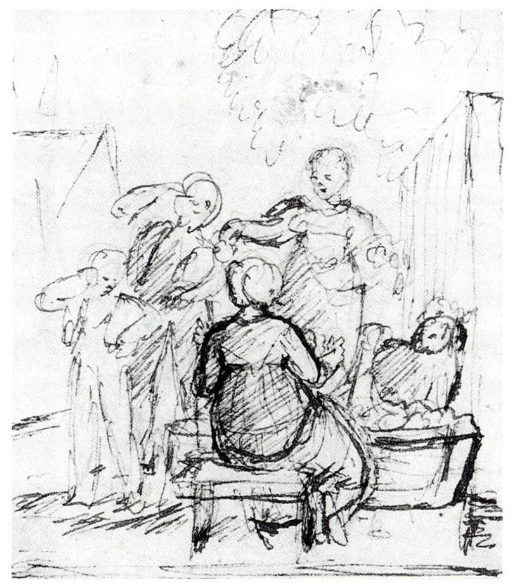

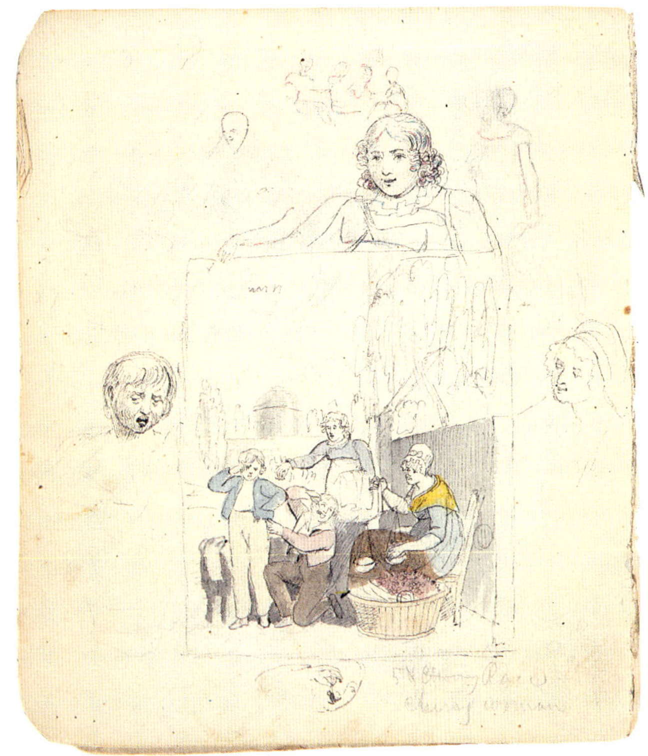

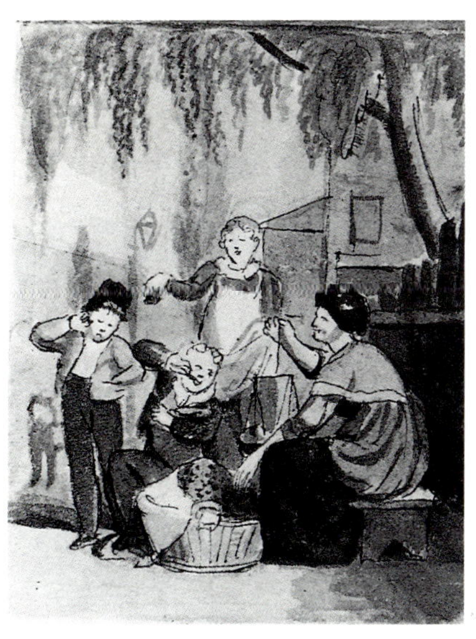

so it parallels the girl's arm and the slant of the roof in the background. The position of the beam also leads the viewer's eye down to the white cloth draped over the edge of the basket, which repeats the shape of the woman's apron. Together these forms create a cascading movement within the image. To further improve the design, Krimmel altered the type of hat worn by the cherry woman by giving it a form that inversely corresponds to the form of the scale pan and making sure the oval rim of the cherry-filled hat echoes the semicircle of the basket handle. The curious angle made by the left arms of the two boys is a visual tie to the triangular shoulder wrap of the woman. The round lines of her basket are repeated in the belt and collar of the girl and in the standing boy's cylindrical hat. These and several other coordinating devices simplify and clarify the design, giving the picture an abstract quality and firm cohesion that monumentalize the scene. In the final painting Krimmel moved the street lantern closer to the front of the picture, which along with the large tree and fencepost, frames the figures. He emphasized the highlights, as is most noticeable on the cherries in the basket and on the hat of the penniless boy.

An 1813–15 date can be assigned to *Cherry Woman with Children* because of the overall skill with which it is designed. (A certain crudeness in the execution of some parts of the picture reveal later overpainting by another hand.) Details such as the basket draped with a cloth, the face and figure of the young girl, and the stance of the dog suggest the painting was composed about the same time as *Quilting Frolic* (1813), and the strongly unified composition and bright color scheme suggest he was working on it about the same time as *Country Wedding* (1814), or shortly afterwards.[39]

An inability to attract buyers for their paintings prompted both Krimmel and Alexander Rider to take positions as "teachers of drawing" during these years, although the dates of these jobs are never specified. Quite possibly Krimmel was teaching in a private school outside the city during the winter and spring of 1815, for he did not participate in the annual exhibition at the Pennsylvania Academy that year.[40] Supporting this assumption is an undated drawing in sketchbook 3 showing a townscape in which one building is labeled "boys" and the other "girls," suggesting a boarding school (fig. 127). A subsequent owner of the sketchbooks identified the location as Chambersburg, a town situated in south central Pennsylvania. A precise outline of the town's architectural features and two separate studies of the steeples testify to Krimmel's close acquaintance with the town. The execution of the image—brushed in a tighter, more minute manner than the topographical landscapes Krimmel had practiced in August and September of 1813 and at a level of skill that is commensurate with (perhaps even slightly better than) that achieved in *Country Wedding*—implies an 1814/15 date.

Yet if Krimmel was in south central Pennsylvania that spring he was quite mobile, for in March 1815 he was also in northeastern Pennsylvania where he produced a small watercolor portrait of a young woman, which has the distinction of being the earliest finished portrait of his to survive (fig. 128). Designed along neoclassical principles, the image presents the subject in strict frontal view sitting on a settee next to an open window. Her face is framed by the spiral curls of her light brown hair and distinguished by the pensive look of her large blue eyes. The bodice of her blue silk dress is covered with a stylishly transparent lace top that is meticulously rendered. The curious draping of her dress suggests she may be pregnant, and her well-groomed fingers and

39. The painting is listed among the works exhibited in the 1821 and 1823 exhibitions at PAFA; see *Tenth Annual Exhibition* . . . (1821), p. 6; *Twelfth Annual Exhibition* . . . (1823), p. 16. When the painting was exhibited in 1823 it belonged to William Strickland, and in 1821 a watercolor identified as "Cherry Woman, sketch in colors" was listed in Krimmel's estate sale listing, *Poulson's American Daily Advertiser*, August 14, 1821. Krimmel's knowledge of neoclassical painting came ultimately from Benjamin West who was among the first to use classical composition for the interpretation of modern life, but Krimmel's application of this was tempered by his understanding of French classical and neoclassical painting with its precise, linear, and geometrical character.

40. Dunlap, *History*, 2:393; *Catalogue of the Exhibition* . . . (1815); *Exhibition at the Pennsylvania Academy* . . . (1816), pp. 6, 7. Naeve (*Krimmel*, p. 22) implies that Krimmel's lack of participation in 1815 had something to do with the end of the joint sponsorship of the exhibitions by the society and the academy; however, I have found no evidence that Krimmel was among those artists upset with these decisions.

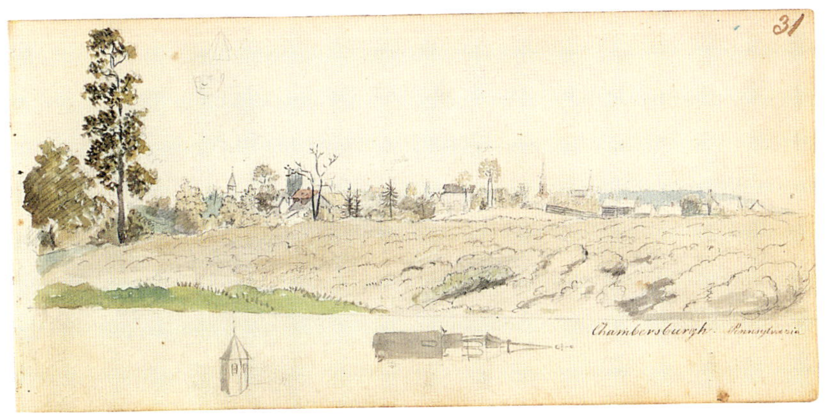

FIGURE 127
View of Chambersburg, Pa., ca. 1815. Watercolor and ink over pencil. Sketchbook 3, leaf 16 recto.

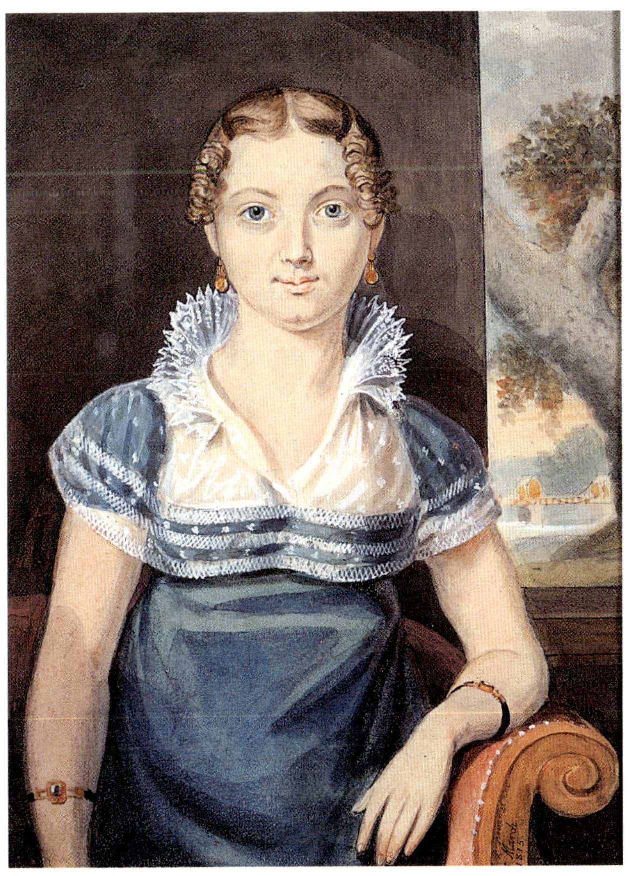

FIGURE 128
John Lewis Krimmel, Young Woman in a Blue Dress, *Easton, Pa., March 5, 1815. Watercolor and gouache over pencil; 6¼ x 4½ in. (Private collection: Photo, Christie, Manson, and Woods, Intl., New York.) Signed lower right.*

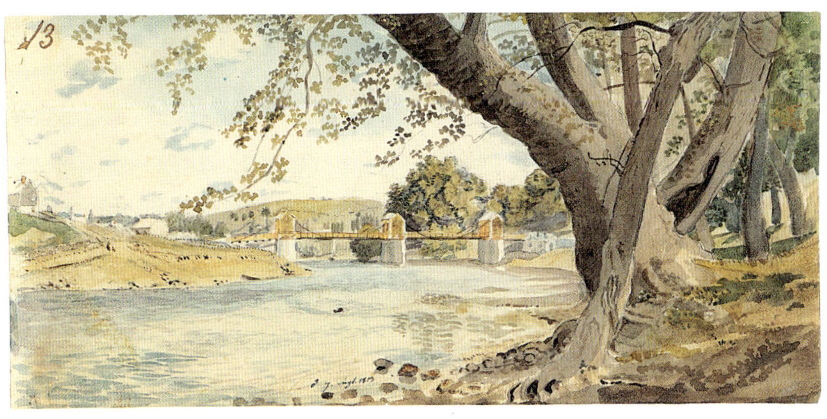

FIGURE 129
View of Easton showing bridge over the Lehigh River, September 7, 1813. Watercolor over pencil. Sketchbook 3, leaf 7 recto.

jeweled armbands and earrings imply that her family is well-to-do. The stiffness of the figure design, the almost vertical right arm, and the sharply vertical background are somewhat relieved by subtle devices: the picturesque bend of the tree beyond the window echoes the curve of the woman's left shoulder and upper arm, and the bracelet on her right arm balances the scrolled armrest on her left.

How Krimmel created this watercolor portrait can be discerned on close examination. First he drew the outlines of the figure with a well-sharpened pencil and then modeled the face and neck with blue-gray watercolor. When he used his brush his strokes were delicate and precise; his touch was sure. To enliven the eyes, ears, and earrings he applied small touches of red; to convey the white of the eyes and the highlights in the pupils he simply refrained from applying paint to those sections of the paper. He deliberately placed a large blue shadow on the right arm to break up its length and to heighten its compositional relationship to the tree trunk.

The view through the open window shows the same bridge framed by the trunk and branches of a tree that Krimmel included in a topographical watercolor a year and a half earlier. The bridge spanned the Lehigh River at Easton (fig. 129).[41] The differences in the way the bridge is depicted in the two images show the increased flexibility in the artist's style. The September 7, 1813, view is done with a light application of watercolors that is lucid and fluid. The March 8, 1815, view of the bridge is done in solid, substantial watercolors or gouache that approximate the effect of oils.

The portrait is clearly different from the examples being produced by Sully and other of Philadelphia's accomplished portraitists; it is also quite different from those created by lesser portraitists such as Jacob Eichholtz who, like Krimmel, was essentially a self-taught artist. Eichholtz, a Lancaster, Pennsylvania, artist of German stock, had studied briefly with Sully and Gilbert Stuart before he began exhibiting at the academy the same time Krimmel did. His portraits are more conventional in style than Krimmel's *Young Woman in a Blue Dress.* Indeed most of Eichholtz's portraits present a more idealized image, and few are strictly frontal—most sitters face left or right. Backgrounds are often unspecific locations or indoor settings that include a classical column. Finally, his workmanlike approach in applying paints created flat textures, especially in textiles.

A review of *Quilting Frolic*, published in *Port Folio* in June 1813, closed with the comment, "if Mr. Krimmell only perserveres in the path he has chosen, we are decidedly of the opinion that his labours and talents will contribute largely toward giving a character in the arts in our own country."[42] By 1816 Krimmel had demonstrated his persistence in the specialty of genre painting and was well on his way to painting pictures that would exert an influence on genre artists who followed in his footsteps. He was more readily experimenting with acutely contemporary subject matter, and his maturing talent gave him the dexterity and confidence to expand and change his compositional schemes. At the special exhibition of May 1816, organized by the academy without the assistance of the Society of Artists, Krimmel displayed two paintings: one drew upon a recent historic event of national importance, the other presented a glimpse of a local event significant to Philadelphia.

Victory on Lake Champlain was Krimmel's first history painting. In it he commemorated the British surrender following an important battle near Plattsburg, New York, in September 1814. The painting, a preliminary watercolor,

41. Uzal W. Condit, *The History of Easton, Penn'a from the Earliest Times to the Present, 1779–1885* (Easton: George W. West, 1885), facing p. 41.

42. M., "Review of the Third Annual Exhibition," p. 140.

and a later engraving made by Alexander Lawson, one of Philadelphia's foremost engravers, have since disappeared.[43] The exhibition catalogue, however, contains a detailed description of the composition and indications of colors:

> The painting represents the quarterdeck of the Saratoga at the time the British officers are delivering their swords. In the centre of the picture, Captain Pring is presenting his sword to Commodore M'Donough, on the left of Captain Pring, is Lieutenant Robinson—Lieutenant M'Gee has his back toward the spectators, and Lieutenant Hicks his hand upon his chain. Lieutenant Fitzpatrick and Lieutenant Giles of the marines are in red; the young men behind them are Midshipmen. The American officers are Lieutenant Valette, on the Commodore's right, and Sailing Master Braum with the trumpet under his arm; behind him, is Lieutenant Montgomery who lost his arm on board the President. Captain Young of marines is beckoning to Montgomery to come forward and receive the swords from the Commodore. Lieutenant Howell of the marines is on the left of Captain Young, with his head inclined a little forward; and Mr. Beale, the Purser, in a round hat behind the Commodore. All the Officers, and many of the common sailors are portraits.[44]

Krimmel had composed his image with concern for historical meaning and visual accuracy yet had retained his penchant for emphasizing the interaction of people. The victory of the young American navy over the powerful British navy was a popular subject among American artists, including friend and colleague Thomas Birch.[45] Most of these artists depicted battle scenes. In contrast Krimmel, perhaps taking his inspiration from Diego Velázquez's *Surrender of Breda* (1636-44), or more likely from John Trumbull's *Surrender of General Burgoyne at Saratoga, New York, October 16, 1777*, commemorated the symbolic surrender of the swords. (Trumbull, in turn, had relied on portraits and drawings by other artists for the faces of officers in his image.) The painting featured specific men who had fought and survived, particularly the young American commander whose courage and strategy had forced the British to retreat to Canada and who in March 1816 had been featured in *Analectic* with an engraving and a biographical sketch.[46]

The artist alluded to the war in his earlier paintings, but *Victory on Lake Champlain* explicitly expressed patriotism and reflected the spirit of national pride that was still running high, although the war had ended in stalemate in December 1814. Only the last military engagement, the Battle of New Orleans (which occurred after the peace treaty had been concluded), had provided an outstanding victory over the British by the American army, and it fostered the notion that the Americans had won the war and were at last independent of the interfering British.

The second canvas Krimmel exhibited in 1816 had political overtones. *Election Day 1815* focused on voter activity in amazing detail and was the most ambitious figural composition the artist had attempted (fig. 130). Dunlap termed it "a great composition . . . executed with a taste, truth, and feeling, both of pathos and humor, that rivals, in many respects, the best works of this description in either hemisphere. . . . It is filled with miniature portraits of the well-known electioneering politicians of the day . . . [and] a portrait of the venerable building within whose walls the independence of America was declared."[47] The scene features an election day crowd gathered on Chestnut Street outside the statehouse polling place.

43. The oil painting was owned by Lawson in 1820 ("*Return from Boarding School*," p. 508) and still in his hands in 1843; see *Catalogue of the Exhibition . . .* (1843). The watercolor remained in Krimmel's hands; estate sale listing, *Poulson's American Daily Advertiser*, August 14, 1821. It was purchased by Nathaniel Devaltooth, taken to Boston, and sold upon his death; J. L. Cunningham, *Executor's Sale Catalogue . . .* (Boston, 1825). The print is referred to in Townsend Ward, "Alexander Lawson," *Pennsylvania Magazine of History and Biography* 28, no. 2 (1904): 206. Lawson emigrated from Scotland in 1794; he gained fame for his plates of Alexander Wilson's *American Ornithology* (1808–14).

44. *Exhibition at the Pennsylvania Academy . . .* (1816), p. 6. To depict the British and American officers, Krimmel relied on engravings.

45. Gerdts, *Birch*.

46. "Biographical Sketch of Captain Thomas MacDonough," *Analectic Magazine and Naval Chronicle*, n.s., 7, no. 39 (March 1816): 201–15.

47. Dunlap, *History*, 2:394–95. Dunlap erroneously identifies this as Krimmel's last painting. It is clearly dated 1815, and others postdate it.

FIGURE 130
John Lewis Krimmel, Election Day 1815. *Oil on canvas; 16⅜ x 25⅝ in. (Winterthur.) Signed at lower left, "I. L. Krimmel pinxit 1815."*

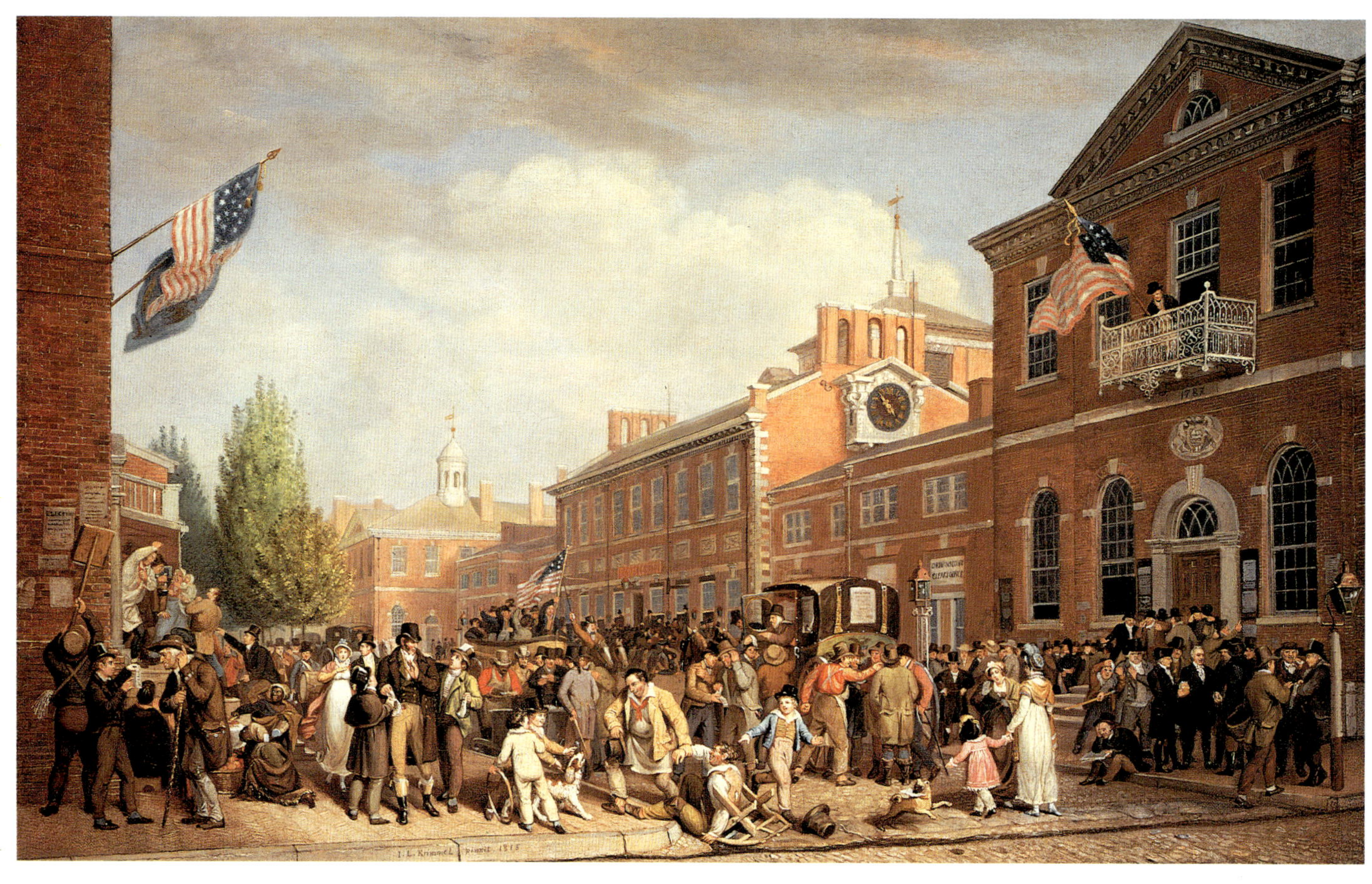

Philadelphia had a history of rowdy elections that stretched back to the late eighteenth century. Krimmel's canvas captures a diversity of simultaneous activities, most but not all of which are related to the election. Krimmel's focus is on the lobbying and other acts of persuasion; for the casting of ballots by voters who jostle each other (and sometimes try to block their opponents) as they mount the wooden platform in front of their ward's polling windows on the first floor of the building occurs somewhat indistinctly in the middle of the image. A variety of voting-related activity occurs across the foreground of the canvas. To the left of the coach, which has just transported an invalid to the polling place, two men huddle over their ballots. Three men in the middle left foreground, two in the left foreground, and three in the right foreground illustrate last minute attempts to change votes: in one instance a voter reaches for one ballot while firmly refusing the other; in other instances the prospective voters listen to the spiel. Within the crowd women and children provide bright accents: on the left an elegant young woman walks in lively steps on the arm of her husband moving past an altercation on the stairway that involves, secondarily, another woman; on the right two well-dressed women, one with a daughter, converse. An exception to this bright clothing is the only female street vendor. She is drably dressed, almost unapparent. Most of the somberly dressed gentlemen stand to the right on the sidewalk watching the hubbub in the street. An equally somberly dressed laborer pastes new posters on the wall to the left. Human interest stories are suggested by the two black youngsters crouching near the street vendor's baskets of fruit and the two men, one holding a bottle of beer, arguing on the steps of a building as a third tries to stop them while a mother and baby pull back in fright. The beer bottle suggests the building houses a tavern, possibly the headquarters of the opposition, because Amos Holahan's tavern at which the Democrats gathered was directly across from the statehouse.[48] The elevated arm of the quarreler on top of the stairs on the left provides a visual link to a figure just beyond the medial point of the painting: the tradesman wearing a red shirt and suspenders who shakes his finger at his listeners.

As in the past, Krimmel borrowed ideas from other artists and converted those ideas into his own idiomatic pictorial language. Krimmel set the architecture in visual motion by using a diagonal perspective in a deliberate departure from the neoclassical planometry with which he had designed his earlier oil paintings. The idea for this may have come from William Birch's 1800 design for a print depicting the Philadelphia procession commemorating George Washington's death, a supposition strengthened by another element: the woman who holds a child by the hand appears in the same pose and position in both pictures. The husky tradesman's wide stance and the outstretched arm suggest that Krimmel also drew upon David's *Oath of the Horatii* (1784). For the two balloters besieging a voter, the motif of a man on a balcony, and possibly the perspective of the buildings, Krimmel drew on Hogarth's *Canvassing for Votes* (fig. 131). The design of the crowd is similar to that used by Hogarth in the *Industry and Idleness* series, particularly *The Idle 'Prentice Executed at Tyburn* and *The Industrious 'Prentice Lord Mayor of London* (figs. 132, 133)—especially the parade marching from the background toward the beholder, the flags and banners, the carriage stopped amidst the voters, the figures tumbling in the center foreground, and the device of presenting figures in mirror image on opposite sides of the scene.[49]

Election Day 1815 is also a good demonstration of Krimmel's ability to paint with great precision and to do so on the scale of a miniaturist. This allowed him

48. A description of the election crowds in the 1815–20 era is provided in Oberholtzer, *Philadelphia*, 2:80–81.

49. Many of Hogarth's designs were derived from old engravings of paintings of multifigural religious and historical scenes.

FIGURE 131
William Hogarth, Canvassing for Votes. *Etching and engraving; 17⅛ x 22 in. (Print Collection, Lewis Walpole Library, Yale University.)*

FIGURE 132
William Hogarth, The Idle 'Prentice Executed at Tyburn. *Etching and engraving. (Print Collection, Lewis Walpole Library, Yale University.)*

FIGURE 133
William Hogarth, The Industrious 'Prentice Lord Mayor of London. *Etching and engraving. (Print Collection, Lewis Walpole Library, Yale University.)*

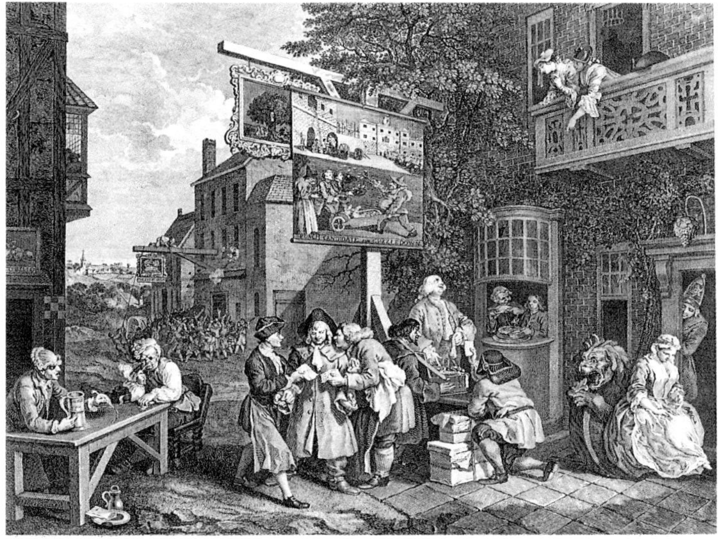

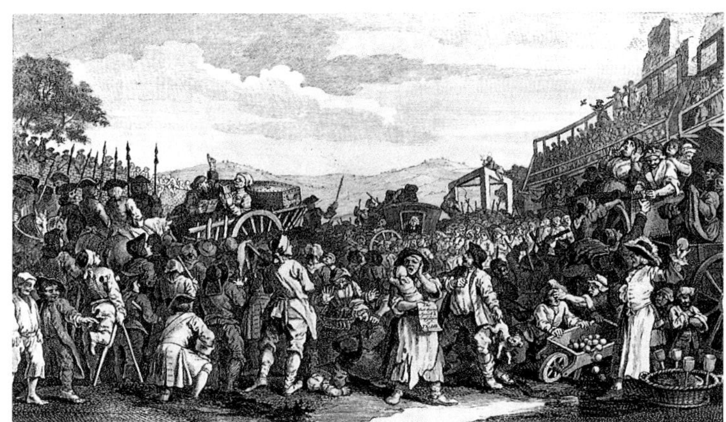

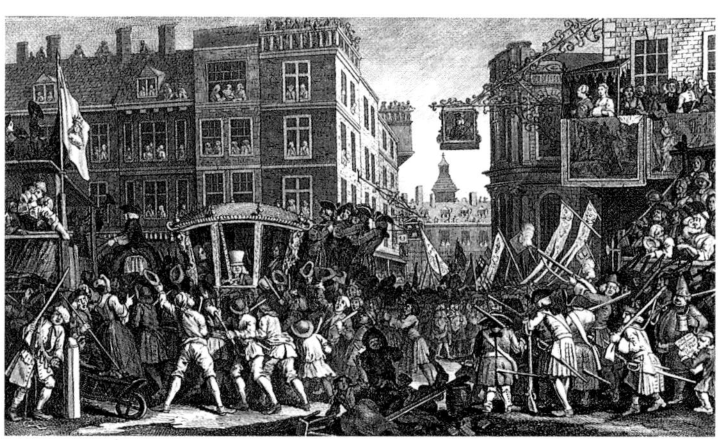

to present the multitude of figures in a diversity of situations, and his dexterity in working with extremely fine brushes enabled him to give lively definition even to figures in the distant background. In this his technique set him apart from contemporaries such as Trumbull and Allston, who were producing quite large canvases to convey their multifigural scenes.

Krimmel's precision allowed him to keep his design clear, stable, and balanced. His crowd is subdivided into recognizable units, and the figures are arranged in a calculated, imaginative manner. Those in the left half of the picture correspond to those in the right half to an amazing degree: the men assembled on the sidewalk and on the steps on the far right visually relate to the groups on the far left gathered near the brick wall and on the steps. The two drunken men in the middle foreground also complement each other in design, as do the boys watching them. The peculiar shape of the man slouched on the curb on the right side is repeated in the figure kneeling at the vendor's basket on the left. The most noticeable juxtaposition involves two women—one shown from the back (on the right) the other from the front (on the left) both of whom are clad similarly and in almost identical colors. Krimmel also used color to relate the oyster vendor in the left center of the scene (a motif taken from the 1812 watercolor *Oyster Barrow in Front of Chestnut Street Theatre*) to the argumentative tradesman behind the carriage: both wear the same type of red shirt, light brown work apron, and hat. Other correlations exist between groups of men; for example, the men gathered behind the coach with their backs to the viewer are markedly similar to the threesome standing next to the streetlamp that are shown facing the viewer.

Despite the deliberate placement of the specific elements, Krimmel's scene looks natural and unarranged, an effect that is enhanced by his new way of handling light. In *View of Centre Square* (1812) the crowd was unevenly lit, a characteristic harkening back to a seventeenth-century convention best exemplified in the painting style of Caravaggio, Rembrandt, and Claude Lorraine and continued by West, whose work was then influencing Krimmel. For *Election Day 1815*, also an afternoon scene (the time is 4:54) in October, the crowd is bathed in an even, rose-tinted light that unifies the complex composition—a Davidian device.

The painting was soon purchased by Alexander Lawson who began to work on an engraving of it. For some reason he never completed the task. Yet as Krimmel's friend and colleague he steadfastly urged the talented genre artist to continue painting "his favorite subjects without waiting for commissions, and take his chance for the sale."[50]

In 1816 Krimmel did just that. He proceeded to make a smaller but highly finished watercolor of the election day activities using the same general design he created for the 1815 scene (fig. 134). It is a later moment—as Krimmel took pains to point out: the tower clock reads 5:40—and the crowd is different. To reflect the later hour of the October day Krimmel lengthened the shadows, a good demonstration of his growing precision and technical skill. He also moved the crowd closer to the viewer and simplified the content of the picture. Many figures, including the marching band, are no longer in view, and others have changed position. The people are even more animated. The group of men standing behind the carriage are closer to the foreground. A small monkey has escaped from Peale's menagerie on the second floor and two men hang out the windows below trying to coax it back. The woman at the vendor's table selling apples is more visible, as are the two young boys who

50. Dunlap, *History*, 2:395. By 1820 Lawson also had this painting in his possession (see "*Return from Boarding School*," p. 508) and was listed as the owner of it when it was exhibited at PAFA in 1843; see *Catalogue of the Exhibition . . .* (1843), p. 4, no. 62. Lawson was thirteen years older than Krimmel. After first working in a Philadelphia firm of engravers he set up his own business sometime between 1795 and 1798; see Mantle Fielding, *Dictionary of American Painters, Sculptors, and Engravers* (New York: Paul A. Struck, 1942), s.v. "Lawson." Dunlap (*Diary*, p. 706) describes Lawson.

FIGURE 134
John Lewis Krimmel, Election Day at the State House, Philadelphia, 1816, *Philadelphia, 1816. Watercolor; 8½ x 13 in. (Historical Society of Pennsylvania, Philadelphia.) Signed at lower right, "J L Krimmel 1816."*

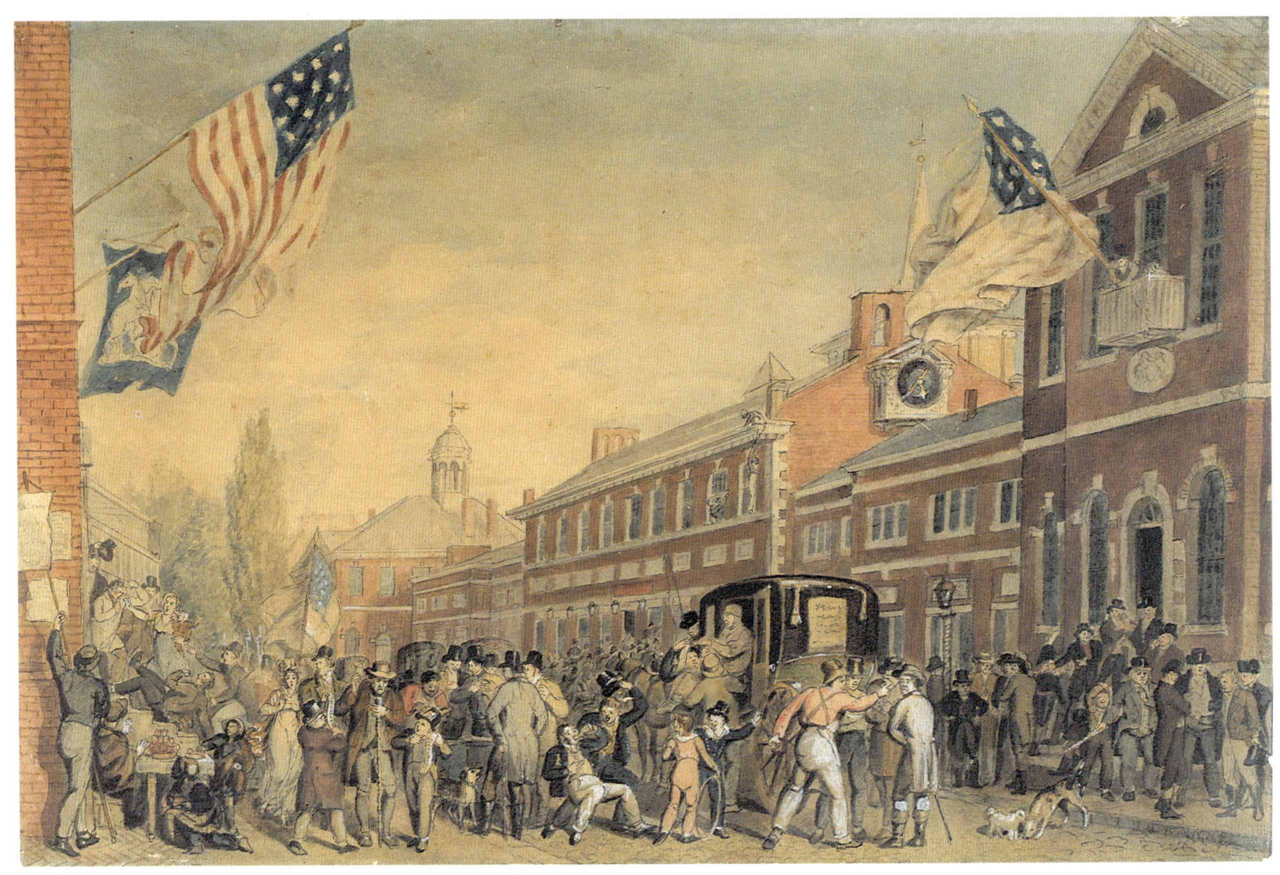

FIGURE 135
Group of men, ca 1813. Wash over pencil. Sketchbook 3, leaf 1 recto.

FIGURE 136
William Hogarth, Rake Surrounded by Artists and Professors. *Etching and engraving; 14 x 16 in. (Print Collection, Lewis Walpole Library, Yale University.)*

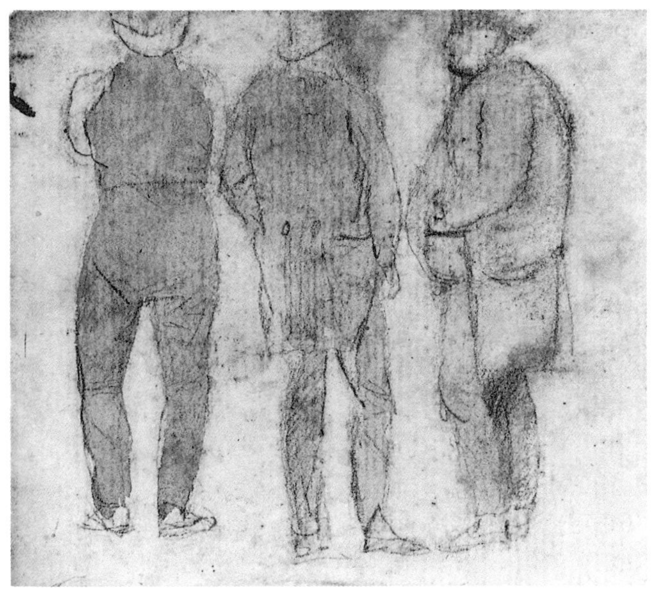

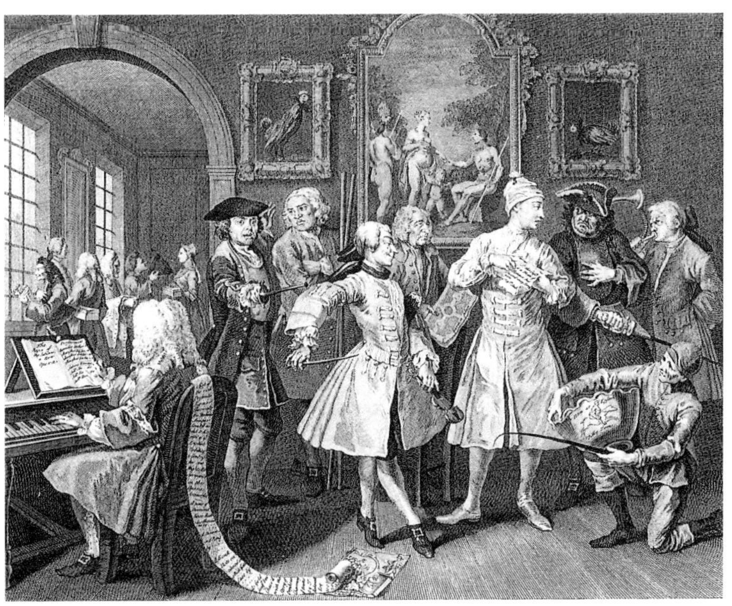

plan to swipe some fruit while she is distracted by the commotion on the steps beside her.[51] Some figures are outlined with a thin-nibbed pen, others with a fine brush. Krimmel relied on his sketchbooks for details such as the group of men in top hats and tail coats standing together in conversation (fig. 135).

Although many scholars and Krimmel's contemporaries have compared him with Hogarth, such a view is too narrow, and it ignores the much stronger influence of other artists, especially Wilkie. The degree to which Krimmel did draw inspiration from Hogarth is illustrated by an examination of *Rake Surrounded by Artists and Professors* (fig. 136). The work probably influenced the kneeling figure, the dancelike stances, possibly some of the lively gestures, and the flying ribbon in *Quilting Frolic* (see fig. 57); the position of the left foreground figure seated with his back to the viewer, and the partial opening up of the background through a view on the left in *Interior of an American Inn* (see fig. 105); and gestures such as pointing to a picture or pointing to one's own chest in *Country Wedding* (see fig. 115). Krimmel also employed such Hogarthian devices as a foreground figure holding a switch or a fiddling stick and a decoration in the background that augments the story line. Yet the way in which Krimmel dealt with human failings such as drunkenness, anger, coercion, and petty theft were not Hogarthian. Wilkie's art appealed more to Krimmel the storyteller, and it did so in a fashion that was more in tune with the style that the German American artist preferred.

Although copying famous pictures may have been the way that Krimmel provided himself with a kind of standard artistic training, his main reason for making copies of Wilkie's genre scenes had a more pragmatic dimension: they sold more readily than his own designs, indeed only one example of his copy work was listed among his effects at his death. Philadelphia's artists were striving to promote original works of art, yet many buyers were only interested in purchasing painted copies of famous pictures. Among the buying public, to own such art was deemed a mark of discernment.[52]

At least one fellow artist lamented Krimmel's excursions into copy work. In 1817 Charles Willson Peale traveled to New York and in May wrote in his journal, "Having leisure, I visit the [American] Academy of [Fine] Arts alone in order to make some remarks on the different pieces. . . . The young bird, [and] Jewsharp, copies by Kremmil are well painted, but I would rather see originals of his pensil as I consider him a prodigy in the art. I have understood that he is gone to Europe."[53]

By 1817 the dean of art in Philadelphia had good reason to regard Krimmel "a prodigy in the art." As to Krimmel's being in Europe, Peale was correctly informed. By May 1817 John Lewis was back in Ebingen.

51. A woodcut engraving of the watercolor was made for J. Thomas Scharf and Thompson Westcott, *History of Philadelphia* (Philadelphia: L. H. Everts, 1884), 3:1844.

52. "The Singing Party, copy from the Flemish" is in Krimmel's estate sale listing, *Poulson's American Daily Advertiser*, August 14, 1821. Krimmel did not sign his copies of other artists' pictures.

53. Charles Willson Peale, Journal to New York, May 28, 1817, Diary No. 22, Peale-Sellers Papers, American Philosophical Society, Philadelphia. The owners are not listed in the American Academy exhibition program. Krimmel may have made a personal visit to New York City. There are three addresses of New Yorkers in sketchbook 3: "John Apple No. 208 Broadway / Mr. Hvcet No. 67 or 76 Pearl Street board / Corns Schroeder of Broadway seminary." Naeve (*Krimmel*, p. 23) speculates that the first is John Appel who owned a music shop at 208 Broadway and that Schroeder is the portrait painter and miniaturist who worked in New York City between 1811 and 1826; see George C. Groce and David H. Wallace, *The New-York Historical Society's Dictionary of Artists in America, 1564–1860* (New Haven: Yale University Press, 1957).

Europe Revisited 1816–1818

The passion for travel that swept Europe in the late eighteenth and early nineteenth centuries soon spread to the United States. Following the Napoleonic Wars, as before them, it became the custom for young, well-to-do Americans to go on a Grand Tour of the Continent. Many went to emulate the educational practices of young British aristocrats, others simply wanted to see the Old World. Artists, however, aspired to go to Europe for quite different, very specific, mostly practical reasons; Europe offered the opportunity for advanced training, and study in England, Italy, and France especially, enhanced artist's chances of gaining commissions when they returned home. Although such considerations may have encouraged Krimmel's decision to travel to Europe, they were not the primary reason. Problems in his sister's family demanded the Krimmel brothers' attention.[1]

Christiane Krimmel Daser had died in Ebingen on October 28, 1815, leaving a husband and five small children, the oldest only 10 years old. Her death required a new legal settlement of the Krimmel family estate because the two brothers in America still owned nearly two-thirds of it. In addition, an emergency had arisen that threatened the loss of the long-held family business and all the property. The confectionery, still managed by brother-in-law Paul Daser, had developed serious financial troubles, the result of circumstances beyond Daser's control. The Napoleonic Wars and very poor harvests in 1814 and 1815 had created great food shortages all over Germany, and Württemberg suffered severely. The total failure of the harvest in 1816 threatened famine as the nearly complete lack of flour increased the price of an ordinary loaf of bread 500 percent. Among bakers, fine-pastry bakers were hit hardest, for most people could no longer afford even small baked luxuries. During 1816 Daser was forced to declare bankruptcy, and the Krimmel property was to be put up for auction. When the Krimmel brothers learned that the financial security of their sister's children was at stake, they decided to find a way to keep the house and confectioner's shop as well as most of the other real estate in the family; to accomplish this, one of them had to go to Ebingen.[2]

With a family to support and a business to manage in Philadelphia, George could not absent himself for an extended trip to Ebingen. John Lewis, on the other hand, was unmarried, and his profession did not tie him down to one particular place. In 1816 he was 30 years old and had been a professional painter for six years. Although he could not claim financial success, he had gained recognition as an artist specializing in genre scenes. Recently he had demonstrated his ambition to tackle challenging themes in compositions of greater complexity. An extended European trip might make him lose the foothold he had gained in the art world of Philadelphia, but it would also enrich his professional knowledge and further his artistic development.

Carrying a letter from George Krimmel to Paul Daser, John Lewis Krimmel boarded a ship that sailed to Europe by way of Bermuda, the chain

1. Dunlap (*History*, 2:393) wrote: "Such was Krimmel's strict economy, that at the end of a few years, he found himself enabled to visit his dear *faderland*. . . . the steeple of [Ebingen's] church appeared much lower to him than when he had looked back on it from Philadelphia, and probably many other things had diminished in the same proportion; and after seeing many good pictures and good people he appears to have been content to return to America as the land of his choice." Dunlap's version indicates that Krimmel (or perhaps his friends) chose to reveal little about his personal life. The archives in Albstadt-Ebingen are a good deal more informative.

2. In 1816 there was no summer. Cold steady rains prevailed from May to September; winter started in October. The correspondence from Daser has not survived; however, the nature of it can be deduced from George Frederick Krimmel to Paul Daser, October 16, 1816, Gerichtsprotokolle, Stadtarchiv, Albstadt-Ebingen.

of small islands situated in the western Atlantic Ocean about 600 miles east of Philadelphia. That he chose to sail via Bermuda to carry out some business for his brother is at best speculative, but the island's economy had long been closely linked to that of the American continent, and in 1816 it was recovering from the commercial disaster brought by the War of 1812. Although trade with the United States had resumed on a grand scale, it was the scenery, rather than business, that kept Krimmel's hands busy in Bermuda. During the week the ship was docked near Hamilton he did considerable sightseeing and took his sketchbook with him (figs. 137–143). On December 3, when the ship was in the middle of the Atlantic Ocean, Krimmel did a pencil sketch of the seemingly endless water and a dramatic sky in which the sun was hidden behind huge clouds, but its rays produced such a beautiful multicolored sight that Krimmel even took color notes. On the same page, he also sketched some of the passengers sitting and lying on the ship's deck.

The ship's next port of call was probably France, for sketchbook 4, newly purchased and made of paper from European—most probably French—mills, opens with drawings made in Paris.[3] Some numbered pages among the Parisian sketches have been torn out of the book, but those still in place show that once again the artist was uninterested in either famous buildings or historic sites but fascinated by the everyday life of ordinary people who, after the downfall of Napoleon in 1815, saw the restoration of the Bourbon monarchy (figs. 144, 145). Louis XVIII was sitting on the throne of France when Krimmel passed through the capital city, and in one composed picture, an image surely based on observation, Krimmel seems to hint at the king's moderately liberal attitude. The young woman collecting money for the old musician (who is playing the harp and the flute) is wearing the bonnet rouge, the symbol of the French Revolution, and a soldier apparently policing the area is about to join the group. The curbstone, which he employed as trompe l'oeil in *Election Day 1815*, also leads the eye into the background.

There is no pictorial record in the sketchbooks of Krimmel's journey from Paris to Ebingen, but the trip could only have been made by coach, and the usual route went via Strassburg through a pass in the Black Forest to Balingen, northwest of Ebingen. In all likelihood, the short stops afforded few opportunities to sketch.

Krimmel probably reached his hometown in late January or February 1817 because the first Ebingen references to him occur in early March and specifically note his recent arrival. One reference is a compendium of local events kept by Bleacher Johannes Jerg, a local tradesman with a propensity for writing. He recorded and expounded upon almost everything that happened in the town between 1771 and 1825. For March 7, 1817, he wrote:

> There is an exodus going on to other parts of the world, like America, Russia, and the Caucasus, many unmarried persons have departed; although preceptor Höcklin's son urged the country folks to go to America, the sugar baker's son [Krimmel], when he came home, spoke differently; he said [that] while the country was good, it required the gift of good health to undertake such a long sea voyage. He said [that] the trip could be made in four weeks but storms at sea can get the ship off course, causing it to search about for two, three, four months until it finds again the correct way. He said that rich and poor people live there, just as here among us; he also said, whoever was nobody in his fatherland will also amount to nothing in America.[4]

3. Dunlap's sources concur with this itinerary; Dunlap, *Diary*, p. 705. The watermarks in all the sketchbooks were examined by watermark specialist Tom Gravel. On the inside cover Krimmel wrote the address of a man with a Germanic name: "Dr. Zugenbühler près la porte St. Denis No. 2 Paris," which also implies that Krimmel was conversant in French too, further supporting the conclusions drawn in chap. 1 about Krimmel's education.

4. *Chronik des Bleichers Johannes Jerg, 1771–1825* (Balingen, Ger.: Hermann Daniel, 1952), pp. 135–36.

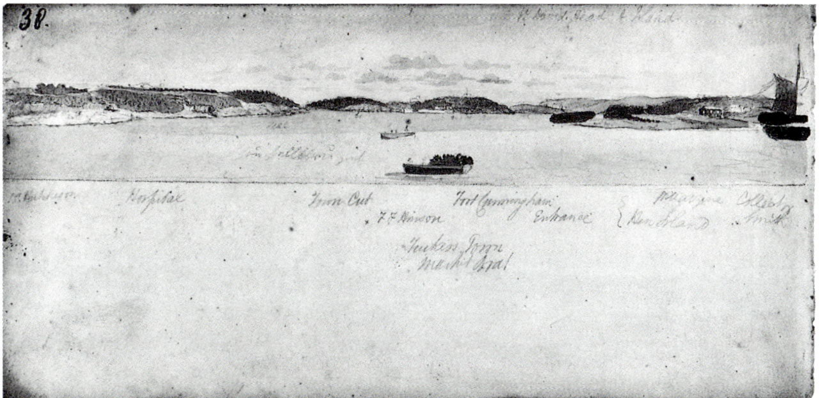

FIGURE 137

View of the main section of the chain of coral islands that form Bermuda, October 1816. Watercolor over pencil. Sketchbook 3, leaf 19 verso. Color notes in German; pencil inscriptions for points of interest not by Krimmel.

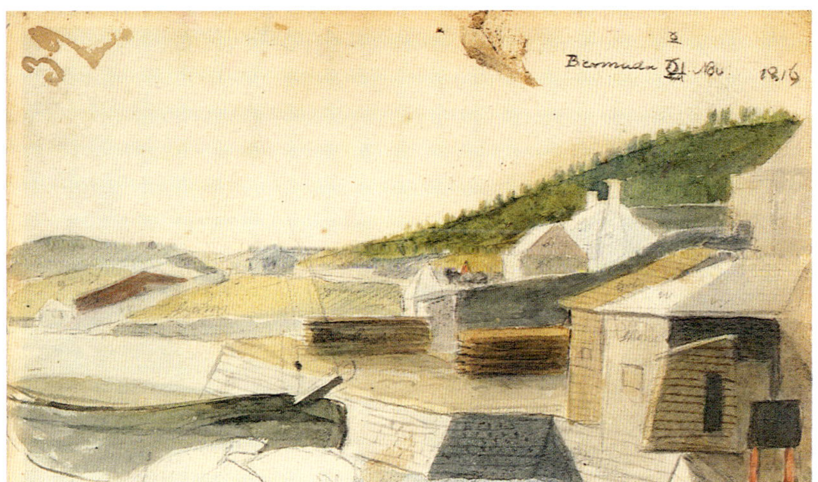

FIGURE 138

Bermuda, November 6, 1816. Watercolor over pencil. Sketchbook 3, leaf 20 recto. Color notes in German.

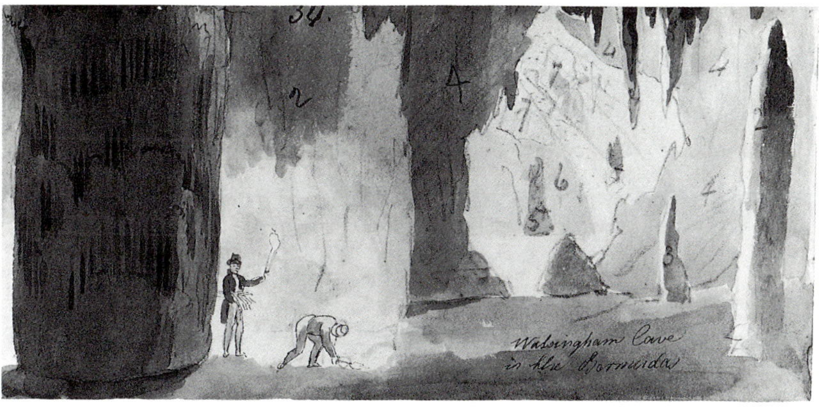

FIGURE 139

"Walsingham Cave in ——— Bermuida," November 1816. Watercolor and ink over pencil. Sketchbook 3, leaf 17 verso. The cave is located in Hamilton Parish and has long been known for its stalactites and stalagmites. Similar caves also existed near Ebingen. The numbers on the various formations are color notes.

FIGURE 140
Ocean view from Bermuda, November 1816. Watercolor over pencil. Sketchbook 3, leaf 18 verso. Color notes in German; identification of locations in pencil not by Krimmel. The top is labeled "sugar loaf hill." The point of land on the left is Spanish Point, the land in the middle distance is Somerset, and to the right is Ireland Island. Krimmel's vantage point must have been a hill in Pembroke or Devonshire.

FIGURE 141
Bermuda farm, November 1816. Watercolor. Sketchbook 3, leaf 17 recto.

FIGURE 142
Coconut palm, November 1816. Watercolor and ink over pencil. Street studies of figures, ca. 1813. Pencil and ink over pencil. Sketchbook 3, leaf 18 recto.

FIGURE 143
Bermuda vista looking back on St. David's Island, 1813. Watercolor over pencil, pencil inscription. Sketchbook 3, leaf 21 verso. Identification of locations not by Krimmel. The date in the upper corner, now partially obscured, is "Monday 11. 9br." (November). The date "7. 7bris" in the lower left accompanies a larger image of a tree (only part of which is shown here), probably drawn during Krimmel's visit to the Lehigh Valley in 1813; see chap. 2.

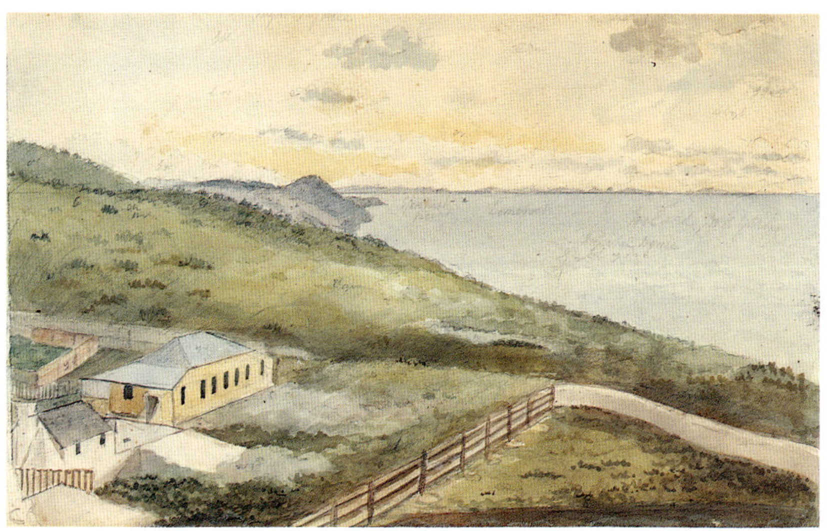

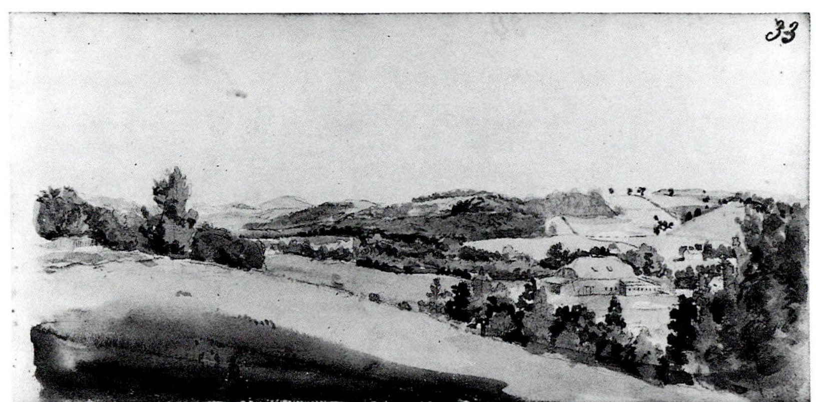

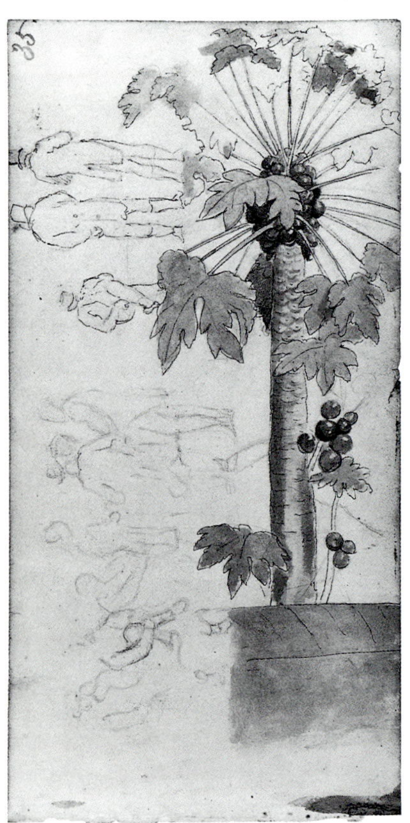

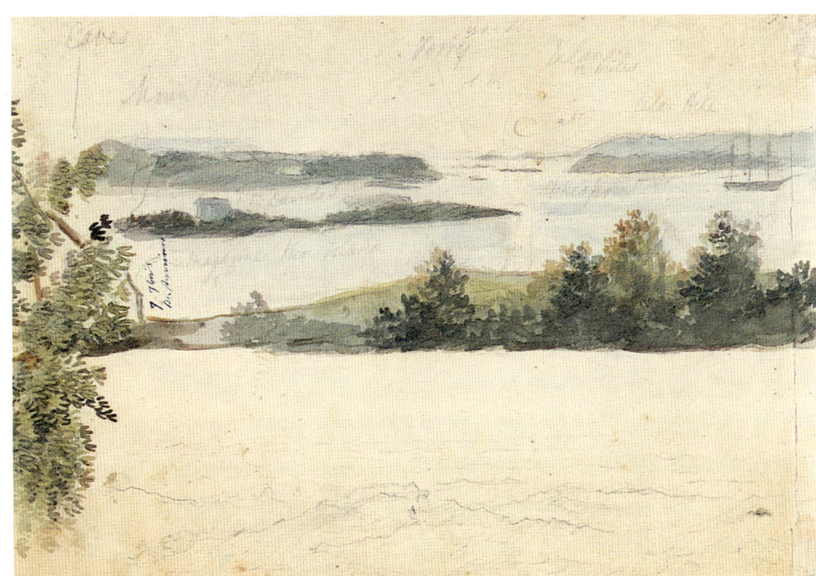

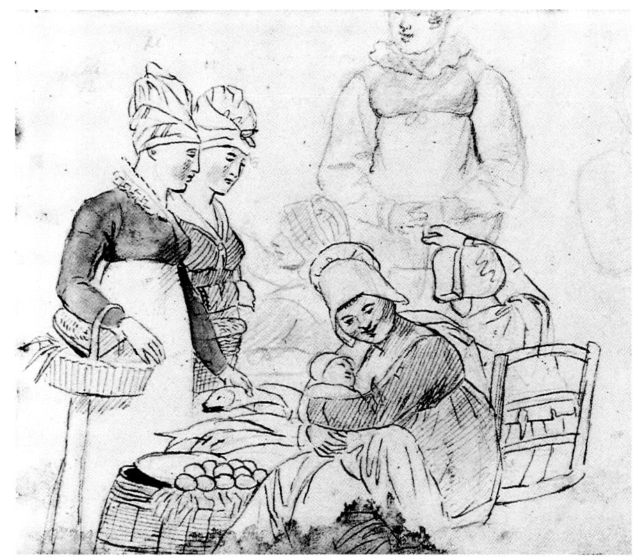

FIGURE 144
Parisian women, December 1816–January 1817. Watercolor over pencil. Sketchbook 4, leaf 2 recto.

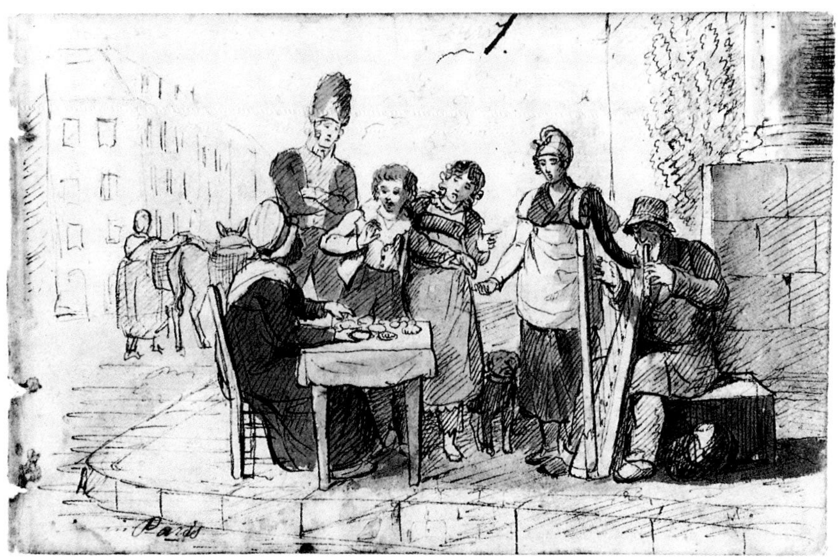

FIGURE 145
Paris street scene, December 1816–January 1817. Ink and wash with pencil. Sketchbook 4, leaf 1 recto. Krimmel composed this scene as a neoclassical frieze similar to that he used in Cherry Woman.

Krimmel's cautionary remarks about the hazards of a transatlantic voyage may have reflected his own recent experience, for he seems to have been on his way from America for nearly three months. If the ship that took him from Bermuda soon after November 11 to the coast of Europe had traveled at the customary speed, and even if the artist spent a few weeks making his way across France to Paris, he should have arrived in Ebingen around New Year's Day instead of weeks later.

Krimmel's first task in Ebingen was to deliver his brother's letter to Daser.

> My dear brother-in-law
>
> Since my last letter to you written in April of this year, I have heard nothing further from you.
>
> This time I will write briefly because my brother, through whom this letter reaches you, will serve for me instead of a long letter, and I wish, because it does not cost me anything at all, that you will fully take his advice. Anyway, an opportunity like this will not present itself to you in the near future. Therefore, take advantage of it!
>
> Since the death of our dear and unforgettable sister you were obliged to make a new legal inventory, how did you handle my end of it? As concerns my share with you, if it is to remain in your hands, it must remain assured to my sister's children in one way or another. Putting aside that I have suffered severely from the recent hard times [the War of 1812] and that I cannot spare anything in this world on account of my rapidly growing family, still, for the sake of my sister, I will gladly forget my claim as long as her children will profit by it. Since in this way you, yourself, will be taken care of at the same time, work with my brother and make secure in the most advantageous manner for these children alone, not only what you owe me, but also what is due to the children [from their mother] according to the law.
>
> As regards my brother's share in your hands, you two should come to an agreement about it. I have nothing from it to claim.
>
> It is my deeply felt wish always to receive good news from you and your dear children. May God preserve all of you. Farewell! My wife sends her regards to all of you. Your faithful brother-in-law,
>
> George F. Krimmel
>
> Philadelphia, October 16, 1816[5]

Immediately afterward Krimmel began drawing on his experience in the business world to secure his nieces and nephews' inheritance. He appeared before the Orphans Court on March 2, 1817, and signed a document affirming "the two brothers of the deceased wife of Daser, George Frederick, merchant in Philadelphia, and John Lewis, painter, relinquish their inheritance, due to them according to the court rulings of 1805 after the death of their mother, in favor of their deceased sister's children." By this step George Frederick's claim to 659 guilders and John Lewis's to 652 guilders were terminated. As proof of George Frederick's consent, his October 16 letter to Daser was entered in the files of the case.[6]

Next, in the names of his sister's children, Krimmel purchased all the family real estate by combining the money that he and his brother were relinquishing (1,311 guilders) with the inheritance Christiane's children had received after their mother's death (1,328 guilders). Thus the Daser children became the owners of the Krimmel house and confectionery, and their father

5. Krimmel to Daser, October 16, 1816, Gerichtsprotokolle. Ritter ("Recollections," p. 120) describes George as well educated and well read, which the letter confirms. George's confidence that his brother's on-site analysis would be adequate also confirms conclusions in chap. 1 about Krimmel's level of education.

6. Waisengericht [Orphans Court], March 2, 1817, Stadtarchiv, Albstadt-Ebingen.

was given the right to use the facilities. Since Daser had been declared bankrupt, a local citizen, *Zeugmacher* (cloth or textile manufacturer) J. M. Weinheimer, was appointed legal guardian of the five Daser children.[7]

The court dealings relating to the complex procedures of this case took more than a year, and during this period Krimmel sketched local subjects in his spare time. His earliest drawings, done shortly after he arrived in the late winter of 1817, depict indoor scenes, rooms with tall tiled stoves and women spinning, a typical cold-weather activity (fig. 146). As the weather improved he made watercolors of the town and the nearby countryside (figs. 147–150).

Ebingen is situated on a plateau surrounded by steep hills with limestone outcroppings. Originally a fortified town, it still had remnants of the old wall, two late medieval gate towers, many half-timbered houses, and a late Gothic church with a baroque spire. On the inside back cover of sketchbook 5, Krimmel itemized the locations of eight different Ebingen views: the church, the marketplace, Ebingen from Techtelfingen, Ebingen from Lautenberg, goats' pulpit, lower meadow, pointed rock, and upper gate. Seven exist as finished or partially finished watercolors in sketchbooks 4 and 5; only the marketplace, which might have included the Krimmel house, is missing (figs. 151–158). In these and other images, Krimmel's choice of vantage points, his general compositions, and his careful delineations of natural and architectural details demonstrate that he was quickly adapting his style to the type of landscapes and town vistas then being produced by contemporary southern German artists such as Johann Georg von Dillis and Wilhelm von Kobell in Munich.[8]

In the summertime, Krimmel added watercolor studies of flowers and farm animals to his repertoire. These he rendered with the precision of a botanist and the delight of a nature lover. Compared with the images he had produced in 1813 when he was sketching near the Lehigh River of Pennsylvania, the 1817 drawings are systematic. The botanical studies are done with close scrutiny and include flowers in different stages of bloom and at various angles (figs. 159–161). The animal studies are likewise far more specific than those done between 1810 and 1813 and focus on characteristic activities such as eating or sleeping (figs. 162, 163).

In autumn Krimmel journeyed southwest as far as Ebnat, which is close to Schaffhausen, the point at which the Rhine cascades over a ledge of hard Jura limestone some sixty feet high to create the largest and most picturesque of Europe's waterfalls. No record is known of Krimmel sketching the famous site, but it is inconceivable that he would not have depicted the falls if he had reached them, and certainly on November 10, 1817, he was in the general area (figs. 164–167).

Krimmel also sketched the people of Ebingen—old and young, in work clothes and in Sunday best (figs. 168–176). The bachelor painter especially delighted in sketching young women and girls in their regional dress, identifying many by name and their fathers' occupations. In the most finished of these watercolors, eight slender Ebingen maidens stiffly pose in two groups that totally occupy the foreground. The friezelike composition together with the fastidious rendition of different fabrics and patterns imply that Krimmel emphasized their costumes because he intended to use the watercolor as the basis for a print (fig. 177). Indeed a few years later, aquatints and hand-colored lithographs of people in national and regional garb sold readily in markets across Europe.[9]

7. Waisengericht, March 19, 1817.

8. Sketchbook 5, inside back cover. *Münchner Landschaftsmalerei, 1800–1850* (Munich: Städtische Galerie im Lembachhaus, 1979), pp. 237, 273.

9. *Ländliche Gebräuche*, a portfolio of 10 colored aquatints, exemplifies the expanding market for pictures of people in regional garb and the fostering of local traditions.

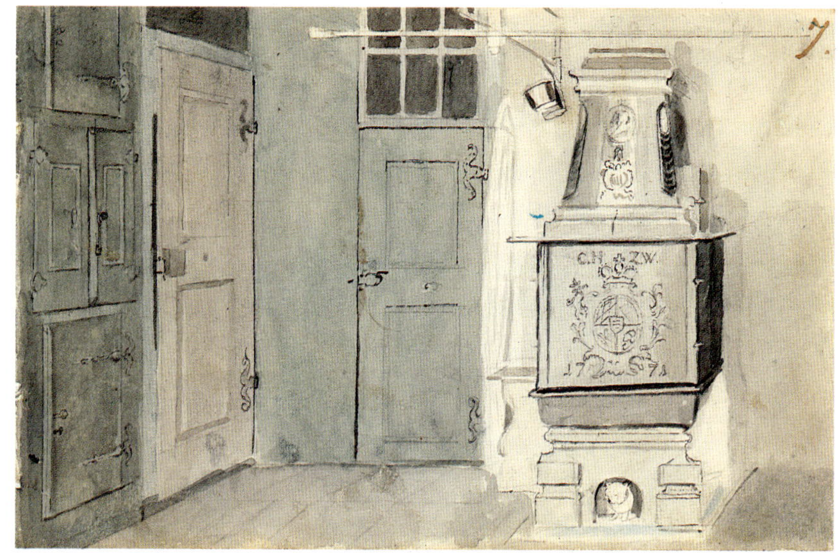

FIGURE 146
Interior corner of Ebingen room, 1817. Watercolor and ink over pencil. Sketchbook 4, leaf 3 recto. The same stove is depicted in fig. 180. This cat appears on top of the stove in figs. 179 and 183.

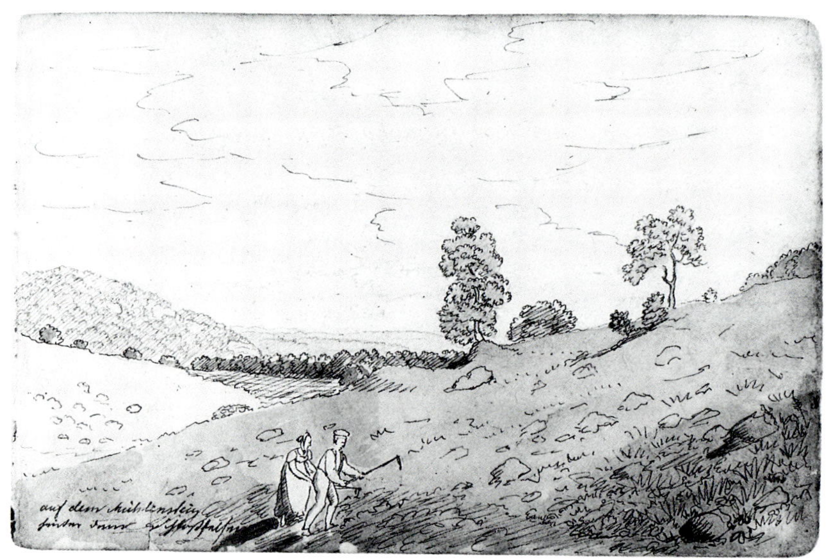

FIGURE 147
Auf dem Mühlensteig hinter dem Schlossfelsen, 1817. Ink and wash over pencil, ink inscription. Sketchbook 5, leaf 39 verso.

FIGURE 148
Landscape near Ebingen, 1817. Ink and wash over pencil. Sketchbook 5, leaf 40 recto.

FIGURE 149
Landscape near Ebingen, 1817. Watercolor and ink over pencil, ink inscription. Sketchbook 5, leaf 41 recto.

FIGURE 150
Lang's paper mill near Laufen, summer 1817. Watercolor and ink over pencil, ink inscription. Sketchbook 5, leaf 7 recto.

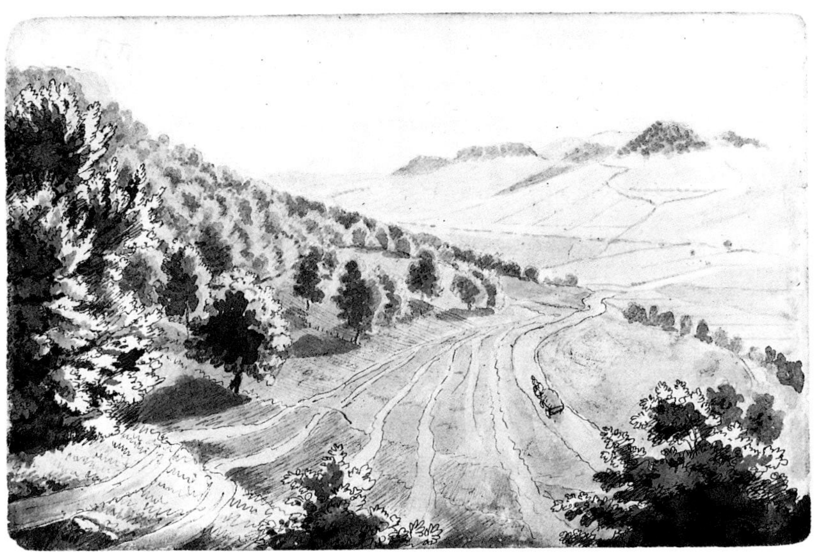

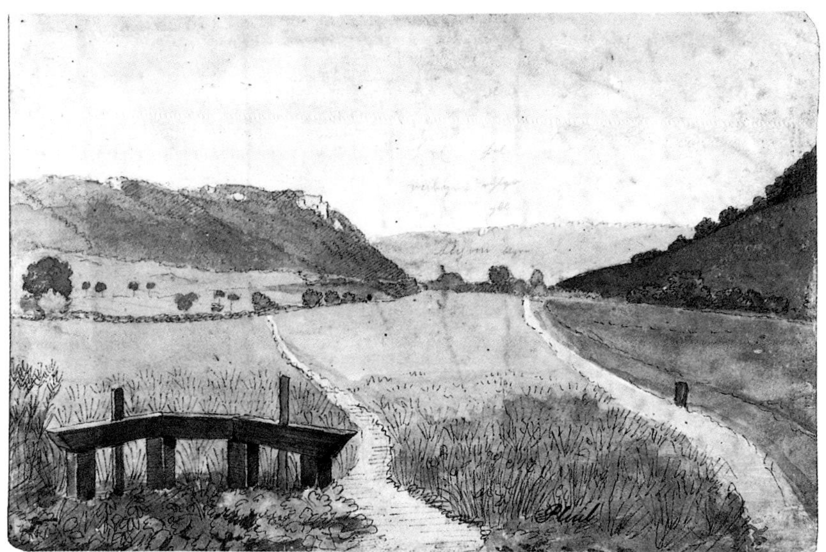

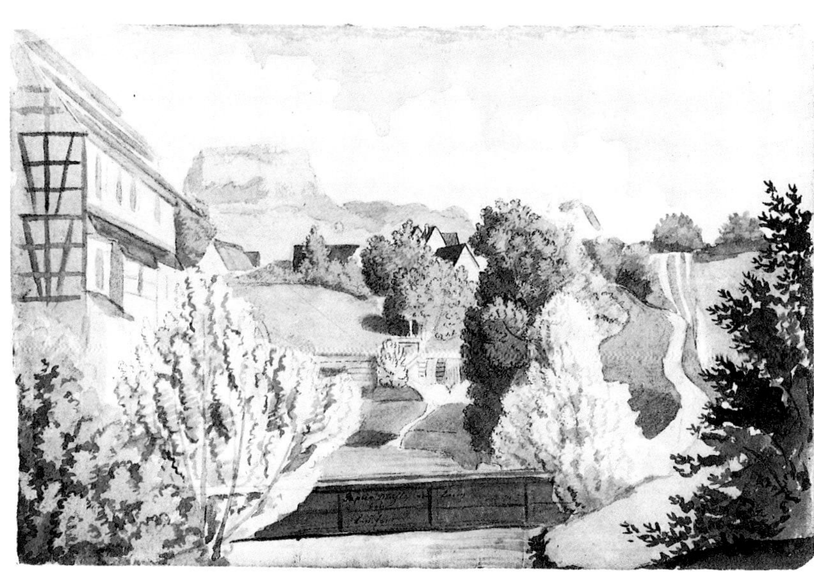

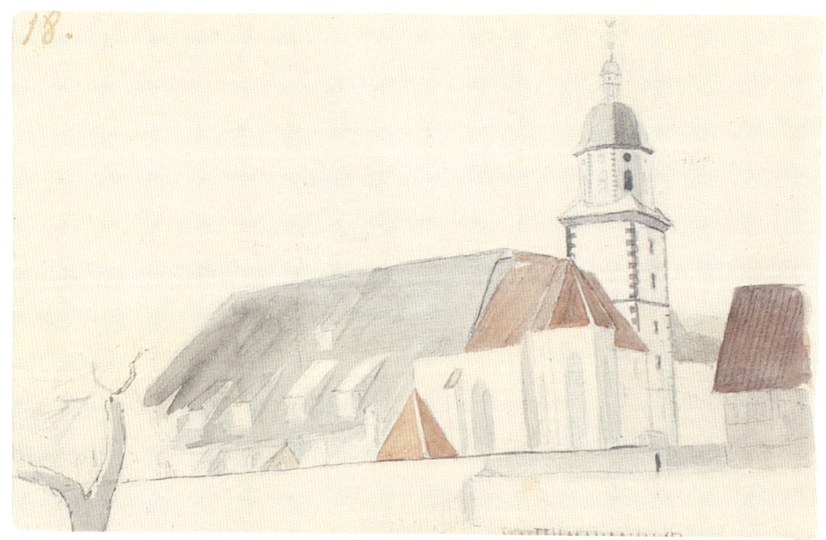

FIGURE 151
St. Martin's Lutheran Church, 1817. Watercolor and ink over pencil. Sketchbook 4, leaf 7 verso. The same church tower is in several other sketches.

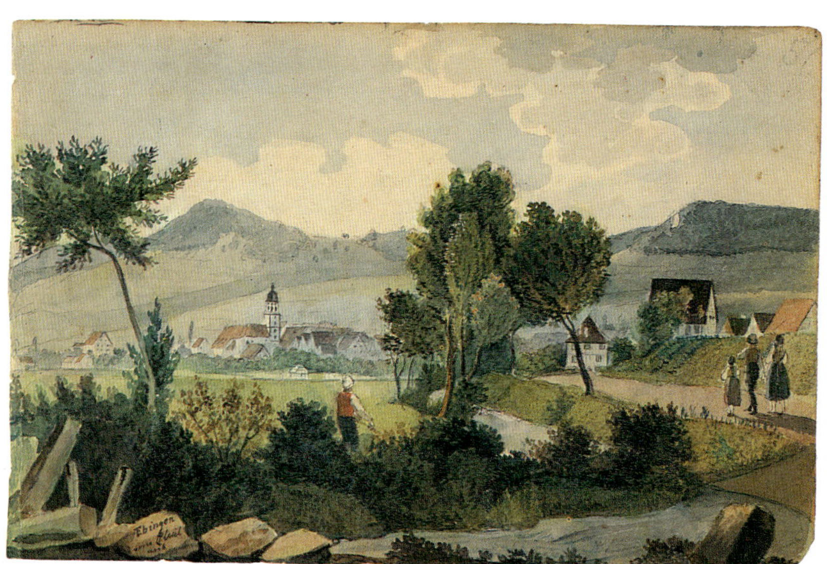

FIGURE 152
Ebingen vom Pluil aus [Ebingen seen from Pluil], 1817. Watercolor and ink over pencil, watercolor inscription. Sketchbook 5, leaf 3 recto. The tower is that of St. Martin's Church.

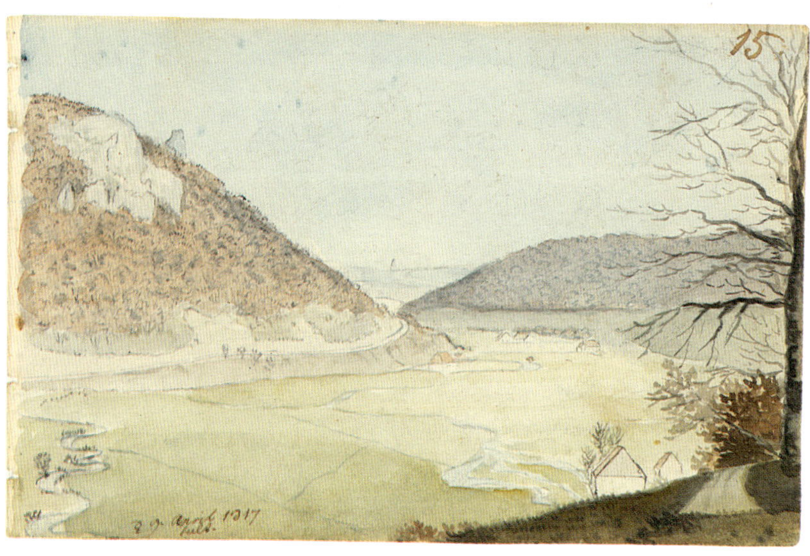

FIGURE 153
Distant view of Ebingen, Friday, April 9, 1817. Watercolor and ink over pencil, ink inscription. Sketchbook 4, leaf 6 recto. Most likely this is the view coming from Lautlingen, northwest of Ebingen.

FIGURE 154
View near Ebingen, 1817/18. Watercolor and ink over pencil. Sketchbook 4, leaf 15 recto.

FIGURE 155
Geissenkänzele [Goat's pulpit], 1817. Watercolor over pencil, ink inscription. Sketchbook 5, leaf 7 verso.

FIGURE 156
Heidenstein, der Spitze Felsen [Pagen rock, pointed rock], 1817. Watercolor over pencil, watercolor inscription. Sketchbook 5, leaf 1 recto.

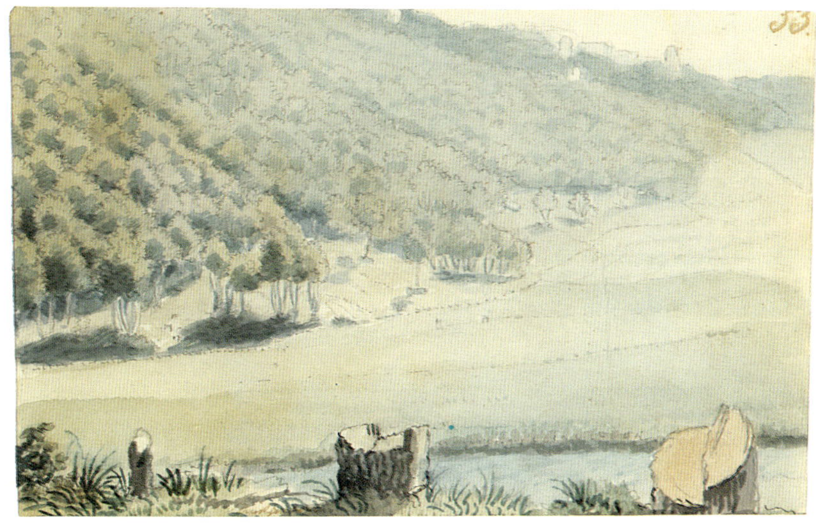

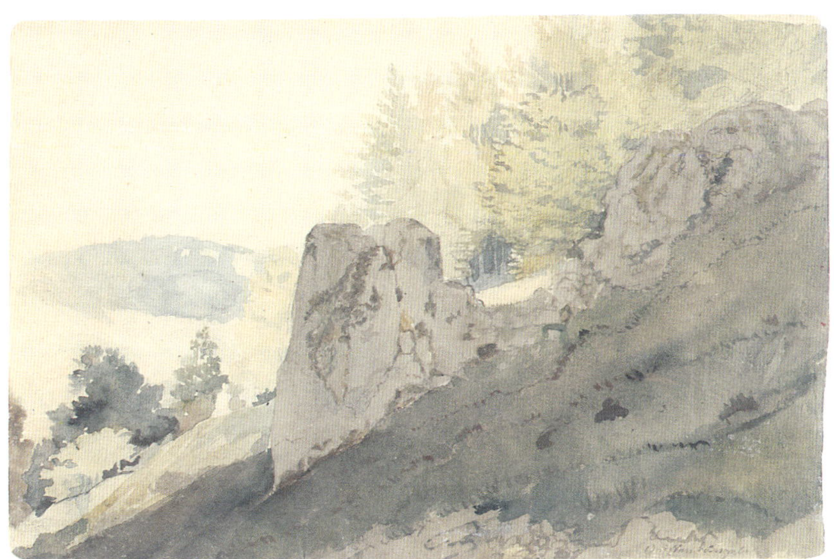

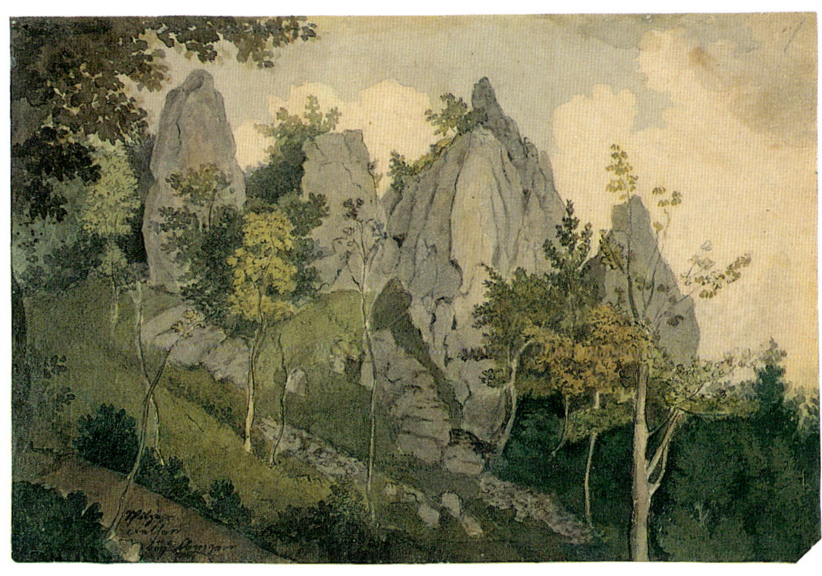

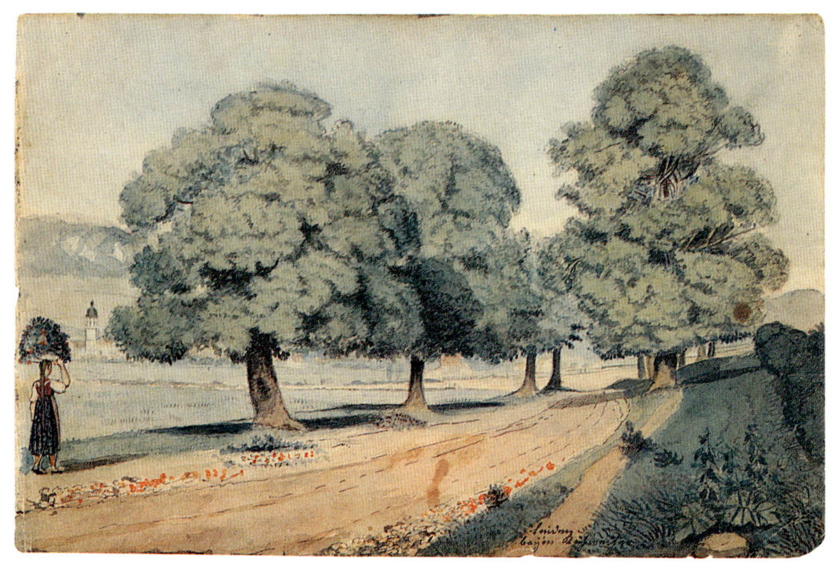

FIGURE 157
Linden beym Kuhweiher [Lindens near the cow pond], 1817. Watercolor and ink over pencil, ink inscription. Sketchbook 5, leaf 5 recto.

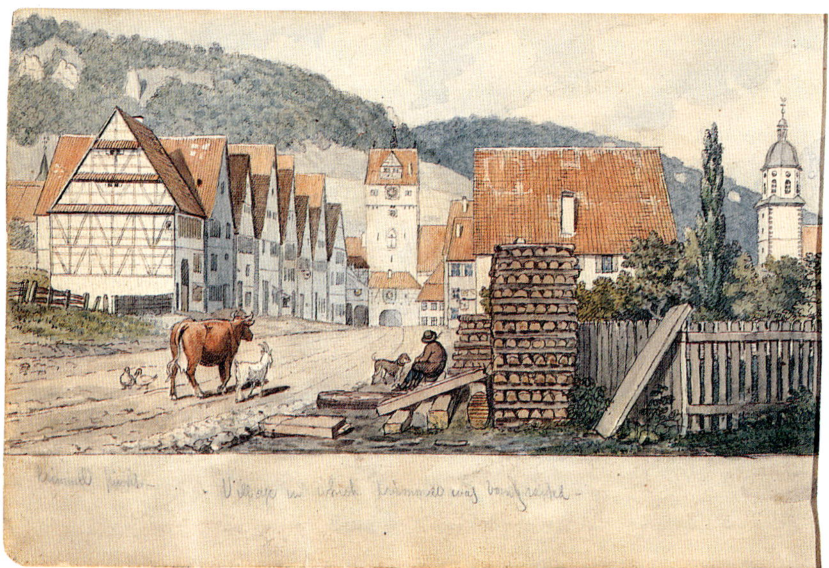

FIGURE 158
Das Obere Thor [Sonnenstrasse leading to the upper gate], 1817. Watercolor and ink over pencil, pencil inscription. Sketchbook 5, leaf 16 verso. This is the only pictorial record of a part of town that no longer exists.

FIGURE 159
Roses, 1817. Watercolor over pencil. Sketchbook 5, leaf 4 recto.

FIGURE 160
Flowers, July 10, 1817. Watercolor over pencil. Sketchbook 5, leaf 3 verso.

FIGURE 161
Flowers, 1817. Watercolor over pencil. Sketchbook 5, leaf 4 verso.

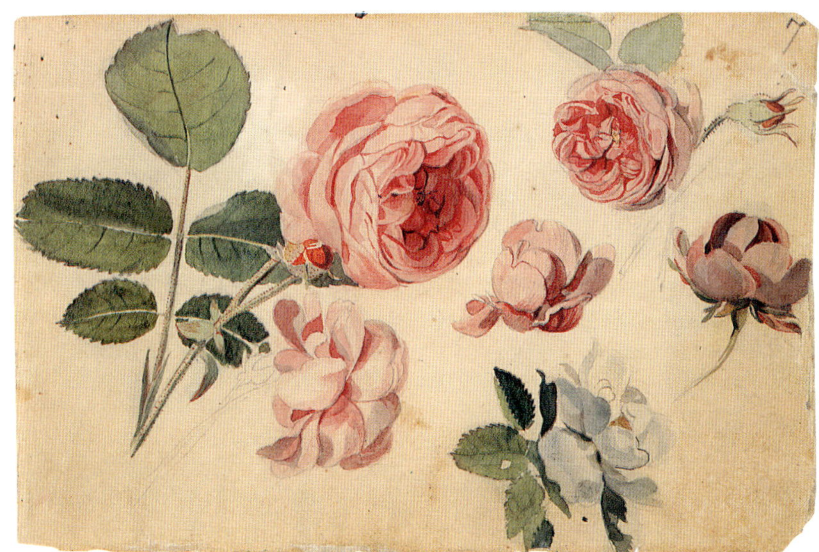

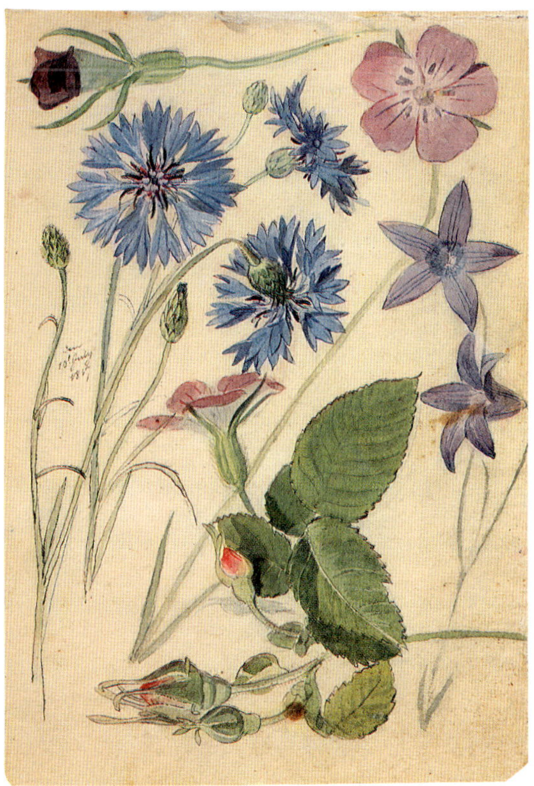

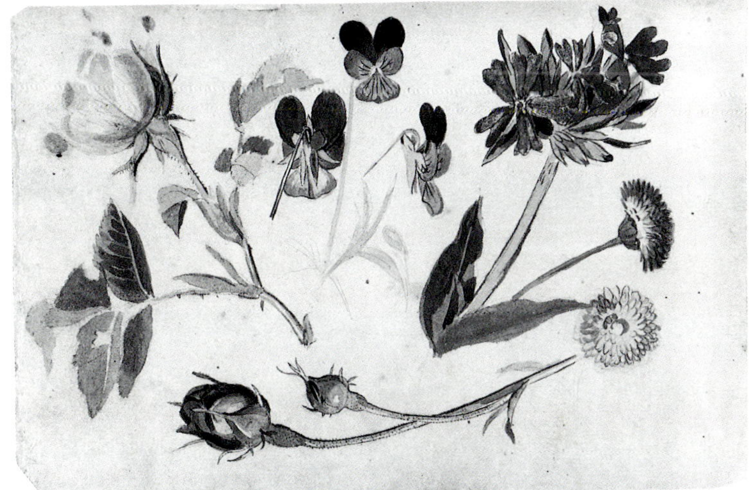

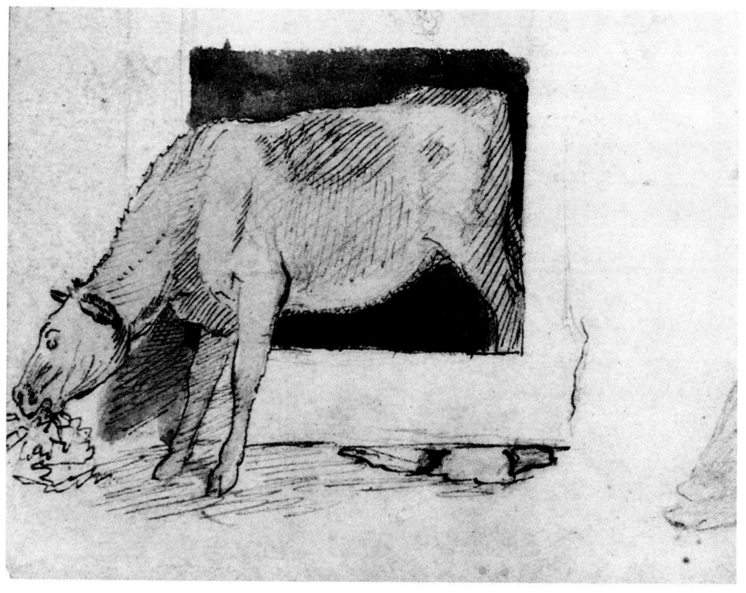

FIGURE 162
Calf feeding, 1817. Watercolor over pencil. Sketchbook 5, leaf 11 verso.

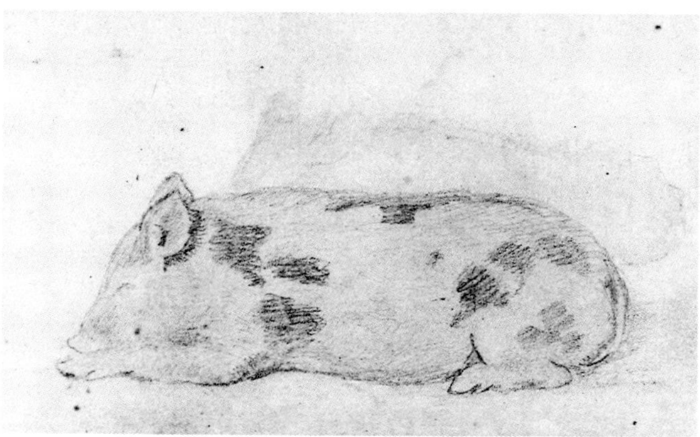

FIGURE 163
Pig, 1817. Watercolor over pencil, faint wash. Sketchbook 5, leaf 11 verso.

FIGURE 164
Southwestern Württemberg, November 3, 1817. Watercolor over pencil, ink inscription. Sketchbook 5, leaf 38 verso.

FIGURE 165
Southwestern Württemberg, November 4, 1817. Watercolor over pencil. Sketchbook 5, leaf 36 verso.

FIGURE 166
Liechtenst, Monday, November 10, 1817. Watercolor and ink over pencil, ink inscription. Sketchbook 5, leaf 10 recto. Lichtenstein near Ebnat was once a fortified town.

FIGURE 167
View near Ebnat with the Jura Mountains in the middle ground and the Swiss Alps in the background, November 10, 1817. Watercolor over pencil, ink inscription. Sketchbook 5, leaf 21 recto.

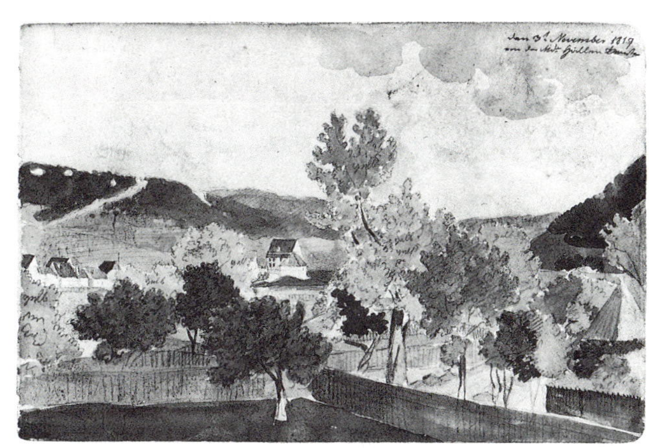

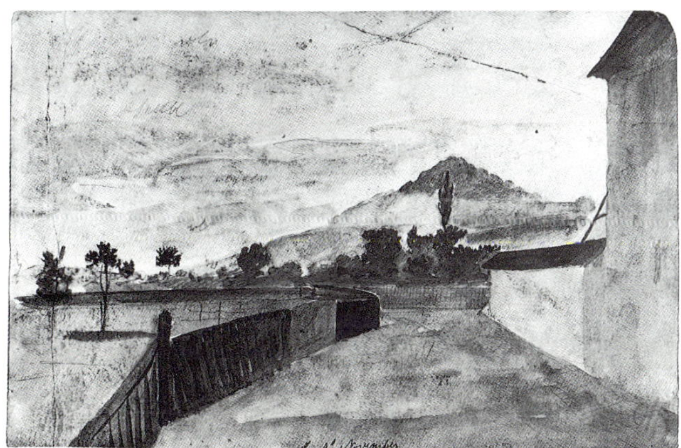

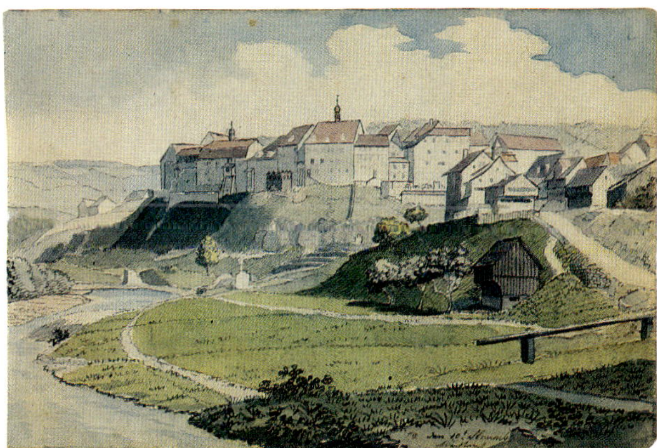

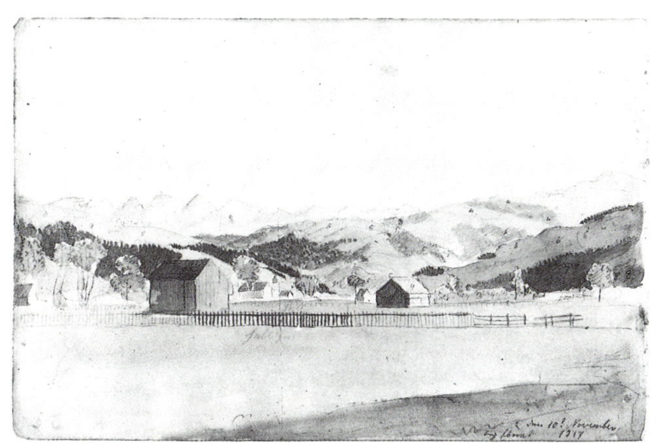

FIGURE 168
Women and tradesman, 1817 or 1818. Watercolor over pencil, pencil. Sketchbook 5, leaf 8 verso.

FIGURE 169
Two Ebingen women and a man, 1817 or 1818. Ink over pencil, watercolor over pencil. Sketchbook 5, leaf 6 verso.

FIGURE 170
Man on horseback, 1817 or 1818. Pencil, watercolor over pencil. Sketchbook 5, leaf 13 recto. The pencil outline of the horse's back is barely visible.

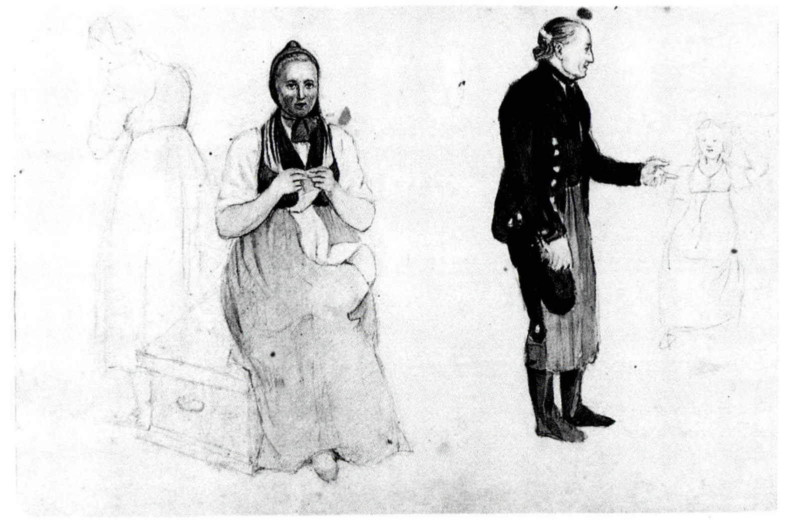

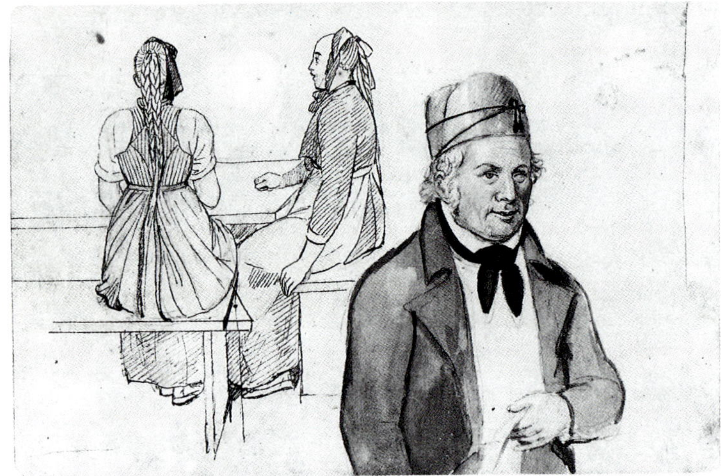

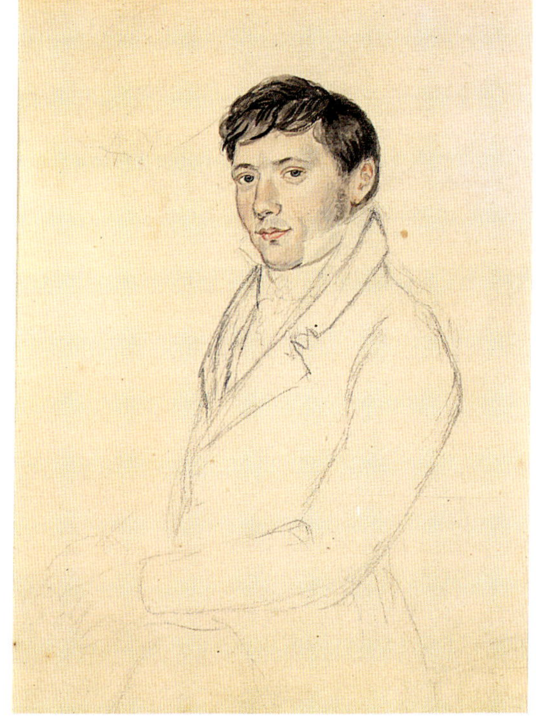

FIGURE 171
Man and young woman, 1817 or 1818. Watercolor over pencil, pencil. Sketchbook 5, leaf 9 recto.

FIGURE 172
Women, 1817 or 1818. Watercolor over pencil, wash over pencil, pencil. Sketchbook 5, leaf 6 recto.

FIGURE 173
Girl with flowers, 1817. Watercolor over pencil, ink inscription. Sketchbook 4, leaf 8 verso. The inscription translates "Sunday 22d June, rain 1817."

FIGURE 174
Heads and faces, 1817. Ink over pencil, watercolor over pencil, pencil. Sketchbook 4, leaf 3 verso.

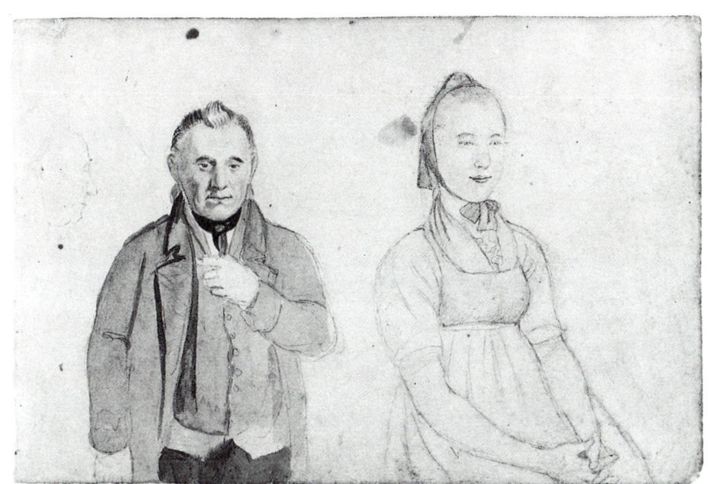

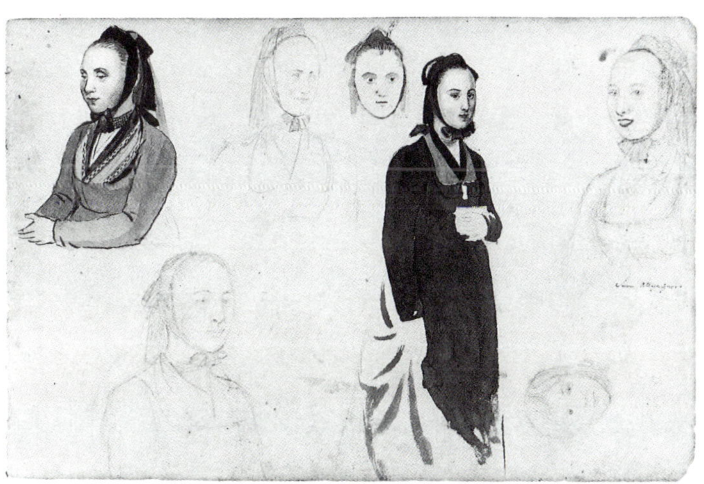

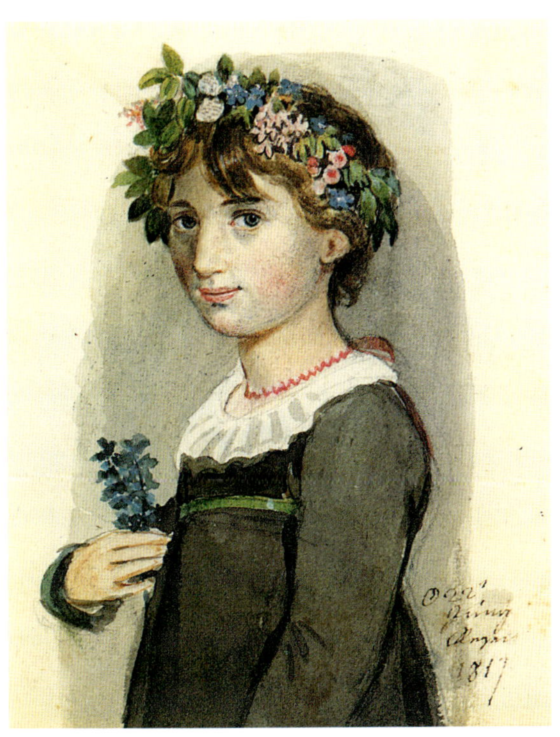

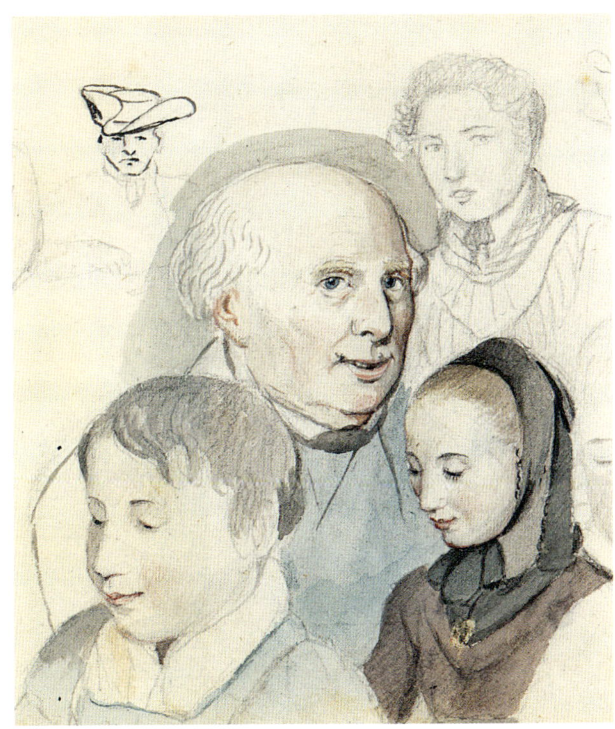

FIGURE 175
Woman with cow, 1817 or 1818. Pencil, watercolor over pencil. Sketchbook 5, leaf 5 verso.

FIGURE 176
Two women, 1817 or 1818. Watercolor over pencil. Sketchbook 5, leaf 9 verso.

FIGURE 177
Group of Ebingen women, 1817 or 1818. Watercolor over pencil, ink inscription. Sketchbook 5, leaf 8 recto. The inscriptions are names, one of which is Sarah; the other two are illegible.

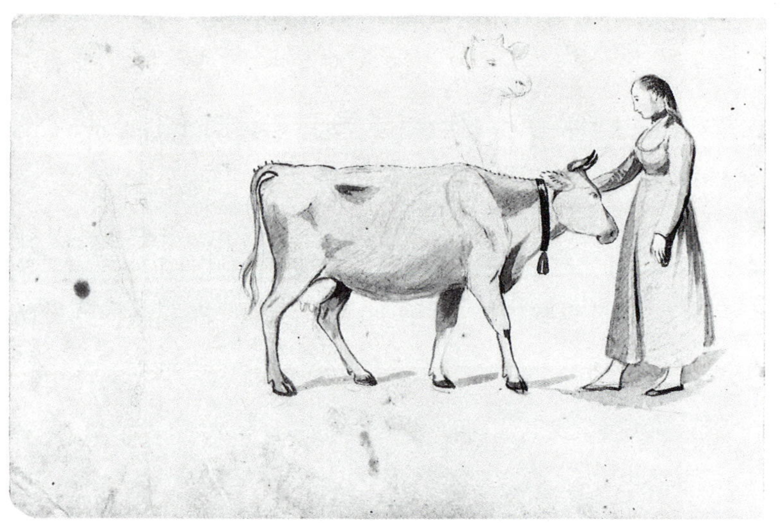

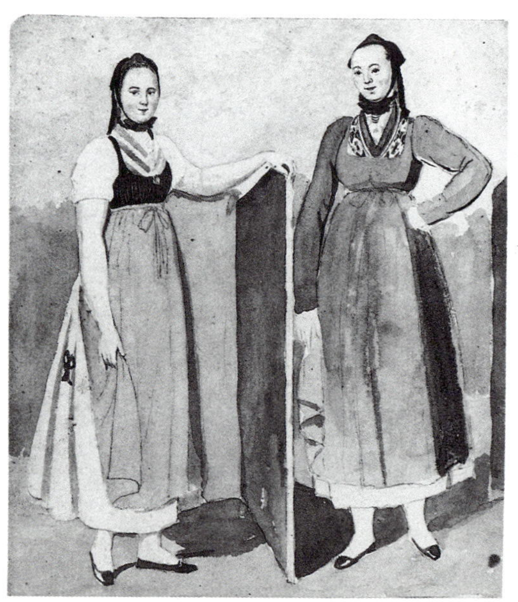

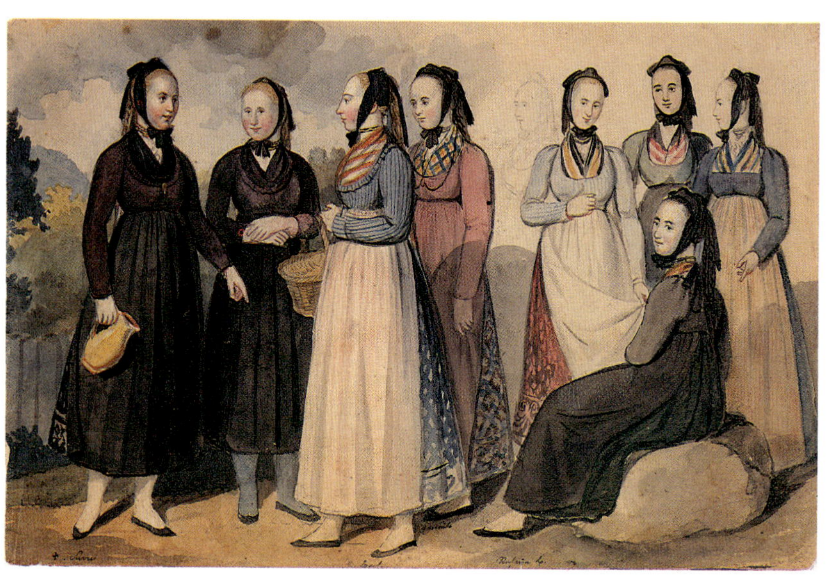

The emphasis on regionalism so apparent in Krimmel's drawings was part of the same romantic movement that had kindled interest in folklore, folk songs, and other aspects of ethnic traditions in many parts of the Western world. German literary historians were in the vanguard of European intellectuals studying regional ethnographic traditions. Out of this had come the 1806 publication of *Der Knaben Wunderhorn*, a selection of folk songs collected by Clemens Brentano and Achim von Arnim and in 1812, the collection of German folklore assembled by brothers Jakob and Wilhelm Grimm. These books had spurred popular appreciation of local traditions and had precipitated a demand for images of people in regional costumes—pictures that appeared in books and magazines in Europe throughout the ensuing century.

Krimmel hoped to capitalize on the romantic enthusiasm. He did a drawing that was subsequently produced as an etching entitled *Der Nachtkartz* that appeared with nine other images in *Ländliche Gebräuche in Württemberg* (Rural Customs in Württemberg). The series was published by Ebner'sche Kunsthandlung of Stuttgart in 1830, but Krimmel's drawing or watercolor dates from late 1817 or early 1818, as does the aquatint etching of it by Joseph Ignaz Hörmann of Augsburg, who died in 1820 (fig. 178). The other nine images in the series date from the 1820s and are attributed to genre and landscape painter Johann Baptist Pflug, who lived in Biberach, about thirty-five miles southeast of Ebingen, and were etched by Eberhard Emminger, a for mer student of Pflug's who worked for Ebner'sche Kunsthandlung. Although Krimmel's and Pflug's manner and style of painting and drawing were very different, both men focused on the same topic—the landscape and the rural customs of Württemberg.[10]

Der Nachtkartz provides an intimate look at Württemberg life. It shows how young people of marriageable age entertained themselves during the long winter evenings by gathering in the *Stube* (living/dining area) of private homes. While the young women spun thread and knit garments, someone read a story aloud. On many occasions young men joined the group, which for the early part of the evening was chaperoned by the master and mistress of the house. That Krimmel's image shows seven women and only three men is illustrative of the shortage of men following the long Napoleonic Wars. Within the scene are several vignettes. Darkness falls through the open door and through the window in the left foreground, which functions as a compositional counterpoint to the door. The clock hung high on the right wall indicates the time is 8:20. If Krimmel worked in his customary manner, his finished image (now lost) was dated on the paper tacked to the hutch; however, in Hörmann's print the paper shows only squiggly lines.

As in his American interiors, Krimmel placed an equal number of figures on either side of the central axis, but there are also signs that he was exploring new methods of composing multifigural images. In this instance he abandoned the homogeneity of the neoclassical frieze and defined each group or single figure with a more pronounced separateness. The motif of the single figure seen from the back, a pictorial device that Krimmel had included in all earlier genre scenes, is much more isolated and therefore particularly well explored.

Sketchbook 4 contains Krimmel's preliminary compositional ink and wash drawing of the scene that became *Der Nachtkartz* (fig. 179). A comparison of it with the engraving indicates that as with his Philadelphia work, the artist made numerous changes between the wash drawing and finished work. It also reveals that for the final image Krimmel had turned to his individual sketches,

10. Augsburg, located about 160 km from Ebingen, was the regional capital of the part of Swabia that belonged to Bavaria and was the major gateway of commerce and cultural exchange between Italy and Germany; see Hans Ulrich Roller, *Volkskultur in Württemberg* (Stuttgart: Württembergisches Landesmuseum; Tübingen: Gulde Druck, 1974), p. 74. Ulrich Thieme and Felix Becker, eds., *Allgemeines Lexikon der bildenden Künstler von der Antike bis zur Gegenwart* (Leipzig, Ger.: W. Englemann, 1907–50), s.v. "Hörmann, Joseph Ignaz," "Pflug, Johann Baptist," and "Emminger, Eberhard." Hörmann, a Swabian like Krimmel, gained renown for his series of botanical prints, genre scenes, landscapes, and city views. Pflug had studied in Munich with court painter Christian von Mannlich before returning to Biberach in 1810; see also Hartmann, *Pflug*. There is no evidence that Krimmel and Pflug collaborated; however, it is plausible that the two met. The two towns were not that far apart; indeed, Johann Paul Bux of Biberach attended Krimmel's August 8, 1818, farewell party (sketchbook 5, inside front cover).

FIGURE 178
J. I. Hörmann, engraver, and J. L. Krimmel, pinxt, Der Nachtkartz, *1818–20. Colored aquatint; 6⅛ x 8 in. (Württembergisches Landesmuseum, Stuttgart.) Etchings of this work are also in the collections of the Staatsgalerie and the Staatsbibliothek, both in Stuttgart.*

FIGURE 179
Compositional sketch for Der Nachtkartz, *late 1817 or early 1818. Wash and ink over pencil. Sketchbook 4, leaf 4 recto.*

FIGURE 180
Woman spinning, probably 1817. Watercolor over pencil. Sketchbook 5, leaf 11 recto. This image employs neoclassical principles of design in an intimate motif.

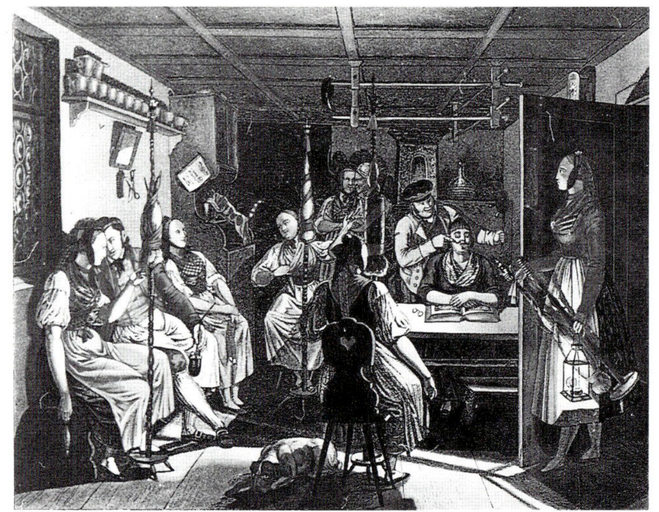

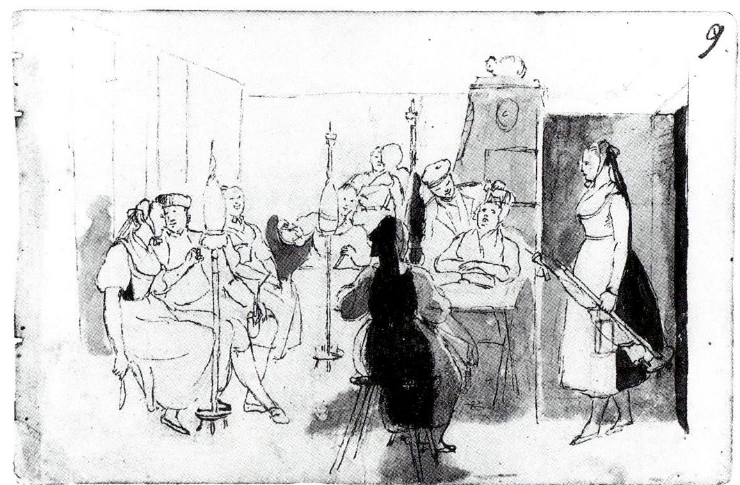

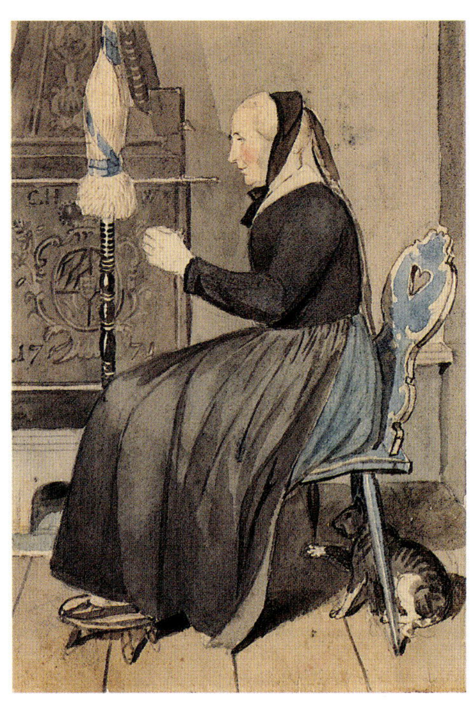

especially for details such as faces, figures, dresses, spinning shafts, chairs, the stove, and the cat (figs. 180–182; see also figs. 168, 169, 172, 173).

Hörmann's etching is not of high quality; nevertheless, it does convey Krimmel's careful rendering of the room's uneven lighting, the shine of the lantern, the highlights on the cups standing on the shelf, the picturesque reflections in the heavy window glass, and the spot of light in the mirror. Compared with the profusion of goods Krimmel depicted in his paintings of the interiors of American houses, this German house has few goods, something the artist has stressed. He seemingly compensates for the spareness by heightening the illusion of depth—emphasizing the ceiling beams and the floorboards, which run perpendicular to the picture space.

The reverse side of the sketch contains an ink and wash drawing of a scene in an Ebingen tavern, which Krimmel may also have intended to have turned into a print (fig. 183). Krimmel's rhythmic spacing of the figures gives simultaneous preeminence to the barmaid and the taverner. Although the subject matter and design of this scene are related to *Interior of an American Inn* (the figure of the barmaid is in almost the same pose as the young mother), the Ebingen tavern scene is more naturalistic, and the concept is calmer and friendlier. The carefully balanced construction intimates that it was designed as a companion piece to *Der Nachtkartz.*

The changes that occurred in Krimmel's style during 1817 and 1818 signify a growing awareness of the currents in German art, especially those that favored relaxing neoclassical principles and abandoning the bilateral symmetry that had dominated artistic design for several decades in favor of romantic spatial concepts. During the two years of Krimmel's visit, German romanticism was reaching its zenith and affecting all areas of life. The extraordinary cultural revitalization coincided with the preeminence of a host of men of genius—Goethe and Schiller, Beethoven and Schubert, Runge and Friedrich, and many other gifted German poets, philosophers, composers, and painters—who in combination made this period one of the most creative times in Western history. Yet Krimmel's exposure to the dynamic developments in Weimar, Dresden, Vienna, Berlin, and Munich was very limited so long as he remained in Ebingen. Stuttgart, the capital of Württemberg, was a two-day coach ride away, and even so, that city was not a particularly vibrant center of romantic painting. On the other hand, Stuttgart did have a great tradition in neoclassical painting, having been the residence of Gottlieb Schick and Philip Friedrich Hetsch, two outstanding German neoclassical painters. Both had studied with David in Paris and had spent long periods in Rome. Whether Krimmel visited Stuttgart in his first year back in Württemberg cannot be deduced from his sketchbooks; he did visit there early in May 1818, at which time Hetsch, acclaimed for his history paintings and portraits, was still alive. In all probability, that visit inspired Krimmel to paint a copy of a picture by Hetsch, simply identified as a female head with flowers, which was exhibited at the Pennsylvania Academy the year following Krimmel's death. He also may have sketched one of the women of the city (fig. 184).[11]

Among the Stuttgart artists whose work appealed to Krimmel was Johann Baptist Seele, a painter and etcher of genre scenes, whose work remained widely known through prints. Seele had studied at the progressive Hohe Carlschule, which offered nobles and talented young men of humble origin, like Seele, the most modern education. In 1804 he was appointed the official court painter and director of the ducal (soon royal) galleries, a move that

11. Hetsch's picture of this subject remains unidentified.

FIGURE 181
Ebingen women, 1817 or 1818. Wash over pencil, watercolor over pencil, watercolor and ink over pencil. Sketchbook 4, leaf 7 recto. Note that Krimmel had used this page earlier, the faint outlines of several figures are discernible underneath these images.

FIGURE 182
Girl with distaff, winter 1817/18. Watercolor over pencil. Sketchbook 5, leaf 12 recto.

FIGURE 183
Interior of Ebingen tavern, 1817 or 1818. Wash and ink over pencil. Sketchbook 4, leaf 4 verso.

FIGURE 184
Young woman seated, probably 1818. Watercolor over pencil. Sketchbook 5, leaf 16 recto. The dress and hair style suggest this woman resided in a town less rural than Ebingen, such as Stuttgart.

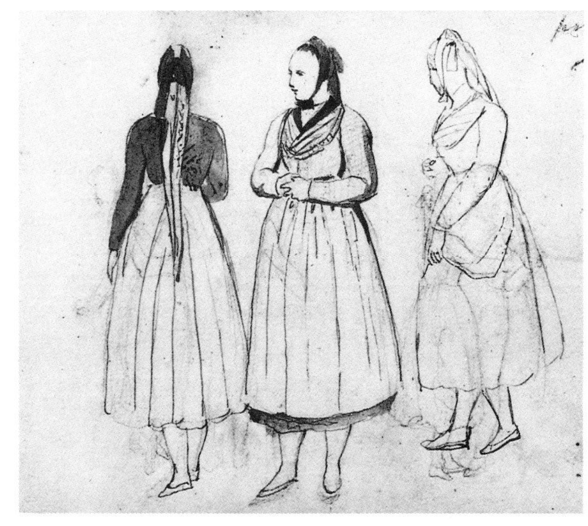

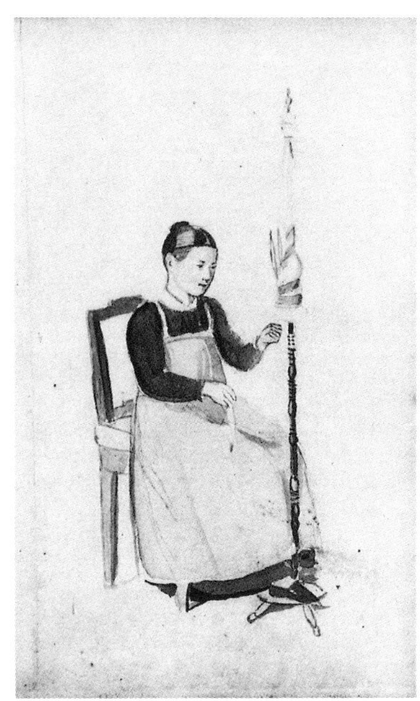

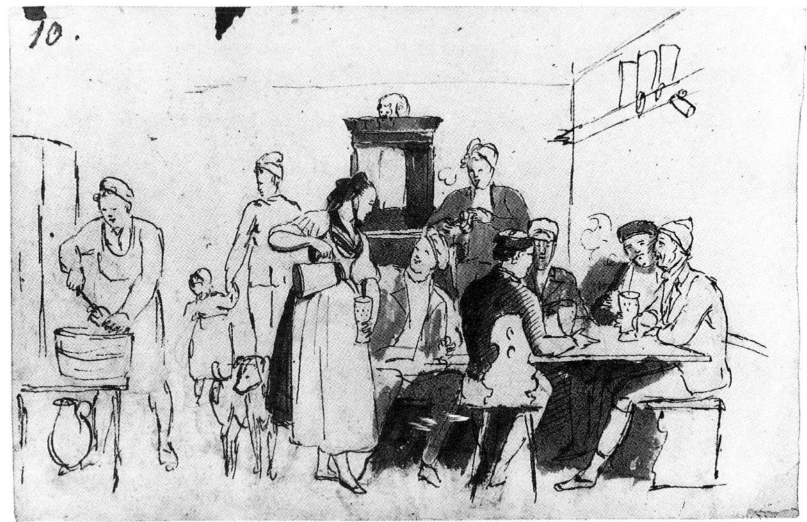

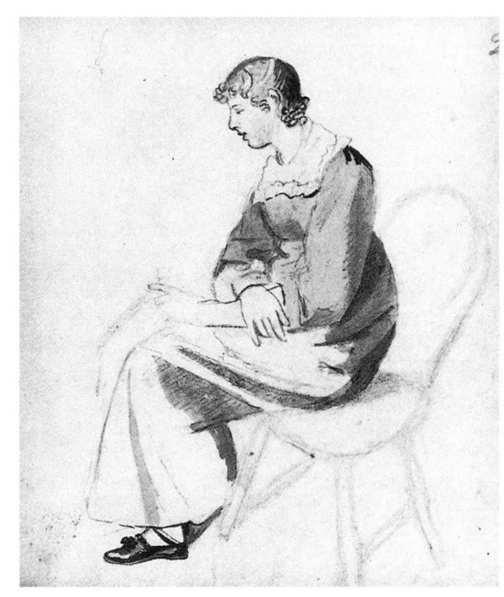

embittered Hetsch (with whom Seele had studied) and Schick, both of whom were better artists. King Frederick of Württemberg, however, preferred Seele's animated, more down-to-earth genre scenes and naturalistic depictions of battles and military life to Hetsch's and Schick's sophisticated neoclassicism. Furthermore, Seele's numerous portraits were painted with striking verity; they exude vitality and avoid idealization. Krimmel's paintings and drawings indicate these same characteristics appealed to him, so although no specific picture links the two artists, their very work demonstrates that they shared an attitude and a determination to take their subject matter directly from life.[12]

Krimmel's decision to move away from the precepts that had informed his art since 1810 was gradual and not linear. Some of his 1817 sketches show experimentation with neoclassical designs (see fig. 179), while others, especially his watercolors (figs. 185, 186), reveal a growing interest in the innovative concepts and spatial patterns of German romanticism. The latter images reveal an intensifying interest in nature; he focused on the structure of plants, trees, and geologic formations as he strove to understand how the parts fit into the larger whole.

Krimmel's artistic output during these months was also varied. In December 1817 he painted two portraits: a musical-instrument maker, Johannes Beck, and Beck's wife Anna Maria, née Rieber (figs. 187, 188), which are still owned by a descendant. The sitters were members of old and prominent Ebingen families: the Becks had produced several mayors (among them Krimmel's godfather); the Riebers had been early schoolmasters and more recently millers and tobacco merchants.[13] Johannes, a handsome young man with fine features, curly hair, and stylish clothes, is depicted playing a keyboard instrument; his bride, Anna Maria, a sturdy, pretty young woman wearing a traditional Ebingen dress and bonnet, holds a prayer book in her right hand and prominently displays her wedding ring on her left hand. In both portraits the artist eschewed the strict frontality he had used in the 1815 portrait of the young woman in blue and also chose not to use the traditional device of a view of the world beyond the sitter. He moved the sitter close to the viewer but at an angle, which strengthened the focus; at the same time his attempt to convey a new kind of picture space resulted in a surprisingly poor perspective.

Unlike the previous year, the harvest of 1817 had been a normal one, bringing to an end the period of starvation, and Krimmel's late 1817 and 1818 sketchbook drawings indicate that life in Ebingen had resumed a proper course. But elsewhere in Germany, particularly in intellectual centers, political tensions had been building following the Wars of Liberation (1813/14). Many people had expected social and political reforms; instead, the German confederation established at the Congress of Vienna (1815) had become an instrument for the suppression of liberal ideas and the repression of those who promoted national unity and civil liberties, particularly in the Rhineland, Prussia, and Saxony. In October 1817 Saxony experienced the "Wartburgfest," the first great national demonstration against the reactionary politics of Prince Metternich, Austrian statesman and leader of the German confederation. Württemberg, however, had adopted a constitution based on representative assemblies and remained relatively calm.

Krimmel continued to focus on the everyday and the ordinary in his art. Then after a year of work the case involving his sister's estate was settled.

12. Staatsgalerie Stuttgart, *Schwaben sehen Schwaben: Bildnisse 1760–1940 aus dem Besitz der Staatsgalerie Stuttgart* (Stuttgart, 1979), pp. 45–50. If Pflug met Krimmel, he may have given him the information about Seele, who had worked in Munich in 1808 while Pflug was there; see Thieme and Becker, *Allgemeines Lexikon*, s.v. "Pflug."

13. Stettner, *Ebingen*, pp. 149, 151.

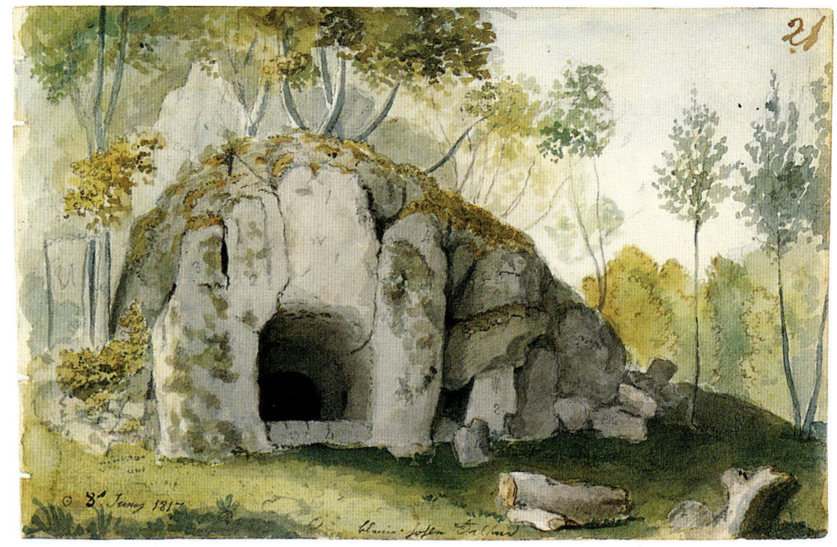

FIGURE 185
Hohle Felsen [Hollow rock], Sunday, June 8, 1817. Watercolor and ink over pencil, ink inscription. Sketchbook 4, leaf 9 recto.

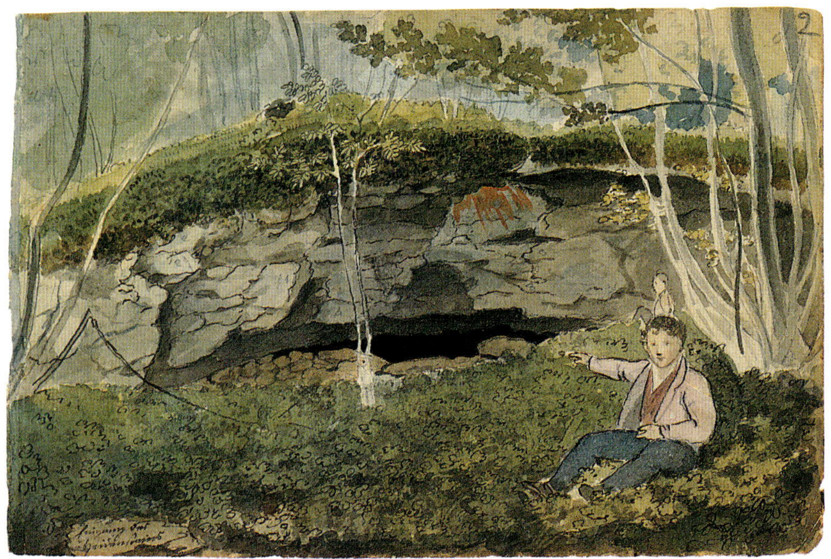

FIGURE 186
Eingang des Heidensteins [Entrance to pagan rock], 1817. Watercolor and ink over pencil, ink inscription. Sketchbook 5, leaf 2 recto.

FIGURE 187
John Lewis Krimmel, portrait of Johannes Beck, December 1817. Watercolor and gouache on paper; 7 1/8 x 5 3/8 in. (Private collection, Albstadt-Ebingen.) Signed above the sitter's left hand, "J. L. Krimmel Dec. 1817."

FIGURE 188
John Lewis Krimmel, portrait of Anna Maria Rieber Beck, December 1817. Watercolor and gouache on paper; 7 1/8 x 5 3/8 in. (Private collection, Albstadt-Ebingen.)

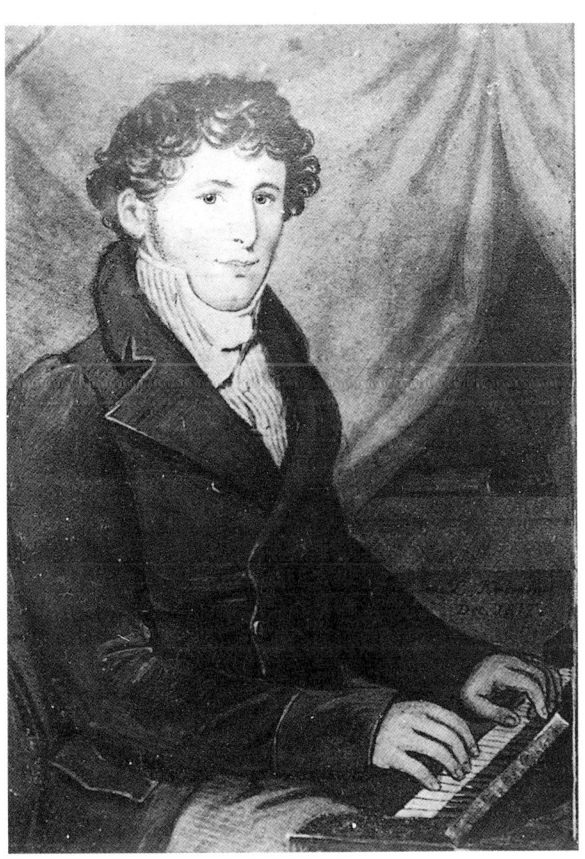

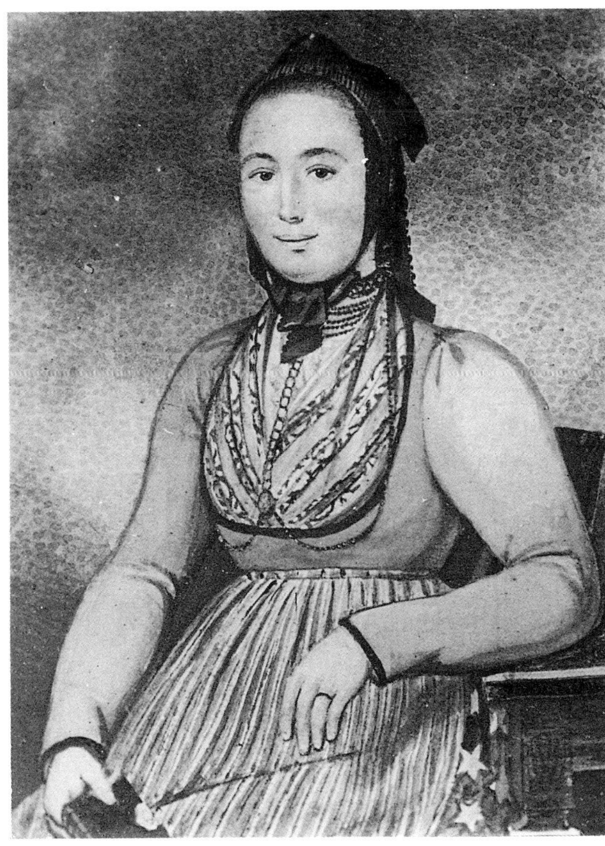

On March 9, 1818, the Orphans Court named Krimmel and cloth manufacturer Weinheimer joint legal guardians of Krimmel's 13-year-old nephew and apparently restored Daser's paternal authority over the younger four children. Less than a month later, on April 5, Paul Daser remarried, bringing into the family a woman who could care for his five children.[14] Because the harvest of 1818 promised to be an exceptionally rich one, flour would be in plentiful supply, which meant that the confectionery business had an excellent chance of recovering. At last Krimmel was free to travel according to his own interests. He chose to make a trip to Vienna, a city with several outstanding collections of art.

On May 1, 1818, Krimmel submitted a detailed account of all legal expenses he had been obliged to pay since March 2, 1817, and two days later he began a ten-week journey through southern Germany and Austria.[15] According to notes in sketchbook 4, the morning he left Ebingen it was raining. He traveled north via Tübingen and arrived in Stuttgart at midnight on May 4. Although the sketchbooks contain no clues as to how long he remained there, it was probably at least a week. While there he visited with Carl Friedrich Heinzmann, a genre and landscape painter and printmaker.

Heinzmann had studied with Seele and after the latter's death (1814) had completed Seele's unfinished etchings of Württemberg regiments, beautifully executed genre scenes that include precise renderings of uniforms and a host of data about early nineteenth-century military life. (Heinzmann had served as an officer in the war against France in 1814 and 1815.) The artist subsequently moved to Munich to study with Wilhelm von Kobell, who taught landscape painting at the art academy. Deeply interested in landscapes, as a lithographer Heinzmann went on to produce a large number of topographic landscape views that he published as a series in the 1820s.[16] It was probably he who encouraged Krimmel to make the systematic sketches of the scenic views that detail the rest of Krimmel's trip to and from Vienna. Krimmel probably stayed in Stuttgart at least until mid May.

From there he traveled southeast to Ulm, where he paused to visit some people or shops near the famous Ulmer Münster, a beautiful fourteenth-century cathedral with a one-tower facade that has the highest steeple in Europe. Ulm was also the terminus for long-distance travel down the Danube, one of the great rivers in Europe, second in size only to the Volga. The river barges known as *Ulmer Schachteln* (Ulm boxes) were long flat boats with pointed bows that were rowed downstream by teams of men and then dismantled. Because the boats lacked sleeping quarters they pulled ashore for the night, but during the daylight hours they covered great distances.

From notes in the sketchbooks and the absence of sketches of sites along this stretch of the Danube, it can be assumed that Krimmel did not take a boat in Ulm but instead traveled by coach to the historic and wealthy city of Augsburg to contact Hörmann, and from there continued to the southeast and Munich, the residence of the kings of Bavaria and an important art center. The city's superb royal art collections and active cultural life offered rich opportunities. Krimmel's sketchbooks contain three addresses in Munich, one of them listing Butta and Bromberger, a shop that sold "pencils, brushes, erasers, watercolors and oil paint," but no drawings of the city.[17] If he made sketches and visited art collections there, he apparently used a larger drawing pad.

From Munich the artist must have traveled northeast to Landshut, a town mentioned in the sketchbooks, and from there he journeyed toward the

14. Waisengericht, March 9, 1818; Ehebuch, April 5, 1818.

15. Waisengericht, May 1, 1818.

16. Kobell's landscapes include people in regional garb, and they are very clear in composition and color. The lithographs of southern Bavaria that Heinzmann published in 1822 included Chiemsee and Rosenheim—places that Krimmel visited and sketched on the return leg of his trip to Vienna; for Heinzmann see Werner Fleischhauer, *Die Schwäbische Kunst, 19. und 20. Jahrhundert* (Stuttgart: Deutsche Verlags Anstalt), p. 84.

17. Sketchbook 4, inside back cover. A second Munich address reads "*Scheuermann, p. ad. 76 E. v. Eichthal München*" (leaf 35 recto).

Danube. Such a route would have brought him to the river below the wide loop to the north through the area of Regensburg (an important city not mentioned by Krimmel) and explains why his first Danube sketch is the area of Straubing. Krimmel spent these next few days on the river drawing precise topographic sketches as his boat passed myriad picturesque sites. Even though the swift current of the Danube rapidly changed his vantage point, Krimmel's remarkable eyesight and powers of concentration allowed him to produce a detailed record of his voyage. Indeed those views that impressed him the most he depicted twice, once in the distance and a second time close up. He continued to sketch after the boat docked each day. These drawings are small in format—some are minute—yet all are exact, and close examination reveals that Krimmel drew the initial images with pencil and later traced over most of them with a fine-nibbed ink pen.

The orderly and systematic nature of the Danube drawings and the precise notes on date and location suggest that they were not meant to be simply a personal pictorial diary but were a sequence of views that Krimmel planned to transform into engravings or lithographs. By 1818 illustrated series of river voyages were popular in Europe because they satisfied people's curiosity about distant places famous for their natural beauty.[18] As if catering to this market, Krimmel depicted the most picturesque stretch of the Danube—river banks with steep cliffs, medieval castles, beautiful monasteries, and wooded hills. In true romantic fashion he chose vantage points that showed the buildings echoing the outlines of the hills and mountains or that showed natural features that enhanced the visual significance of the buildings.

The Danube sketches also demonstrate Krimmel's increasingly commanding way of looking at his subject matter. His new approach was the final step in a long process that had begun with the drawings he did off the coast of Bermuda. He had freed himself, step-by-step, from dependence on the schematic models provided by drawing books he had used in America; he had begun to let the sites dictate the composition of his pictures. As a result his landscapes exhibited greater variety, and his vistas, so tightly packed with detail, became flowing and more naturalistic.

According to Krimmel's notes, his boat passed the area above Straubing on June 1, Straubing on June 2, and Vilzhofen on June 3 (figs. 189, 190). At four o'clock on the afternoon of June 3, he made a close-up and very finished sketch of Castle Krempelstein, which implies the boat had pulled ashore there (figs. 191, 192). The following day Krimmel made drawings of the church at Engelhartszell further downstream (figs. 193, 194). At Odensheim (fig. 195), now in Austria, Krimmel boarded a *Holzschiff* (wooden ship) to travel to Linz, arriving there the same day.

During a day's layover in Linz, Krimmel made several drawings (figs. 196–199). On one of these, made in the evening of June 5 looking down on the town, the artist noted in tiny letters "*mit Erhard von Cs. Neuhaus*" (with Erhard from Castle Newhouse). "Erhard" might well be Johann Christoph Erhard, a talented young artist born and educated in Nürnberg who worked in Vienna from 1816 on, primarily as a draftsman and etcher. He had become part of a close circle of young artists known as the Nazarenes, and during the summers of 1817 and 1818 he and other young painters of Vienna hiked and sketched in the mountains and plains surrounding Linz and Salzburg.[19] Although younger than Krimmel, Erhard's artistic reputation was well established. Krimmel, always eager to improve his skills, would have been receptive

18. Busch-Reisinger Museum, *German Master Drawings of the Nineteenth Century* (Cambridge, 1972), pp. 14, 15, 16.

19. Thieme and Becker, *Allgemeines Lexikon*, s.v. "Erhard."

FIGURE 189
Near Wörth, June 1 and 2, 1818. Ink over pencil, ink inscriptions. Sketchbook 4, leaf 26 recto. Inscriptions translate "Würth," "June 1, 1818, above Straubing," and "Near Bogenberg [at] Wallfürth, 2 hours after Straubing June 2, 1818."

FIGURE 190
Views on the Danube, June 2 and 3, 1818. Ink over pencil, ink and pencil inscriptions. Sketchbook 4, leaf 28 verso. Inscriptions translate "Jedersberg, Tuesday, June 2, evening" and "Passau, June 3, 1818."

FIGURE 191
Views of Castle Krempelstein from the Danube, Wednesday, June 3, 1818, 6 P.M. Ink over pencil, watercolor. Sketchbook 4, leaf 29 recto. Krimmel notes that another name for the castle is Schneider-schlösschen [Little castle of the tailor].

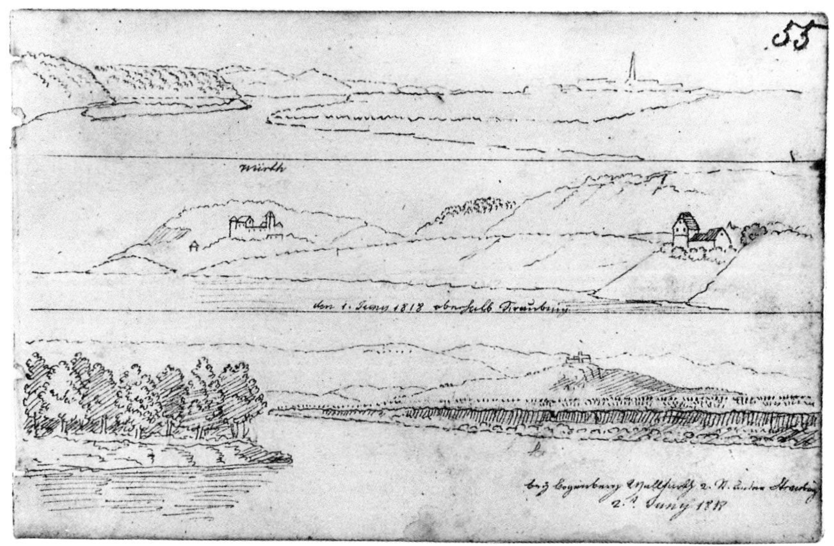

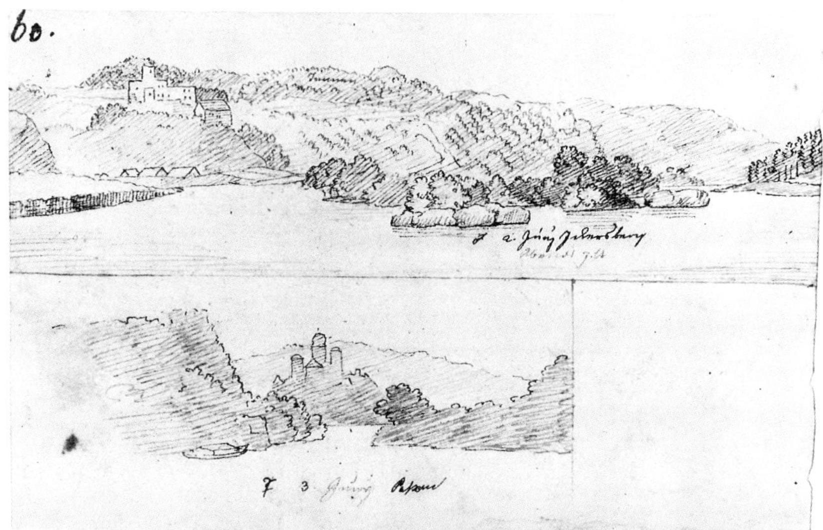

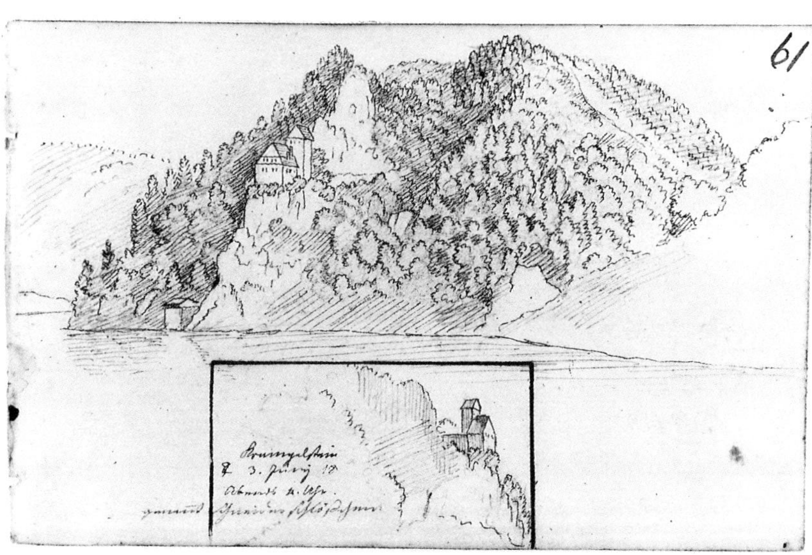

FIGURE 192
Houses in Hafnerzell, June 3, 1818. Pencil, ink inscription. Sketchbook 4, leaf 25 verso. The town is now called Obernzell.

FIGURE 193
Docking near Engelhartszell on the Danube, Thursday, June 4, 1818. Pencil and wash over pencil, pencil inscription. Sketchbook 4, leaf 30 recto.

FIGURE 194
The Danube south of Engelhartszell, June 4, 1818. Ink over pencil, ink and pencil inscriptions. Sketchbook 4, leaf 30 verso. The top image was drawn at 11 A.M. and may be the medieval Castle Ranaried.

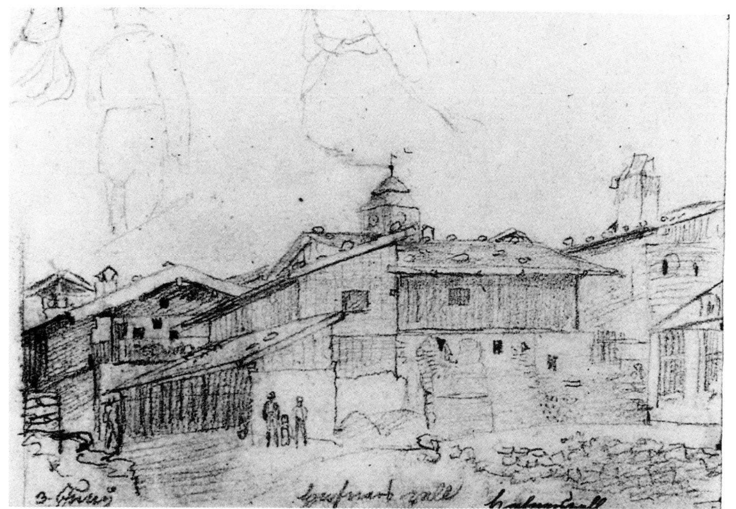

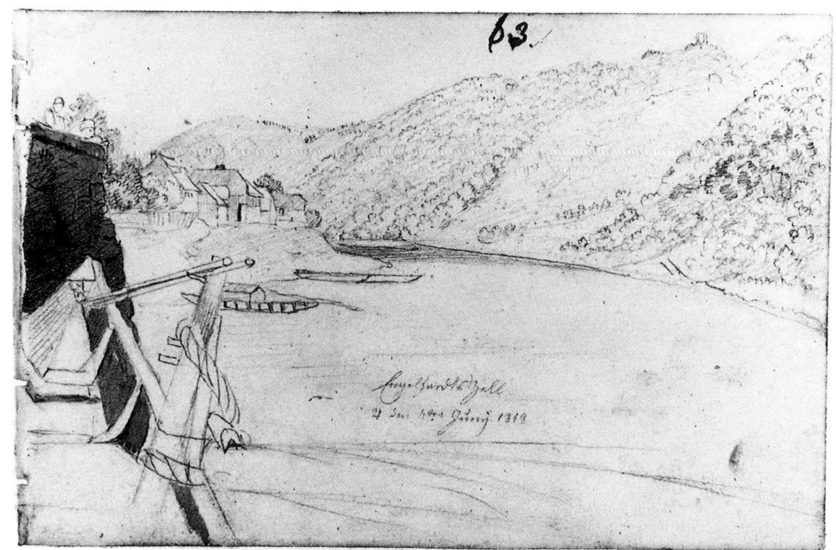

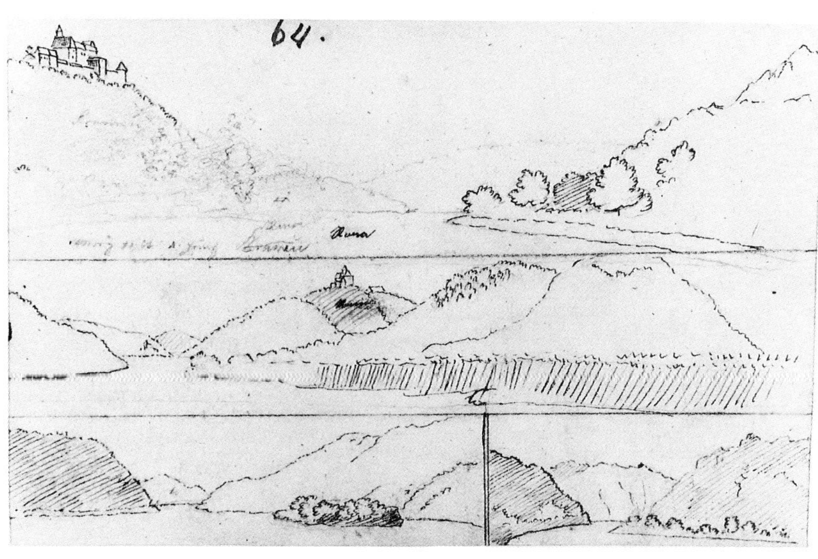

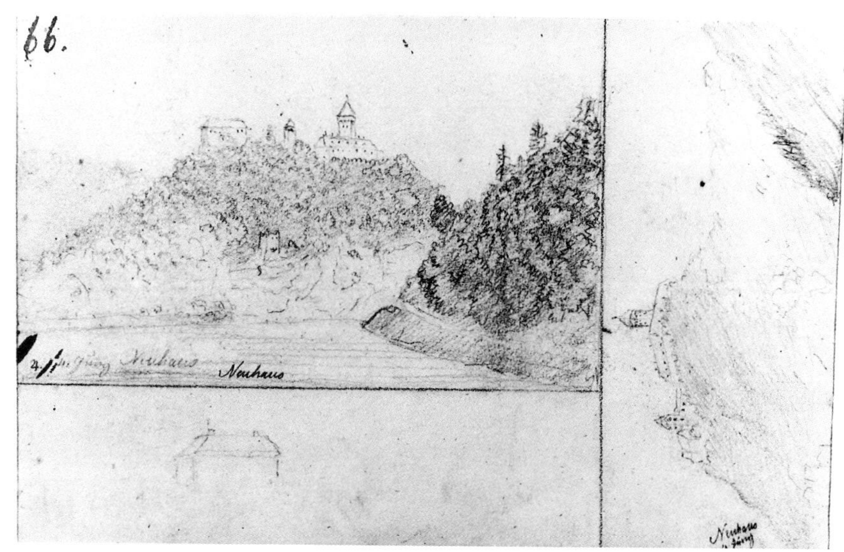

FIGURE 195
View of Castle Neuhaus, Thursday, June 4, 1818. Pencil, pencil and ink inscriptions. Sketchbook 4, leaf 31 verso.

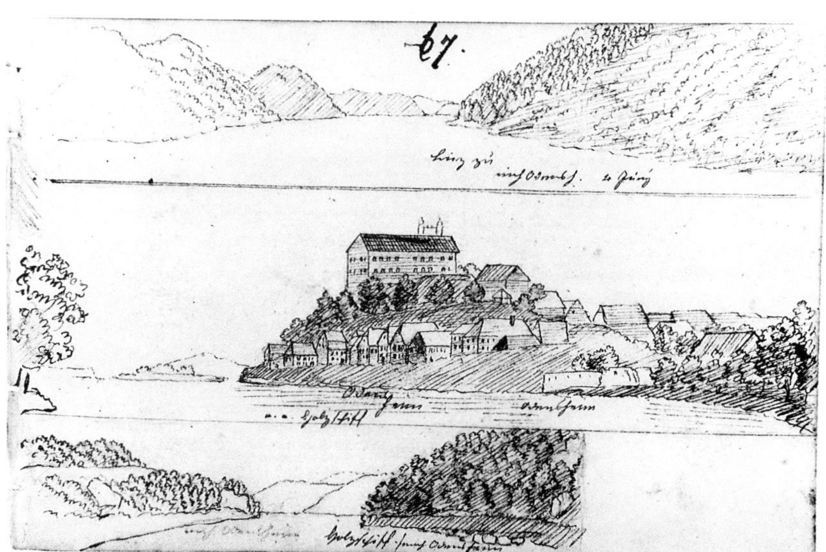

FIGURE 196
Views of the Danube approaching Odensheim, June 4, 1818. Ink over pencil, ink and pencil inscriptions. Sketchbook 4, leaf 32 recto. Two inscriptions state that Krimmel is near Odensheim en route to Linz, and the third specifies he is taking a wooden barge.

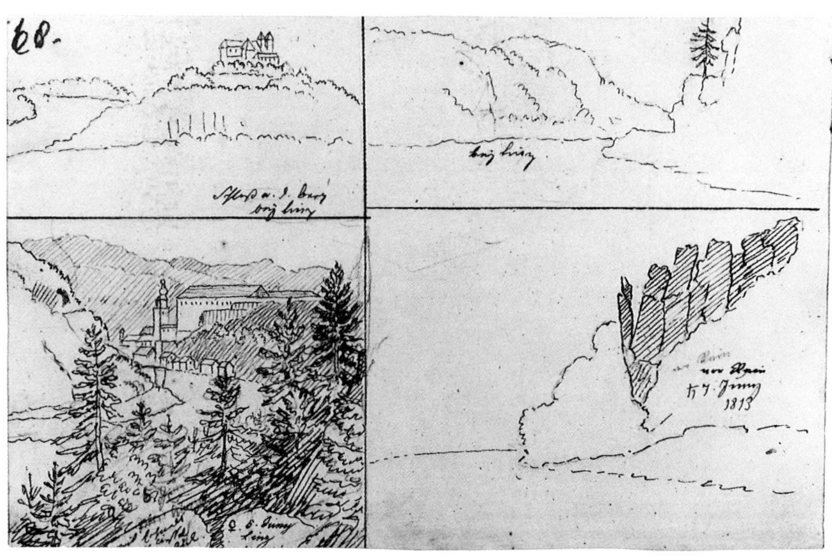

FIGURE 197
Sites in and around Linz, June 5 and [6], 1818. Ink over pencil, ink and pencil inscriptions. Sketchbook 4, leaf 32 verso. The inscription identifying the building in the upper left panel is illegible, but that in the lower left reads "mit Erhardt von Cs Neuhaus." Krimmel's correction of the date on the next page indicates that the 7th in the lower right panel is in error, unless it is one that was drawn later, perhaps at the ridges of rock near Grein. (The ridges were destroyed by blasting in 1866.)

FIGURE 198
Panorama near Linz, Friday, June 5, 1818. Watercolor over pencil, ink and pencil inscription. Sketchbook 4, leafs 15 verso and 16 recto. The inscription translates "Mt. Calvary."

FIGURE 199
The Danube near Linz, June 6, 1818. Pencil, pencil and ink inscriptions. Sketchbook 4, leaf 16 verso. The first inscription on the hillside is illegible; the others translate "Rodenfeld, Saturday, June 6 near Linz."

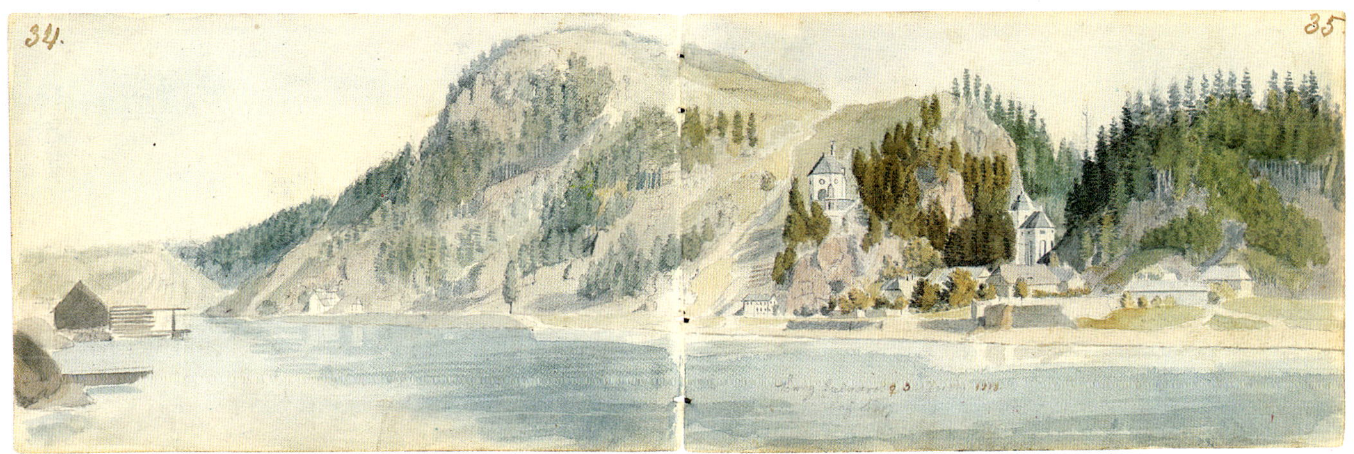

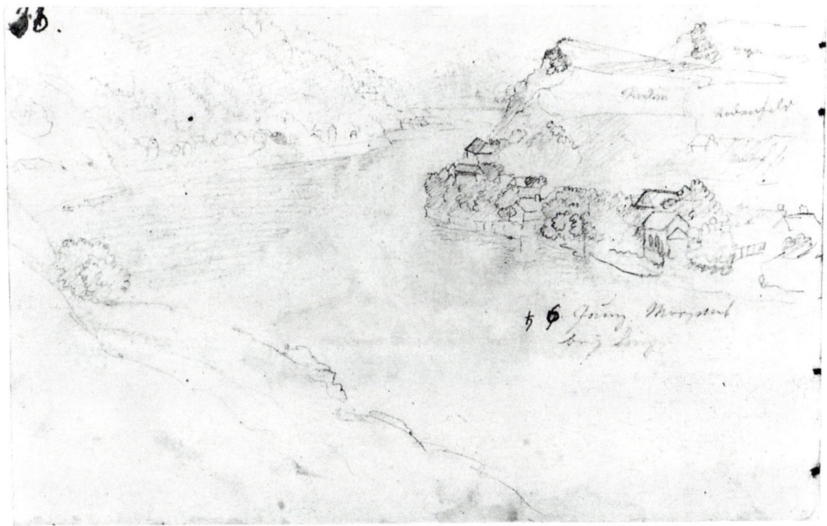

to ideas and suggestions from any talented and experienced artist who shared his sensibility, so even if he spent only a brief time with Erhard, he probably used that time to study and absorb new concepts and approaches.

Erhard's art had been shaped by the latest artistic currents, especially those that emphasized sharply accentuated linear qualities. This was characteristic of south German romanticism, which had been influenced by Austrian-born Joseph Anton Koch, whose work stylistically remained clearly within the classicist mode yet expressed a deep identification with nature that was typically romantic. After living in Rome between 1794 and 1812 Koch had returned to Austria for three years and befriended another highly talented landscape painter, Ferdinand Olivier. Their combined influence on the development of romantic landscape painting in southern Germany and Austria was at its peak in 1817 and 1818. Erhard's work typifies that done by German artists enraptured with nature in its untouched state. Images that he made on his long sketching tours in scenic areas indicate he valued the abstract linear structure of the landscape as much as achieving a realistic depiction.[20] Especially in Vienna and later in Salzburg when he had time to compose his images, Krimmel often chose a scheme much like Erhard used: a strong foreground constructed with an array of rocks, trees, and plants that move from both sides toward the middle of the picture.

Krimmel left Linz early on the morning of June 6, passing through the whirlpool area of the Danube called *Der Strudel.* The next day they went by the Abbey of Melk, an outstandingly beautiful late baroque structure situated high on a bluff above a sharp turn in the Danube (fig. 200). Later that day, as his boat passed the area of Krems, he made a drawing of Castle Dürnstein (fig. 201). Underneath, he wrote in English: "1818. 7 June Castell Diernstein on the Danube where Richard Coeur de Lion was kept prisoner. The rocks are all granit." At that point Vienna was less than a day away.

The few sketchbook drawings that document Krimmel's visit to the imperial city of Vienna include three that are dated—one June 21 and two June 28; thus, Krimmel stayed for about three weeks, from June 8 until nearly June 30 (figs. 202–208). One image is an unfinished sketch of the exterior of the famous *Karlskirche*, an important landmark and the earliest example of German baroque architecture designed with pure classical elements. Most of the others are less readily identifiable.

Krimmel had prepared for his visit by turning one page of sketchbook 4 into a notebook, on which he listed eleven addresses, including eight different art collections owned by aristocratic patrons, about which he added notes:

Gemälde Sammlungen
von Kupferstichen u. Zeichnungen, Herzog Albert von Sachsen Teschen
    in dessen Pallast auf der Bastion
Von Gemälden vom Grafen de Lamberg im 2. Stock des Hauses de Lopresti
    Ecke der Körnerstrasse gegen dem Thore
    —niederländische, sehr ausgesuchte

Von verschiedenen	Kunststudien	Professor von Fries
"	Gemälden	Grafen von Schoenborn
"	Kupferstichen	" von Harrach
ditto		Prinz von Paar
ditto		von der Nutt
Medaillen		Baron von Hess

20. Busch-Reisinger Museum, *German Master Drawings*, pp. 42, 43; Hubert Schrade, *Deutsche Malerei der Romantik* (Cologne: Verlag M. DuMont, 1967), pp. 54–58; Jens Christian Jensen, *Aquarelle und Zeichnungen der deutschen Romantik* (Cologne: DuMont Buchverlag, 1978), p. 20.

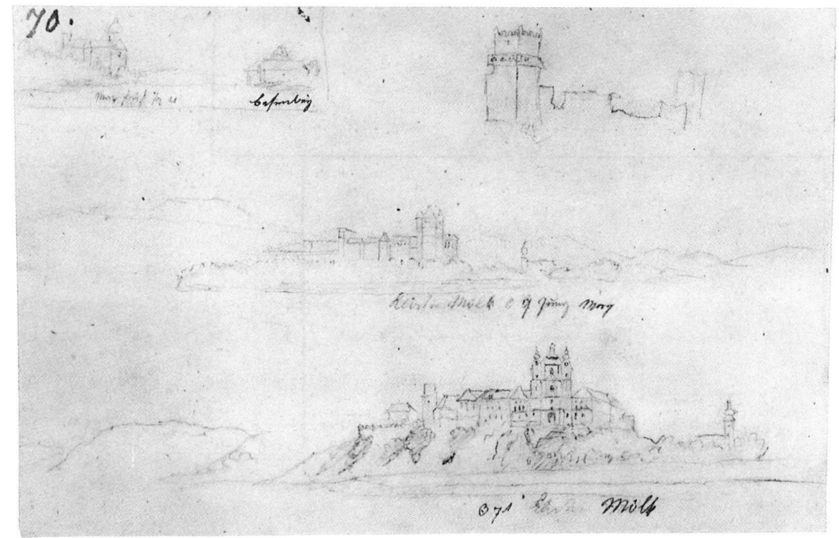

FIGURE 200
The Benedictine Abbey of Melk, Sunday, June 7, 1818. Pencil, pencil and ink inscriptions. Sketchbook 4, leaf 33 verso. The abbey was rebuilt 1701–38 and resembles a palace more than a monastery. The inscription translates "Cloister of Melk."

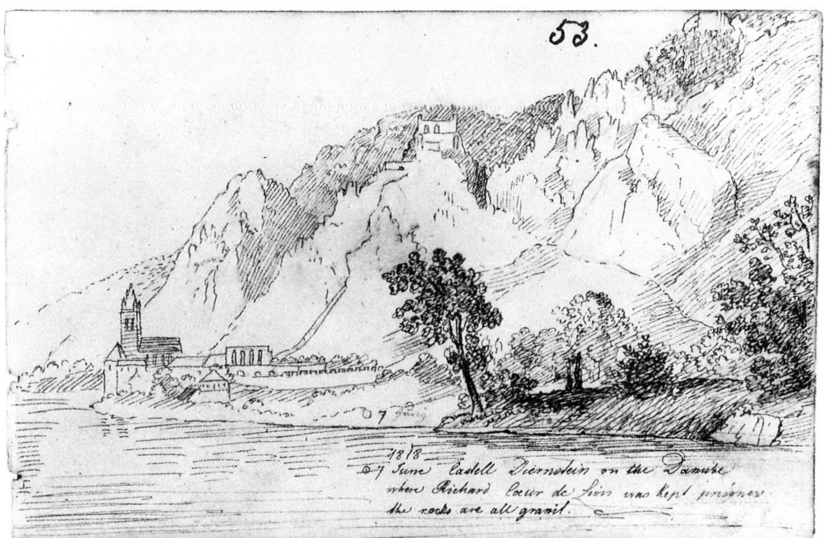

FIGURE 201
View of Castle Dürnstein, Sunday, June 7, 1818. Ink over pencil, ink inscription. Sketchbook 4, leaf 25 recto.

FIGURE 202
A woman and three men, Vienna, Sunday, June 21, 1818. Pencil. Sketchbook 4, leaf 18 recto.

FIGURE 203
Man on hillside looking toward Kahlenberg from Leopoldsberg, Sunday, June 28, 1818. Pencil. Sketchbook 5, leaf 31 verso.

FIGURE 204
Man reading, June 1818. Pencil. Sketchbook 4, leaf 17 verso.

FIGURE 205
Man writing or drawing, probably June 1818. Pencil. Sketchbook 5, leaf 33 recto. This may be Bernhard Freuler of Vienna.

FIGURE 206
Man reading or drawing, June 28, 1818. Pencil. Sketchbook 5, leaf 32 verso.

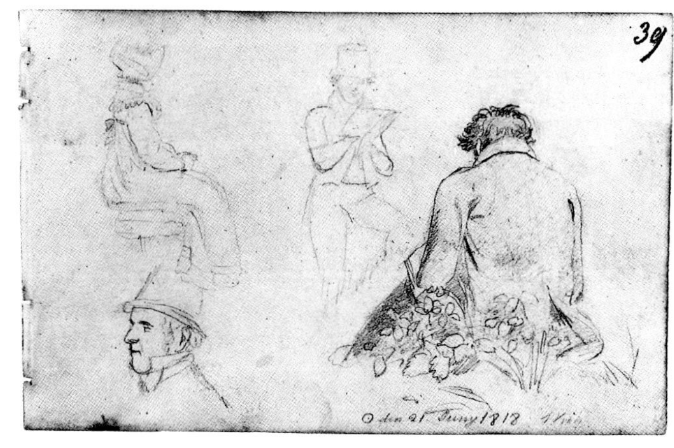

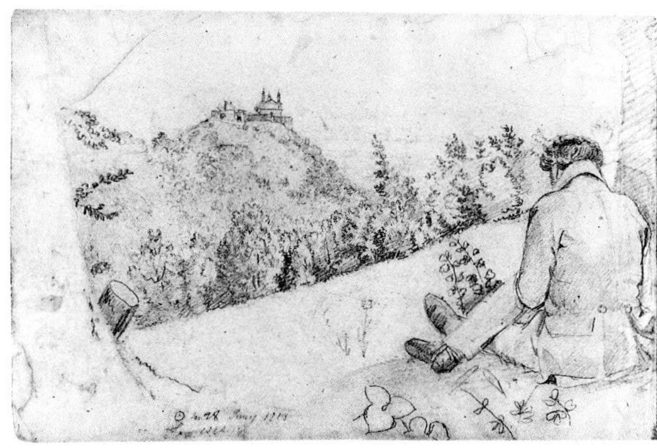

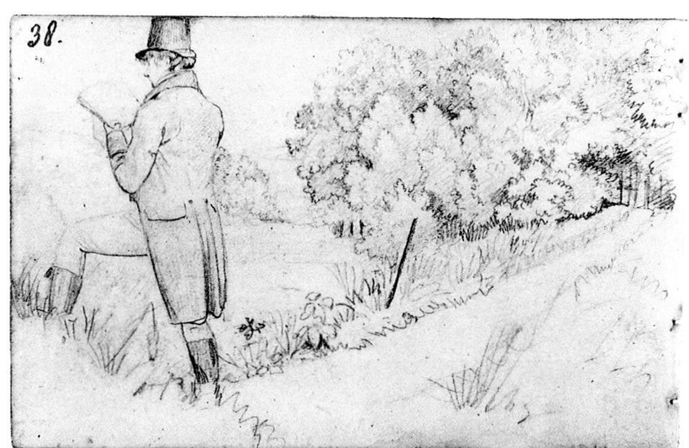

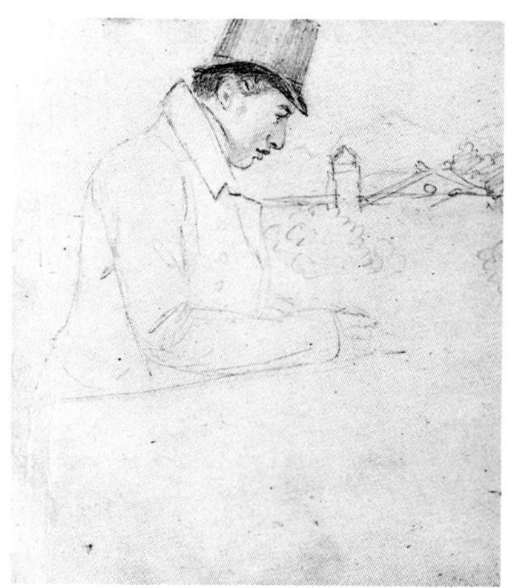

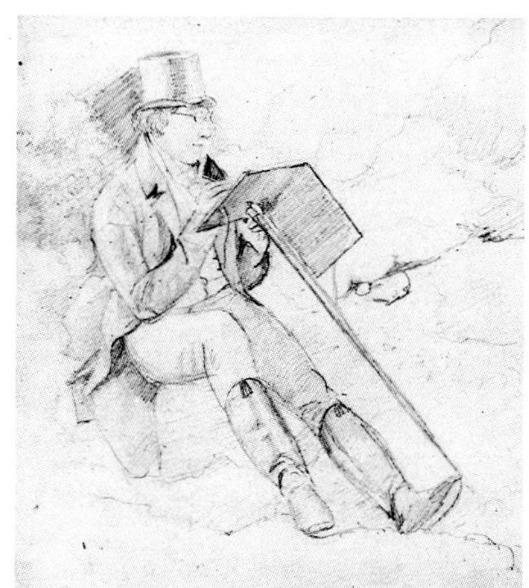

FIGURE 207

Waterfall, probably June 1818. Wash and ink over pencil. Sketchbook 5, leaf 36 recto. The figure on the left may be giving information on the site that the second individual, in a travel coat, is either making notes on or sketching. The couple and child are not travelers, judging from their dress, so the place is probably close to Vienna.

FIGURE 208

Wooded area with templelike structure built in the rocks, probably June 1818. Watercolor over pencil. Sketchbook 5, leaf 30 recto.

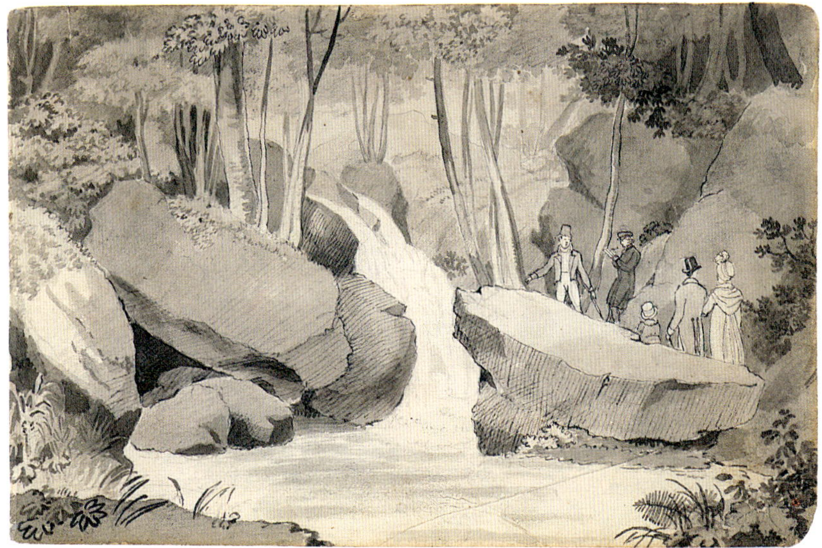

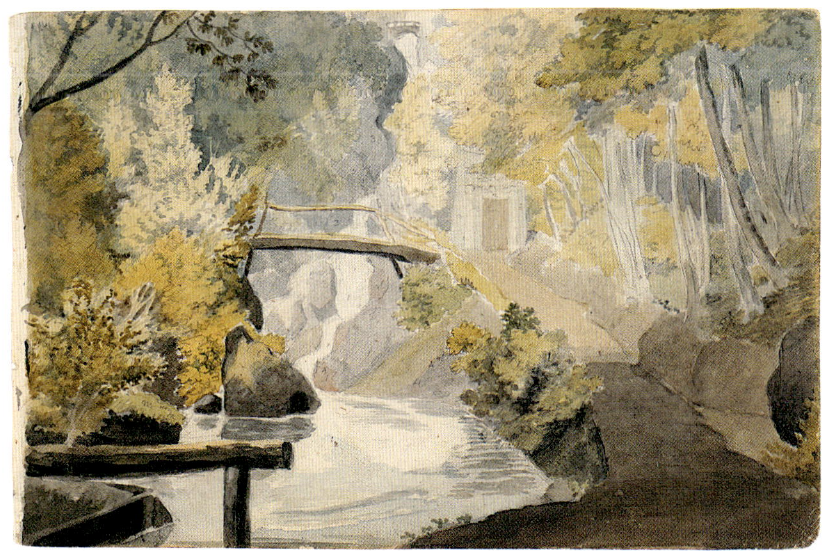

The first item translates as "collection of engravings and drawings of Duke Albert von Sachsen Teschen"—a reference to the collection that later grew into the famous Albertina, one of the world's finest assemblages of drawings and prints. Krimmel was especially interested in paintings of the Flemish and Dutch schools and under the address of the collection of Count de Lamberg wrote "Netherlandish, very choice." For an artist who had demonstrated a penchant for self-instruction, the city offered unparalleled opportunities for studying the designs and methods of other artists. It is surprising, therefore, that the sketchbooks contain not a single record of Krimmel's visit to these art collections. Certainly Krimmel drew more, rather than less, while he had the best opportunity of his life to study great art, so most likely he purchased a larger drawing pad for making copies of pictures that interested him in various collections and for making drawings of people, buildings, and scenery while staying in the city.

As the capital of the Austrian empire and permanent residence of the Hapsburg monarchs, Vienna was incredibly rich in historical architecture, an important center of romantic painting, and indisputably the world center of music (Beethoven and Schubert both resided there in 1818). Just three years earlier it had been the focus of world attention when it hosted the Congress of Vienna (September 1814 to June 1815). The purpose of this important diplomatic convention was to address the territorial problems of Europe after the downfall of Napoleon and to ensure an external and internal peace on the Continent. Chaired by Prince Metternich, the Austrian minister of foreign affairs, and attended by most of the European monarchs including the Russian emperor, the congress began with a round of magnificent balls and other splendid entertainments but settled down to serious business after Napoleon's escape from Elba. Although in a political sense the outcome of the grand international conference was disappointing, the congress's impact on Vienna had been highly beneficial. It boosted progress and created a forum for the exchange of technology and information among countries. In 1816 a Viennese craftsman inspired by the production methods of the English cotton industry was the first to introduce the weaving of silk fabrics on mechanical looms. The changeover from small scale manufacturing to industrial operations in many areas of the economy led to shifts in the social structure. It fostered the emergence of a more powerful and prominent middle class that soon began to rival the upper classes as style setters, patrons of the arts, and promoters of innovations. A new and more practical furniture style came into vogue—Biedermeier—later so named after two popular fictional characters who were thought to personify the typical bourgeois mentality of the period. Biedermeier furniture was not just a pared-down version of empire furniture; it had its own characteristics. Emphasis was on clear and graceful construction, lightweight appearance, and comfort. Chairs followed the contour of the body, and rooms were sparsely furnished, full of light, and decorated in cheerful colors. The bourgeois taste was also expressed in painting. Artists depicted people in cozy, quiet interiors, painted scenes of everyday life with a touch of humor, and portrayed middle-class sitters in an unpretentious manner. In all probability, while in Vienna Krimmel was simultaneously exposed to myriad artistic, cultural, and intellectual stimuli. Getting in touch with a local artist would have been of primary importance, and Stuttgart's Carl Heinzmann had provided Krimmel with the name and address of Bernhard Freuler, a landscape painter residing in Leopoldstadt.[21] As a student

21. See for example, Historisches Museum der Stadt Wien, *Das Wiener Bürgerliche Zeughaus, 1600–1840: Barock und Klassizismus* (Vienna: Eigenverlag des Museums, 1962); sketchbook 4, leafs 34 verso and 35 verso list Leopoldstadter A. Krause, who resided with pharmacist Moser, but no artist of this name is listed in Thieme and Becker, *Allgemeines Lexikon.*

at Vienna's famed academy of painting since 1816, Freuler undoubtedly knew the latest developments in art and could introduce Krimmel to other artists in the city.

On June 28 Krimmel climbed Leopoldsberg at the northern edge of the city to make a drawing of the view toward Kahlenberg in the west, a vista that included the church built to commemorate the successful defense of Vienna against the Turks in 1683 (see fig. 203). In the foreground of Krimmel's sketch is a dark-haired young man making a sketch of the view. He is seated on the ground, his back to the viewer. The same figure appears to be the subject a few pages later in sketchbook 5 (see figs. 204, 205), which suggests that the person was a companion, perhaps Freuler. A second drawing made June 28, 1818, depicts a light-haired man in top hat and tail coat seated atop a hill while writing or drawing (see fig. 206). A man dressed in the same garb is shown in a watercolor of a romantic depiction of an opening in the forest where the waters of a large brook cascade over big rocks. In the latter image, an artist quietly sketches while his companion speaks and gestures. Unlike the companion and the three other stylishly dressed visitors to the site, the artist, a tall, slender man with curly hair, is wearing a long travel coat and a travel cap; this is most probably Krimmel's drawing of himself (see fig. 207).

Notes in sketchbooks 4 and 5 also indicate that Krimmel used his stay in Vienna to do many things on behalf of others. For Johannes Beck of Ebingen, he inquired about round saws "two to three feet in diameter" and sought out a man named Seyffert to obtain the newest drawings of upright instruments (organs and pianos). For John Watts, a stereotype printer in New York, he inquired about lithographic stones and made notes on dimensions and prices. He sought to purchase, either for himself or for others, a geometry book, a world atlas, a book of folk songs, and Friedrich Heinrich Kohlrausch's *Geschichte der Deutschen* (History of the Germans).[22] The note about lithographic stones is particularly intriguing because the first American lithograph was produced by Bass Otis in Philadelphia in 1819. Viennese artists had become interested in lithography only after Aloys Senefelder, the inventor of lithography who lived in Munich, had in 1816 visited Vienna a second time to introduce his invention to the local artists. John Watts, the earliest American stereotype printer, was born in England. He had received a classical education, and in 1806/7 was printing Greek and Latin dictionaries in Philadelphia. When he moved to New York in 1809 he worked as a printer and agent for foreigners. New York City directories for 1814 list him at Broom near Orange Street; in the directories for 1815 and 1816 his foundry was listed at 154 Broadway with a home on Broom. He is not listed again in the directories.[23]

Krimmel also made notes adding new names and specific information, including messages to friends elsewhere in Germany and to distant relatives in America: "*Jonathan Lenz Oeconomie Doctor von Stuttgart reisste 1817 nach Philadelphia*" (Jonathan Lenz, Doctor of Economics from Stuttgart, departed for Philadelphia in 1817); "Bravour Andrew Boys, legations Secretaire in Phila. who got a girl pregnant in Vienna who was chased away by her parents, and lives in great misery with her girl, Magdalena Kohl—her father was Househof Meister beym Graf Amader"; and "*Joseph Diebold lässt wegen seines Bruders Ignatz Diebold der von Hazeln in Baltimore seyn soll nach fragen. März 18*" (Joseph Diebold is asking about his brother Ignatius Diebold, from Hazeln, who supposedly lives in Baltimore. March 1818).[24]

22. Kohlrausch was a member of a distinguished family of scholars and educators. His book, published in Ebersfeld in 1816, traced the history of Germany from ancient times to Napoleon's banishment to Elba. Because his account was highly readable, the book was popular. The first English translation of Kohlrausch's book was published in New York by Appleton in 1822.

23. He had moved to Vienna by 1819; see *American Dictionary of Printing and Bookmaking* (New York: Howard Lockwood, 1894), p. 578; Rollo G. Silver, *The American Printer* (Charlottesville: University Press of Virginia, 1967), p. 60.

24. Sketchbook 5, inside cover; sketchbook 3, inside cover. Sketchbook 5 is made from paper with a German or Austrian watermark.

Leaving Vienna at the end of June, Krimmel struck out on a westerly overland route over Amstetten in the direction of Salzburg. This return trip to Ebingen would take him through the scenic areas that Erhard and other Nazarenes presented in their best-known landscape views. Along the way he stopped to sketch local people as well as groups of travelers in fashionable city dress and did what may be the compositional study for an as-yet-unidentified genre painting (figs. 209–214).

On July 1, a few days out of Vienna, near Sigmarkirchen, Krimmel and a few travelers became passengers on a wagon laden with hay. The weather was very warm, and the travelers slept atop the hay beneath a canopy of woven straw, which Krimmel depicted meticulously. He focused on the wagon's draft horses as they ate from a trough near Sigmarskirchen and again, on July 2, in Amstetten, as they stood in their traces. For the next few days the countryside absorbed his attention. On July 3 and July 4 he sketched the scenic view of a slightly hilly and forested terrain with the Austrian Alps visible in the distance (fig. 215).

Pausing in Salzburg on July 6 and 7, Krimmel made accomplished drawings of important vistas. This city famous for its beautiful setting and its long and rich history was situated along the Salzach River between two mountains, the Mönchsberg and the Kapuzinerberg (also called the Imberg). From their elevations one could see the nearby peaks of the Alps and have a magnificent view over the Salzburger Becken, the plain transversed by the river and interspersed with several lakes. The artist carefully chose his fields of view to produce more dynamic definitions of space than he had in the past—clear evidence that he had achieved a firm understanding of the artistic concepts underpinning German romantic landscapes.

On Monday, July 6, his first working day in Salzburg, the artist selected a moderately elevated vantage point, apparently on a lower path of the Mönchsberg, to make an accurate view of the city's core section (fig. 216). His drawing accurately captures a sense of the historic town's spectacular location and stresses the contrasting relationship of its most important architectural monuments. By structuring the foreground with large rocks and lush summer foliage, Krimmel created a spatial effect that helped convey the nestled-in and tightly built-up character of the old town below.

The vista, however, is dominated by the striking juxtaposition of Salzburg's most prominent landmarks. On the left and seen from above is the Gothic church of the Franciscans and behind it the cluster of cupolas and spires of an imposing cathedral built in the baroque style. This grouping of gracefully rising and handsomely rounded shapes is contrasted on the right by the towering angularity and massive compactness of the medieval fortress called Hohensalzburg. The seat of the region's independent-minded, powerful archbishop/princes for more than a thousand years, it was the largest medieval stronghold in central Europe. In outline and sturdiness the citadel and the cliff on which it stands relate to the layers of the mountains rising in the background. The care with which Krimmel designed and executed this drawing seems to indicate that he found the intellectual exercise in geometry and abstract relationships as important as the topographical correctness of his depiction.

On the same day, after completing the drawing of Salzburg that had required such intense concentration, he produced a more relaxed vista of the nearby countryside, now using watercolor over pencil (fig. 217). Remaining on

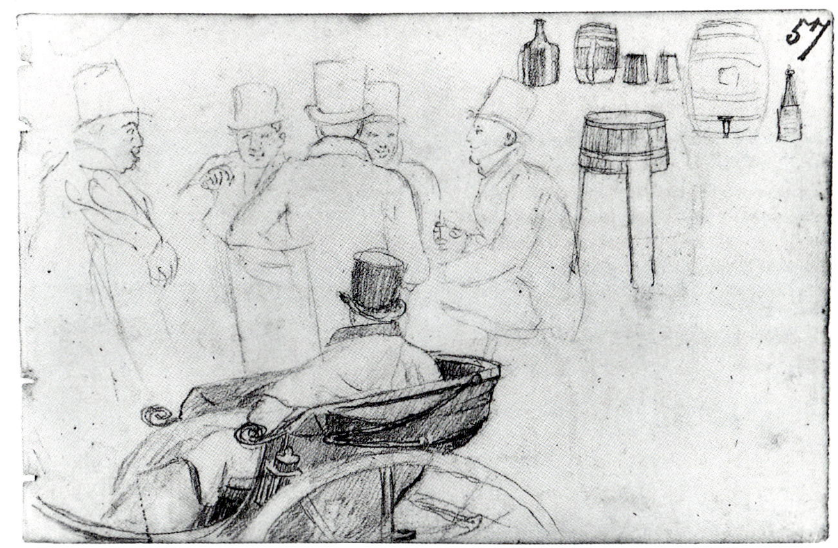

FIGURE 209
Man in carriage, men talking, bottles and barrels, 1818. Pencil. Sketchbook 4, leaf 27 recto.

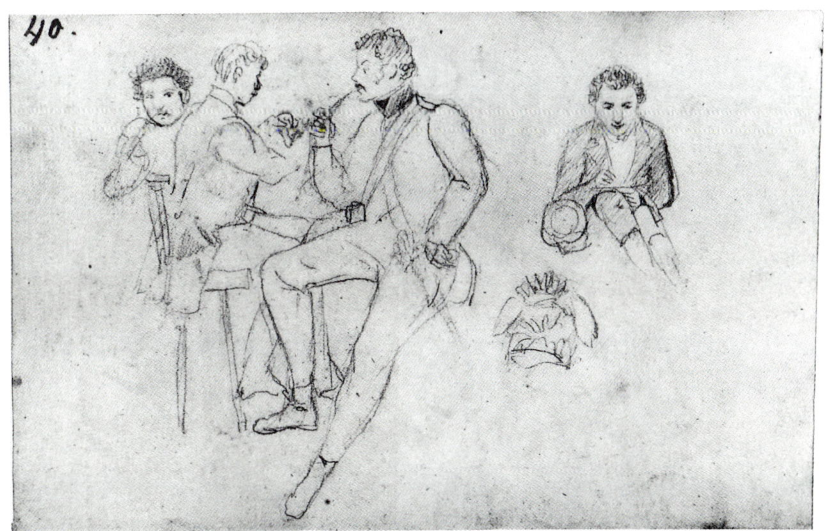

FIGURE 210
Fellow travelers in fashionable dress, 1818. Pencil. Sketchbook 4, leaf 18 verso.

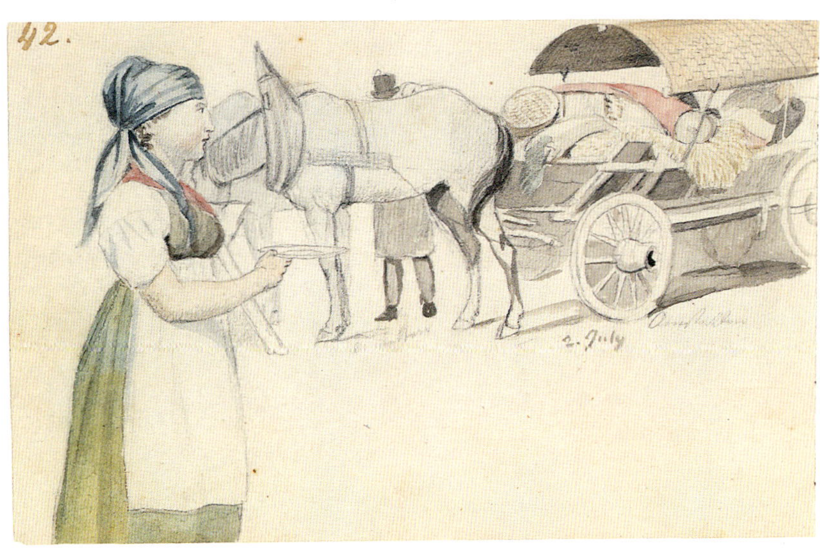

FIGURE 211
Woman near farm cart, Amstetten, July 2, 1818. Watercolor over pencil, watercolor and pencil inscription. Sketchbook 4, leaf 19 verso. Amstetten lies southwest from Vienna on the way to Salzburg.

FIGURE 212
Draft horses feeding, Amstetten, July 2, 1818. Pencil. Sketchbook 4, leaf 19 recto.

FIGURE 213
Farm cart, Amstetten, July 2, 1818. Watercolor over pencil, watercolor and pencil inscription. Sketchbook 4, leaf 20 verso. The pencil sketch in the lower left is reminiscent of the court session drawings in sketchbook 2; see fig. 47. The inscription translates "Thursday, July 2, 1818, ~~Sigmarskirchen~~, very warm."

FIGURE 214
Two travelers, probably July 1818. Pencil. Sketchbook 4, leaf 26 verso.

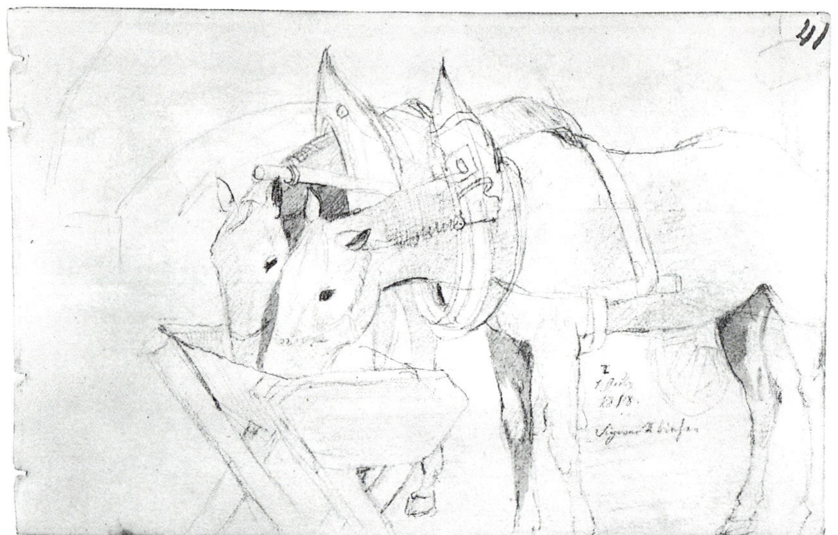

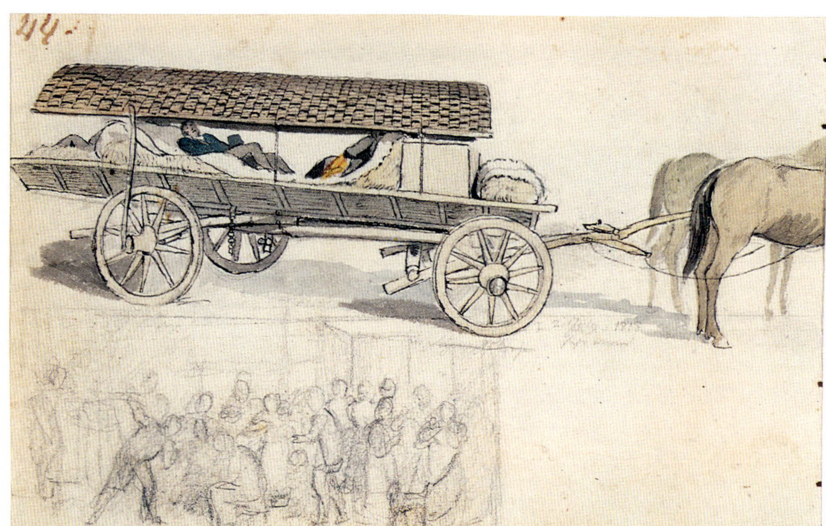

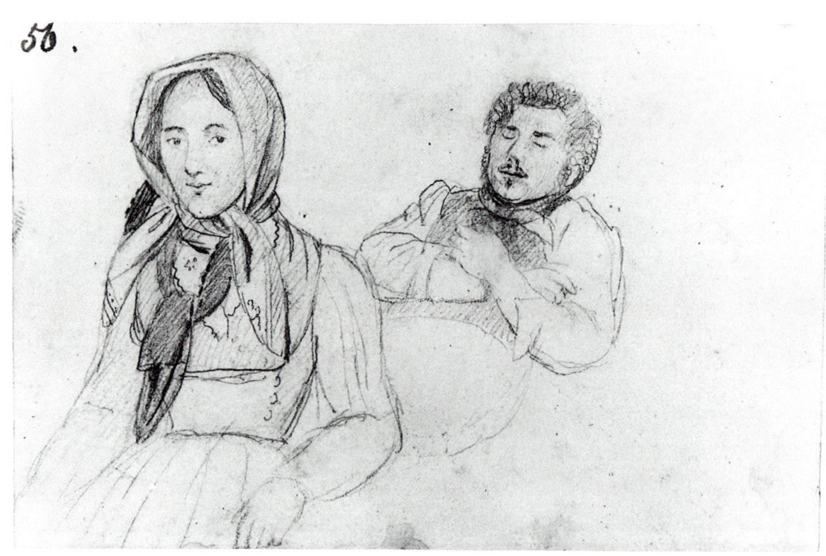

FIGURE 215
Panorama of landscape between Amstetten and Salzburg, July 3 and 4, 1818. Watercolor over pencil, ink inscriptions. Sketchbook 4, leaf 21 recto.

FIGURE 216
View of Salzburg, Monday, July 6, 1818. Ink and wash over pencil, ink inscriptions. Sketchbook 5, leaf 29 verso.

FIGURE 217
View from the Mönchsberg bastion, overlooking Richterhöhe toward the Hochstaufen, Monday, July 6, 1818. Watercolor and ink over pencil, ink and pencil inscriptions. Sketchbook 5, leaf 30 verso. The label above the mountain on the right reads "Staufenberg."

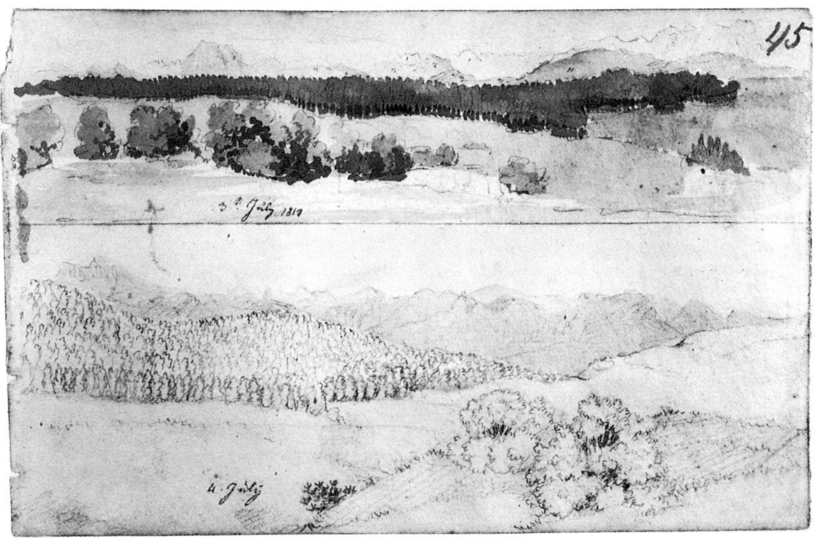

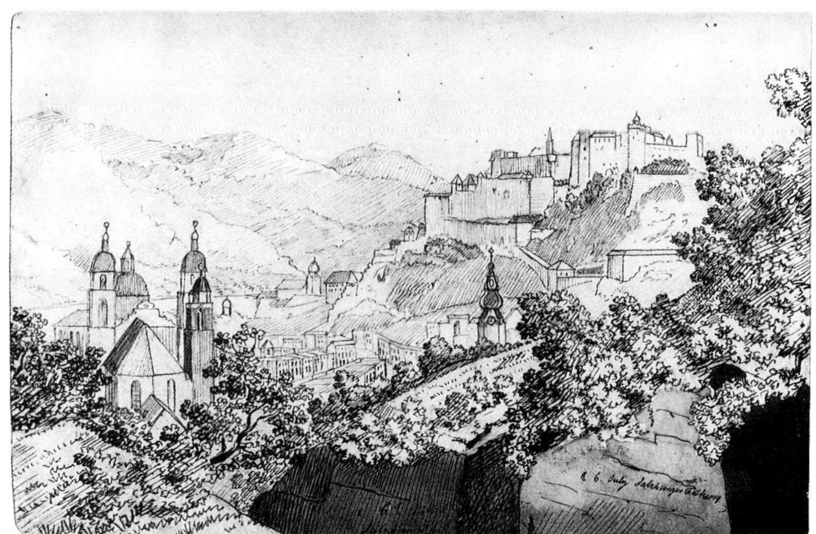

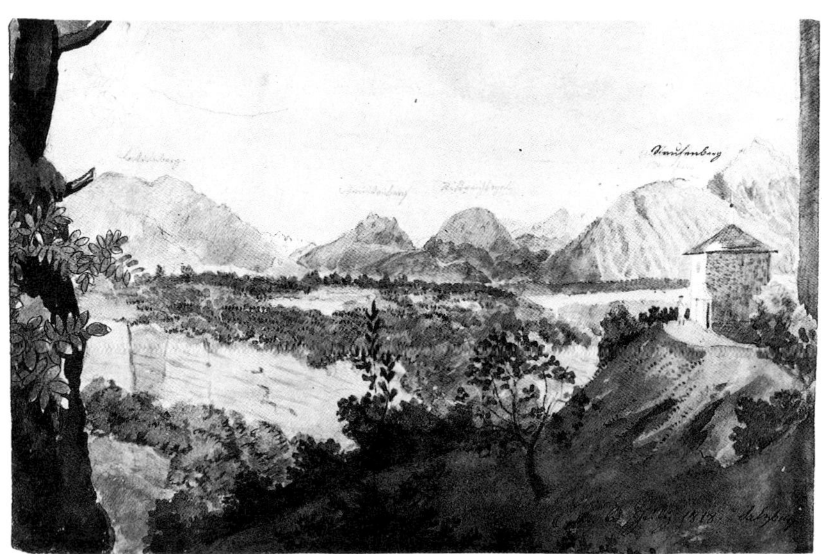

the Mönchsberg, he positioned himself on the other side of the hill, near one of the towers of the lower fortifications, to depict the view overlooking Richterhöhe toward the Hochstaufen or Staufenberg, a famous mountain in the range of the Voralpen.

On the following day Krimmel made a pencil and watercolor sketch of the Neutor (New Gate), the outer entrance to the tunnel built through the Mönchsberg in 1764 to connect Salzburg to Riedenburg (fig. 218).[25] Though the portal occupies the central area of the sketch, it does not face the viewer. Instead, as in some of Krimmel's Vienna woods watercolors, the design is constructed with diagonals. A road coming from the left foreground and partially lined with poplars leads to the walled-in area that controls the tunnel entrance. The thrust of this diagonal is continued in the giant volumetric cuts in the rock from which the tunnel's path can be deduced. The Neutor so impressed Krimmel that some time later he developed his sketch of the site into a more finished and larger watercolor (fig. 219). The later watercolor may have been intended for a printmaker and was perfected to appeal to contemporary taste. The differences between the two Neutor images are consistent with the type of changes Krimmel had demonstrated in his American genre scenes: invariably the final image was more neoclassical than the life sketch from which it had originated. The later Neutor scene is a frieze-like composition with a deliberate coordination of shapes. Because the perspective has been flattened, the hill seems much nearer. The Neutor, although moved from the center to the right third of the composition, has increased in size and importance. The curve of the tunnel entrance is echoed in the much higher arch of the recess. The same monumental arch is repeated in other rock formations. Another indicative change lies in the arrangement of the poplars that in the sketch stood in a diagonal row leading to the Neutor; in the final version they are moved further back, into the plane of the mountain, and function as an extension of the horizontal at the base of the hill that spans the width of the picture. This more unified and lively composition is complemented by a more picturesque lighting that gives a stronger presence to the details of the scene.

The artist's new approach to landscape is also evident in the watercolors he made of other Salzburg panoramas. On July 7 he climbed the mountain on the other side of the Salzach River, the Kapuzinerberg (Mountain of the Capuchin Monks). Stationing himself on the bastion high above the town, Krimmel sketched the commanding view on the small pages of his pocket-size sketchbook, creating an illusion of vast space (fig. 220). He also made a watercolor sketch of the legendary Untersberg, the site of many local legends and tales (fig. 221). In a long, unbroken line he traced the lofty mountain from its slow beginning in the plain to its gradual rise, gaining in steepness over several ridges to its majestic height of 1,853 meters. Its characteristically shaped peak called the Geiereck (Hawks' Corner) is clearly recognizable. The rampart towers on the right, placed in the middle distance of the drawing, are part of the citadel's low fortifications and function here as a diagonal counterbalance to the mighty Untersberg. Between lies the flat plain. This enclosure of open space was a favorite scheme of romantic landscape painters.

Working in minute scale with pencil and fine brushes, he carefully applied his watercolors to precisely define each mountain in outline and formation, an effort that demonstrates a new fascination with distance and atmospheric hues. This was clearly a departure from his earlier landscape representations in

25. Betwen 1763 and 1766 a simple tunnel was carved through the Mönchsberg to permit foot traffic. After it was enlarged to accomodate vehicles, it opened in 1774 to the public. The statue over the entrance (by Johann B. Hagenauer) represents Saint Sigismund, the patron saint of Archbishop Sigismund von Schrattenbach who reigned during the period of the tunnel's construction.

FIGURE 218
The Neutor in Salzberg, Tuesday, July 7, 1818. Watercolor and ink over pencil, ink inscription. Sketchbook 5, leaf 27 verso.

FIGURE 219
Ausseres Neutor, 1818. Pen and ink with wash, ink inscription; 11⅝ x 19 in. (Salzburger Landesarchiv.) Inscription reads "Salzburg gate, through rock—400 feet wide."

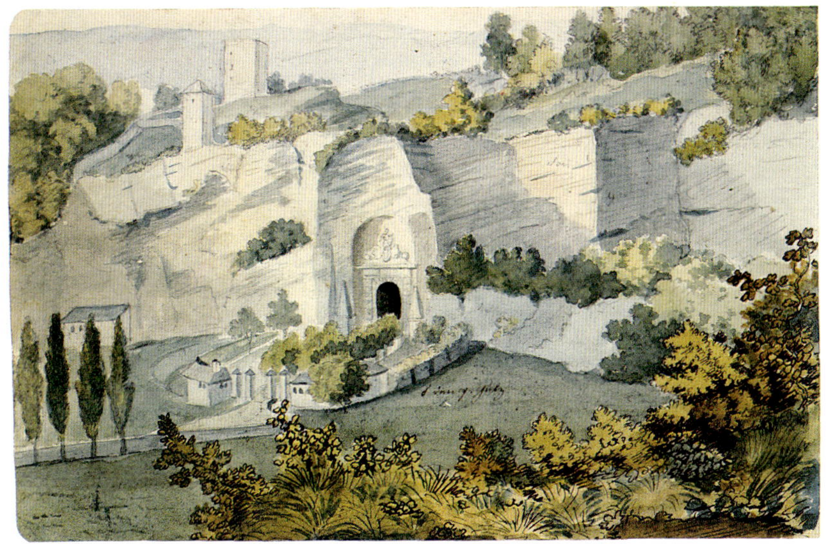

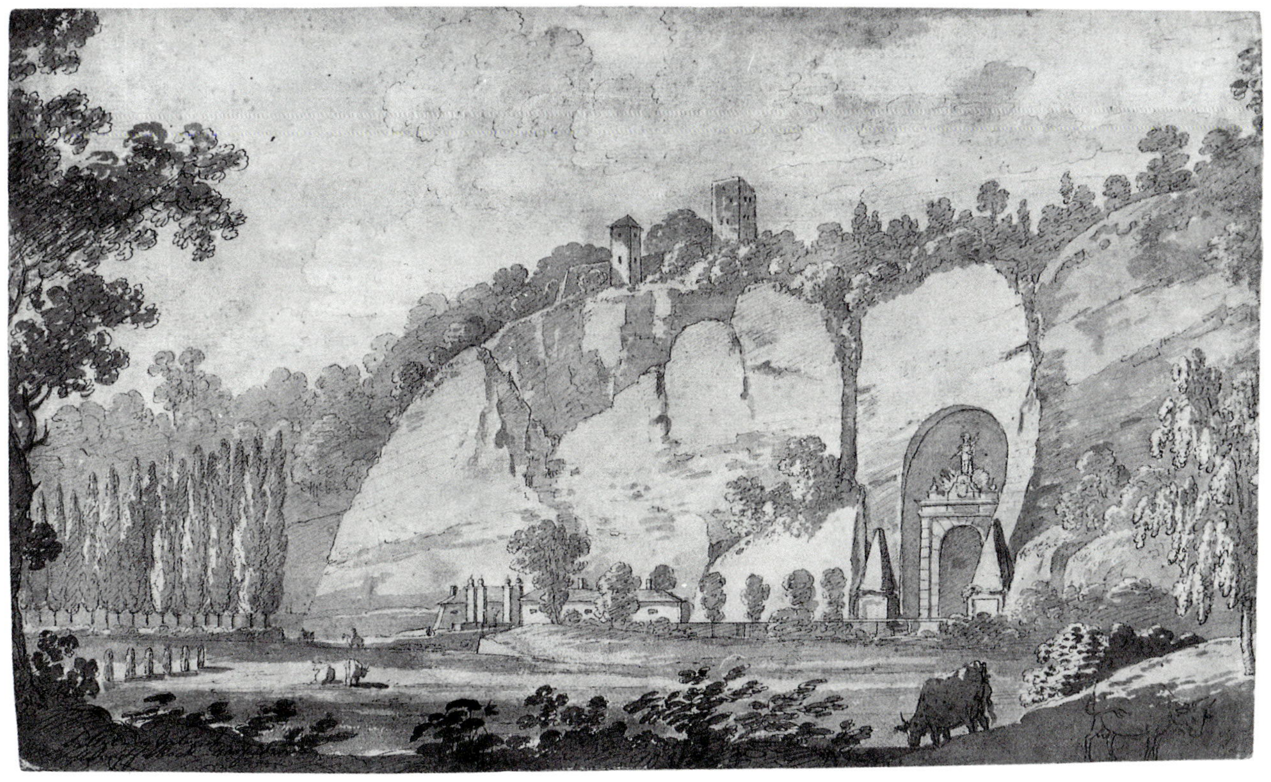

FIGURE 220

View from Salzburg's Kapuzinerberg, looking to the Alps, July 7, 1818. Watercolor and ink over pencil, pencil and ink inscriptions. Sketchbook 5, leaf 28 verso. The inscriptions translate "on the mountain of the Capuchin monks, Tuesday, July 7." "Hohengehl," written over one of the peaks is also known as Hohe Göll. In the middle distance, about 3 miles south of Salzburg, is the grove of trees labeled Hellbrun, a reference to Schloss Hellbrunn, built in the early baroque style for Archbishop Marcus Sitticus by Santino Solari in 1613–15.

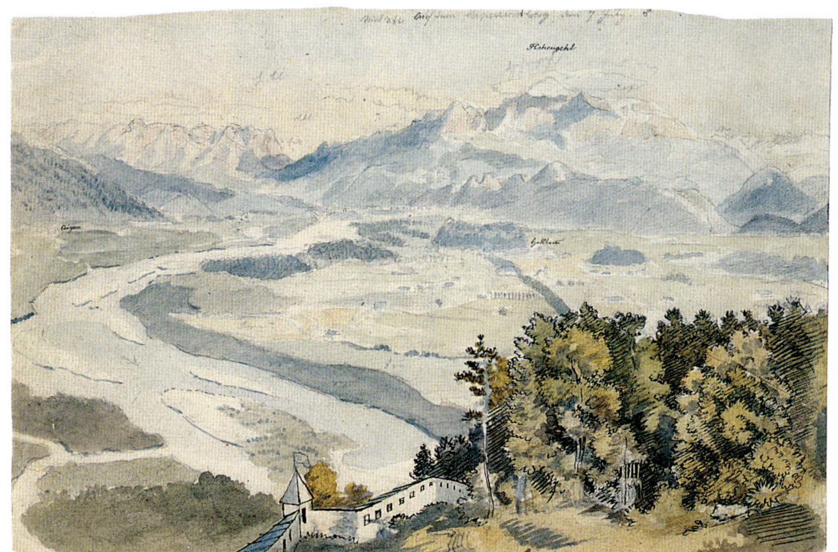

FIGURE 221

View from Salzburg's Mönchsberg, looking toward the Untersberg, Tuesday, July 7, 1818. Watercolor and ink over pencil, ink inscription. Sketchbook 5, leaf 17 verso. The lower fortifications of the citadel are visible at the left.

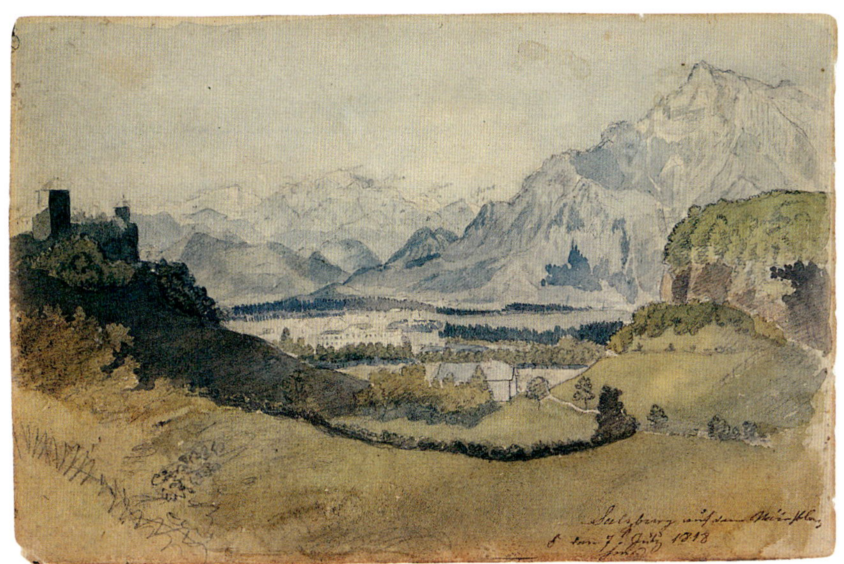

which he had built the view through successive layers of depth and had relied on conventional perspective arrangements predicated on a foreground, a middle ground, and a background (see, for example, figs. 143, 152, 156, 167, 185, 186). Thus in a few short weeks Krimmel's handling of perspective had become surer and bolder, his juxtaposition of the near and the far more dramatic and more dynamic. Every element is an essential part of the whole. The creation of images with strongly unified landscapes was the special accomplishment of artists working in the German romantic mode, especially Johann Christoph Erhard.

While in Salzburg Krimmel's eye for the charm and distinctive design of regional costumes produced a very small half-length portrait of a young woman wearing a customary large hat (fig. 222). This finished watercolor portrait shows that Krimmel had not lost his ability to produce a likeness on a miniature scale.

While following the Salzach upstream from Salzburg, Krimmel came to a site that struck him as an ideal, wild romantic vista (fig. 223). Although his composition seems emphatically symmetrically structured, it is not rigid. Shown is the Salzach encroached by cliffs at a point where it is forced to flow through a narrowing of its bed. On the right a rugged path winds upward to the open gate of a building that leads to Pass Lueg, a passageway through the mountains. Reaching beyond the height of the picture, the outlines of the cliffs and the trees clinging to the rocks give the image a strong vertical dimension. The funnel-shape opening between the cliffs offers a glimpse of a village. Ready to head for Pass Lueg, a traveler is given directions from a local workman. The positioning of the two figures reveals that Krimmel was familiar with the compositional figural conventions of contemporary German painting. C. D. Friedrich and other contemporary painters used the human figure seen from the back as a symbol for man's deep spiritual contemplation of nature; but Krimmel is less metaphysically inclined. In this drawing, the two men give scale to the natural site and perhaps refer to the artist's personal travel experience.

On July 9 he paused in Rosenheim and attended a country fair that featured exotic animals. Using a sharply pointed pencil he sketched an elephant and made additional studies of the animal's head and legs, and on the opposite page he drew a young kangaroo (fig. 224). The people who attended the fair interested him too, especially a hefty man and group of young Bavarian women, wearing fur-trimmed hats and small graceful bonnets. From Rosenheim it was at least a three-day journey to Ebingen, which would have brought him back to his hometown before the middle of the month.

Earlier that day in Chiemsee Krimmel had produced a panoramic sketch (fig. 225) that visually unified the extraordinary width of the vista, emphasizing the geometric lines of the long bridge connecting the island of Frauen Chiemsee on the left with the lake shore of Seebrück on the right.

During the latter part of July, Krimmel executed a number of sketches with Ebingen views. They too indicate that the experience of the previous ten weeks had altered his style. On Friday, July 17, he made a double-page watercolor of Ebingen's main streets: Schütte and Langewarte, not far from where the Krimmel house/confectionery was located (fig. 226). Relying on his newly developed approach, Krimmel chose to contrast the open space of the foreground with the unbroken row of half-timbered houses that tightly lined one side of the street. The sense of abstraction he imparted to the image

FIGURE 222
Woman, 1818. Watercolor over pencil. Sketchbook 5, leaf 17 recto. This medallion is pasted onto the page.

FIGURE 223
Pass Lueg, July 1818. Pen and ink with wash, ink inscriptions; 11 5/8 x 19 in. (Heimatmuseum Golling.) Inscription reads "Pass near Hallein, Saltzburg 1818." The drawing depicts the pass that separates the plain of the Salzachtal from the mountains. The church visible in the background is Maria Brunneck, a church of pilgrimage.

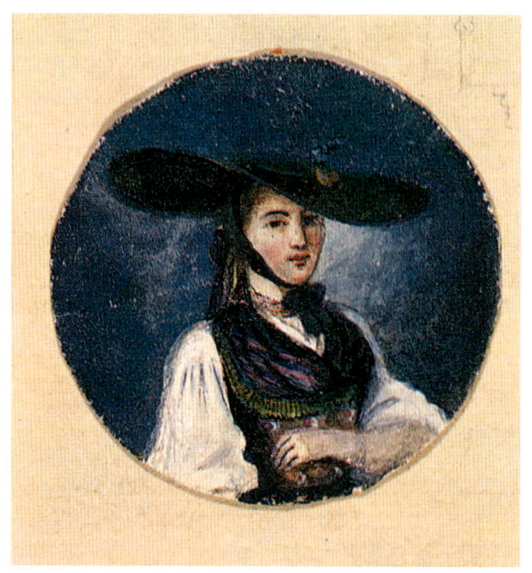

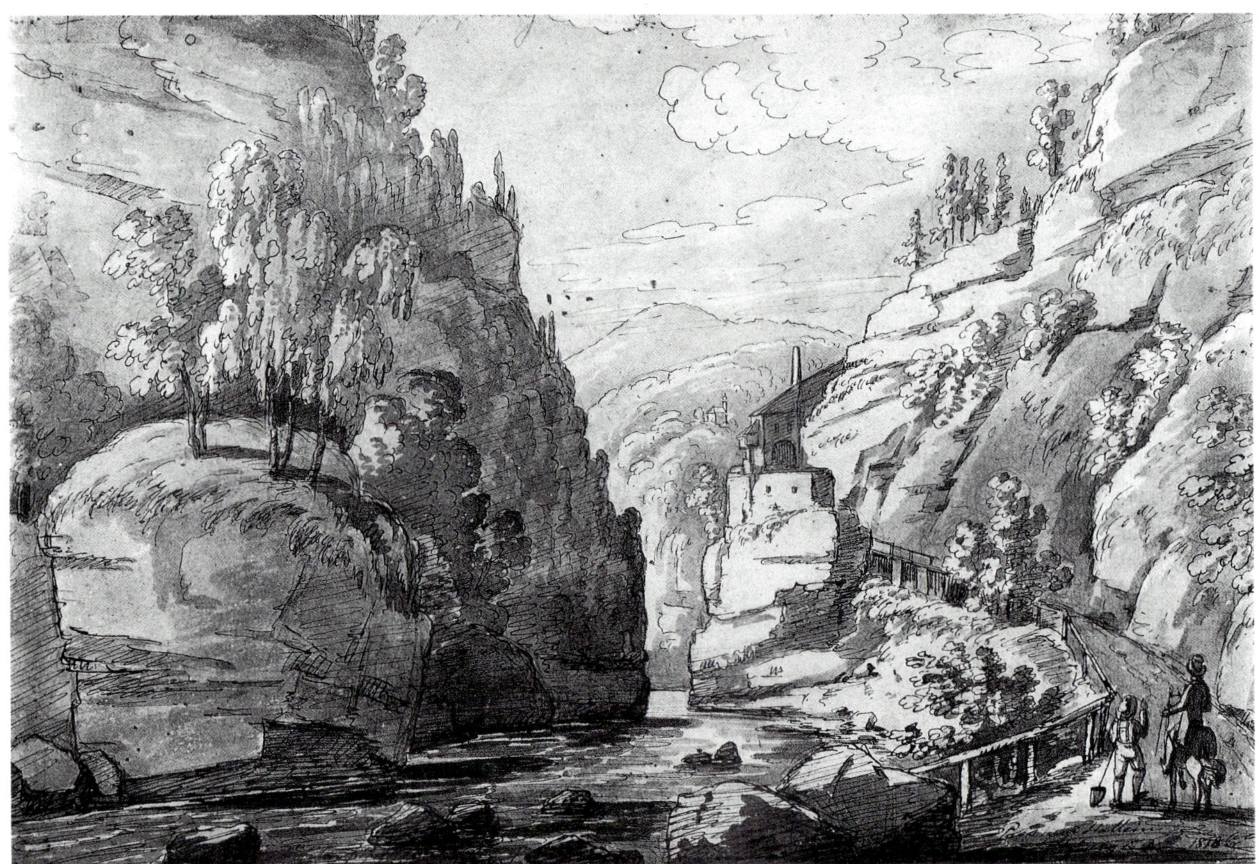

FIGURE 224

People and kangaroo at a country fair in Rosenheim, July 9, 1818. Watercolor and ink over pencil, pencil. Sketchbook 5, leaf 35 recto.

FIGURE 225

Panorama of Chiemsee, July 9, 1818. Watercolor and ink over pencil, ink inscription. Sketchbook 5, leafs 33 verso and 34 recto. The bridge is probably to one of the three islands located in the southwest section of the 7-by-7½-mile lake, possibly to 22-acre Frauen Insel, which attracted many artists and was also the site of a Benedictine nunnery.

FIGURE 226

Panorama of Schütte and Langewarte, Friday, July 17, 1818. Watercolor and ink over pencil, ink inscription. Sketchbook 5, leafs 26 verso and 27 recto.

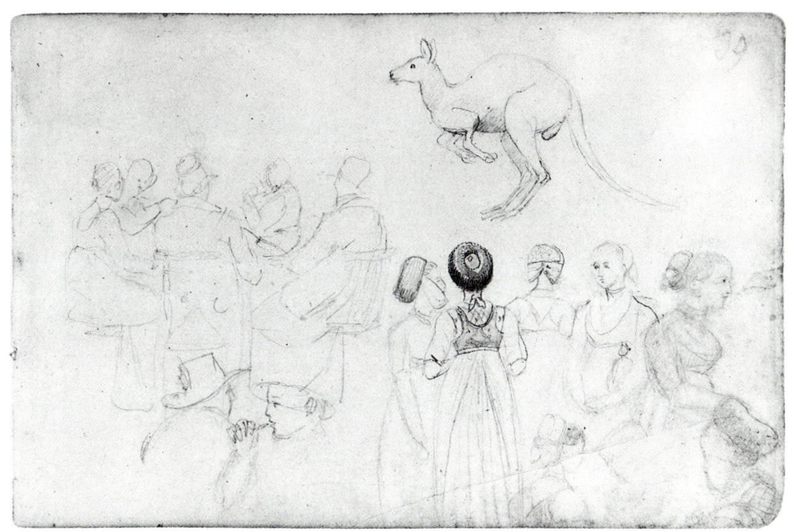

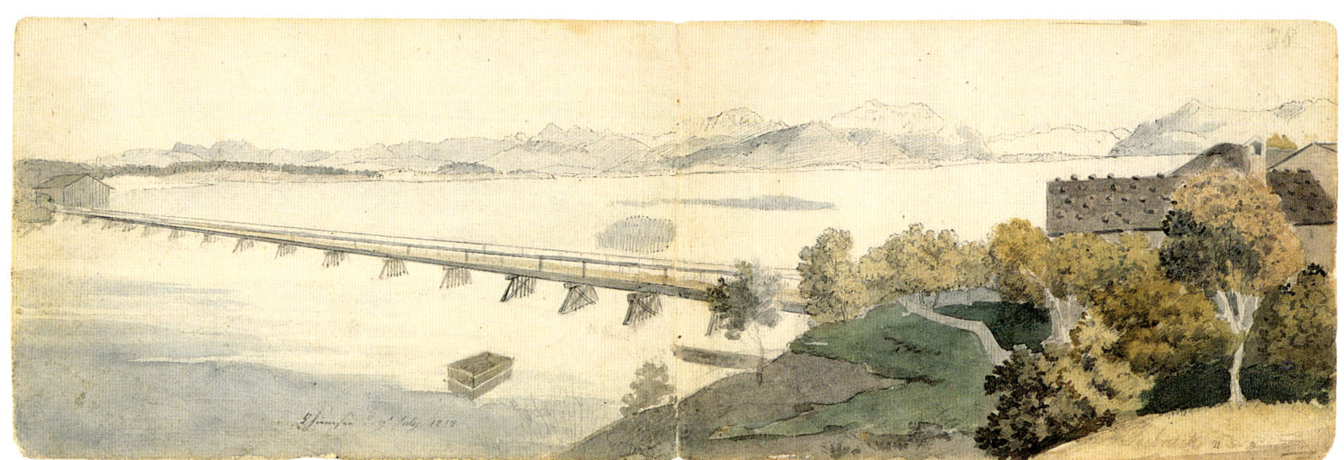

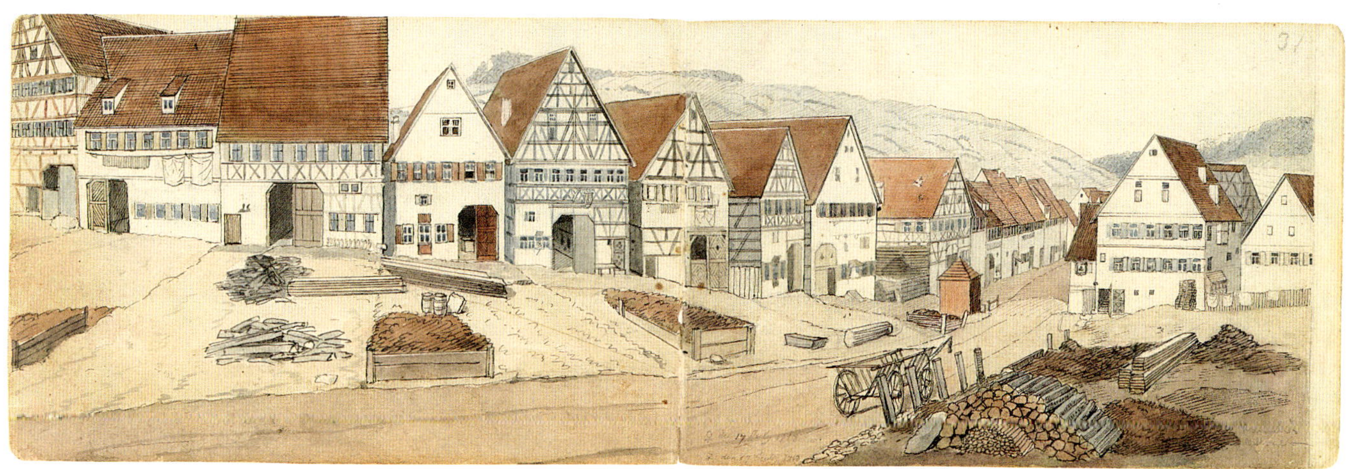

FIGURE 227
Hillside scene, Sunday, July 19, 1818. Pencil. Sketchbook 5, leaf 19 recto.

FIGURE 228
Vendor's table, Ebingen, Wednesday, July 22, 1818. Wash over pencil, pencil inscription. Sketchbook 4, leaf 20 recto.

FIGURE 229
Ebingen woman, Saturday, July 25, 1818. Watercolor over pencil, ink inscription. Sketchbook 5, leaf 10 verso.

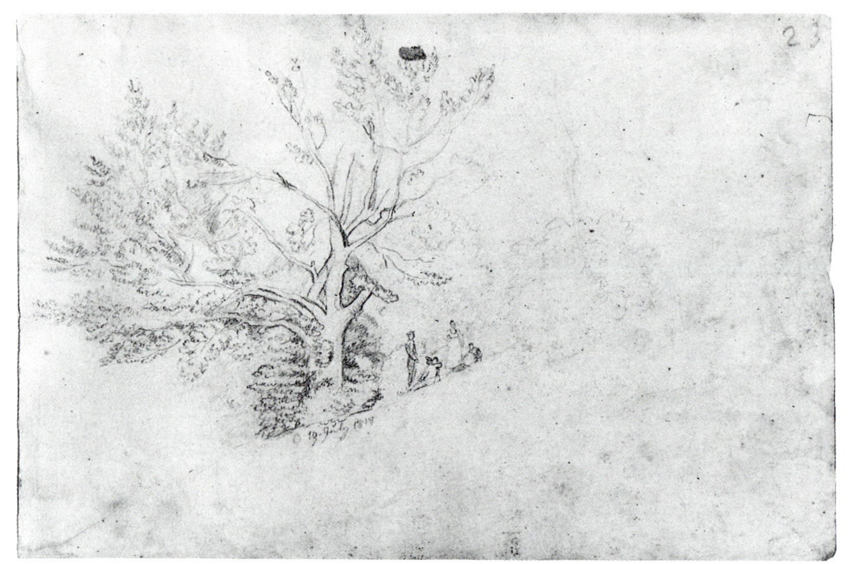

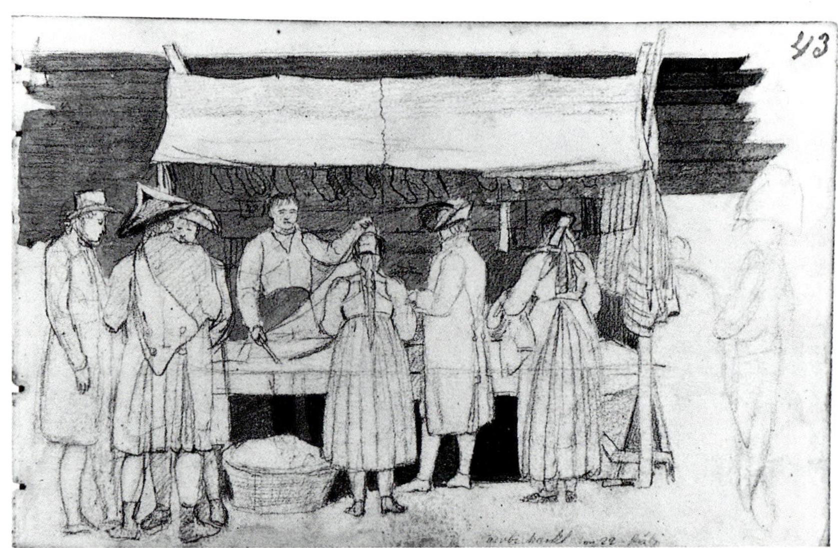

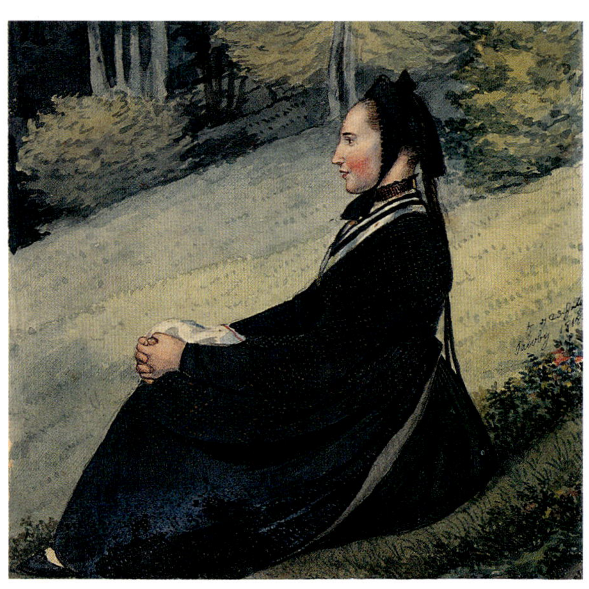

enhanced the illusion of three-dimensionality on the pages. Another view in which Krimmel employed a favorite motif of romanticism is a particularly fine pencil drawing of a large oak tree under which three young couples have stopped to rest (fig. 227).

On Wednesday, July 22, Ebingen's *Jacobimarkt*, a two-day summer fair, began, and Krimmel executed a wash drawing of a stand at which yard goods and stockings were sold (fig. 228). On the following day, the feast day of Saint James, he depicted a young woman seated near the woods (fig. 229). His composition, presenting her in strict profile and firmly outlined, at first glance appears to be regressive; however, it is modern in the relationship of the figure to the bushes, trees, and the incline stretch of meadow. The strong formal unification of figure and surroundings is typical of romanticism, and this differentiates the image from the neoclassical precepts that dominated his construction of earlier images, for example the elderly spinner (see fig. 180). On the same day, he made a watercolor of three half-timbered houses and part of the watchtower called *untere Thor* (lower gate), a remnant of the old fortification of the town that is today in the very center of Ebingen (fig. 230).

Twenty-one months had elapsed since Krimmel had left Philadelphia, but in terms of his artistry a great deal had changed: he had arrived in Europe firmly grounded in the neoclassical tradition, which emphasized balance and symmetry; he was ready to leave Europe with a grounding in German romanticism, which emphasized depth, spatial effects, and a deeper identification with nature.

During the many months in Ebingen, Krimmel had revived many old friendships and established new ones. At ten o'clock on the evening of August 8, 1818, about a dozen friends—teachers, tradesmen, and town officials—assembled in a local tavern, *Die Kanne* (The Pitcher), to bid the artist farewell. Krimmel probably left early the next morning and headed straight north, most likely once more via Tübingen and Stuttgart, and then followed the Neckar River downstream to Heilbronn, about fifty kilometers north of Stuttgart. Heilbronn was the major commercial town of Lower Swabia, and while there Krimmel may have looked up a resident whose name was listed in sketchbook 5. His next stop may have been Heidelberg, for he had also made a note of the names of two aristocrats—General zur Westen and Count Widenberg—who might have owned art collections and lived in the famous university town idyllically located some fifty kilometers northwest of Heilbronn. Next he paused in Frankfurt, a Free City of historical fame and great wealth, eighty kilometers north.[26]

On September 1, after three weeks of travel, Krimmel reached Mainz, 300 kilometers from Ebingen. This important ancient town, located at the confluence of the Main and Rhine, was the upper terminus for long-distance travel on the Rhine. From there boats could transport goods and people to the North Sea relatively quickly and inexpensively because all passengers rode on deck, protected from the sun and rain by an awning or wooden enclosure that stretched across the middle section of the barge (fig. 231). The artist sketched two of them, one a burly man seated on a trunk he identified as merchant Vetter, an indication that he had made his acquaintance (figs. 232, 233).

The artist started sketching scenery on September 3 after his boat had passed Bingen, about six hours from Mainz. The river entered a narrow gorge of the Rhenish Slate Mountains, presenting a sequence of exceptionally scenic

26. His friends signed their names and occupations in sketchbook 5, inside front cover and back cover. Krimmel's visit to Frankfurt is documented by the labeled sketch of a dog in sketchbook 5 (see fig. 231).

FIGURE 230
Watchtower, lower entrance to Ebingen, labeled Tuesday, July 23, 1818, but more correctly Tuesday, July 21, or Thursday, July 23. Watercolor and ink over pencil, ink inscription. Sketchbook 5, leaf 37 recto.

FIGURE 231
Rhine River barge, horse, woman, two dogs; Germany; probably September 1818. Pencil, ink inscription. Sketchbook 5, leaf 38 recto. The inscriptions translate "J. Beck's poodle; Brecht's pomeranian in Frankfurt."

FIGURE 232
Fellow travelers on the Rhine, September 1818. Ink over pencil, ink inscription. Sketchbook 5, leaf 20 recto. The inscription translates "Merchant Vetter, September 5."

FIGURE 233
Fellow travelers on the Rhine, 1818. Pencil. Sketchbook 5, leaf 31 recto.

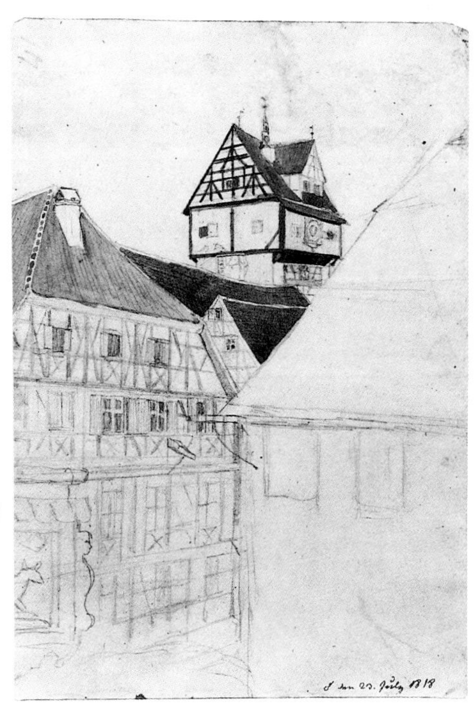

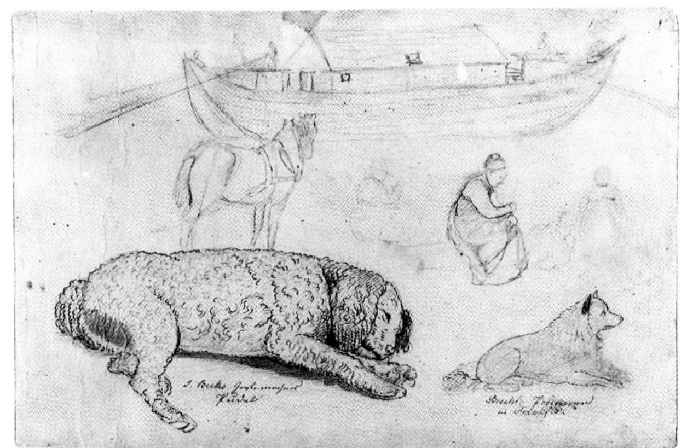

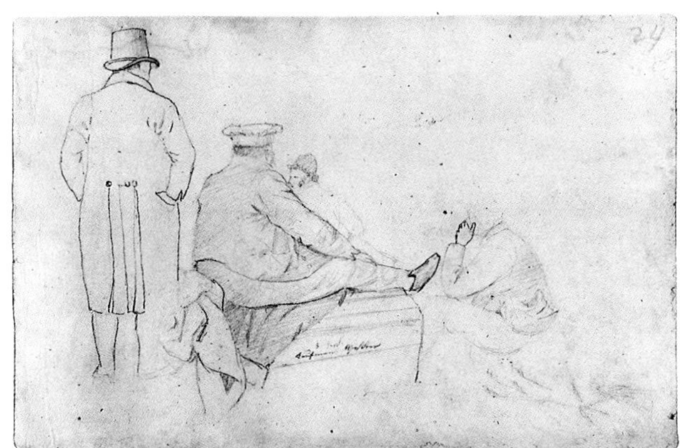

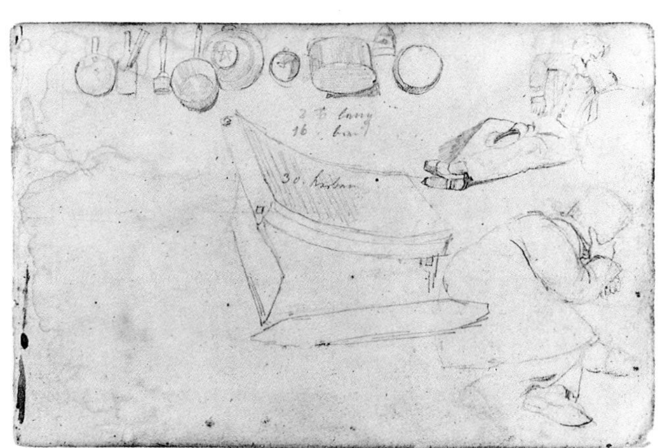

FIGURE 234
Views from the Rhine: Tower of Ehrenfels, Mouse Tower, Castle near Bingerbrück, September 3, 1818. Ink over pencil, ink inscriptions. Sketchbook 5, leaf 21 verso.

FIGURE 235
Falkenberg (also known as Trechtlingshausen) and St. Clemens, Bauzberg, unidentified view, September 3, 1818. Ink over pencil, ink inscription. Sketchbook 5, leaf 22 recto.

FIGURE 236
Approach to Sonneck; view of Stahleck, across from Lorch with Bacharach in the distance; view of the ruins of Fürstenberg; September 3, 1818. Ink over pencil, ink and pencil inscriptions. Sketchbook 5, leaf 22 verso.

FIGURE 237
Approach to Caub [Kaub] with the hexagonal thirteenth-century Castle Pfalz (also known as Pfalzgrafenstein) on the left and possibly thirteenth-century Castle Gutenfels on the right; close-up of Castle Pfalz; approach to Schönberg and Oberwesel with its early fifteenth-century Frauenkirche; September 3, 1818. Ink over pencil, ink inscriptions. Sketchbook 5, leaf 23 recto.

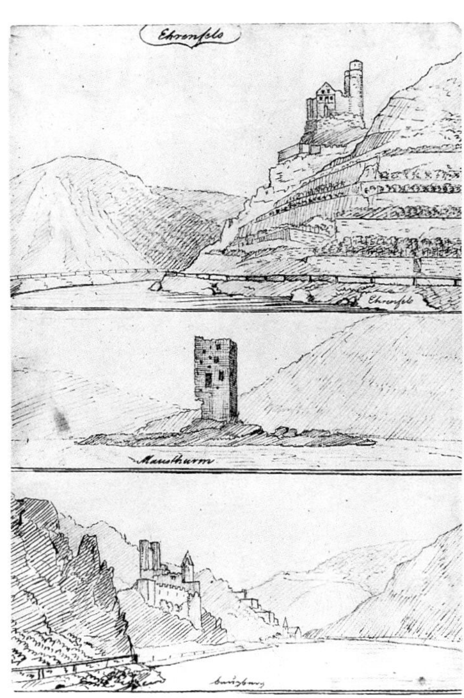

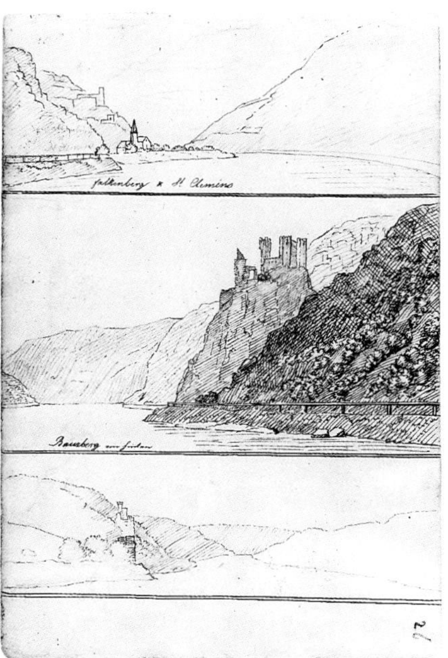

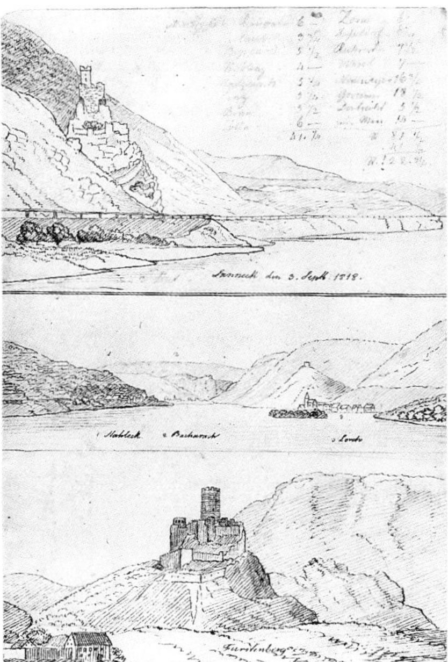

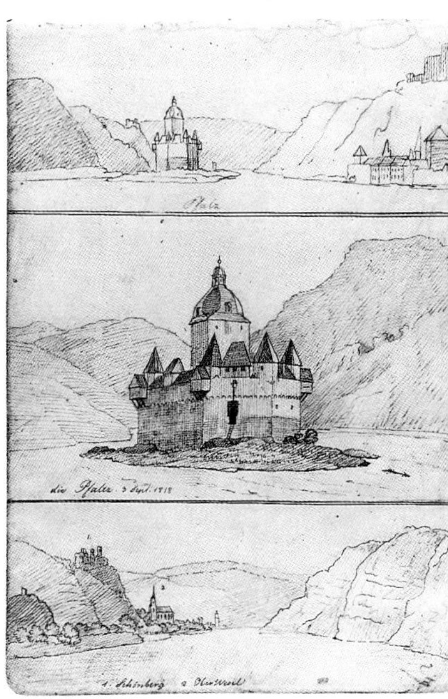

views that have long fascinated artists. Ruins of lofty castles, sunbaked vineyards, and old towns nestled at the foot of giant rocks kept Krimmel's pencil busy.

Krimmel's first sketches show the vineyards and the ruins of Ehrenfels, once a large medieval citadel built high on the river bank. Next came the "Tower of the Mice," a medieval tollhouse erected in the middle of the river, and which, according to a legend, took its name from the hordes of mice that killed the cruel Archbishop Hatto there. Soon the boat passed *Burg Pfalz*, a particularly picturesque castle also built on an island in the middle of the flowing stream. Krimmel sketched it twice (figs. 234–237).

At one point the river curled around the massive cliff. Krimmel drew the outlines and geologic formations with great care—but added: "*Lureley Felsen nicht gewiss*" (Rock of the Lorelei, not certain). It was indeed the rock made famous by the myth of the beautiful siren (fig. 238).

As Krimmel's barge floated downstream, the sharp-eyed artist focused on castles and ruins, defining their architectural outlines precisely, even at considerable distances (fig. 239).[27] Late in the afternoon of September 3, the barge reached an area of Bornhofen that so fascinated him that he delineated the approach to the town from two different angles and distances, thus the details become larger and clearer in the second image (fig. 240). He also drew Boppard, a typical old town with a church built in the Rhenish Gothic style (fig. 241). During some eighteen hours of travel on September 3, Krimmel depicted twenty-two different sites, the last of which is Märzburg, the only surviving old citadel on the Rhine, built on the tip of a mountain in the vicinity of Koblenz, an ancient city at the juncture of the Moselle and the Rhine rivers. There the barge probably stayed for the night, and Krimmel and his fellow travelers slept ashore. While there he sketched the facade of a tall, half-timbered house.

When Krimmel resumed sketching on September 4, it was nine o'clock in the morning, and the boat was approaching the town of Andernach some five hours down the stream from Koblenz, indicating that their night's stay had been a short one (fig. 242). He wrote underneath his first sketch of that day: "Sunshine, in the morning fog." The silhouette of Andernach appears in three of the sketches, each time from a different vantage point (fig. 243). In contrast to the exceptionally rich output of the previous day, Krimmel produced only eleven sketches on September 4. The Rhine had entered a different geographical region and was flowing through a wider bed surrounded by a less scenic landscape (fig. 244). The artist depicted the whole panorama of the *Siebengebirge* (Seven Mountain Range) in one meticulously outlined vista and then concluded his Rhine sketches with a drawing of the site of Drachenfels, a large ruin on the very top of a mountain not far from Bonn (fig. 245).

The thirty-three Rhine sketches occur in jumbled sequence in sketchbook 5. The book no longer had a group of blank pages, so the artist sketched the scenes wherever there was an unused page or half page. When rearranged in geographical sequence, the drawings communicate his journey like a film strip. These images show a greater pictorial continuity than do his Danube sketches, yet Krimmel could not have produced his Rhine sketches with such efficiency and skill had he not practiced drawing from a moving boat on his way to Vienna. The Rhine sketches demonstrate that Krimmel's approach had become increasingly methodical, almost scientific, a different level of competence. In contrast to his earlier drawings, this sequence attests that his

27. "He could stand at a great distance and count the different courses of bricks in a building without a glimmer before the eyes" (Dunlap, *History*, 2:394).

FIGURE 238
Approach to St. Goar, view of the Rock of the Lorelei, approach to St. Goarshausen with a view of Neu Katzenellbogen (colloquially known as The Cat, built 1393), September 3, 1818. Ink over pencil, ink and pencil inscriptions. Sketchbook 5, leaf 23 verso.

FIGURE 239
Approach to Welmich with a view of the ruins of Thurenberg (colloquially known as The Mouse, built before 1636), view of Castle Rheinfels near St. Goar, unlabeled view, September 3, 1818. Ink over pencil, ink inscription. Sketchbook 5, leaf 24 recto.

FIGURE 240
Two views downstream near Bornhofen, September 3, 1818. Wash and ink over pencil; ink over pencil, ink inscriptions. Sketchbook 5, leaf 24 verso. The castles above Bornhofen's 1435 Gothic church are Sterrenberg and Liebenstein (colloquially known as The Brothers).

FIGURE 241
Approach to Boppard and the Castle of Märzburg overlooking Braubach, September 3, 1818. Ink over pencil, ink inscriptions. Sketchbook 5, leaf 25 recto.

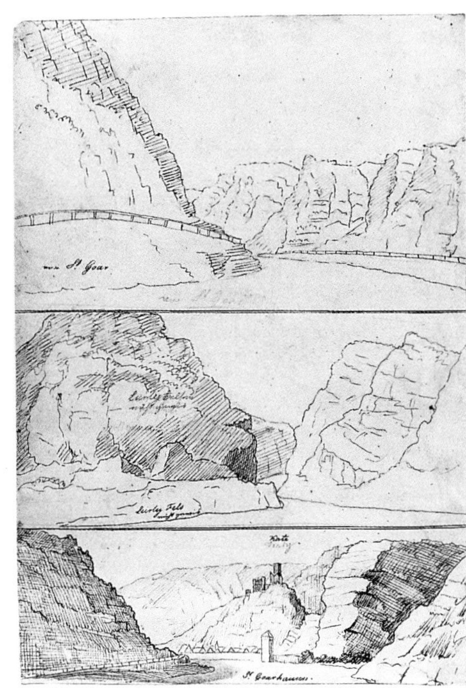

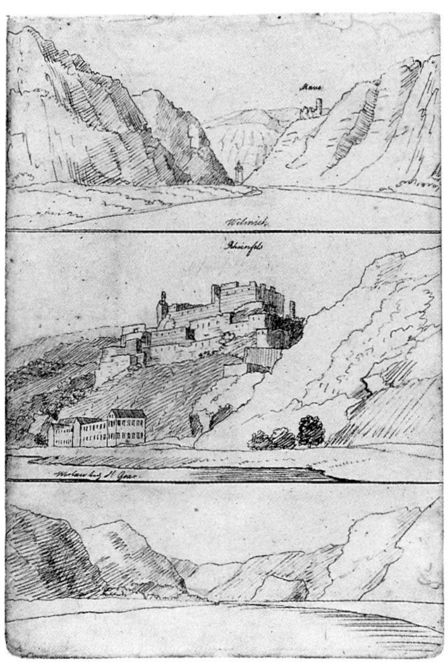

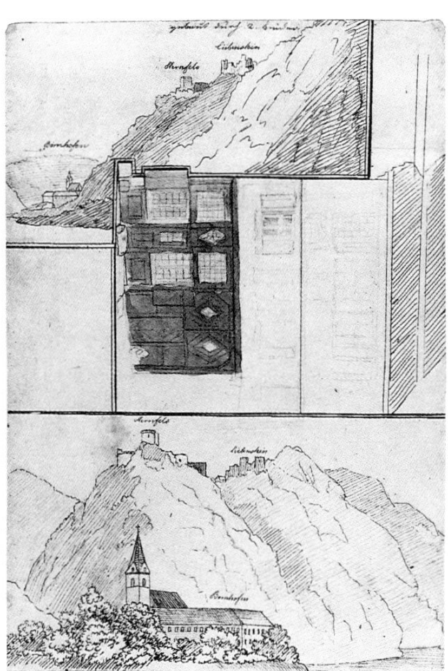

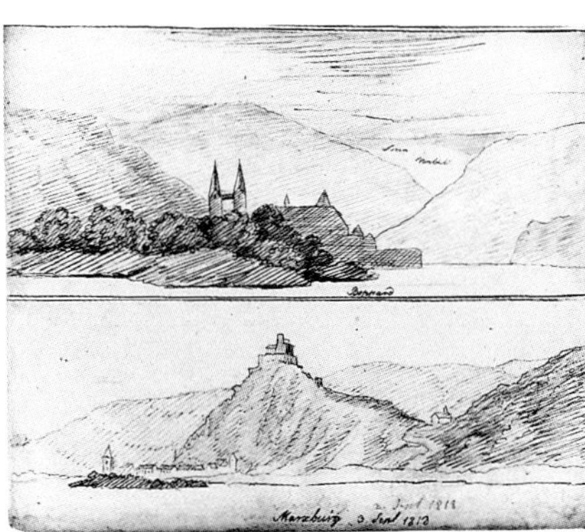

FIGURE 242
Three views of Andernach, September 4, 1818. Ink over pencil, ink and pencil inscriptions. Sketchbook 5, leaf 25 verso. The octagonally topped, round watch-tower was built between 1414 and 1468; the church with four towers dates from 1206.

FIGURE 243
Four views near Andernach: view downriver toward Hammerstein at top; view downriver at Rheineck at bottom; September 4, 1818. Ink over pencil, ink and pencil inscriptions. Sketchbook 5, leaf 26 recto.

FIGURE 244
Views from the Rhine near Bad Godesberg-Bonn: view toward Hammerstein; view toward Rheineck and Hammerstein; September 4, 1818. Ink over pencil, ink inscriptions. Sketchbook 5, leaf 19 verso.

FIGURE 245
Siebengebirge [Seven Mountain Range] near Bonn with closer view of the first mountain on which twelfth-century Castle Drachenfels [colloquially known as Dragon's Rock] is located, September 4, 1818. Ink over pencil, ink inscriptions. Sketchbook 5, leaf 20 verso.

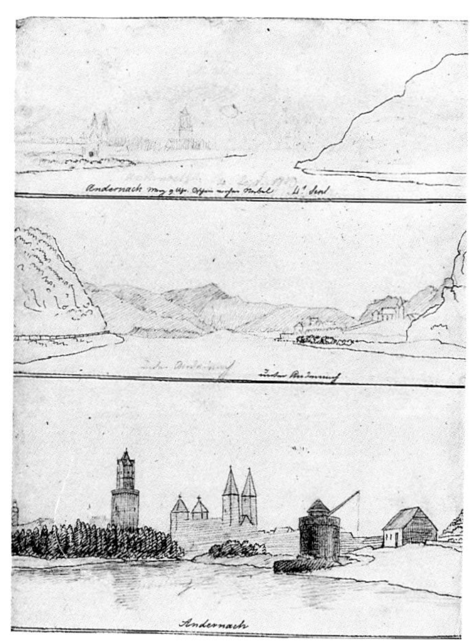

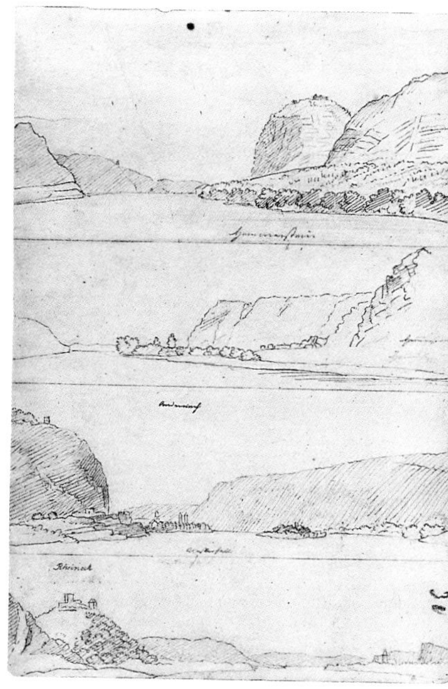

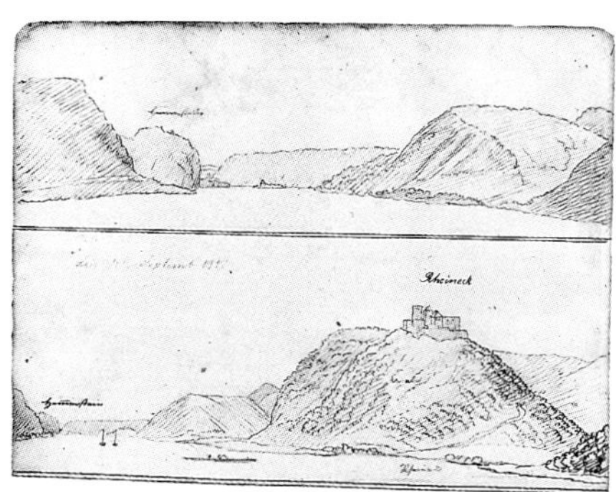

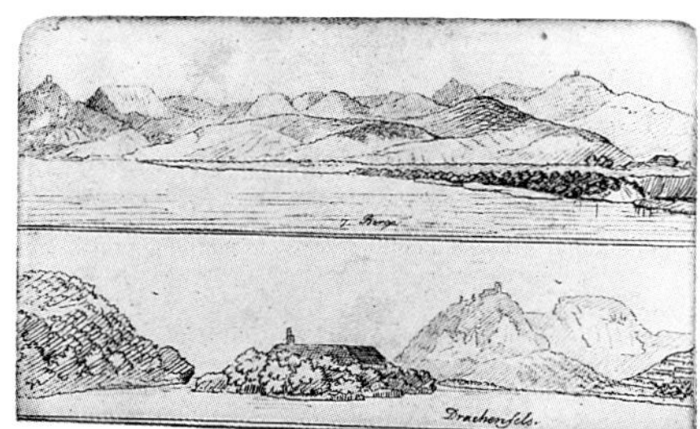

FIGURE 246
Fellow travelers, September 1818. Watercolor over pencil. Sketchbook 5, leaf 19 verso.

FIGURE 247
Man standing beside horse-drawn sleigh, coast of Cape Henry, Virginia, late 1818. Pencil. Sketchbook 4, leaf 22 verso. House, sideboard, woman, horse, sleigh, early 1819. Pencil, wash over pencil. Sketchbook 4, leaf 23 recto. Krimmel may have drawn the coast as early as mid October 1818 and the sleighs as late as March 1819.

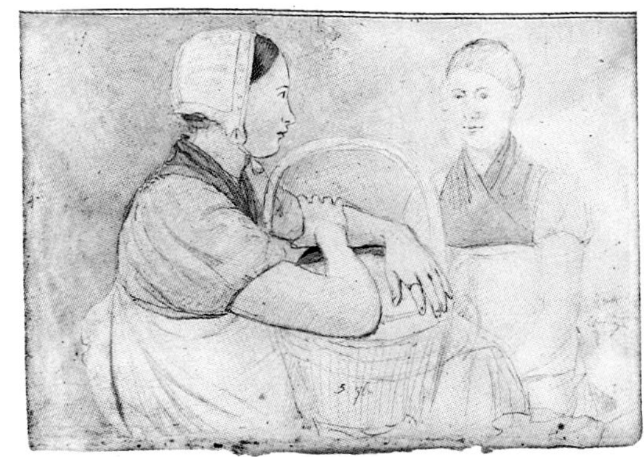

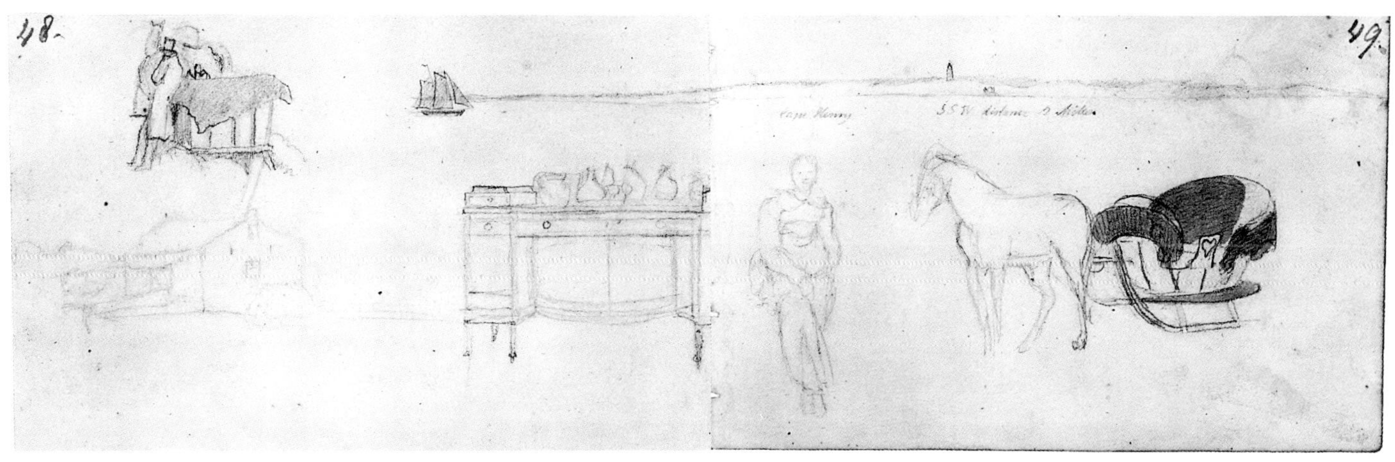

ability to define geological formations had become stronger and his representation of architectural elements more three-dimensional. The way these images convey distance and space, preeminent concepts in German romantic painting, demonstrate that Krimmel had achieved a thorough understanding of those precepts.

Krimmel also left a record of how long it took the barge to travel from one major town to the next. It took 6 hours to travel from Mainz to Bingen and a total of 41 ½ hours to reach Cologne. Proceeding to Düsseldorf, Nijmegen, and Dordrecht took another 81 hours. All in all, the artist calculated that the river barge took 123 hours to go from Mainz to the North Sea. Assuming that the boat traveled 18 to 24 hours each day, this journey down the Rhine took 5 to 7 days. Notes and addresses on the inside cover of sketchbook 5 suggest that Krimmel was prepared to sail for America from either Rotterdam or Amsterdam.

Good planning brought Krimmel to the coast about mid September, and the most favorable periods for crossing the Atlantic were the weeks immediately following the spring or autumn equinox. Still, depending upon the winds, the voyage could last from twenty-five to sixty days. As an experienced traveler, he probably found passage on a ship relatively quickly, perhaps in one or two weeks. But in 1818 emigration had resumed vigorously, and he had to compete with the new tide of emigrants, most from German states, that flooded into Dutch ports following the end of the Napoleonic Wars (fig. 246). The shipping companies were unprepared for such a rush, and the ports were enormously overcrowded with people. Ships were often overloaded and set sail even in unsafe weather. As a result the normal hardships of an overseas voyage were much increased.

If Krimmel's contemporaries were correct about his careful handling of money, Krimmel probably traveled in steerage, which even in the best of conditions could make for a tedious and difficult voyage in overcrowded, cramped quarters. Steerage passengers were required to supply their own provisions, a folding table-knife, and bedding (mattress and blankets). Tea and coffee, without sugar, were furnished by the captain. The fare would have been about $75.[28]

Sketchbook 4 includes a few images of distinctly American motifs. One of a distant coastline and a lighthouse labeled "Cape Henry, SSW distance 7 miles" extends over two pages and is his recognition view of the Virginia coast (fig. 247). A schooner is in the left foreground, apparently a pilot boat designed to operate with little wind and typical of the boats used on the Virginia coast.[29] The same page contains a sketch of a horse-drawn sleigh, which suggests that season's first snowfall came shortly after Krimmel's return to Pennsylvania.

28. "The store of gold with which he left Pennsylvania was not great, yet, with honest pride he threw a portion of it on his friend's table at his return, as proof of his prudence, temperance and economy" (Dunlap, *History*, 2:393). The cost of the voyage is inferred from Joseph Jobé, ed., *Extended Travels in Romantic America*, trans. D. B. Tubbs (Lausanne, Switz.: Edita, 1818), p. 8.

29. The same type of vessel, a Virginia pilot boat, was depicted by Benjamin Henry Latrobe on March 7, 1796, and described in his journal; see Carter, Van Horne, and Brownell, *Latrobe's View*, pp. 60–61, 150–51, 154–55.

Back in Philadelphia 1819–1820

After an absence of two years Krimmel returned to Philadelphia eager to resume his career and to see friends and relatives. In the interim, changes had occurred on both the national and local levels, some of which affected the artist and his adopted city. Manufacturers, aided by the protective tariff of 1816, were seeking to expand their domestic markets; improved roads and an interest in constructing canals was spurring interstate commerce; and a general sense of optimism and patriotism, dubbed the "Era of Good Feelings" by Boston's *Columbian Centinel*, suffused the nation. Tempering this were growing sectional differences and the deepening postwar economic depression the nadir of which is termed the Panic of 1819. Businesses were failing, and unemployment was rising, and there was a large increase in the number of homeless poor.[1]

Although the problems were visible in autumn of 1818, Krimmel decided not to let them intrude upon his art. He probably arrived in high spirits, buoyed by the successful accomplishment of his familial duties in Ebingen and by the opportunities he had been able to take advantage of in the months between the final settlement and his autumn departure.

Such optimism was quickly dampened by the tragic personal news that met him as he disembarked. On August 25, Susana Krimmel had died suddenly at the age of 36.[2] Although he had not lived with his brother's family since 1810, the ties between them had remained strong, as many watercolors of what are presumed to be his brother's wife and children in sketchbook 3 indicate. The only record of how Krimmel dealt with the grief he felt is a single allegorical family portrait that took more than a year for him to compose and execute. While he was formulating the ideas for this canvas and while he was painting it, he also had to earn a living and resume his place in Philadelphia's artistic community.

Before his departure for Europe Krimmel had been the only painter in town to receive recognition for his genre scenes of contemporary life, and fortunately for him, no other artist had replaced him in this specialty. By spring 1819 he was once again actively painting, but because buyers for his American scenes of ordinary life were few, he was also taking on portrait commissions and teaching drawing at a local school.

The first of the portrait commissions may have been for Mary Poulson. According to a calendar Krimmel penned on the inside back cover of sketchbook 6, on May 27, 1819, she stopped by his studio; her parents, Zachariah and Susanna Poulson, visited the following day, probably to make financial arrangements and to inspect Krimmel's work. Little is known about Mary, and it can only be assumed that she was then in her twenties and living at home. Her father was editor and publisher of *Poulson's American Daily Advertiser*; had served for twenty-one years as librarian of the Library Company of Philadelphia; actively supported prison reform, antislavery, and the banning of gambling in the city parks; and promoted civic improvements and the establishment of a fire

1. Many authors have researched the economic developments in and around 1819, and their conclusions about the degree of severity of the depression are by no means unanimous. For an assessment of the impact on Philadelphia, see J. Thomas Jable, "Aspects of Moral Reform in Early Nineteenth-Century Pennsylvania," *Pennsylvania Magazine of History and Biography* 102, no. 3 (July 1978): 344–63, esp. 351–53.

2. Susana was to be buried August 27 at 10 A.M. "from their dwelling" at "the Southwest corner of Pine & 7th Street" (*Poulson's American Daily Advertiser*, August 26, 1818, p. 3). There was no reference to the cause of death.

insurance company (the Philadelphia Contributorship).[3] The nature of the image and the disposition of Mary Poulson's portrait are unknown.

In June 1819, and perhaps even earlier, Krimmel also was working on a portrait of Jacob Ritter, Sr., who years before also had emigrated from Württemberg (fig. 248). In this canvas the artist captured more of the physical and intellectual presence of the sitter than he had with the Becks or the young woman in the blue dress. He rendered an unidealized likeness that suggests a straightforward presentation of character: the subject sits against a plain background, his body positioned so that the composition is triangular, and he looks pensively in the direction of the viewer, his head turned slightly to the left. The colors are warm and rich, the textures are rendered naturalistically, the lighting is effectively handled, and the surface is highly finished.

Ritter, then 65 years old, was a shopkeeper and an elder of the Moravian Church, but in the painting he is presented as a man of botanical interests. He holds a specimen of veronica, a genus of the speedwell family used to treat several ailments as a stomachic tonic, laxative, and antiperiodic; the same plant illustrates the page of the book on which his hand rests. Although the hand-held flower echoes a northern European tradition that American artists had adopted in the previous century (a flower alluded to the sitter's betrothal or a special virtue), Krimmel used it differently. He employed it to indicate his sitter's inquisitive mind, possibly his pharmaceutical business, and quite probably the republican ethos that valued learning and enterprise more than social position. On July 3, 1819, the portrait was finished, for Krimmel noted "Alt Ritters Portr. hgbn." (old Ritter's portrait handed over).[4]

Later in 1819 or early in 1820 Krimmel began work on two more portraits, both apparently on speculation. His subjects were also German Americans who were members of the Moravian community, and both lived in Bethlehem, fifty-three miles north of Philadelphia. The first was John Gottlieb Ernestus Heckewelder, ethnologist, missionary, and author who was then in his late seventies and suffering from severe arthritis. Krimmel's finished canvas conveys Heckewelder's physical frailty, age, and strength of character, and it was achieved by working from a preliminary sketch that the artist probably made during a visit to Bethlehem, possibly during August or September 1819 (fig. 249).

Heckewelder, a man of calm and simplicity who is "at peace with God, with himself, and with all men," squarely faces the viewer, his hands clasp his walking staff, and one elbow rests on a thick book positioned just in front of his hat. Countering the foreground symmetry of the sitter's figure is a background scene that includes a diagonal cliff near the base of which are three Native Americans at a settlement and mountains in the distance. This device was a variation on the eighteenth-century convention of an enclosed background view that provided a space in which the painter added an image that alluded to a sitter's successes, often with reference to real estate. Heckewelder had spent nearly fifty years among the Native Americans, specifically with the Delaware and Mahican, doing most of his missionary work on foot, hence the walking stick and hat; after his final retirement to Bethlehem in 1813 he had devoted himself to writing. Of Heckewelder's essays and books published by Philadelphia's American Philosophical Society, *Account of the History, Manners, and Customs of the Indian Nations Who Once Inhabited Pennsylvania and the Neighboring States* (1819) was the most important, and that is the book Krimmel features in the painting.[5]

3. City directory for Philadelphia, 1819; *Dictionary of American Biography*, s.v. "Poulson." See also Isaiah Thomas, *The History of Printing in America with a Biography of Printers and an Account of Newspapers*, 1874, 2d ed., ed. Marcus A. McCorison (New York: Weathervane Books, 1970), pp. 428, 439, 454–55; Scharf and Westcott, *History*, 3:1967–68. In 1800 Susanna was 44 and presumably near the end of her childbearing years, thus one may speculate that in 1819 Mary was at least 20 and, because her parents were involved in the transaction, still living at home.

4. Sketchbook 6, leaf 14 verso. City directory of Philadelphia, 1819; Charles F. Millspaugh, *The Medicinal Plants: An Illustrated Descriptive Guide*... (Philadelphia: J. C. Yorston, 1892), p. 114. Naeve (*Krimmel*, p. 79) claims Ritter was an importer/druggist; 1819 and 1820 city directories list him as a storekeeper at 70 N. Front Street. Abraham Ritter describes his father as experimenting with "the mysteries of animal magnetism" and hypnotism, with druggist Samuel Wetherill; *History of the Moravian Church in Philadelphia from Its Foundation in 1742 to the Present Time* (Philadelphia: Hayes and Zell, 1857), pp. 278–79. Wetherill ran one of two stores nearby at either 65 N. Front (Samuel Wetherill and Sons) or 76 N. Front Street (Samuel P. Wetherill) and is undoubtedly related to the Wetherill who subsequently acquired the Krimmel sketchbooks. Son Jacob Ritter, Jr., was George Krimmel's business partner; Naeve, *Krimmel*, p. 79. A lithograph, which Abraham Ritter terms a "very correct copy from a portrait by the late J. F. Krimmel" is in Ritter, *History of the Moravian Church*, p. 90, but shows only the face and upper shoulders from the painting; Ritter misdates it as 1818.

5. Edward Rondthaler, *Life of John Heckewelder*, ed. B. H. Coates (Philadelphia: T. Ward, 1847), p. 148; Paul A. W. Wallace, ed., *Thirty Thousand Miles with John Heckewelder* (Pittsburgh: University of Pittsburgh Press, 1958). Heckewelder was born in England of German immigrant parents; they moved to Bethlehem, Pa., in 1754. His expeditions began in the 1760s. His *Account*... was volume 1 of the *Transactions of the American Philosophical Society* in 1819; a German translation was published in Göttingen in 1821, and a French translation was published in Paris in 1822.

The Heckewelder portrait was completed during 1820 because in January 1821, the then ailing Heckewelder wrote to Philadelphia lawyer Peter S. DuPonceau, a longtime friend and supporter who was also a vice-president of the American Philosophical Society: "You astonish me by saying that You had got my picture up in Your Office . . . —'and that it is much admired'— If it is a *good* likeness, Mr. Kremel must be an ingenious Man in the Art of painting, for I never sat half an hour for him to take my likeness. Yet I have within 12 month been told by several Gentlemen who had seen the picture *at* Kremmels, that it was a very good likeness. If I live to go to Philada. once more, I will do myself the pleasure, & call to see it." In 1824, the year after Heckewelder's death, DuPonceau donated the portrait to the Philosophical Society. In 1823 portraitist Jacob Eichholtz executed a posthumous painting of the famous missionary/author, basing his composition on Krimmel's image.[6] Eichholtz's portrait has an idealized yet generalized visage that is far different from the plain and pensive face Krimmel painted.

By early 1821 Krimmel had also finished the portrait of a second Bethlehemite, Francis "Daddy" Thomas, and it had been acquired by P. A. Brown, Esq., in Philadelphia. It was based on a full-page watercolor portrait Krimmel had made in sketchbook 6 (figs. 250, 251). The *Gemeinrath* (common council) had appointed the sprightly but aged Thomas to serve as *Cicerone*, or *Fremdendiener* (strangers' servant), and escort all visitors desiring to see the church, school, and various buildings of the society. He also served as steward of the Moravian Seminary for Young Females.[7]

The drawing of Thomas is a fine example of Krimmel's ability to capture both physique and character. Thomas sits with his legs spread wide apart and hands resting on his knees, his 88-year-old face deeply furrowed and wrinkled, his eyes lively with a slight twinkle. Close comparison of the drawing and the portrait shows how Krimmel transformed his image of the patiently seated, obviously posing sitter into a depiction of a "man on the job," a congenial soul who rests on his walking stick while he talks to the visitors he is escorting about the town. Thomas's face, which was the most detailed part of the drawing, is even more lively in the painting. The curve of his mouth implies he is in midsentence, his dark and bushy eyebrows are emphatic, his wide-open eyes are energetic. As in the Heckewelder portrait, Krimmel positioned Thomas centrally in a frontal view and incorporated background elements to refer to the sitter's achievements.

The marked similarity in the designs of the Thomas and Heckewelder portraits reinforces the presumption that they were done at the same time.[8] Yet why they were done remains less clear. Heckewelder's statements argue that his portrait was not a commission. Because the two portraits were quickly acquired by DuPonceau and Brown, the logical presumption is that Krimmel painted both in the hope that he could find a buyer, just as he had painted his genre scenes.

Although Krimmel adhered to established Anglo-American conventions in his portraits of Ritter, Heckewelder, and Thomas, in his genre work he was abandoning compositional arrangements based on neoclassical precepts that previously had been so satisfactory. This is readily apparent in the genre work he completed and was exhibiting within a few months of his return to Philadelphia.

To the disappointment of the directors of the academy, in Spring 1819 the Society of Artists decided not to organize an annual exhibition, but encouraged

6. Heckewelder to DuPonceau, January 11 and March 31, 1821, Peter S. DuPonceau Papers, American Philosophical Society, Philadelphia; *Who Was Who*, s.v. "DuPonceau"; city directories for Philadelphia, 1819, 1820. The existence of a preliminary drawing of Heckewelder is based on two assumptions: 1) a drawing of the second Moravian, Daddy Thomas, was made in sketchbook 6, and it served as the basis for his portrait; 2) some of the nearby leaves in the sketchbook have been removed. Until recently the painting by Krimmel was misattributed; see *A Catalogue of Portraits and Other Works of Art in the Possession of the American Philosophical Society* (Philadelphia, 1961), pp. 45–46. The Eichholtz picture, signed "J. E. 1823," is now in PAFA; I thank Frank Goodyear, former director, for information about it.

7. John Hill Martin, *Historical Sketch of Bethlehem in Pennsylvania with Some Account of the Moravian Church* (1872; reprint, New York: AMS Press, 1971), pp. 61, 93; Levering, *History*, pp. 550, 632. The second image, long out of public view, was offered for sale by Christie's on May 26, 1988, lot 2. P. A. Brown is listed in the city directory in 1819 and in 1820 as an attorney at law and conveyancer.

8. Because the Thomas sketch is in the sketchbook and the Heckewelder sketch is not, it is likely that one of the later owners of the sketchbook removed it. Winterthur museum records indicate that the donor and possibly prior owners removed some of the pages of the sketchbook and gave them away. The verso leaves were numbered in sketchbook 6 at some time during the nineteenth century, possibly by Krimmel; using that as a guide one can conclude that several pages have been removed.

FIGURE 248
John Lewis Krimmel, Jacob Ritter, Sr., *Philadelphia, 1818/19. Oil on canvas; 29½ x 24½ in. (Kennedy Galleries, New York.)*

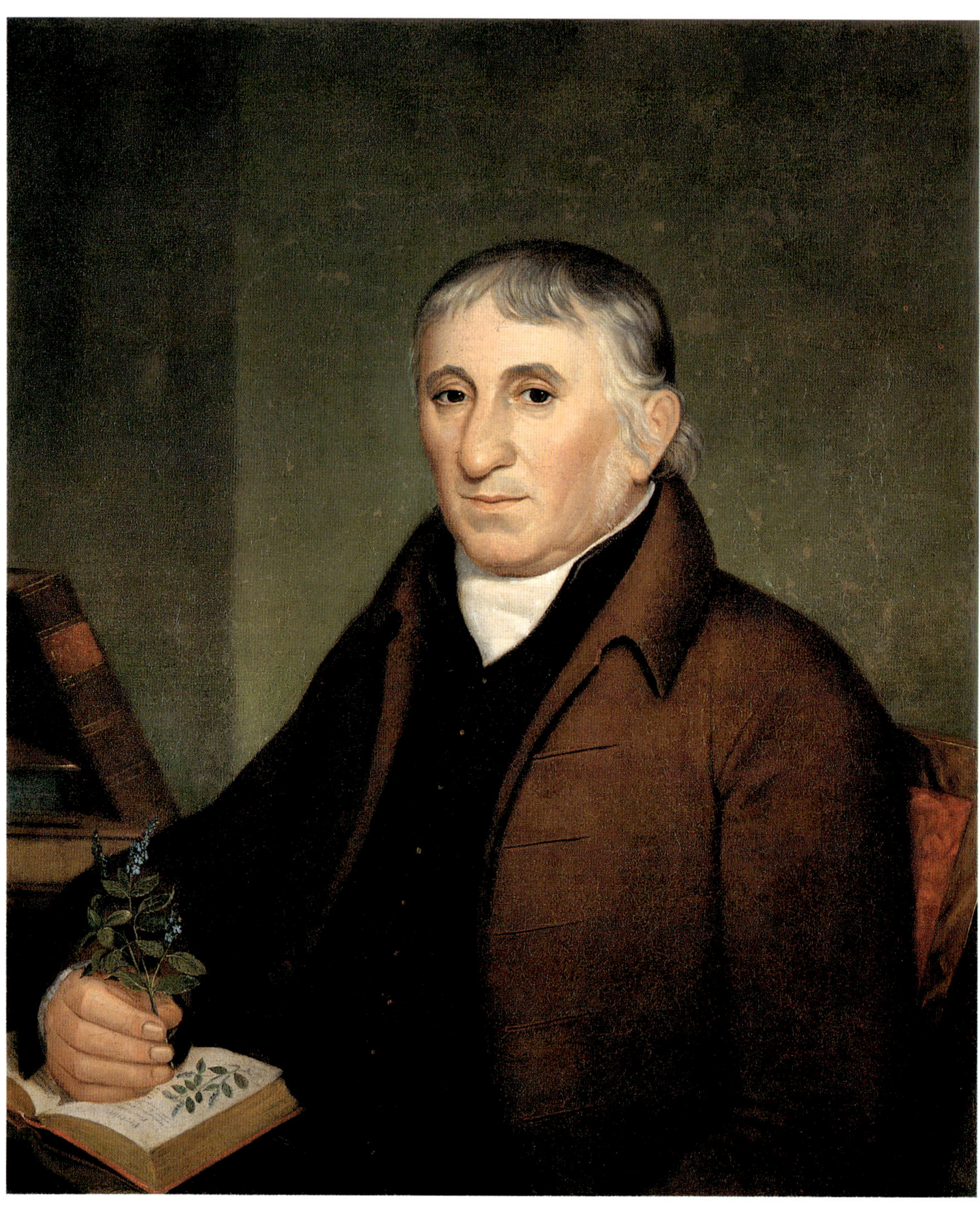

FIGURE 249
John Lewis Krimmel, John Gottlieb Ernestus Heckewelder, *1820. Oil on canvas; 14 5/16" x 12 1/4 in. (American Philosophical Society, Philadelphia.)*

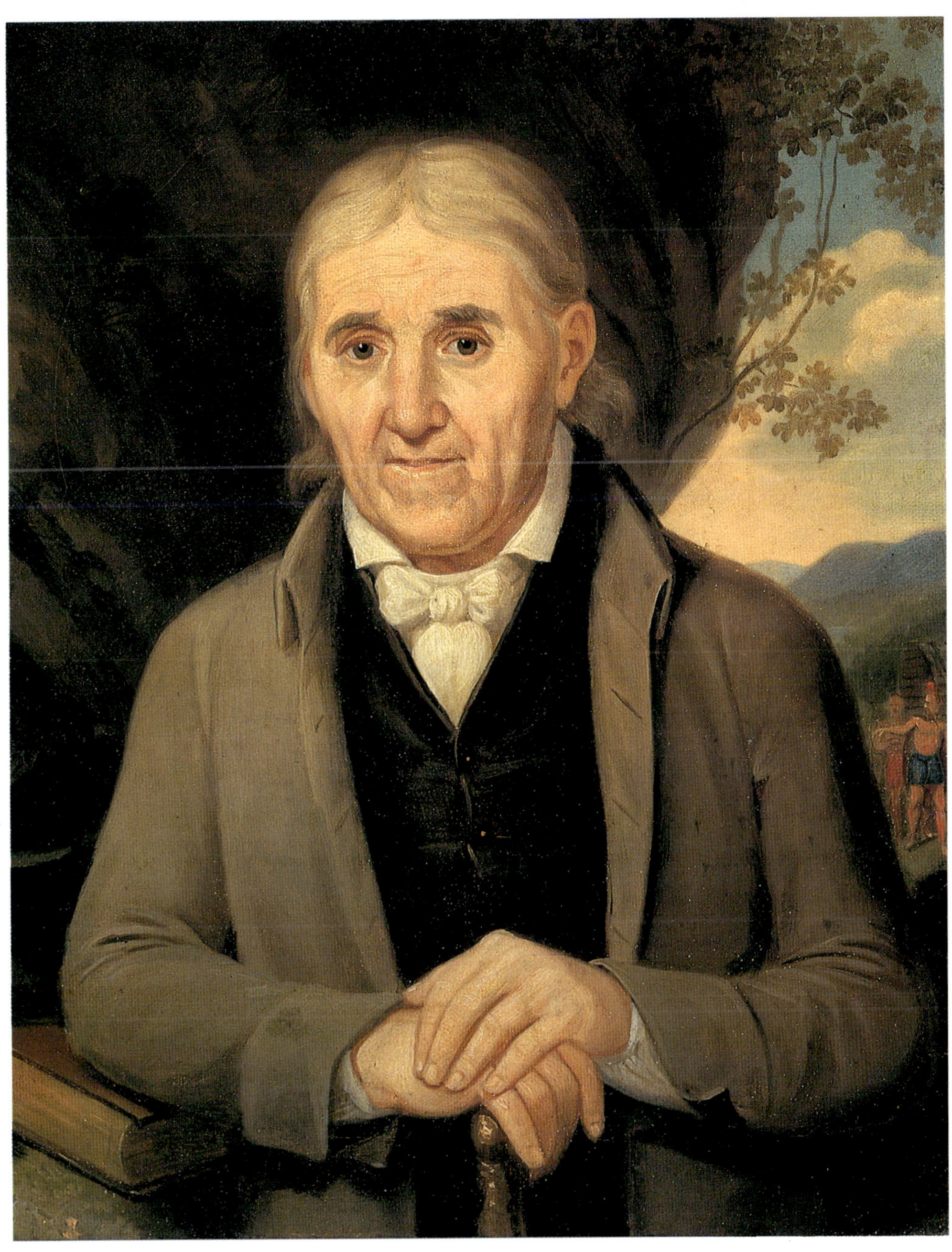

FIGURE 250

Portrait sketch of Francis Thomas, 1819. Watercolor over pencil. Sketchbook 6, leaf 3 recto. Some thirty years later Charles M. Wetherill, who then owned the sketchbooks, added a pencil inscription: "Daddy— oldest inhabitant of Easton."

FIGURE 251

John Lewis Krimmel, Francis Thomas, *1819/20. Watercolor, gouache, and pencil on paper; 5 1/8 x 4 1/8 in. (Photo, Christie, Manson, and Woods, Intl., New York.) The buildings are the Moravian Church at Bethlehem (left) and the Moravian Seminary for young women (right).*

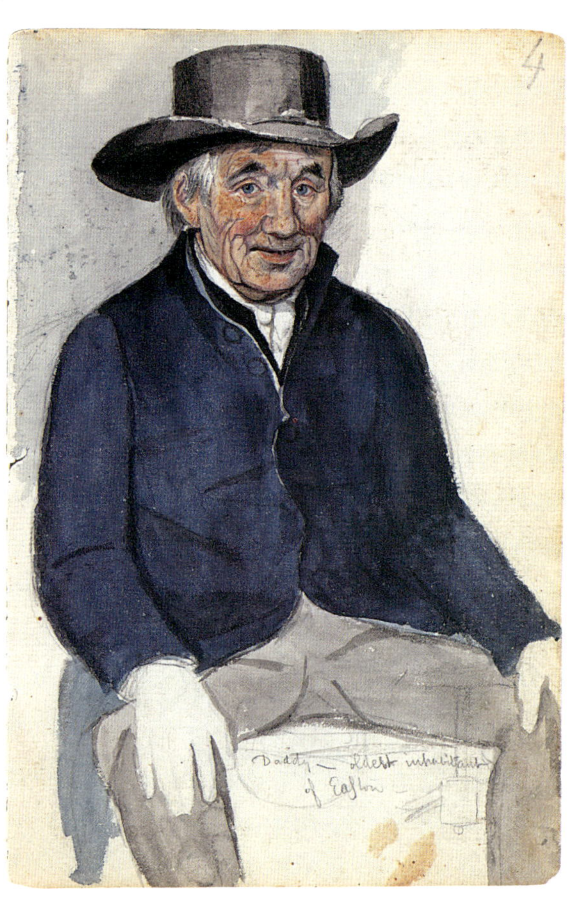

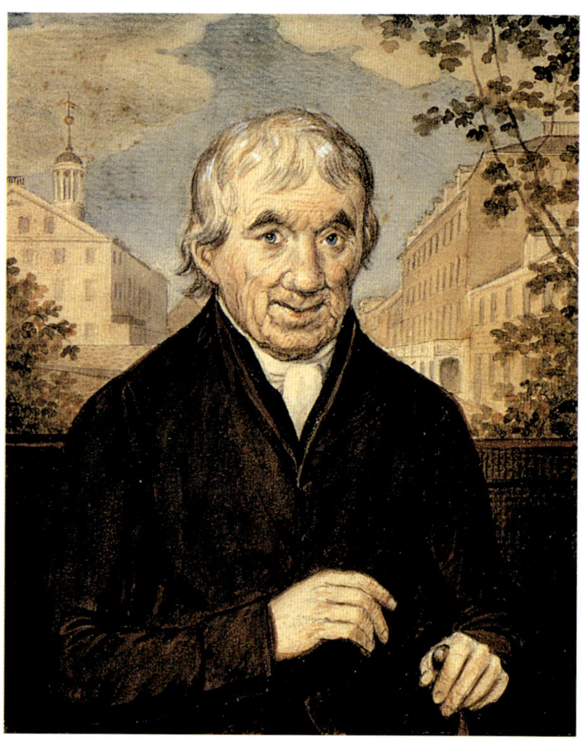

the directors of the academy to organize one. The directors promptly appointed three members, William Rush, Thomas Sully, and John Vaughan, as a committee "to examine the arrangement of the Paintings at the Exhibition at the Academy and to direct such alterations as they may deem necessary."[9]

Among the paintings was Krimmel's *Return from Market*, a simple story extolling rural life and family happiness. Charles Willson Peale, who had deplored Krimmel's pre-1816 decision to do and exhibit copy work, was delighted with the image and described the scene in detail in a letter to his son Rembrandt, then living in Baltimore:

> Crimmel has a cart returned from Market—a story well told. The Cart in front of a farm hou'se, unloading; a young woman receiving her fine bonnet in dancing attitude; Panier on the ground with children overhalling it, they find Cakes, china etc., a strong young man carrying some of the load into the portico; a Woman in the Waggon holding out a rattle to a young child in its mothers arms standing in the Portico, the child eagerly reaching to get the rattle, the Master of the family of Venerable Visage, eager to see the contents of a news paper. Other appendages of a farm are a hen and her chickings and a Cat watching to catch her prey; & a riving of wood in a corner, represented by an axe in a slit of a log, some of the grunting animals in the distant part of the yard—but I had like to have forgot that a pair of Pidgeons billing in the eves of the Portico that covers the heads of the family.

The canvas has since disappeared, but an engraving and mezzotint survive (figs. 252, 253).[10]

Krimmel began with two compositional drawings in sketchbook 2 in 1813 (figs. 254, 255). A drawing in the same book, *Going to Market*, suggests that he planned a companion picture (fig. 256). When Krimmel turned to the subject anew in 1819, he retained the narrative content of the two earlier sketches and the figure types and even paraphernalia that he had used in his pre-1816 paintings, but he rearranged the composition in significantly different ways that demonstrate the thoroughgoing influence of ideas he had absorbed while in Europe. The most obvious change is the increased prominence given to nature and to animals; even more meaningful is the change in definitions of space and structure. In the 1813 sketches of the scene, verticals and horizontals prevail; in the finished painting diagonals dominate—the roof line, the strong contrapposto of the father, the children's raised arms, and the lines of the horse. In the sketches, neoclassical notions of bilateral symmetry, horizontal orientation, and centripetal gestures determine the figural composition; in the painting the composition is organized through pyramidal groups of figures that interlock from left to right and from front to back. To strengthen the coherence of the design the artist placed the kneeling children in line with the figure of the mother and repeated the shape of the basket in the hatbox, an element introduced only in the final version of the image. He increased the depth of the scene by playing foreground figures against those in the middle ground and by expanding the design at both sides—to the right, a view of the kitchen; to the left, a view of the fences and farm buildings. The careful placement of two seemingly minor elements—the broom and the ax—directs the viewer's eye beyond the picture frame. The clothesline across the porch and the bird cage hanging next to it effect a trompe l'oeil quality that reinforces the illusion of pictorial depth.

9. Minutes of the Board of Directors, April 7, May 12 and 19, 1819, PAFA, microfilm. The society's lack of interest in organizing an annual exhibition coincides with their efforts to open an exhibition and sales gallery elsewhere in the city.

10. Charles Willson Peale to Rembrandt Peale, May 22, 1819, typescript, Peale-Sellers Papers, American Philosophical Society, Philadelphia. Note that Peale misidentified the grandparents as parents and made no mention of the black boy. The 1819 exhibition records in Rutledge, *Cumulative Record*, p. 116, omit Krimmel's name from the exhibitors list. In 1820 Lawson possessed and possibly owned *Return from Market*; see "Krimmel's Picture—*Return from Boarding School*," pp. 507–8. Lawson lent the painting to PAFA in 1843 and presumably also for the 1831 exhibition, but no owners are credited in that catalogue. In the 1850s J. A. Brown lent it to PAFA. Lawson's engraving, *Happy Family*, illustrated "Happiness," a poem in G. T. Bedell, ed., *The Religious Souvenir: A Christmas, New Year's and Birthday Present for 1834* (Philadelphia: Key and Biddle, 1834), p. 254. He reissued the plate as *The Farmer*, accompanying "The Happy Farmer," in Edward C. Biddle, ed., *Selected Poems by Mrs. L. Sigourney* (Philadelphia: Edward C. Biddle, 1842), facing p. 103. The Sartain mezzotint, *Home Scene with Presents: Returned from Market*, was a premium from *Eclectic Magazine of Foreign Literature, Science, and Art*.

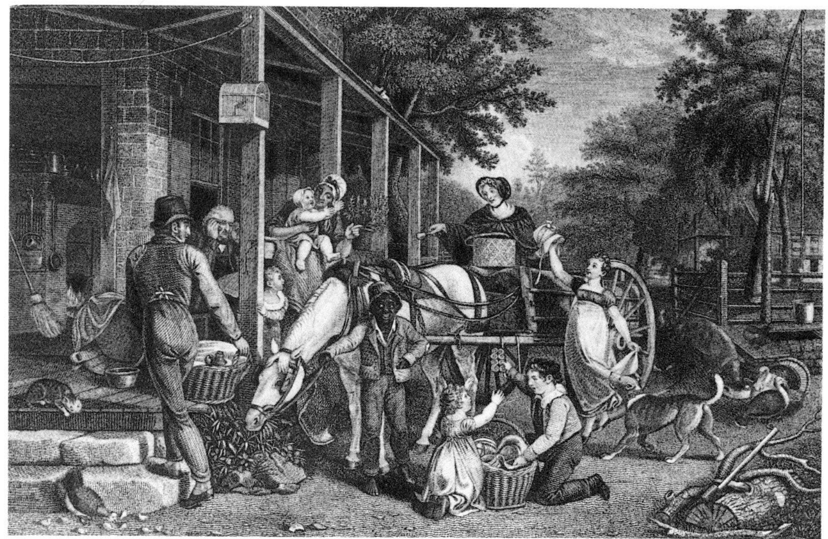

FIGURE 252
Alexander Lawson, The Happy Family, *1832–34, after Krimmel,* Return from Market *(1819). Engraving; 4 3/8 x 6 1/2 in. Published by Key and Biddle, Philadelphia. (Joseph Downs Collection of Manuscripts and Printed Ephemera, Winterthur.)*

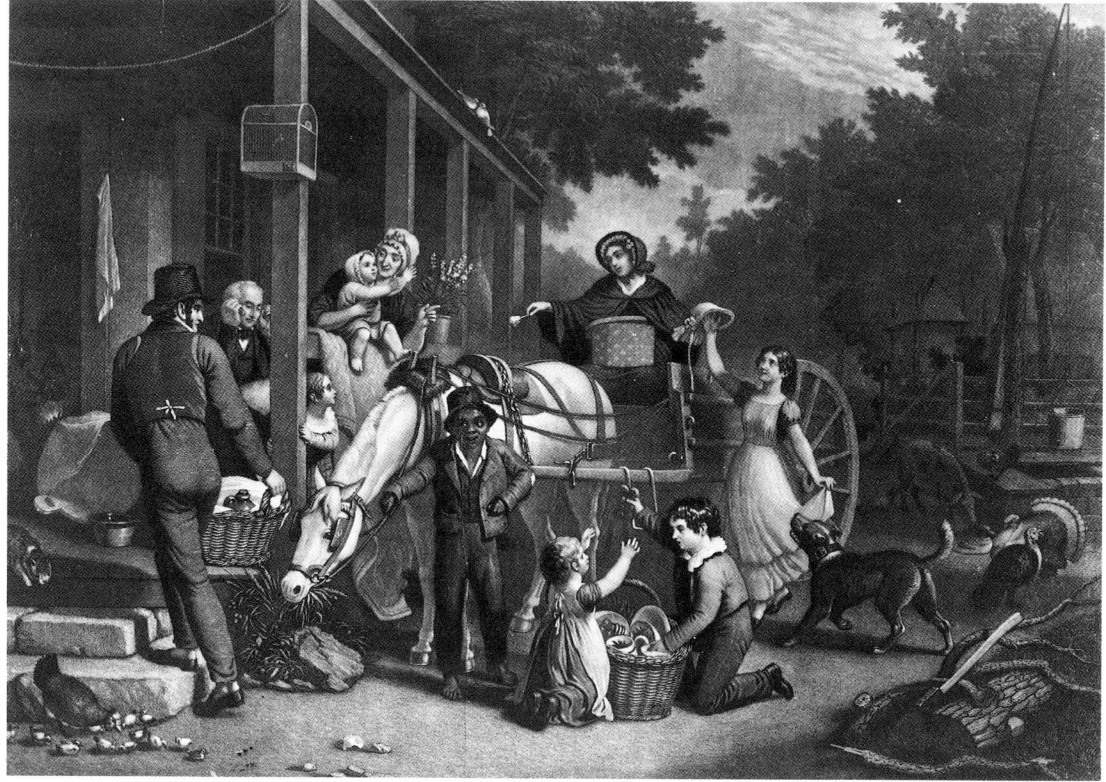

FIGURE 253
John Sartain, Home Scene with Presents: Returned from Market, *ca. 1850. Mezzotint engraving; 9 3/8 x 13 9/16 in. Published by W. Bidwell, New York. (Private collection.) Although Sartain updated Krimmel's image by altering clothing and hair styles, it has a rich differentiation of light and dark and probably more closely approximates the original painting than the Lawson engraving.*

FIGURE 254
Compositional sketch for Return from Market, *ca. 1813. Ink and ink wash over pencil. Sketchbook 2, leaf 3 recto.*

FIGURE 255
Compositional sketch for Return from Market, *ca. 1813. Ink and ink wash over pencil. Sketchbook 2, leaf 5 recto.*

FIGURE 256
Study for Going to Market, *ca. 1813. Pencil. Sketchbook 2, leaf 9 recto.*

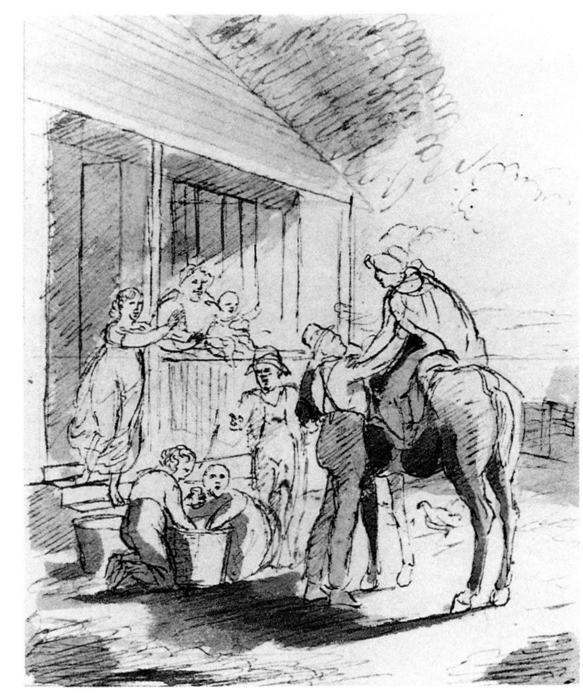

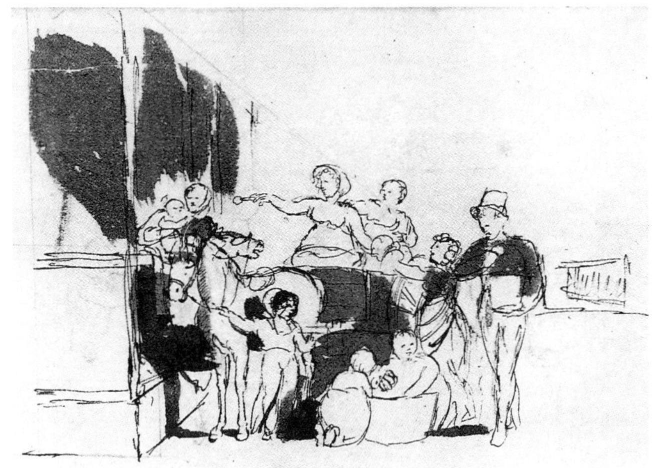

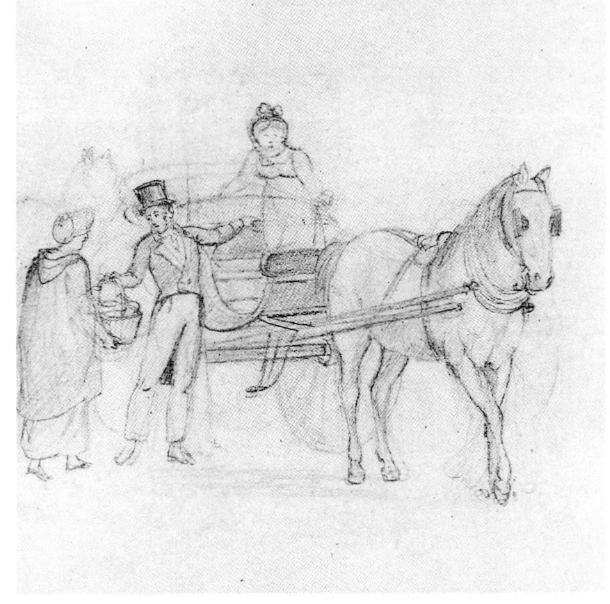

The outwardly casual 1819 figural arrangement is deceptive. The lively actions of the ten figures are bound by a circulating movement that starts on the left with the father carrying a basket up the stairs. The lines of his energetic contrapposto travel to the grandfather who puts on his glasses to read the newspaper, to the grandmother who points to the bell and the baby who reaches for it, and to the little boy who looks toward the mother standing with outstretched arms in the carriage. The mother as the apex of a pyramid turns the direction of rotation toward the older daughter whose raised hand and exuberant gesture correspond to the elevated arm of the kneeling boy. The motion of his arm visually connects with the upheld hands of his little sister on the other side of the basket. The boy holding the feeding horse acts as a stable middle amidst the excitedly stirring family, and his function as a still focus is reinforced by the post behind him, which extends the vertical line to the top of the image.

The artist conveys vigorous motion by reusing old figure types with greater effectiveness. The father moves with greater vitality than does a similarly drawn figure who steps onto the curb in the right foreground of *Election Day 1815* or the man twisting his body as he pastes a poster in the left foreground of *Election Day 1816.* The artist also added details he had recently drawn in his sketchbooks (figs. 257–260). In the painting Krimmel has conveyed an exceptional, almost euphoric spirit. The artist's emphasis on emotions is shown in the excitement prompted by the parents' arrival home, their pleasure in bringing supplies and gifts, and the delight these elicit from those who receive them. The well-orchestrated vitality of this scene is further enhanced by the profuse foliage of the trees in the background and the abundance of barnyard animals.

Compared with Krimmel's earlier scenes of family life in interior settings, this idealized vision of family life in the country suggests the influence of romanticism he had absorbed in Europe. The subject also reflects the artist's own rural background and demonstrates his belief in the strength of familial ties. Although the painting does not hint at the postwar economic depression that wracked the United States or even the hardship of farm work, it conveys Krimmel's sensitivity to extremes in economic and social position—it is the black farmhand who stands barefoot and poorly dressed and looks troubled in a pose reminiscent of the penniless boy in *Cherry Woman with Children.* This is Krimmel's first overtly rural exterior scene filled with people, but it by no means reflected an only recent exposure to rural life. Krimmel knew the rural Pennsylvania countryside, as is apparent from his sketchbooks and what we know of his travels during his first six years in his new homeland. Although he lived in the nation's largest city, he knew that most people lived in rural settings and was likewise aware of the power that the mental image of starting anew further West held for most Americans. This may well explain why the image was reissued later in the century.

It was about this time that Krimmel painted another rural image, this one an interior scene, and it too demonstrates the impact of his trip to Europe on his approach to art. The painting, *Country Frolic and Dance*, may be the image referred to as "Country Dance" in the February 1820 issue of *Analectic*. If so, it was begun soon after Krimmel set foot on shore, freshly impressed with design concepts of Netherlandish genre art he saw in Vienna or during his brief stay in Amsterdam in September 1818. The structural composition seems to paraphrase Flemish and Dutch models, for example Jan Steen's *Dancing Couple*,

FIGURE 257
Horses, ca. 1819. Watercolor and ink over pencil. Sketchbook 6, leaf 4 recto.

FIGURE 258
Horse, ca. 1819. Watercolor over pencil. Sketchbook 6, leaf 4 verso.

FIGURE 259
Young rooster, hen, dog, ca. 1819. Watercolor over pencil. Sketchbook 7, leaf 19 verso.

FIGURE 260
Barnyard fowl, ca. 1819. Ink over pencil, watercolor, watercolor over pencil. Sketchbook 7, leaf 16 verso.

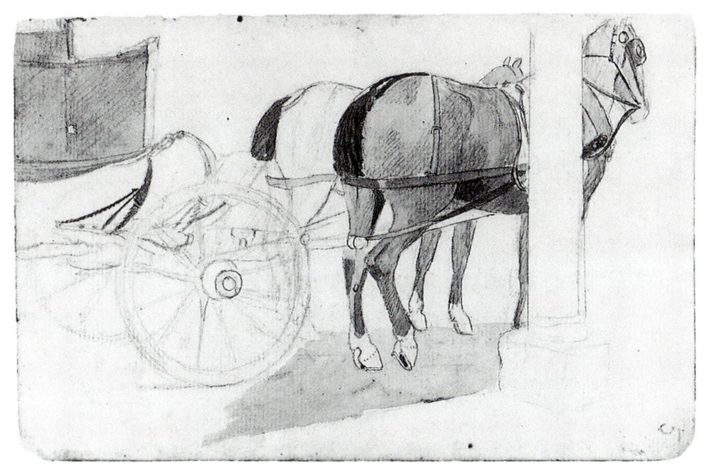

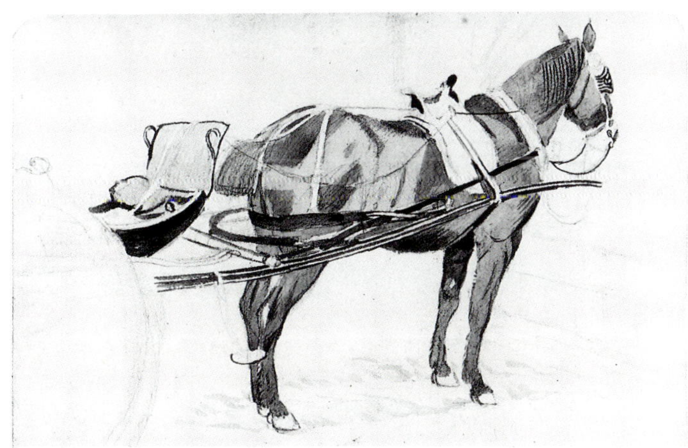

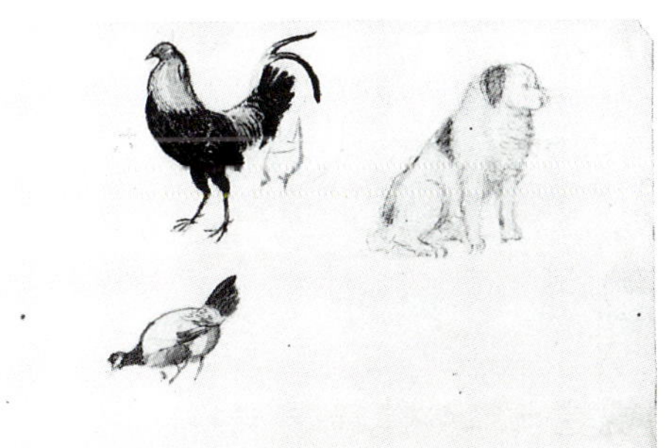

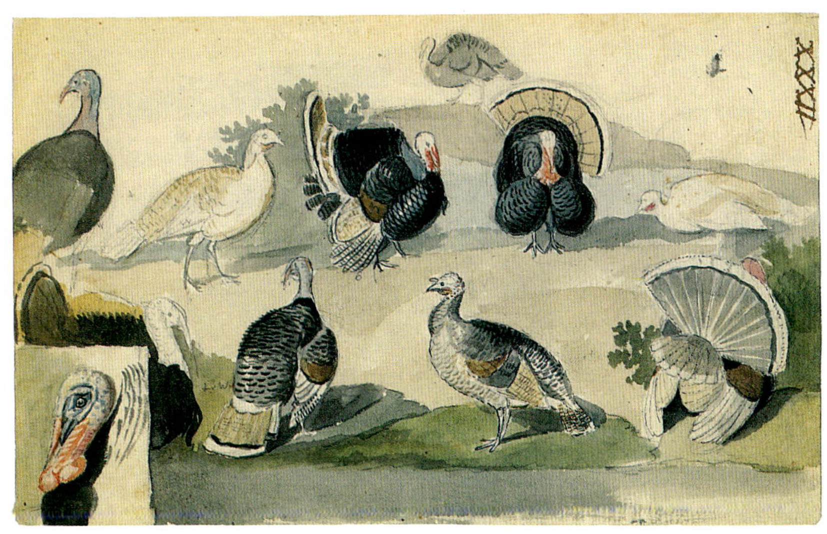

which also depicts a central dancing couple, figures and furniture aligned on a diagonal to the left side, clear verticals and horizontals on the right side, a seated figure shown in rear view, a man standing in an open door, and a suspended bird cage in the left background. Krimmel adopted the Netherlandish formula to American subject matter when he decided to present the manner in which people in Pennsylvania amused themselves while at an inn, a topic he had explored six years earlier in a watercolor he had sold to Pavel Svinin (see fig. 70). This earlier image was seemingly based on firsthand observation and depicted two young couples dancing in the waiting room of a coach station, but the setting in the 1819 painting is more obviously the main room of a tavern, and only one couple dances (fig. 261). Many elements are not new. The portrait of George Washington is the same one Krimmel used in his 1819 Fourth of July picture. The broadside with the image of a horse, the fiddler's chair, and the tavernkeeper's wooden stall had appeared in the 1813 tavern painting. The bird cage is similar to those in *Quilting Frolic* (1813) and *Return from Market* (1819), and the rifle over the door can be found in *Quilting Frolic* and *Dance in a Wayside Inn.* The figure types of the dancers, fiddler, and flirting couple in *Country Frolic and Dance* are basically the same as those he used six years earlier in *Dance in a Wayside Inn*, but they function differently. The fiddler is positioned to the same side and holds the bow in the same manner as the musician in Wilkie's *Blind Fiddler*, of which Krimmel had painted a copy.[11]

Krimmel's improved ability to handle interior space is obvious. *Country Frolic and Dance* is designed around an invisible central axis with open space in the middle. The viewer's eye moves easily from foreground to background, from the main focus—the dancers—to secondary narratives that involve the other figures. The figures are interspersed consecutively from foreground to middle ground to background. Depth is further articulated by their movements: people turn and gesture in many directions, carrying the motion from front to back through the scene.

The following year Krimmel produced a watercolor copy of *Country Frolic and Dance*, and he made subtle but important improvements (fig. 262). The configuration of the advertisements on the chimney breast is more effective, and the fire burns more brightly and throws stronger and more effective reflections across the room. His figures display his progressively better understanding of anatomy and movement. The figures and faces are more expressive; this is particularly noticeable in the dancers who are more slender, more elongated, and more graceful. The posture of the flirting couple is more convincing: the man holds his head a bit back and his right shoulder further forward; the woman's head is slightly more inclined. The flowing contrapposto of the male dancer is a posture Krimmel was working at refining, for it appears in the figure of the father in *Return from Market*, also painted in 1819.[12]

Although the subject of country dances had a long history in European art (earlier examples are in the works of Brueghel, Rubens, Teniers), it had not existed in American art. Krimmel introduced it and used it as an opportunity to present a slice of American life. He chose not to stress rural aspects but instead focused on the variety of people who might belong to a sleighing party or be waiting for the next stage to arrive or for nightfall to come.

Krimmel's 1819–21 sketchbooks give further evidence of his changed approach to defining pictorial depth. A full-page watercolor in sketchbook 6 dated Sunday, July 4, 1819, depicts two people in an interior (fig. 263).[13] Krimmel has focused on elements that deepen the pictorial space: along the

11. An intriguing coincidence is that Krimmel's copy of Wilkie's *Blind Fiddler* was exhibited at the academy in New York in 1820. Perhaps his reexamination of that picture in order to adapt some features to his new composition sparked his decision to exhibit it in New York; see Mary Bartlett Cowdrey, *American Academy of Fine Arts and American Art-Union: Exhibition Record, 1816–1852*, Collections of the New-York Historical Society, vol. 76 (New York, 1953), p. 218.

12. In 1835 or 1836 Philadelphian George Lehman made a lithograph based on the 1820 watercolor version of *Country Frolic and Dance* and marketed it with his partner, Cephas Grier Childs.

13. On the same day Krimmel was in Centre Square, where he sketched Philadelphia's Fourth of July celebration.

back wall is a door, slightly ajar, and a tall hutch; against the adjacent wall is a cast-iron cookstove (disconnected and pushed aside for the summer). The perspective, showing part of the ceiling, conveys both size and scale. Clearly the artist was more interested in exploring ways of defining the space than in depicting the activity of the figures. His approach is comparable to that practiced by contemporary German artists such as Friedrich Georg Kersting and Franz Seraph Stirnbrand. Kersting, who worked mostly in Dresden, became known for his intimate but spacious interiors with one or two figures quietly engrossed in a task or by a thought. His rooms are always shown with part of the ceiling visible, and there is always a large, empty foreground floor space. Krimmel's art is even closer in style and spirit to that of Stirnbrand, a Stuttgart artist, who painted *Eine Familie Baumeister* (The Baumeister Family) (1815), which likewise has but a few individuals in a large spacious interior, and in it the ceiling and an open foreground floor space are important elements. Krimmel may well have seen this 1815 canvas while in Stuttgart.[14]

In another watercolor of a room in which a woman irons and folds laundry, Krimmel focused more obviously on abstract design qualities (fig. 264). Yet despite the attention Krimmel gave to the details of the activity, he was less concerned with describing the woman's work procedure than with conveying the geometry of the scene. What fascinated him more were the volumetric shapes of the furnishings and the perspective lines he could achieve by incorporating the views beyond the large open windows. In other drawings Krimmel focused solely on architecture or nature in an effort to refine further his new ideas about conveying space (figs. 265–267).

Similar spatial concepts exist in a contemporaneous watercolor entitled *The Watercolor Class* (fig. 268), by an anonymous artist. Similar to Krimmel's view of the Pennsylvania kitchen, it has a rhythmic punctuation of space, achieved by the long curtains and tall window frames. The somewhat askew perspective lines of the benches and tables and views through the windows compare with Krimmel's sketch of the woman ironing laundry. The preponderance of geometric lines in *The Watercolor Class* also compares with another Krimmel watercolor of a yard scene (fig. 269), completed the same day as the full-page interior in sketchbook 6. Further, a similar type of young woman appears in Krimmel's sketchbooks (figs. 270–274). While *The Watercolor Class* is intriguing because its artist was simultaneously exploring the same concepts as Krimmel, the happenstance is all the more interesting because Krimmel also helped support himself by teaching drawing.

One of Krimmel's teaching stints in private schools occurred in the spring immediately following his return from Germany. Beside May 17, in the calendar he had penned for May 1819 in sketchbook 6, he wrote: "Anf. d. Examination v.d. Schule" (start of the school examination). But according to Dunlap, in at least one instance this artist-turned-drawing-teacher resigned after discovering that he and his employer disagreed:

> Krimmel, like an honest and conscientious man, was in the habit of teaching the girls what to do, how to do, and then leaving them to do it, under instruction. The consequence was, that his pupils did not produce, in a given time, such pretty pictures as were presented to their parents by the young ladies of a rival establishment, where the cunning and complaisant teacher put his lessons in practice by finishing the work his pupils were utterly incompetent to the production of, and thus cheating papas

14. *Eine Familie Baumeister* is illustrated in Staatsgalerie Stuttgart, *Schwaben sehen Schwaben*, p. 78.

FIGURE 261
John Lewis Krimmel, Country Frolic and Dance, *1819. Oil on canvas; 16½ x 22½ in. (Private collection.) The painting is dated on the almanac suspended from the corner post of the taproom.*

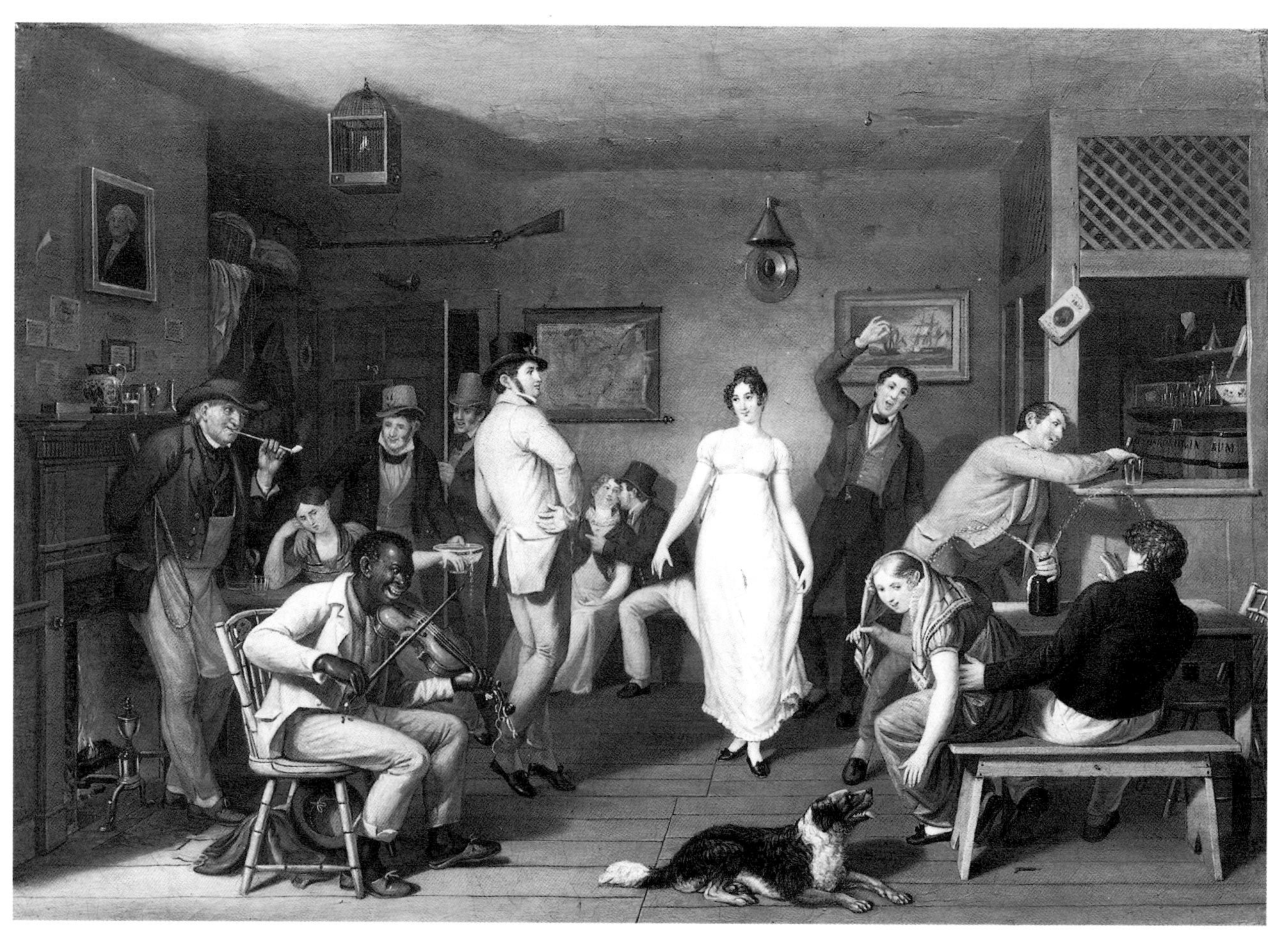

FIGURE 262
John Lewis Krimmel, Country Frolic and Dance, *1820. Watercolor over pencil and ink. (Library of Congress, Prints and Photographs Division.)*

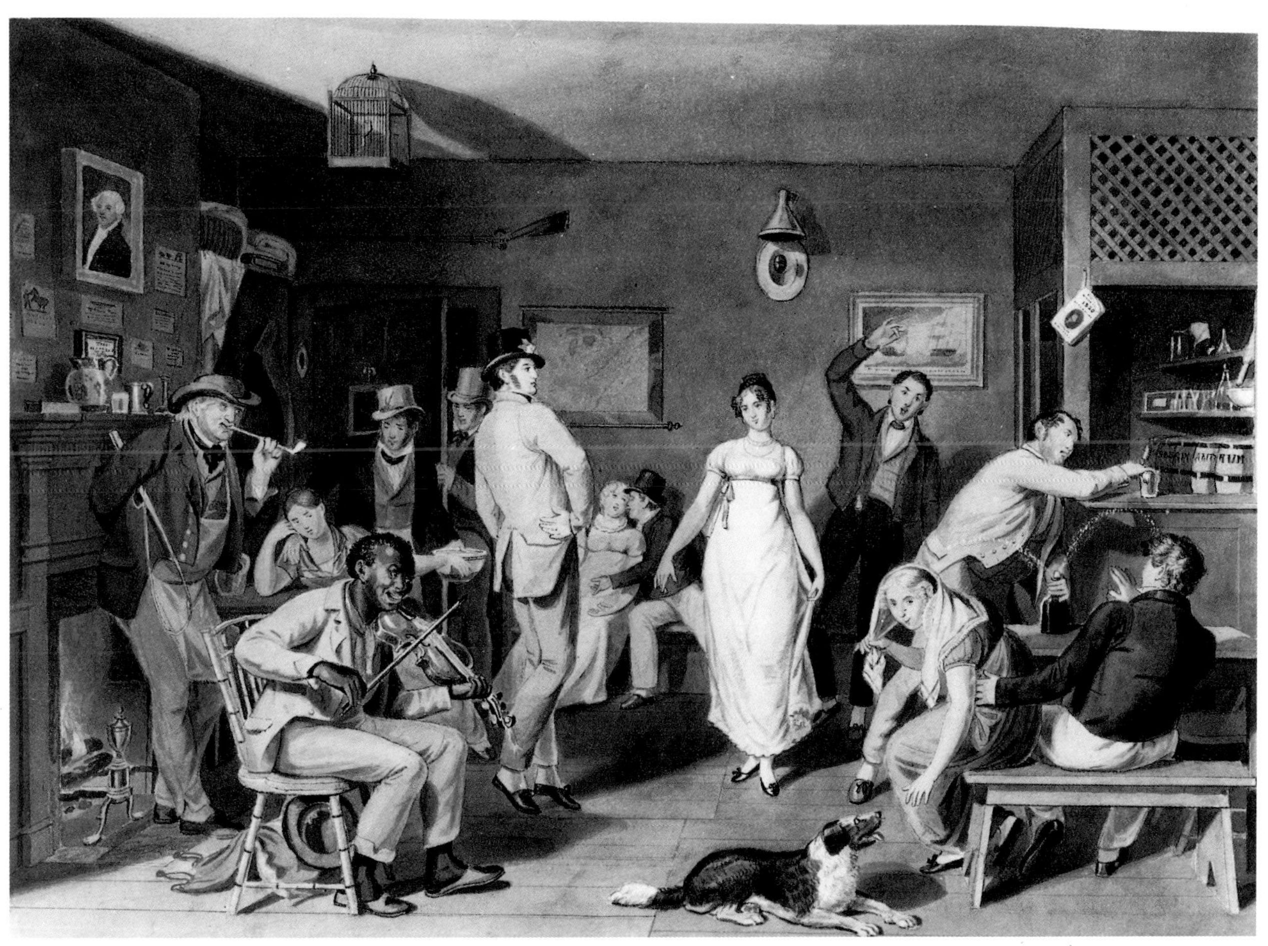

FIGURE 263
View into kitchen of a house, Sunday, July 4, 1819. Watercolor over pencil, pencil inscription. Sketchbook 6, leaf 3 verso.

FIGURE 264
Woman pressing and folding laundry, ca. 1819/20. Watercolor over pencil. Sketchbook 7, leaf 9 verso.

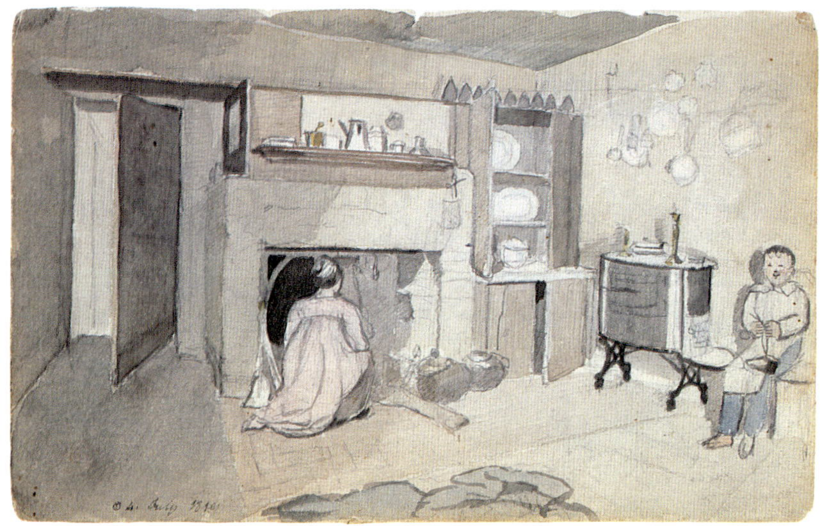

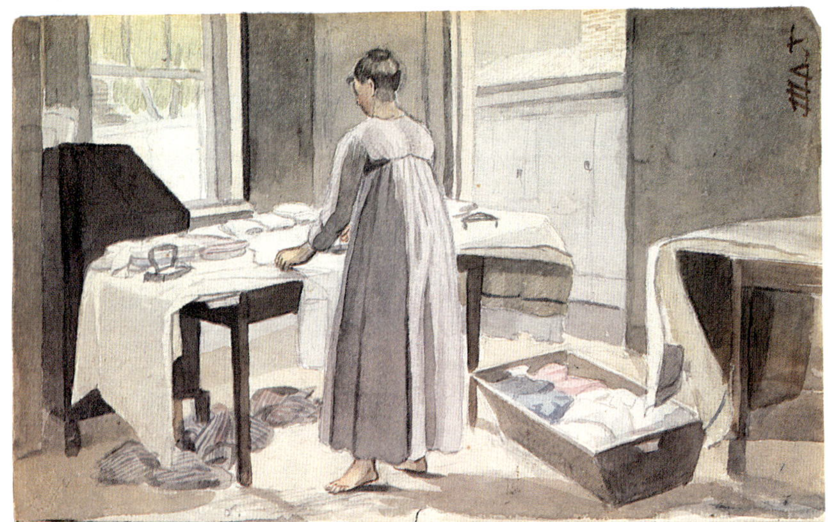

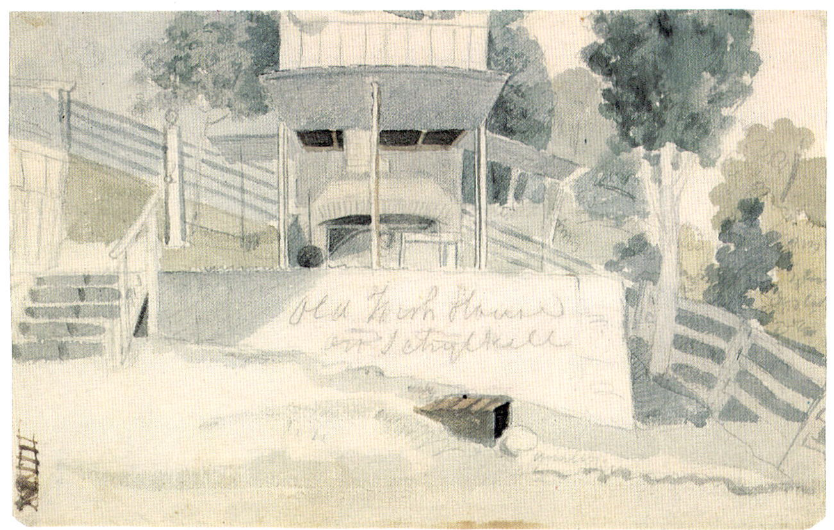

FIGURE 265
Old Fish House on Schuylkill, 1819–21. Watercolor over pencil, pencil inscription. Sketchbook 7, leaf 22 verso.

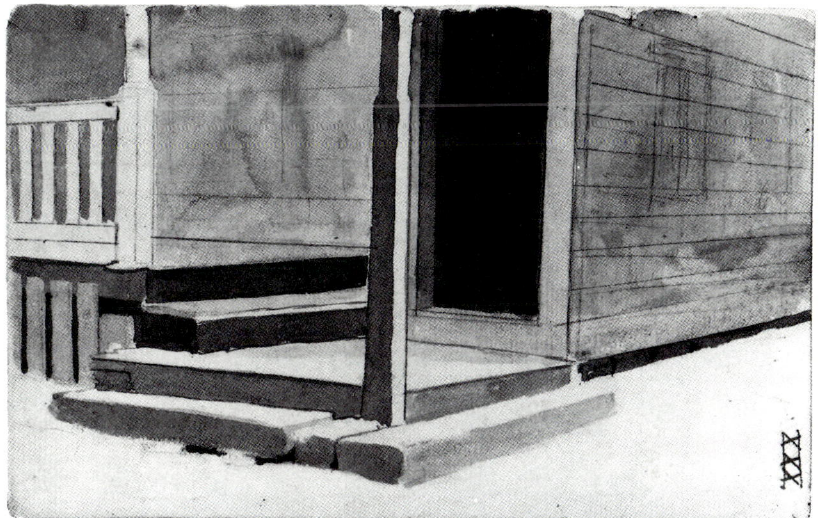

FIGURE 266
Front corner of porch, 1819–21. Watercolor over pencil. Sketchbook 7, leaf 16 recto.

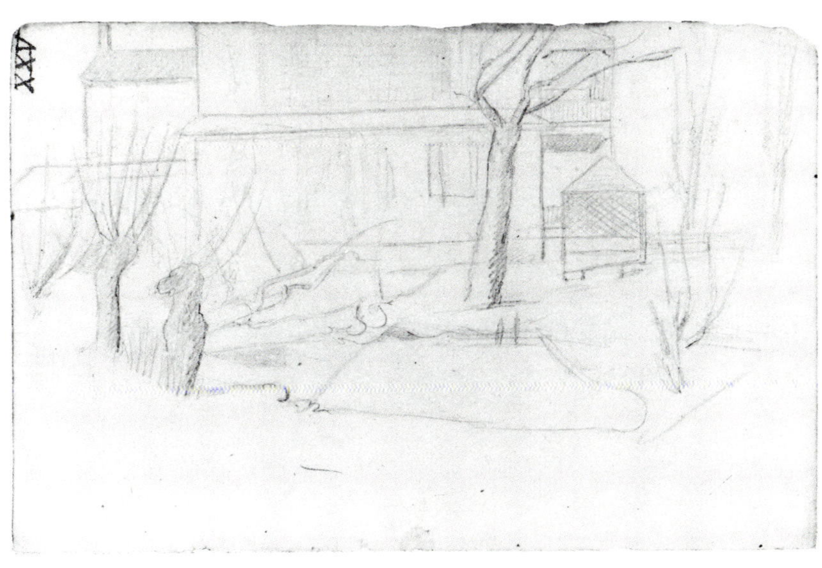

FIGURE 267
House, 1819–21. Pencil. Sketchbook 7, leaf 13 recto.

FIGURE 268
The Watercolor Class, *1819/20. Watercolor; 14 3/8 x 22 in. (Emily Crane Chadbourne Collection, The Art Institute of Chicago.)*

FIGURE 269
Yard at Bushhill, Sunday, July 4, 1819. Watercolor over pencil, pencil inscription. Sketchbook 6, leaf 11 recto.

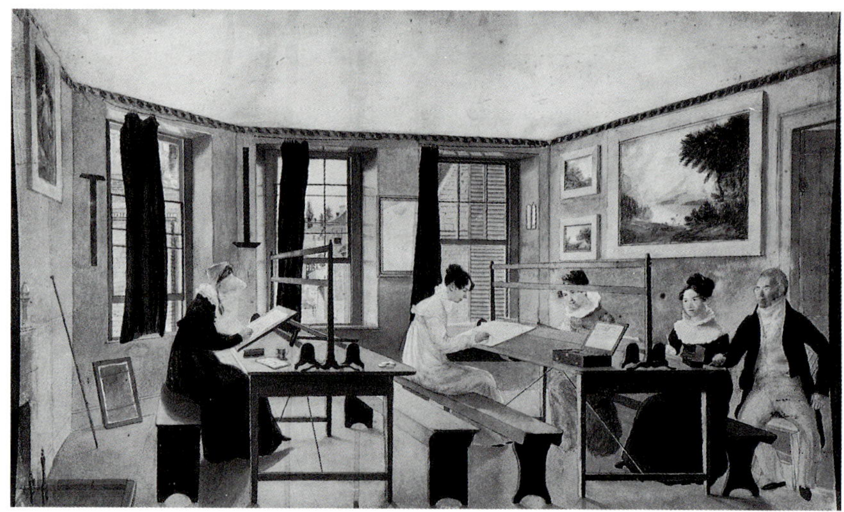

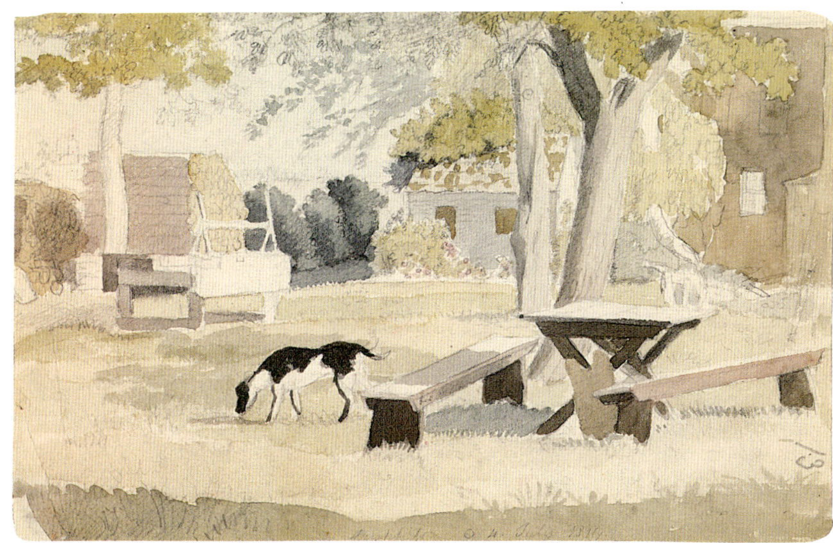

FIGURE 270
Woman sewing, boy eating, girl sitting, ca. 1819. Watercolor over pencil. Sketchbook 6, leaf 8 recto.

FIGURE 271
Two needleworkers, ca. 1819. Watercolor over pencil, pencil inscription. Sketchbook 6, leaf 2 recto. Inscription reads: "Mrs Jones—with whom Krimmell boarded."

FIGURE 272
Two needleworkers, ca. 1819. Watercolor over pencil. Sketchbook 6, leaf 9 verso.

FIGURE 273
Woman, faces, ca. 1819. Pencil. Sketchbook 7, leaf 18 recto.

FIGURE 274
Two women, ca. 1819. Pencil and watercolor over pencil. Sketchbook 7, leaf 21 recto.

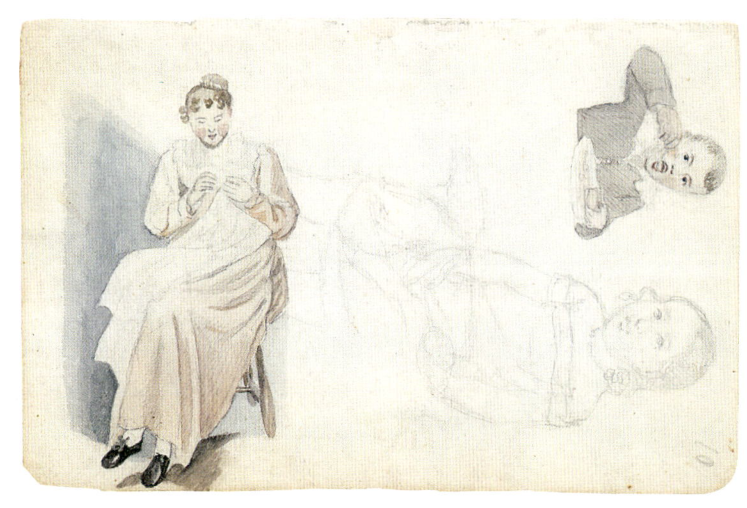

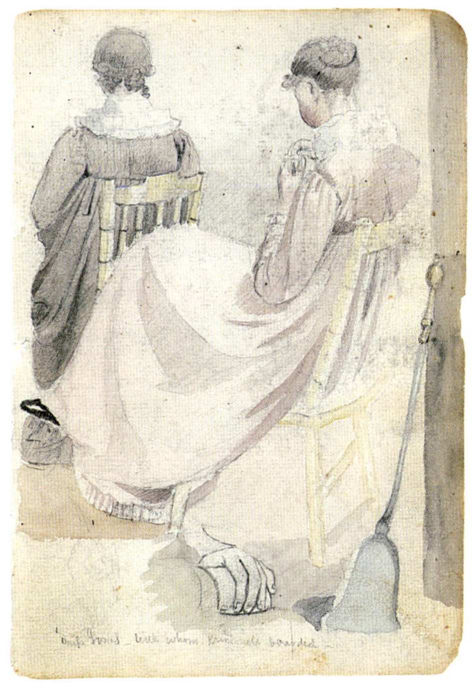

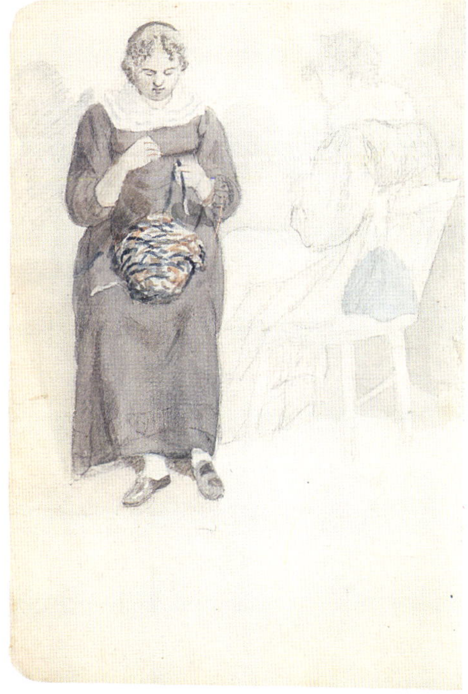

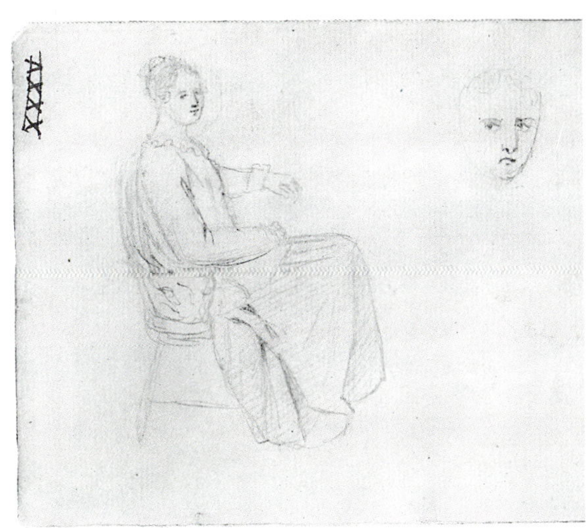

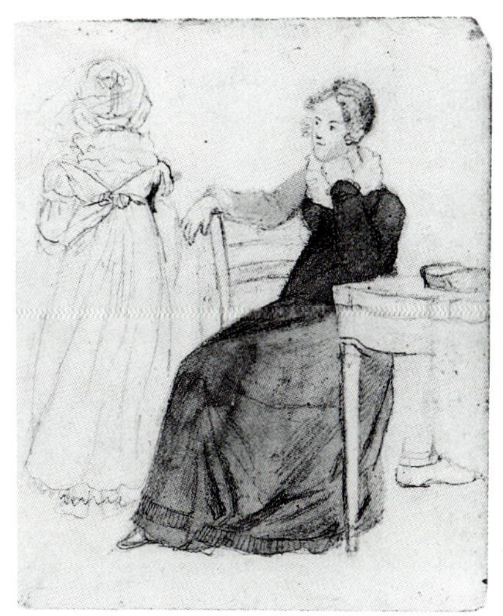

and mamas, and increasing the reputation of the school. Krimmel was told by the proprietor of the establishment that he must not only teach her scholars to draw and paint, but must draw and paint for them, or give up the school. The unbending Württemberger did not choose to be an agent in deceit, and chose the latter part of the conditions. Honesty, poverty, a clear conscience and independence were preferable, in his mind, to money, servility and falsehood.[15]

Whenever he could, Krimmel studied and drew, continually working at conveying the illusion of depth. An opportunity to hone his skills arrived with a traveling exhibition of *The Choir of the Capuchin Church in Rome*, a painting acclaimed for its deep spatial perspective and classically balanced design (fig. 275). It was the most famous of many interiors of churches and monasteries by François Marius Granet, who had studied with David. While living in Rome Granet depicted an interior view of a church in the Piazza Barberini during a worship service. The picture proved so successful that he received orders for at least ten copies, one of which came from Benjamin Wiggins of Boston. The Wiggins version was sent on tour in the United States and was probably in Philadelphia in summer or autumn of 1819, at which time Krimmel made a watercolor sketch, which he identified as "Grenet 1818," perhaps signifying the year that Granet painted this particular copy (fig. 276).[16]

The compositional rules underlying the painting, especially the organization of the figures along the lines of perspective, had considerable impact on the way Krimmel designed his paintings in the 1819–21 period—even his portraits. The change becomes clear when the Ritter portrait (see fig. 248) is compared with the Heckewelder and Thomas portraits (see figs. 249, 251). The earlier painting has a shallow background space; the other two have great depth.

Granet's dynamic geometry had an even stronger influence on Krimmel's genre paintings, as *Fourth of July Celebration in Centre Square, Philadelphia, 1819* demonstrates (fig. 277). In this image Krimmel applied Granet's concepts of symmetrical balance, strong centrality, and stability to give a firm structure to an extraordinarily busy scene. The perspective lines of the tents converge on the domed pumphouse in much the same way the perspective lines of the walls converge in the vaulted area at the rear of Granet's chapel. The calculations necessary to achieve this composition are readily evident in a comparison of the finished image with the preparatory sketches. The sketches are, quite simply, records of what the artist observed and not part of his design process; the finished picture has a very different structure.

Krimmel walked to Centre Square on July 4, 1819, with a specific objective in mind: to find an idea for a genre painting. As he scrutinized the people and the place, he sketched whatever caught his eye. He later organized these elements and created a scene featuring a vigorous, milling crowd—a watercolor that in its rich variety of genre elements surpasses all previous images.[17]

Seven years earlier Krimmel had depicted the observance of the same holiday in the same square. A comparison of the two pictures reveals the dramatic changes that had taken place both in Americans' life-styles and the artist's painting style during the intervening years. The 1812 holiday was a pleasant gathering of a small group of city folk—more sedate than the rowdy celebrations of the previous decade, which had prompted the city to ban gambling in public parks. Adults in their best clothes politely conversed with their social peers. Only young boys and dogs moved about, and a single vendor's table was the

15. Dunlap, *History*, pp. 393–94. His experiences prompted him to draw and possibly to paint a pair of satirical pictures about the value of boarding school education (see chap. 5).

16. Thieme and Becker, *Allgemeines Lexikon*, s.v. "Granet, François Marius"; Naeve, *Krimmel*, p. 175; Dunlap, *History*, 1:274; Dunlap, *Diary*, p. 704. The Wiggins copy may have been the only one in America. During July 1821 Thomas Sully went to Boston to paint a finished copy of the Wiggins painting. Granet's picture was also a design model for Henry Sargent's *Dinner Party* (ca. 1821; Museum of Fine Arts, Boston) and *Tea Party* (ca. 1823; Museum of Fine Arts, Boston).

17. The watercolor remained in his studio until his death two years later. Quite possibly he intended to use it as the source for either an oil painting or a large print, such as an aquatint that could be hand-colored.

FIGURE 275
François Marius Granet, The Choir of the Capuchin Church in Rome, *Rome, 1815. Oil on canvas; 77½ x 58¼ in. (The Metropolitan Museum of Art, gift of L. P. Everard, 1880.)*

FIGURE 276
Sketch after François M. Granet, The Choir of the Capuchin Monastery in Rome, *ca. 1819. Ink and watercolor over pencil, ink inscription. Sketchbook 7, leaf 11 verso.*

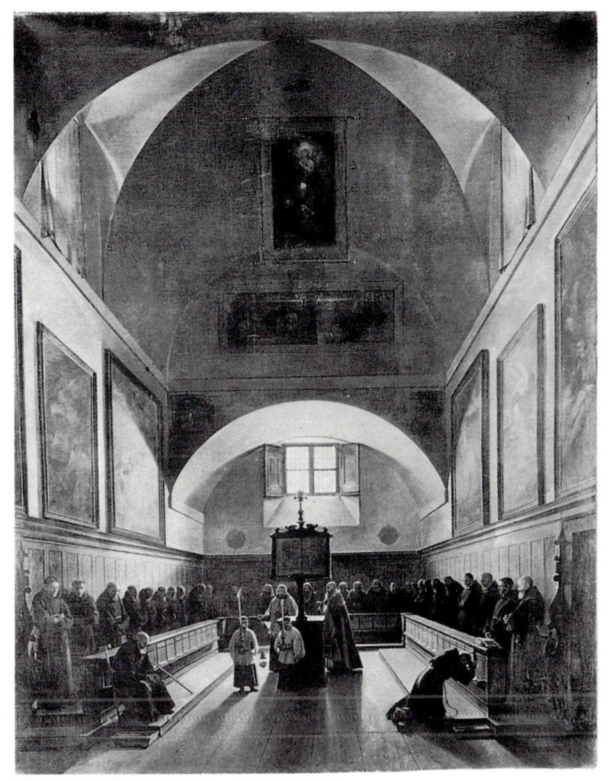

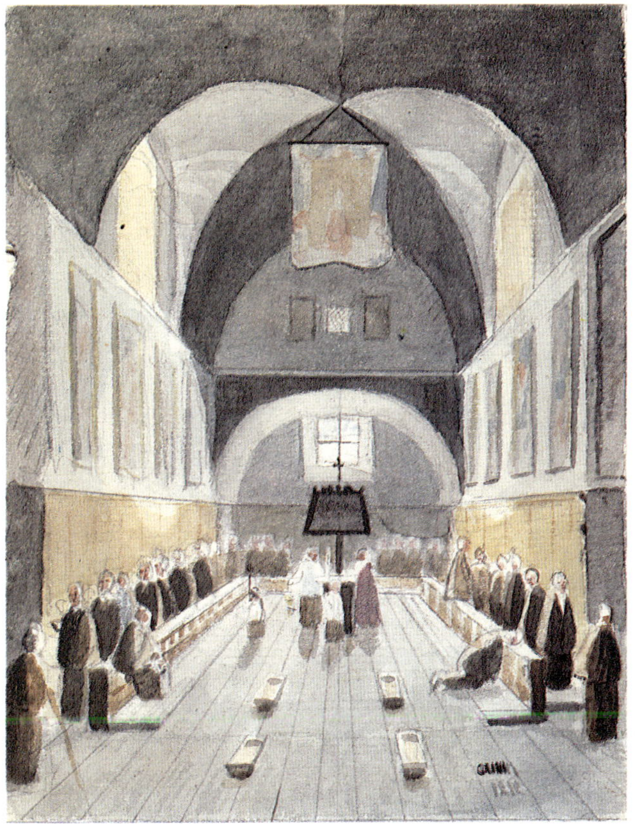

FIGURE 277

John Lewis Krimmel, Fourth of July Celebration in Centre Square, Philadelphia, 1819, *1819. Watercolor over pencil and ink; 12 5/16 x 18 1/8 in. (The Historical Society of Pennsylvania, Philadelphia, gift of James Claghorn.) Signed "J. L. Krimmel 1819."*

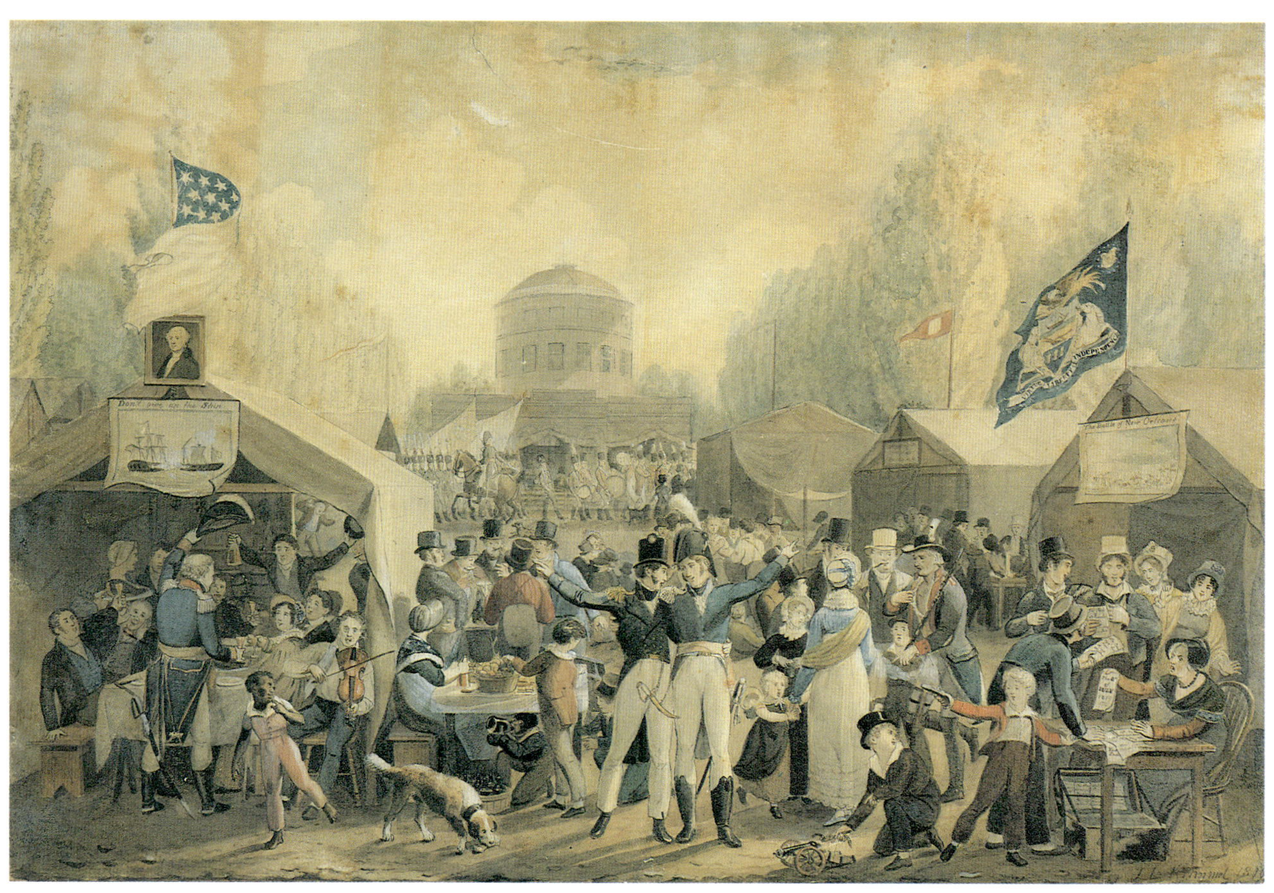

commercial component. The 1819 holiday has the dimensions of a summer fair. It has attracted a large and boisterous crowd; the clothing shows less obvious class differences and suggests that people of different walks of life and of different ages mingle in a more egalitarian manner. Celebrants in military uniforms dominate the festivities, and young boys brandish toy pistols and canons. Black adults are absent—possibly an indication that relations between whites and blacks had worsened in the postwar years, as jobs for all people, especially the disadvantaged, became increasingly scarce. Quakers are also absent. Fashions have changed: women's hats have cylindrical backs; their dresses have larger collars that closely encircle the neck and somewhat shorter skirts with decorations near the hemline; men wear long pants; boys wear shirts open at the neck.

Krimmel's preliminary drawings of the site are dated July 4 and 5 and accompanied by notations. He began by sketching several tents set up beneath large trees, paying special attention to their wooden frames (fig. 278). At the bottom of the page he added a rough, small sketch of a design from a banner depicting the death of General Mercer, a design that may have been derived from John Trumbull's painting of the subject, beside which he wrote: "Battle of Trenton / Death of Gen'l Mercer / General Jackson the Hero of the South." The first two refer to events that had occurred during the revolutionary war; the third alluded to the War of 1812 and perhaps Andrew Jackson's more recent role in the Seminole War of 1818 and his February 1819 visit to Philadelphia. On the same page Krimmel also itemized the food and beverages for sale, mixing German and English terms—seville oranges, lemons, pies and breads, gingerbread, oysters, stewed oysters, lobsters, crayfish, pretzels, sausages, lemonade, and beer—and two activities—dice throwing and an optic show.

Monday, July 5, he returned to the site to make two new sketches. In sketchbook 7 he divided one page into an upper and lower half and sketched two wide-angle views with tents in the foreground and the cylindrical drum of the pumphouse station in the middle background (fig. 279). Underneath he wrote: *"Die Zelte waren mit quilts, rag carpets, Fussteppichen and Semmeltüchern bedeckt"* (the tents were covered with quilts, rag carpets, foot rugs, and bakers' sacks), elements that are not included in the finished image.

When the artist started on the final watercolor version he predictably gave primacy to the spirited interaction among the people, using his site sketches for general ideas while resorting to his well-tested formulas for portraying a crowd in order to summarize the full experience of the event. Familiar figure types and details from his earlier paintings reappear: an old woman sits at a table selling fruit and beverages to a child, while a boy kneels underneath her table guzzling what is more probably either hard cider or beer than lemonade; that boy is spied by a lad who has dropped to one knee nearby, and yet another boy moves away with amusement; an oyster vendor has positioned his barrow nearby and has attracted a group of men who stand absorbed in conversation as they eat; a couple flirts; a well-dressed woman stands with her back to the viewer; a man stands with his arm raised high; the man who plays the fiddle holds it vertically; a dog wanders freely; and pictures of George Washington and a war scene are prominently displayed. To these stock figures and devices Krimmel added some totally new types in the foreground. Most prominent are two young men standing side by side with their arms around each other. Both are military men—one from the navy, the other from the army—who together symbolize national unity, and they are presented with the wide stance and broad gestures introduced by David, for each officer has one arm stretched out to the fullest. Similar gestures

FIGURE 278

Tents erected for the Fourth of July celebration, Centre Square, Philadelphia, July 4 and 5, 1819. Ink and watercolor over pencil, ink and pencil inscriptions. Sketchbook 6, leaf 12 verso.

FIGURE 279

Two views of Centre Square, Philadelphia, Monday, July 5, 1819. Watercolor and ink over pencil, ink inscription. Sketchbook 7, leaf 6 recto. Although the holiday had passed, the tents were still standing, and some vendors were selling wares.

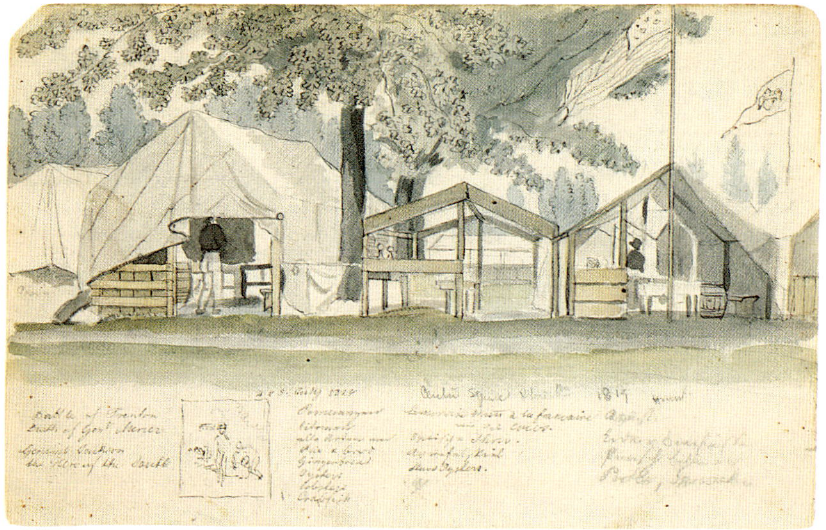

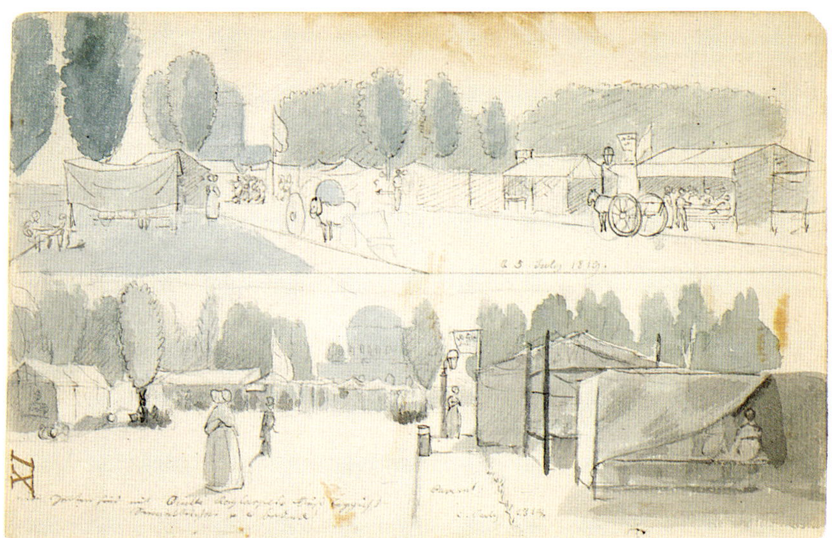

are given to the men in the tent. Other figures are based on Krimmel's recent sketches; for example, the young boy igniting a toy cannon is derived from a study dated July 7 (fig. 280), the older man and the old soldier in conversation with the woman are derived from Krimmel's portrait of tobacconist Hamilton and his companions (fig. 281), and two men at a table near a tree are from sketchbook 6 (fig. 282).

Overall, the watercolor suggests that by 1819 Krimmel owned a print of David's *Sabines*, possibly acquired while in France (see fig. 112). This assumption is reinforced by the increased number of Davidian devices that appear in his pictures after 1819. In this instance they include strong directional lines that emanate from the design of the central figures and visually draw the image together. Emulating the French model, Krimmel constructed two parallel friezes: the lower one consisting of the playing and kneeling boys and the dog, and the main one across the middle ground. In the latter the figure of the fashionable woman is a restatement of David's Roman with a large shield. Both figures are depicted from the back and at the same spot in the composition; the circular back of the woman's hat and the lines of her shawl are a free paraphrase of the curves of the Roman's helmet and shield.

Many details in the painting help to create an extraordinarily lively crowd, and the composition conveys a sense of the shouting and shooting, talking and drumming, singing and barking that filled the afternoon and continued into the evening. Krimmel directly referred to his notes when including the two vendors, the dice throwing at the table between the two tents on the right, and the optic show in the second tent; but he also included other activities that must have been so common they needed no special research, such as the wrestling contest and the parade. Against the teeming activities in the middle and foregrounds, the towering drum of the pumphouse provides a steady but distant focal point. Krimmel created the depth and balance necessary to include all these activities in a single scene by employing a calculated compositional symmetry. A succession of planes lead the eye from front to back and make it impossible for the strong foreground elements to overpower the image or to foil the deliberately contrived sense of depth, a device also inspired by David's *Sabines*.

Perhaps because the only version of the 1819 Fourth of July scene was a watercolor, Krimmel did not submit it for the May 1820 exhibition at the academy. Instead he entered *Soldier Taking Leave of His Family*, *Country Frolic and Dance*, and *A Dutch Country Girl*, the last of which was undoubtedly based on a sketch the artist had made during his visit to Europe and probably depicted a young woman in regional garb.[18]

The canvas *Soldier Taking Leave of His Family* is now known only through a reproduction made later (fig. 283).[19] The scene is a variation on the theme of familial love in its many manifestations. Emphasizing emotion, Krimmel gave a broad representation to nature within the framework of his modest subject, a technique often used by German romantic painters. His drawing of an Ebingen bride and groom provided the basis for the central couple (fig. 284), late Gothic Madonnas provided the model for the baby on the mother's arm, and Wilkie's *Blind Fiddler* was the source for the younger girl's pose and the position of her apron. To these he added details drawn recently in his sketchbooks (figs. 285–292; see also figs. 259, 280).

Soldier Taking Leave of His Family illustrates the rapidity with which Krimmel's conceptual approach to genre representation was changing. Just a

18. *Ninth Annual Exhibition . . .* (1820), p. 7.

19. "Krimmel's Picture—*Return from Boarding School*," p. 508, lists the painting as being in New York City. Lawson may have started the engraving soon after the exhibition ended, for by December the painting was in New York and at the disposal of business partners Pierre Flandin and Francis B. Winthrop; alternatively, Flandin and Winthrop or subsequent owners may have loaned the picture to Lawson between 1820 and 1833. The first mention of the engraving is under the title *Frederic and Ellen*, accompanying a poem of the same title by C.W. T. in Bedell, *Religious Souvenir*, p. 166. The plate was reissued eight years later with Lydia H. Sigourney's "The Volunteer," in Biddle, *Selected Poems*, pp. 200, 201–2.

FIGURE 280
Studies of cat, asparagus, various household utensils and cooking implements, child, July 7, 1819. Watercolor over pencil, ink inscription. Sketchbook 7, leaf 9 recto.

FIGURE 281
Tobacconist Hamilton, Jimmy Cox, unidentified companion, late 1818. Watercolor over pencil. Sketchbook 4, leaf 24 recto.

FIGURE 282
Two men, tree, peacock, ca. 1819. Pencil and watercolor over pencil. Sketchbook 6, leaf 16 verso.

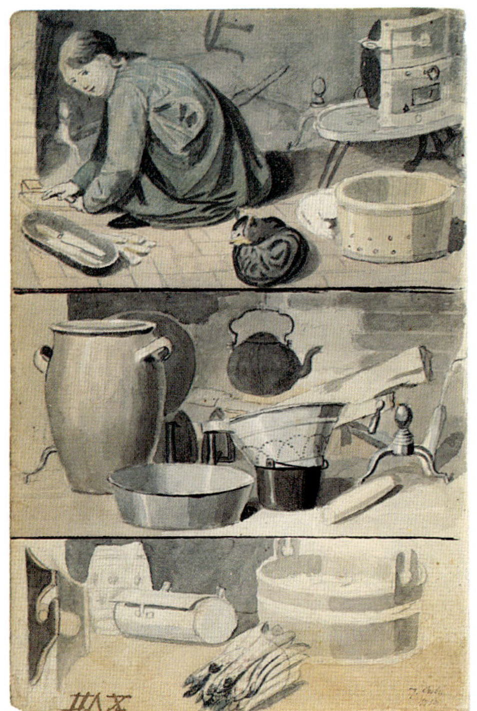

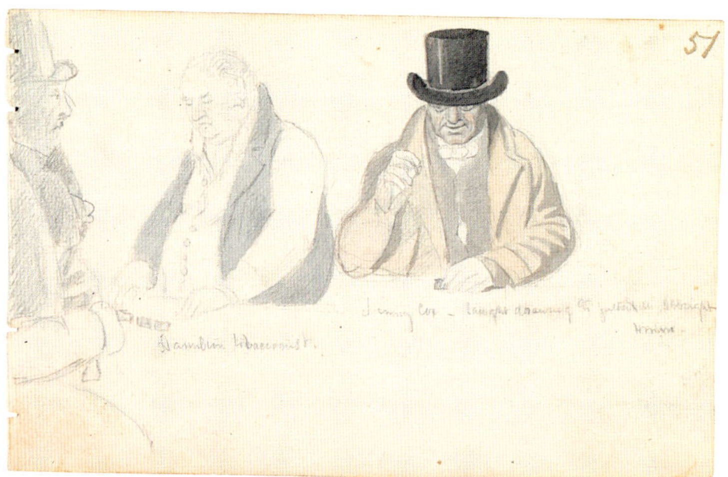

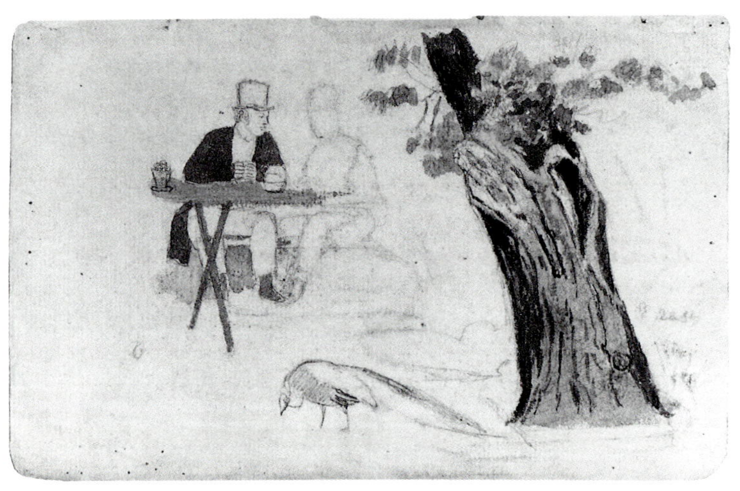

FIGURE 283
Alexander Lawson, Frederick and Ellen, *Philadelphia, 1833–34, after John Lewis Krimmel,* Soldier Taking Leave of His Family *(1820). Engraving; 2 $\frac{15}{16}$ x 4 $\frac{7}{16}$ in. Published by Key and Biddle, Philadelphia. Inscription reads: "Painted by J. L. Krimmel. Engraved by Alexander Lawson. B. Rodgers Printer."*

FIGURE 284
Ebingen couple, 1817. Watercolor over pencil. Sketchbook 5, leaf 12 recto.

FIGURE 285
Studies for the oldest girl, grandfather, and bugle in Soldier Taking Leave of His Family, *1820. Pencil, watercolor over pencil. Sketchbook 7, leaf 12 recto.*

FIGURE 286
Study for grandmother in Soldier Taking Leave of His Family, *1820. Pencil. Sketchbook 6, leaf 15 verso.*

FIGURE 287
Study for baby in Soldier Taking Leave of His Family, *1820. Watercolor over pencil. Sketchbook 7, leaf 20 recto.*

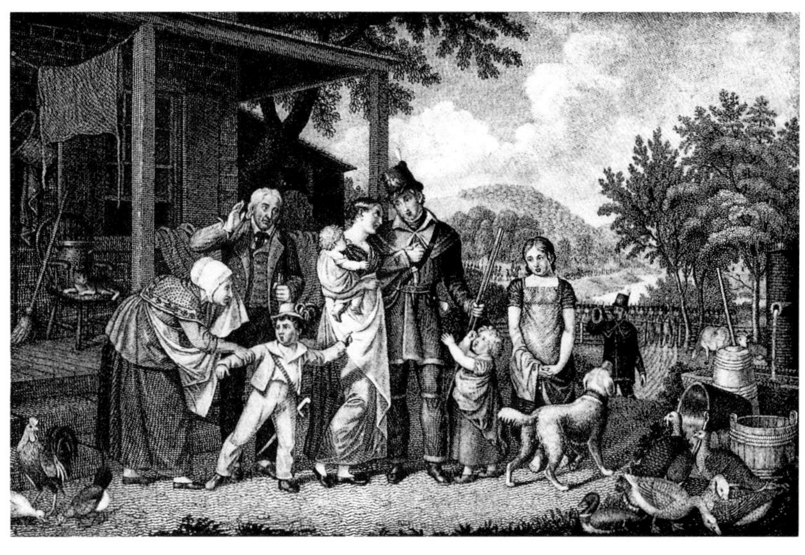

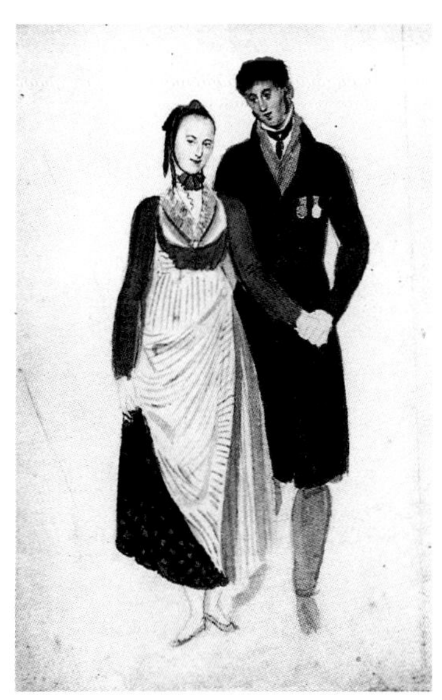

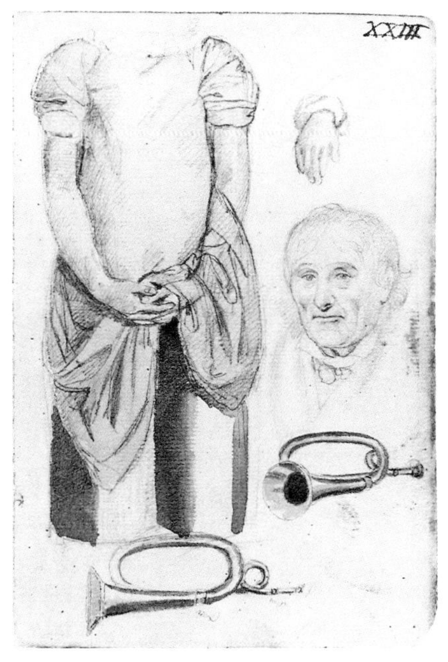

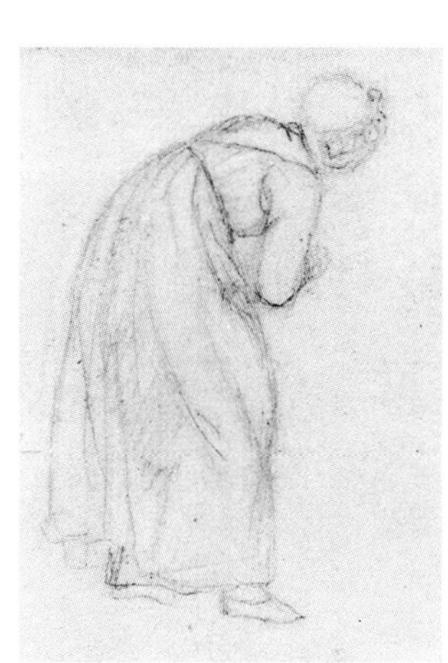

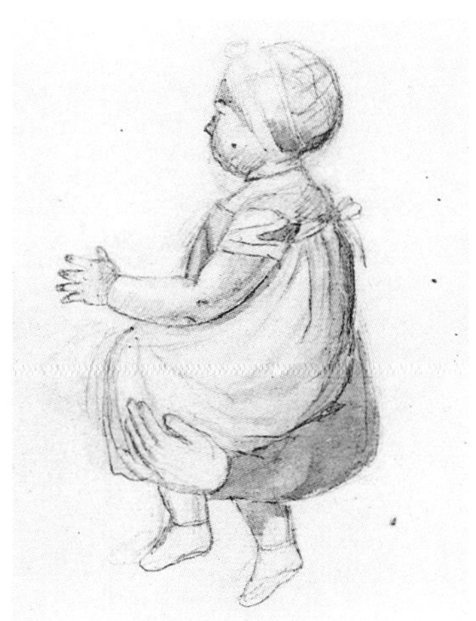

FIGURE 288
Landscape and cow, leaf and horse, 1812/13. Pencil and watercolor over pencil, ink and pencil inscriptions. Sketchbook 3, leaf 1 verso.

FIGURE 289
Rooster and barnyard fowl, plants, top of chicken coop, 1820. Watercolor and ink over pencil, wash over pencil, pencil. Sketchbook 6, leaf 17 verso.

FIGURE 290
Cows, 1820. Watercolor over pencil. Sketchbook 6, leaf 9 recto. Inscription reads: "Sketched behind the arsenal, Philada in Company with Wm Albright Esqr."

FIGURE 291
Goats, geese, 1820. Watercolor and pencil, watercolor and ink over pencil. Sketchbook 7, leaf 13 verso.

FIGURE 292
Woman's head, various household furnishings and utensils, 1819. Pencil and watercolor over pencil. Sketchbook 7, leaf 17 recto.

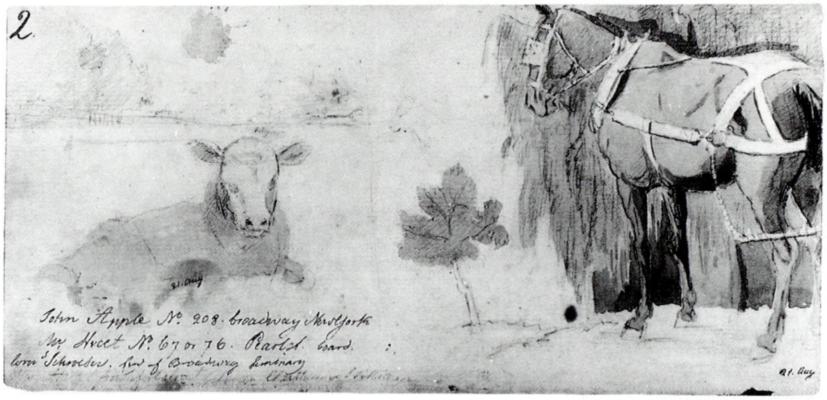

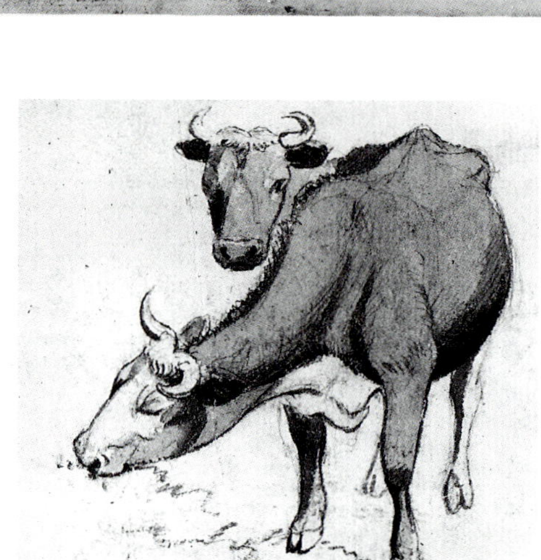

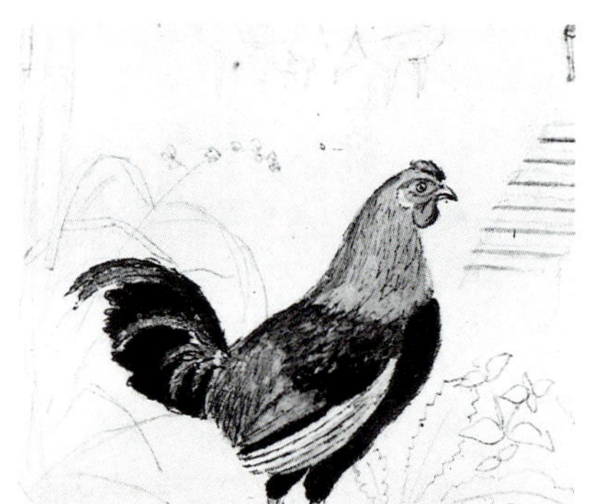

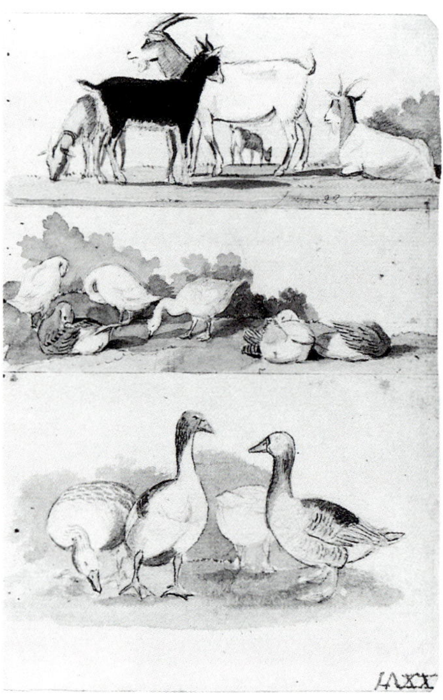

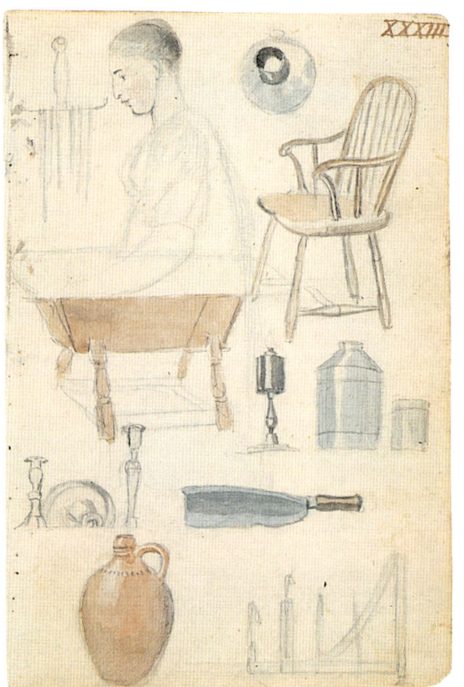

year before, in *Return from Market*, Krimmel had created a family scene set before a landscape with a diagonally positioned modest house and used farm animals and household items as accoutrements. In *Soldier Taking Leave of His Family* Krimmel deliberately simplified and tightened the external action and concurrently deepened the moral content. The setting is the yard of a small farm at the moment a bugle call summons a young father back to his militia unit, which is standing in the background. Each member of his family reacts differently to his imminent departure.

The humble setting belies the sophistication with which the picture is designed. The figures of the grandparents and grandson and those of the parents and their younger children form two interlocking pyramids firmly bound together by their gestures and motions. Krimmel's arrangement is compact, yet each figure is clearly outlined and connected. His vertical axis runs between the husband and wife and up the porch post directly behind them, emphasizing the central importance of their figures.

The idea behind *Soldier Taking Leave of His Family* was not new in the United States or Europe. In several respects the image is similar to one that appeared twenty years earlier and that may have influenced Krimmel's design: an engraving of John James Barralet's *MacPherson's Blues: Taking Leave*, which depicts a soldier embracing his sweetheart before rejoining his unit, a comrade-in-arms urging him to hurry, and an officer on horseback waiting in the background (fig. 293). In both pictures the background narrative plays against a foreground scene, yet the foreground figures dominate, and the background scene is visually no more significant than a view through a window. Both pictures also share specific details: for example, the angle of the architecture, a long rifle, and, most precisely, the position of hands folded over the stomach. Barralet used the gesture to express the plaintive emotion of the sweetheart, and Krimmel used it to express the worries of an adolescent daughter.

In European art the scene was often depicted in a barnyard, and the soldier was always surrounded by his family. *The Conscript's Departure* (ca. 1807) portrays a Bavarian and his lamenting family as the bugle summons him to the waiting wagon. Its companion piece, *The Conscript's Return from Battle* (ca. 1807), presents the same man, a new corporal wearing a handsome uniform with military decorations, being welcomed by his happy family.[20]

Krimmel may have been inclined to make the picture because of recent events. The War of 1812 had been over for four years; however, relations with the Spaniards who controlled East Florida had been acrimonious since July 1816, and border raids were common by each side. These had culminated in the First Seminole War in which Gen. Andrew Jackson led the Tennessee militia in a successful campaign against both Native Americans and Spaniards. In 1819 East Florida was ceded to the United States, and the Seminoles were seemingly vanquished. Nonetheless, a long-lasting mistrust of Native Americans had been reinforced, and most people still perceived the state militia (rather than the federal army) as defenders. The vague location in which Krimmel situated his scene gave it a general character and made it possible for a viewer to infer that this could be any nearby rural homestead and nearly any family.

The changes that Krimmel was making in his choice of genre subjects and in their composition was netting him no more sales in Philadelphia than his earlier ones had. He decided to test the market for his art in New York, a city that was rapidly growing because eastern merchants, especially those who were

20. These paintings are now in Osterreichische Galerie des 19. u. 20. Jahrhunderts, Vienna, and reproduced in Richard R. Brettell and Caroline B. Brettell, *Painters and Peasants in the Nineteenth Century* (New York: Rizzoli, 1983), p. 123. Precisely contemporary with Krimmel's picture are *Departure of the Militiaman* and *Return of the Militiaman* (1820; Osterreichische Galerie) by Peter Kraft.

FIGURE 293
Alexander Lawson after John J. Barralet, MacPherson's Blues: Taking Leave, *1796. Engraving; 11¾ x 9¼ in. (Library, Academy of Natural Sciences of Philadelphia.)*

FIGURE 294
Abraham Raimbach after David Wilkie, The Cut Finger, *London; January 16, 1819. Engraving. (Photo, © British Museum.)*

FIGURE 295
Plucked goose, 1819. Pencil. Sketchbook 6, leaf 6 recto.

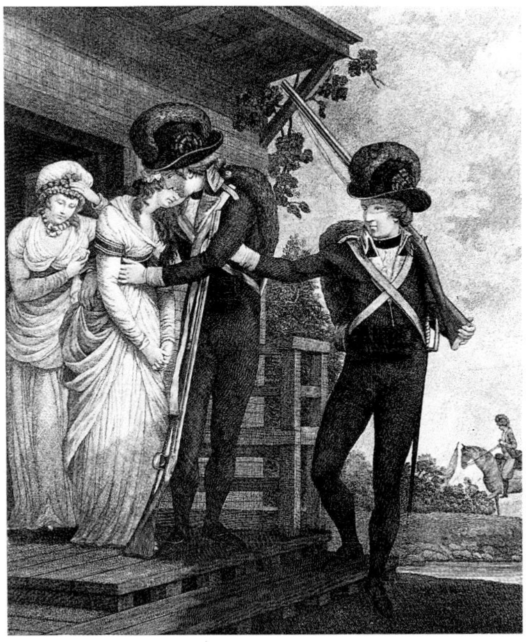

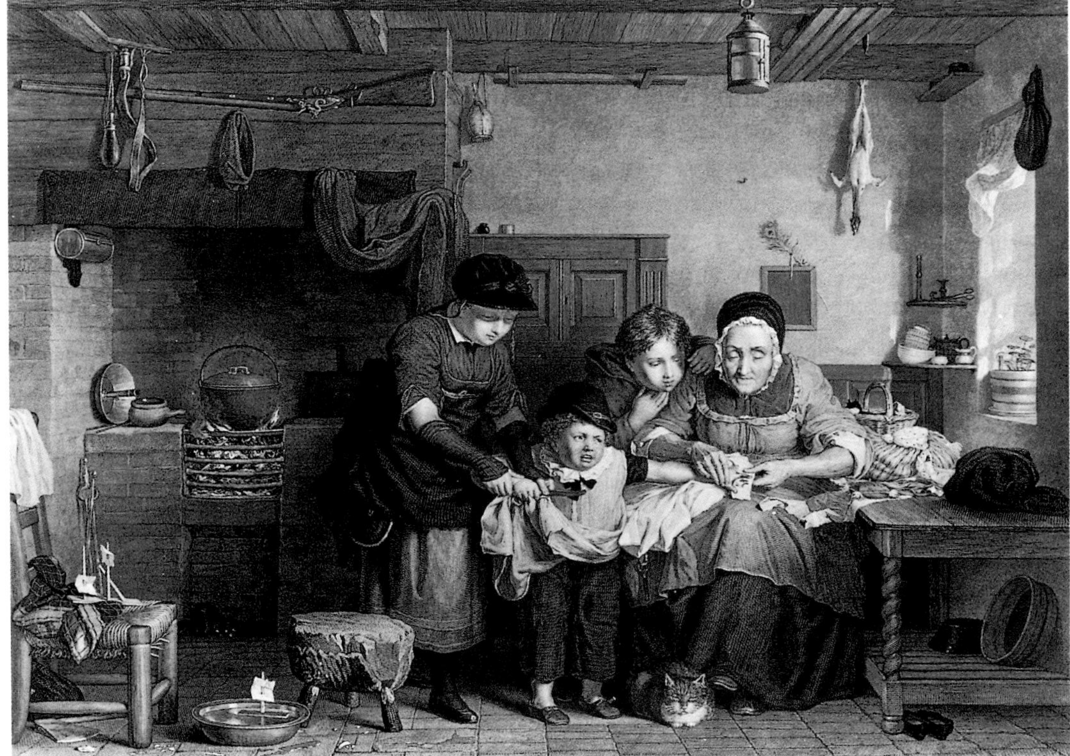

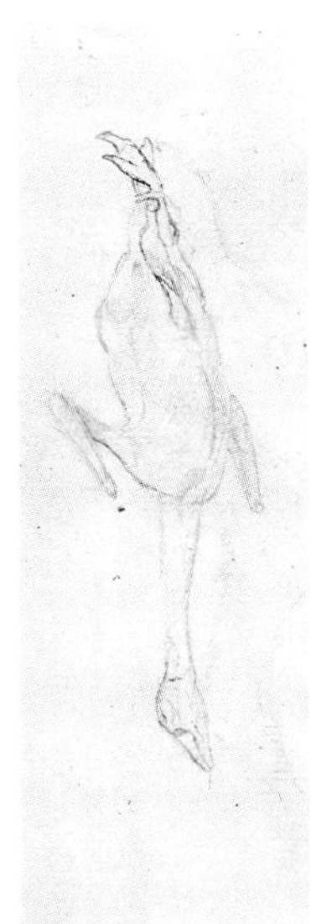

active in the transatlantic trade, had decided to settle there with their families and take advantage of its ice-free port, opening warehouses and offices in Manhattan. Among these men were merchants Francis B. Winthrop and Pierre Flandin, both of whom became active lenders to exhibitions at New York's American Academy of the Fine Arts in 1817 and were elected as patrons in 1820. The two men were also business partners. A letter written by Krimmel to Flandin provides insights on the business relationship Krimmel had established and his aspirations.

Philadelphia October 8th 1820

> Dear Sir
> Friday evening I returned to this City, and yesterday I learned from Mr. Birch that he sent you the 3 pictures.
>
> I am very anxious to know, how you are pleased with them; if they were varnish'd, they would show to better advantage. You might give them; after exposing them for about half a day to the Sun, a slight Coat of Varnish now; and then you would better judge of the Effect and Finish.
>
> I took the liberty, to send an Order of $35 balance. due on these 3 pictures, to a particular friend of mine Mr. F. A. Schneider; who will present it to You—Would you think it advisable for me to pay a Visit there, with my Pictures of *the dance* and *sleighing Party?* Did any of your Amateurs see your Pictures, and is there any hope of encouragement?
>
> I expect your candid Remarks and Opinion with your next letter.
>
> I am Yours
> J.L. Krimmel
>
> No. 233 Spruce Street[21]

Because Krimmel speaks of a balance due, the three unnamed paintings must have been commissions rather than paintings done on speculation, and because he suggests drying them in the sun a half day and then lightly varnishing them, the paintings were unquestionably done in oil and very recently finished. Behind this is a tone that betrays the still-precarious nature of his existence: Krimmel was seeking the public recognition—financial and artistic—so necessary for his career.

Five months earlier three of Krimmel's paintings had been exhibited at the New York academy's annual show: *The Blind Fiddler*, *Blind Man's Buff*, and *The Cut Finger*. The first was designated in the catalogue as "after Wilkie," and was probably the same canvas Krimmel had first exhibited in Philadelphia in 1813. The second, lent to the academy show by Winthrop, was Krimmel's own 1814 composition.[22] The identity of *The Cut Finger* is less clear. The exhibition catalogues usually specified which paintings were copy work, and no such designation is given to this painting, which makes it likely it was Krimmel's 1814 painting; however, on July 3, 1819, Krimmel noted he had "Contour Cut Finger schattiert [shaded in]," which suggests he was working on a new picture. This could mean he was doing an ink drawing, watercolor, or oil version of the earlier image (precedent for which exists in the two election scenes dated a year apart, or that he was making a copy after a recently published engraving of Wilkie's 1809 *The Cut Finger* (fig. 294). Drawings in the sketchbooks depict discrete elements that are also in the Wilkie image—a cylindrical metal salt holder; a sleeping cat; and a plucked goose, its elongated scrawny body strung up by its feet (fig. 295, see fig. 280). But in the past Krimmel had not drawn

21. Krimmel to Flandin, October 8, 1820, Dreer Autograph Collection, Historical Society of Pennsylvania, Philadelphia. In July 1813 Krimmel did a watercolor of a meadow and labeled it *Schneiders Wiese* [Schneider's meadow]; this may be the same F. A. Schneider.

22. Cowdrey, *American Academy*, 2:218. *Blind Man's Buff* and *Blind Fiddler* reappeared together in 1983 after many years in a private collection, which suggests they went into the same private collection 160 years earlier; see Christie, Manson, and Woods, Intl., *Important American Paintings*, sale of December 9, 1983, p. 14.

FIGURE 296
Household implements, 1819–21. Watercolor over pencil, pencil inscription. Sketchbook 6, leaf 1 verso.

FIGURE 297
Cooking fireplace and kitchen implements, bonnet, July 4, 1819. Pencil and watercolor over pencil, ink inscription. Sketchbook 7, leaf 17 verso.

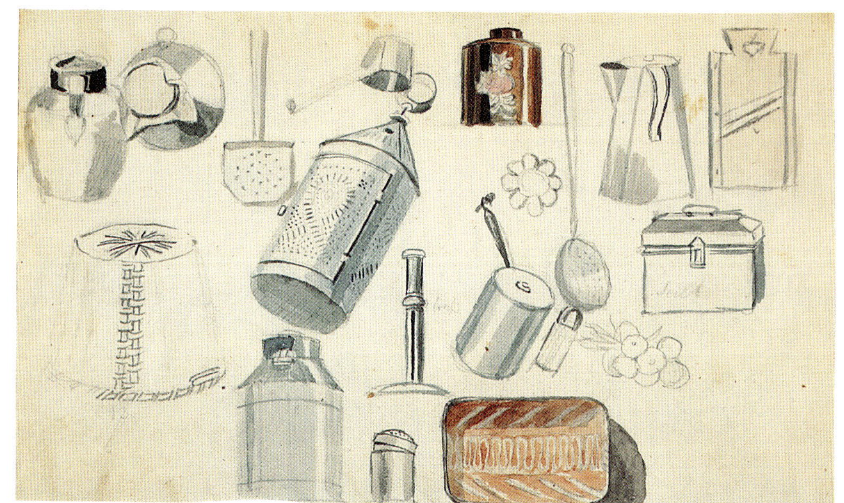

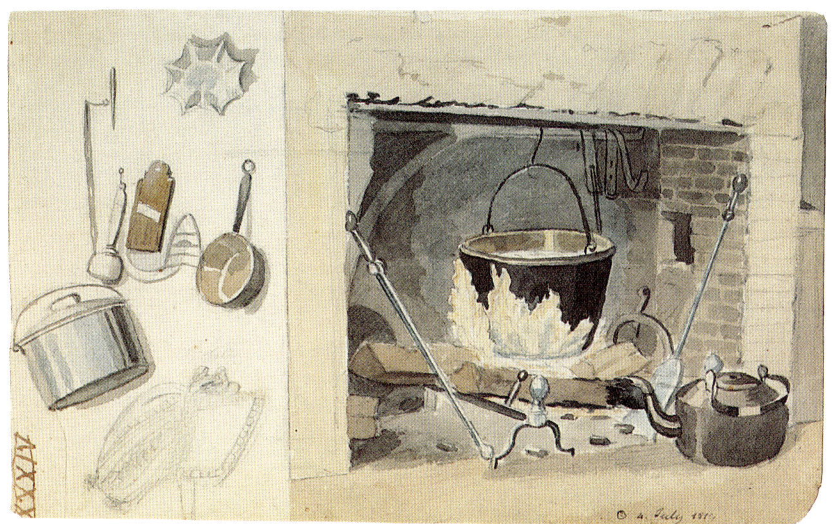

details for his copy-work paintings in the sketchbooks; furthermore, these very elements were commonplace in American households, and Krimmel had no need to rely on Wilkie for their configuration. Indeed Krimmel was still actively drawing many household implements in greater detail, even if they did not have ready application in a genre scene at hand (figs. 296, 297).[23]

The New York venture yielded only a few sales. Winthrop (who had already purchased *Blind Man's Buff*) and Flandin apparently jointly purchased *The Cut Finger* and *Soldier Taking Leave of His Family* later that year or the following year.[24]

Given the many drawings in sketchbooks 6 and 7 that range from cursory to very finished (figs. 298–304), it is curious that Krimmel, who had recently been elected president of the Society of Artists, entered just two genre paintings at the 1821 annual exhibition at the Pennsylvania Academy: *Cherry Woman with Children* (1814–15), which by no means exemplified his latest work, and *The Sleighing Frolic*, a recently finished image of an idea he had sketched out seven years earlier (fig. 305). The latter depicted a fashionable winter pastime that had caught the attention of many visitors to Pennsylvania, for example Englishman William Priest, who several years earlier had written a fulsome description of it:

> Every moment that will admit of sleighing is seized on with avidity. The tavern and innkeepers are up all night; and the whole country is in motion. . . . Our planters daughters provide hot sand, which they place in bags at the bottom of the sleigh. Their sweethearts attend with a couple of horses and away they glide with astonishing velocity; visiting their friends for many miles round the country. But in large towns, in order to have a sleighing frolic in *style*, it is necessary to provide a *fiddler*, who is placed at the head of the sleigh and plays all the way. At every inn they meet with on the road, the company alight and have a dance.[25]

A passage from popular literature was likely the source for Krimmel's first depiction of a sleighing scene, a cursorily drawn compositional sketch of two sleighs moving through a countryside with trees and a house in the background (fig. 306). In all probability, he did this while a member of Sully's sketch club, where the artists practiced compositional sketching after a text was read aloud. As had Priest a generation earlier, Krimmel noted the association of sleigh rides and dances in taverns, specifically in his pairing of the 1820 sleighing picture and the 1819 *Country Frolic and Dance*. (This was first noted in his letter to Flandin and reinforced by the listings of items for sale from Krimmel's estate.) The same pairing of paintings occurred in 1825 when the two canvases were offered by Nathaniel Devaltooth's estate, and when *The Sleighing Frolic* emerged from a private collection in 1991, the coupling of the two paintings was confirmed: the two have the same dimensions.[26]

Of Krimmel's two earlier sleighing scenes, an 1813 watercolor representing a single-passenger sleigh passing the building of the Bank of the United States in Philadelphia was unavailable because it had been purchased by Pavel Svinin who took it to Russia in 1814. The other, an 1813 sketch in his sketchbook, showed two sleighs loaded with passengers traveling in opposite directions, one pictured from the back, the other from the front, both drawn the same size. Balanced into a symmetrical composition, the sleighs pass each other in a shallow space, approximating the neoclassical ideal of a frieze to which Krimmel was subscribing at the time. Seven years later when he designed the 1820 painting, he depicted the same types of sleighs pulled by very similar teams of horses

23. Perhaps what Krimmel exhibited in 1819 and subsequently sold or consigned to Flandin and Winthrop was his 1814 painting, and what he shaded in on July 3, 1819, was the india ink drawing entitled *The Cut Finger* that was among the artist's studio effects in 1821; if so Krimmel may have been making a drawing of his painting for an engraver. The only mention of the art for two Krimmel images that were engraved in 1820 is the Krimmel estate sale listing: "Departure for a Boarding school, sketch in india ink" and "return from Boarding School, d[itt]o" (*Poulson's American Daily Advertiser*, August 14, 1821).

24. "Krimmel's Picture—*Return from Boarding School*," pp. 507–8.

25. William Priest, *Travels in the United States of America* (London, 1802), p. 47.

26. The finishing date of *The Sleighing Frolic* is inferred from Krimmel to Flandin, October 8, 1820, Dreer Collection; estate sale listing, *Poulson's American Daily Advertiser*, August 14, 1821; Cunningham, *Executor's Sale Catalogue*, pp. 153, 154.

FIGURE 298
House, 1819–21. Pencil. Sketchbook 7, leaf 7 recto.

FIGURE 299
People, clothing, 1819–21. Pencil. Sketchbook 7, leaf 21 recto.

FIGURE 300
Cookstove, probably 1819. Watercolor over pencil. Sketchbook 6, leaf 5 verso. The artist depicted the same stove in fig. 14.

FIGURE 301
Street scene, 1819–21. Pencil. Sketchbook 6, leaf 11 verso.

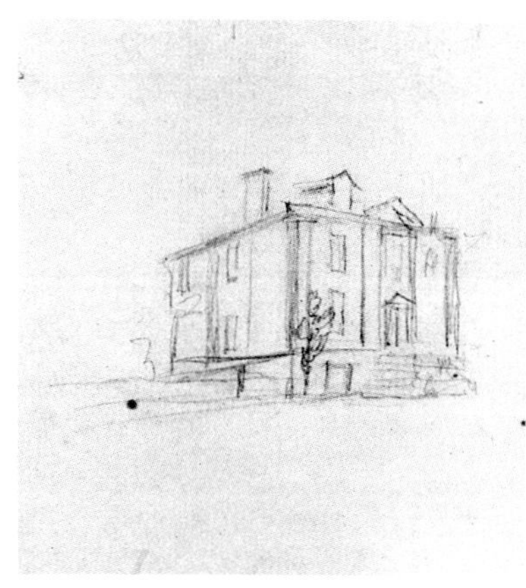

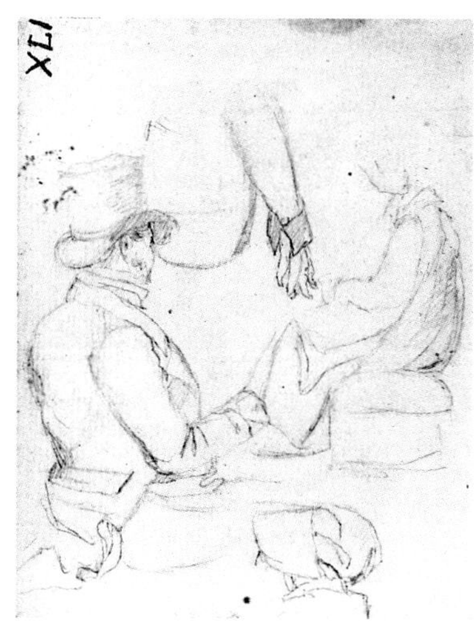

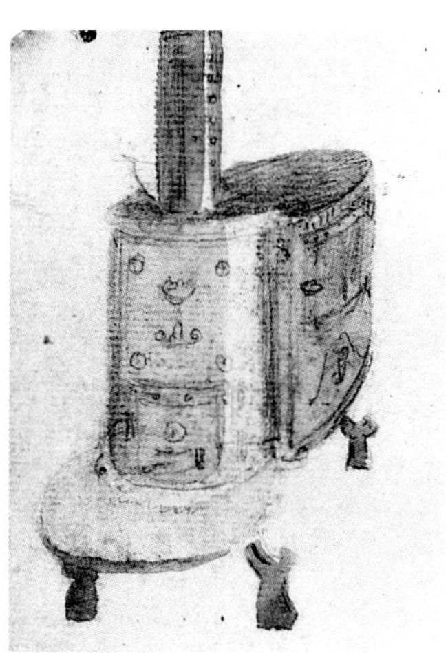

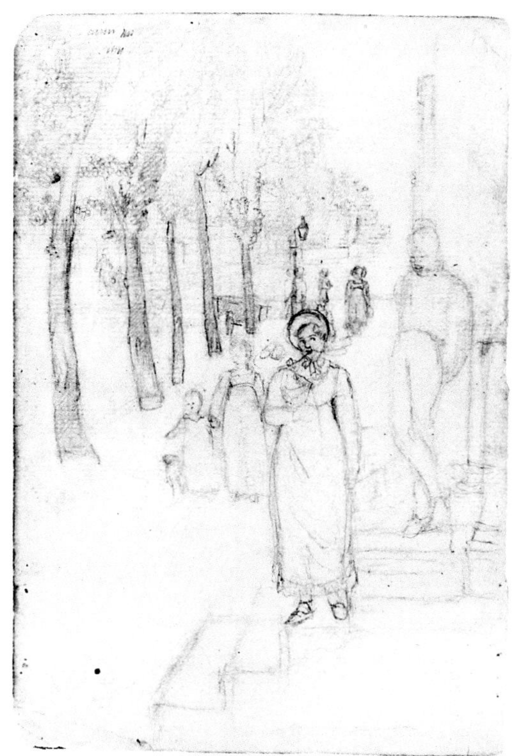

FIGURE 302
Barn with carriage porch, 1819–21. Watercolor over pencil. Sketchbook 6, leaf 17 recto.

FIGURE 303
Lilacs, 1819–21. Watercolor over pencil. Sketchbook 6, leaf 7 recto.

FIGURE 304
River bluff, 1819–21. Watercolor over pencil. Sketchbook 7, leaf 10 verso.

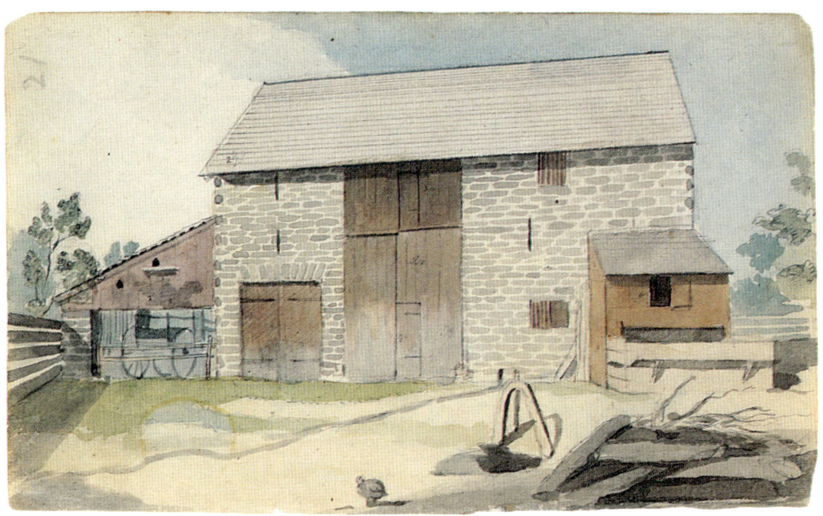

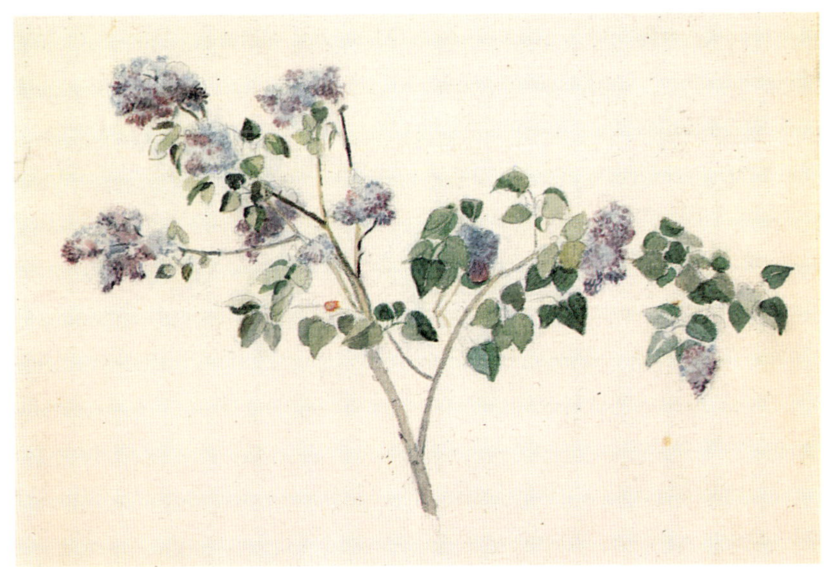

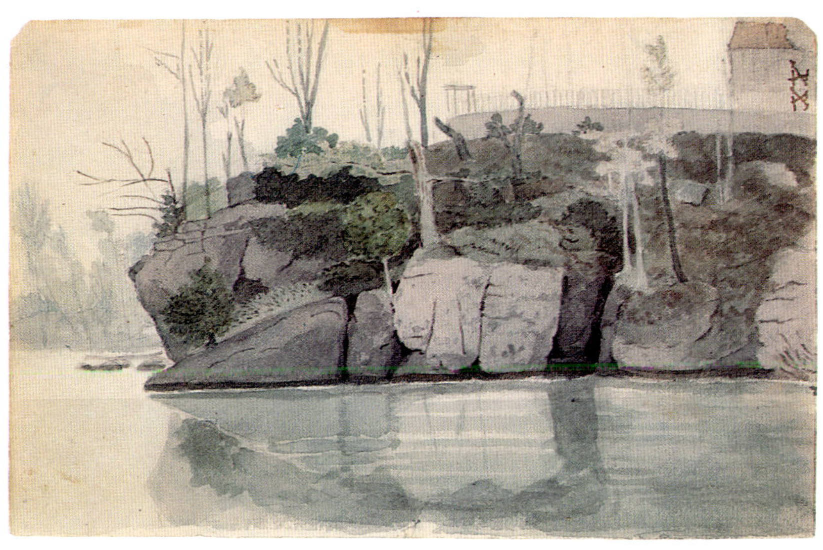

FIGURE 305
John Lewis Krimmel, The Sleighing Frolic, *1820. Oil on canvas; 16 x 24½ in. (Collection of the Browne family: Photo, Kurt A. Dolnier.)*

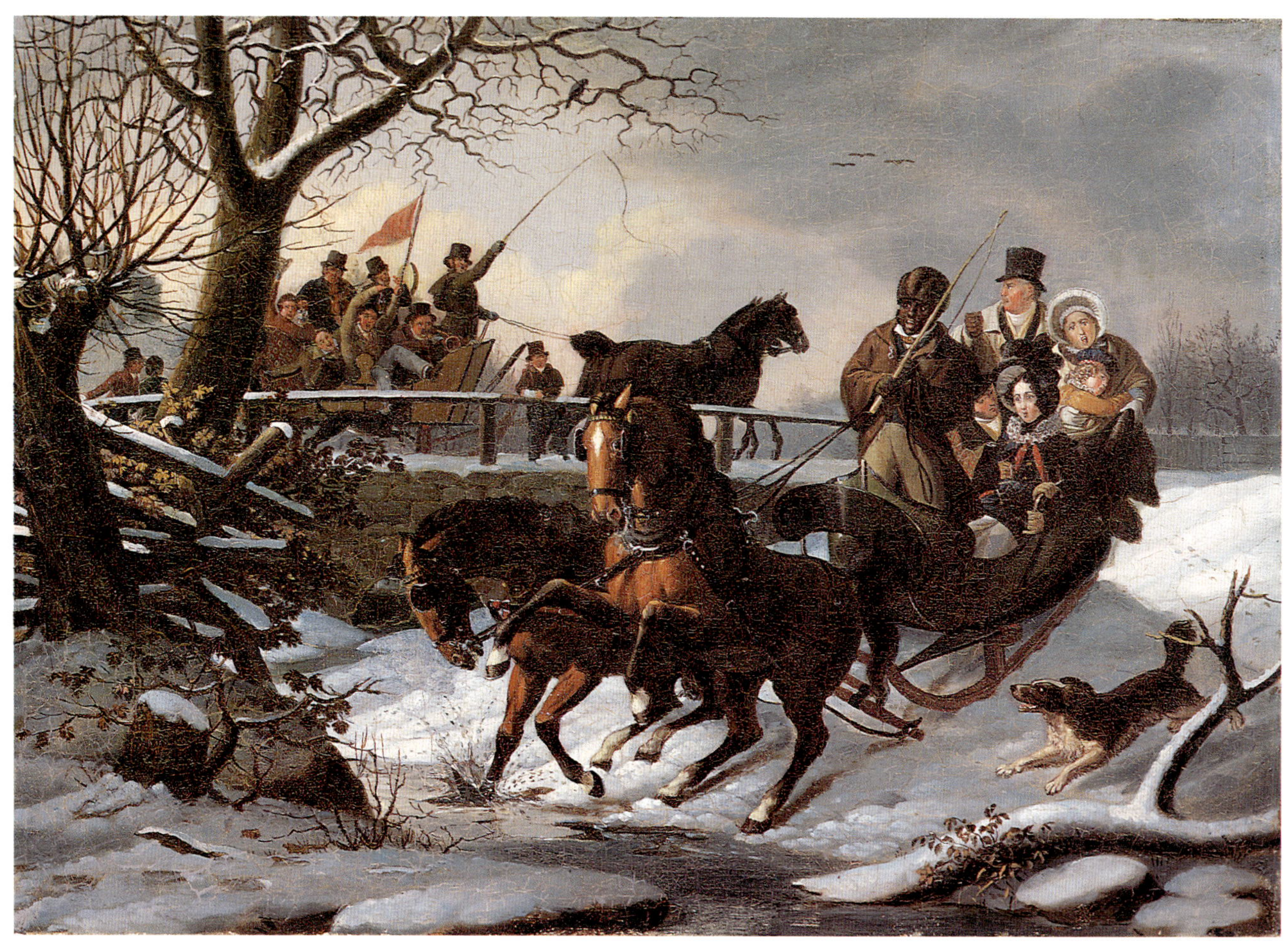

FIGURE 306
Compositional sketch for sleighing scene, ca. 1813. Pencil, ink. Sketchbook 2, leaf 4 verso.

FIGURE 307
Stationary sleigh with horses hitched to it, 1819/20. Pencil. Sketchbook 6, leaf 18 verso.

FIGURE 308
Horse hitched to wagon, 1820/21. Pencil. Sketchbook 6, leaf 16 recto.

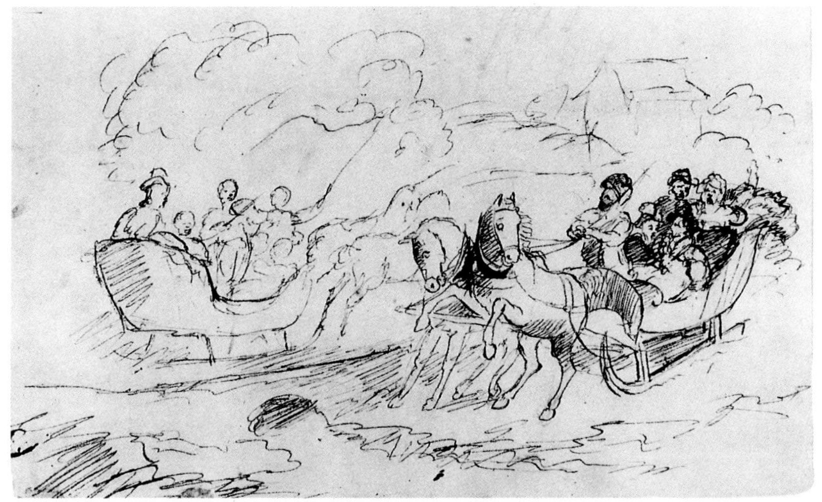

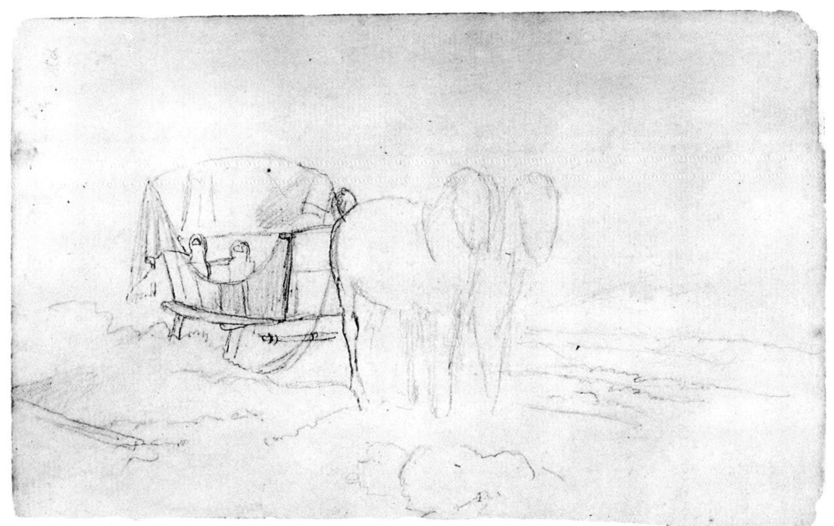

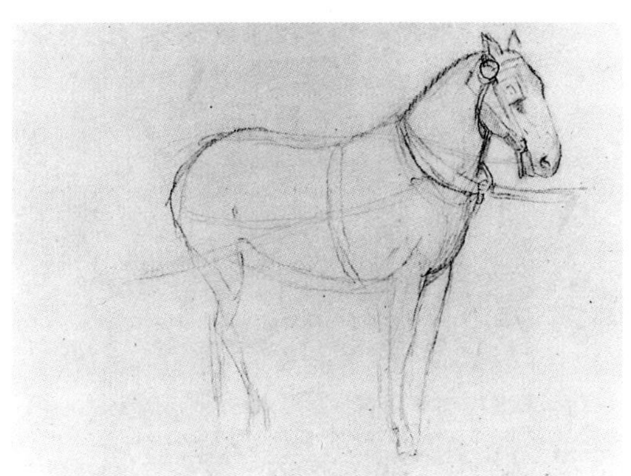

and occupied by the same type and number of passengers; however, he shifted the location of the sleighs, put more distance between them, and abandoned the homogeneity of the frieze. The sleigh on the right, which he had earlier depicted riding at a flat angle, comes down the slope of a small bank with a steeper diagonal and a more foreshortened perspective. The second sleigh, positioned approximately forty-five degrees from the first, is depicted from the front instead of the back, and its design is based on two recent studies (figs. 307, 308). Krimmel accented the horizontality of the midground design with the long bridge railing and continued it to the right with the faint lines of a far away fence. Because Krimmel was aiming for greater pictorial depth while maintaining a balanced composition, he designed the split rail fence on the left so that its lines mirror the diagonals of the foreground sleigh. These two laterally balanced diagonals, together with the horizontal of the bridge railing demarcate a trapezoidal space bisected by an imaginary line that runs through the highlighted forehead and muzzle of the rearing horse. The horse's raised left leg is the middle axis of the picture. The brute strength and wild energy conveyed in the delineation of this horse demonstrate Krimmel's outstanding ability for animal representation. His many studies of horses had served him as details in several of his genre pictures; here, however, he made the team of horses the centerpiece of his genre scene.

In the 1813 sketch the front seat passengers were engaged in lively conversation, and in the watercolor sold to Svinin the front passengers were holding hands, but in the 1820 painting the artist defined their relationship with a finely tuned sense of the comical. The suitor is ardent and smiles as he whispers into the ear of his pretty companion; what she has heard has given rise to an expression of shocked amusement. Thus preoccupied, the two are oblivious to the racket made by the occupants of the second sleigh, whose earsplitting noise is painfully upsetting the mother and her little daughter in the back seat and angering the father. The offending sleigh is packed with a group of high-spirited young men, possibly college students, judging from their pennant, who are singing, shouting, and trumpeting along with music provided by the fiddler and the cymbalist. As in the winter scene he sold to Svinin, Krimmel has placed a couple of boys around the sleigh; one has wiped the snow from the bridge railing and is prepared to pelt the occupants with snowballs. In 1820 Krimmel has represented the driver as a black man and changed the behavior of the horses. In the ink sketch the horses pulling the right sleigh have come to a dead stop before the partially frozen brook, but in the painting one horse is bucking and the other has stepped into the icy water.

In spite of Krimmel's otherwise excellent draftsmanship a shortcoming in the representation of the foreground sleigh makes the back-seat passengers look as if they are atop the sleigh instead of within it, and thus they look as if they are in danger of falling off. Although his more distinct differentiation of the two sleighs successfully contrasts the abruptly arrested movement of the nearer one and the gliding motion of the distant one, it does not convincingly present the space between them. This struggle with perspective is one Krimmel shared with most artists in America; it was at least partially due to a lack of opportunity to study the works of old masters and to understudy great contemporary artists. (Krimmel's awareness of the problem can be inferred from the lack of confidence in the quality of his work, which he voices in his letter to Flandin in which he pleads for the New York art merchant's candid critique and advice and asks, "Is there any hope of encouragement?")

These deficiencies notwithstanding, Krimmel did achieve the illusion of an expansive winter landscape in *The Sleighing Frolic*. Contributing to this are the repoussoires of the fallen bough and the running dog, the sturdy tree trunks marking the midground distance, and the unifying light of the weak winter sun hanging low in the western sky. Because he was working with the precepts of romantic landscape design, Krimmel made the painting compositionally more accessible than his earlier neoclassical sleighing scenes. The middle section of the foreground is wide open, the diagonal of the brook draws the viewer's eye toward a central, brightly lit area from which one may proceed further into the scene, either by way of the sleigh on the right or the fence on the left, where trees visually connect to the second sleigh. The thrust of their large boughs is echoed in the pennant, in the poses of the three men standing in the sleigh, and in the outlines of the horses (the entangled lines of their small branches relate to the design of the wildly behaving sleigh riders). In the oil painting the artist eschews any representation of the house and trees that appeared in the background of his 1813 image but paints a shadowy image of a larger building as seen through the branches of the lower tree. The successful construction of a single comprehensible picture space is largely attributable to the long horizontal that transverses the width of the canvas, and in the spirit of the romantic, leads the viewer's imagination beyond the border of the picture. With this image Krimmel introduced a genre motif that later became very popular in American art and is best known through the lithographs of Currier and Ives, for example, *Road Winter* published in 1853 and *Sleigh Race* of a few years later.

When applying his oil colors, Krimmel gave the warm brown coats of the two foreground horses a polished smoothness that differs from the uneven surface of the partially melting snow. He used small brushes to achieve a closed surface and to catch effectively the light in areas of emphasis, such as the faces of the passengers on the nearer sleigh. In contrast with the wide array of bright colors that he had used, for instance, in *Cherry Woman*, a painting he exhibited 1820, in *The Sleighing Frolic* Krimmel worked with the variations and gradations of whites, grays, and browns to achieve a unified atmosphere in his landscape. Red and green appear only as small details, such as the pennant, the scarf of the young woman, and the cap of the girl. (Krimmel's prediliction for satirizing the fashion conscious, detectable in many of his genre scenes, is evident in the extravagant bow on the young woman's hat and the stylish coat of her suitor.)

Krimmel's sensitive rendering of the winter sky and its light reflected on the snow, together with the charming delineation of the bare trees, represent in 1820 a rare achievement in American landscape painting and a seldom-depicted motif. The design of the two trees, the lone bird perched on a long branch, and the swarm of birds suggest an influence of two paintings by Pieter Brueghel the Elder. The taller tree is reminiscent of *The Hunters in the Snow* (1565); the shorter tree is almost identical with one near the center of *A Gloomy Day (February)* (1565).[27] Both Brueghel pictures were genre paintings as well as landscapes, and both came into collections of the princes of the House of Austria in the late sixteenth century; they were in Vienna when Krimmel spent three weeks there in 1818, and he may have made drawings of them.

One plausible explanation for Krimmel's referral to his old canvases and for recycling his earlier ideas in 1819 and 1820 is that he was spending considerable time and effort on a personal project, a canvas that he had no intention of offering for public sale. This canvas is a group painting in which Krimmel demonstrated his wholehearted embrace of romanticism. It is one of the few

27. F. Grossman, *Brueghel's Paintings: Complete Edition of the Paintings* (London: Phaidon Press, 1966), pp. 8, 198.

paintings to impart fully Krimmel's capabilities as a mature artist. Because the history of the painting is clouded, an explanation of it as an image that expressed the influences he absorbed from German romantic painting requires a detailed discussion.[28]

On first viewing, the well-balanced portrayal of four adults and six children in their "Sunday best" with a recumbent dog in a pleasant family gathering is a typical conversation piece in an interior setting (fig. 309). The image is distinctly middle class, largely because of the natural looks of the sitters and informal poses of the children. It is a seemingly quickly staged, unpretentiously arranged group, and it almost presages images captured in group photographs at midcentury, but the painting exudes a peculiar seriousness and stillness. No one "speaks." It is an image of restrained inaction rather than narrative action. The figures have a quiet presence that is heightened by the artist's clean, linear handling of form. Intense colors and special lighting contribute to the mood, and they relieve the static nature of the design. Each figure is clearly contoured and strongly differentiated by color. As with the designs that dominate Krimmel's 1819 and 1820 genre paintings, the figures are arranged in measured spatial intervals that create a convincing illusion of progression within the space. Each person is rendered a distinct individual, but in the aggregate they all bear a strong family resemblance. And although each figure reflects the artist's intimate knowledge of the person, the figures have also been elevated to a higher, symbolic level. Their faces are accented, their eyes possess special intensity.

Only by contemplating the details does one acquire an appreciation of the subtle symbolism and deep meaning in the picture, for there is no trace of the sentimentality so often seen in other family pictures of the period, particularly with regard to the children. The key to understanding the peculiarity of this picture is the knowledge that the central figure, the young mother, and the four children next to her are dead. The other three adults and two children are alive. The living persons are depicted at their ages when the mother died, and the dead are depicted according to their ages at death.[29]

Susana Krimmel is the mother who gazes directly at the viewer. Krimmel had sketched her and three of her daughters in sketchbook 3 (figs. 310, 311). To emphasize Susana's primacy the artist has painted her in crimson and placed her chair on a dais.[30] She holds a baby on her lap, and the composition of these two figures is similar to that used by Nazarenes in Germany and Austria when depicting a Madonna. Krimmel made it anatomically explicit that the baby is male, and he parted the infant's hair on the side to distinguish it from that of the girls', which is uniformly parted in the middle.

One daughter links arms with her mother, symbolizing their unity, and she visually connects the other two girls in this half of the painting to their mother. Further, the angle of the mother's left arm is precisely repeated three times in these daughters' arms, a deliberate repetition that conjures the image of links in a chain. The kneeling daughter looks on as her little sister carefully unfolds a paper. Strewn on the floor next to them are two other pieces of unfolded paper, possibly a combined reference to her few years of life. In the foreground, precisely at midpoint, is a black poodle in a posture suggestive of that of a guardian.[31] Krimmel's 1818 sketch of instrument-maker Beck's poodle may have served as the basis for the design of this dog (see fig. 231). Behind the dog is a doll whose prostrate position is reminiscent of that of a dead person, the angle of its pose points to the mother, her infant, and the three girls to her left.

28. For a discussion of the introduction of romanticism, see Nygren, *Views and Visions*, p. 49.

29. My reading of this picture is bolstered by the Verzeichnis Register, the records of the Krimmel's church and information in George's 1830 will that specified his heirs. "J" Krimmel, a daughter born in Europe, possibly Basel ca. 1802, died age 11 on July 1, 1813, five years after her parents emigrated in 1807; Heinrich (Henry), born October 1, baptized November 12, 1807, was age 11 at time of mother's death and still alive in 1830; Catharina (Catherine), born September 16, 1808, baptized September 27, 1809, date of death unrecorded but probably about the time of mother's death, not alive in 1830; Frederika (Fredericka), born May 11, 1810, baptized May 28, 1811, age 8 in 1818 and still alive in 1830; Georg Friedrich (George Frederick), born August 17, 1811, died age 5 months on January 22, 1812; Susana, born February 10, 1814, baptized November 10, 1815, age 4 in 1818 and still alive in 1830; a daughter born in Europe, possibly Basel, in 1804 or 1805, died age 2 or 3 before the family emigrated (she is unmentioned in American records but explains the gap between the births of "J" and Heinrich).

30. Red is traditionally associated with the person of greatest importance because the color is a signal of eminence; see George Ferguson, *Signs and Symbols in Christian Art* (New York: Oxford University Press, 1954), pp. 47, 180.

31. Because of their watchfulness and faithfulness, dogs are traditional symbols of fidelity; see Eva C. Hangen, *Symbols: Our Universal Language* (Wichita, Kans.: McCormick-Armstrong, 1962), p. 90; Ferguson, *Signs and Symbols*, p. 9. Most of Krimmel's genre paintings included a dog; the posture and placement of this one is reminiscent of the dogs in *Country Frolic and Dance*, *Interior of an American Inn*, and *Country Wedding*.

FIGURE 309
John Lewis Krimmel, Portrait of the Artist and the Krimmel Family *(called by the museum* An Artist and His Family), *ca. 1820. Oil on canvas; 29½ x 25 in. (The National Gallery of Art, Washington.) On the back of the painting in a nineteenth-century hand is "J. L. Krimmel" and "Portrait of the Artist with the Krimmel Family."*

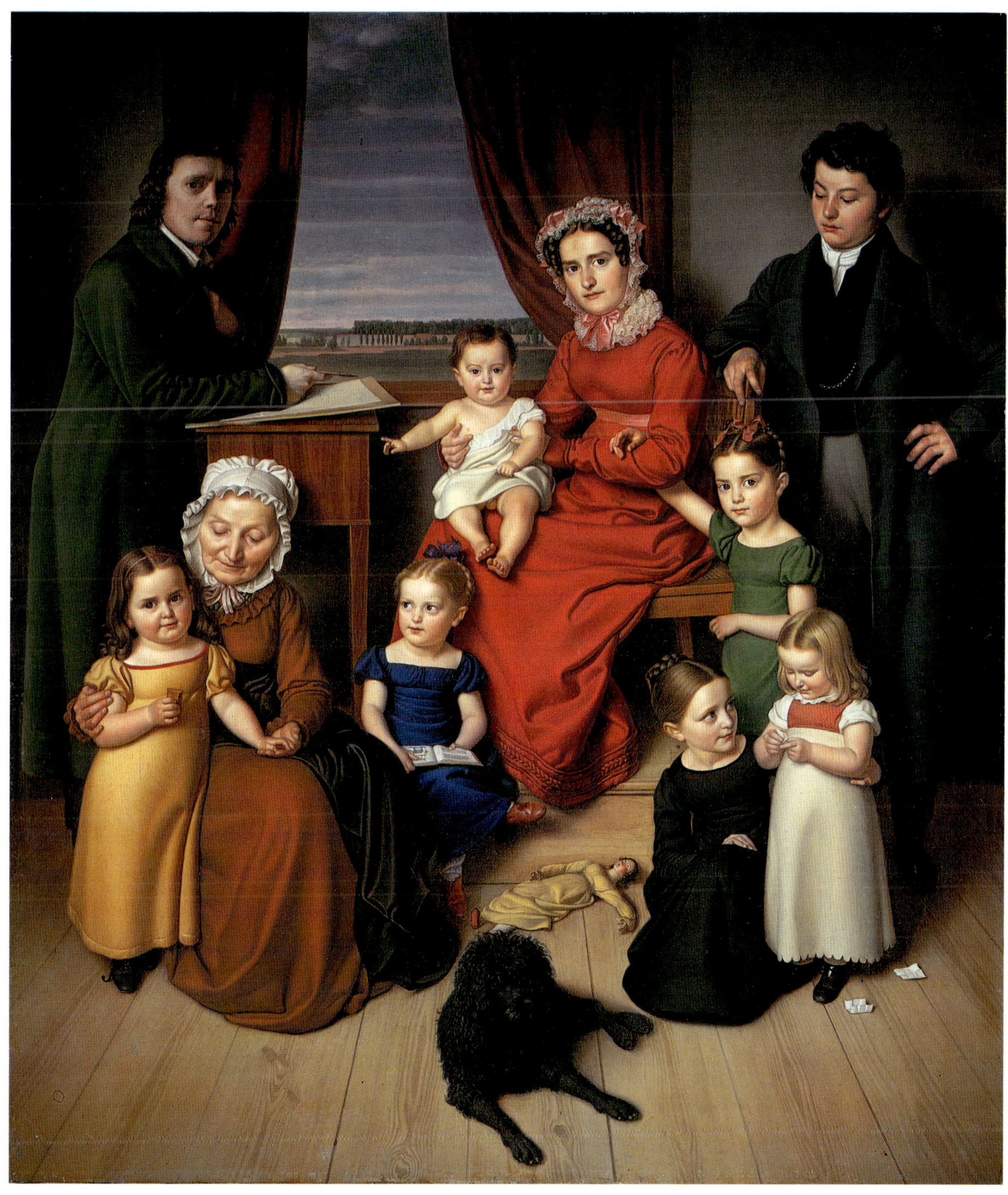

FIGURE 310
Seated girl, September 9, 1813 or 1814, watercolor over pencil; young girl, back of head, 1813 or 1814, watercolor over pencil; head of child, head and upper body of child, head and shoulders of woman, 1813, pencil. Sketchbook 3, leaf 22 recto.

FIGURE 311
Studies of little girls, September 1, 1813. Watercolor and ink over pencil; pencil. Sketchbook 3, leaf 4 verso.

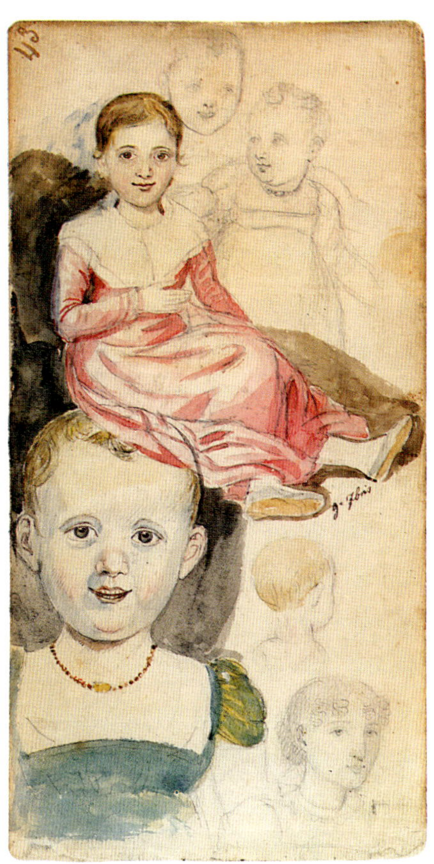

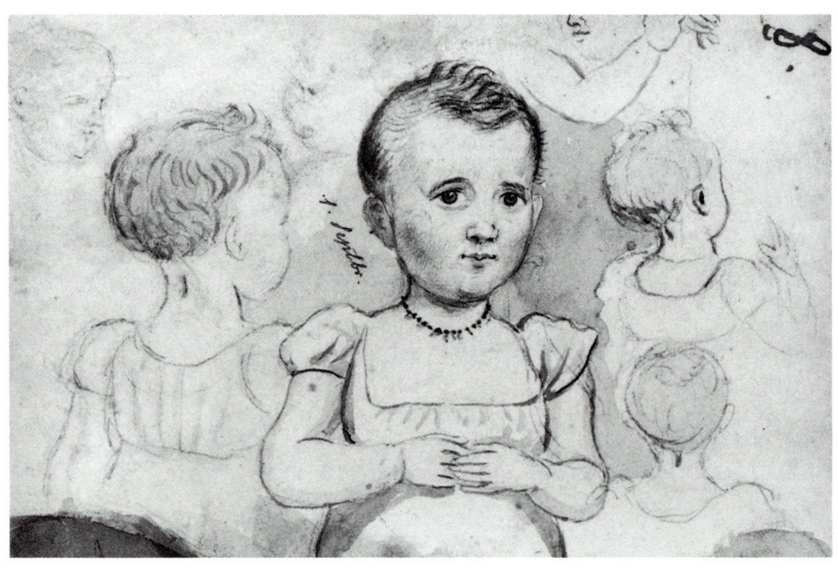

From the perspective of the sitters, the decedents are on the sinister (or left) side. Behind and somewhat above the decedents stands the sorrowing husband/father. In the dexter (or right) realm of the living sits a pale grandmotherly woman flanked by two girls, each of whom holds an object symbolizing continued involvement with life: food (chocolate), and a picture book (in which one of the two illustrations is an elephant similar to the one Krimmel drew in July 1818). Behind these three figures and somewhat above stands the draftsman artist. The features of the older child are strikingly similar to the blonde child Krimmel sketched in the summer of 1813 (see figs. 95–99). This may be Frederika Krimmel who in 1813 was 3½ years old and 8 at the time of her mother's death. Her younger sister Susana was born in 1814 and was only 4 at the time of her mother's death. The older woman is probably the children's maternal grandmother; her dark clothes signaling mourning, her downcast eyes and face expressing resignation.

At the time of his wife's death George was 43 years old, which is consonant with the image on the canvas. In the painting this bereft husband rests his right arm on the back of Susana's chair, yet he is separated from her and signals this by the unnatural separation of his index and middle fingers. His general demeanor is characteristic of a "sorrowing figure," a type often represented in American memorial pictures of the period.[32]

To the left stands John Lewis Krimmel (in 1818 only 32 years old and, as Ritter recalled, "5 ft 9 in. high. Slim and of very elastic, wiry motions. Light complexion. Hair Light Brown & curling, Blue Eyes. . . . Pleasing expression of countenance"), brush in hand at a tall work table. He stares at the viewer in a manner typical of a self-portrait made by an artist who was using a mirror to capture his visage on canvas.[33] His left hand, partially slipped inside his coat, presses against his breast in a gesture of love. His drafting paper is seemingly marked with the design of a memorial stone.

The antecedents for the design and figure placement on this canvas can be traced to various Krimmel works. Using juxtaposed figures—in this case, the two brothers—to stabilize an otherwise flowing design was a compositional rule Krimmel liked to observe. The outlining of Susana's head and shoulders in three-quarter profile as well as the extended sweep of her right arm were techniques he had used in his portrait of Ritter. The symmetrically balanced composition, stratified into a foreground occupied by figures, a thin midground that functions like a frame, and a background with a distant view, was a design he had recently applied in his portraits of Heckewelder and Thomas and in *The Sleighing Frolic*. The reliance on a circular cohesion, here tying the women, children, dog, and doll together in the foreground, was a design he had used in *Return from Market* and in *The Sleighing Frolic*. And, although he placed the figures in a relatively compressed arrangement, the painting has some structural similarities to Granet's *Choir of the Capuchin Church in Rome*, a design firmly closed on each side, with figures grouped in juxtaposition and oriented toward an open space in the middle, the floorboards running perpendicular to the picture frame, and strong horizontals stabilizing the background.

Specific details also have counterparts in Krimmel's other pictures, for example the ruche collar and hairstyle of Susana are the same as that of the young woman in *The Sleighing Frolic*, the white scarflike cravats of George Krimmel and Francis Thomas are the same, and, as in all his finished portraits, the artist gives life and expression to the eyes by adding a spot of light in the upper part of the eye, just above the pupil (*Young Woman in a Blue Dress*, and

32. Anita Schorsch, "A Key to the Kingdom: The Iconography of a Mourning Picture," *Winterthur Portfolio* 14, no. 1 (Spring 1979): 41–71; Jean Lipman and Tom Armstrong, eds., *American Folk Painters of Three Centuries* (New York: Hudson Hills Press, 1980), p. 147; John Ebert and Katherine Ebert, *Old American Prints for Collectors* (New York: Charles Scribner's Sons, 1974), p. 72.

33. Ritter, "Recollections," p. 120. Krimmel had done what may be a tiny self-portrait in sketchbook 5, leaf 36 recto (see fig. 207). In 1831 a portrait by Krimmel titled *Portrait of Himself* was exhibited at PAFA; in 1843 *Portrait of the late L. Krimmel*, owned by Alexander Lawson, was exhibited; the whereabouts of these are unknown.

the portraits of Ritter, Heckewelder, and Thomas). The dresses, bonnets, and hairstyles of the women and children are based on his sketchbook studies, especially those in sketchbooks 6 and 7, which contain distinctly similar details (figs. 312–314).

Krimmel was adroit at painting recognizable portraits without the benefit of a sitter in front of him. In *Victory on Lake Champlain* he had depicted at least fifteen identifiable men, none of whom sat for him; *Election Day 1815* was similarly distinguished by its inclusion of identifiable local politicians. For both, Krimmel relied on existing prints, paintings, and his memory to paint a recognizable visage. His portraits of Heckewelder and Thomas were done from sketches. To be sure, the family portrait was a larger undertaking and required greater accuracy, but Krimmel had a good resource. Krimmel had previously painted Susana and her children in a group portrait that still hung in his brother's house, thus he could refer to it as necessary.[34] An artist depicting himself with other family members was a favorite motif of German romantic painters whose double and triple portraits often included themselves with sisters, brothers, or friends. One of the most famous of these is Philipp Otto Runge's *Wir Drei* [The Three of Us] (1805), which portrays Runge, his wife, and his brother. Memorial pictures had become popular in America following the death of Washington in 1799, but most images were stylized rather than specific. Few artists in the United States undertook to paint a family group with a self-portrait as a memorial picture. An exception was Robert Peckham of Massachusetts, who in late 1817 or 1818 portrayed four generations of his wife's family at a special occasion. They are grieving for a little girl who died in 1817. She is included in the painting, standing at the corner of the table (fig. 315). In contrast German romanticism encouraged artists to express their feelings in their art and promoted allegory and symbolism, precepts of traditional art, to modern compositions.[35]

Accepting these directives, Krimmel conceived a painting that reunited the members of his brother's family—living and dead—a pictorial symbol of family love and binding spiritual unity. This was an adaptation of a distinguished fifteenth-century convention in northern European art that had found expression in altarpieces and epitaphs. Such canvases often depicted both the surviving and deceased members of a donor's family in a single composition, and the dead were usually identified by small crosses painted above their heads. Hans Holbein the Younger broke with that convention and painted *Madonna des Bürgermeister Meyer* (1526) in which husband, second wife, children, and deceased first wife kneel side by side without any clear indication that one was dead. German romantic painters, particularly the Nazarenes, often took the works of fifteenth- and sixteenth-century masters as models following the guidelines set forth by W. H. Wackenroder in *Herzensergiessungen eines kunstliebenden Klosterbruders* (Effusions from the Heart of an Art-Loving Friar) a small but influential book published in 1796. Wackenroder urged artists to rediscover early German art, to banish preconceived ideas of any style or manner, and to commit themselves to an emotional expression in art. An example is Friedrich Overbeck's *Christ Visiting Mary and Martha* (1810). Among the paintings in Vienna at the time of Krimmel's visit was *The Holy Kinship* (1515) by Lucas Cranach the Elder, depicting a gathering of the relatives of Jesus—it includes a self-portrait of the artist as a bystander. A Württemberg artist now known only as Dietrich followed these rules when he painted a memorial picture of the Kurz family (fig. 316). His group portrait depicts the father seated

34. Heckewelder to DuPonceau, January 7, 1821, DuPonceau Papers; Ritter, "Recollections," p. 120; Dunlap, *History*, 2:395. Ritter stated, "In this residence [George Frederick's house], over the door of the entrance from the back building, there hung a family picture of our artist, representing his entrance into the room with a newspaper in his hand, smiling as he was wont at the group of Mrs. K and her children as they stood by her lap in which every likeness was to the very life" (Naeve, *Krimmel*, p. 19). I thank Naeve for alerting me to the Ritter quote, which is not on the page he cites and is not in the microfilm copy.

35. Phoebe Lloyd Jacobs, "John James Barralet and the Apotheosis of George Washington," in *Winterthur Portfolio 12*, ed. Ian M. G. Quimby (Charlottesville: University Press of Virginia, 1977), pp. 115–37; Carol Troyen, *The Boston Tradition: American Paintings from the Museum of Fine Arts, Boston* (New York: American Federation of Arts, 1980), p. 91.

FIGURE 312
Studies of young girl, ca. 1820. Watercolor over pencil, pencil. Sketchbook 6, leaf 14 recto. Krimmel seems to have made these studies to plot out the design of Susana Krimmel's dress and the pose of the second oldest girl.

FIGURE 313
Study of young girl, ca. 1819/20. Watercolor over pencil. Sketchbook 6, leaf 15 verso.

FIGURE 314
Head and shoulders of young girl, ca. 1819/20. Watercolor and pencil. Sketchbook 7, leaf 7 verso.

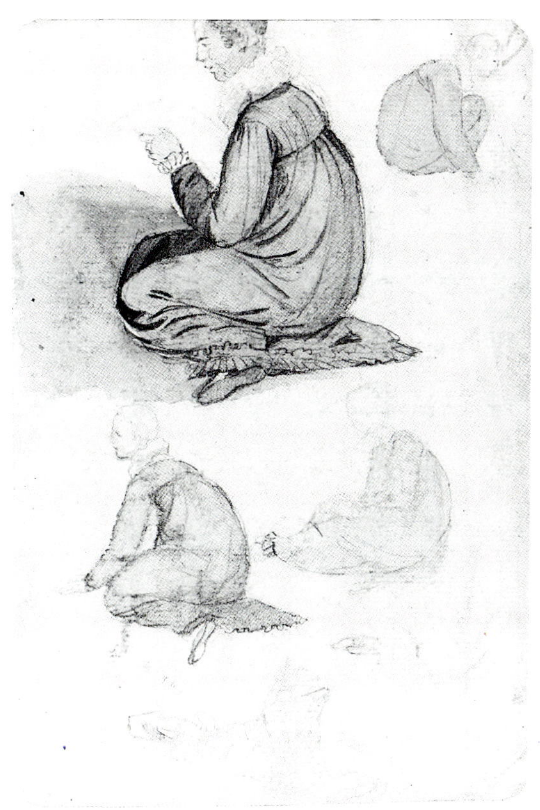

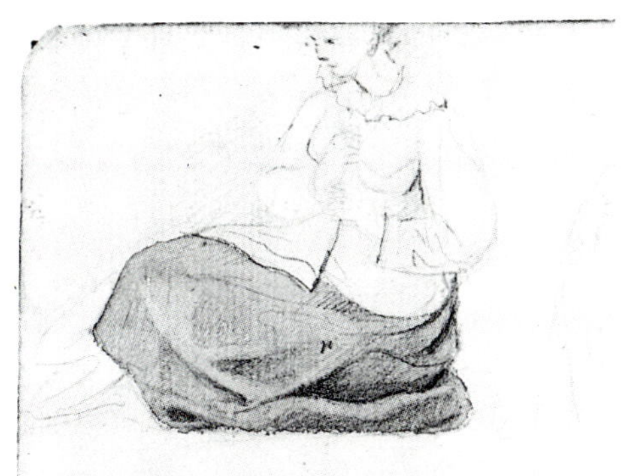

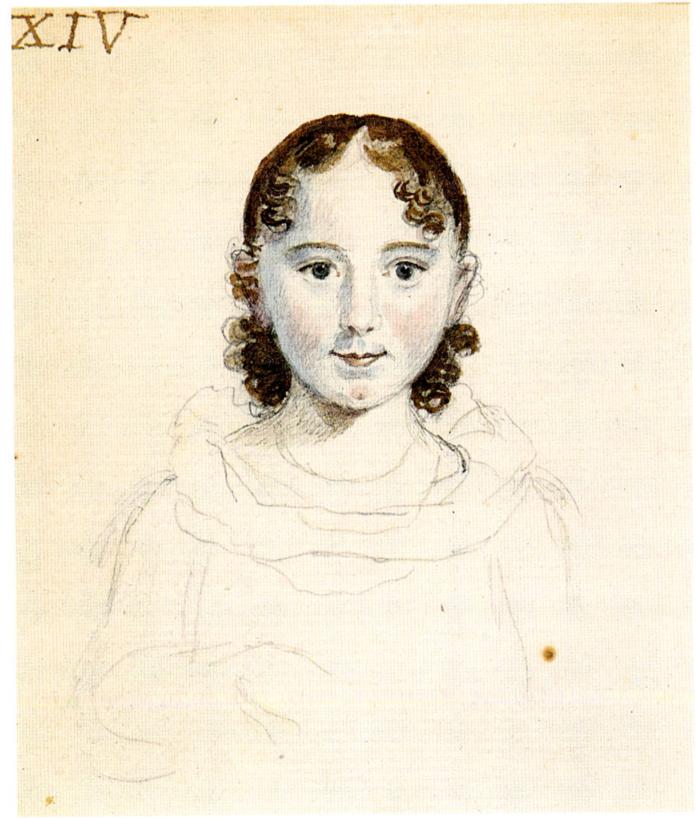

FIGURE 315
Robert Peckham, The Peckham-Sawyer Family, *ca. 1817. Oil on canvas; 29 x 34 in. (The Hayden Collection, Museum of Fine Arts, Boston.)*

FIGURE 316
Dietrich, Familie Kurz, *Württemberg, ca. 1815. Oil on canvas. (Galerie der Stadt Stuttgart.)*

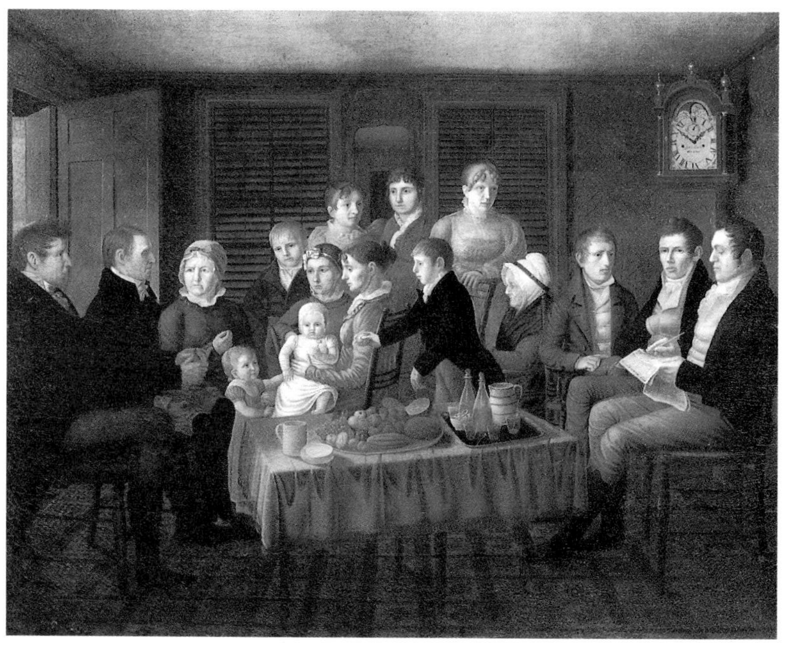

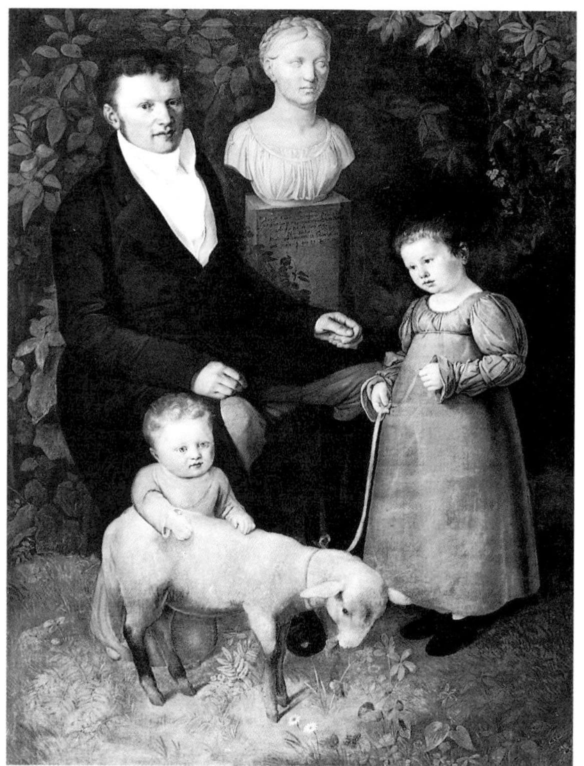

beside a marble bust of his deceased wife while their two children play with a lamb in front of him.[36] Given Krimmel's probable exposure to the Nazarenes in 1818, it is not surprising that he decided to design a memorial portrait that drew upon older German religious paintings, especially those representing the holy kinship.

Once he had settled on the composition and elements, Krimmel began applying the techniques he had learned in Europe. To increase the sense of volume and mass he painted large areas of pure, intense colors and achieved a closed enamel-like surface, such as he had seen in Nazarene art. He also adopted their emphasis on strong outline and preference for stylized realism, although not their fervent religiosity and penchant for softness of expression. But meticulous and impersonal application of color, seemingly done without the intervention of the artist, was a hallmark of all German romantic painting.

Making use of the romantic prerogative of expression through allegory, Krimmel referred to death through the posture of the doll, the guarding position of the dog, the strewn paper, and the colors. He assigned each figure a different color and gave the dress of Susana and those of the youngest children the largest areas of luminescence with varying degrees of intensity, thereby creating a strong pictorial presence for each individual figure.

As in the portrait of Ritter, Krimmel applied the colors with fine brushes and repeatedly overlaid them with thin glazes and scumbles to achieve a polished surface that conveys the nature of textures—in this instance the smoothness and sheen of heavy silk, the soft touch of woolen, and the grain of wood. Light is seemingly trapped between the transparent layers. Minutely added highlights play on skin, hair, and eyes, creating a naturalistic, three-dimensional effect. Brush strokes are nearly invisible.[37] Krimmel had been practicing with a closed, polished style in the oil portraits he completed following his return from Europe, although in watercolor he had retained the loosely brushed style in which his hand—the characteristic stroke of his brush—remained apparent (see figs. 248–251).

To achieve the illusion of pictorial space, Krimmel gave special attention to the position of the figures, the sculptural presence with which he defined each one, and the rhythmic pattern of the floorboards. In contrast to his interior genre scenes, which were rich with still-life elements, the connotative nature of this group portrait demanded a minimum of furnishings. Heavy drapes flank an open window with its view of a flat landscape with only two isolated buildings. (This portion of the painting is partly restored.) The landscape, defined in strong horizontals and accented by trees and shrubs, seems to extend beyond the picture as does the long horizontal view in *The Sleighing Frolic*.

Since 1955 the authorship of the family portrait has been disputed. Krimmel authority Milo M. Naeve has argued that the painting is not by Krimmel. He bases his conclusion on technical differences apparent between this canvas and the aggregate of Krimmel's paintings and on details in the will of George Frederick Krimmel. Most of the technical distinctions he draws are based upon comparisons of the family portrait and Krimmel's pre-European-trip paintings, rather than a close study of the 1819–21 images. Second, he interprets the image as a standard portrait and points out that although the picture was titled *An Artist and His Family* when it emerged from a private collection in 1922, J. L. Krimmel was a life-long bachelor. To this he adds facts drawn from the few records left by or about the Krimmels that were written in English. Because Susana died while Krimmel was abroad, she could not

36. I thank Dr. Ulrike Gauss, National Galerie Stuttgart, for bringing *The Kurz Family* (Galerie der Stadt Stuttgart) to my attention.

37. Dunlap (*History*, 2:394) notes that Krimmel preferred special fine brushes and includes artist John Neagle's comment: "His [Krimmel's] acute vision led him to the use of very small brushes, some no thicker than a common pin. After his death I purchased, at a sale of his effects, all his brushes, many were so small as to be useless to me, and I gave them to his friend Rider, who works with the same kind of tools."

have posed for the portrait, and because at the time of George Frederick's death in 1830 only three children were mentioned in his will (two daughters and a son), Naeve rules out the possibility that the picture represents the artist and his brother's family.[38]

There is, however, other material of which Naeve was not fully aware. Records of Philadelphia's St. Michael's and Zion Lutheran Church, of which George and Susana were members, document the births of three daughters—Katharina, Frederika, Susana—and two sons—Heinrich and Georg; and the deaths of two children—11-year-old "J", who was born in Europe, and 5-month-old Georg. The age of "J", who died in 1813, makes it possible to impute the birth of one other child from what we know of Susana's age, probable date of marriage, and normal childbearing patterns. The main problem that emerges from this assemblage of facts and presumptions is that the oldest son, Henry, who was 11 years old at the time of his mother's death and who is mentioned in his father's holographic will, is not included in the portrait. His absence is inexplicable.

George Krimmel had become a land surveyor and had moved to Northern Liberties. He signed a will on October 6, 1830, on the same day he died, in which he bequeathed to his son Henry (age 23) $5 and to his youngest daughter Susana (age 16) all of his household goods. The remainder of the estate was to be divided equally between Susana and his elder daughter Frederika (age 21 and probably married since she was not given his household goods). The gender disparity in the settlements may indicate that Krimmel had already settled property on Henry; conversely it may be a signal of a family dynamic about which no record has survived. Henry's absence does weaken the case for this painting being a full representation of George and Susana's family. Henry may be the boy asleep on a chair in sketchbook 3; however, that drawing is amidst the series done in Bermuda. It would have to have been done in 1815 or 1816 when Henry was 8 or 9 years old.[39]

Because of the objections raised by Naeve in the late 1950s, the picture was reattributed to the "German School," but there are clear differences between this painting and those painted by Germans working in the romantic idiom.[40] The clothes worn by the sitters are neither Germanic nor Continental. The dresses and types of bonnets worn by the women and children in the painting are the sort found throughout Krimmel's sketchbooks (see figs. 118, 271, 299, 312–314).[41] The painter of the family portrait has identified himself with the romantic movement but with restraint. There is no outpouring of emotion; instead there is an adherence to the formal tradition of the Anglo-American family portrait as introduced by John Smibert in *Bermuda Group: Dean George Berkley and His Entourage* (1729), and continued by Robert Feke, Joseph Blackburn, Charles Willson Peale, and others. German artists in the early nineteenth century tended to depict family portraits like genre scenes, showing sitters in spacious, well-furnished settings that provided information about the family's life-style. These objects and furnishings are often so elaborately rendered that they compete with the sitters for the viewer's attention. The German overtones in the image are most explicable if the canvas is seen as the product of an artist whose general development was shaped by an Anglo-American approach to art and had recently been exposed to trends in Germany's romanticism, rather than as the product of an artist who trained in Germany and then had adapted his style to Anglo-American tastes.

38. Naeve, "Krimmel," pp. 197–98; Naeve, *Krimmel*, p. 186.

39. The executor of the will was Krimmel's partner Abraham Ritter. The most valuable item listed was George's surveyor's gear, at $60; George Frederick Krimmel, Will, 1830, Book 9, p. 592, Register of Wills, City Hall, Philadelphia.

40. Karl Begas, *Familie Begas* (1821; Wallraf-Richartz Museum, Cologne) is a group portrait depicting nine members of the artist's family, including himself and is an apt example of a contemporaneous painting.

41. The two early nineteenth-century fashion centers were Paris and London. Most middle- and upper-class people in the United States followed English styles; men and women in Germany, especially in the south and the Rhineland, emulated French fashions. German men wore higher collars than men in England and the United States; German women preferred a hairstyle that featured small curls hanging from the middle of the crown extending over the forehead and the temples, or they wore their hair straight, parted in the middle and softly drawn over the ears; see examples in Schrade, *Deutsch Malerei*; William B. Vaughan, *German Romantic Painting* (New Haven: Yale University Press, 1980).

FIGURE 317
A German Funeral, *1820. Oil on wood panel; 8¼ x 11¼ in. (Private collection: Photo, Winterthur.)*

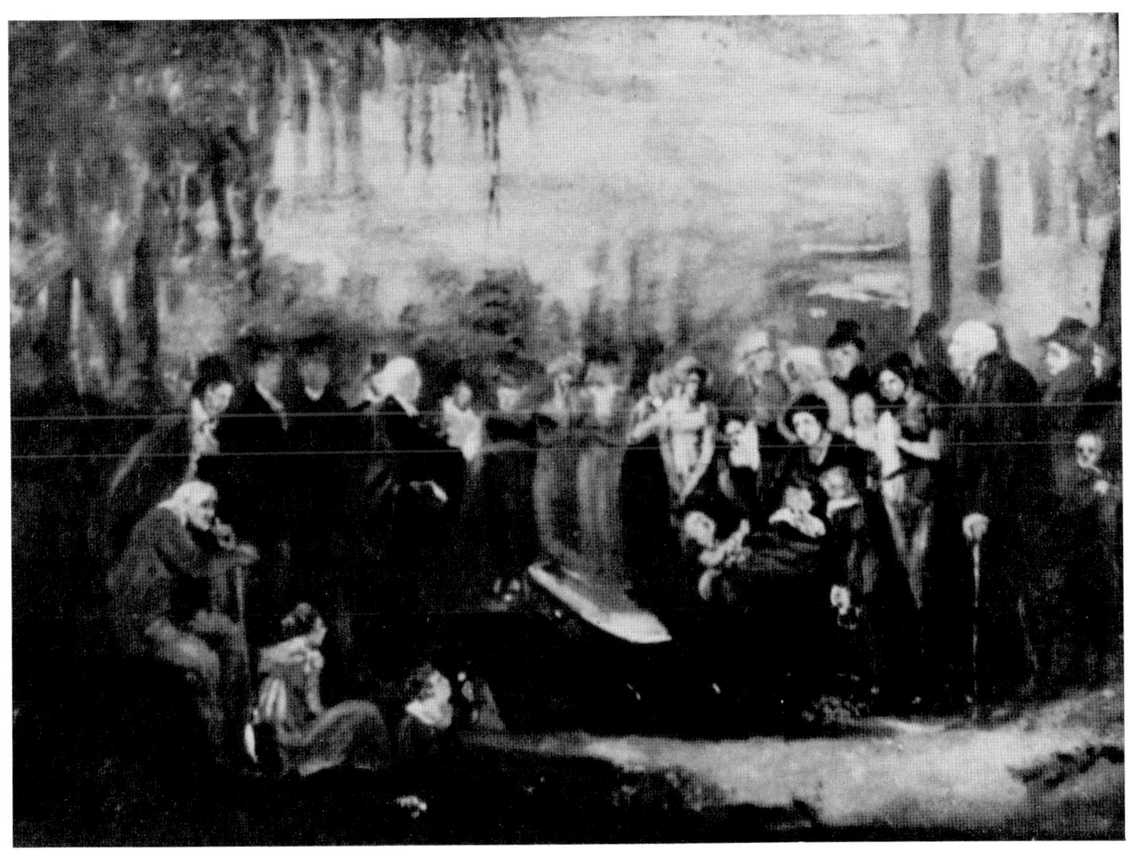

In 1819 and 1820 Krimmel tackled a scene that dealt overtly with death—an especially bold choice of subject matter. (One of the first Europeans to pursue this theme was Gustave Courbet, whose 1850 *Burial at Ornans* was deemed an act of defiance by the art establishment.) The graphic qualities of Krimmel's painting were apparently compelling. Abraham Ritter maintained that "Funeral" was one of two paintings that would "live to his [Krimmel's] fame as long as canvass or paper project their charge."[42]

If the oil on panel sketch that survives in a private collection is an index, the image was indeed striking (fig. 317). The setting is a cemetery late in the summer. A bereaved woman and children stand next to a long coffin ready to be lowered into a grave. A clergyman is flanked by men who stand quietly, in contrast to the women and children who are in great emotional distress. A tall, elderly gentleman to the right rests on his walking stick in a pose reminiscent of the one Krimmel used for Heckewelder. Several bystanders are individualized, as if the artist was intent upon making them identifiable, and a great variety of expressions emphasize the participants' emotions in a manner similar to *Soldier Taking Leave of His Family.* Krimmel framed the closely gathered figures with trees and architecture and again used his stock figure types—for example, a woman with downcast eyes and clasped hands. Thus *A German Funeral* was a combined group portrait and genre painting, which in style corresponds to other works painted by Krimmel during 1819/20 that employed a romantic emphasis on feelings and on the use of a deeper pictorial space.

The painting did not attract a buyer, if indeed he even offered it for sale. *A German Funeral,* identified as a sketch in oil, was among his studio effects in 1821; in 1834 Krimmel's *Sketch of a German Funeral* was exhibited at the academy and identified as belonging to John Vaughan, long-time treasurer and librarian of the American Philosophical Society. The small oil on panel may be the sketch in oil listed in the inventory of Krimmel's goods or the preparatory study for the painting Vaughan owned.[43]

By 1821 Krimmel had replaced neoclassical tenets with those of romanticism and was creating images that had greater variety in design, deeper spatial concepts, and more expressive colors. More important, he had expanded his ability to convey a broad range of human feelings: joy of life in *Return from Market, Country Frolic and Dance, The Sleighing Frolic, Fourth of July Celebration 1819;* sorrow of death and separation in *Soldier Taking Leave of His Family, Portrait of the Artist and the Krimmel Family,* and *A German Funeral.*

The same artistic independence that had prompted Krimmel a decade earlier to paint genre pictures of recognizably American scenes at a time when the people were being fed a steady diet of portraits, still lifes, history paintings, and copy work, in 1819 also motivated him to apply his talents in new directions, to fresh opportunities that helped him weather the severe economic depression. No longer was he content to confine himself to the traditional work of the easel painter. He began to explore collaborative and innovative projects that involved new technology. Krimmel may have hoped that the role of the painter would change as technological advances occurred in reproductive illustrations. For in the same years that he was resuming his career as a genre painter in Philadelphia and was undertaking portraits and the memorial picture, he was also shifting part of his attention to projects that capitalized on new economic developments and yet would allow him to continue to construct the genre scenes at which he excelled. In 1819 Krimmel strove mightily to keep his career afloat.

42. Ritter, "Recollections," p. 119.

43. *Poulson's American Daily Advertiser,* August 14, 1821; *Twenty-third Annual Exhibition . . .* (1834), no. 11. According to Naeve, *Krimmel,* p. 94, Vaughan bequeathed his painting to Joseph Sill. The oil on panel was acquired by its current owner about 1940 in a sale in New York City (owner to A. Harding, January 12, 1982).

New Avenues—Collaborations

Krimmel's efforts to depict scenes that were clearly identifiable as Philadelphian or American coincided with the efforts by writers and others to develop a cultural identity for the United States that was distinct from England's and continental Europe's. While politicians tried to chart a national course that steered clear of European dominance, poets and essayists began to look to the New World for inspiration and settings for their stories.[1] Among these writers was Washington Irving, whose *Knickerbocker Tales* was followed by "Rip Van Winkle," and "The Legend of Sleepy Hollow," which appeared in serial and book form. The public response was enthusiastic. In the meantime, Europeans who were infused with the romantic spirit strove to preserve their distinct cultural heritages. Perhaps because he had so recently returned from Germany, Krimmel saw possiblities that applied to his own work. He calculated that American passion for indigenous subject matter would spill into the artistic realm—were the images affordable to a general public—and accordingly began investigating ways to translate his images of everyday life into the print medium.

Printmaking required a collaborative effort by painters, engravers, and publishers. Ideally each print could be issued as an illustration in a book or magazine and then sold separately as an image suitable for framing or hanging on the wall. This would take advantage of the rapidly expanding publishing network in and around Philadelphia.

One of Krimmel's first prospects in collaborative work came in the form of copy work. The board of managers of Philadelphia's Pennsylvania Hospital wanted an engraving of Benjamin West's *Christ Healing the Sick in the Temple* (fig. 318). Krimmel decided to pursue the commission to produce the drawing from which the engraver would work because to be identified with this sensationally popular painting would unquestionably enhance his reputation.

The painting had been done by West in response to a request in 1800 from the managers of the hospital for an image that could be used to raise money for "the relief of the sick poor." It took him more than a decade to complete the canvas, and before shipping it to the States he exhibited it at the gallery of the British Institution, which then offered to buy it for 3,000 guineas (£3,150), an unusually high price, and West, greatly pressed for money, accepted the offer but reserved the right to paint a copy for the Pennsylvania Hospital.[2] The copy was completed in 1815 and shipped to Philadelphia in 1817.

To display the painting the hospital constructed a separate building. Admission fees were 25¢ for a one-time viewing, $10 for a life-ticket. Before the year was out, the hospital had earned a profit of $15,000. When the managers of the hospital voted to have an engraving of the image made, they decided to offer the project only to the most renowned of Philadelphia's artists. They awarded the commission to Thomas Sully, but he soon decided that "the money [$500] would not pay him & beg'd off the bargain [unless they made] an addition of 200 to the price—they chose to let him off. . . . This was in 1818

1. In the first decade of the century Philadelphian Charles Brockden Brown (1771–1810) was the first author to use American settings for his novels.

2. Robert C. Alberts, *Benjamin West: A Biography* (Boston: Houghton Mifflin Co., 1978); Allen Staley, *Benjamin West, 1738–1820: American Painters at the English Court* (Baltimore: Baltimore Museum of Art, 1989). The British Institution, a picture gallery established in 1806, is described in Whitley, *Art in England*, p. 106.

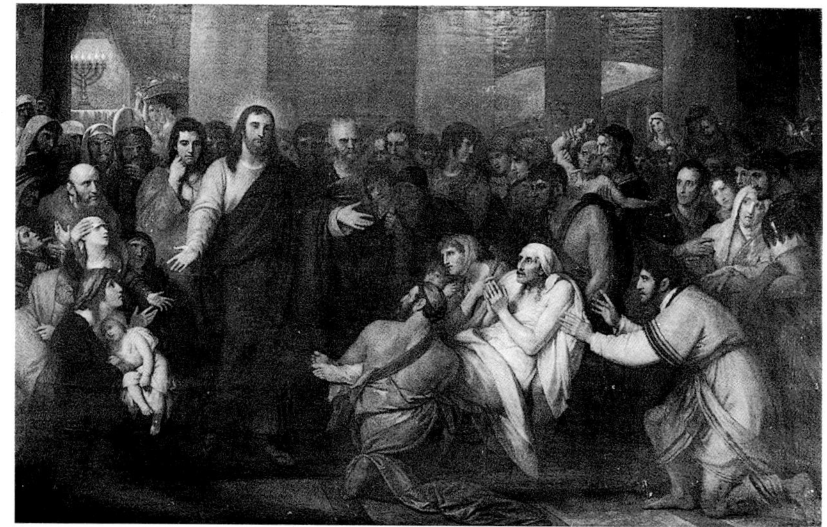

FIGURE 318
Benjamin West, Christ Healing the Sick in the Temple, *London, 1815. Oil on canvas; 120 x 180 in. Signed "Benj. West 1815." (Pennsylvania Hospital, Philadelphia.)*

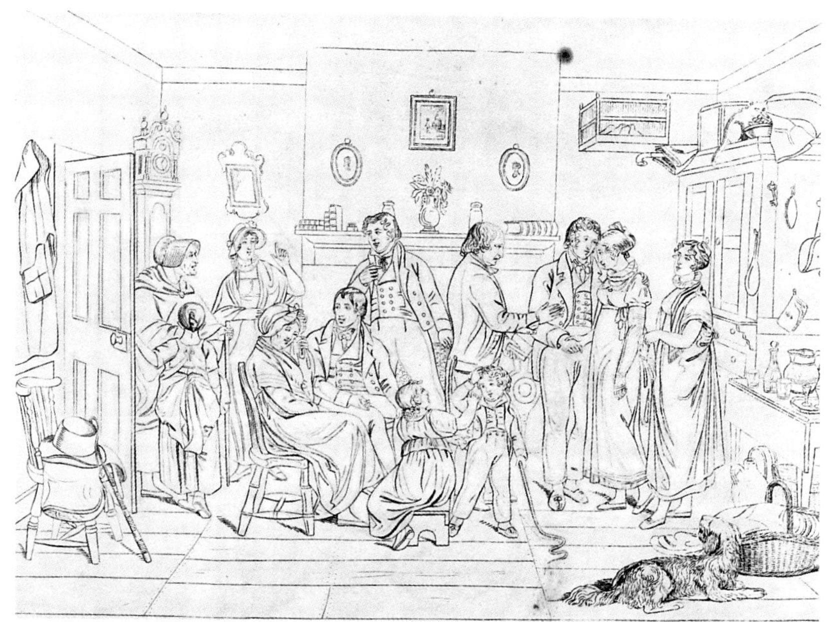

FIGURE 319
Unidentified engraver, John Lewis Krimmel pinxt, Country Wedding, *probably Philadelphia, 1819/20. Line engraving; 4 x 7 3/16 in. From* Analectic, *n.s., 1, no. 2 (February 1820): facing p. 176. (Joseph Downs Collection of Manuscripts and Printed Ephemera, Winterthur.)*

July." Nine months later the board had still not found a suitable artist for the project. On April 5, 1819, Sully informed Samuel Coates, president of the hospital, "that Mr. Krimmel the Painter has a desire to undertake the copy of Wests painting for the Hospital in order that it may be engraved." Believing "that my recommendation of his talent would have some weight," Sully continued, "I am happy to have it in my power to bear testimony to his ability as an Artist; and I am convinced that he will do justice to the undertaking. I beg you to make known to the Board of Management that this opinion is given by me without Mr. Krimmel's application for it."[3] Sully's endorsement suggests that he had followed Krimmel's career with interest in the years since inviting him to join the informal sketch club in 1812.

Two weeks later Krimmel sent a letter to Coates.

> Sir:
>
> Having understood, that you and the Honorable board of Managers of the Hospital contemplate to have a Print taken from West's celebrated Painting of "Christ healing the Sick" and Mr. Sully, on account of important engagements having declined to finish the Copy, I take liberty to offer my services for drawing an accurate Copy of the Same, in any manner desired.
>
> As to my abilities for accomplishing this task in the most satisfactory manner, I refer you to the board of the Academy of fine Arts, or any Artist of this City.
>
> Should you after a Satisfactory testimony, be inclined, to honour me with your confidence, please have the Goodness to give me notice, and I shall immediately wait upon you.[4]

On May 5, his offer was rejected. The board continued (without success) to seek the interest of an artist of greater stature.[5]

Undaunted, Krimmel explored other printmaking avenues, ones that would use his images rather than his copies of other artists' works. In this he was more successful. In 1820 three engravings of Krimmel's genre pictures were featured in *Analectic*, a Philadelphia-based monthly that catered to a national readership by publishing "original reviews, biographies, analytical abstracts of new publications, translations, and selections of foreign periodicals" and one or two engravings, usually of important buildings, sculptures, or paintings. The February 1820 issue included an engraving of *Country Wedding*, which it termed "a scene of no rare occurrence," and added, "the furniture and decorations of the room, the costume and attitudes of the characters show, perfectly the inside of a farmer's dwelling, and the business that occupies the group" (fig. 319). Recommending the picture to readers and to amateur painters, the magazine's editor, James Maxwell, gave Krimmel extraordinary but also much-needed publicity by specifying that the original canvas on which the engraving was based and three others—*Return from Camp, Country Dance* (probably *Country Frolic and Dance*), and *Return from a Boarding School*—were then in (thus presumably for sale at) Krimmel's studio located on Spruce Street above Seventh.[6]

Return from Camp has not survived, but it was probably a companion piece to *Soldier Taking Leave of His Family*, which indicates that Krimmel, like his European counterparts, saw the initial image as one half of a larger story. *Return from a Boarding School* was definitely one of a pair of images, both of which were printed in *Analectic* later in the year. Whether an oil or watercolor version of this image ever existed is unknown.[7]

3. Dunlap, *Diary*, p. 703; Sully to Samuel Coates, April 5, 1819, Joseph Downs Collection of Manuscripts and Printed Ephemera, Winterthur.

4. Krimmel to Samuel Coates, April 22, 1819, Downs Collection. Although Krimmel had undoubtedly studied the painting to learn how West handled a multifigured scene, in his own work he refrained from adopting West's style of sentimental proto-romantic, religious art.

5. No other artist was awarded the commission during Krimmel's lifetime; an engraving after the painting, drawn by Philadelphia artist James B. Longacre (a member of the AAA in 1819) was published in Bedell, *Religious Souvenir*, p. 176; a mezzotint was made in the 1850s by John Sartain. In 1822 Charles Heath did an engraving of the version of the painting that remained in London.

6. *Analectic*, n.s., 1, no. 2 (February 1820): 175–76.

7. Although *Analectic* mentioned that "Return from boarding school" was on view in Krimmel's studio, it is not specified as a painting. *Departure for a Boarding School* and *Return from a Boarding School* are referred to as ink drawings in Krimmel estate sale, *Poulson's American Daily Advertiser*, August 14, 1821. Naeve (*Krimmel*, pp. 111–14) points out that the engravings were later republished in *The Elements of Drawing . . .* (Philadelphia: Robert Desilver, 1823). The drawing *Return* seems to have remained in Philadelphia, although it was not listed in the March 1825 Cunningham catalogue for the auction of the Devaltooth estate; *Means for Boarding School* (No. 155), which can only have been *Departure for a Boarding School*, was. A copperplate of *Return* is owned by the Library Company of Philadelphia and bears the stamp "J. B. Keim" on the back. Keim, who worked in the city ca. 1815–45, used a larger plate for the etching of Krimmel's image (11 ¼ x 15 in.) and made his aquatint from either the original drawing or the published print. After 1964 some prints were made from Keim's plate; I thank Naeve for calling my attention to this.

The two boarding school images provide a scathing commentary about the problems caused by the wrong sort of education. When *Departure for a Boarding School* (fig. 320) appeared in the November 1820 issue of *Analectic*, Maxwell appended a lengthy descriptive text, lest any reader miss the point of Krimmel's story:

> The view now presented, shows the successful farmer counting over the *golden* returns of his harvest; the implements of husbandry close at hand, and the rustic decorations of the room are all indicative of his occupation. The old grandmother withdraws her attention from her bible, and raises her spectacles to gaze on the splendid heaps of money. The wife reproves the farmer's incivility, and removes his hat in compliment to the presence of the mistress of the boarding school, who having called to take her intended pupil to the city, looks with great scorn upon the vulgar rustics among whom she is obliged to pass a few moments. The girl appears to be taking leave of her lover, and is seen in all the simplicity of mien characteristic of a farmer's daughter. The stage coach is seen through the open door, and the driver is urging the departure of his passengers. The little girl packing up her young mistresses trunk, which seems to be providently furnished with a large bible, forms also a consistent part of the scene.[8]

As was customary, Krimmel blended many ideas in the image and used various pictorial models. To express the sweet innocence of the departing girl he turned to the modest maiden in *Autumn*, one of the prints engraved by Alexander Lawson to illustrate Thomson's epic poem *Seasons* (fig. 321). For the pose of the young woman and her sweetheart, he turned to his European sketches, adapting the watercolor of a bride and groom he had made at an Ebingen wedding (see fig. 284). He based the spinning wheel on a recent study in sketchbook 6 (fig. 322). *Return from Market*, which he had completed by May of 1819, provided him with other elements: the kneeling girl, the basket, the cat, the gesture of the schoolmistress, and her hat. Indeed, similarities between *Return from Market* and *Departure for a Boarding School* are so strong that they suggest Krimmel began *Departure* soon after completing *Return from Market*.

The composition of the eight figures, which are evenly divided into two groups, is asymmetrical. Gestures and movements string the scene together in a continuous harmoniously undulating silhouette. The ceiling beams, floorboards, and view beyond the open door enhance the pictorial depth. Various furnishings and decorations provide information about the family's life-style and the girl's character (note, for example, the image of a guardian angel that hangs above the mantel).

The companion picture, *Return from a Boarding School*, is executed in an equally meticulous and precisely defining manner that evinces Krimmel's knowledge of human nature (fig. 323). It depicts the same people in the same setting a school term later. The themes are simple—the wrong kind of education has ruined the young woman, and rural life is best when simple and unaffected by the trappings of wealth or of bourgeois urban taste—yet editor Maxwell felt the need to explain this scene to his readers:

> Decked in the most fashionable attire, and seated in the midst of luxurious articles of furniture, that appear to have been brought with her or for her from the town—her dress and figure form a striking contrast

8. "Going to Boarding School," *Analectic*, n.s., 2, no. 5 (November 1820): 421.

FIGURE 320
Charles Goodman and Robert Piggot engravers, John Lewis Krimmel pinxt, Departure for a Boarding School, *Philadelphia, 1819. Line engraving; 5 ¼ x 8 in. From* Analectic, *n.s., 2, no. 5 (November 1820): facing p. 420. (New-York Historical Society.)*

FIGURE 321
Alexander Lawson after William Hamilton, Autumn, *Philadelphia[?], ca. 1796. Engraving; 4 ½ x 3 ⅛ in. (Private collection.)*

FIGURE 322
Spinning wheels and niddy noddies, ca. 1819. Watercolor over pencil, pencil inscription. Sketchbook 6, leaf 1 recto.

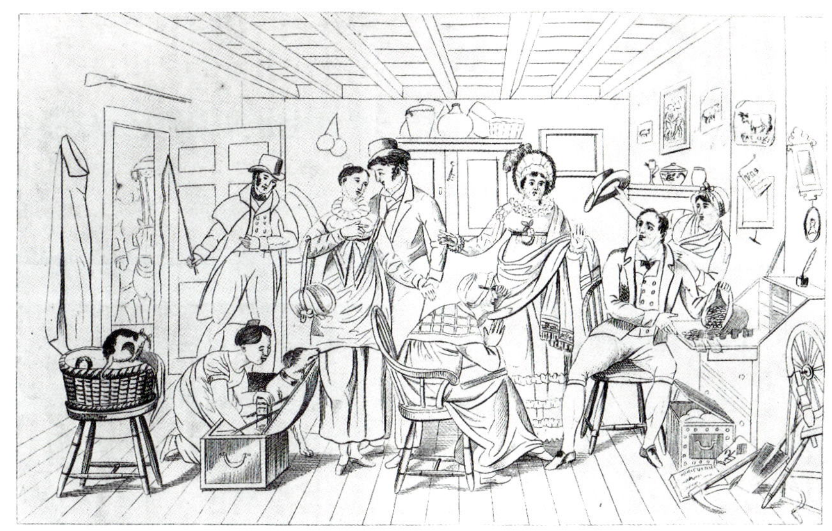

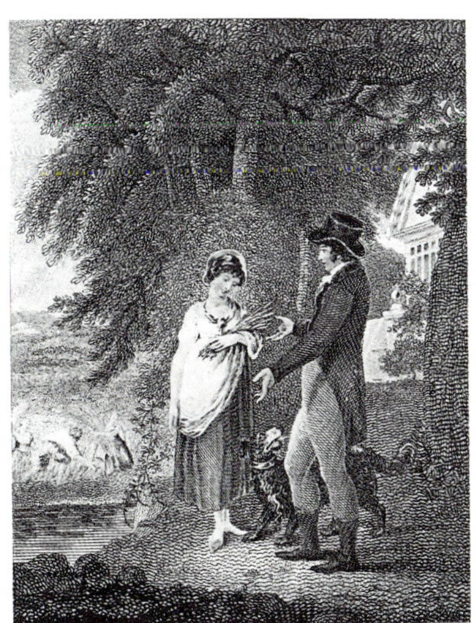

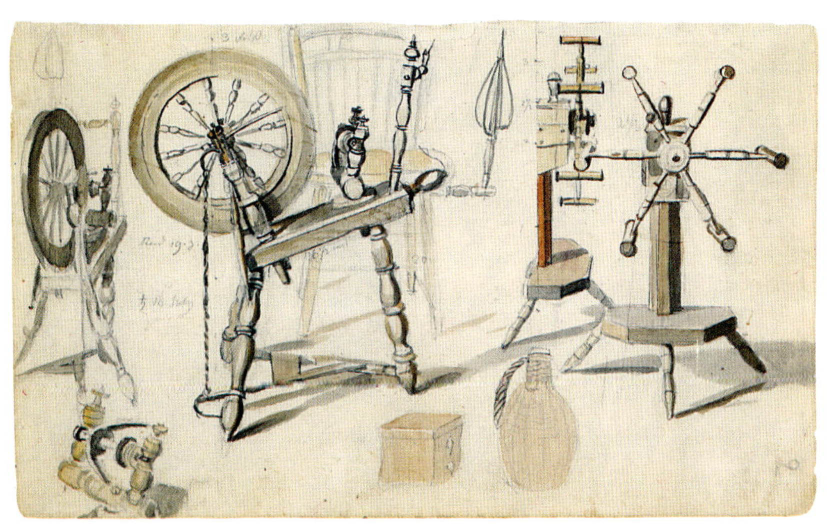

with the rusticity of the other members of the family;—while the indications of her newly acquired accomplishments, and *improved* taste—the piano, work-table, foot-stool, lap-dog—mirror, carpet—the mantle ornaments, and drawings over the fire-place, present an incongruous medley with the remaining furniture and decorations of the apartment. An incongruity, however, not unfrequently to be seen in the parlours of our wealthy farmers.

> Her foot on the overturned spinning-wheel indicates her contempt for the morning occupations of former days, now laid aside in favour of the piano. And the miniature depending from her left hand, shows that the attractions of an epaulette and regimentals have been too powerful for her constancy, and explains why the plain dressed lover advancing to make the salutations of his first visit since her return, is scornfully repulsed by his fickle mistress.

> The next most conspicuous figure is that of the father, reading with vexation and astonishment the various items of the "bill of tuition," while his attention is vainly called to the neglected breakfast by the girl in waiting.

> The background contains three figures in excellent *keeping,* with the more important personages of the scene. The mother points with great complacency to the drawings over the mantel piece, and the stupid admiration of the elder visitor, as well as the envy of the younger, are distinctly marked by the expression of their countenances.—The old grandame also, and her astonishment at the reception met with by the lover, and all the minor and even minute objects are perfectly consistent with the main design.

Maxwell closed the discussion by focusing on the artist:

> Mr. Krimmel's style of painting is the same in which Wilkie has gained a celebrity that places him among the first artists of the age; and that has given immortality of fame to Hogarth. Whenever the present insensibility to the interest of the fine arts shall have passed away, and the American public have learned to appreciate the labours of the pencil, Krimmel's name will rank high as an artist of great ingenuity of design, and truth and delicacy of delineation. And perhaps a future generation will pay honors to his talent that are now withheld from his living worth.[9]

The parlor in which Krimmel has reassembled the eight people is differently furnished, and the door to the outside world is no longer open, which, pictorially speaking, concentrates attention on the commotion within the room. There are now three separate groups of people, and their movements and gestures direct the viewer's eye toward the protagonist of the story and her new possessions. For various elements in the picture Krimmel once again delved into his sketchbooks, his paintings, and images by other artists. The sewing cabinet was the product of a recent study (fig. 324). The young woman's pose is similar to Brutus's in David's *Brutus and His Return Home after Condeming His Sons,* an image that had recently appeared in *Port Folio,* and to studies Krimmel was making in his sketchbooks.[10] The rifle, chairs, mirror, bird cage, and broom were among the items he had used in previous pictures. The design of the bewildered suitor and his dog is based on Lawson's *Autumn* (see fig. 321). The allegorical objects strewn in the right foreground are reminiscent of those in Hogarth's *Marriage à la Mode.*

9. "Krimmel's Picture—*Return from Boarding School,*" p. 507, pl. facing p. 507.

10. For an illustration of a contemporaneous sewing cabinet made in Philadelphia, see Garvan, *Federal Philadelphia,* p. 34. "The Fine Arts; . . . David," pp. 388–89.

FIGURE 323
Unidentified engraver, John Lewis Krimmel pinxt, Return from a Boarding School, *probably Philadelphia, 1820. Line engraving; 4 ½ x 7 ³⁄₁₆ in. From* Analectic, *n.s., 2, no. 6 (December 1820): facing p. 507. (New-York Historical Society.)*

FIGURE 324
Sewing table, ca. 1819. Watercolor over pencil. Sketchbook 7, leaf 5 verso.

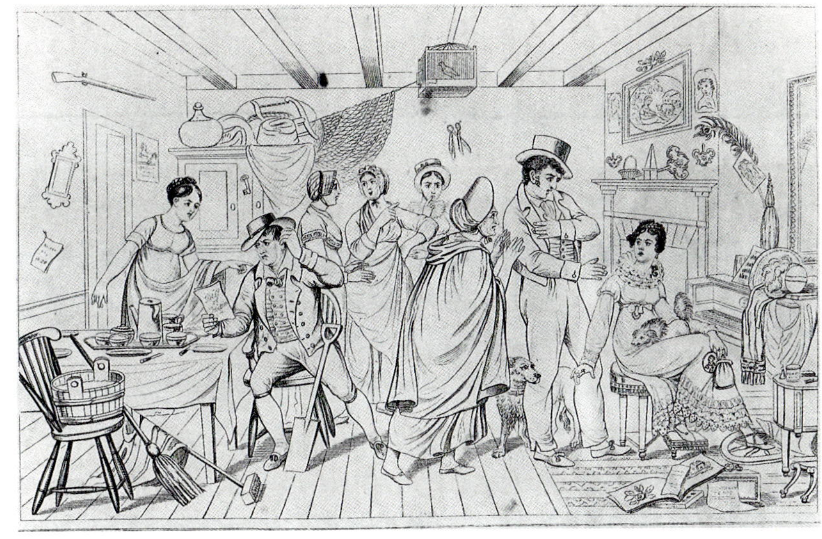

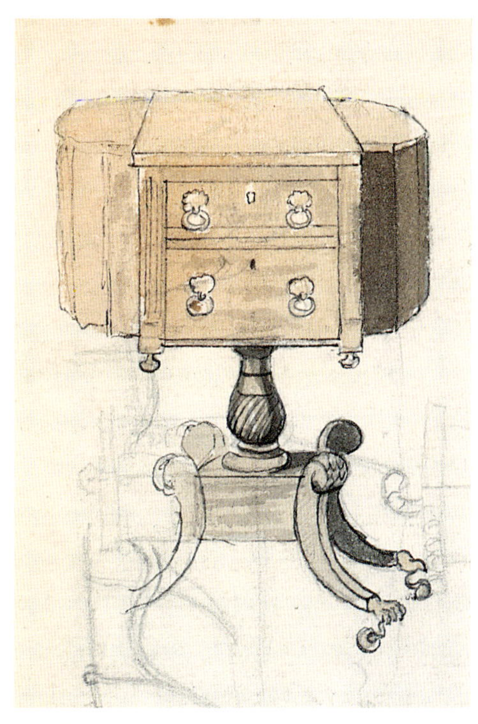

The 1820 publication of *Country Wedding, Departure for a Boarding School,* and *Return from a Boarding School* brought Krimmel's art and his name to a wide audience. The exposure that he received from these three engravings gave him more publicity than most other local artists received; however, Krimmel did not rely on this to make his way and spread his fame. Soon after he had approached Coates about reproducing the West painting, and perhaps about the same time that he began working on the boarding school images (as well as the portraits of Poulson and Ritter), he became involved in an innovative project.

In the spring of 1819 Krimmel and other Philadelphia artists began an endeavor aimed at increasing the public's awareness of pictures local artists had ready for sale or would be able to execute on commission. Working through a private businessman, who happened to be an officer of their society, they rented a room in his store for use as a gallery; in return he agreed to promote the works of art they hung there. They took out a full-page advertisement in *Paxton's Philadelphia Annual Advertiser* and announced: "The Association of American Artists have opened a room for the sale and exhibition of American Works of Art, in Painting, Sculpture, Architecture, Engraving, Drawing, &c. &c. at Samuel Kennedy's No. 72, Chestnut Street, Where visitors may behold the advanced state of the arts in this country, purchase Paintings, Prints, or Drawings, and where any person desirous of having any thing done in the Fine Arts may see specimens of the abilities of the different artists in this city, know their address, prices, &c."[11]

A second advertisement, which appeared daily in the *Aurora General Advertiser* between April 19 and June 28, 1819, gave specific information and blatantly appealed to patriotism.

> AT THE ASSOCIATION OF AMERICAN ARTISTS SALE AND EXHIBITION ROOM NO 72 Chestnut Street, between Second and Third Streets there are constantly for sale, nearly 200 specimens of works exclusively of Artists in this country. Purchasers from this institution will have the gratification of not only procuring what they want on the lowest terms, but that of serving the Fine Arts in America.
>
> Orders for portraits or miniatures; views of landscapes in oil or water colors; likenesses of animals etc. marine pictures; architectural designs for building; sculpture in its various branches; designs for the illustration of any written work; p do. engraved; portrait or ornament engravings for books etc. by being left with Samuel Kennedy, Secretary to the Association, will be promptly attended to, and executed to the satisfaction of those who wish thus to patronize this effort to promote the fine Arts in the United States.

Sales were the primary objective, but the artists also hoped the centrally located gallery shop would attract a steady stream of viewers. To defray expenses visitors were charged 25¢ per visit, or an annual fee of $2 per person ($4 per family) and, as Kennedy assured prospective customers, the annual fee was well worth paying, for consigned items would sell so quickly that the display would be ever-changing. Kennedy's own shop, in which "carving, gilding, looking glass manufacturing, and framing" were done, was in the same building, so customers' art works could be suitably framed before they were carried home.[12]

The collaborative venture worked to Krimmel's advantage by bringing him an important commission when Kennedy became the driving force behind the production of *The Conflagration of the Masonic Hall,* a print of topical interest.

11. Kennedy advertisement, *Paxton's Philadelphia Annual Advertiser,* 1819, n.p.

12. Kennedy advertisement, *Paxton's Advertiser,* 1819.

FIGURE 325
Samuel Jones, The Conflagration of Masonic Hall, Chestnut Street, Philadelphia, 1819. *Oil on panel; 19 1/16 x 22 1/16 in. (The Art Institute of Chicago, restricted gift of Wesley M. Dixon, Jr., Jamee J. and Marshall Field, Gloria and Richard Manney, Hope B. and Brooks McCormick Foundation, Mrs. Phillip D. Sang, and Jeffery Shedd; Emily Crane Chadbourne, Leon Mandel.)*

FIGURE 326
John Hill sculptor, Samuel Jones and John Lewis Krimmel pinxt, The Conflagration of the Masonic Hall, Chestnut Street, Philadelphia, *Philadelphia, 1819. Aquatint; 21 1/2 x 17 1/4 in. (Photo, Winterthur.) The monumentalizing of the buildings, the sharper definition of the architecture, and the effective cropping of the view suggest that Krimmel made the final drawing for the engraver to copy.*

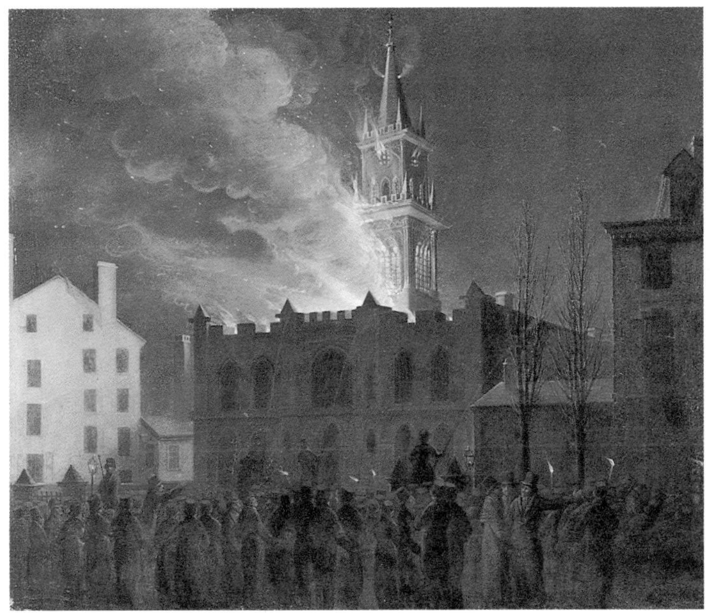

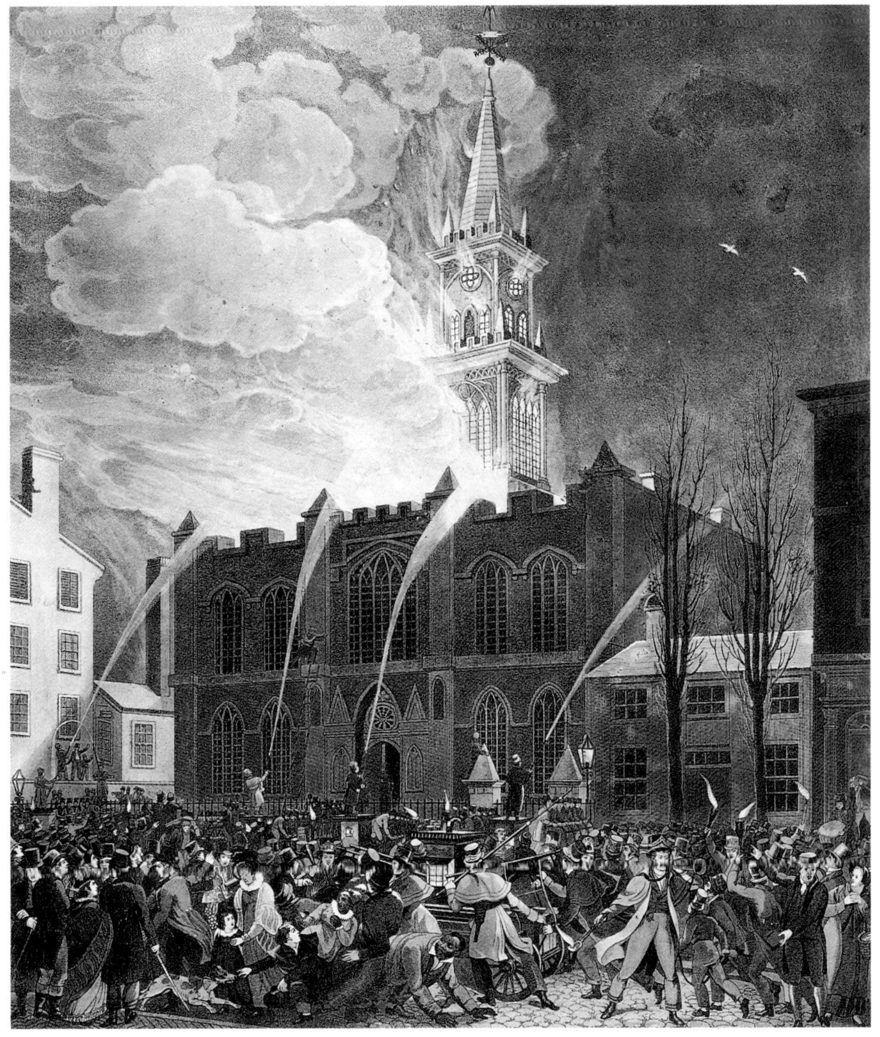

Philadelphia's Masonic Hall, an imposing edifice the design of which is attributed to William Strickland, had been built near Centre Square in 1811. On the evening of March 9, 1819, the structure was completely gutted by a fire that started just before a cotillion was to begin. The fire attracted a large crowd.

Just who decided that the sensational event should be commemorated as a print is unclear. Samuel Jones, a Philadelphia artist, initially depicted the spectacular fire in a painting.[13] His canvas became the basis for the print, but Jones's rendition of the figures needed improvement before an etcher could begin work on the project (fig. 325). Krimmel was commissioned to produce the drawing for reproduction and to create a new crowd scene; John Hill, who had recently emigrated from London, was hired to do the etching. Kennedy chose to have the image reproduced as an aquatint because its painterly techniques would better convey the spectacular nighttime fire (fig. 326). Etching was also much faster and easier than engraving, which meant that the print would be produced quickly—an important consideration for the backer of a topical image.

On May 26, 1819, just two and a half months after the fire, Krimmel noted on the inside cover of sketchbook 6, *"Skizze für Kennedy"* (Sketch for Kennedy). Within a month Kennedy and Samuel West, who was also a member of the Society of American Artists, advertised that they were taking subscriptions for the "just published" print, "A CORRECT REPRESENTATION OF THAT AWFUL & SUBLIME SCENE." Their notice continued: "The Publishers have spared neither pains nor expense to produce a truly interesting print, and in addition to the terms of their prospectus, have increased its size, and added the abilities of Mr. J. L. Krimmel whose grouping and drawing of figures is not surpassed, not withstanding this considerable additional expense, they will continue the price to subscribers the same as proposed, until the 21st of July, when subscription lists will be closed, and the price considerably advanced."[14]

Below the print image is a legend, the text of which explains the publishers' decision to reorient Jones's image: "The Conflagration of the MASONIC HALL Chestnut Street Philadelphia which occurred on the night of the 9th of March 1819 This Plate is respectfully dedicated to the active and much esteemed FIRE ENGINE & HOSE COMPANIES, by their Obedt Servts S. Kennedy and S.S. West." Kennedy and West were purposely wooing an influential sector of the city. Fire fighters, largely volunteers, had formed numerous companies. In 1819 they were becoming increasingly vocal about the costs of maintaining fire-fighting strength and equipment and as a united group they began flexing their muscles in civic affairs. Krimmel's version of the scene focused on the fire-fighting aspects of conflagration, rather than the loss of the building. In some ways the reorientation is surprising, for immediately after the fire, Masons began holding benefits to raise money for a new temple. Their efforts were quite successful and the new temple, which cost an estimated $55,000 was finished and dedicated in 1820.[15]

The differences between Jones's version and Krimmel's version are revealing. In Jones's image, a picture of horizontal format, only three hoses are trained on the fire, and two firemen climb a ladder to the second floor. The spectators, men in top hats and long coats, watch with little or no animation. They are indistinctly seen in the reflections of the fire and create a dark wall across the foreground width of the painting. To achieve a dominant horizontal, Jones had designed the image using the neoclassical precept of isocephaly, keeping the heads about the same level.[16] In contrast, Krimmel's design for the

13. Samuel Jones was a member of AAA and treasurer of the American Beneficial Society, which provided a form of workmen's insurance for its members.

14. Kennedy and West advertisement, *Aurora General Advertiser*, Philadelphia, June 28, 1819.

15. Oberholtzer, *Philadelphia*, 2:63.

16. Krimmel had used isocephaly only once—in *View of Centre Square on the Fourth of July* (1812).

FIGURE 327
Fire-fighting equipment, 1819. Pencil. Sketchbook 7, leaf 5 verso.

FIGURE 328
Pumpmen, 1819. Watercolor over pencil. Sketchbook 7, leaf 2 verso.

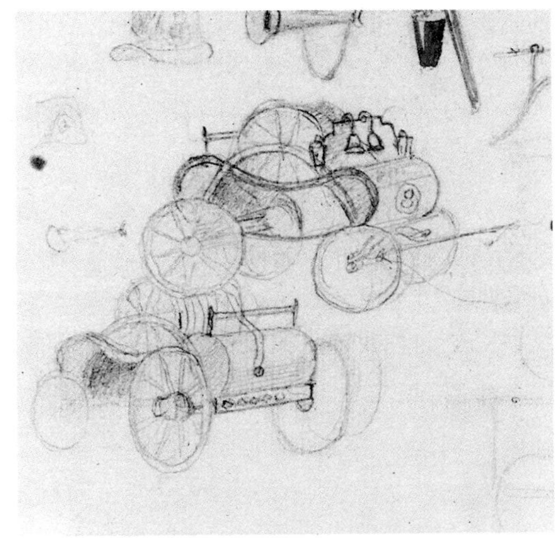

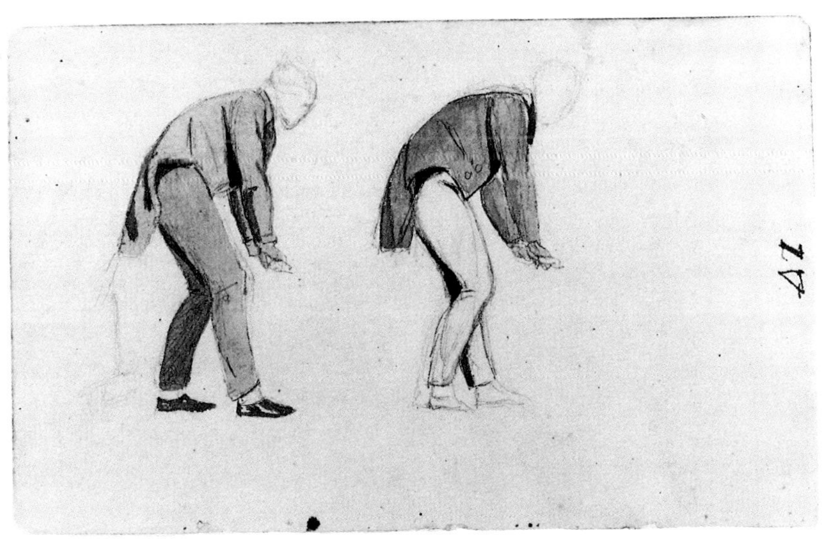

print has a vertical format and is based on very different spatial concepts. Krimmel narrowed Jones's original composition and heightened the drama: the architectural setting is monumentalized and concentrated on Masonic Hall. More important, the foreground scene is differently organized, brightly lit, dramatically animated, and executed with a higher level of skill. It stresses the firemen's dynamic actions and the crowd's varied responses to the blaze. The artist juxtaposed a tightly packed frieze of spectators on the left with an open frieze on the right—space has been cleared for the firemen and their equipment (figs. 327, 328). A woman and daughter, the conversing group of men, and the tumbling bodies are reworked figure types from Krimmel's earlier pictures, and the postures of the firemen are reminiscent of David's *Sabines*, which also depicts an excited multitude in front of a structure engulfed in flames. Like David, Krimmel presented principal figures in mirror images and other figures in rapid motion with wide stances, devices that generate a centrifugal force in the composition. Given that Krimmel was using the same elements to compose *Fourth of July Celebration, 1819*, which he began shortly after finishing the conflagration drawing, it is likely that he then owned an engraving of David's picture.[17]

About a year after *Conflagration* was issued, Krimmel received a commission for a straightforward form of advertising, perhaps not coincidentally, from Sellers and Pennock, a Philadelphia manufacturer of fire engines and fire hoses. The item was a business card. Krimmel did the design and William Kneass, longtime secretary of the artists' association, produced the engraving (fig. 329).[18] The small-scale image depicts twenty-one firemen in action, using the riveted hose recently invented by James Seller and the "Hydraulion," a wagon with a pumping engine and a hose reel recently invented by Abraham Pennock. Sixteen fire fighters operate the pump handles; three fill the pumper's tank from the nearby stream and from the hydrant (the latter symbolizing the city's running water system, an element that set Philadelphia apart from all but one other North American city—Bethlehem, Pennsylvania); two have snaked the hose into the burning building. Krimmel's design has a distinctly decorative, highly balanced quality. The curves of the hoses and wheels connect the groups of men and unify the composition, and the rhythmic spacing of the figures mimics the pulsating pattern of the pumping process. Preliminary sketches of a pumpman in position and studies of fire engines and a fire bucket are in sketchbook 7; a faint drawing of a fire engine is on the cover of sketchbook 6 (fig. 330; see also figs. 327, 328).

Krimmel's success with providing images for printmaking prompted him to explore other possibilities in advertisements and related areas. A number of ink and pencil drawings in sketchbook 7 show his experiments with decorative allegorical designs in 1819/20. Like other artists he derived his symbols from classical imagery, principally the ornamental traditions of the baroque style, and he may have intended to produce designs for documents such as organizational certificates, stocks, or mastheads.[19] Sketchbook 7 opens with an ink drawing of the Pennsylvania state emblem (fig. 331). This is followed by allegorical sketches—personifications of Columbia, Liberty, and Wisdom (figs. 332–335).

Krimmel constructed the images in what was the typical working method for him but one that was an unusual approach for the creation of allegorical designs—he worked from observation. In three instances a sketch of a young woman seated on the ground served as a model for an allegorical figure. With slight modifications, the same image became part of the decorative design of

17. *The Conflagration of the Masonic Hall* proved popular—during the nineteenth century, the plate was republished in Philadelphia three times with the image left unchanged, but the inscription underneath varied according to the name of the printer/publisher. In 1854–55 the print was republished by William H. Morgan, a looking-glass maker, and between 1867 and 1885 by William Barber and between 1862 and 1891 by William Smith.

18. In 1812 Kneass and Krimmel had collaborated on an allegorical print of religious content (see chap. 1).

19. At this point their exact application cannot be determined. Commercial illustrations appeared in *Paxton's . . . Advertiser* (1819, 1820) and in daily newspapers to draw attention to shops and other business enterprises with decorative designs that included emblematic motifs.

FIGURE 329
William Kneass sculptor, John Lewis Krimmel pinxt, trade card or advertisement for Sellers and Pennock, Philadelphia, 1820. Engraving; 3 11/16 x 5 3/4 in. (American Philosophical Society.)

FIGURE 330
Leather fire-fighting bucket, 1819/20. Watercolor and ink over pencil, pencil inscription. Sketchbook 7, leaf 15 verso.

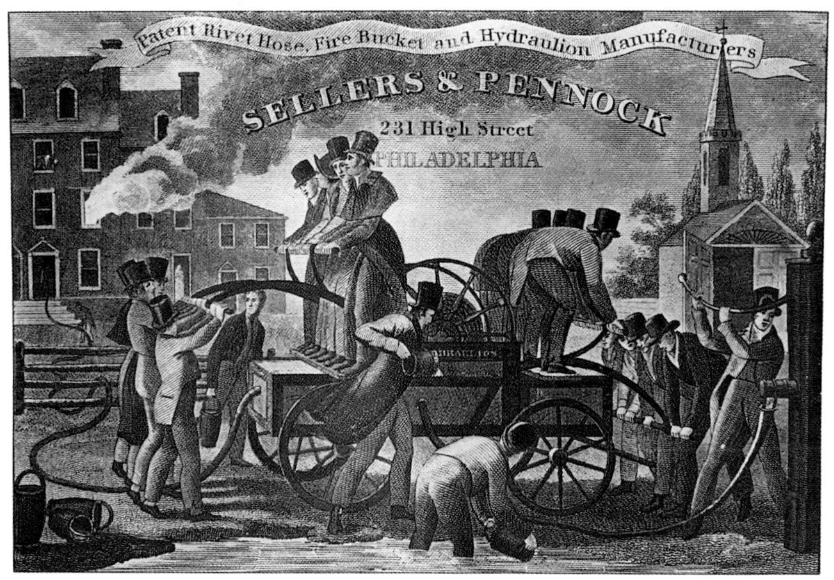

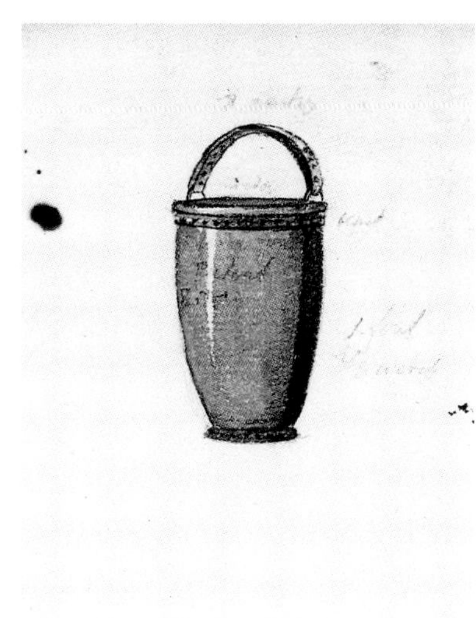

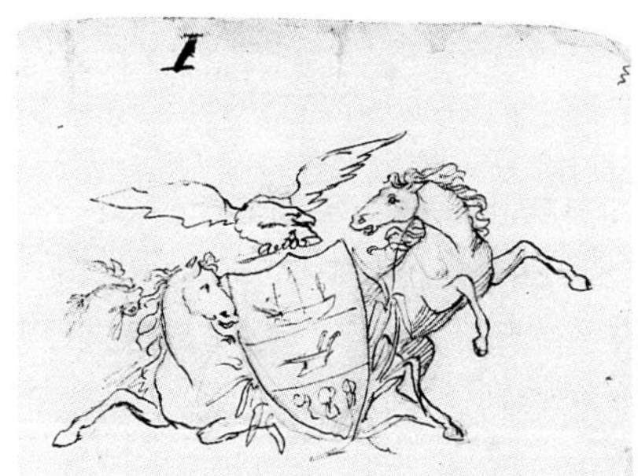

FIGURE 331
State seal of Pennsylvania, ca. 1819. Ink over pencil. Sketchbook 7, leaf 1 recto. The seal was adopted in 1809. Krimmel used the seal in the 1819 Fourth of July picture.

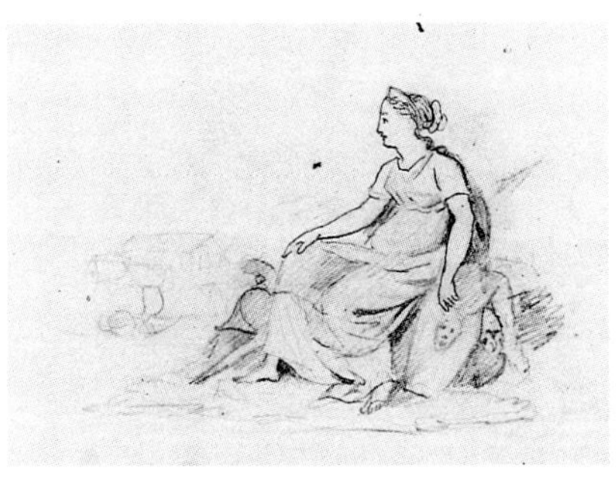

FIGURE 332
Columbia, ca. 1819. Ink over pencil. Sketchbook 7, leaf 1 verso. Columbia, symbolizing the United States, has put aside the tools of war. She is accompanied by an owl, an attribute of Wisdom.

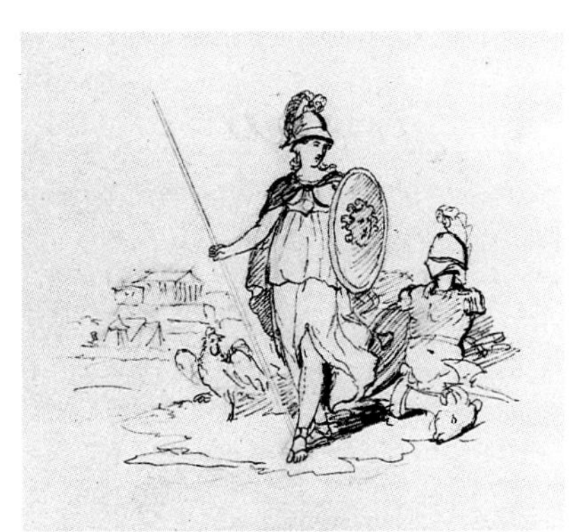

FIGURE 333
Liberty as Minerva (Athena), goddess of wisdom, patroness of the arts and many household trades, especially spinning and weaving, 1819/20. Ink over pencil. Sketchbook 7, leaf 1 verso. Liberty is dressed in armor and holds the Rudis, the rod signifying the freeing of slaves. Beside her are the trophies of war. The rooster symbolizes lust; the ram's head may symbolize the tumbling of old gods. The background tents and temples signify trade, the arts, and glory.

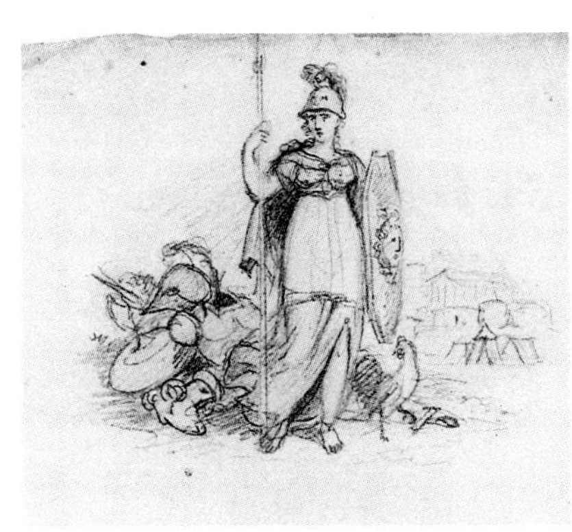

FIGURE 334
Liberty as Minerva (Athena), patroness of the arts and trade, 1819. Pencil. Sketchbook 7, leaf 25 recto.

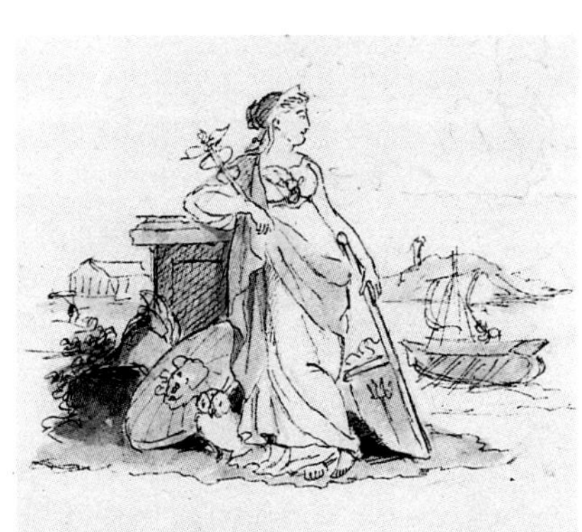

FIGURE 335
Columbia, 1819/20. Ink and wash over pencil. Sketchbook 7, leaf 25 recto. Columbia holds a caduceus in her right hand, signifying the flowering of science, and rests her left hand on a plow, signifying agriculture. The owl perched next to her signifies wisdom. The buildings and the ship in the background symbolize trade and commerce.

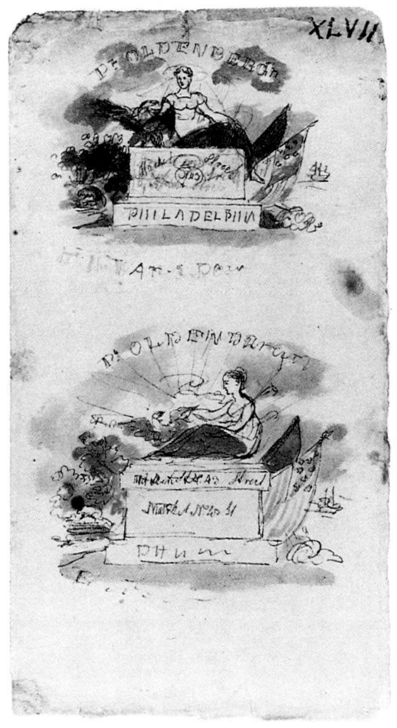

FIGURE 336
Sketches for a trade card, letterhead, or advertisement for Daniel Oldenbergh, 1820/21. Wash and ink over pencil. Sketchbook 7, leaf 24 recto.

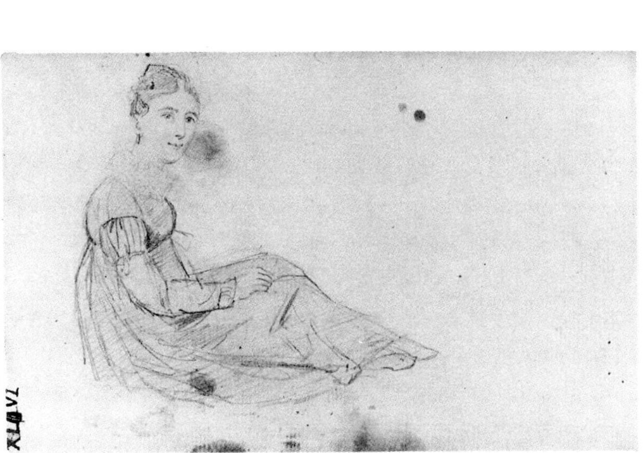

FIGURE 337
Seated female figure, 1820/21. Sketchbook 7, leaf 23 verso. This design served as a basis for fig. 332.

two different sketches in which Krimmel explored possible compositions for Daniel Oldenbergh, whose hatting business was located on Market Street in 1819 (figs. 336, 337; see also the similarities to the posture of the young woman in *Return from a Boarding School*, fig. 323).

The wider recognition that prints of his designs brought to Krimmel may have had some bearing on his election to the post of president of the Association of American Artists early in 1821. The functions and duties of this position must have been a challenge to him, especially where they required public speaking in the English language, for the directors of the academy requested that the director of the society deliver introductory remarks at the opening of the annual exhibition. It seems inconsistent with what is known of Krimmel's character and the "simplicity of manner" that he could have sought after or been available for such a conspicuous and demanding position. But Krimmel may have decided that to receive important commissions, he needed to be recognized as an artist who played a prominent and active part in Philadelphia's art life. Both Thomas Sully and Charles Willson Peale may have set rather persuasive examples for him to emulate.[20]

Although when commissioned Krimmel could produce excellent images, such as the *Conflagration*, those that he chose to construct on his own initiative brought out his best talents. In 1821 he composed a genre scene of exceptional scope—throngs of people in the streets of Philadelphia responding to an annual commercial celebration, and in 1821 the procession was of unprecedented proportions. In the number of people, the precisely rendered details, and the sweeping spatial design, Krimmel's depiction of the parade surpasses anything that had been attempted in American topographic views. The parade took place March 15, 1821, and less than six weeks later Krimmel had finished a richly detailed and well-designed watercolor that rendered the parade as a grandiose and remarkable event and synthesized its many activities in a highly successful manner (fig. 338).

The design precepts of romanticism encouraged artists to present spirited events taking place in vast spaces. To expand the spatial illusion, Krimmel depicted one portion of the two-mile-long procession as it turned the corner of Fourth and Chestnut streets. He balanced a long asymmetric street vista with strong middle and foreground designs. Thus the dense row of houses, the compactly moving factions of the marchers and riders, and the closely gathered groups of spectators are juxtaposed with a large area of open space in the middle of the picture—a device typical of romanticism.

A small ink sketch on the leather cover of sketchbook 6 is Krimmel's first conception of the design and was probably drawn as he watched the parade (its location may signify that the book no longer had any blank leaves left). Working in a cursory fashion, he differentiated wagons, long lines of marchers, and riders in a procession moving from the distant right to the left foreground, set against a row of houses on the left side of the street and spectators in the right foreground. The artist then expanded the initial sketch into a small watercolor, retaining the basic layout and buildings that identified the location.

When Krimmel made his final, much larger watercolor known as *Parade of the Victuallers*, he depicted the procession at a later moment, a decision that produced significant changes in his composition: two diagonals form the thrust of the design, and the vantage point is the southeast corner of the intersection of Fourth and Chestnut streets, the center of Philadelphia's mercantile district (fig. 339). For his basic formula, the artist turned to an important European

20. Minutes of the Board of Directors, April 21, 1821, PAFA, microfilm; Dunlap, *History*, 2:395–96.

FIGURE 338
John Lewis Krimmel, A Patriotic Society Parading Past Independence Hall, *Philadelphia, March or April 1821. Watercolor and ink over pencil; 7 5/8 x 11 3/4 in. (Springfield Art Museum, Springfield, Mo.)*

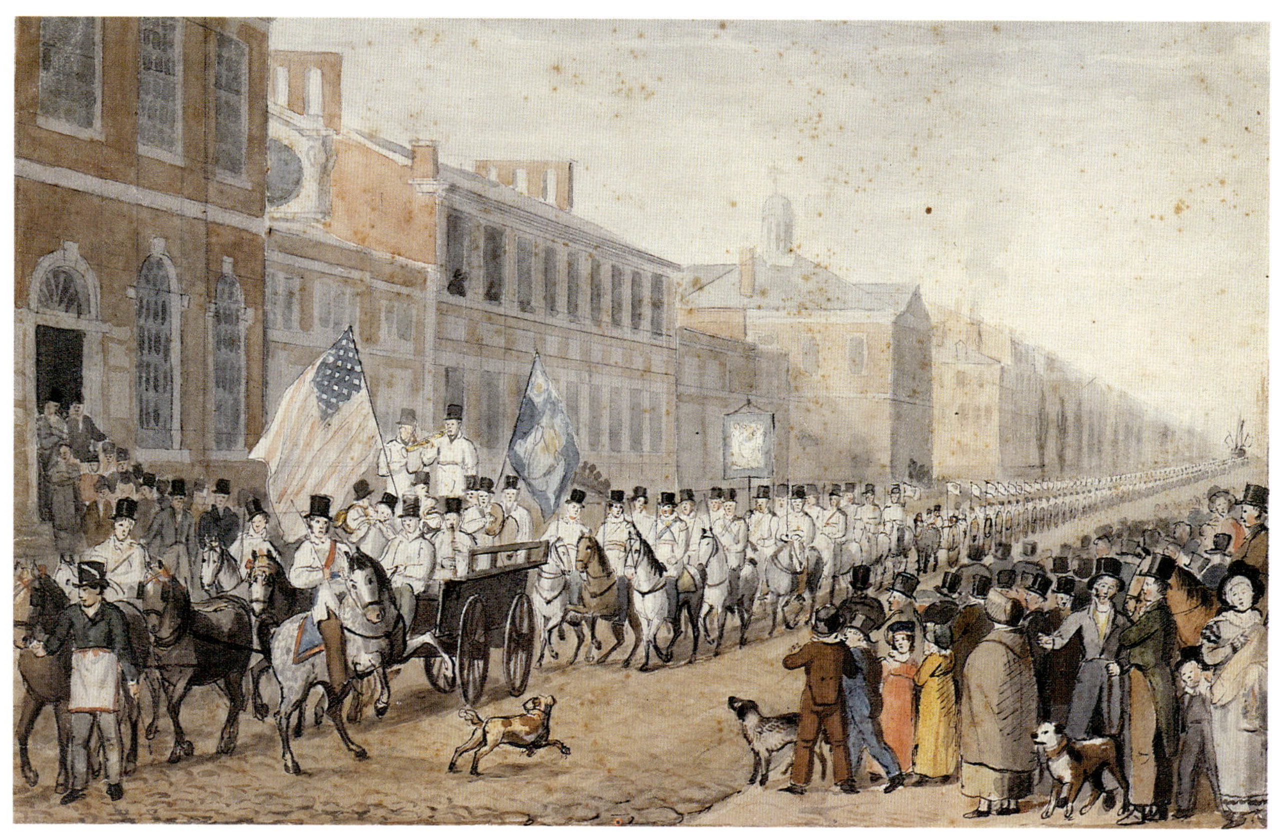

FIGURE 339
John Lewis Krimmel, Parade of the Victuallers, *Philadelphia, April 1821. Watercolor over ink and pencil; 14 ½ x 24 in. (Private collection.) Signed and dated.*

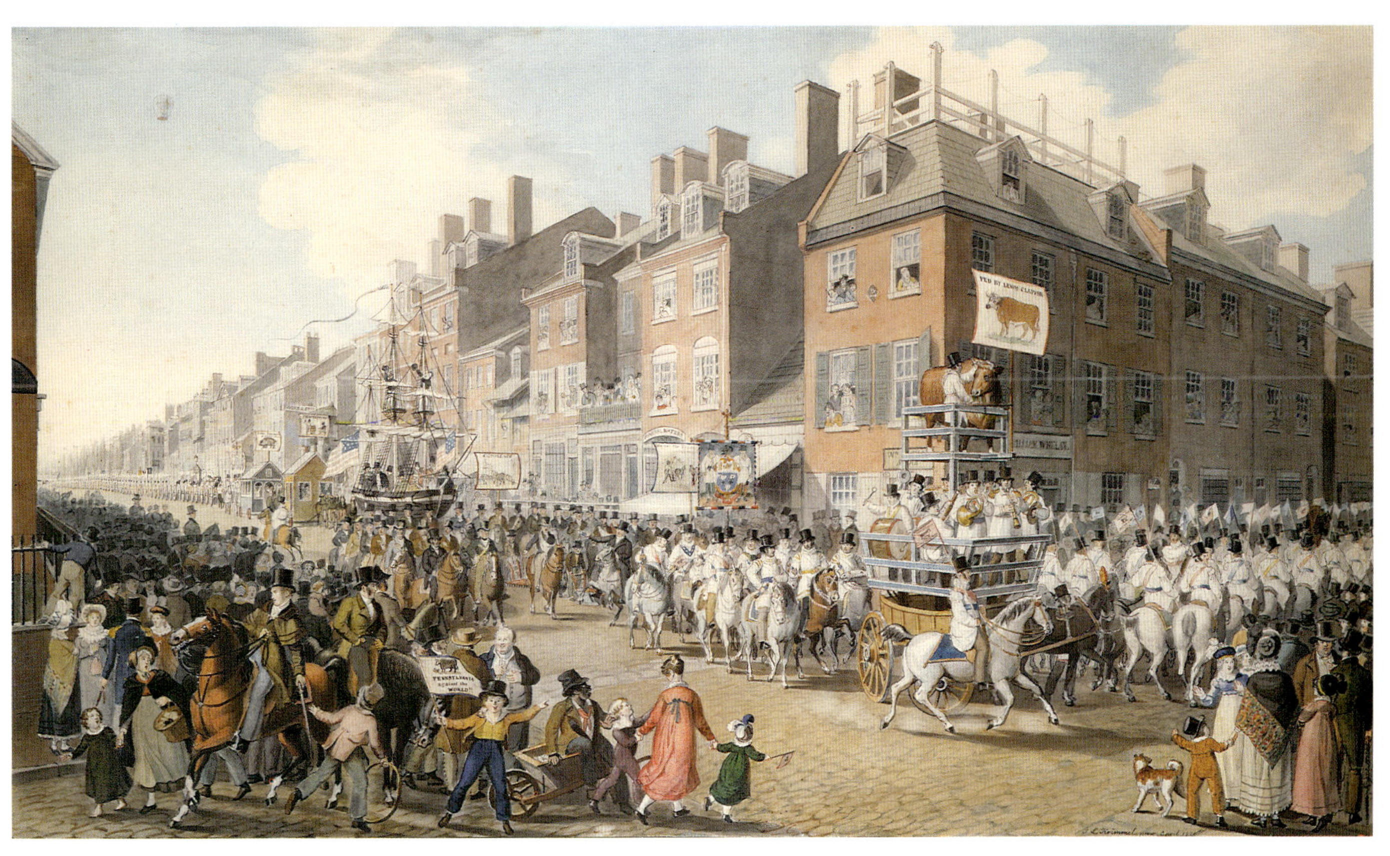

tradition—the depiction of pageants, religious processions, and triumphal marches of emperors and conquerors and also to William Russell Birch's engraving of the Philadelphia procession commemorating Washington's death. As in Birch's image the parade moves from left to right, and Krimmel adopted Birch's figures watching the demonstration as spectators in his own picture. The representation of horses is given even billing with that of the riders and marchers. Their astonishing number and naturalistic depiction is the more remarkable since at the time horses appeared infrequently in American art, except in military scenes. The first stretch of houses on the right side of the street are visible in sharp detail as is the main throng of spectators on the left. The new vantage point enabled the artist to show part of the procession turning and marching away, and this extra spatial extension added a three-dimensional effect that dramatically enlivened the scene. Krimmel further improved his rendition of the parade by including two of its highlights in close-up. A carriage platform is turning the corner: a band plays on the lower level, and a man stands on the upper level holding a prize bull (possibly stuffed) by the horns, above which rides a sign reading "Fed by Lewis Clapier." Close behind comes a float with a replica of a ship, *The Louis Clapier*, jammed with men. The many banners and pennants punctuating the procession proclaim the quality of the livestock and the skill of the breeders and butchers.[21]

Krimmel based many of the elements in his picture on studies he made the day of the parade that he then combined with his existing pictorial vocabulary. Sketchbooks 6 and 7 contain drawings of people and animals, many of which he integrated into his final version of the parade (figs. 340, 341). He turned to sketchbook 4 for the visages of three elderly men; tobacconist Hamilton is the huge bare-headed man in the crowd to the left, and Jimmy Cox and an unnamed companion are two of the men conversing in the crowd on the right (see fig. 281).

Both *Parade of the Victuallers* and *Election Day 1815* depict a large number of people in the streets, and a comparison of the two demonstrates the changes and growth that had occurred in Krimmel's style within a six-year period. In the 1815 picture a continuous friezelike composition extends across the foreground; in the later picture the foreground figure frieze opens in the middle and shifts the most important aspect of the picture content to the middle ground. In the 1821 image the emphasis is on pictorial space, as expressed by the exceedingly long view of the parade and reinforced by the volumetric and monumentalized definition of the houses. Space is rendered in a clear and tautly organized manner, correctly calculated in its systematic progression, suggesting Krimmel used the set of mathematical instruments and the camera obscura that he still owned at the time of his death. The buildings loom tall and have pronounced sculptural plasticity, their height accentuated by the chimneys and the rooftop laundry porches. The grand facades are well integrated with the genre scene—people watch the parade from the windows. The definition of the people in the middle ground is more intelligible than in *Election Day 1815*, and foreground figures are better separated. Stock figures such as the mother holding her child by the hand and the oyster vendor that appear in both images possess livelier and more spirited movements in the 1821 picture. Indeed in the later picture few figures are still, and some seem to step in rhythm with the band. A comparison of *Parade* and *Conflagration* is also instructive. In *Parade* Krimmel made more dramatic use of pictorial space and presented figures in a more natural manner and better distributed fashion.

21. Descriptions of the parade are in Oberholtzer, *Philadelphia*, 2:85; Scharf and Wescott, *History*, 1:602; Philadelphia Museum of Art, *Philadelphia: Three Centuries*, p. 254. For a European example, see Robert Waissenberger, ed., *Vienna in the Biedermeier Era, 1815–48* (New York: Rizzoli, 1986), ill. 78.

FIGURE 340
Cows, dog, horse, 1821. Pencil, watercolor over pencil. Sketchbook 7, leaf 5 recto.

FIGURE 341
Bull, 1820/21. Wash over pencil. Sketchbook 7, leaf 22 recto.

FIGURE 342
Hogs, 1820/21. Watercolor and ink over pencil, ink inscription. Sketchbook 7, leaf 8 verso. The inscription reads: "700 # / A Hog weighing 700 lb exhibited from the 5th to the 8th of March 1820 at "Bulls Head" N[orthern] L[iberties] Phila". The artist drew the hogs while they were on exhibit at this popular inn just outside of Philadelphia.

FIGURE 343
Pig roasting on spit, 1820/21. Watercolor over pencil. Sketchbook 7, leaf 7 recto.

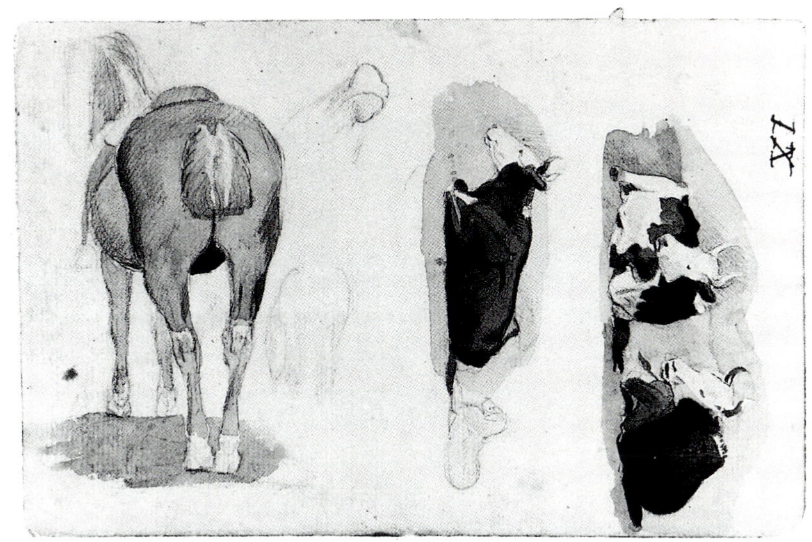

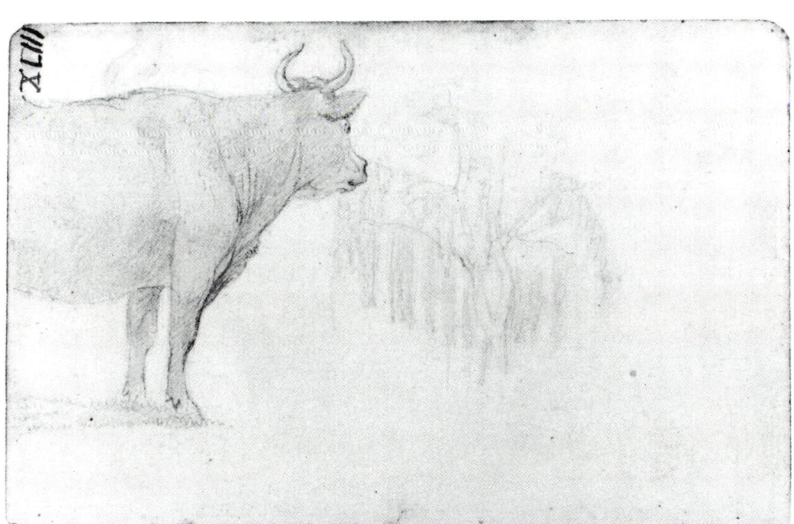

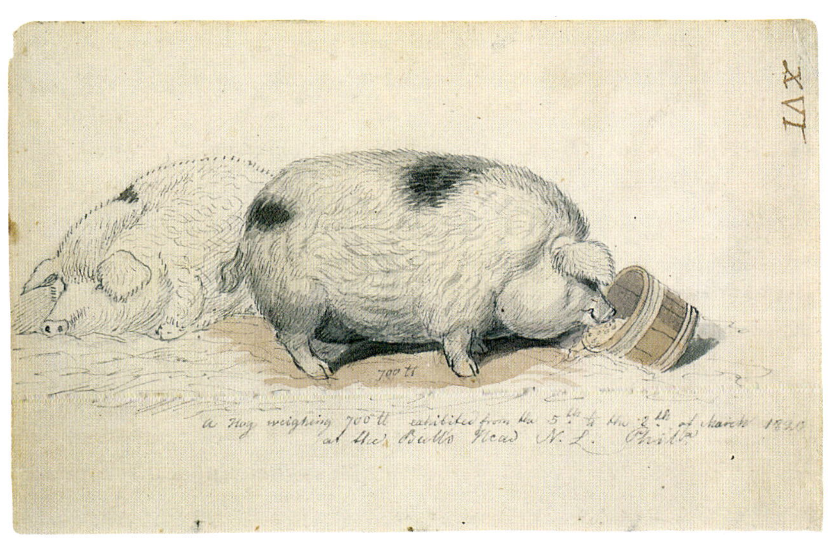

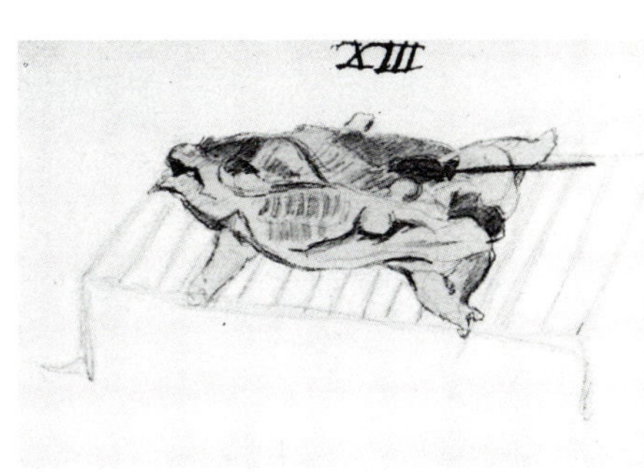

Krimmel's two images of the parade were a modern version of the *vedutti* that had flourished in eighteenth-century Europe, especially as depicted by Venetian artists Francesco Guardi (1712–93) and Bernardo Bellotto (called Canaletto Bellotto [1720–80]). But Krimmel reversed the European formulation. Rather than give primacy to the meticulously articulated buildings and make the crowd mere staffage, he created a detailed description of the people and the event. The result was unquestionably successful. The composition speaks volumes about optimism, civic pride, commercial progress, idealism, and the concept of what constituted good peaceful life, and as was typical for Krimmel, he makes no mention of the region's recent economic problems—unemployment, poverty, rising taxes. A slightly different but also optimistic perspective is that in a poem published in the newspapers the day after the parade:

> We have plenty of money and plenty of meat,
> We have nothing to do, yet plenty to eat;
> Patriots to whom Pennsylvania is dear;
> Yes many we hope like Louis Clapier:
> We have sailors and soldiers all willing to fight,
> Who will never want beef while exists Wm. White.
> We have favorites of fortune, both Allen and Hope,
> Whose luck's so proverbial, none with them can cope,
> Internal improvements, too, when happy and free,
> We'll plough inland rivers, give Neptune the sea.[22]

The parade followed several days of activity. The 87 animals that White had sponsored had been exhibited in the Northern Liberties area of the city for several days. Once slaughtered their meat was arranged on 200 carts were interspersed among floats, farm implements, marchers, and riders constituting the procession that attracted an audience estimated at 300,000. As in previous years, after the parade, the meat was sold to the public (figs. 342, 343).

Philadelphia engraver Joseph Yeager (ca. 1792–1859) made an aquatint of the Krimmel's watercolor and sold it at his 37 Chestnut Street shop (fig. 344). Yeager's generally faithful copy (which has somewhat stiffer figures) has different slogans on the banner held by the boy and on the hot-air balloons, which were still very much a novelty.[23] In Krimmel's watercolor they read "Pennsylvania against the World!" In Yeager's print they read "Fed by William White." The commercial nature of the parade, the extraordinary effort Krimmel invested in this image, and the minuteness of description that he rendered suggest that he intended it as the drawing for the print. Yeager may have begun work on the aquatint as early as April or as late as autumn 1821. Given the topical nature of the print the earlier of the months is more likely.[24] Even less clear is who orchestrated the venture. It could have been Yeager; Yeager and printer Charles Woodward, whose partnership ended in 1822/23; or possibly William White, who directed the "mammoth parade." It is unlikely that Krimmel invested anything beyond his finished watercolor in the project.

Krimmel, Yeager, and White had different sets of rules by which each assessed the image, but all three came together well in this picture. The artist was concerned with achieving an effective composition that presented the multitude and setting with clarity in a modern, innovative design. The etcher was concerned with making an accurate, identifiable, and salable image. The sponsor was concerned with commemorating his achievements and those of the men who worked in the meat trades.[25]

22. *Relf's Philadelphia Gazette and Daily Advertiser*, March 16, 1821; I have been unable to clarify the references to "Allen" and "Hope" in line 7.

23. In 1819 a series of balloon ascents was marked by riots in Philadelphia and across the Delaware River in Camden. On two occasions crowds of 30,000 or more grew restive after the weather prevented the ascent; see Scharf and Westcott, *History*, 1:598.

24. J. L. Cunningham advertisement for the executor's sale of the Devaltooth estate, *Columbian Centinel*, Boston, March 30, 1825, specifies "Original Drawings in water colors by Krimmel."

25. Thirty years after the parade, Krimmel's watercolor, as preserved in the Yeager print, was still well known. Two other printmakers produced lithographs: one by George DuBois, a German-born artist active in Philadelphia ca. 1850, the other by Louis Haugg, who worked in the city 1856–94. At midcentury the original commemmorative, promotional, and financial aims of the printmakers were no longer pertinent; by then the picture was a fascinating record of a historical event and was an image appreciated and reproduced for its artistry.

FIGURE 344
Joseph Yeager sculptor, John Lewis Krimmel pinxt, Procession of Victuallers, *1821. Aquatint; 19 15/16 x 25 3/4 in. (plate). (Philadelphia Museum of Art, gift of the estate of Charles M. B. Cadwalader.)*

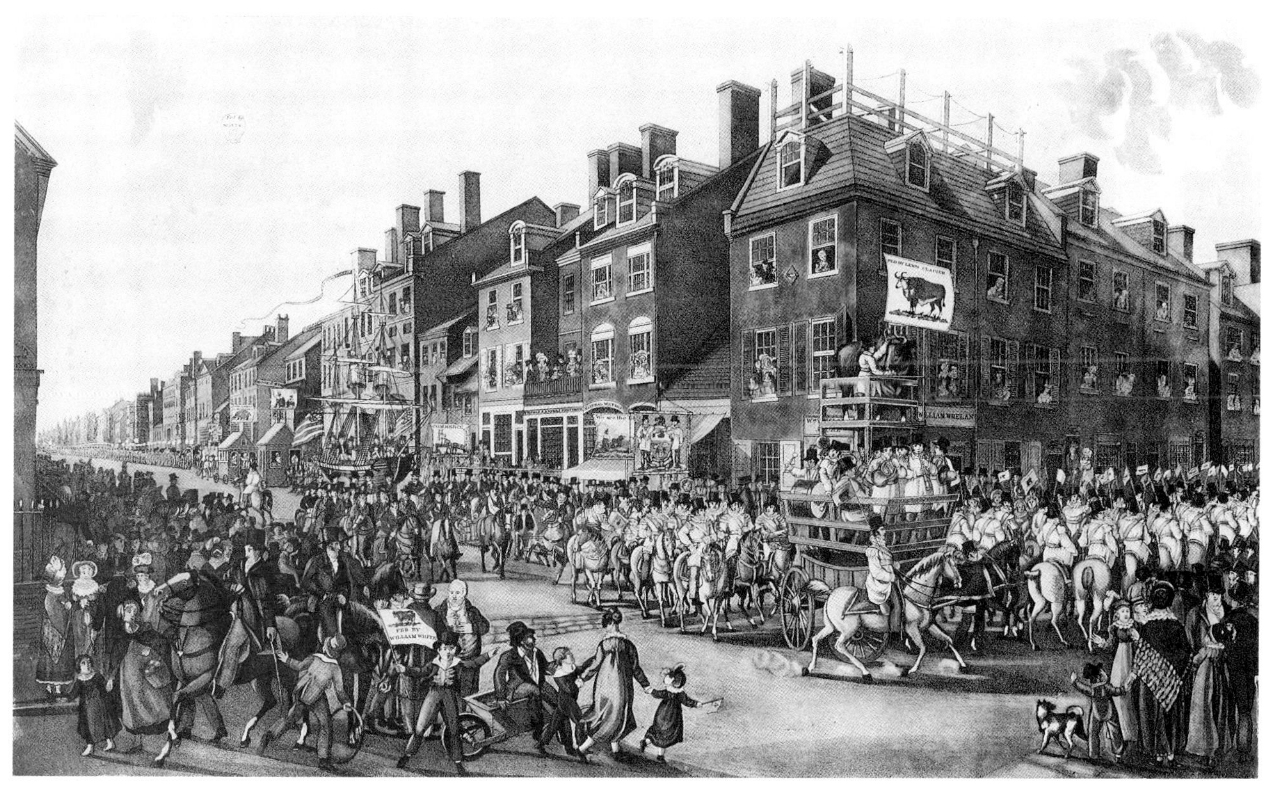

White had unquestionably demonstrated an energetic approach to business. On March 13, 1821, two days before the parade, he announced the exact route of the procession in *Relf's Philadelphia Gazette and Daily Advertiser* and explained: "The object of the [livestock display] . . . is not gain, but for the encouragement of the breed of Cattle, so essential in every country. The meat will be sold at a low market price, and it is desirous to be disposed in one city."

Soon after finishing the watercolor of the procession, Krimmel received a commission for an important historical painting, *The Landing of William Penn at Newcastle in October 1682*. The project was financed by subscription, and the key supporters were seventeen distinguished Philadelphians, among them Peter S. DuPonceau, Joseph P. Norris, and Roberts Vaux. They specified that the canvas was to measure six feet by nine feet, much larger than any painting Krimmel had done before. Thus in subject matter and size it was to measure up to Benjamin West's *William Penn's Treaty with the Indians* (1771–72). West's painting belonged to the Penn family in England, but the image was known in America through John Hall's engraving (published by John Boydell in London in 1775) and numerous derivative prints.[26]

Krimmel's companion painting was to depict Penn's Quaker settlers welcoming him to his colony in New Castle, Delaware, in October 1682, after a harrowing fifty-six-day voyage in which a third of Penn's hundred would-be colonists had died of smallpox. The terms of the commission allowed Krimmel the right to exhibit the finished painting for six months before it became the property of the subscribers who would then present it to the academy.

The commission also guaranteed Krimmel greater public prominence. The subject had local historical appeal, and if Krimmel's image proved successful, no doubt an engraving would be made of it, further enhancing his reputation and his income. In the meantime the size of the project would require painstaking consideration of how the multifigural scene should be composed.

His main supporter in obtaining this commission was DuPonceau, who had firsthand knowledge of Krimmel's talent because he owned the portrait of Heckewelder that Krimmel had made from a sketch in 1819 or 1820. DuPonceau, who later founded a society commemorating the landing of William Penn, gathered the historical documents that Krimmel might need to create an accurate image. On June 28 he wrote a fellow committee member, "The picture will, I hope, be executed in a manner that will do us honor. I am going in a few days to New Castle with the painter to examine the site and obtain local information. You see I neglect nothing for what I have at heart."[27] Steamboats and coaches traversed the thirty or so miles from Philadelphia to New Castle daily. If the two men made the trip, Krimmel may have taken a sketchpad rather than his sketchbook, for no images relating to the scene survive.

Then, two weeks later, "while preparing for the arduous task, [Krimmel] went to visit a friend in Germantown; and going with the children of the family to bathe in a neighboring mill pond, he strayed from his young companions, and they having finished their sport waited for him a long time to accompany them home—as he did not return they sought him, but only found his corpse."[28]

26. Naeve (*Krimmel*, pp. 26, 33n) is the source of the names Roberts Vaux and Joseph P. Norris, and he points out that the society was established in 1825 and that DuPonceau served as the first president; see also Henry Simpson, *The Lives of Eminent Philadelphians Now Deceased* (Philadelphia: William Brotherhead, 1859), 1:330–31. Thomas Penn, the son of William Penn, had commissioned West's picture. It had been exhibited at the Royal Academy in 1772. The painting (today in PAFA) did not come to the United States until 1852, when it was hung in Philadelphia's Independence Hall; see Von Erffa and Staley, *Paintings*, p. 207. "Sketches of the most celebrated of the works of Sir Benjamin West engraved," was in Krimmel's estate sale *(Poulson's American Daily Advertiser*, August 14, 1821).

27. Peter DuPonceau to Roberts Vaux, June 28, 1821, Vaux Papers, Historical Society of Pennsylvania, as cited in Naeve, *Krimmel*, p. 26.

28. Dunlap, *History*, 2:305.

A detailed description of the accident was given in the lengthy eulogy published in *Poulson's American Daily Advertiser* on July 20, 1821:

> He had dined on Sunday last near Mount Airy College, and early after dinner, on his return stop't at a friend's house, near Germantown, where, surrounded by those by whom he was esteemed, he remained until five o'clock, in social and animated conversation—At this time, he and two friends left the company for the purpose of bathing in Mr. Thorpe's mill dam near the house, and was observed by a lad on a rock, from which he plunged, his two friends having previously gone in, to strike his stomach forcibly on the surface of the water, to which probably his premature death is attributable, as his immersion was not deep, for he rose directly, but with a gurgling noise in his throat, and a confused movement of his arm, when the lad prudently extending a board to him, which he grasped, but soon relinquished . . . the cries of the boy instantly brought his friends to the spot, one of whom had twice dived for him.

The efforts to resuscitate Krimmel, who had drowned "in a depth of not more than eight feet water," proved futile. Years later, a subsequent owner of the sketchbooks provided another bit of information about that day. He penned a note along the inside edge of a leaf in sketchbook 6, referring to a leaf that he had just removed: "The above is a likeness of Miss Miller at Mt. Aery near Germantown—Krimmel was making a visit to the above when he was drowned in the Wissahickon—The likeness was torn out & presented to Mr. F. B. Gowan in 1883 by me. It proved to be a likeness of his mother's sister—." According to Henry Simpson, who wrote a brief biographical sketch of Krimmel in the nineteenth century, the artist was "engaged to be married at the time of his death."[29]

The accident occurred on Sunday afternoon, July 15, 1821, two weeks after Krimmel's thirty-fifth birthday. His death struck both those who knew him or his work as a great loss. He had been a painter for eleven years and recently had been elected to the presidency of the Association of American Artists. His images were reaching the attention of the middle class at long last. Prospects for sales were finally looking up. And he had just received an important commission.

George Krimmel reacted to the news of his brothers' fatal accident with grief and anger. Three decades later Abraham Ritter still recalled his words: "'Mein Gott (My God), gone what a pity! Why I ask, he needn't have gone to Germantown to get drowned, he might have done it here, . . . in the Schuylkill or the Delaware.'" Colleagues termed Krimmel's death nothing short of tragic. The day after the accident the Association of American Artists held a special meeting, and the day before the funeral the local newspaper carried instructions: members of both the Association of American Artists and of the Pennsylvania Academy were "particularly requested . . . to attend the funeral," and members of the association were to "wear crape on the left arm for six weeks," as a token of respect for their late president.[30]

The funeral commenced Tuesday morning at ten o'clock from Krimmel's dwelling at 198 Chestnut Street. The charges suggest that it was neither unpretentious nor outstandingly elaborate: $10 for a coffin, $18 for the rental of a hearse. After the body was placed on the hearse, the procession walked behind it to the cemetery plot at St. Michael's and Zion Lutheran Church.[31] If customary burial rites were observed, the pastor read prayers while the coffin was

29. *Poulson's American Daily Advertiser*, July 20, 1821; sketchbook 6, leaf 17 recto; Simpson, *Eminent Philadelphians*, p. 630.

30. Ritter, "Recollections," p. 119; *Poulson's American Daily Advertiser*, July 17, 1821.

31. *Relf's Philadelphia Gazette and Daily Advertiser*, July 28, 1821, as cited in Naeve, *Krimmel*, p. 27. The charges are itemized in the estate settlement records. My conclusions on the relative value of the expenses are drawn from Oberholtzer, *Philadelphia*, 2:110.

lowered into the ground, a scene similar to the one Krimmel had depicted about a year earlier in *A German Funeral*.

Mourning continued. Sunday evening, July 29, two weeks after the accident, Krimmel was eulogized in a German-language ceremony held at Zion Lutheran Church on North Fourth Street. On August 6, *Poulson's American Daily Advertiser* carried yet another eulogy, this one signed G. M. (probably George Murray, vice-president of the Association of American Artists). Reflecting on the irony of death coming just as success was nearly in the grasp of the painter's hands, he wrote:

> The pictures of Mr. Krimmel have long been considered by Artists and men of taste as works of great merit; yet this painter with more than ten years in the populous and wealthy city of Philadelphia (the Athens of America) could barely obtain the means of subsistence. His extraordinary merit at last attracted the notice of some of our most distinguished and intelligent citizens who, a few weeks previous to his immature death, liberally engaged him to paint a picture of the landing of William Penn. Thus the sun of prosperity was just beginning to shine on this unfortunate artist. Already had the chilling fogs of poverty which had so long hovered over him, began to disperse, and the high road of fame and fortune appeared before him, when in the prime of life, and in the full enjoyment of health and vigour of mind, the cold hand of death shut his eyes forever.

Calling the tragedy "a public loss," the eulogy summed up the feelings of his fellow artists and friends. "The death of Mr. Krimmel is a severe loss to the arts. He was in every sense a man of worth. In delineating character he stood pre-eminent. He possessed a comprehensive and penetrating mind. In fact he had every qualification to make a great painter."[32]

32. Krimmel eulogy, *Poulson's American Daily Advertiser*, August 6, 1821.

Evaluation and Legacy

Krimmel's genre pictures blazed a new trail across the art scene of Philadelphia. His influence on later American artists far exceeded what one could expect from a painter who had such a short career and produced barely two dozen finished paintings.

Krimmel was one of the few professional artists who chronicled ordinary life in the United States in the 1810s and the only one who did so consistently. His engaging and often humorous images often also contained serious commentary on contemporary life and, at times, gently moralizing details. His art, known to the picturemakers of the next generation of American artists through paintings, watercolors, or prints, inspired those who firmly established genre subjects as acceptable art in the United States. By introducing and legitimizing contemporary local topics Krimmel nudged American art out of the provincial shadows toward the mainstream of western painting.

The significance of Krimmel's drawings and paintings is heightened by the era in which they were created—precisely in the same decade that important social and political developments were fostering a distinct American culture and art. Whereas his sketchbook drawings show Krimmel more often attracted to rural subject matter, many of his finished genre scenes depict life in Philadelphia, then the largest city in the United States. The urban and rural elements in his sketches and paintings are a general reflection of life in the young republic. For although the nation was and would remain for most of the century overwhelmingly rural, in the United States as in Europe city life "formed the core of its civilisation," and "urban society [exerted] a disproportionately large influence in the formation of American culture."[1]

In a historical sense Krimmel lived at a crossroads upon which a variety of cultural influences converged, and his art looked both backward and forward. In the design of his pictures he adhered to respected eighteenth-century modes and even much older pictorial traditions, yet his acute awareness of his time and place enabled him to reinvigorate their increasingly outmoded formulas. Prints from the English school of painting provided the most important models for his early genre scenes, and prints of contemporary French painting taught him to successfully structure his multifigural compositions according to the latest neoclassical fashion; however, Krimmel's artistic sensibility was Germanic. This is most apparent in his sketchbook drawings and pictures of his last years, *A German Funeral, Portrait of the Artist and the Krimmel Family, Parade of the Victuallers*—images created after spending eighteen months in Europe. Because his principal inspiration came from observing people, animals, and objects, his sketches and pictures gave the social and political developments of the decade a seemingly authentic pictorial affirmation. Art-historically, neoclassicism enriched his knowledge of composition and drawing, and romanticism encouraged him to increase the spiritual depth of his images by adding to them the qualities of "motion, growth, chang[e], adaptation, diversity and love

1. Russel Blaine Nye, *The Cultural Life of the New Nation, 1776–1830* (New York: Harper and Row, 1960), p. 124.

of nature and of fellow man."[2] Krimmel, who was more himself as a draftsman than a painter, considered his most articulate medium—watercolor—an art form in its own right, and he used it to produce finished pictures of great significance.

Ironically, Krimmel is best known for a few works from his early years (*View of Centre Square on the Fourth of July* [1812], *Quilting Frolic* [1813], *Interior of an American Inn* [1814], and *Country Wedding* [1814]) when he was struggling to achieve technical proficiency as he sought to compose a genre picture and to master the challenge of adapting the lofty neoclassical style to scenes featuring commonplace activities. Because these best-known pictures were done within two years of each other, they have many of the same models and props and obvious similarities, which have led some critics to conclude that the artist always worked in a slightly stereotyped manner.[3]

When his work is examined chronologically, Krimmel's paintings show striking stylistic differences—these are so great between his early and later pictures that a comparison of one of the earliest images with one of the latest makes it hard to believe that they were the product of the same artist. These dissimilarities in Krimmel's work can be explained by a developmental path that was marked by several well-defined turning points, such as his participation in Sully's sketch club and his visit to Europe. His style varies from a two-dimensional orientation and stiffness in his early pictures (*Pepper-Pot: A Scene in the Philadelphia Market, View of Centre Square on the Fourth of July* [1812], and watercolors in the Svinin Portfolio) and easy-flowing compositions in complex designs at midcareer (*Election Day 1815*), to a rhythmic interplay of outlines and a plasticity of individual forms (*Return from Market; Soldier Taking Leave of His Family; Country Frolic and Dance; The Sleighing Frolic; Fourth of July Celebration in Centre Square, Philadelphia, 1819; Portrait of the Artist and the Krimmel Family;* and *Parade of the Victuallers*) in his post-European-trip paintings. During his eleven-year career, his picture structure becomes bolder and clearer, his concept of volume becomes better understood, the effects of perspective and spatial depth are more expressively explored, and the delineation of character is more sensitively realized. But the most noticeable change between his early and late pictures is in his use of color and the role of light. His first pictures were colorful in a busy manner; his later ones are dominated by relatively large areas of pure luminous color, and in them the quality of light is more subtly and effectively rendered. Although many sources provided him with prototypes for his genre pictures, Krimmel was most significantly inspired by Wilkie and Hogarth. Yet he rarely quoted these artists directly, preferring instead to extract those ideas he found congenial. These he then amalgamated with his own observations and with other European and American pictorial traditions to achieve a creative synthesis depicting new topics and fresh aspects of human experience. He did this with the same rules and principles his fellow artists were applying to their canvases of mythological and historical subjects. What set Krimmel apart from his American contemporaries was his belief that art should depict aspects of contemporary life with authenticity and verisimilitude. His advanced design concepts placed him among the most progressive artists in Philadelphia, which may have played a part in his election to the presidency of the artists' society.

During his lifetime Krimmel found few buyers for his own genre paintings; his images ultimately won more ready acceptance as prints and magazine illustrations. His pictures anticipated American taste by at least a decade and

2. Nye, *Cultural Life*, pp. 7–13.

3. Williams (*Mirror*, pp. 42, 43) writes that Krimmel had two formulas for his genre work, one used for indoor and one used for outside scenes, and that his faces appear stereotyped.

prepared the way for the proliferation of anecdotal themes in nineteenth-century popular art.

The continued interest in exhibiting Krimmel's paintings at the Pennsylvania Academy of the Fine Arts and the Boston Athenaeum allowed Krimmel's images to exert a direct influence on other American painters. About five years after the artist's death, genre painting began to win acceptance in America and flourished in an extraordinary way within the realistic tradition. During these decades William Sidney Mount (1807–68) and Richard Caton Woodville (1825–56) produced their finest pictures. These artists became better known than Krimmel and made strong contributions to the development of American genre painting by extracting inspiration from Krimmel's images.

The compelling visual parallels between Mount's *Rustic Dance after a Sleigh Ride* (1830, and subsequent versions that date from 1831 to 1845) and Krimmel's *Country Frolic and Dance* (1819/20) are "arresting evidence" (figs. 345, 346). Visiting Philadelphia in September 1836 (about the same time Childs and Lehman issued their lithograph of Krimmel's *Country Frolic and Dance*), Mount met Thomas Birch and Alexander Lawson, the latter of whom had in his engraving studio several Krimmel paintings, much to Mount's delight.[4] The lithograph may also have inspired *Kitchen Ball at White Sulphur Springs* (1838), an unusual genre scene painted by German emigrant Christian Mayr that betrays a fascination with black culture. Among the features that are parallel to Krimmel's design are its spatial configuration, the primary dancing couple, the seated fiddler, the foreground figure bending toward a dog, and the objects suspended from the ceiling.

Other artists were inspired by Krimmel's multifigured urban genre scenes. Missouri's George Caleb Bingham studied at the Pennsylvania Academy of the Fine Arts in 1838. He subsequently made his reputation as a genre painter, reaching the height of fame with *County Election* (1851–52) and *Verdict of the People* (1854–55), both of which are related in subject matter, definition of picture stage, and depiction of a multitude of figures to Krimmel's *Election Day 1815*, *Election Day 1816*, and *Parade of the Victuallers*. There are also similarities to Krimmel's works in Bingham's grouping of figures; depictions of inebriated voters, carefree boys, and a street vendor; use of dogs; and images of the flag.[5]

In the 1870s Krimmel's pictures exerted a remarkable influence on Thomas Eakins. When contemplating the design for *William Rush Carving His Allegorical Figure of the Schuylkill River* (1876–77), Eakins turned to Krimmel's *View of Centre Square on the Fourth of July* (1812) then on display at the academy. Next, according to art historian Darrel Sewell, Eakins "made costume studies" using prints and the Krimmel painting, the latter of which "provided Rush's costume, taken from the central figure of the group of two men and a woman." On one pencil study for this work Eakins noted, "The female figure of the group has only a light lace falling over the head for head dress and long yellow gloves. Holds in right hand a green parasol and a red net bag. The nearest man to her has buff vest and buff breeches, white frilled shirt, dark brown coat brass buttons. The other a green coat whitish breeches and fair top boots. One woman seems to wear an India shawl. 4th of July Centre Square. Krimmel, Cope Gallery, Exhibited 1812." Under a drawing depicting an elderly woman, Eakins commented: "White veil often used like in Krimmel." The final image reveals the evident connection to Krimmel's 1812 painting.[6]

Krimmel's artistic legacy also directly and indirectly shaped images marketed by printmakers and magazine publishers throughout the second half of

4. First noted by Donald Keyes, the intermediary role of Krimmel's pictures between the works of Wilkie and Mount is also discussed in Hoover, "Influence," pp. 6, 7, 12, 15, 17, 18, 19. A number of American art historians have pointed to Krimmel's influence on Mount; see for example, Williams, *Mirror*, p. 69. The election scene was among the paintings in the studio and Mount termed it "worth going the whole distance to see" (Alfred Frankenstein, *William Sidney Mount* [New York: Harry N. Abrams, 1975], pp. 19, 45).

5. Russell Lynes, *The Art-Makers of Nineteenth-Century America* (New York: Athenaeum, 1970), p. 249: "When [Bingham] visited Philadelphia on his second trip East, he almost surely saw two pictures by John Lewis Krimmel. . . . The paintings which impressed Bingham (and which had a direct influence not only on his subject matter but on his composition) were 'Election Day at the State House' and 'Fourth of July in Center Square.'" See also Maurice E. Bloch, *George Caleb Bingham: The Evolution of an Artist* (Berkeley and Los Angeles: University of California Press, 1967), p. 129. Another important source was Hogarth, specifically *Canvassing for Votes*, an image that Krimmel had also used some thirty-five years earlier.

6. Darrel Sewell, *Thomas Eakins: Artist of Philadelphia* (Philadelphia: Philadelphia Museum of Art, 1982), pp. 48, 49, 52.

FIGURE 345
William Sidney Mount, Rustic Dance after a Sleigh Ride, *1830. Oil on canvas; 22 x 27 ¼ in. (M. and M. Karolik Collection, Museum of Fine Arts, Boston.)*

FIGURE 346
John Lewis Krimmel, Country Frolic and Dance, *1819. Oil on canvas; 16 ½ x 22 ½ in. (Private collection.)*

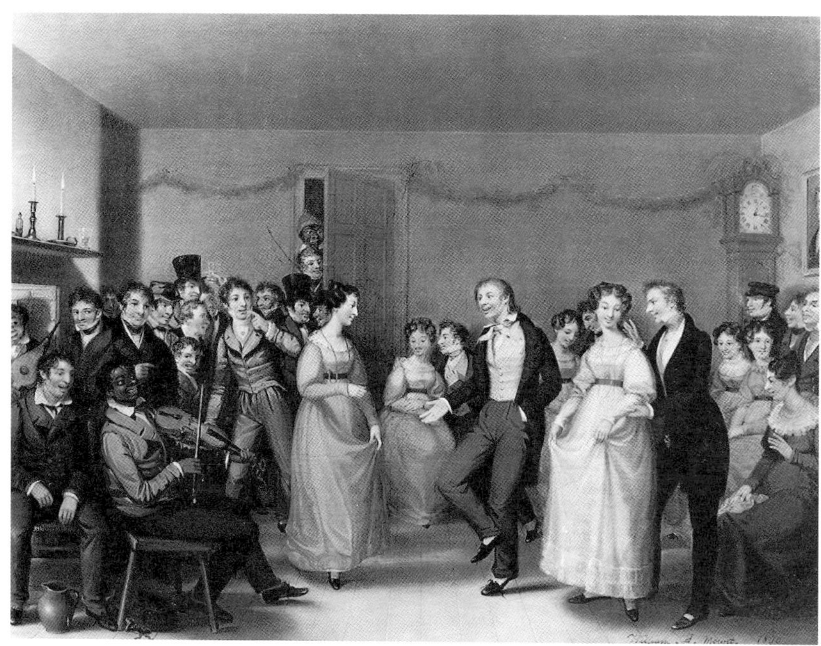

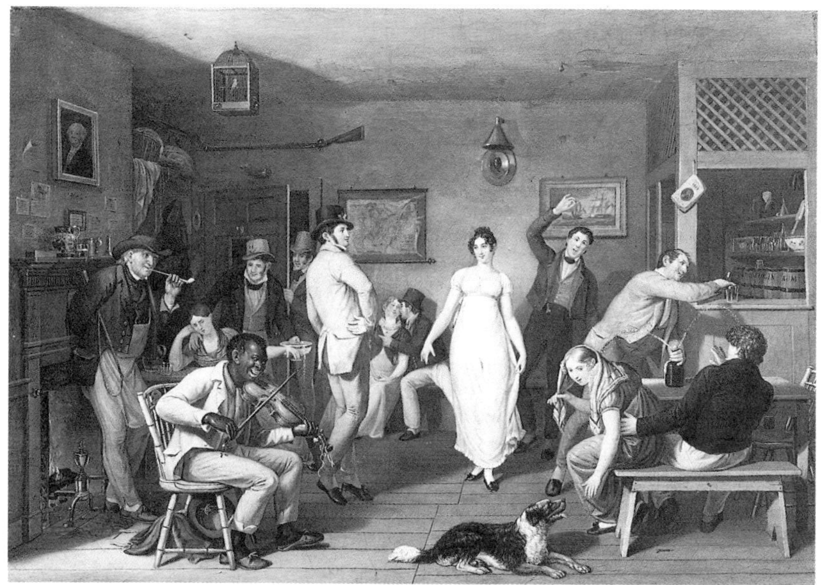

the nineteenth century. *The Conflagration of Masonic Hall* was reissued three times, long after the event had lost its immediacy.[7] Yeager's aquatint plate *Procession of Victuallers* was both reused and translated into lithography in the 1850s and again in the 1860s.[8] During the third quarter of the century, printmaker and illustrator John Sartain produced a mezzotint version of Lawson's line engraving of *Return from Market.* Toward the end of the century, the Pennsylvania Academy of the Fine Arts was given Lawson's unfinished plate of *Election Day 1815* and had prints pulled from it to present as gifts. During the 1880s, woodcuts of *Election Day 1815* and *Fourth of July Celebration* (1819) were used to illustrate Scharf and Westcott's monumental three-volume *History of Philadelphia.*

Finally, Krimmel's images exerted a subtle but wide influence on the formation of a national visual culture. His type of subject matter became favorite themes for images issued by Nathaniel Currier and James Ives—sleighrides, family gatherings, going to market, firemen in action. When the New York–based lithographic firm began producing prints for a national market, among the artists, draftsmen, and lithographers they hired were German immigrants Louis Maurer and Otto Knirsch, whose designs, such as the 1856 *Preparing for Market,* are strongly reminiscent of Krimmel's, perhaps because the men easily identified with Krimmel's artistic sensibility.

The lasting appeal of Krimmel's pictures for fellow American artists and eventually the public reflects the recognition that the images present positive aspects of life with an appealing freshness and convincing authenticity. Krimmel had eschewed the high-flung mystical spirit and poetic imagination of a Washington Allston or a Rembrandt Peale. His down-to-earth, slightly jocose and at times gently moralizing approach successfully linked the neoclassicist's sense of realism and structure with the romantic's dedication to nature and humanity. By devoting his professional career to the representation of ordinary life in the young republic, Krimmel introduced genre images as an acceptable art form for generations of American painters to come.

7. Naeve, *Krimmel,* p. 109.

8. Naeve, *Krimmel,* p. 116, assumes the lithographs were made from the original watercolor. I disagree. The Yeager print was the source that was used for the lithographs because it and the lithographs have the identical slogan, the balloon, and the banner; the slogan is different on the watercolor.

APPENDIX I

Krimmel's Estate

Krimmel's artwork was rapidly dispersed. His belongings had been inventoried immediately after his death, and later in the summer most were auctioned off to pay his debts, both standard procedures for the time. The list of goods itemized in the sale advertisement that appeared in *Poulson's American Daily Advertiser*, from August 7 to 14, 1821, furnishes valuable information about the state of Krimmel's studio in 1821:

Dance at a Country Tavern, in oil framed
Sleighing Frolic, d[itt]o, d[itt]o
Fourth of July, watercolor, do
Head of a young Female, oil
German peasant Girl, do framed
Scene in a Country Tavern during the late war, oil, unfinished
The Tea Party, sketch in oil
The Honey Pot, do
German Funeral, do
Departure for a Boarding School, sketch in india ink
Return from Boarding School, do
Cherry Woman, sketch in colors
Cut Finger, India ink
The General Election at the State House, in colors
Butcher's Procession, do
Pepperpot, a scene in the Philadelphia Market, do
Mc Donough's Victory on the Lakes do

---

also
A landscape from the Italian School, framed
The Singing Party, copy from the Flemish
Sketches from Ancient Masters by Wertmüller, 1 Vol. folio
Sketches of the most celebrated of the works of Sir Benjamin West, engraved
A Port Folio of Studies from the Human Body, drawn from Life, by Krimmel
Engravings from the works of Hogarth
A set of Gil Blas, 4 volumes additional of plates
A Port Folio of Engravings
A handsome Secretary
Camera Obscura
Case of Mathematical Instruments
12 dozens of painter's brushes and a variety of other Articles.[1]

Of the 18 pictures, 5 survive as listed, and 3 others survive in a different medium or as prints. It is difficult to understand the distinctions drawn between

1. Items "144 & 145 View of State St. Boston" are omitted because they are not by Krimmel, and a close reading of the catalogue reveals that the auction house did not indicate that Krimmel had done these.

watercolors and oils by the advertisement, leaving the term "in colors" ambiguous. Other parts of the advertisement are more illuminating and add to or confirm our understanding of Krimmel, his way of working, and his art. Among the artists whose work he admired were Hogarth, West, Wilkie, and Hetsch. The Wertmüller sketches suggest that Krimmel may have turned to this particular copyist for designs perfected by the great masters. The set of Gil Blas—a picaresque romance set in Spain revolving around the adventures of a rogue—is intriguing. The books were the masterpiece of French novelist and dramatist Alain René Le Sage and were issued in parts between 1715 and 1735. Krimmel may have found the story both appealing to his sensibilities and compatible with his art.

The secretary desk indicates that however scarce sales may have been, the artist had acquired a few moveable goods. Most of his money, however, was tied up in his professional activities—the set of mathematical instruments, the 12 dozen brushes, and the camera obscura.

Only a few of the purchasers are known—primarily those who acquired pictures prior to the auction, which meant that their names were recorded for the legal accounting. The financial portion of the estate records show that Thomas Birch, William Strickland, and George Murray purchased one or more items prior to the sale, and Krimmel's brother George bought two paintings. James McMurtie, artist, merchant, art dealer, and a friend of Krimmel later interviewed by Dunlap for his biographical sketch of Krimmel, purchased the "Port Folio of Studies from the Human Body drawn from Life." Nathaniel Devaltooth, an English-born merchant and framemaker in Boston, bought more of Krimmel's pictures than anyone else. Whether Devaltooth alone was instrumental in taking many of Krimmel's pictures to New England is not clear. Only three months later 9 were listed in a catalogue issued by Blake and Cunningham for a November 22, 1821, sale at Doggett's Repository of the Arts in Boston. Only 1 of the 9, *The Tea Party* (no. 32) had been listed among the studio effects offered in August. The other 8 included "Interior, the Country Stage-House Tavern and Post Office, with the News of Peace" (no. 119) and its "companion," *Quilting Frolic* (no. 120), which according to *Analectic* belonged to Alexander Murray along with several others, none of which were in the auction. The remaining 6 were: *Dogs Fighting, and Overturn of the Apple Stall* (no. 28), *Two Female Heads as Studies* (no. 30), *A Portrait of the Artist Painted by Himself* (no. 33), and three copy works—*Interior of a Cottage; A Man Plays the Jews Harp* (no. 26), *Interior of a Cottage; Feeding the Young Bird* (no. 27), and *The Blind Fiddler* (no. 31).[2]

The success of this sale is unrecorded. At least 2 of these were purchased by Nathaniel Devaltooth, who died in Havana about six months later in the spring of 1822. It took three years for his estate to be settled. A final sale of his goods was held by J. L. Cunningham for the estate in Boston on March 30–31, 1825. The advertisement in the March 30 *Columbian Centinel* made special mention of "original Drawings by Krimmel" among the artworks being disposed. The catalogue listing included at least 27 Krimmel works and perhaps 30:

30 A Portrait of the Artist by himself. J. L Krimmel
32 Two Female Heads as Studies, by J. L. Krimmel
45 Dogs Fighting—Overturn of the Apple Stall, by Krimmel
132 Cherries—Krimmel's Water cols

2. Naeve, *Krimmel*, pp. 65–108.

133 The Concert	
134 Pepper Pot	
135 Village Post Office, &c	
136 The Gamblers	Krimmel
137 Fruiterers (In Gilt)	"
138 Milk (Frames)	"
139 A Music Party	"
140 A Barber Shop	"
141 The Walking Party	"
142 The News-Paper	"
143 Returning from Market	"
146 The Cut Finger	Krimmel
147 The Robbers	"
148 Election Day, Philadelphia	"
149 Do & View of State House	"
150 McDonough's Victory	"
151 The Goat	"
152 Oysters	"
153 The Village Dance	"
154 The Sleighing Party	"
155 Means for Boarding School	"
156 Victuallers Procession	"

Of those listed without an artist's name, 3 have titles that suggest they were by Krimmel:

104 Blind Man's Buff
105 Cart Horses
106 Going to Market.

Commencing in May 1827, the Boston Athenaeum opened a series of three-month-long exhibitions of paintings in private collections. Among these were Krimmel's *Cottage Dance* (lent in 1827 by C. Torry), *Cattle Watering* (lent in 1828 by Josiah Bradlee), *Pennsylvania Quilting Scene* (lent in 1829 by T. H. Swett), and *News of Peace* and *Happy Family* (both lent in 1832 by Samuel Swett). These exhibitions were initiated to promote interest in local artists and to regularly introduce Bostonians to the appreciation of the fine arts as a public rather than a private pastime. Clearly the definition of "local" was wider than Boston and New England, and the term may have been a euphemism for artists who had resided anywhere in the young republic.[3]

Although more than 30 of his images went to New England, at least inititally, many of Krimmel's paintings and watercolors remained in the Philadelphia area. Some were exhibited and reexhibited at the academy, and these were some of the very ones that had been offered at the 1821 auction of his estate: *The Honey Pot*, a pair; *Female Head; Dance in a Country Tavern* (oil); *Cherry Woman;* and *German Funeral.* Several new titles also appeared on the exhibition lists: *Sweeps Importuning for Cold Provisions* (1822); *The Fighting Dogs, or the Cake Woman in Distress* (1823); *Winter Scene in Philadelphia—Children Sliding* (watercolor, 1825); *Portrait of a Gentleman* (1828); and *Portrait of Himself* (1831).

3. Robert F. Perkins, Jr., and William J. Gavin III, comps. and eds., *The Boston Atheneum Art Exhibition Index, 1827–1874* (Boston: Library of the Boston Atheneum, 1980), p. 89.

APPENDIX 2

The Winterthur Sketchbooks

Krimmel's seven sketchbooks are now in the Joseph Downs Collection of Manuscripts and Printed Ephemera at Winterthur. The preservation of these books and the identification of the artist is primarily due to Henry M. Wetherill of Philadelphia's Wetherill Brothers, who billed themselves as druggists, chemists, and color merchants. On November 24, 1850, he wrote on the front cover of each of the seven sketchbooks: "Scetches by Joh. Ludw. Krimmel," thus registering the name of the artist, and underneath, he added his own name, indicating he owned the books. The artist himself had signed only the cover of sketchbook 6, as "J. L. Krimmel."

Vivid depictions of ordinary people and objects, such as Krimmel produced in his sketchbooks, were exceedingly rare in early nineteenth-century America, for the flood of illustrations that later inundated the printed world had not yet started. For Wetherill, Krimmel's sketches depicted the world Wetherill knew as a young person, and his remarks and explanations written in the books indicate that he spent considerable time contemplating the images. In addition to Wetherill's hand, those of at least two other people are apparent. Whether these were earlier or later owners of the books is unclear.

Regrettably, the seven sketchbooks have not been kept complete. Several pages have been torn out, so one may speculate that some of the finest drawings were removed to be framed. Wetherill himself wrote in sketchbook 7 that he had taken out a certain leaf to give it away. Precise dates are in all the sketchbooks except sketchbook 2; however, the approximate origin of the drawings can be deduced by relating them to the firmly dated paintings for which they are preliminary studies. When Krimmel added a date, he often indicated the day of the week with the medieval identifications of the days derived from ancient astronomical symbols:

Sunday (Sun) ☉
Monday (Moon) ☾
Tuesday (Mars) ♂
Wednesday (Mercury) ☿
Thursday (Jupiter) ♃
Friday (Venus) ♀
Saturday (Saturn) ♄

These seven characters served as a kind of shorthand in many fields but have not been found in the work of any other American artist. Krimmel may have learned to use them while he worked in the European mercantile trade where their application was common.

Because the artist was in the habit of using his books concurrently, he did not always complete one book before moving to another. Book 2 overlaps book 3, books 3, 4, and 5 overlap, and books 6 and 7 overlap.

SKETCHBOOK 1

Winterthur library 59 x 5.4, book of 48 pages, laid paper (7 ½" x 4 ¾"). Watermarks of two English mills: (1) "J. Whatman," apparent in a number of incomplete marks but best seen on pages 3 and 36; and (2) "Budgen," which is best seen on pages 10 and 36. Whatman and his son owned mills, including Turkey Mill, in Kent, between 1747 and 1794. Thomas Budgen operated Dartford Mill, Kent, between 1790 and 1800.[1] The 47 pages of drawings were executed between May 1810 and July (or slightly later) 1812.

The images show the artist in his initial learning period in Philadelphia as he made random, very small sketches while observing people at work and rest. Many small figure studies closely match details in the watercolors he sold to Pavel Svinin (see app. 3). Others are clearly preparatory studies for his oil paintings, for example the study of the nymph and bittern that he then incorporated in *View of Centre Square on the Fourth of July* (1812).

Once he began to study human proportions and movements systematically, the artist adopted a larger sketching style. Following a long-established method for the training of artists, he first drew from classical sculpture and copied the anatomical engravings of Andreas Vesalius, a standard reference for the study of the human body, and then practiced sketching from live models.

Eight small portraits drawn with pencil or with watercolor over pencil, support Dunlap's contention that Krimmel began to make a living from his art by painting miniature portraits.[2]

SKETCHBOOK 2

Winterthur library 59 x 5.7, book of 24 pages, wove paper (6 ¼" x 7 ½"). No watermarks. The drawings occupy 22 pages and were executed ca. 1813. The book's label reads "sold by David Hogan," and Hogan's shop was located in Philadelphia at that time. Unlike the other sketchbooks, this one is almost square in format and too large to fit into a coat pocket; it also differs in the nature of the sketches. Most are compositional drawings, and many are only defined in outline and are executed in a cursive, very loose style; nevertheless they are clearly recognizable as genre scenes. The artist drew in ink, using a quill pen, a very pliable instrument that produces a flexible line. Many compositions involve several figures. The most well-developed sketches are in watercolors or wash, indicating that Krimmel's conceptual process toward the depiction of a story had reached an advanced stage.

The sketches that directly relate to four of Krimmel's known canvases demonstrate how certain pictures evolved. Of these there are two wash drawings for *Interior of an American Inn;* three ink sketches and a finished watercolor for *Country Wedding;* three ink sketches for *Return from Market;* and three ink sketches and a watercolor for *Cherry Woman with Children.* In addition, the book contains two ink sketches that relate to two watercolors he sold to Svinin: *Winter Scene with the Bank of the United States in the Background* and *Dance in a Wayside Inn.* Among the well-developed sketches are at least three pen and ink drawings that seem to be preparatory studies for *The Tea Party*, one of Krimmel's unlocated oil paintings twice listed for sale in Philadelphia. Three small ink drawings seem to be Krimmel's experimental sketches for the design of *The Cut Finger*, apparently an original painting that Krimmel exhibited in 1814.

1. I thank Anne Clapp for all information on watermarks and paper mills.

2. Dunlap, *History*, 3:392.

SKETCHBOOK 3

Winterthur library 59 x 5.1, book of 44 pages, wove paper (4 3/8" x 8 7/8"). "Canson Frères" watermark is complete on page 15. The Canson mill was French. The drawings occupy all 44 pages plus both inside covers and were executed between 1813 and early November 1816. Most reveal Krimmel as a skillful landscape artist who dated a great number of his sketches, particularly those produced in the area of the Lehigh Valley during late summer 1813. Although in the topographical views Krimmel patterns his designs after drawing book examples, he is amazingly progressive in the depiction of intimate spots in the woods, rocks, and single trees.

Figure sketches are few. Many are portrait sketches of little girls, presumably the children of his brother, and one is of a young boy asleep in a chair. Some of the pencil sketches of men, obviously observed from life, Krimmel used as the basis for his figure types in the paintings *Interior of an American Inn* and *Election Day 1815*. Among the watercolors, two are of exceptional importance because they show Krimmel as one of the first artists in America fascinated by the invention of the steamboat. In November 1816, while on his way to Europe, his ship docked in Bermuda, and the artist made watercolors of the panorama of the many islands and depicted harbor sites, which might be the first of their kind in American art.

SKETCHBOOK 4

Winterthur library 59 x 5.2, book of 75 pages, wove paper (4 7/8" x 7 1/2"). "730" watermark found on pages 6, 35, and 37. "CS" watermark, enclosed in a cup of crossed laurel branches, found on pages 1 and 32. The "CS" watermark is French. Drawings occupy 67 pages, all were executed between December 1816 and December 1818.

This book was purchased in Europe. On the first pages the artist sketched scenes of ordinary life he observed while in Paris. Although he probably arrived in Ebingen in February 1817, the earliest dated outdoor sketch is April 3. While drawing the people and the nearby vistas, he also sketched Ebingen from several vantage points and made a listing of eight of them. In May 1818 he set out on his journey to Vienna via Stuttgart. On June 1 he boarded a boat to complete his travel to the Austrian capital on the Danube River. As the vessel passed the most picturesque sites, he made many pencil sketches that he later traced with ink. When the boat landed, he produced close-up sketches of the sites, some in watercolor, among them the view of Mount Calvary, near Linz.

The many notes written on the cover and last pages of this book provide information on Krimmel's careful preparations for his visit to Vienna. They include eight private art collections and the address of landscape painter Bernhard Freuler (1796–1858) to whom he carried greetings from Stuttgart painter Carl Friedrich Heinzmann (1795–1846). It is likely that Freuler advised Krimmel to return to Württemberg by way of Salzburg, and on that route Krimmel produced some of his most advanced landscape views.

SKETCHBOOK 5

Winterthur library 59 x 5.3, book of 82 pages, wove paper (5 1/8" x 7 1/2"). Made of papers from two different mills: pages 1–22 have watermarks "IF"

(p. 2) or "FI" (p. 7) and are probably German, but they are not found in books on watermarks; "Brielmaier" (pp. 23–41 with the best rendering on p. 41), is surely German or Austrian, but it is not listed in books on watermarks.

This book contains 72 pages of drawings executed between spring 1817 and autumn 1818 plus many notes, which the artist mainly jotted down on the inside cover. Krimmel used the book on his return trip from Vienna to do views at Salzburg, Chiemsee, and Rosenheim, among other places. What Krimmel had gained from his trip to Vienna in terms of professional knowledge is apparent from his double-page watercolor of an Ebingen streetscape dated July 17, 1818—it demonstrates his changed concept of pictorial space.

The book also supplies information about the painter's final departure from Ebingen. On the inside cover ten men signed their names, some also their professions, at the artist's farewell party on August 8, 1818. By September 1 Krimmel had reached Mainz and embarked down the Rhine River to the sea. As his boat passed castles and other famous romantic sites, he drew 33 sketches in just 2 days. He also sketched fellow passengers standing, sitting, or sleeping during the long hours on the boat.

Krimmel's European sketches, particularly those in sketchbook 5, make clear that while in Germany the artist gradually absorbed new formal concepts and ideas. His art underwent a transformation from the neoclassical aesthetic to romanticism.

Sketchbooks 6 and 7 show that Krimmel was back in Philadelphia during 1819, 1820, and until March 1821. Again, Krimmel used both books alternately, as can be seen by the sketches he produced on July 4 and 5, 1819, depicting the same site and the same event at Centre Square, Philadelphia, in each of the two books. Preparatory figure studies for *Soldier Taking Leave of His Family* are also in both books.

SKETCHBOOK 6

Winterthur library 59 x 5.6, book of 36 pages, laid paper (5 ⅛" x 7 ½"). Watermarked "Brandywine," pp. 10–13 have a crowned shield holding a post horn and with a pendant monogram "TG," the mark of the Gilpin Mill on the Brandywine from 1787 to 1837. Drawings are on 32 of the pages and were executed between spring 1819 and spring 1821.

Many images are watercolors over pencil. A small watercolor portrait of a young girl and a number of larger watercolors of fashionably dressed female figures—kneeling, sitting, or crouched down—seem to be preparatory studies for the Krimmel family portrait, which the artist worked on during 1819 and 1820. Other sketches are sensitive observations of flowering plants or precise studies of objects, mainly household tools. The artist's accurate and analytical approach in depicting the different parts of the spinning wheel, for example, is almost that of a mechanical engineer. His heightened interest in geometric shapes and perspective lines is apparent in a beautifully finished watercolor of a large barn built of stone with a carriage porch. The sketchbook also contains several watercolors of seated young women, silently occupied with sewing or other needlework. A very different type is represented in a pencil study of a fashionably dressed woman who smokes a pipe while walking down a Philadelphia street. The leather of the front cover of book 6 has a faint pen and ink sketch that appears to have been made during the parade of the victuallers in March 1821. The inside back cover contains Krimmel's personal calendar for the period May 15 to May 30, 1819, and suggests that he was again teaching in a school.

SKETCHBOOK 7

Winterthur library 59 x 5.5, book of 50 pages: first and last two pages are wove paper, all others are laid paper (7 ⅛" x 4 ¾"). The papers are from two different mills: pp. 1, 2, 49, 50 have the watermark "J. Green/1815" signifying John Green's Hayle Mill, which operated in Maidstone, Kent, between 1815 and 1827; all other pages (except 41–42) have the watermark "Thomas Gilpin & Co," "Brandywine" with crowned shield holding a post horn and with a pendant monogram "TG"; pp. 41–42 have "TG" in large double capital letters. Drawings are on 37 pages and were executed between spring 1819 and April 1821.

This book differs from the others in that it has several pages of emblematic designs, including a precise rendering of the Pennsylvania state seal. The exact meaning of Krimmel's allegorical females is not clear, but their attributes seem to refer to Philadelphia as a city of art, commerce, and trade. As a whole the designs suggest Krimmel's growing interest in commercial commissions, for example the design for D. Oldenbergh, 43 Market Street, Philadelphia. The same is true of the drawings directly related to the watercolor *Parade of the Victuallers* and to the trade card for Sellers and Pennock fire equipment company.

In contrast, a beautiful watercolor of a river bank with reflections in the water shows a very progressive, almost impressionistic use of color. A watercolor of a small room where a barefoot woman is pressing laundry is drawn with an acute geometric vision and a dynamic sense of space. In this same sketchbook, Krimmel drew a copy of François Granet's *The Choir of the Capuchin Church in Rome*, and that painting's perspective and stagelike space influenced the design of his genre scenes from the 1819/20 period.

In this last book, the artist's long-practiced habit of making studies of horses, dogs, cows, hens, geese, and other farm animals helped him build an excellent vocabulary of this kind, for animals continued to play a significant role in all of his genre scenes. Krimmel's enduring sense of humor comes through in a drawing of two huge hogs that he saw displayed at an inn.

The sheer number of Krimmel's drawings in these seven sketchbooks emphasize their great importance, especially when compared to the scarcity of Krimmel's paintings. His watercolor and wash drawings seem to occupy a place intermediate between pure drawing and oil painting, revealing their dual nature where the pencil or pen lines remain visible under the transparent color. Although the drawings in the seven sketchbooks are significant by themselves, they are even more important in their relationship to the artist's extant and lost paintings and as the key to reconstructing Krimmel's development as an artist.

APPENDIX 3

The Svinin Portfolio

Strange but fortunate circumstances have substantially enriched the number of surviving works produced by Krimmel, all dating from early in his career. Among the portfolio of 52 watercolors that once belonged—and hence were largely attributed—to Pavel Svinin, a Russian on diplomatic assignment to Philadelphia from 1811 to 1813, are several genre scenes of Philadelphia, which Krimmel's sketchbooks and paintings demonstrate were made by Krimmel. The attempt to tell the story of this portfolio and to explain the wide variety of watercolors in it—many of which may have been done by artists other than Svinin—must begin with the story of Svinin himself.

Pavel Petrovich Svinin (1787–1839) arrived in America in summer 1811 as secretary to the Russian consul general in Philadelphia and remained at this post for almost two years.[1] The young diplomat had received a fine education: he attended a boarding school for nobility that was attached to the University of Moscow and after graduating briefly studied drawing at the Academy of Fine Arts in St. Petersburg before entering the Foreign Office. Conversant in several languages, he became "Translator and Cavalier of the State Board of Foreign Affairs" and, at the age of 18, diplomatic officer attached to Admiral Senyavin. His new position took him first to the Mediterranean and then, in spite of the ongoing Napoleonic Wars, to almost every important country on the European continent and to England. When this well-seasoned, 23-year-old traveler disembarked at Philadelphia he had already cultivated the habit of keeping a journal. While in the United States his journal rapidly grew in size because he planned to turn it into a travel book when he returned to his homeland.[2]

Svinin was well suited to writing an account of his travels; his bold and energetic personality complemented an inquisitive mind that was "bent on knowing everything." These qualities included an alert eye for the contemporary scene and a gift for vivid description. The Philadelphia post provided him with the chance to collect information about life in the United States, a nation that remained a source of curiosity to most Europeans. Philadelphia's libraries gave him easy access to books about North America, and its artistic community gave him an opportunity to acquire watercolors to illustrate his travelogue.

Because his diplomatic duties were not heavy, Svinin spent much time at his avocations, which, he claimed, included painting; however, he chose not to share any of his visual observations of this new nation with the public, although he did display several images of Russian scenes under his name at one of the two exhibitions at the Pennsylvania Academy of the Fine Arts during his period of residence. This reticence may have been because he realized his limitations as an artist, for as he later wrote: "'I often regretted that I did not possess the brush of a Hogarth!'" He also regretted that he did not possess the "'pen of a Sterne,'" however, when he commissioned the painter Vasili Andreyevich Tropinin to do his portrait he chose to be depicted working on a large

1. Yevgenia Petrova, *Traveling across North America, 1812–1813: Watercolors by the Russian Diplomat Pavel Svinin* (1815; facsimile ed., New York: Harry N. Abrams, 1992), p. 28.

2. The definitive study is Avraham Yarmolinsky, *Picturesque United States of America, 1811, 1812, 1813; Being a Memoir on Paul Svinin* (New York: William Edwin Rudge, 1930); see also Margaret Jeffery, "As a Russian Saw Us in 1812," *Metropolitan Museum of Art Bulletin* 1, no. 3 (November 1942): 134–40; D. Fedotoff White, "A Russian Sketches Philadelphia, 1811–1813," *Pennsylvania Magazine of History and Biography* 75, no. 1 (January 1951): 1–24; Abbott Gleason, "Pavel Svin'in 1787–1839," in *Abroad in America: Visitors to the New Nation, 1776–1914* (Washington, D.C.: National Portrait Gallery, 1976), pp. 12–22.

manuscript, for he spent the years after his return to Russia in late 1814 or early 1815 primarily as an editor and writer.[3] Apparently as soon as he discovered a publishing opportunity in Philadelphia, the young consulate officer wrote two articles for *Port Folio* "to enable Americans to see . . . Russia in its true light." His writing style was that of a natural raconteur, but it is the artwork that accompanied these essays that is of interest here.

The first essay, "The Emperor Alexander," was illustrated with an unsigned copy of a portrait of the reigning czar that was engraved by David Edwin; the second essay, "Memoir on the Cosacks," had an engraving entitled *A Cosack of the Don in his Military Dress* credited "P. Svinin Esqr. pinxt." The following year, 1813, Thomas Dobson of Philadelphia republished Svinin's essays as *Sketches of Moscow and St. Petersburg Ornamented with Nine Coloured Engravings Taken from Nature.* Eight of the nine plates were engraved by Philadelphia artist William Kneass; the exception was Edwin's engraving of the czar.[4]

At the 1812 exhibition at the Pennsylvania Academy of the Fine Arts, Svinin had displayed 7 small watercolors—5 of St. Petersburg and 2 of Russian peasants, which the reviewer for *Port Folio* deemed "very superior to the general products of amateurs. From the manner of finish and correctness of outline, we should have been inclined (without particular information) to have attributed them to a professional artist of great merit." During the exhibition Svinin had gained notoriety by casting aspersions on the originality of Rembrandt Peale's design for *Roman Daughter.* Young Peale, an academician and member of the board of the Pennsylvania academy, had recently returned from France, and his new style and manner of painting quite clearly showed the influence of current French religious and history paintings. He was deeply offended by Svinin's rumormongering and, with Sully at his side, confronted the Russian, whereupon Svinin retracted his comments. Once back in Russia, Svinin again raised questions about Peale's ability to create original works of art.[5]

Svinin did not show any pictures at the exhibition of May 1813. This is all the more noteworthy in light of his later publication (in Russia) illustrated with engravings of genre scenes that have such specificity that they could only be based on watercolors done while he was in the United States.

Svinin had left Philadelphia with the party of Gen. Jean Victor Moreau on June 21, 1813, to join the campaign against Napoleon and took with him 52 watercolors of North American subjects. Within weeks of arriving in Europe, the general was mortally wounded in the battle of Dresden, dying September 2, 1813. Svinin remained with the military command unit until he was dispatched to England to convey official condolences to Mme Moreau the following March.

For the next several months, Svinin lived in London and while there published *Sketches of Russia,* a small book that was a revision of *Sketches of Moscow and St. Petersburg.* This expanded book had 15 plates:

1. Portrait of the Emperor Alexander
2. Portrait of the Empress of Russia
3. View of the Monument of Peter the Great
4. View of Mr. Paschkoff's House in Moscow
5. Sketch, representing a Cozak, Killing a Tyger in Syberia, with an Account of the Cozaks
6. View of the Cazan's Church in St. Petersburg, with a Description of It
7. View of the Field of Mars in St. Petersburg, with an Account of Its Principal Edifices, and Objects

3. Yarmolinsky, *Picturesque United States,* pp. 4–5, 10.

4. Pavel Petrovich Svinin, "The Emperor Alexander," *Port Folio,* n.s., 7, no. 3 (March 1812): 197–201; Pavel Petrovich Svinin, "Memoir on the Cosacks," *Port Folio,* n.s., 7, no. 4 (April 1812): 353–57; Yarmolinsky, *Picturesque United States,* pp. xvi, 6.

5. *Second Annual Exhibition* (1812), pp. 23, 24; "Review of the Second Annual Exhibition," pt. 2, *Port Folio* 8, no. 2 (August 1812): 143–44; Dunlap, *History,* 2:53; Yarmolinsky, *Picturesque United States,* pp. 36–37.

8. A Circassian in His Military Costume with Brief Account of that People
9. General View of the Kremlin
10. The Palace of the Czars in the Kremlin
11. View of the New Exchange in St. Petersburg with a Description of the Edifice
12. Representation of the Russian Winter Amusement on the Ice Mountains
13. Russian Mode of Travelling in Summer
14. Russian Mode of Travelling in Winter
15. View of a Summer Garden, in St. Petersburg ill. with an Account of It and a Specimen of Russian National Poetry and Music.

Most likely the portrait of the czar and five views of St. Petersburg (nos. 1, 3, 6, 7, 11, and 15) were the ones Svinin had exhibited at the academy in 1812—listed in the exhibition catalogue as "Portrait of Alexander I, Emperor of Russia" (no. 74), "Views in St. Petersburg" (nos. 126, 127, 135, 141), and "Winter-scene in St. Petersburg" (no. 136).

The 15 illustrations are dissimilar and exceedingly uneven stylistically, ranging from very loosely brushed definitions to stiffly drawn images of precise linear execution that suggest the tools and skills of a specialist in architectural drafting. None of the architectural views contain figures, and only 4 of the illustrations can be called genre scenes—the cossack killing a tiger, winter amusement, and the 2 travel scenes (nos. 5, 12–14). The illustration of a cossack killing a tiger is, according to the accompanying footnote, a copy after Russian artist Alexander Orlovsky, and it is totally different in style from the picture of winter amusements. Had Svinin been actively painting as an amateur and had he studied the paintings he had purchased, any of his post-1813 images should have been more adeptly done.[6]

Soon after Svinin returned to Russia he wrote and published *Opyt zhyvopisnavo puteshestviya po severnoi Amerike* (A Picturesque Voyage in North America) (1815), which contains seven unrelated essays about the United States, parts of which Svinin had also published in the St. Petersburg monthly, *Syn Otechestva* (*Son of the Fatherland*), in 1814. The essays are written with a positive attitude toward the United States and contain astute observations about the economic and political climate, although Svinin's penchant for bragging led him to make some absurd statements. All 6 of the book's engraved illustrations are based on the watercolors Svinin collected while in the United States. One is of a ship surrounded by whales near the coast of Newfoundland, another is a view of Niagara Falls based on a print by Alexander Wilson (but not so-credited by Svinin), a third is of a ferry crossing the Susquehanna River at Havre de Grace, Maryland. The remaining 3—*Tableau of Indian Faces, Black People's Prayer Meeting* and *Deck Life on One of Fulton's Steamboats*—are based on watercolors made by Krimmel. Svinin's book was reprinted in 1818, and German and Dutch translations without illustrations appeared in 1816 and 1818 respectively.

With only 6 engravings illustrating his book, Svinin had made use of only a small portion of his collection and was anxious to have additional engravings made from other pictures in his portfolio. For such an expensive undertaking, he needed generous financial support. Hoping for the patronage of Empress Elizaveta Alexeyevna, he presented to her in the summer of 1816 a copy of his recently published book and also sent to her two portfolios of American images. That he did not submit these pictures as a gift is evident from the letter that accompanied the return of them. In this letter the spokesman for the empress

6. Pavel Petrovich Svinin, *Sketches of Russia* (London: R. Ackermann, 1814), p. 47 n.

wrote, "Her Majesty's curiosity was satisfied to the fullest and perusal of this collection of pictures afforded her great pleasure."[7] Implicitly, the empress declined to finance the engravings.

Aside from the 6 illustrations in his book, he had not been able to reap more benefit or any financial profit from his collection of North American images. Apparently he did not have the opportunity to sell them, a perplexing fact in view of the czar's 1817 request for immediate delivery of views of American cities and their environs. Dispatches of inquiry on the czar's behalf were sent to Russian embassies in England and America, and apparently no consideration was given to Svinin's American pictures.[8]

Svinin retired from diplomatic service in 1824 at the age of 37, ostensibly for health reasons, but he continued to write and to serve as editor of the St. Petersburg periodical until shortly before his death in 1839. He did nothing with the portfolio of North American watercolors except to mention it in passing in *Picturesque Voyage.*

Nothing more was known about the portfolio until shortly after the Russian Revolution. Then in 1930 R. T. H. Halsey, a New York–based collector, revealed:

> Seven years after the war [World War I] ended, there was brought to me a large leather-bound folio containing fifty-two watercolors. Its title page . . . was in French and showed them to be sketches by "Paul Svignine" made in the United States in 1811, 1812, 1813. The tooling of the leather was of the character of that of the late eighteen thirties, and the gilt lettering on the cover was in Russian. It had been purchased in Russia by one of those American Red Cross workers who did such heroic work there in those dreadful days that followed the revolution.[9]

Halsey brought the watercolors to the attention of Avrahm Yarmolinsky, curator of the Slavonic language department of New York Public Library, who did considerable research on Svinin and wrote *Picturesque United States of America, 1811, 1812, 1813; Being a Memoir on Paul Svinin.* This book, published in 1930, includes reproductions of all 52 watercolors in the portfolio, but only one was reproduced in color. Yarmolinsky's text focuses on Svinin's life rather than the images. After careful study he concluded that when convenient, Svinin had freely manipulated the truth and had liberally and directly borrowed from other works, especially from Charles William Janson's *Stranger in America* (London, 1807), presenting other authors' experiences and investigations of the fledgling nation as his own.[10]

Because there is no English translation of the Svinin text, few historians have studied his work. Art historians who have used the portfolio (which in 1942 became part of the collection of the Metropolitan Museum of Art), have gravitated to the images of the genre scenes, which center on Philadelphia. It was my attempt to place Krimmel's work in the context of his contemporaries working in America that prompted a detailed examination of the imagery in the portfolio. This came at a point following considerable research in the Krimmel sketchbooks and after I had developed a stylistic chronology for both the individual images within the sketchbooks and his paintings.

In their research Halsey and Yarmolinsky had discovered that the watercolor depicting a crowd before the pumphouse station in Philadelphia was a copy of Krimmel's well-known painting at the Pennsylvania Academy of the Fine Arts. They had also identified other drawings in the portfolio as copies: a

7. Petrova, *Traveling across North America*, p. 16.

8. Petrova, *Traveling across North America*, p. 7.

9. Yarmolinsky, *Picturesque United States*, p. xiv.

10. Yarmolinsky, *Picturesque United States*, pp. 7, 8–9, 10, 14–15, 21–22, 25, 26, 30, 31, 32, 34–35; Charles William Janson, *The Stranger in America; Containing Observations Made during a Long Residence in That Country . . .* (London: J. Cundee, 1807). Yarmolinsky also noted that Svinin made claims about the honors he received in America, claims that are unsupported by the records.

portrait of an Osage warrior and one of an Osage chief are copies of watercolors by Charles Balthazar Julien Fevret de Saint-Mémin (1770–1852) that had been in the possession of Rt. Hon. Sir Augustus John Foster, Minister Plenipotentiary to the United States from Great Britain from 1811 to 1814, but were otherwise not publicly known until 1926; a scene of Niagara Falls was a copy of a sketch by ornithologist Alexander Wilson (1766–1813) that had been published in *Port Folio* in 1810; and a picture of three pottery vessels was a copy of an illustration that had appeared in *American Medical and Philosophical Magazine* in 1812.[11] A close look at those images in comparison with Svinin's copy work as exemplified in the Fourth of July watercolor, however, throws doubt on the presumption that Svinin possessed the skill to draw even these copies.

Ironically, it was close study of Svinin's watercolor copy of Krimmel's *View of Centre Square on the Fourth of July* (1812) (figs. 347, 348) that first suggested to me in 1978 that Krimmel might be the artist who produced most of the other genre scenes in the portfolio. In time, further investigation may prove that Krimmel did some of the other images as well.

When Svinin copied Krimmel's picture his primary concern had been the anecdotal information, not the style, and he copied the narrative content fairly accurately. The few alterations are minor and probably unintentional. For example, the woman in the original painting who uses her right hand to shield her eyes from the sun, in the watercolor wears a hat and clings to the arm of her neighbor; also, the Quaker father steps forward with his right leg instead of his left as in the original painting. Svinin was more careless in copying the background. He changed or deleted some of the figures and made mistakes, including not completing the left side of the architecture and omitting the semicircular window in the entrance. He also altered the height and width of the station's drum, leaving barely enough room to show the steam rising from the opening in the roof, an element that Krimmel had effectively worked into his composition because it shows the function of the building. Compared to Krimmel's oil painting the picture space in Svinin's copy is noticeably shallower, the figures are larger, and their movements are wooden. The watercolors are crudely and thickly applied, and in many instances sloppily so. In sum, Svinin's copy of *View of Centre Square* is noticeably different from the light-handed and meticulous execution that characterizes the other Philadelphia genre scenes in the portfolio. The Russian's working method was highly schematic: first he drew the main figures, architecture, and trees with solid continuous lines, and then he brushed on watercolor in broad strokes. In contrast to Svinin's two-step procedure, Krimmel simultaneously created design and color and achieved a plastic unity of differentiated surface and naturalistic effect. When he outlined in pencil he did so lightly, and when he traced in ink he used thin, short, discontinuous strokes. Although Svinin was sufficiently proficient in watercolor to make a nearly faithful copy of the narrative content of Krimmel's painting, he was unable to capture Krimmel's artistic sensibility, his passion for precision, his delicate and minute manner of drawing, and his exquisite application of color ranging from translucent to opaque; nor could Svinin project a sense of the comical side of people's behavior, a sense gently present even in Krimmel's early scenes. The combinations of these are distinctive and typical Krimmel qualities; they are not present in the work of Krimmel's contemporaries in America. The working method with which Svinin produced his copy of Krimmel's *View of Centre Square* is also unlike that displayed by the other Philadelphia genre scenes in the same portfolio.

11. Yarmolinsky, *Picturesque United States*, pp. 43, 32, 25.

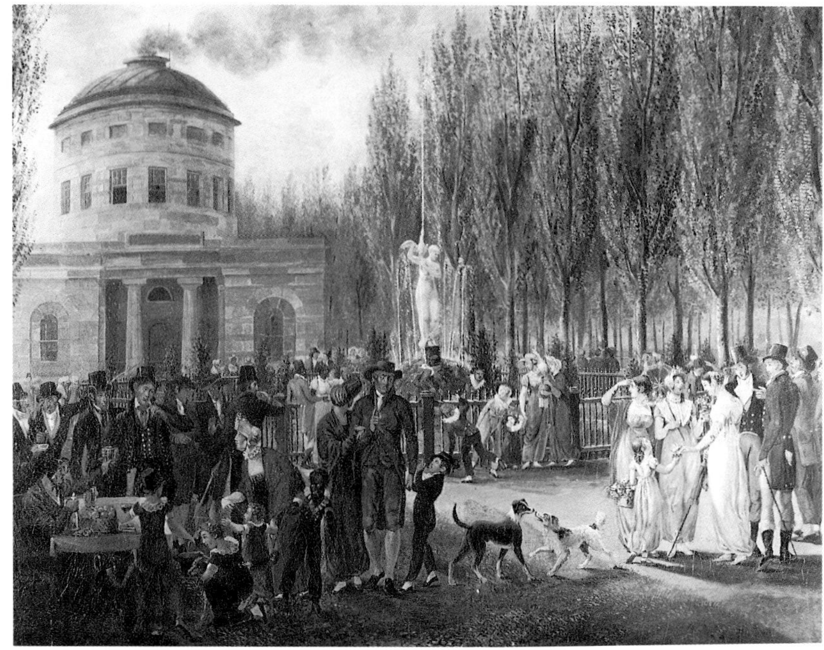

FIGURE 347
John Lewis Krimmel, View of Centre Square on the Fourth of July *(now called* Fourth of July in Center Square*), Philadelphia, 1811/12. Oil on canvas; 23 x 28 ½ in. (The Pennsylvania Academy of the Fine Arts, Philadelphia, Pennsylvania Academy purchase from the estate of Paul Beck, Jr.)*

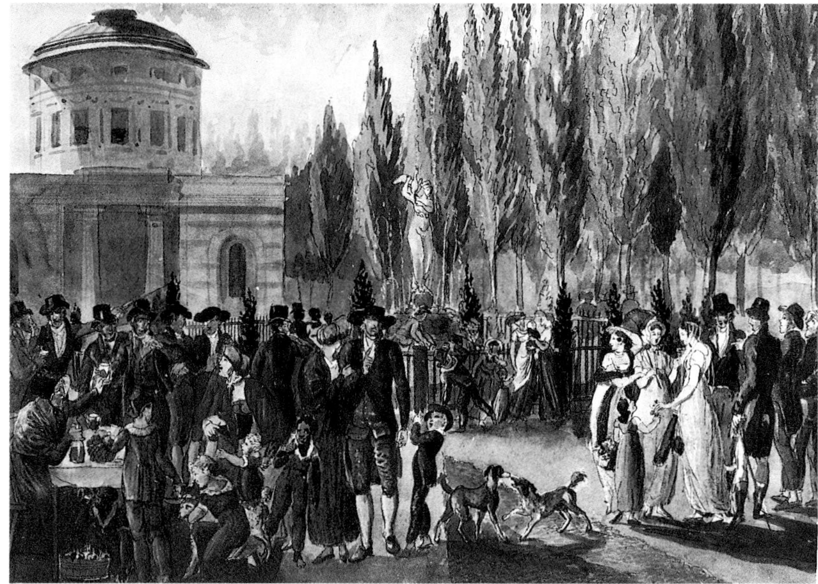

FIGURE 348
Pavel Petrovich Svinin after John Lewis Krimmel, View of Centre Square on the Fourth of July, *1812. Watercolor; 7 ⅛ x 9 ⅞ in. (The Metropolitan Museum of Art, New York, Rogers Fund, 1942.)*

Soon after making his copy of *View of Centre Square*, Svinin decided it would be easier to buy art for his book rather than copy or create it. He may well have continued to buy and even commission images over the next twelve months, at which point he sailed for Europe. Krimmel would have found nothing unusual in Svinin's plans to use local artists' pictures because many European writers published illustrated accounts of their travels using pictures derived from various painters and prints. When Svinin approached Krimmel in 1812, the young painter had already in his studio or rooms a number of watercolors depicting a variety of genre images from which the Russian could choose.

The first conclusive evidence that it was Krimmel who produced the genre scenes in the Svinin portfolio emerged from an examination of *Sunday Morning in Front of Arch Street Meetinghouse*, which is the frontispiece and only color image in the initial study of Svinin written by Yarmolinsky in the late 1920s. There are striking similarities, down to the color of specific details, that exist between this watercolor and images in sketchbook 1 that clearly were drawn from life on the streets of the city (see figs. 31–34). These correlations go far beyond mere coincidence, and what differences there are suggest that the sketchbook was the source from which Krimmel adapted material to make a composition suitable for a genre scene. Furthermore, many of the poses in this scene recur in other of Krimmel's well-known canvases, pictures painted years after Svinin had sailed for Europe with this image. The delineation of the man's leg, the foot position of the young boy, and the motif of a woman with an open parasol, all reappear in *View of Centre Square* (1812). The hats, which are based on drawings Krimmel made in sketchbook 1, appear in the two Fourth of July pictures, *Country Wedding*, the two election scenes, and the tavern scenes; the umbrella appears in *View of Centre Square* (1812) and is transformed into a walking stick carried by a woman in *Country Wedding*. Details suggest that the Sunday morning watercolor predates the Fourth of July scene: its overall effect is awkward, despite the boy's forward tilt and outstretched arms, and perspective and anatomy are less competently handled.

The sheer number of correspondences between details in *Sunday Morning in Front of Arch Street Meetinghouse* and the drawings in Krimmel's first sketchbook prompted a thorough reexamination of the remaining genre scenes in Svinin's portfolio. A second set of correlations emerged from an examination of *Black Sawyers Working in Front of the Bank of Pennsylvania* in conjunction with Krimmel's sketches (figs. 349, 350). Although the figures lack refinement and thus probably predate the Fourth of July image by several months, the stance of the sawyer on the right is identical to one of Krimmel's life sketches, as is the grasp on and angle of the saw, the roll of the shirtsleeve, and the shape of the shoes. The motif of a woman holding a child on one arm is one he continued to refine; he used it more effectively in other paintings—*View of Centre Square* (1812), *Election Day 1815*, and *Soldier Taking Leave of His Family* (1820)—and his sketchbooks. Although in this early image Krimmel had found a way to work the monumental building in the background so that it gives strength to the image, he had not yet mastered how to integrate it into the scene.

The correlations between a third watercolor, *Elegant Couple Meets Chimney Sweeps in Front of Christ Church*, and Krimmel's paintings and drawings strengthen the case.[12] Similar to the Fourth of July scene, this image relies on humor in its depiction of a chance encounter between people of different social ranks, and in both images the figure types and clothing are similar (see fig. 35). The upright format of the scene and the use of architectural features to frame

12. The watercolor may be related to *The Contrast*, one of the three pictures Krimmel exhibited in 1812, or to *Sweeps Importuning for Cold Provisions* that was posthumously exhibited at PAFA in 1822.

FIGURE 349
John Lewis Krimmel, Black Sawyers Working in Front of the Bank of Pennsylvania, *late 1811–early 1812. Watercolor; 9 ¼ x 6 ¾ in. (The Metropolitan Museum of Art, New York, Rogers Fund, 1942.)*

FIGURE 350
Sawyer, ca. 1812. Pencil. Sketchbook 1, leaf 10 recto.

FIGURE 351
Unknown engraver after John Lewis Krimmel, Frenzied Methodists . . ., *1814/15. Woodcut engraving; 3 ¾ x 5 in. From Pavel Svinin,* A Picturesque Voyage in North America *(St. Petersburg, 1815), facing p. 1.*

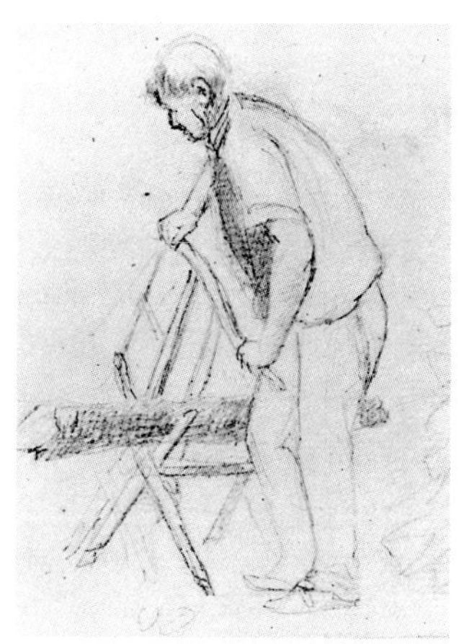

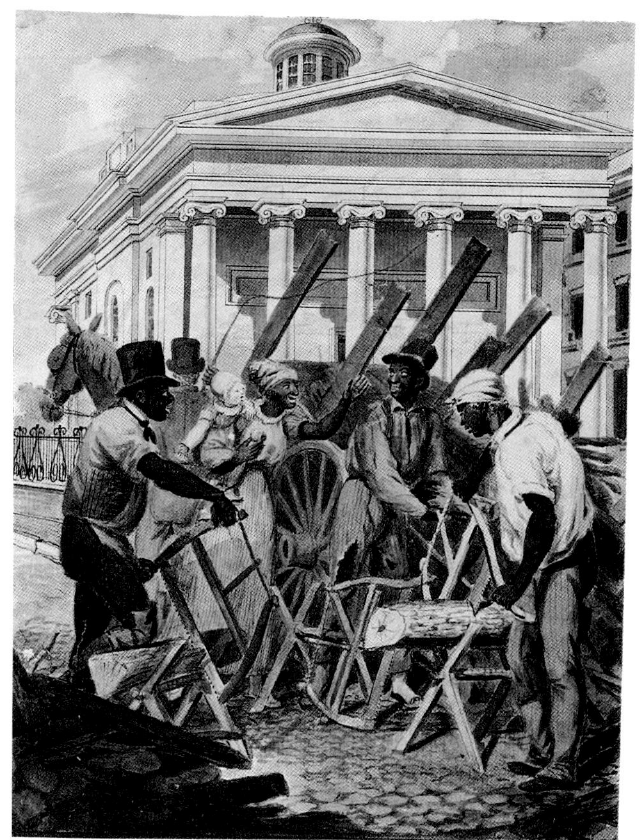

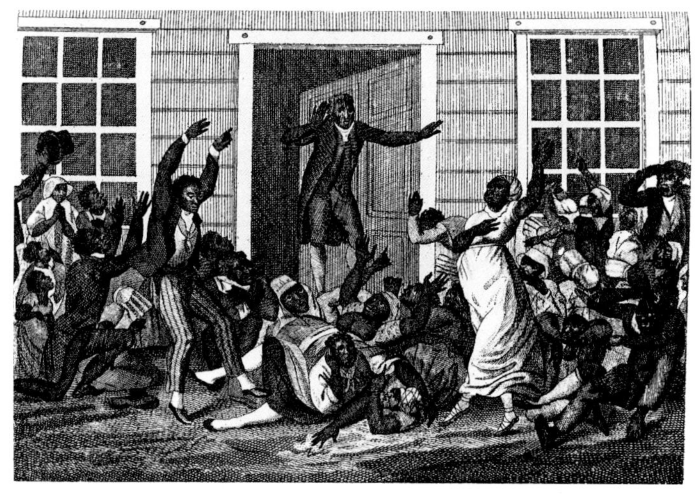

the figures are similar to *Pepper-Pot* (see fig. 17). In the painting, it is the brick pillar that rises the full height of the picture; in the watercolor, it is the corner of a brick building. The design for the street corner scene is intentionally congested and rests upon the strong diagonal of the curbstones, a tromp l'oeil device that Krimmel expanded four years later in the left foreground of *Election Day 1815* (see fig. 130). He reused the idea of giving a street lamp pictorial prominence in *Cherry Woman with Children* (1815) (see fig. 122). Finally this image also has what became one of Krimmel's hallmarks—architectural details drawn with an extraordinarily fine and sharply pointed brush.

Having firmly tied these 3 watercolors to Krimmel, it became possible to identify 11 other watercolors in the portfolio as the product of his hand and to assign approximate dates to each of them. One of the earliest is *Stage Coach Travel on the Trenton Diligence* (see fig. 20), in which the ineptly drawn figures date it closer to *Pepper-Pot* (see fig. 17) than to more polished watercolors in the portfolio, such as that of the sawyers. The horses are based on a study of a stationary horse (see fig. 24) drawn on a page dated September 17, 1811. The arm position of the man reaching for his hat seems derived from the watercolor of a man seated at a table dated August 15 (see fig. 21). Between 1811 and 1812 Krimmel's adeptness at drawing the movement of people and horses improved.

The neoclassical arrangement of *Anabaptist Baptism* (see fig. 25) suggests it dates from about the time of *View of Centre Square* (1812), and the execution of the elements, especially the definition of hands, suggests that it predates that oil painting.[13] Designed with a relatively shallow spatial arrangement, the figures are aligned on two levels. The group standing in the river is organized into a classical frieze. The verticality of the figures forms right angles with the horizontals of the dock. On the upper level, the numerous spectators are grouped into smaller units of varying size. The keen observation of human nature and the slightly humorous touch of this scene are typical of Krimmel's genre scenes. The figure types, poses, and garb are all closely related to the small images drawn from life in sketchbook 1. Among the specific details that reappear in Krimmel's later paintings is the man leaning on his walking stick in the two election scenes, the portrait of Heckewelder (1820), and *A German Funeral* (1820) (see figs. 130, 134, 249, 317). The hand and arm poses of the men waiting to be baptized and the slight tilt of their heads are the same as that of the boy and the blonde girl in *Pepper-Pot.*

Blacks constituted a visible sector of Philadelphia's residents (slightly over 5,000 in 1810) but were virtually unknown in Northern Europe. Krimmel produced an image populated solely by blacks, *Black People's Prayer Meeting,* which became one of the 6 watercolors Svinin chose to illustrate his book (see figs. 62, 351). Many of the ecstatic gestures and poses are related to life studies in sketchbook 1 and reappear in Krimmel's paintings (for example, *View of Centre Square* [1812], *Quilting Frolic* [1813], and *Interior of an American Inn* [1813/14]). In principles of construction the watercolor relates to Krimmel's 1813 oil paintings—*Quilting Frolic* and *Interior of an American Inn*—with lively gesturing figures in front of a background that stresses clear horizontals and verticals. It also shares specific details with *Interior of an American Inn,* such as a man swinging his hat, a man resting his head on his right hand, and a man raising his hand (palm toward the viewer) in a gesture of appeasement. The motif of the raised hand is based on Krimmel's hand sketches and is also used in the raised hand of the joyful girl, the prayerfully outstretched hands of the large woman on the ground, and the upstretched hands of the kneeling man.

13. In 1855 a picture titled *Baptism at Jones Falls, Maryland,* identified as a Krimmel painting, was exhibited at the Pennsylvania Academy. It was lent by T. A. Waterman, as was a second Krimmel painting, *The Soldier's Return from the Revolutionary War.*

A fallen figure also marks the mid foreground of *Election Day 1815* (see fig. 130) and *The Conflagration of Masonic Hall, Chestnut Street, Philadelphia* (see fig. 326). The figure of the dancing girl first appeared in *Quilting Frolic* and then again some years later as the elder girl in *Return from Market*. The emphatic gesturing in this scene suggests that it was made in late spring 1813, following Krimmel's enrollment in the life model class.

Svinin also recognized that he could not write a book about the United States without making reference to the Native Americans, whose appearance and customs fascinated Europeans; however, events offered him little opportunity to observe them firsthand. Although his text states that on August 9, 1812, a delegation of Native Americans passed through Philadelphia on the way to Washington to conclude a treaty with the United States government, no such delegation came through Philadelphia while Svinin resided in America. As biographer Yarmolinsky points out, Svinin relied on descriptions of visits by Osage leaders to New York and Washington in 1804.[14]

Svinin probably commissioned Krimmel to produce the 2 watercolors of Indian groups in the portfolio, an assumption bolstered by the use of one of them for an engraving in the Russian version of the book (fig. 352, see also figs. 53, 54). Because Krimmel had had no opportunity to sketch Native Americans from life, as his sketchbooks attest, he concocted images in a time-honored fashion—by relying on other artists' depictions. He turned to Benjamin West's *William Penn's Treaty with the Indians* and *The Death of General Wolfe* to produce *Tableau of Indian Faces* and *Indian Council*.

Indian Council shows the influence of *Penn's Treaty* in the hand movement of one chief and in several tribal head dresses, and *The Death of General Wolfe* provided the inspiration for the left foreground seated figure who rests his head on his hand as well as the recumbent figure to his left. For the middleground figure pointing toward the dais, Krimmel relied on his sketches of Vesalius's skeletons (see figs. 12, 13). The composition of the watercolor is balanced without being symmetrical and is unified by a strong horizontal. Krimmel reprised the more successful motifs from this picture in later canvases: one of the dogs underneath the speakers' platform reappears in the same position under the table in *Interior of an American Inn* (1813/14), and both pictures have a man resting his head on his hand.

For *Tableau of Indian Faces*, Krimmel adopted a general compositional idea from Hogarth and applied specific details from West's and other artists' paintings. The figures in the right foreground—specifically the young mother nursing her papoose and the girl and boy standing next to her—are from the center group in *Penn's Treaty*. He also maximized his limited sources by reusing the same facial type repeatedly but giving it a different expression in each instance, much in the manner of late eighteenth-century studies of physiognomy. Finally, he emphasized the middle and foreground faces, placing the idealized noble savage close to the viewer, and making those in the background look, by contrast, fierce and unkempt.

Svinin was professionally interested in military subjects, so it is likely that he also specifically asked for a picture of soldiers. Krimmel provided him with *Members of the City Troop of Philadelphia* (see fig. 66). The figure types Krimmel used for the watercolor of the city troop are richly varied and individualized but possess the same elongated proportions and long, picturesque shadows that he used in his Fourth of July painting. The stances of the officer and the drummer are derived from studies in sketchbook 1.

14. Yarmolinsky, *Picturesque United States*, p. 26.

Svinin also may have commissioned *Winter Scene with the Bank of the United States in the Background*, for the man in the back seat of the sleigh looks like Svinin, if D. Koch's engraving of Vasili Tropinin's painting is an accurate rendering (compare fig. 353 with fig. 69). The preliminary compositional sketch of another winter scene is in sketchbook 2, and the sleighs in these images are strikingly similar (see fig. 306).

The composition of *Oyster Barrow in Front of Chestnut Street Theatre* is likely Krimmel's own, although the oyster vendor motif may have come from the woodcut in *The Cries of Philadelphia*. The figure types are related to those in the sketchbooks, and the grouping is very similar to that in the left foreground of *View of Centre Square* (1811/12); the figure of the woman holding the candle is similar to the woman shading her eyes in the right foreground of the same painting. In conjunction with *Pepper-Pot* and *Cherry Woman, Oyster Barrow* indicates a consistency—Krimmel found outdoor food vending a convenient device around which to depict the interaction of different sorts of people. It also is a subtheme in the two election scenes and the two Fourth of July pictures, and the specific motif of a black vendor selling oysters from a wheelbarrow recurs in *Election Day 1815* and in *Parade of the Victuallers* (1821).

Another Krimmel watercolor in Svinin's portfolio, *Dance in a Wayside Inn*, has a typical Krimmel conceit, an open door revealing part of the outside world. The figure types, gestures, and props reappear in Krimmel's early paintings, as do the distinctions between city and country folk. But the strongest connection is to *Country Frolic and Dance* (1819), due to the nearly identical poses of the dancers and the similarity in the characterizations of the fiddler and of the flirting couple. Even minor details are comparable such as the rifle above the door, the type of chair, and the draped towel, which is a compositional element in several of Krimmel's genre scenes.

If Svinin's book was to discuss life in the United States, it had to include a picture of the newly introduced steamboats, a mode of travel that so passionately interested Svinin that he went so far as to take credit for some of Robert Fulton's ideas and achievements.[15] For Svinin, Krimmel completed a polished and detailed watercolor of a steamboat cutting speedily through the waters of the Hudson River. Svinin chose to have an engraving made from this watercolor to illustrate his book, yet the engraving is distinctly different from the watercolor: the boat is shorter, has fewer windows, and has only a working crew on deck (fig. 354). These changes are additional evidence that the image was not produced by the Russian amateur artist: were the watercolor his own design, Svinin would have insisted on a more faithful rendering of the original image.

Another of Krimmel's watercolors in the Svinin portfolio is not a genre picture but an allegorical triple portrait. *Moravian Sisters* (fig. 355) depicts three women of different ages standing closely together, each turned in a different direction, each wearing the typical bonnet of their religious community. However, the dress, shawl, and facial expressions of each are individualized to personify a particular age. The arrangement of a young, middle-aged, and old woman shown together is a very old one, occurring in German art as the popular staircase of life *(Lebenstreppe)* from the early sixteenth century through the nineteenth century.[16] Used as an allegory for the three stages of life, it also served as a reminder of the vanishing quality of physical beauty and the transience of life. The sensitive characterization of each face shows Krimmel more accomplished as a portraitist, which suggests a date of origin for this image in late 1812 or early 1813. The young woman's arm and hand pose is based on a

15. Yarmolinsky, *Picturesque United States*, pp. xvi, 8–9; see also Alice C. Suttcliffe, *Robert Fulton and the Clermont* (New York: Century, 1909), pp. 296–97.

16. *Die Lebenstreppe: Bilder der manschlichen Lebensalter* (Köln: Rheinland-Verlag, 1983), pp. 21, 75.

FIGURE 352
Unknown engraver after John Lewis Krimmel, Tableau of Indian Faces, *1814/15. Woodcut engraving; 4 ¾ x 3 ½ in. From Pavel Svinin,* A Picturesque Voyage in North America *(St. Petersburg, 1815), p. 11.*

FIGURE 353
D. Koch after Vasili Andreyevich Tropinin, Pavel Svinin. *Engraving. From Avraham Yarmolinsky,* Picturesque United States of America 1811, 1812, 1813; Being a Memoir on Paul Svinin . . . *(New York: William E. Rudge, 1930), p. 2.*

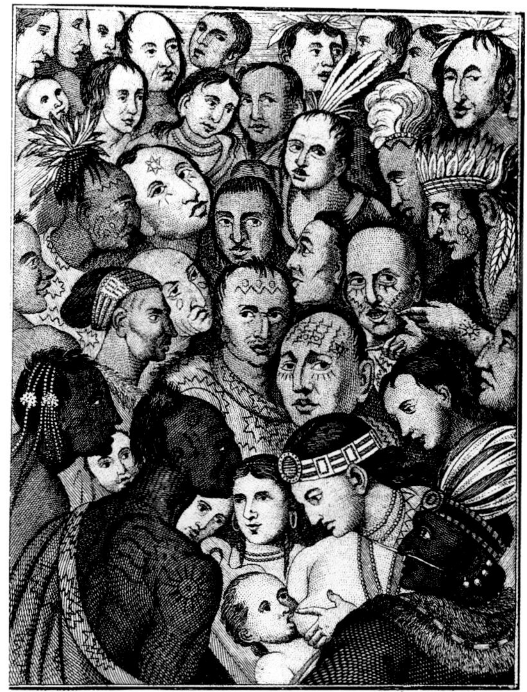

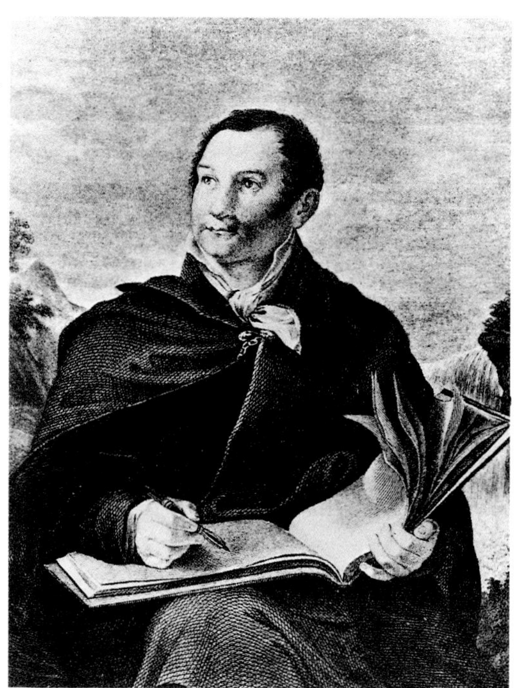

FIGURE 354
Unknown engraver after John Lewis Krimmel, Steamboat Travel on the Hudson River, *1814/15. Woodcut engraving; 3 x 4 ⅞ in. From Pavel Svinin,* A Picturesque Voyage in North America *(St. Petersburg, 1815), facing p. 5.*

FIGURE 355
John Lewis Krimmel, Moravian Sisters, *1812/13. Watercolor; 6 x 8 in. (The Metropolitan Museum of Art, New York, Rogers Fund, 1942.)*

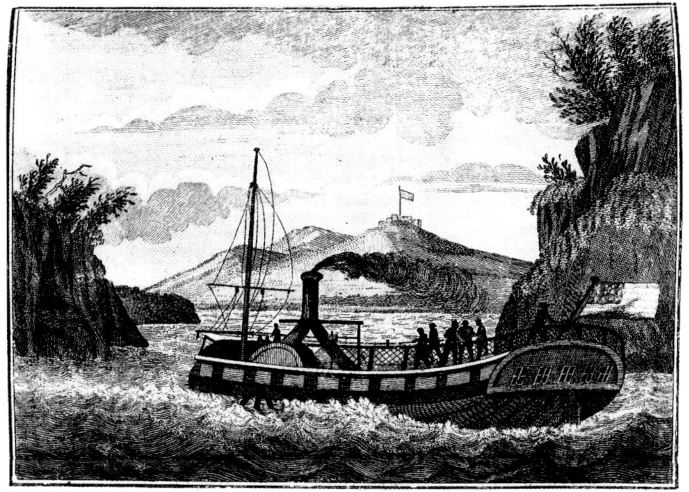

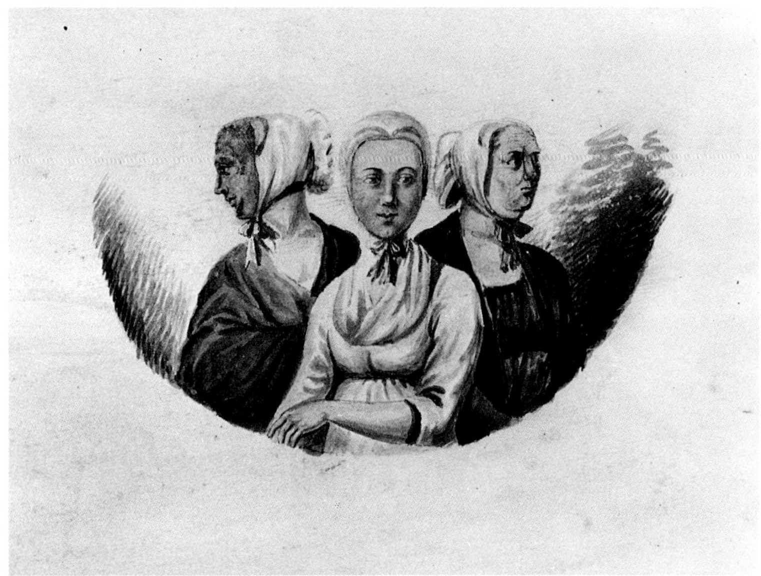

life study drawn in sketchbook 1, but applied here in reverse. The youngest woman in *Moravian Sisters* and the subject of *Young Woman in a Blue Dress* are strikingly similar (see fig. 128).[17]

Each of Krimmel's 14 watercolors in Svinin's portfolio is executed with an exquisite sense for naturalistic configurations, a sense not present in most other watercolors in the portfolio. Each also exhibits a touch of humor and a strong interest in depicting ordinary and characteristic aspects of contemporary American life, a habit that was uniquely Krimmel's (an achievement that Svinin was unable to emulate even in his close copy of Krimmel's *View of Centre Square* [1812]). In spite of the unpretentious subject matter, the pictures manifest the artist's well-developed concern for decorative aspects of pictorial design. Figures and animals are individualized. As was typical of Krimmel's other genre scenes, many of the figures in these images have slightly elongated proportions and relatively small heads. The watercolors, in a rich choice of colors and shades, are delicately and neatly applied, usually masking the pencil underdrawing, and most figures are outlined by strokes of a fine brush. The artist's sensitive handling of the brush is particularly evident in the manner in which light modifies and enlivens the colors. He repeatedly combined luminescent blue and bright yellow accented with red. He was less skillful and much less sure when attempting to convey perspective, and his struggle to correctly define picture depth and space reinforces what his early oil paintings demonstrate: although he found opportunity to study anatomy during his first years in Philadelphia, he had not found systematic instruction in perspective.

When the Philadelphia watercolors are compared with each other, it becomes obvious that they were produced over a period of time, a period that corresponds to the months when Krimmel was making the transition from amateur to professional painter. These were the years of his most intensive studies as he sought to attain competency as an artist. Using the exhibition of 1812 as a dividing line and the firmly dated oil paintings of 1812 and 1813 and the drawings in the first 3 sketchbooks as points of reference, it is possible to separate the 14 watercolors into two groups and to roughly arrange them within each.

Group 1: Produced in the period 1811 until May 1812, these watercolors relate to drawings in sketchbook 1 and to the oil paintings *Pepper-Pot* and *View of Centre Square on the Fourth of July.*

1. Stage Coach Travel on the Trenton Diligence (9 ¾" x 6 ⅞")
2. Black Sawyers Working in Front of the Bank of Pennsylvania (6 ¾"x 9 ¼")
3. Sunday Morning in Front of Arch Street Meetinghouse (7 ⅜" x 9")
4. Elegant Couple Meets Chimney Sweeps in Front of Christ Church (6 ⅞" x 9¼")
5. Anabaptist Baptism (9 ¾" x 7")
6. Oyster Barrow in Front of Chestnut Street Theatre (6 ⅞" x 9 ¼")

Group 2: Produced between June 1812 and June 1813, these watercolors relate to drawings in sketchbooks 1, 2, and 3 and to *Quilting Frolic* (1813) and *Interior of an American Inn* (1813/14).

7. Members of the City Troop of Philadelphia (7 ¼" x 9")
8. Winter Scene with the Bank of the United States in the Background (9 ¾" x 7 ⅜")
9. Dance in a Wayside Inn (9 ⅛" x 7 ⅛")

17. This similarity was first realized by Kevin Avery, assistant curator in the Department of American Painting, Metropolitan Museum of Art, New York.

10. Black People's Prayer Meeting (9 ⅞" x 8 ½")
11. Tableau of Indian Faces (7" x 9 ¼")
12. Indian Council (9 ¼" x 7")
13. Steamboat Travel on the Hudson River (14 ¼" x 10")
14. Moravian Sisters (8" x 6")

Neither Halsey, who then owned the portfolio, nor Yarmolinsky mentioned that Svinin's text does not match the pictures that are attributed to him; indeed, not a single depiction of an action in the watercolors has an equivalent description in Svinin's book. Even the watercolor about the congregation depicts them joyously undulating with religious enthusiasm in front of a sunlit, well-kept wooden structure, an image incongruent with the following account in Svinin's text:

> We entered a large hall or chamber, lighted very dimly by torches. Walls black with smoke, dilapidated benches and broken windows made at the outset a disagreeable impression upon us. We went up close to the platform and sat down on a bench in the third row. The hall was full of blacks; the men were on the right, the women on the left. The frightful countenance and the sparkling eyes of the Africans, staring at us in the dim light, filled us in spite of ourselves with a dread which increased even further when they began to howl with wild and piercing voices. I believed myself to be in Pluto's kingdom, amongst all the monsters of hell, and, when the doorman, greatly resembling Cerberus, locked the door, lest anyone depart, I secretly repented my curiosity.
>
> On the platform a terrible black skeleton was reading psalms from Holy Writ. At the end of every psalm the entire congregation, men and women alike, sang verses in a loud, shrill monotone. This lasted about half an hour. When the preacher ceased reading, all turned toward the door, fell on their knees, bowed their heads to the ground and started howling and groaning with sad, heart-rending voices. Afterwards, the minister resumed the reading of the psalter and when he had finished sat down on a chair; then all rose and began chanting psalms in chorus, the men and women alternating, a procedure which lasted some twenty minutes. Then silence fell, a deep, terrible silence such as precedes a storm, when all things grow mute and when the air trembles in expectation of something dreadful and inexplicable.
>
> In an even, hoarse voice the preacher began his sermon, expatiating in a high-flown style upon *the terrors of hell* and *the wrath of God.* At first all was fairly calm, but little by little the preacher warmed up and by means of terrible pictures and gestures fired the imagination of his hearers. Soon the groans of penitents were heard on every side, and the outcries and ejaculations of the possessed; finally, when in a strong impressive voice the preacher spoke of *the destruction of the Universe,* pointed to *the black cloud* pregnant with all-shattering thunders and described the tortures and sufferings awaiting the sinners, they loosed such a howl that the very foundations of the hall shook and the vaulted ceiling trembled. I confess, at the moment I myself feared the destruction not of the universe, but of the gallery under which I sat and which threatened momentarily to collapse with the convulsions of the possessed, who leapt and swayed in every direction and dashed themselves to the ground, pounding with hands and feet, gnashing their teeth, all to show that the

evil spirit was departing from them. Imagine, then, my joy when I heard the church doors creak on their ponderous hinges. I think some beneficent spirit helped me to fight my way through the crowd which thronged even the entrance to the church.[18]

Realizing that his extensive and detailed description did not match the illustration in his book, Svinin added one sentence to justify the image. "Often in Philadelphia, in the summer, the Methodists gather out of doors and, from a narrow alley way, direct their prayers toward heaven, which is depicted in this picture." Similar disparities exist between the written description and visual image of the baptism. Svinin described a baptism taking place during a thunderstorm as a choir sang. The watercolor shows no choir and no thunderstorm; instead, the sun shines so brightly one of the women has opened her parasol.

Svinin, an enthusiastic proponent of the steamboat, claimed that stage coach travel had been "entirely abandoned on the New York, Albany and Philadelphia routes," yet one watercolor in the portfolio features the "Trenton Diligence," a four-horse stagecoach that carried passengers between Philadelphia and Trenton on the New York–Philadelphia route during these same years.[19]

Finally, the portfolio of watercolors as a whole raises several questions. Why are the only genre scenes in the portfolio the ones from the Pennsylvania region? Although Svinin traveled widely—according to his text he traversed the area from the Carolinas to Maine—why is none of the other 39 watercolors a genre scene? If he was capable of producing such vivid genre scenes of Philadelphia, why did he refrain from entering them at the 1812 or 1813 exhibition or in similar exhibitions in Russia? Why was he never again mentioned as an exhibiting artist in America or Russia? Why is he not listed in Thieme and Becker's *Allgemeines Lexikon*, the most complete and reliable compendium of information about artists? Why does E. Bénézit's *Dictionnaire* mention Svinin only in connection with the sketches in the book on Russia that he published in England?[20]

A Russian art historian has tried to tackle the problem of Svinin's contradictory personality in the context of two albums containing 68 small sketches of American views now in the collection of the Russian Museum of St. Petersburg and attributed to Svinin.[21] Seventeen appear to be copies made from the much larger watercolors in the Svinin Portfolio in New York. They have the identical picture content, but in drafting style, watercolor technique, and artistic sensibility are distinctly different, facts not acknowledged by the Russian author. All executed by the same hand and apparently during the same span of time, they could not be the work of the same artist or group of artists who made the watercolors in New York. Because some of the sketches in the Russian albums were made not from the original watercolors but from the engravings in Svinin's book, including the 3 based on Krimmel's pictures, there is no possibility that they could have been preparatory sketches for the watercolors and must have been made after the first publication of Svinin's book in 1815.

Of the 52 watercolors in the Svinin Portfolio in New York, only the 13 Philadelphia sketches have aroused interest and widespread attention. Several have become familiar illustrations in books on Philadelphia and American cultural history of the late federal and early national periods. In contrast the landscape views, 24 in number, are never reproduced because they present a superficial definition of nature that is boring. They are rendered competently but without distinction, indicative of a minor talent capable of copying from

18. Pavel Petrovich Svinin, *Opyt zhyvopisnavo puteshestviya po severnoi Amerike* [A Picturesque Voyage in North America] (St. Petersburg, Russia, 1815), pp. 47–51, as quoted in Yarmolinsky, *Picturesque United States*, p. 20.

19. Yarmolinsky (*Picturesque United States*, p. 10) notes that Svinin was in error on this point.

20. "Ssvinjin (Pavel Pétrovitch), peintre, né en 1787, mort le 9 avril 1839 (Ec. Rus). Il dessina des vues de Saint-Pétersbourg" (E. Bénézit, *Dictionnaire des Peintres, Sculpteurs, Dessinateurs, et Graveurs* [Paris: Librarie Gründ, 1955], p. 69).

21. Petrova, *Traveling across North America*.

FIGURE 356
Pavel Svinin, Sketch of Svinin and Two Indians. *Watercolor; 5 ⅞ x 8 ⅝ in. (The Metropolitan Museum of Art, New York, Rogers Fund, 1942.)*

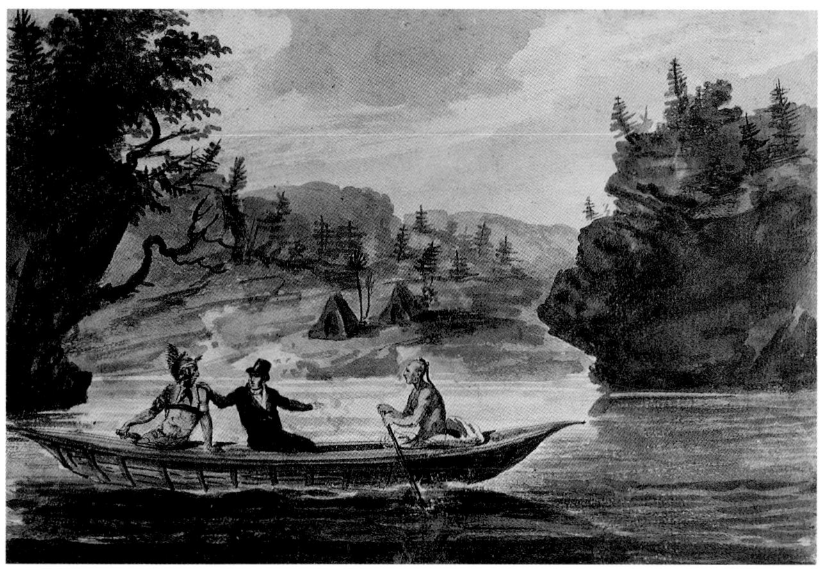

drawing-book models. Some of the sweepingly brushed landscapes may have been produced by Svinin himself. For example, in the foreground of one a boat moves across the water (fig. 356). It is occupied by three awkwardly positioned figures—two Indians who do the rowing and a man who sits between them: the man looks like Svinin, the heads of the Indians are taken from the St.-Mémin images, and the bodies of all three are poorly rendered.

In the preface to his book Svinin stated that while in London in 1814 he received repeated offers of 25,000 rubles for his portfolio of watercolors. These he declined.

> The thought that I would have to write, not in my native tongue, and often contrary to my inclinations and ideas, and indeed unfairly, not as I felt, but as the policy of England demanded, or to gratify the desires of my publishers, who would perhaps use me as a tool of their hatred for the United States, finally the thought that not my country, but a foreign land would reap the first-fruits of my labors, that my fatherland would be indebted to foreigners and not foreigners to my fatherland for detailed information about America—all these sentiments of justice, honor, and patriotism forced me to reject these advantageous offers and occupy myself here [in Russia] with the description of my picturesque travels in the United States, which, in case of successful completion, I intend to lay at the feet of our Most August Monarch.[22]

The charge of self-aggrandizement was leveled at Svinin during his lifetime, and in the following century Yarmolinsky expressed the opinion that Svinin's "sycophancy . . . may have been due in part to the mawkish and blatant variety of patriotism . . . he displayed."[23]

Paradoxically, thanks to Svinin's self-promotional inclinations coupled with his literary aspirations, the portfolio of watercolors he collected in the United States remained complete and well preserved. Inadvertently he provided American art with a set of important pictures and the opportunity to study the early efforts of America's first genre painter, John Lewis Krimmel.

22. Svinin, *Opyt zhyvopisnavo puteshestviya*, pp. 2–4, as quoted in Yarmolinsky, *Picturesque United States*, p. 18.

23. Yarmolinsky, *Picturesque United States*, p. 44.

APPENDIX 4

Paintings of Disputed Attribution

An oil on panel painting of *Return from Market* has been misattributed to Krimmel. The sloppy painting style is not typical of Krimmel's work nor is the unfinished state. Krimmel seldom painted on wood panels—the only other example is a pre-1817 copy after Burnet's *Young Bird* that is painted with finer brushes in a tighter, firmer style that is more consistent with Krimmel's other oils. Evidence in the oil on panel version of *Return from Market* suggests it is was made by a copyist who worked from Lawson's engraving or Krimmel's original oil well after Krimmel's death; the clothing of the kneeling boy dates to the mid nineteenth century.[1] The copyist lacked Krimmel's facility in drawing animals, and although the unfinished state of the panel might explain the absence of some details, the omission of one child, the cat, and the flowerpot and the repositioning of the hen and her chicks and the bonnet are evidence that the copyist also misunderstood Krimmel's design principles.

PORTRAITS

Two large portraits attributed to Krimmel could only date from the 1819–21 period, if indeed they were painted by him. They are known only through photographs made when the canvases were offered on the New York art market in 1945 and 1946 (figs. 357, 358).[2] The paintings were commissioned and in approach are rather conventional. They are designed as companion pieces, composed so that the man should hang to the right of the woman. The portraits adhere to the English formula successfully utilized by Sully, King, and other local portraitists, but the earnest, unidealized representations and fastidious rendition of details are Germanic characteristics and are found in Krimmel's images, for example *Young Woman in a Blue Dress.* Meticulous attention is given to the woman's clothes and accessories: the areas of transparent ruche on the woman's sleeve and jewelry are painted with the same exquisite description as were the lace top and jewelry in Krimmel's 1815 portrait of a young woman. Most artists in this period were following Stuart and Sully and painting in a looser style with regular or wider brushers; however, Krimmel was painting with extraordinarily fine brushes that helped create a closed surface and eliminated traces of brush strokes. As in other firmly documented examples of Krimmel's work, the delineation of these portraits is careful, and light reflects in the sitters' eyes and plays on precious stones and embellishments. Nonetheless a firm attribution to Krimmel cannot be made until it is possible to examine the paintings directly for style, technique, and application of paint.

FAMILY PORTRAIT

The tradition that surfaced with this canvas early in the twentieth century claimed that the picture was painted in Germantown, circa 1820. The canvas

1. The copy lacks the alterations found in the Sartain print of the scene. For a different point of view, see Naeve, *Krimmel*, p. 98; "Study for Return from Market," *Kennedy Quarterly* 8, no. 4 (January 1969): 257.

2. The pair was first offered for $698 (*New York Times*, March 11, 1945), and a year later for $449 (*New York Times*, April 21, 1946). Each frame bore a plaque identifying Krimmel as the painter, but the wording of the advertisements implies that neither portrait was signed.

FIGURE 357
Attributed to John Lewis Krimmel, Portrait of a Gentleman, *ca. 1819–21. Oil on canvas; 27 ¾ x 22 in. (Photo, Frick Art Reference Library.)*

FIGURE 358
Attributed to John Lewis Krimmel, Portrait of a Lady, *ca. 1819–21. Oil on canvas; 27 ¾ x 22 in. (Photo, Frick Art Reference Library.)*

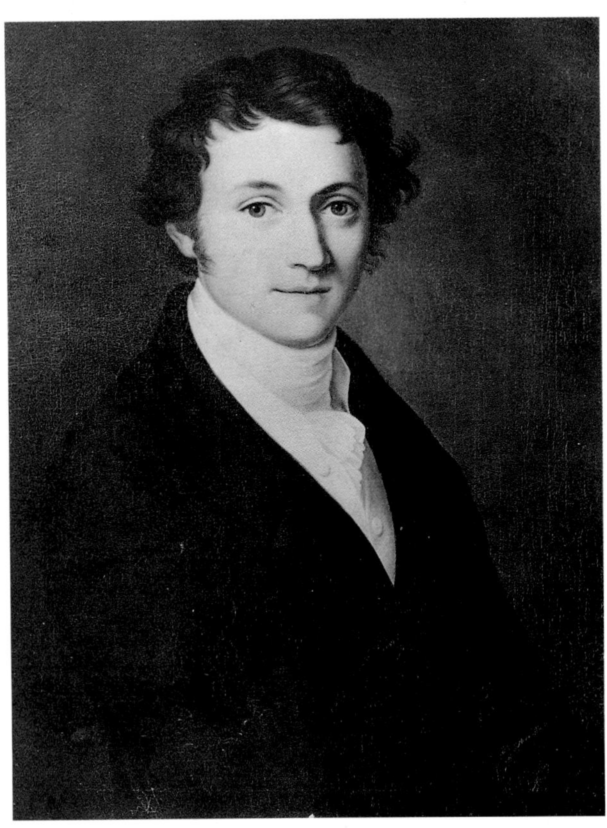

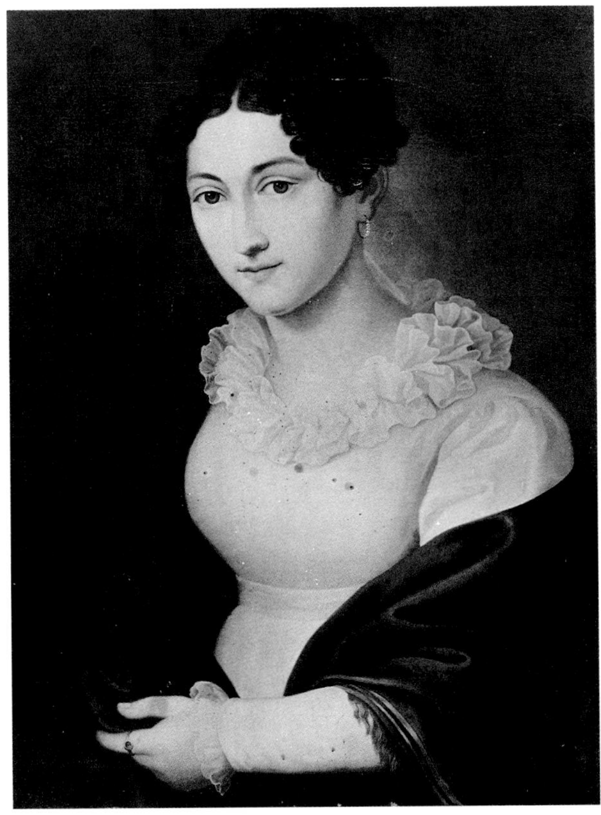

is not signed or dated, but there is evidence that it was cut down to fit the current frame. On the wooden stretcher in dark crayon is "J. L. Krimmel, Portrait of the Artist with the Krimmel Family" in a nineteenth-century hand.

The association with Krimmel was first made in 1859 when biographer and local historian Henry Simpson credited the artist with a painting called *A Family Group* and added "[Krimmel] resided with his brother, George Frederick Krimmel, for a number of years, in Philadelphia. He was a bachelor, but was engaged to be married at the time of his death."[3] Although Simpson exaggerated the time Krimmel lived with his brother, it is most probably an image of the artist's brother's family.

In 1921 art collector Thomas Benedict Clark (1848–1931) acquired the portrait from dealer August de Forrest and lent it for display in an exhibition of early American portraits at the Union League Club in New York City the following year, identifying it as a work of Krimmel entitled *An Artist and His Family.* The painting was placed on an easel in the middle of an exhibition space and was framed by drapes that duplicated those in the picture. Portraits by Thomas Sully and James Peale hung to the right of it; portraits by Chester Harding and James Lambdin hung to the left. The reviews were generally positive: "This month the minor men are most numerous in the exhibition. The artist Krimmel painted himself and his family with extraordinary skill and simplicity. That the heads are too big and the hands and feet too small [both of which are characteristic of Krimmel's style] fails to destroy the general effect of good workmanship, and the color is mellow and strong." Another wrote, "Krimmel painted a self-portrait with his family of nine, exclusive of the dog and doll, which are given incidental places. The costumes are painted in brilliant colors." Soon afterward an essay on Krimmel appeared in an art journal, and the painting was twice illustrated. Six years later the canvas was shown in an exhibition at the Pennsylvania Museum of Art. Paul Mellon subsequently acquired the Clark collection, including Krimmel's painting, which he donated to the National Gallery of Art in 1942. From all indications and comments, its role as a memorial picture and as an allegory of family love was recognized by no one.[4]

In the mid 1950s Milo Naeve, while working on his master's thesis devoted to Krimmel, became convinced that the disparity between Krimmel's genre scenes and this group portrait was so great as to merit the removal of the attribution to Krimmel. Although professor Werner Haftmann, a prominent German art historian whose books on twentieth-century art are standard works and a staff member of the Berlin National Gallery, demurred, maintaining that the painting was not by a German or other European artist but looked more like the product of an American-trained artist; the National Gallery of Art changed the attribution to "German school."[5]

The evidence presented in chapter 4 details the reasons that it is time for the National Gallery of Art to reassess the painting and reattribute it to Krimmel.

3. Simpson, *Eminent Philadelphians*, pp. 630–31.

4. *New York Times*, March 9, 1922; *New York Evening World*, March 10, 1922. Frederic Fairchild Sherman, "John Lewis Krimmel's Portrait Group of Himself and Family," *Art in America and Elsewhere* 11, no. 1 (December 1922): 57–58. The clipping file on Krimmel, Print Room, New York Public Library, contains a pamphlet titled *Inspiration for Printers* 180, a 1950 advertisement printed by Westvaco company; one of the illustrations is the family portrait. Curatorial Files, National Gallery of Art.

5. Naeve ("Krimmel," pp. 197–99) provides the most cogent explanation of his point of view, an argument that is not as well developed in Naeve, *Krimmel*, p. 186. Curatorial Files, National Gallery of Art.

SELECT BIBLIOGRAPHY

Alberts, Robert C. *Benjamin West: A Biography.* Boston: Houghton Mifflin Co., 1978.

"American Biography—For the Port Folio: Life of Commodore Murray." *Port Folio,* 3d ser., 3, no. 5 (May 1814): 399–409.

American Dictionary of Printing and Bookmaking. New York: Howard Lockwood, 1894.

American Philosophical Society. *Historic Philadelphia: From the Founding until the Early Nineteenth Century.* Philadelphia, 1953.

Andrews, Dee. "The African Methodists of Philadelphia, 1794–1802." *Pennsylvania Magazine of History and Biography* 108, no. 4 (October 1984): 471–86.

Andrews, Keith. *The Nazarenes: A Brotherhood of German Painters in Rome.* Oxford: Clarendon Press, 1964.

Bantel, Linda. "William Rush, Esq." In *William Rush: American Sculptor.* Exhibition catalogue. Philadelphia: Pennsylvania Academy of the Fine Arts, 1982.

Bauer, Herman. *Niederländische Malerei des 17. Jahrhunderts.* Munich: Verlag F. Bruckmann, 1982.

Baumgart, Fritz Erwin. *Vom Klassizismus zur Romantik.* Cologne: DuMont Schauberg, 1974.

Bayne, William. *Sir David Wilkie R.A.* London: Walter Scott Publishing; New York: Charles Scribner's Sons, 1903.

Beal, Rebecca J. *Jacob Eichholtz, 1776–1842: Portrait Painter of Pennsylvania.* Philadelphia: Historical Society of Pennsylvania, 1969.

Bedell, G. T., ed. *The Religious Souvenir: A Christmas, New Year's and Birthday Present for 1834.* Philadelphia: Key and Biddle, 1834.

Bénézit, E. *Dictionnaire des Peintres, Sculpteurs, Dessinateurs, et Graveurs.* Paris: Librarie Gründ, 1955.

Benisovich, Michael. "The Sale of the Studio of Adolph-Ulrich Wertmüller." *Art Quarterly* 16, no. 1 (Spring 1953): 20–39.

Bernhard, Marianne. *Deutsche Romantik Handzeichnungen.* 2d ed. 2 vols. Munich: Rogner and Bernhard, 1974.

Biddle, Edward C., ed. *Selected Poems by Mrs. L. H. Sigourney.* Philadelphia: Edward C. Biddle, 1842.

Biddle, Edward, and Mantle Fielding. *The Life and Works of Thomas Sully (1783–1872).* 1921. Reprint. New York: Kennedy Graphics and Da Capo Press, 1970.

"Biographical Sketch of Captain Thomas MacDonough." *Analectic Magazine and Naval Chronicle,* n.s., 7, no. 39, (March 1816): 201–15.

Bloch, Maurice E. *George Caleb Bingham: The Evolution of an Artist.* Berkeley and Los Angeles: University of California Press, 1967.

Boime, Albert. *The Academy and French Painting in the Nineteenth Century.* London: Phaidon Publishers, 1971.

———. *Art in the Age of Revolution, 1750–1800.* Chicago: University of Chicago Press, 1987.

Börsch-Supan, Helmut. *Deutsche Romantiker zwischen 1800 und 1850.* Munich: Prestel-Verlag, 1972.

Brettell, Richard R., and Caroline B. Brettell. *Painters and Peasants in the Nineteenth Century.* New York: Rizzoli, 1983.

Brown, Milton W. *American Art to 1900: Painting, Sculpture, Architecture.* New York: Harry N. Abrams, 1977.

Budd, Henry. "Thomas Sully." *Pennsylvania Magazine of History and Biography* 42, no. 2 (1918): 121–25.

Busch-Reisinger Museum. *German Master Drawings of the Nineteenth Century.* Exhibition catalogue. Cambridge, 1972.

Carter, Edward C., II, John C. van Horne, and Charles E. Brownell, eds. *Latrobe's View of America, 1795–1820: Selections from the Watercolors and Sketches.* New Haven: Yale University Press, 1985.

A Catalogue of Portraits and Other Works of Art in the Possession of the American Philosophical Society. Philadelphia, 1961.

Champa, Kermit Swiler, with Kate Champa. *German Painting of the Nineteenth Century.* Exhibition catalogue. New Haven: Yale University Art Gallery, 1970.

Chiego, William J., et al. *Sir David Wilkie of Scotland (1785–1841).* Raleigh: North Carolina Museum of Art, 1987.

Christie, Manson, and Woods, Intl. *Important American Paintings, Drawings, and Sculpture of the Nineteenth and Twentieth Centuries.* Sale of December 9, 1983.

Christie, Manson, and Woods, Intl. *Important American Paintings, Drawings, and Sculpture of the Nineteenth and Twentieth Centuries.* Sale of May 26, 1988.

Chronik des Bleichers Johannes Jerg, 1771–1825. Balingen, Ger.: Hermann Daniel, 1952.

Cikovsky, Nicolai, Jr., with Linda Bantel and John Wilmerding. *Raphaelle Peale Still Lifes.* Exhibition catalogue. Washington, D.C.: National Gallery of Art, 1988.

Cincinnati Art Museum. *Masterpieces of American Painting from the Pennsylvania Academy of the Fine Arts.* Exhibition catalogue. Cincinnati, 1974.

Clark, H. Nichols B. *Francis W. Edmonds: American Master in the Dutch Tradition.* Exhibition catalogue. Washington, D.C.: Smithsonian Institution Press, 1988.

Coke, Desmond. *The Art of the Silhouette.* 1913. Reprint. Detroit: Singing Tree Press, 1970.

Condit, Uzal W. *The History of Easton, Penn'a from the Earliest Times to the Present, 1779–1885.* Easton: George W. West, 1885.

Cosentino, Andrew J. *The Paintings of Charles Bird King (1785–1862).* Washington, D.C.: Smithsonian Institution Press, 1977.

Cowdrey, Mary Bartlett. *American Academy of Fine Arts and American Art-Union: Exhibition Record, 1816–1852.* With a history . . . by Theodore Sizer. 2 vols. Collections of the New-York Historical Society, vol. 76. New York, 1953.

The Cries of Philadelphia: Ornamented with Elegant Wood Cuts. Philadelphia: Johnson and Warner, 1810.

Cunningham, J. L. *Executor's Sale Catalogue of Valuable Cabinet and Other Old Paintings* and *A Large Number of Superior Engravings to be Sold at Joy Building at Public Auction March 30/31, 1825.* Boston, 1825.

Davidson, Marshall B. *The Drawing of America.* New York: Harry N. Abrams, 1983.

Dickson, Harold E. *Arts of the Young Republic: The Age of William Dunlap.* Chapel Hill: University of North Carolina Press, 1968.

Directory to the Bicentennial Inventory of American Paintings Executed before 1914. New York: Arno Press, 1976.

Drawing Book of Landscapes. Philadelphia: Johnson and Warner, ca. 1810.

Drepperd, Carl W. *American Pioneer Arts.* Springfield, Mass.: Pond-Ekberg, 1942.

———. *Early American Prints.* New York: New Century, 1930.

———. *Pioneer America: Its First Three Centuries.* Garden City, N.Y.: Doubleday, 1949.

———, comp. *Early American Advertising Art . . ., 1750–1850.* New York: Youth Group of Magazines, 1943.

Dunlap, William. *Diary of William Dunlap (1766–1839) . . . The Memoirs of a Dramatist, Theatrical Manager, Painter, Critic, Novelist, and Historian.* 3 vols. in 1. 1931. Reprint. New York: Benjamin Blom, 1969.

———. *A History of the Rise and Progress of the Arts of Design in the United States.* 3 vols. Rev. ed. Ed. Frank W. Bayley and Charles E. Goodspeed. Boston: C. E. Goodspeed, 1918.

Ebert, John and Katherine Ebert. *Old American Prints for Collectors.* New York: Charles Scribner's Sons, 1974.

Egle, William Henry. *An Illustrated History of the Commonwealth of Pennsylvania.* Harrisburg: De Witt C. Goodrich, 1876.

Elements of Drawing Illustrated by Eleven Elegant Copper Plates. New York: John Low, 1804.

The Elements of Drawing, Illustrated by Views, Landscapes, Human Figures, Etc., Explanatory of the Different Directions in the Text. Philadelphia: Robert Desilver, 1823.

Engelhardt, Ottmar. *Albstadt im Herzen der Schwäbischen Alb.* Stuttgart: Konrad Theis Verlag, 1982.

"Explanation of the Plates." *Analectic,* n.s., 1, no. 2 (February 1820): 175–76.

Fàbian, Monroe H. *Mr. Sully, Portrait Painter: The Works of Thomas Sully (1783–1872).* Exhibition catalogue. Washington, D.C.: Smithsonian Institution Press, 1983.

Faust, Albert Bernhard. *The German Element in the United States: With Special References to Its Political, Moral, and Educational Influence.* New York: Steuben Society of America, 1927.

Ferguson, George. *Signs and Symbols in Christian Art.* New York: Oxford University Press, 1954.

Fielding, Mantle. *American Engravers upon Copper and Steel.* Philadelphia: Burt Franklin, 1917.

———. *Dictionary of American Painters, Sculptors, and Engravers.* New York: Paul A. Struck, 1942.

"The Fine Arts; . . . The Modern French School: Life of David." *Port Folio,* 3d ser., 1, no. 4 (April 1813): 388–89.

"The Fine Arts; . . . The Life of Poussin." *Port Folio,* 3d ser., 1, no. 1 (January 1813): 52–59.

Fink, Lois Marie. "Rembrandt Peale in Paris." *Pennsylvania Magazine of History and Biography* 110, no. 1 (January 1986): 71–90.

Fisher, Stanley. *Dictionary of Watercolor Painters, 1750–1900.* London: W. Foulsam, 1972.

Fleischhauer, Werner. *Die Schwäbische Kunst, 19. und 20. Jahrhundert.* Stuttgart: Deutsche Verlags Anstalt.

Flexner, James Thomas. *The Light of Distant Skies: History of American Painting, 1760–1835.* 1959. Reprint. New York: Dover Publications, 1969.

"For the North-American Journal: On the Fine Arts." *North American Review and Miscellaneous Journal* 3, no. 8 (July 1816): 194–201.

Fox, James Edward. "Iconography of the Black in American Art, 1710–1900." Ph.D. diss., University of North Carolina, Chapel Hill, 1979.

Frankenstein, Alfred. *Painter of Rural America: William Sidney Mount.* Exhibition catalogue. Stony Brook, N.Y.: Suffolk Museum of Stony Brook, 1968.

———. *William Sidney Mount.* New York: Harry N. Abrams, 1975.

Friedländer, Walter. *David to Delacroix.* 1952. Reprint. Cambridge: Harvard University Press, 1977.

Fries, Adelaide L. *Customs and Practices of the Moravian Church.* Rev. ed. Winston-Salem, N.C.: Board of Christian Education and Evangelism, 1964.

Garvan, Beatrice B. *Federal Philadelphia, 1785–1825: The Athens of the Western World.* Exhibition catalogue. Philadelphia: Philadelphia Museum of Art, 1987.

Gerdts, William H. *Thomas Birch, 1779–1851: Paintings and Drawings.* Exhibition catalogue. Philadelphia: Philadelphia Maritime Museum, 1966.

———. "Washington Allston and the German Romantic Classicists in Rome." *Art Quarterly* 32, no. 2 (Summer 1969): 167–96.

Gleason, Abbott. "Pavel Svin'in, 1787–1839." In *Abroad in America: Visitors to the New Nation, 1776–1914,* pp. 12–21. Exhibition catalogue. Washington, D.C.: National Portrait Gallery, 1976.

Godcharles, Frederic A. *Chronicles of Central Pennsylvania.* 4 vols. New York: Lewis Historical Publishing, 1944.

Gordon, Thomas F. *A Gazetteer of the State of Pennsylvania.* Philadelphia: T. Belknap, 1832.

Groce, George C., and David H. Wallace. *The New-York Historical Society's Dictionary of Artists in America, 1564–1860.* New Haven: Yale University Press, 1957.

Grossman, F. *Brueghel's Paintings: Complete Edition of the Paintings.* London: Phaidon Press, 1966.

Hangen, Eva C. *Symbols: Our Universal Language.* Wichita, Kans.: McCormick-Armstrong, 1962.

Harding, Anneliese, comp. *John Quincy Adams: Pioneer of German-American Literary Studies.* Exhibition catalogue. Boston: Goethe Institute, 1979.

———. *Eden Revisited: Graphic Works by German Romantic Artists.* Exhibition catalogue. New York: Goethe House, 1981.

———. *The Edible Mass Medium: Traditional European Cookie Molds of the Seventeenth, Eighteenth, and Nineteenth Centuries.* Exhibition catalogue. Cambridge: Busch-Reisinger Museum, Harvard University, 1975.

Hart, Charles Henry. *Catalogue of the Engraved Portraits of Washington.* New York: Grolier Club, 1904.

Hartmann, Julius B. *Johann Baptist Pflug (1785–1866): Gemälde und Zeichnungen.* Biberach, Ger.: Verlag Biberacher Verlags druckerei, 1985.

Heckewelder, John Gottlieb Ernestus. *Account of the History, Manners, and Customs of the Indian Nations Who Once Inhabited Pennsylvania and the Neighboring States.* Transactions of the American Philosophical Society, vol 1. Philadelphia, 1819.

Henry, James. *Sketches of Moravian Life and Character.* Philadelphia: J. B. Lippincott, 1859.

Hevner, Carol Eaton. *Rembrandt Peale, 1778–1860: A Life in the Arts.* Exhibition catalogue. Philadelphia: Historical Society of Pennsylvania, 1985.

Hills, Patricia. *The Painters' America: Rural and Urban Life, 1810–1910.* Exhibition catalogue. New York: Praeger Publishers, 1974.

Historisches Museum der Stadt Wien. *Das Wiener Bürgerliche Zeughaus, 1600–1840: Barock und Klassizismus.* Vienna: Eigenverlag des Museums, 1962.

Honour, Hugh. *Romanticism.* New York: Harper and Row/Icon, 1979.

Hoopes, Donelson F. "The Emergence of an American Medium." In *American Traditions in Watercolor: The Worcester Art Museum Collection,* edited by Susan E. Strickler. Exhibition catalogue. New York: Abbeville Press, 1987.

Hoover, Catherine. "The Influence of David Wilkie's Prints on the Genre Paintings of William Sidney Mount." *American Art Journal* 13, no. 3 (Summer 1981): 4–33.

"Illustrations of the Graphic Art: Exemplified by Sketches from the National Museum at Paris." *Port Folio,* n.s., 6, no. 6 (December 1811): 568–75.

In This Academy: The Pennsylvania Academy of the Fine Arts, 1805–1976. Exhibition catalogue. Philadelphia, 1976.

Jable, J. Thomas. "Aspects of Moral Reform in Early Nineteenth-Century Pennsylvania." *Pennsylvania Magazine of History and Biography* 102, no. 3 (July 1978): 344–63.

Jackson, Joseph. "Iconography of Philadelphia." *Pennsylvania Magazine of History and Biography* 59, no. 1 (1935): 57–70.

———. "Krimmel, The American Hogarth." *International Studio* 93, no. 385 (June 1929): 33–36, 86, 88.

Jacobs, Phoebe Lloyd. "John James Barralet and the Apotheosis of George Washington." In *Winterthur Portfolio 12*, edited by Ian M. G. Quimby, pp. 115–37. Charlottesville: University Press of Virginia, 1977.

Janson, Charles William. *The Stranger in America; Containing Observations Made during a Long Residence in That Country . . . .* London: J. Cundee, 1807.

Jeffery, Margaret. "As a Russian Saw Us in 1812." *Metropolitan Museum of Art Bulletin* 1, no. 3 (November 1942): 134–40.

Jensen, Jens Christian. *Aquarelle und Zeichnungen der deutschen Romantik.* Cologne: DuMont Buchverlag, 1978.

Jobé, Joseph, ed. *Extended Travels in Romantic America.* Translated by D. B. Tubbs. Lausanne, Switz.: Edita, 1818.

Keller, Kenneth W. "Cultural Conflict in Early Nineteenth-Century Pennsylvania Politics." *Pennsylvania Magazine of History and Biography* 110, no. 4 (October 1986): 509–30.

Kohlrausch, Friedrich Heinrich. *Die Geschichte der Deutschen.* 2d ed. Elberfeld: Büschler, 1816.

"Krimmel's Picture—*Return from Boarding School.*" *Analectic,* n.s., 2, no. 6 (December 1820): 507–8.

L. "Going to Boarding School." *Analectic,* n.s., 2, no. 5 (November 1820): 421.

Latrobe, B. Henry. "Anniversary Oration Pronounced before the Society of Artists of the United States." *Port Folio,* separately issued with n.s., 5, no. 6. (June 1811): 3–31.

Leslie, Charles Robert. *Autobiographical Recollections.* Edited by Tom Taylor. 2 vols. Boston: Ticknor and Fields, 1860.

Levering, Joseph Mortimer. *A History of Bethlehem, Pennsylvania, 1741–1892 . . . .* Bethlehem: Times Publishing Company, 1903.

Lipman, Jean and Tom Armstrong, eds. *American Folk Painters of Three Centuries.* Exhibition catalogue. New York: Hudson Hills Press, 1980.

"List of Passengers on Board Ship Frederick Augustus, Capt. Robinson Potter, from Amsterdam, Sept. 15, 1807." *Pennsylvania Archives.* Edited by William H. Egle. 2d ser., vol. 17. Harrisburg, 1890.

Lister, Raymond. *Silhouettes; An Introduction to Their History and to the Act of Cutting and Painting Them.* London: Pitman, 1953.

Lynes, Russell. *The Art-Makers of Nineteenth-Century America.* New York: Atheneum, 1970.

M. "Review of the Third Annual Exhibition of the Columbian Society of Artists and Pennsylvania Academy of Fine Arts." *Port Folio,* n.s., 2, no. 2 (August 1813): 122–41.

M., G. "Review of the Second Annual Exhibition." *Port Folio* 8, no. 1 (July 1812): 17–28.

Martin, John Hill. *Historical Sketch of Bethlehem in Pennsylvania with Some Account of the Moravian Church.* 1872. Reprint. New York: AMS Press, 1971.

Melish, John. *Travels in the United States of America in the Years 1806 and 1807, and 1809, 1810 and 1811 . . . .* Philadelphia, 1812.

Metropolitan Museum of Art. *German Masters of the Nineteenth Century: Paintings and Drawings from the Federal Republic of Germany.* Exhibition catalogue. New York, 1981.

———. *Nineteenth-Century American Paintings and Sculpture.* Exhibition catalogue. New York: New York Graphic Society, 1969.

Miller, Lillian B. "In the Shadow of His Father: Rembrandt Peale, Charles Willson Peale, and the American Portrait Tradition." *Pennsylvania Magazine of History and Biography* 110, no. 1 (January 1986): 33–64.

Millspaugh, Charles F. *The Medicinal Plants: An Illustrated Descriptive Guide to Plants Indigenous to and Naturalized in the United States Which Are Used in Medicine.* Philadelphia: J. C. Yorston, 1892.

Moltmann, Günter, ed. *Germans to America. 300 Years of Immigration.* Stuttgart and Bonn Bad Godesberg: Institute for Foreign Relations and Inter Nationes, 1982.

Moure, Nancy Dustin Wall. *American Narrative Painting.* Exhibition catalogue. Los Angeles: Los Angeles County Museum of Art, 1974.

Naeve, Milo M. *John Lewis Krimmel: An Artist in Federal America.* Newark: University of Delaware Press, 1987.

Nash, Gary B. *Forging Freedom: The Formation of Philadelphia's Black Community, 1720–1840.* Cambridge: Harvard University Press, 1988.

Novak, Barbara. *American Painting of the Nineteenth Century: Realism, Idealism, and the American Experience.* New York: Praeger Publishers, 1969.

Nye, Russel Blaine. *The Cultural Life of the New Nation, 1776–1830.* New York: Harper and Row, 1960.

———. *Views and Visions: American Landscape before 1830.* Washington, D.C.: Corcoran Gallery of Art, 1986.

Oberholtzer, Ellis Paxson. *Philadelphia: A History of the City and Its People; A Record of 225 Years.* 4 vols. Philadelphia: J. S. Clarke, 1912.

Oedel, William T. *Philadelphia Portrait, 1682–1982: Catalogue of an Exhibition Celebrating the Three Hundredth Anniversary of Philadelphia.* Exhibition catalogue. Philadelphia: Historical Society of Pennsylvania, 1982.

Oedel, William T. "Review Essay: Krimmel at the Crossroads." *Winterthur Portfolio* 23, no. 4 (Winter 1988): 273–81.

Oldschool, Oliver. "Pennsylvania Academy of the Fine Arts." *Port Folio*, n.s., 1, no. 6 (June 1809): 461–62.

Parke-Bernet Galleries. *Part Two Final of the Collection of the Late John Kenneth Danby, Wilmington, Delaware* . . . . Auction catalogue. Sale of December 13–15, 1956.

Pauli, Gustav. *Die Kunst des Klassizismus und der Romantik.* Berlin: Propylaen-Verlag, 1925.

Paulson, Ronald. *Hogarth: His Life, Art, and Times.* 2 vols. New Haven: Yale University Press, 1971.

Perkins, Robert F., Jr. and William J. Gavin III, comps. and eds. *The Boston Athenaeum Art Exhibition Index, 1827–1874.* Boston: Library of the Boston Athenaeum, 1980.

Peters, Harry T. *America on Stone.* Garden City, N.Y.: Doubleday, 1931.

Petrova, Yevgenia. *Traveling across North America, 1812–1813: Watercolors by the Russian Diplomat Pavel Svinin.* 1815, facsimile ed. New York: Harry N. Abrams, 1992.

Philadelphia Museum of Art. *Philadelphia: Three Centuries of American Art.* Exhibition catalogue. Philadelphia, 1976.

Pochmann, Henry A. *German Culture in America: Philosophical and Literary Influences, 1600–1900.* Madison: University of Wisconsin Press, 1957.

Priest, William. *Travels in the United States of America.* London, 1802.

"Review and Register of the Fine Arts." *Literary and Philosophical Intelligence* 1, no. 2 (June 1817): 131.

"Review of the Fourth Annual Exhibition of the Columbian Society of Artists and the Pennsylvania Academy." *Port Folio*, n.s., 4, no. 1 (July 1814): 94–100.

"Review of the Second Annual Exhibition" pt. 2. *Port Folio* 8, no. 2 (August 1812): 142–50.

Richardson, Edgar P. *American Romantic Painting.* New York: E. Weyhe, 1944.

———. *Painting in America: The Story of 450 Years.* New York: Thomas Y. Crowell Co., 1956.

Richardson, Edgar P., Brooke Hindle, and Lillian B. Miller. *Charles Willson Peale and His World.* New York: Harry N. Abrams, 1983.

Ritter, Abraham. *History of the Moravian Church in Philadelphia from Its Foundation in 1742 to the Present Time.* Philadelphia: Hayes and Zell, 1857.

———. *Philadelphia and Her Merchants, as Constituted Fifty [to] Seventy Years Ago.* Philadelphia, 1860.

Roller, Hans Ulrich. *Volkskultur in Württemberg.* Exhibition catalogue. Stuttgart: Württembergisches Landesmuseum; Tübingen: Gulde Druck, 1974.

Rondthaler, Edward. *Life of John Heckewelder.* Edited by B. H. Coates. Philadelphia: T. Ward, 1847.

Rosenblum, Robert. "German Romantic Painting in International Perspective." *Yale University Art Gallery Bulletin* 33, no. 3 (October 1972): 23–36.

Rosenblum, Robert, and H. W. Janson. *Nineteenth-Century Art.* New York: Harry N. Abrams, 1984.

Rutledge, Anna Wells. *A Catalogue of Portraits and Other Works of Art in the Possession of the American Philosophical Society.* Philadelphia: American Philosophical Society, 1961.

———, comp. and ed. *Cumulative Record of Exhibition Catalogues: The Pennsylvania Academy of the Fine Arts, 1807–1870; The Society of Artists, 1800–1814; The Artists' Fund Society, 1835–1845.* Philadelphia: American Philosophical Society, 1955.

Scharf, J. Thomas, and Thompson Westcott. *History of Philadelphia.* 3 vols. Philadelphia: L. H. Everts, 1884.

Schefold, Max. *Alte Ansichten aus Württemberg.* 2 vols. Stuttgart: Kohlhammer, 1956.

———. *Alte Ansichten der Schwäbischen Alb.* Stuttgart: Kohlhammer, 1954.

Schorsch, Anita. "A Key to the Kingdom: The Iconography of a Mourning Picture." *Winterthur Portfolio* 14, no. 1 (Spring 1979): 41–71.

Schrade, Hubert. *Deutsche Malerei der Romantik.* Cologne: Verlag M. DuMont, 1967.

Sealsfield, Charles (Karl Anton Postl). *United States of North America as They Are.* 1828. Reprint. New York: Johnson Reprint Corp., 1970.

Segal, Sam. *A Prosperous Past: The Sumptuous Still Life in the Netherlands, 1600–1700.* The Hague: SDU Publishers, 1988.

Seidensticker, Oswald. *The First Century of German Printing in America, 1728–1830.* 1893. Reprint. Millwood, N.Y.: Kraus Reprint, 1966.

Sellers, Charles Coleman. *Charles Willson Peale.* New York: Charles Scribner's Sons, 1969.

———. "Joseph Sansom, Philadelphia Silhouettist." *Pennsylvania Magazine of History and Biography* 88, no. 4 (October 1964): 395–438.

Sewell, Darrel. *Thomas Eakins: Artist of Philadelphia.* Exhibition catalogue. Philadelphia: Philadelphia Museum of Art, 1982.

Sherman, Frederic Fairchild. "John Lewis Krimmel's Portrait Group of Himself and Family." *Art in America and Elsewhere* 11, no. 1 (December 1922): 57–58.

Silver, Rollo G. *The American Printer.* Charlottesville: University Press of Virginia, 1967.

Simpson, Henry. *The Lives of Eminent Philadelphians, Now Deceased.* Philadelphia: William Brotherhead, 1859.

Smith, Billy G. *The Lower Sort: Philadelphia's Laboring People.* Ithaca, N.Y.: Cornell University Press, 1990.

Snyder, Martin. *City of Independence: Views of Philadelphia before 1800.* New York: Praeger Publishers, 1974.

Sotheby's. *Important American Nineteenth- and Twentieth-Century Paintings, Drawings, and Sculpture.* Sale of December 8, 1983.

Staatsgalerie Stuttgart. *Neue Meister.* Handbook. Stuttgart, 1968.

———. *Schwaben sehen Schwaben: Bildnisse 1760–1940 aus dem Besitz der Staatsgalerie Stuttgart.* Exhibition catalogue. Stuttgart, 1979.

Stadel (Stadtische Galerie im Stadelschen Kunstinstiut). *Die Nazarener.* Exhibition catalogue. Frankfurt am Main, 1977.

Städtische Galerie Albstadt. *Das Landschaftsbild der Schwabischen Alb.* Albstadt-Ebingen, 1980.

Städtische Galerie im Lenbachhaus. *Münchner Landschaftsmaleri 1800–1850.* Exhibition catalogue. Munich, 1980.

Staley, Allen. *Benjamin West, 1738–1820: American Painters at the English Court.* Exhibition catalogue. Baltimore: Baltimore Museum of Art, 1989.

Stebbins, Theodore E., Jr. *American Master Drawings and Watercolors: A History of Works on Paper from Colonial Times to the Present.* New York: Harper and Row, 1976.

———. *A New World: Masterpieces of American Painting, 1760–1910.* Exhibition catalogue. Boston: Museum of Fine Arts, 1983.

Stettner, Walter. *Ebingen, die Geschichte einer Württembergischen Stadt.* Sigmaringen, Ger.: Jan Thorbecke Verlag, 1986.

"Study for Return from Market." *Kennedy Quarterly* 8, no. 4 (January 1969): 257.

Suttcliffe, Alice C. *Robert Fulton and the Clermont.* New York: Century Co., 1909.

Sutton, Peter C. *Masters of Seventeenth-Century Dutch Landscape Painting.* Boston: Museum of Fine Arts, Boston, 1987.

Svinin, Pavel Petrovich. "The Emperor Alexander." *Port Folio,* n.s., 7, no. 3 (March 1812): 197–201.

———. "Memoir on the Cosacks." *Port Folio,* n.s., 7, no. 4 (April 1812): 353–57.

———. *Sketches of Russia.* London: R. Ackermann, 1814.

———. *Opyt zhyvopisnavo puteshestviya po severnoi Amerike* [A Picturesque Voyage in North America]. St. Petersburg, Russia, 1815.

Tatum, George B. *Penn's Great Town: 250 Years of Philadelphia Architecture Illustrated in Prints and Drawings.* Philadelphia: University of Pennsylvania Press, 1961.

Taylor, Joshua C. *America as Art.* Exhibition catalogue. Washington, D.C.: Smithsonian Institution Press, 1976.

———. *The Fine Arts in America.* Chicago: University of Chicago Press, 1979.

Thomas, Isaiah. *The History of Printing in America with a Biography of Printers and an Account of Newspapers.* 1874. 2d ed., edited by Marcus A. McCorison. New York: Weathervane Books, 1970.

Trautmann, Frederic. "Pennsylvania through a German's Eyes: The Travels of Ludwig Gall, 1819–1820." *Pennsylvania Magazine of History and Biography* 105, no. 1 (January 1981): 35–65.

Vaughan, William B. *German Romantic Painting.* New Haven: Yale University Press, 1980.

———. *German Romanticism and English Art.* New Haven: Yale University Press, 1979.

Von Einem, Herbert. *Deutsche Malerei des Klassizismus und der Romantik, 1760 bis 1840.* Exhibition catalogue. Munich: C. H. Beck, 1978.

Von Erffa, Helmut, and Allen Staley. *The Paintings of Benjamin West, 1738–1820.* New Haven: Yale University Press, 1986.

Wallace, Paul A. W., ed. *Thirty Thousand Miles with John Heckewelder.* Pittsburgh: University of Pittsburgh Press, 1958.

Ward, Townsend. "Alexander Lawson." *Pennsylvania Magazine of History and Biography* 28, no.2 (1904): 204–8.

Weigley, Russell F. *Philadelphia: A 300 Year History.* New York: W. W. Norton, 1982.

White, D. Fedotoff. "A Russian Sketches Philadelphia, 1811–1813." *Pennsylvania Magazine of History and Biography* 75, no. 1 (January 1951): 1–24.

Whitley, William T. *Art in England, 1800–1820.* Vol. 1. New York: Macmillan Co., 1928.

Whitney Museum of American Art. *American Genre: The Social Scene in Painting and Prints.* Exhibition catalogue. New York: Whitney Museum of American Art, 1935.

Williams, Hermann Warner, Jr. *Mirror to the American Past: A Survey of American Genre Painting, 1750–1900.* Greenwich, Conn.: New York Graphic Society, 1973.

Wolf, Edwin, II. *Philadelphia, Portrait of an American City: A Bicentennial History.* Harrisburg, Pa.: Stackpole Books, 1975.

Wolf, Stephanie Grauman. *Urban Village: Population, Community, and Family Structure in Germantown, Pennsylvania, 1683–1800.* Princeton, N.J.: Princeton University Press, 1976.

The Works of William Hogarth . . . . 2 vols. London: n.p., n.d.

Württembergisches Landesmuseum Stuttgart. *Volkskultur in Württemberg.* Stuttgart, 1974.

Wust, Klaus, and Heinz Moos, eds. *Three Hundred Years of German Immigrants in North America, 1683–1983.* Baltimore: Heinz Moos Publishing Co., 1983.

Yarmolinsky, Avrahm. *Picturesque United States of America, 1811, 1812, 1813; Being a Memoir on Paul Svinin.* New York: William Edwin Rudge, 1930.

Zweihundert Jahre englische Kunst. Munich: Haus der Kunst, 1976.

NEWSPAPERS

Aurora General Advertiser, Philadelphia.

Columbian Centinel, Boston.

Paxton's Philadelphia Annual Advertiser.

Poulson's American Daily Advertiser, Philadelphia.

Relf's Philadelphia Gazette and Daily Advertiser.

CITY DIRECTORIES

The Philadelphia Directory, 1809–30.

Longworth's Directory, New York City, 1825–43.

Doggett's New-York City Directory, 1842–53.

Trow's City Directory, New York City, 1852–64.

Wilson's Business Directory of New-York City, 1851–52.

EXHIBITIONS AT THE ACADEMY

First Annual Exhibition of the Society of Artists of the United States, 1811. Philadelphia, 1811. Microfiche.

Second Annual Exhibition of the Society of Artists of the United States, 1812. Philadelphia, 1812. Microfiche.

Third Annual Exhibition of the Columbian Society of Artists and the Pennsylvania Academy, 1813. Philadelphia, 1813. Microfiche.

Fourth Annual Exhibition of the Columbian Society of Artists and the Pennsylvania Academy, May, 1814. Philadelphia, 1814. Microfiche.

Exhibition at the Pennsylvania Academy of the Fine Arts . . . . Philadelphia, 1816. Microfiche.

Ninth Annual Exhibition of the Pennsylvania Academy of the Fine Arts, June 1820. Philadelphia, 1820. Microfiche.

Tenth Annual Exhibition of the Pennsylvania Academy of the Fine Arts, May 1821. Philadelphia, 1821. Microfiche.

Catalogue of the Paintings, Statues, Prints . . . Exhibiting at the Pennsylvania Academy of the Fine Arts, July 1821. Philadelphia, 1821. Microfiche.

Eleventh Annual Exhibition of the Pennsylvania Academy of the Fine Arts, May 1822. Philadelphia, 1822. Microfiche.

Plus all subsequent exhibiton catalogues on microfiche up through 1865. Titles vary slightly.

MANUSCRIPTS

Ehebuch der Evangelischen Kirchengemeinde Ebingen. Spitalhof, Albstadt-Ebingen, Germany.

Estate of John Lewis Krimmel. Administration no. 187. Department of Wills, County Court House, Philadelphia.

Gebäudekataster [register of buildings], Ebingen, ca. 1840, Stadtarchiv Albstadt, Germany.

Geburts- und Taufregister, Stadtarchiv, Albstadt-Ebingen, Germany.

Gerichtliche Protokolle [record of court hearings], 1806–1809, Stadtarchiv, Albstadt-Ebingen, Germany.

Grundbesitzurkunde [real estate documents], Stadtarchiv, Albstadt-Ebingen, Germany.

Heckewelder-DuPonceau correspondence, Peter S. DuPonceau papers. American Philosophical Society, Philadelphia.

Inventuren und Teilungen, vol. 1184, Stadtarchiv, Albstadt-Ebingen, Germany.

Kaufprotokolle [sale and purchase records], Ebingen, 1817–1818. Stadtarchiv, Albstadt-Ebingen, Germany.

Krimmel, George Frederick, to Paul Daser, October 16, 1816. Gerichtsprotokolle, Stadtarchiv, Albstadt-Ebingen, Germany.

Krimmel, George Frederick, Will 137, 1830. Book 9, p. 592. Register of Wills, City Hall, Philadelphia.

Krimmel-Birch correspondence. [1812 or 1813.] Charles Henry Hart Autograph Collection. Archives of American Art. Microfilm.

Krimmel, John Lewis, to Samuel Coates, April 22, 1819. Joseph Downs Collection of Manuscripts and Printed Ephemera, Winterthur.

Krimmel, John Lewis, to Pierre Flandin, October 8, 1820. Dreer Autograph Collection, Historical Society of Pennsylvania, Philadelphia.

Krimmel, John Lewis, curatorial files, National Gallery of Art, Washington, D.C.

Krimmel, John Lewis, sketchbooks, spring 1810–summer 1821. Joseph Downs Collection of Manuscripts and Printed Ephemera, Winterthur.

Murray, George. Address of August 1, 1810, as transcribed on December 19, 1810. Minutes, Society of Artists. Archives of American Art. Microfilm.

Naeve, Milo Merle. "John Lewis Krimmel: His Life, His Art, and His Critics." Master's thesis, University of Delaware, 1955.

Naturalization Record 582. District of Pennsylvania, U.S. District Court Records, Philadelphia.

Nygren, Edward J. "Art Instruction in Philadelphia, 1795–1845." Master's thesis, University of Delaware, 1969.

Peale, Charles Willson. Journal to New York, May 28, 1817. Diary No. 22. Peale-Sellers Papers, American Philosophical Society, Philadelphia.

Peale, Charles Wilson, to Rembrandt Peale, May 22, 1819. Peale-Sellers Papers, American Philosophical Society, Philadelphia. Typescript.

Peale Papers, related to exhibitions at Pennsylvania Academy of the Fine Arts. Microfiche 6:A-2.

Records of the Society of Artist, records of the Academy. Pennsylvania Academy of the Fine Arts. Microfilm.

Ritter, Abraham. "Recollections of the Village of Nazareth, Northampton Co., in the More Primitive and Unsophisticated Times of 1809–10 & 11," 1855. Historical Society of Pennsylvania, Philadelphia. Microfilm.

Seelenregister der Evangelischen Kirchengemeinde Ebingen, Familienbuch A2, Evangelisches Kirchenregisteramt Spitalhof, Albstadt-Ebingen, Germany.

Sully, Thomas to Samuel Coates, April 5, 1819. Joseph Downs Collection of Manuscripts and Printed Ephemera, Winterthur.

Sully, Thomas. Journal of May 1792–1846. New York Public Library. Archives of American Art. Microfilm.

St. Michael's and Zion Lutheran Church, Philadelphia. Verzeichnis der Tauf- Trauungs- Begräbnis Register der St. Michaelis und Zion Gemeinde. Historical Society of Pennsylvania, Philadelphia. Microfilm.

Waisengericht [orphans' court], 1817, 1818. Stadtarchiv, Albstadt-Ebingen, Germany.

INDEX

Page numbers in *italics* indicate illustrations.

John Lewis Krimmel: Genre Artist of the Early Republic

Editor: Catherine E. Hutchins
Copy Editor: Lisa L. Lock
Sketchbook photographer: Wayne B. Gibson
Typeface: Adobe Garamond
Paper: 90 lb. Gardamatt Brillante
Endleaves: 80 lb. Nettuno
Designed and composed by Katy Homans and Deborah Zeidenberg
Printed and bound by Arnoldo Mondadori Editore S.p.A., Verona, Italy